Also by Bernard Gwertzman and Michael T. Kaufman

THE COLLAPSE OF COMMUNISM

THE DECLINE AND FALL
OF THE SOVIET EMPIRE

THE
DECLINE
AND
FALL
OF THE
SOVIET
EMPIRE

EDITED BY
BERNARD GWERTZMAN
AND
MICHAEL T. KAUFMAN

TIMES BOOKS

Library of Congress Cataloging-in-Publication Data

The Decline and fall of the Soviet empire / edited by Bernard
Gwertzman and Michael T. Kaufman.—1st ed.
      p.   cm.
Includes index.
ISBN 0–8129–2046–5
1. Soviet Union—Politics and government—1985–1991.
I. Gwertzman, Bernard M. II. Kaufman, Michael T.
DK288.D43 1992
947.085′4—dc20   91–51038

Manufactured in the United States of America
9 8 7 6 5 4 3 2
First Edition

CONTENTS

INTRODUCTION

By Bernard Gwertzman

After delaying the inevitable for several days, Mikhail S. Gorbachev announced over television on the evening of December 25, 1991, that he was giving up trying to hold the Soviet Union together. "I hereby discontinue my activities at the post of president of the Union of Soviet Socialist Republics," he said.

"I am making this decision on considerations of principle," he explained, saying that he could not support a policy of "dismembering this country and disuniting the state."

And so, at 7:32 P.M., the red flag with hammer and sickle, which had flown over the Kremlin for most of this century, was lowered, and the white-blue-and-red flag of the Russian federation rose in its place. It marked not only the breakup of one of the world's superpowers, but also the early retirement of one of this era's most interesting political figures. What emerged from the wreckage of the Soviet Union are 15 separate national states, whose future association is still uncertain, and whose overall political, economic, and military power has been dramatically reduced.

"There was no ceremony, only the tolling of chimes from the Spassky Gate, cheers from a handful of surprised foreigners, and an angry tirade from a lone war veteran," reported Serge Schmemann of *The New York Times* that day.

Seventy-four years earlier, after the czar abdicated in the midst of a punishing and increasingly unpopular war, there was also astonishment at the speed with which the Russian empire fell apart. Richard Pipes, the historian, recalled the comment of Kerensky, who led the provisional government which replaced the monarchy and held power until it, in turn, was ousted by the Bolsheviks in November 1917. Kerensky noted that as soon as Nicholas II withdrew, "a whole world of national and political relationships sank to the bottom, and at once all existing political and tactical programs, however bold and well conceived, appeared hanging aimlessly and uselessly in space."

There was much that same sense of shock over the rapid decline in Gorbachev's fortunes, which were so intertwined with those of the Soviet Union. Although his popularity had long since waned in his own country, Gorbachev was still revered abroad as the most imaginative leader ever to be produced by the Soviet system.

The catalyst for his resignation, of course, was the ill-planned effort by some of his top aides in August 1991 to carry out a coup, which collapsed within days. The Gorbachev appointees, who ran the K.G.B., the police, and the defense forces and included the vice president and former prime minister, had hoped by their plot to stem the disarray in the central authority, to block the plan to grant more authority to the national republics, and to prevent the demise of the Communist Party. In the aftermath, of course, not only did the disarray continue, but the national republics, one after another, all broke with finality from the Soviet Union, and both the Communist Party and Gorbachev were discredited.

Boris N. Yeltsin, Gorbachev's chief political rival, since he had the affrontry to criticize Gorbachev in late 1987, zoomed in popularity for his courage during the brief coup when he stood outside his "White House" Russian republic headquarters and rallied the opposition. As these words are written in the spring of 1992, Yeltsin remains the most prominent public figure in the former Soviet Union, but it is uncertain whether his economic reforms, meant to shock the Russians out of their lethargy, will succeed.

Of course, the underlying reasons for the U.S.S.R.'s collapse are many—a broken-down economy, a political system based largely on fear, and the bankruptcy of the Communist ideology which for a time in this century had attracted millions to its banners. What Gorbachev did was loosen the controls enough to end the decades of fear and unleash a Soviet equivalent of the popular will; which was, very simply, that the Soviet Union should die. It was similar to what had happened in 1989 in Eastern Europe, and in 1979 in Iran. It recalled the words of Alexis de Tocqueville about the French Revolution:

"Thus it was precisely in those parts of France where there had been most improvement that popular discontent ran highest. This may seem illogical—but history is full of such paradoxes. For it is not always when things are going from bad to worse that revolutions break out. On the contrary, it oftener happens that when a people which has put up with an oppressive rule over a long period without protest suddenly finds the government relaxing its pressure, it takes up arms against it."

But Gorbachev's distinct personality also played a major part in his own downfall. Like the last czar, Gorbachev tried to conciliate and shied away from brutal force. In Eastern Europe, he almost seemed to support the downfall of Communist regimes in 1989, and shocked the West by doing nothing to prevent the collapse of the Berlin wall, something which had stood as a fortress symbol of the dividing line between East and West for nearly 30 years, and which Western leaders had been convinced would have been defended by nuclear arms if they had tried to breach it. At home, Gorbachev wavered between trying to invigorate the society with freedoms totally lacking in the Soviet Union, with constant talk of reforms and democratization, while at the same time trying to reassure the Communist Party that he would not undercut its well-established interests as the ruling force. The effort to be both a good democrat and a good party man in the end proved impossible.

And on one issue he seemed absolutely insensitive: the historic grievances of the peoples of the non-Russian republics for more independence. Adam Ulam of Harvard University believes that if Gorbachev had moved with a concrete plan of increased autonomy for the Baltics and others earlier in his term he could have avoided the rapid slide to independence that occurred at the end, and which ultimately forced Gorbachev to acknowledge the Soviet Union no longer could exist.

What was so surprising about the fall of the Soviet Union was not only that it was so rapid, but also that it went so gently into the night. As Ulam has noted, both German Nazism and Italian fascism died after catastrophic military defeats. The common wisdom for years had been that the Soviet system, with its centralized totalitarian wings, the Communist Party, the K.G.B., the enormous military, and the controlled media would never topple from within, and that any attempts from the outside to bring about the collapse of the empire would lead to nuclear war. The common wisdom proved to be utterly wrong.

The focus of this book is on the events in the Soviet Union from March 1985, when an exuberant and relatively youthful Mikhail S. Gorbachev was anointed as the new general secretary of the Communist Party, until his grudging recognition six years later that the Soviet Union and the Communist Party, which he had vowed to protect, no longer existed.

Throughout this period, *The New York Times* paid almost day-to-day attention to the rapidly unfolding events, not only in the Soviet Union, but also in the Eastern European states which made up what amounted to a Soviet empire. The paper was fortunate in having exceptionally skilled correspondents not only in Moscow but also in Eastern Europe.

Most of these same reporters contributed to *The Collapse of Communism,* published in two editions, in 1990 and 1991, which dealt primarily with the disintegration of Communism in the so-called Soviet bloc. This volume is exclusively on the Soviet Union.

In a sense, looking back from the vantage of even a few months in the spring of 1992, what happened before can seem like a blur. Events run into each other, and it can be difficult to sort through the chronology of events, which are covered at length in this book, with material reprinted from the articles published at the time in *The Times.*

On March 11, 1985, Gorbachev was chosen as general secretary of the Communist Party, within hours after the announcement that Konstantin U. Chernenko had died. In a remarkable three-year period, the Soviet Union had seen three leaders die in succession: Leonid I. Brezhnev, Yuri V. Andropov, and now Chernenko. There was a palpable desire in the country for a more vigorous leadership to step forward. Gorbachev, who had been groomed for a top post by Andropov, had little experience at the center, but had just turned 54 and was the youngest man to take charge of the Soviet Union since Stalin. And that alone made him more acceptable to the nation's peoples.

"I promise you, comrades, to do my utmost to faithfully serve our party, our peoples, and the great Leninist cause," he said on taking over. Gorbachev spoke of giving economic enterprises more independence and of increasing production, and said people should have more information. He called for better relations with the West and China. These themes of loyalty to the party, a need for economic reform, increased popular participation, and an end to international tensions were to mark Gorbachev's entire tenure.

His first priority was to repair the strained ties with Washington, thereby reducing the need for such large expenditures on the military. He agreed to a Geneva summit meeting with President Reagan which occurred that November, saying that "confrontation is not an inborn defect of our relations." He said, "We regard the improvement of Soviet-American relations not only as an extremely necessary but also as a possible matter."

By October 1986, when Reagan and Gorbachev held their second summit, in Iceland, it was evident that Gorbachev was willing to make major sacrifices in Soviet nuclear and other force levels, well beyond any that Western powers had thought possible. In fact, Gorbachev regularly was offering concessions that the United States was too wary to accept, wondering what the loopholes were.

Within months of taking office, Gorbachev's seeming zest for change had attracted wide and favorable attention from Moscow's intelligentsia.

Taking note of Gorbachev's first 100 days in power, Serge Schmemann wrote that he had tapped a popular "depth of excitement and hope. After years of viewing their doddering chiefs with disdain and embarrassment, ordinary people were once again discussing their leader's doings and appearances, and even some cynical intellectuals cocked a hopeful eye to the young man in the Kremlin."

"For now," he wrote, "the honeymoon was on and the new style was the talk of the town. Mr. Gorbachev's readiness to go into the streets and to speak off the cuff in public, his modesty and relative candor, his bright and attractive family, all seemed to come as revelations to a public accustomed to dreary ritual and pomp."

Of more importance than words to the West were the concrete steps Gorbachev took in the human rights area. Anatoly B. Shcharansky, one of the leading Jewish protesters, was freed from prison on February 11, 1986. His mother said, "I think there has been a liberalization. There was a man who realized it was necessary." And toward the end of 1986, Gorbachev telephoned Andrei D. Sakharov, the physicist and human rights activist, who had been in exile in Gorky, and told him he could return to Moscow.

"The news of his impending return sent a thrill through the dissident community, a group that had been depleted and demoralized by imprisonments, deaths, or deportations," Bill Keller wrote on December 21.

It was in February 1986 that Gorbachev began pushing for some changes in the economic system. Schmemann described Gorbachev's speaking to a party conference "like a preacher trying to fire a somnolent congregation."

"Mr. Gorbachev pressed his case before the 5,000 delegates and the nationwide television audience with a blend of fiery rhetoric, tantalizing hints of bold new policies, exhortations, and reprimands. Ears perked in the hall as he ticked off the buzzwords of the advocates of economic change—market forces, financial incentives, local autonomy, and even a bit of private enterprise."

It was at this conference that he began to promote regularly the Russian word *glasnost,* which means "openness," as a policy.

Schmemann wrote in November that the *glasnost* campaign was a spectacular success. Although some with long memories recalled how an earlier "thaw" under Khrushchev ended up in a freeze, Schmemann said that "the frontiers of the permissible are still expanding day by day, and there are heady feelings in the theaters and living rooms of Moscow."

But an early disaster took some of the initial bloom off Gorbachev's image and suggested that there were still limits to his openness. A catastrophe at a nuclear reactor in Chernobyl in the Ukraine, not far from

Kiev, occurred on April 26, 1986, and the authorities were very slow in getting the news out. It was not until May 14 that Gorbachev spoke to his nation about the disaster. The slowness of Moscow's reaction fed the simmering discontent which would explode in the independence drive in Ukraine.

The emphasis on *glasnost* and democracy inevitably began to trouble the more traditional Communist Party members who were more aware, perhaps, than Gorbachev that once the levers of power were discarded, it might be impossible to control the future. Gorbachev began in early 1987 to try and assuage these concerns.

At a labor union convention in February, he sought to assure his right-wing critics. "Greater democratization may prompt some people to ask whether we are not disorganizing society, whether we shall not weaken management and lower the standards for discipline, order, and responsibility," he said. But he made it clear he was not about to change his efforts at democratization of society. "So it is either democracy or social inertia and conservatism," he said. "Nothing will come of it if we do not fully break the forces of inertia and deceleration, which are dangerous in their ability to draw the country back again into stagnation and dormancy, threatening a freezing up of society and social corrosion." He also warned that there already existed "a revolution of expectations" that had to be met.

As some of his party critics had warned, the new liberalization made it easier for nationalists to speak openly against Moscow. In the past, even the smallest glimmer of anti-Moscow nationalism usually led to K.G.B. actions and arrests. There were two kinds of nationalism being noted by 1987. One was the discontent in non-Russian areas. The other was a kind of primitive Russia-First movement that became vocal in Moscow. Felicity Barringer reported in May that "Pamyat is the first grass-roots organization to invoke the official watchword of *glasnost,* or openness, in support of a decidedly unofficial political agenda, in which a yearning for a return to traditional Russian values has become inextricably intertwined with a darker nationalism that sees the Russian homeland beset by enemies, chiefly 'international Zionism.' "

Into the summer, there was talk of reform in the economic sphere, but it was apparent that despite the proposals, opposition from those who did not want to upset the established system had blocked change. This led to the first major political sensation of the Gorbachev regime. Boris N. Yeltsin, who was head of the Moscow party organization and who had been seen earlier as a staunch Gorbachev supporter, was removed from office and publicly humiliated on November 11 because he had spoken out at a Central Committee meeting on October 21, criticizing Yegor K.

Ligachev, a leading conservative in the ruling Politburo, and Gorbachev for the slow pace of change. Yeltsin was to show himself politically resilient and would eventually outlast Gorbachev.

"In a sense, Gorbachev is a victim of his own *glasnost,*" Bill Keller quoted a Western diplomat as saying in early 1988. "The press focuses on all the problems in the economy and pushes for changes, and that raises people's expectations. People expect something short-term, and if they don't get it, cynicism may set in before the real reforms get off the ground."

In February 1988, there were two developments that were to prove crucial in the future. Early in the month, Gorbachev announced that he envisaged ordering the start of a withdrawal of Soviet troops from Afghanistan in three months. And midway through the month, demonstrations erupted in the south that pitted the rival claims of nationalistic Armenians against nationalistic Azerbaijanis. Like earlier protests by Lithuanians and Estonians, the outburst was seen by some in Moscow as both a portent of spreading troubles and a direct consequence of the Kremlin's policy of loosening reins. It seemed to suggest that among the first things that a people did with the freedom they gained was to proclaim their particular identity by stressing their differences with their immediate neighbors. It was at this time that the outside world, and indeed, many in the Soviet Union, first took note of Nagorno-Karabakh, the autonomous region inside Azerbaijan, populated mostly by Armenians who wanted to be united with Armenia.

The crisis posed acute political problems for Gorbachev as he tried to steer a middle course between those who wanted faster change in the Soviet Union and those who feared his programs would produce a breakdown in order.

With President Reagan due to visit the Soviet Union in June 1988, further liberal steps were taken. Gorbachev held a well-publicized meeting with the hierarchy of the Russian Orthodox Church, and the Communist Party Central Committee approved proposals to curtail the power of the party and limit the term of party and government officials.

The proposals, sponsored by Gorbachev, would expand the authority of popularly elected legislatures and make them more democratic by requiring competitive elections by secret ballot. Similar procedures would govern the election of party officials. The broad changes, if put into practice, would leave the party as the ultimate source of authority and policy, but would reduce its ubiquitous involvement in the day-to-day management of government and economic institutions and almost every aspect of Soviet life.

But the new proposals fell far short of true democracy, since they underlined Gorbachev's often-stated allegiance to the principles of Communist governance, including the leading role of the party. The new electoral regulations, however, were to backfire on the party because they opened the way to allow the public for the first time by the ballot box to show their contempt for the Communists. A similarly "safe" plan put forth by Communists in Poland in 1989 had proven their undoing, but the message had obviously not been assimilated by Gorbachev.

At the national Communist Party conference that summer, Gorbachev set forth a new political framework that he clearly hoped would provide him with the support for the economic reforms he was pressing. But in doing so, he opened up a Pandora's box he could not control. As Philip Taubman reported in July: "More than any even since Mr. Gorbachev took office in March 1985, the conference shattered the stifling political customs of the Soviet system, making candor, pointed debate, even public confrontation between party leaders acceptable."

In October, Gorbachev took over the formal powers of chief of state, and in December his reorganization plan was accepted by the Soviet legislature, creating a more powerful presidency and national legislature. The year ended on a sour note for him. In New York to attend a special United Nations session, he had to rush back to deal with a severe earthquake in Armenia, which only further provoked nationalist grievances in that republic.

In the summer of 1988, Gorbachev got approval for elections to a new national Congress of People's Deputies, a body that he evidently thought he could control. But as the election campaign for that body began in early 1989, it was clear that it was out of his control. For one thing, as Esther B. Fein reported, it marked the return from the political dead of Boris N. Yeltsin, who ran and won the single at-large seat from Moscow.

Bill Keller reported that when the elections were held at the end of March 1989, it turned out that the electorate dealt "a mortifying rebuke to the high and mighty in elections for a new national congress, including stunning upsets of a Politburo member and several other senior Communist Party officials who ran without opposition." Keller speculated correctly that Gorbachev would find that a free-thinking legislature would make his life more difficult, with some nationalist deputies threatening to bolt from the Soviet Union and reformers impatient for more radical change than even he wanted.

This in turn provoked concern by conservative party members that Gorbachev was opening the floodgates to disaster. Meanwhile, the economy continued to cause serious problems for Gorbachev. In July, some 100,000 miners in the western Siberian region went on strike for money and more liberalization in the political sphere. Keller in July said that "as wildcat strikes and nationalist violence broke out across their domain, besieged party leaders met to share their fears that the party's prestige is plummeting and that the pace of political change is beyond the party's ability to keep up."

August marked the fiftieth anniversary of the Hitler-Stalin secret agreement to carve up separate areas of influence, which included Hitler's allowing Stalin to absorb Lithuania, Latvia, and Estonia. Over a million people in the Baltic states were reported to have joined in a 400-mile human chain linking Estonia, Latvia, and Lithuania in a symbol of solidarity and a call for their independence. Other nationalist movements were reported in Central Asia. Even the Ukraine was not immune from the nationalist movements. Keller reported in March that one of Gorbachev's nightmares should be the evident nationalism in the Ukraine. One leader told him in Lvov that "here we're not talking about 1.5 million people, as in Estonia, but 50 million, a nation the size of France or Italy. We think the question of the Soviet Union, whether it survives or not, will be resolved not in Estonia, but in the Ukraine." But Gorbachev seemed to think that these were transitory developments and did not appear to realize the dangers the separatist forces were for his government.

In addition to his frequent travels to the West, Gorbachev also paid the expected visits to the Communist states of Eastern Europe, whose leaders were completely dependent on the Soviet Union for their existence. In the past, Soviet armed forces had been used to quell liberal moves in Hungary in 1956 and Czechoslovakia in 1968, and it was Soviet pressure that forced the imposition of martial law in Poland in 1981. Nevertheless, to the disquiet of the Eastern European Communists, Gorbachev's message on his visits was to hasten reform. He acted, not as the head of an empire, but as one foreign leader to another. It seemed evident that Gorbachev would have easily countenanced the kind of Prague spring of 1968 that led Brezhnev to send in troops. But Brezhnev realized what Gorbachev apparently didn't, that once Eastern Europeans were allowed to choose freely, they would choose to break with Communism and with the Soviet Union.

The changes at first were gradual—elections in Poland and Hungary, the two most "liberal" states in Eastern Europe. But starting in August and September, thousands of East Germans were fleeing via Hungary and Czechoslovakia to the West. When nothing was done to stop this, people took to the streets in Czechoslovakia, East Germany, and Bulgaria. By the end of the year, all the former members of the Soviet bloc had in one way or other done away with the ruling Communist Party and their close links to Moscow. Rumania, which was independent of Moscow, also came apart. Gorbachev's response was almost nonchalant. While in Helsinki on October 25, Gorbachev's spokesman jokingly declared that Moscow had adopted the "Sinatra doctrine," in Eastern Europe. "You know the Frank Sinatra song, 'I did it my way,' " said Gennadi I. Gerasimov. "Hungary and Poland are doing it their way."

"I think the Brezhnev doctrine is dead," he added, referring to the armed intervention to stifle liberalism in Eastern Europe which had been used in the past. In trying to answer why Gorbachev was so relaxed about the loss of Soviet domain, Bill Keller speculated that the Soviet Union had drastically redefined its security interests, recognizing that halting its own economic decline was more important to the ultimate survival of Soviet power than enforcing an unpopular Communist gospel. And to some extent, Gorbachev made a policy of the inevitable, realizing that even if he wanted to stop the transformations of Eastern Europe he could not do so without endangering his support at home and abroad. Better to claim the initiative, winning admiration in his own bloc and credibility in the West.

With Moscow's acquiescence toward Eastern Europe's independence, it was perhaps inevitable that this would only fan the nationalists within the Soviet Union who had even larger grievances. The Eastern Europeans, after all, never were incorporated into the Soviet Union. But virtually every one of the non-Russian republics had a past history of independence, even if for only a few years, before being incorporated into the Soviet Union.

At the start of 1990, Gorbachev went to Vilnius to implore Lithuanians to remain within the Soviet Union, warning that secession would mean economic calamity for this tiny republic, while weakening Soviet security and endangering his own position and program. But his words had no impact on the crowds, who continued to foment for independence. There were new reports of moves for independence in Moldavia and in Azerbaijan, where there were mob killings of Armenians, which the Soviet forces could not prevent. Lithuania on March 11 proclaimed itself a sovereign state and named a non-Communist government headed by Vytautas Landsbergis to negotiate their future relations with Moscow.

On April 13, Gorbachev issued an ultimatum to Lithuania saying that if the republic did not rescind its strongest independence measures within 48 hours, he would order other republics to start cutting off needed supplies. But in the end, Lithuania withstood the boycotts, and the actions only made Gorbachev less popular overseas and in other parts of the country.

And in Moscow, in advance of a party Central Committee meeting, some 100,000 people marched to the Kremlin walls to demand that the Communist Party surrender its monopoly of power. Francis X. Clines quoted a man who said, "We started the revolutionary events in Eastern Europe, and now they are finally having a reverse effect on us." Clearly, Communism seemed on its last legs as a real force, even in the Soviet Union. On February 7, the party leadership agreed to surrender its historic monopoly of power and accept a program that recommended the creation of a Western-style presidency and cabinet system of government. This became law in early March.

The decline in Gorbachev's popularity, which came even as he was instituting increasingly bold measures to reduce the power of the party, had the effect of enhancing the standing of Yeltsin, who was working adroitly through the Russian parliament, positioning himself to challenge Gorbachev for the top job in the country. On May 29, 1990, Yeltsin, in fact, was elected by his parliament as president of the largest republic, despite Gorbachev's lobbying against it. And by June, the Russian republic's parliament passed a law saying that its laws took precedence over Soviet ones—another challenge to Gorbachev. In 1991, Yeltsin was to be elected by the population as Russian president, which was a signal event in Gorbachev's slide downward.

In July 1990 it was the turn of the conservatives to lambast Gorbachev. His main rival within the party, Yegor K. Ligachev, roused delegates to the nationwide party congress by deploring the five years of Gorbachev's rule as a period of wavering and "blind radicalism."

His lament for the undermining of old values was reinforced by the chief of the K.G.B. and the defense minister, who both warned against efforts to divorce their institutions from the party. Gorbachev's main support came from his foreign minister and friend, Eduard A. Shevardnadze, who declared that the country would benefit from German reunification, and said the military had spent the country into ruin. It was at this party congress that Gorbachev was reelected leader, but Yeltsin and other liberals resigned from the party.

For much of the rest of 1990, the debate was over how drastic an economic reform to push through the country. At first, Gorbachev seemed to favor a crash program of 500 days drawn up by Stanislav S. Shatalin but opposed by his prime minister, Nikolai I. Ryzhkov. In the end, Gorbachev prevaricated, and took no firm step.

"No single plan can be finally adopted. It is my deep conviction that we have to unite forces at this decisive moment. If we split up, if we clash, we will ruin this historic turning point," Gorbachev said.

On October 15, at a time when Gorbachev's standing in his own country had dropped significantly, Gorbachev was elected as the Nobel Peace Prize winner. But the prize was regarded as something of a joke by many Soviet people who by this time were openly mocking him in the streets for his words instead of deeds. By the end of the year, the Soviet Union was being rent apart by recriminations by various political factions, and ever more loudly by various nationality groups increasingly seeking more independence for their republics.

Against this background, on December 20, one of Gorbachev's closest allies, Foreign Minister Shevardnadze, abruptly resigned with an impassioned warning that "reactionaries" threatened his country with dictatorship. "The reformers have gone into hiding. A dictatorship is approaching—I tell you that with full responsibility. No one knows what this dictatorship will be like, what kind of dictator will come to power, and what order will be established." He set the scene for the climactic events of 1991.

However important the developments in the Soviet Union, world attention in January 1991 was on the looming war in the Persian Gulf, caused by Iraq's occupation of Kuwait the preceding summer. Moscow had quickly backed the United States' moves to send troops to Saudi Arabia, and had fully supported the Security Council warnings to Iraq. But if Gorbachev had no problems with the West, the same could not be said of the growing pressures on him brought about by Lithuania's continuing secessionist moves.

For reasons not altogether clear even as these words are written, Gorbachev either ordered or agreed to the intervention of Soviet troops in strength in Lithuania and Latvia, where they seized buildings and in doing so caused many casualties. Yeltsin flew to Vilnius to show support for the independence-minded government. He said that the fate of democratic movements in Russia and elsewhere hinged on the outcome of the confrontation in the Baltics. Sensing that the future was being decided now, 100,000 people marched in Moscow in support of Lithuania, putting Gorbachev clearly on the spot to either reaffirm his democratic moves or continue a crackdown.

President Bush, who was supposed to meet with Gorbachev in Moscow in February, postponed his visit on January 28, ostensibly to direct the war effort; but it was clear that concern about the Baltics also contributed. The issue was even further drawn when Lithuanians voted overwhelmingly on February 10 for independence. On February 19, Yeltsin on television called for Gorbachev's resignation for amassing "absolute personal power" and "deceiving the people." In mid-March, the Soviet people voted in a referendum sponsored by Gorbachev on the question: "Do you support the preservation of the union as a renewed federation of sovereign republics in which the rights of a person of any nationality are fully guaranteed?" The results favored Gorbachev, but Yeltsin, who put his own question on the ballot, also won a strong mandate for a direct election for the Russian presidency.

Meanwhile, on March 28, defying a ban by Gorbachev, and despite a show of military force, some 100,000 Muscovites rallied in support of Yeltsin. Serge Schmemann reported that "as the day drew to a close, the consensus was that Mr. Gorbachev had suffered a serious political setback." By the spring, Gorbachev was reaching out to the republics to fashion some kind of union accord, but meanwhile Yeltsin in June was elected president of Russia, the first time there had been a popularly elected leader in Russian history. Gorbachev by comparison was elected only by his parliament.

On July 24, Gorbachev announced that he had worked out a draft treaty for a decentralized system of power sharing with nine of the 15 republics, including Russia. He was to sign the treaty on August 20. On July 25, Gorbachev told the party Central Committee that to survive it would have to jettison some of its most hallowed principles, even Marxism-Leninism. This paved the way for a visit at the end of July by Bush, a visit marked by an agreement on scaling down nuclear arsenals.

This done, Gorbachev went on vacation in the Crimea, where he was when the coup occurred against him on August 18 and was announced to the Soviet people on August 19. It was evident that whatever other complaints the main plotters had against Gorbachev, they wanted to ensure he did not sign the treaty giving the republics more power. By August 21, the coup had failed. With Yeltsin preaching defiance, the military did not back the coup, and the seemingly inept plotters gave in to public pressure and allowed Gorbachev to return to the capital.

As Schmemann noted, "It was evident that the balance of power and the course of the Soviet Union's history had shifted, that the Communists, who had fought a rearguard action against change, had suffered a potentially fatal blow, that Mr. Gorbachev himself was now beholden to the anti-Communist forces that had rescued him, and above all, to Mr. Yeltsin." Gorbachev did not improve his situation by refusing on August 22 to join with Yeltsin in condemning the party. He said he was determined to remain as party leader; but on August 24, he reversed himself and issued a statement quitting as party leader and calling for the seizure of party property.

By August 25, it was evident that the Soviet Union had crumbled and Gorbachev could not put the U.S.S.R. back together. Byelorussia and the Ukraine both announced independence; and one by one, the other republics followed suit. Gorbachev still tried to fashion another union treaty to replace the one which was never signed on August 20. A State Council was set up to act in place of the Supreme Soviet. One of its first actions was to recognize on September 6 the independence of the three Baltic states, and the Russian republic officially accepted the name change of the city of Leningrad back to St. Petersburg.

The coup de grace to the Soviet Union followed on December 8, when without any prior warning, the heads of the three Slavic states—Russia, Byelorussia, and Ukraine—announced in Minsk that the Soviet Union had ceased to exist and that they had formed a new "Commonwealth of Independent States." Because only three republics signed that statement, it was repeated on December 21 by 11 of the remaining 15 republics—only Georgia, caught up in its own civil conflict, did not sign—which formally issued a new statement proclaiming the end of the Soviet Union and the formation of the Commonwealth of Independent States. But it was clear that the commonwealth was only a handy title to allow some form of united army to remain and for an Olympic team to be formed. There was no central organizing force behind it, and as the former Soviet Union entered into 1992, there were indeed many questions as to how such neighbors as Russia and Ukraine were going to coexist.

The decline and fall of the Soviet Union was a breathtaking story of enormous consequence. Mikhail S. Gorbachev had come to power determined to help save Communism from itself. In the end, it would be his fate to preside over its demise. The manner of its dissolution occurred in a way that no one had predicted. History, it turned out, was still full of surprises, and had in no sense ended. Indeed, for the peoples of the former Soviet Union, it may have just begun.

THE DECLINE AND FALL
OF THE SOVIET EMPIRE

1985

K onstantin U. Chernenko died on **March 10, 1985.**

**Chernenko Is Dead in Moscow at 73; Gorbachev Succeeds Him and
Urges Arms Control and Economic Vigor; Transfer Is Swift**
By Serge Schmemann

MOSCOW, MARCH 11—The Kremlin today announced the death of
Konstantin U. Chernenko and, within hours, named Mikhail S. Gorbachev to succeed him as Soviet leader.

The announcement said Mr. Chernenko died Sunday evening after a
grave illness at the age of 73. He had been in office 13 months, and had
been ill much of the time, leaving a minor imprint on Soviet affairs.

The succession was the quickest in Soviet history, suggesting that it had
been decided well in advance. Whereas the Central Committee had taken
several days to name a successor to Leonid I. Brezhnev and Yuri V.
Andropov, Mr. Gorbachev was confirmed in his new job four hours and
15 minutes after Mr. Chernenko's death was announced.

Mr. Gorbachev became, at 54, the youngest man to take charge of the
Soviet Union since Stalin and the seventh to head the Soviet state.

"I am well aware of the great trust put in me and of the great responsibility connected with this," he said. "I promise you, comrades, to do my
utmost to faithfully serve our party, our people, and the great Leninist
cause."

In his acceptance speech on being named general secretary, he showed
his impatience to start working.

"We are to achieve a decisive turn in transferring the national economy to the tracks of intensive development," he said. "We should, we are bound to attain within the briefest period the most advanced scientific and technical positions, the highest world level in the productivity of social labor."

In world affairs, he said he valued the "successes of détente, achieved in the 1970s." Referring to the Soviet-American arms talks starting Tuesday in Geneva, Mr. Gorbachev said the Soviet Union sought a "real and major reduction in arms stockpiles, and not the development of ever-new weapon systems, be it in space or on earth."

The speech was one sign that the leadership intended to pursue business as usual despite Mr. Chernenko's death. The period of official mourning for Mr. Chernenko, who will be buried Wednesday in Red Square, is shorter than those of his predecessors.

The Geneva talks are to proceed as scheduled, and Prime Minister Nikolai A. Tikhonov and Foreign Minister Andrei A. Gromyko met today with Roland Dumas, the visiting French foreign minister.

The businesslike approach seemed to underscore the Kremlin's confidence in handling the third transition in two and a half years, this time to a new generation of Soviet leaders whose careers have been formed since the Stalin era.

The transfer of power was dramatized by the fact that Mr. Gorbachev was nominated in the Central Committee by Mr. Gromyko, 75, the most influential of the older leaders.

The loss of Mr. Chernenko brought the number of full members in the Politburo down to 10, half of them 70 or older.

His death was announced at 2 P.M. (6 A.M. New York time), although it had been signaled by the curtailment of several high-level Soviet missions abroad and the playing of somber music on radio stations.

A medical report confirmed that Mr. Chernenko suffered from pulmonary emphysema and heart problems, and it revealed that he had also been afflicted by chronic hepatitis, which worsened into cirrhosis of the liver.

The first hint that Mr. Gorbachev had been selected as successor was the announcement of the membership of the funeral commission, with Mr. Gorbachev at its head. In the past the chairman has been the successor.

Mr. Chernenko will lie in state in the Hall of Columns of the House of Unions on Tuesday and Wednesday, and will be buried behind Lenin's Mausoleum.

The television news showed Mr. Chernenko laid out in the Hall of Columns. Politburo members led by Mr. Gorbachev stood a minute before the bier and then expressed condolences to Mr. Chernenko's wife, Anna, and other family members.

Mr. Chernenko was eulogized in terms reserved for senior officials as an "outstanding party and state figure, patriot and internationalist, consistent fighter for the triumph of the ideals of Communism and peace on earth."

The stress in the statements was on forming united ranks behind the Politburo and the party.

But beyond the familiar rites, the emphasis seemed to be on Mr. Gorbachev and the future.

Little known internationally as recently as three years ago and brought to the Politburo with the politically thankless task of overseeing the Soviet Union's problem-ridden agriculture, Mr. Gorbachev reached the forefront of Soviet politics through his association with Mr. Andropov.

Mr. Andropov had come to power determined to shake up the bureaucracy, discipline workers, and jar the laggard economy into action. But as his health ebbed, he turned to Mr. Gorbachev for help.

On Mr. Andropov's death on February 9, 1984, the Old Guard in the Politburo evidently chose to extend its hold on power a bit longer and picked Mr. Chernenko to be general secretary. But Mr. Gorbachev emerged as the second in command of the party and as the heir to Mr. Andropov's unfinished program.

Although the pace of the experiments initiated by Mr. Andropov slowed under Mr. Chernenko, none was abandoned and some were actually extended, testifying both to the strength of Mr. Andropov's legacy and to Mr. Gorbachev's influence.

In his speech today and in the hurry he demonstrated to get moving, Mr. Gorbachev made clear his legacy. While formally paying tribute to Mr. Chernenko's memory, he pointedly listed Mr. Andropov by name as architect of the strategy he would adopt.

He spoke of giving enterprises more independence and of increasing their interest in higher production. Sounding another theme raised by Mr. Andropov, Mr. Gorbachev talked of the need to provide people with more information. In foreign affairs, Mr. Gorbachev stressed the need for improved relations with China and with the West.

At the same time, Mr. Gorbachev took care to assure the military that it would receive "everything necessary" to maintain its defense capacity.

The shape of Mr. Gorbachev's program could become clearer next month, when a regular Central Committee meeting is scheduled. The session is expected to deal with science and technology, and could give the new leader an opportunity to bring new people into the Kremlin hierarchy.

Mr. Gorbachev also has more than eight months to plan for the next party congress, which is to approve a new party program, the next five-year plan—1986 to 1990—and a new Central Committee, giving Mr.

Gorbachev an opportunity to shape the ranks of the party elite to his taste.

The rush to move ahead suggests that Mr. Chernenko will fade into relative historic obscurity. His achievements included a restructuring of education, to channel more students into vocational schools; an expansion of economic experiments; and a land reclamation program.

But Western diplomats believe he will be best remembered for keeping alive the changes initiated by Mr. Andropov, maintaining the campaign against corruption and the drive for labor discipline. In so doing, he may have supplied a smooth transition between the old generation and the new.

In foreign affairs, Mr. Chernenko presided over the return of the Soviet Union to negotiations with the United States after years of chill. The policies were associated more with Mr. Gromyko than with Mr. Chernenko, but, as in his economic policies, he was credited at least with not standing in the way of the revival of talks.

Bush Has Meeting with Gorbachev; Is Hopeful on Ties
By Seth Mydans

MOSCOW, MARCH 13—Vice President Bush met today with the new Soviet leader, Mikhail S. Gorbachev, and came away saying he believed "we can move forward with progress."

The government press agency Tass said that Mr. Gorbachev, in the 85-minute meeting, had affirmed Soviet readiness "to work in practice" to improve relations with the United States.

Mr. Bush said he had delivered a letter from President Reagan that American officials said contained an invitation to a meeting.

The Vice President declined to discuss the content of the letter, but said:

"I believe the President does feel that a meeting will be useful. I think he would be ready as soon as the Soviet leadership is ready."

Mr. Bush declined to comment on Mr. Gorbachev's reaction.

The Soviet press agency said Mr. Gorbachev had noted the importance of relations with the United States and had "reiterated the Soviet Union's readiness to work in practice to improve them, provided the United States side was also ready."

At the same time, Tass said, "it was stressed anew that the U.S.S.R. would never forsake its legitimate security interests or the interests of its allies."

The Vice President called the meeting constructive and nonpolemical and said that it had touched on a wide array of issues. He declined to discuss the substance.

"If there ever was a time when we can move forward with progress in the last few years, I would say this is a good time for that," he said. "Our aspirations for that are high. We are not euphoric. We are realistic."

From the outset, Gorbachev projected a high-profile vitality.

Gorbachev Pushes Corruption Drive
By Serge Schmemann

MOSCOW, MARCH 25—Today it was the Coal Ministry that came under attack in *Pravda,* and the head of the Bratsk city party committee who was dismissed.

On Sunday, an outspoken economist, Abel G. Aganbegyan, said in *Izvestia* that it was time to start training young managers in Western-style business schools instead of relying on workers promoted from factory ranks.

Before that the minister of electric power and the Kirov provincial party chief were dismissed, and *Izvestia,* the government daily, published letters from readers urging less restriction on public information.

Two weeks after coming to power, Mikhail S. Gorbachev seems intent on confirming his advance image as a young man on the move, eager to resume the fight his mentor, Yuri V. Andropov, had begun against corruption, sloth, and inefficiency.

The changes, Western diplomats said, are not revolutionary—ministries were criticized and party secretaries dismissed in the past. At least one Central Committee official, Vadim V. Zagladin, scorned any thought of moving toward a Western-style market economy or pluralism.

"Such a path," he wrote in the foreign affairs magazine *New Times,* "is excluded for us."

But as the layered snow and ice from an unusually harsh winter dwindled under a warming sun, the signs of change seemed unmistakable.

Mr. Gorbachev had given the signal in his first speech to the Central Committee on March 11, calling for a "decisive breakthrough" in production, for "resolute measures" against corruption, and for more public information.

Those themes have become the stuff of editorials and party conferences as the propaganda apparatus has swung into action behind a new leader. Mr. Gorbachev's name is rarely mentioned. The new slogans are being attributed to the Central Committee session that approved Mr. Gorbachev's assumption of office.

The initial changes were the dismissal of Pyotr S. Neporozhny, the 74-year-old minister of electric power, and of Ivan P. Bespalov, the 69-year-old party chief of Kirov Province. Though planning for such moves would have begun before the death of Konstantin U. Chernenko on March 10, they would have been approved, and probably hastened, by Mr. Gorbachev.

The dismissal of Mr. Neporozhny was preceded by an editorial in *Pravda* criticizing the performance of the Electric Power Ministry in rural electrification. Today, *Pravda* signaled that more heads may roll with a critique of the coal industry, whose output has been lagging for several years.

Meanwhile, regional party meetings are being called around the country to discuss the themes of the Central Committee session. Three regional reports appeared in *Pravda* today about meetings in Ufa, Volgograd, and Irkutsk.

In Ufa, according to *Pravda,* "officials who have committed serious misdeeds were being protected." The report identified local officials who had been dismissed or reprimanded. In Volgograd, officials were accused, among other things, of being "more concerned with building homes for themselves" than with public housing.

In Irkutsk, the *Pravda* report listed instances of embezzlement and poor work at Bratsk, the aluminum and wood pulp center based on a large hydroelectric station. *Pravda* said the city's party secretary, A. Yelokhin, Mayor V. Korshunov, and others had been dismissed "for gross abuse of their positions."

A critical report in the daily *Sotsialisticheskaya Industriya* about a party meeting in Yaroslavl noted that "the loss to the state from embezzlement in the past year grew by 42 percent over the previous year."

Other articles have been calling for party discipline. One item in *Izvestia* reported a speech by the minister of justice of the Russian republic, the largest of the Soviet Union's 15 states, admonishing his staff to "strengthen the struggle against malingering, embezzlement, mismanagement, and abuse of official position."

According to Western diplomats, Mr. Gorbachev's coming to office at a time when preparations are under way for a party congress that is to approve a new party program and the five-year plan for 1986–1990 gives him an opportunity to consolidate his power early.

The revived anticorruption drive has been coupled in the press with a renewed debate on ways to "intensify" the economy. The word, which has become a byword of Mr. Gorbachev's campaign, means achieving efficiency through modernization of existing plants instead of building ever more production capacity.

One approach was described by Mr. Aganbegyan, an influential Siberian economist. Writing in *Izvestia,* he noted that most plant managers had received their engineering education some 20 years earlier and had risen through the ranks. Advances in automation and management techniques, he said, require a new type of manager.

His institute, Mr. Aganbegyan said, has organized a three-month seminar that not only includes lectures but also has executives working directly with computers.

"If the capitalists don't skimp on means for training businessmen through active methods," Mr. Aganbegyan said, "why should we think that we can get away with lectures alone?"

In terms of foreign initiatives, Gorbachev set out to leap boldly over the technical details and qualifying clauses that lay at the heart of slow negotiations to raise very big thoughts and very big challenges.

Gorbachev Ready for Reagan Talks; Freezes Missiles
By Seth Mydans

MOSCOW, APRIL 7—Mikhail S. Gorbachev said today that he was prepared to hold a summit meeting with President Reagan and announced a moratorium on the deployment of Soviet medium-range missiles in Europe. He called on the United States to respond with a similar freeze.

In his first major foreign policy statement since taking office a month ago, Mr. Gorbachev said the Soviet Union, "starting with this day," would halt deployment of its SS-20 medium-range missiles, as well as "other reply measures in Europe."

He said the moratorium would hold until November, when Moscow would see whether the United States had responded by stopping deployment of Pershing 2 and cruise missiles in the nations of the North Atlantic Treaty Organization.

In addition, Mr. Gorbachev said that while arms talks are under way in Geneva, the Soviet Union supports a freeze on strategic nuclear weapons and on the research, testing, and development of space weapons.

His remarks were read on nationwide television in the form of answers to questions from the Communist Party newspaper *Pravda*. The interview was to be published in the Monday issue of the newspaper.

The remarks came as House Speaker Thomas P. O'Neill, Jr., Democrat of Massachusetts, arrived in Moscow at the head of a congressional delegation that was expected to meet with Mr. Gorbachev later in the week.

Mr. Gorbachev said he did not believe confrontation was the natural state of relations between Moscow and Washington.

"Confrontation is not an inborn defect of our relations," he said. "It is rather an anomaly. There is no inevitability at all of its continuation. We regard the improvement of Soviet-American relations not only as an extremely necessary but also as a possible matter."

He said that he had corresponded with Mr. Reagan about the possibility of a summit meeting and that "I can say that a positive attitude to such a meeting being held was expressed from both sides."

"Its time and place will be the subject of subsequent arrangement," he said. No mention was made of a possible agenda.

Gorbachev, Receiving O'Neill, Urges U.S. to End "Ice Age"
By Seth Mydans

MOSCOW, APRIL 10—The Soviet leader, Mikhail S. Gorbachev, told a visiting congressional group today that United States–Soviet relations had been suffering an ice age, and he urged Washington to show the political will to overcome it.

In remarks reported by the Tass press agency, he told Thomas P. O'Neill, Jr., the Speaker of the House of Representatives, that the Soviet Union favored détente and that "our nations can gain much from the development of broad and fruitful cooperation."

Later, at a news conference, Mr. O'Neill said he and three other House members had met with Mr. Gorbachev in the Kremlin for three and three-quarter hours, more than twice the planned time, and had been impressed by his toughness, knowledge, and persuasiveness.

The Speaker, who is a Massachusetts Democrat, said the Americans had delivered a letter from President Reagan, though he declined to disclose the contents.

Representative Robert Michel of Illinois, who is the House minority leader, said at the news conference that Mr. Gorbachev had been "most interested" in receiving the letter, but was still awaiting a "full response" to a letter he had sent to Mr. Reagan.

Mr. O'Neill said the talk with Mr. Gorbachev had covered arms control, trade, cultural exchanges, and human rights, but he declined to go into detail.

The Speaker said he was impressed with the Soviet leader's ability, talents, frankness, and openness.

"He appeared to be the type of man who would be an excellent trial lawyer, an outstanding attorney in New York had he lived there," Mr. O'Neill said. "There is no question that he is a master of words and a master in the art of politics and diplomacy. Was he hard? Was he tough? Yes, he is hard; he is tough."

When asked whether he believed that Mr. Gorbachev was taking "propaganda positions," the Speaker said: "I like to believe that the General-Secretary was speaking his mind and his heart and his feeling for world peace, and I don't want to look at it as merely propaganda."

The Soviet press agency, in summarizing Mr. Gorbachev's remarks, quoted him as having said: "The world situation is disquieting, even dangerous, and a kind of ice age is being observed in relations between the U.S.S.R. and the United States; at least it has been until recently."

A genuine improvement in relations "requires political will on the part of the leaders of the two countries," Mr. Gorbachev said.

"From the Soviet side, such a will exists," he added. "If it is displayed by the American side as well, then many concrete questions separating our countries gradually will begin to find their solution."

The Soviet leader said he was disturbed at the prompt rejection of his overture Sunday for a freeze on deployment of medium-range missiles in Europe. Mr. Gorbachev had announced a moratorium until November on deployment of SS-20 missiles and called on the United States to halt deployment of its medium-range missiles in Europe.

The White House promptly rejected the idea on the ground that such a freeze would preserve Soviet superiority in these weapons.

"The administration displayed absolutely incomprehensible haste and promptly declared its negative attitude, describing our actions as propaganda," Mr. Gorbachev said. "How can one, under these conditions, not feel doubt about the sincerity of United States' intentions at the Geneva talks?"

The two sides have been meeting in Geneva in an attempt to limit or cut back medium-range weapons, strategic, or long-range, weapons, and space weapons.

Mr. Gorbachev repeated his position that the détente of the 1970s showed mutually beneficial cooperation was possible.

From the outset there were critics who contended that Gorbachev's innovations were only matters of style and would soon come to nothing. As months went on, this sort of criticism subsided while the Gorbachev style spread, inspiring long-inert sectors of Soviet society to believe that reform might be possible.

First 100 Days of Gorbachev: A New Start
By Serge Schmemann

MOSCOW, JUNE 16—Mikhail S. Gorbachev may have had little or nothing to do with the recent release of the film *Agoniya*.

Yet it was symptomatic that people were quick to credit the new leader with being responsible for bringing out the film, which is about the last days of the Romanov dynasty. It had lain on the censor's shelf for more than a decade—because, in the view of many here, the Soviet authorities were not willing to have Czar Nicholas II portrayed as a bewildered human being overwhelmed by history.

In the past, Muscovites would have said that the film had been released despite the leader. Now they seemed anxious to treat the event as added evidence that a new day had dawned in the Kremlin.

It was a reaction that spoke of the depth of excitement and hope that Mr. Gorbachev seems to have tapped across the land in his first 100 days in office. After years of viewing their doddering chiefs with disdain and embarrassment, ordinary people were once again discussing their leader's doings and appearances, and even some cynical intellectuals cocked a hopeful eye to the young man in the Kremlin.

In Moscow, Roy A. Medvedev, the historian and dissident, reported that Mr. Gorbachev had met with "goodwill and hope in almost all circles of Soviet society."

In Soviet Central Asia, Nur T. Tabarov, the young editor of the paper *Soviet Tadzhikistan,* spoke with elation of a new style of leadership, "profoundly unconstrained and bold."

What had captivated the popular imagination above all was the novelty of an energetic, bright, and youthful presence in an office filled so long by frail, aged men. One new joke asked, Who supports Gorbachev in the Politburo? Answer: Nobody has to. He can move around on his own.

He may be moving on his own, but he is not moving alone. Since he was officially named leader of the Soviet Communist Party on March 11, Mr. Gorbachev has gathered his own team around him and has declared his program with extraordinary speed. He brought three allies to full Politburo membership in April, he launched a major campaign against drunkenness, and he demanded an urgent modernization of the economy.

In a major economic speech last week, Mr. Gorbachev flashed some sharp teeth through his normally affable smile. He sent the draft of a major national development program back for rewriting because it fell short of his ambitious standards, and he sent tremors throughout the bureaucracy by heaping scorn on four government officials for failing to get in step with his fast new pace.

After striking a mild tone initially toward the United States, he toughened up considerably. In a speech on April 23, he charged that the first round of the Geneva talks "already gives ground to say that Washington does not seek agreement with the Soviet Union." At that time he accused the United States of imperialist policies across the globe.

"Certain circles in the U.S.A. still want to attain a dominant position in the world, especially militarily," he said. "We have told the American side more than once that such ambitious plans are hopeless."

In the long run, the success of Mr. Gorbachev's domestic initiatives is likely to hinge on whether he proves to be capable of meeting the high goals he set for the economy. Some Western diplomats believe that achievement of his goals would require a far deeper restructuring of the heart of the Soviet system, the centralized economic planning organs.

For now, however, the honeymoon was on and the new style was the talk of the town.

Mr. Gorbachev's readiness to go into the streets and to speak off the cuff in public, his modesty and relative candor, his bright and attractive family, all seemed to come as revelations to a public accustomed to dreary ritual and pomp.

Popular legends, some apocryphal and some not, spread about the new leader—that he had ordered his driver to keep to the speed limit instead of screaming down the center lane as some of his predecessors did, that he had banned vodka from the Kremlin buffet, that he had told newspaper editors to stop the personal adulation.

His wife, Raisa, and their daughter, Irina, and granddaughter, Oksana, have emerged as something of an American-style first family, appearing at parades, party meetings, and official receptions. The Gorbachevs were spotted at a new production of *Uncle Vanya* at the Moscow Art Theater, sitting in the stalls like ordinary theatergoers rather than in the balcony, and at the opera in Leningrad.

It is said that on arrival in Leningrad in May, Mr. Gorbachev refused the proffered flowers, saying, "I'm here on business, not as a guest."

That trip to Leningrad seemed especially to catch the public fancy. The nationwide evening news program on May 17 showed something Russians had not seen since Nikita S. Khrushchev: there was their leader, mingling and bantering with a jostling crowd in the street.

"I'm listening to you," Mr. Gorbachev told the people. "What do you want to say?"

Someone shouted back, "Continue as you began!"

A little later a woman's voice broke in: "Just get close to the people and we'll not let you down."

Mr. Gorbachev, hemmed in tightly, came back with a smile, "Can I be any closer?" The crowd loved it.

Even more striking for many was a speech Mr. Gorbachev made to Leningrad Communists that night at the Smolny Institute. The speech was not shown on television until four days later, reportedly because Mr. Gorbachev himself helped edit it.

The theme was Mr. Gorbachev's familiar call for intensified work, rejuvenated managerial ranks, and an end to waste and sloth. But the style was entirely new: for more than an hour Mr. Gorbachev spoke largely off the cuff, referring only occasionally to a television prompter and regaling the party organization with statistics, humor, praise, and threats.

"Those who do not intend to adjust and who are an obstacle to solving these new tasks must simply get out of the way," he said. Then he repeated with emphasis: "Get out of the way. Don't be a hindrance."

That quotation harked back to something Andrei A. Gromyko, the longtime foreign minister, reportedly said when he nominated Mr. Gorbachev to be general secretary of the Soviet Communist Party the day after Konstantin U. Chernenko died.

"Comrades," Mr. Gromyko reportedly said, "this man has a nice smile, but he's got iron teeth."

It was a trait Mr. Gorbachev has demonstrated by assembling his team faster than any of his recent predecessors were able to do. He thrust two allied party secretaries directly to full membership in the Politburo. One of them, Yegor K. Ligachev, said to be a humorless and tough party stalwart, has taken charge of personnel and ideology, effectively becoming the second in command in the Politburo.

The other, Nikolai I. Ryzhkov, has apparently been charged with formulating an economic revival strategy. A third ally, Viktor M. Chebrikov, the chairman of the K.G.B., was promoted from candidate to full membership in the Politburo.

Mr. Gorbachev has also shaken up the bureaucratic ranks farther down. Most recently, he sent into retirement one of the late Leonid I. Brezhnev's political buddies, Ivan I. Bodyul, a deputy prime minister.

In moving quickly to consolidate power, Mr. Gorbachev clearly benefited from his position as the political heir to Yuri V. Andropov, who in his brief 15 months in office initiated many of the economic and organizational changes that Mr. Gorbachev champions. It was notable that all three men brought to full Politburo membership by Mr. Gorbachev had been raised to political prominence by Mr. Andropov.

But Mr. Gorbachev, at age 54, stood poised to consolidate a degree of power few of his forerunners even came close to at so early a stage of their administrations. The natural demise of the Old Guard and Mr. Gorbachev's control over the Politburo are expected to help assure him of a thoroughly rejuvenated and loyal Central Committee and Council of Ministers by the time of the twenty-seventh Soviet Communist Party congress, scheduled for February.

If there has been a central theme to all of Mr. Gorbachev's work in his first three months, it has been his urgent demand for a thoroughgoing change in the way the Soviet economy is run. In speech after speech, he has hammered away at the necessity of yanking the country from its

15-year doldrums and raising the economy to Western levels of efficiency and quality.

Sprinkling his speeches with terms like "revolutionary" and "historic" and notions like altering the "very psychology of economic activity," Mr. Gorbachev has linked his leadership inextricably with the idea of a radical change in the way Russians work.

The Soviet leader has called for a minimal growth rate of 4 percent a year without reducing the military budget or social welfare programs. To achieve this, he has outlined measures for an immediate kick to the economy like the antidrinking laws, coupled in the longer term with a major shift of investment into reequipment of existing plants and machine building.

Mr. Gorbachev has also proposed giving individual enterprises greater autonomy to determine their budgets, and to tie pay to quality production. At the same time, he has proposed that the central planning agencies and the ministries should spend less time supervising details of production and concentrate on long-term planning and technical innovation.

The program is ambitious. But many of its details remained vague, and Western diplomats said the plan was still short of a real overhaul of the central planning mechanism, one that would give plants the autonomy to decide what they produce and what they charge for it.

"He's setting loose a lot of dynamics and aspirations," one diplomat said. "But I wonder if he can sustain the fever pitch. A few years down the road the pace will start to drop, and then he'll either have to go far deeper—or to start lying."

Western diplomats believe that Mr. Gorbachev's preoccupation with domestic affairs has restricted his participation in foreign affairs so far.

From his first days in office, Gorbachev set out to synchronize his domestic and international agendas. Breakthroughs abroad stimulated innovations at home, and these in turn brought him credit for further ventures in foreign policy.

Soviet to Stop Atomic Tests; It Bids U.S. Do Same
By Seth Mydans

MOSCOW, JULY 29—The Soviet Union announced today that it was suspending the testing of nuclear weapons, beginning August 6, the fortieth anniversary of the bombing of Hiroshima.

In making the announcement, the Soviet leader, Mikhail S. Gorbachev, said the moratorium would last until the end of the year. He said it could be extended if the United States also halted testing.

He said a suspension of the moratorium was being announced to "set a good example" for the United States and for other nations possessing nuclear weapons.

The Soviet Union had proposed such a ban in the past and had mentioned the Hiroshima anniversary as an appropriate date.

The announcement appeared timed to coincide with the opening of a ceremony in Helsinki, Finland, marking the tenth anniversary of the Helsinki accords on East-West cooperation in Europe.

Mr. Gorbachev's announcement, carried by the government press agency Tass, said: "It is our conviction that ending all tests of nuclear weapons would become a major contribution to consolidating strategic stability and peace on earth."

The announcement followed an invitation by the United States for the Soviet Union to send a team of experts to monitor an underground nuclear explosion in Nevada.

The Tass press agency, in reporting the American invitation, said it was intended to divert attention from what it called the United States' reluctance "to reach agreement on the question of limiting and banning nuclear weapon tests."

"By again inviting the Soviet Union to exchange 'observers' at nuclear weapon tests," it said, "the American administration suggests actually only to register nuclear blasts and thus to legalize them."

The Soviet Union has been reluctant to invite observers to its secret underground tests, which are conducted in desert proving grounds west of Semipalatinsk, in Kazakhstan.

Underground tests are the only ones conducted by the United States and the Soviet Union under the 1963 treaty on a limited nuclear test ban, which prohibited testing in the atmosphere, in outer space, and under water.

Mr. Gorbachev, alluding to the proposed American program of space-based defense weapons, said: "It is no secret that new, ever more perilous kinds and types of weapons of mass annihilation are developed and perfected in the course of such tests."

The Soviet Union has been mounting a campaign to try to halt the American space-based program, called officially the Strategic Defense Initiative and known popularly as "Star Wars."

Mr. Gorbachev's statement said: "In the interests of creating favorable conditions for concluding an international treaty on a comprehensive ban on nuclear weapons tests, the U.S.S.R. has repeatedly proposed that the nuclear states agree on a moratorium on nuclear explosions, starting from a mutually agreed date. Regrettably, it has not been possible to make this important step."

Therefore, he said, the Soviet Union is making the gesture on its own, "starting from this date, which is observed worldwide as the day of the Hiroshima tragedy."

"Striving to facilitate the termination of the dangerous competition in building up nuclear arsenals and wishing to set a good example," Mr. Gorbachev said, "the Soviet Union has decided to stop unilaterally any nuclear explosions starting from August 6 this year."

Shultz Rejects Test Ban

HELSINKI, FINLAND, JULY 29—Secretary of State George P. Shultz today rejected the Soviet idea of a ban on nuclear tests, saying that such a ban would be difficult to verify and adding that the Russians had violated similar agreements in the past.

Arriving for a conference marking the tenth anniversary of the Helsinki accord on East-West cooperation in Europe, Mr. Shultz said: "To have a moratorium that does not have in it the proper means of verifiability would not be in our interests at this time."

The Gorbachev style was continuing to develop, laying stress on spontaneity, sophistication, and candor.

Gorbachev Meets the Press: A Bantering Style and an Echo of Khrushchev
By Serge Schmemann

MOSCOW, OCT. 4—The spectacle of Mikhail S. Gorbachev tangling with the press in the ruthless forum of a Western-style news conference marked a Soviet leadership finally arrived in the television age.

Not since Nikita S. Khrushchev harangued and bantered with Western reporters 25 years ago had a top Soviet leader submitted himself directly to the massed world press, and never had one handled himself with such self-confidence.

Today's news conference, which was broadcast in its entirety in Moscow, showed an animated Mr. Gorbachev preaching, cajoling, joking, thundering, and stonewalling in a manner than had long been thought the preserve of the West.

Mr. Khrushchev also confronted reporters in Paris, on May 18, 1960, soon after the U-2 incident. *The New York Times* reported at the time that he did so with "a rolling barrage of threats, menaces, and insults," brandishing his fist, heaping vitriol on President Dwight D. Eisenhower, and stunning those present with his crude force and fury.

There were echoes of that at times in Mr. Gorbachev's performance, especially when he brusquely rejected questions on Soviet violations of human rights, when he assailed American policies on disarmament of the Middle East, when he declared what he thought of Prime Minister Margaret Thatcher's expulsion of Soviet officials from Britain, or when, bringing his hand down sharply on the table, he angrily shouted, "If necessary the Soviet Union will put anyone at all in his place." Mr. Gorbachev even lapsed at times into a Ukrainian-influenced accent, with the particular *g* sound that had marked Mr. Khrushchev's speech.

The assertive, well-tailored Soviet leader facing the cameras 25 years later was a far cry from the rumpled, volcanic Mr. Khrushchev, whose swaggering, bullying, and fiery diatribes through two and a half hours at the Palais de Chaillot provoked catcalls from the reporters. But Mr. Gorbachev's swift reaction to a challenge, his indignation at what he felt were slights to Soviet dignity, and his combative stance kindled the memory of many a Moscow old-timer.

The more dramatic contrast, however, was between Mr. Gorbachev and the leaders who followed Mr. Khrushchev. In the two decades that separated them, the world grew accustomed to impassive, often barely mobile men like Leonid I. Brezhnev or Konstantin U. Chernenko, who seemed to be incapable of making the simplest announcement without a script, of taking a single step without guidance.

Their appearance at a news conference was simply unthinkable, and of the senior leadership only the man who was long foreign minister, Andrei A. Gromyko, occasionally took on Western reporters.

On coming to power six months ago, Mr. Gorbachev quickly demonstrated a knack for public relations, making frequently televised forays into the provinces to press the flesh and preach his economic gospel. In Paris he confirmed that he could do it on Western television as well.

The echoes were of Mr. Khrushchev's day, but the impact of Mr. Gorbachev's performance seemed closer to that of the Kennedy-Nixon debates of 1960, when America woke up to the power of television in shaping public opinion.

In effect, Mr. Gorbachev seemed to be giving notice to the West that its dominance of the airwaves in the East-West contest were at an end.

In its eagerness to bridge the gap between theory and practice, the new leadership was prepared to modify the ideological blueprints of the past.

Moscow Offers More Modest Plan for Achieving True Communism
By Serge Schmemann

MOSCOW, OCT. 25—In a major departure from its traditional goals, the Soviet Communist Party today published a new draft program that abandons predictions of quickly overtaking the West or of soon achieving a true Communist society.

The central pledge of the last program, adopted under Nikita S. Khrushchev in 1961, that "the present generation of Soviet people shall live in Communism" has been dropped. Instead, the new draft asserts that attempts to move too fast in introducing Communism, "without due account taken of the level of material and spiritual maturity of society, are, as experience shows, doomed to failure."

And where Khrushchev's program exuded certainty about the imminent demise of capitalism, pledging to leave the United States "far behind" in industrial output and labor productivity by 1980, the new draft states that capitalism, although still doomed, "is constantly maneuvering to adjust itself to the changing situation."

In addition to abandoning much of the bombast of the last program, Mikhail S. Gorbachev has elevated his own economic goals and ambitions to the level of party policy. While dismissing the projections in the earlier document as "groundless fantasies," Mr. Gorbachev made it a formal party goal to double production potential by the end of the century and to increase labor productivity by as much as 150 percent within 15 years.

The new draft program was approved last week by the Central Committee and is to be debated across the country until adopted, probably largely intact, by a party congress in February. Once adopted, it will become the main theoretical document on the goals and strategies of the party.

Only three programs have been used by the party. The first, adopted by the Bolshevik party in 1903, called for the overthrow of the czarist regime and a dictatorship of the proletariat. The second, adopted after the Revolution, in 1919, set out the plans for installing socialism. The program adopted in 1961 was intended to guide the final transition to full Communism.

The current draft is formally only a revision of the third program. But in introducing it, Mr. Gorbachev made it clear that one of his primary goals was to replace the ideological hyperbole of the earlier document with a more practical program.

The drafters of the new version, Mr. Gorbachev said, "rethought those formulations that had not stood the test of time." He said the new program was "a clear and precise presentation of what the party is striving for."

The new document maintains the basic definition of Communism, and much of the prose is still in the grandiloquent and self-congratulatory tradition of Communist Party manifestoes. "The party," one passage declares, "has become the living symbol of scientific socialism with the workers' movement, of unbreakable harmony of theory and practice."

Yet in its sections about the prospects of the Communist system it is considerably briefer, more pessimistic, and less categorical than the earlier document.

Where the 1961 document boldly proclaimed that "a Communist society will in the main be built" in the Soviet Union by 1980, the new draft says that "the advance of humanity toward socialism and Communism, though uneven, complex, and controversial, is inexorable."

While the Khrushchev document set a specific timetable for introducing Communism—down to promises that "the entire population will be able adequately to satisfy its need in high-quality and varied foodstuffs" and that life expectancy will be increased, neither of which has occurred—the new draft says the party "does not set itself the aim of foreseeing in detail the features of full Communism."

In addition, while the earlier program painted an unblemished and uniformly triumphant Communist Party record, Mr. Gorbachev's draft implicitly criticizes virtually all his predecessors except Lenin.

The draft program pledges to "remove the consequences of the personality cult, the deviations from the Leninist norms of party and state guidance"—the official euphemisms for the Stalinist terror—"and to rectify errors of a subjectivist, voluntaristic nature." The last phrase is an allusion to the faults attributed to Khrushchev.

The draft also says that "the party takes into account the fact that in the 1970s and the early '80s there were certain unfavorable trends and difficulties." This was the era of Leonid I. Brezhnev, the party leader for 18 years before his death in 1982.

The new document also reflects a change in the assessment of capitalism's demise. In 1961, enjoying rapid economic growth and still basking in postwar optimism, the Kremlin asserted that "the world capitalist system as a whole is ripe for the social revolution of the proletariat."

The program introduced today takes a much gloomier view of the prospects for the collapse of capitalism, and it takes considerable pains to put into ideological perspective why the inevitable has not happened.

The world of capitalism, the draft asserts, "is yet strong and dangerous, but has already passed its peak."

"In conditions of world socialism's growing influence," it says, "the class struggle of working people at times compels the capitalists to make partial concessions, to grant certain improvements in conditions of labor and its remuneration, and social security. This is being done to preserve the main thing—the domination of capital."

As President Reagan and Gorbachev were preparing to meet at a disarmament summit in Geneva, expectations were fluctuating wildly. Moscow was insisting that there could be no deep reductions in offensive strategic forces until the United States abandoned all efforts to develop "space strike weapons." Washington, meanwhile, wanted immediate deep cuts in offensive weapons.

The Russians Make Their Entrance; Gorbachev, in Geneva, Asks for End to the Arms Race
By Serge Schmemann

GENEVA, NOV. 18—Mikhail S. Gorbachev arrived here today and said that the "first and foremost" issue facing his meetings with President Reagan starting Tuesday was how to halt the arms race "and its extension to new spheres."

The allusion was evidently to the United States' space-based missile defense program, which has been a target of Soviet diplomacy.

Swiss sharpshooters scanned surrounding buildings and a Soviet émigré shouted protests as Mr. Gorbachev stepped out of his Aeroflot airliner at Cointrin Airport, holding the arm of his wife, Raisa. A stiff, cold wind blew across the runway and swirled the skirts of Mrs. Gorbachev's ankle-length, fox-trimmed gray coat.

In a statement, Mr. Gorbachev said the Soviet and American people expected "positive results" from the summit meeting.

"I can assure you that on our part we shall seek precisely such an outcome of this important meeting," he said.

His sentiments for arms control were relayed to Mr. Reagan by reporters as the Soviet leader made a ceremonial visit to the Swiss President, Kurt Furgler.

"We must both have the same intention," Mr. Reagan said. "If he feels as strongly that way as I do, we will end the arms race."

When Mr. Reagan was told that Mr. Gorbachev also wanted an end to "Star Wars," as the American missile-defense program is popularly known, the President replied: "I think when it is explained to him, he will find that it can help us end the arms race."

Mr. Reagan added that the Soviet leader should stop "calling it 'Star Wars' and call it what it is—a defensive shield, instead of an offensive weapon."

Reagan and Gorbachev Optimistic after Meeting; Russian Appears Upbeat

By Serge Schmemann

GENEVA, NOV. 21—Mikhail S. Gorbachev conceded today that he had failed to budge President Reagan from his commitment to space-based missile defenses, but the Soviet leader said their meeting had left him optimistic.

Mr. Gorbachev appeared upbeat and animated as he delivered an hour-long opening statement and then answered questions for 45 minutes at a news conference at the Soviet Mission after appearing with Mr. Reagan in a concluding ceremony.

It is "unfortunate," Mr. Gorbachev said, that no agreement had been reached on arms control, a development for which he laid the blame on the American side. But he called the meeting "the beginning of a dialogue aimed at improving the situation and changing it for the better."

After the news conference, Mr. Gorbachev flew to Prague to brief the other Warsaw Pact leaders on the summit meeting. He spent the night in the Czechoslovak capital.

In the news conference, which was shown on Soviet television, Mr. Gorbachev focused on what he said had been the absence of movement on arms control, and specifically on the United States' missile-defense program, known officially as the Strategic Defense Initiative and popularly called "Star Wars."

Before the summit meeting, Mr. Gorbachev had insisted that movement on arms control and a halt to the American missile defense program be the foremost goal.

Today, while maintaining that arms control had been the "pivotal" question at every session of the summit meeting, he sought to explain the absence of progress and to report at least qualified success for the summit meeting as the start of a process toward improved relations.

"We see that the Americans did not like the logic that we presented," Mr. Gorbachev said about the space-based defense issue. "But we did not see any logic in their position."

Although he avoided personal criticism of Mr. Reagan, Mr. Gorbachev struck a didactic and frustrated note on the missile-defense issue.

"We felt that the idea was something that had taken hold of the President as a person," Mr. Gorbachev said. "But as a politician responsible for such an important country, such a powerful country, and for its security, I could not understand his actions."

More broadly, Mr. Gorbachev placed the fault for the absence of progress on arms control entirely on the Americans.

"Of course, it would have been much better if, in Geneva, we could have reached an agreement on the key problem of stopping the arms race," he said. "Unfortunately this did not happen. It turned out the U.S. side was not yet prepared to make major decisions."

In their joint statement, Mr. Gorbachev and Mr. Reagan "agreed to accelerate the work" of the Geneva arms negotiators, who are seeking accords on strategic nuclear weapons, medium-range nuclear weapons, and space weapons. The statement did not mention Soviet insistence that progress on nuclear missiles be linked to progress on space weapons, although Mr. Gorbachev reiterated the point at his news conference.

In the balance of his presentation, Mr. Gorbachev sought to paint a positive and favorable image of the meeting.

"I would assess the meeting as something that creates possibilities for moving ahead," he said. "This makes it possible for me on leaving Geneva to look to the future with optimism."

Mr. Gorbachev spoke with satisfaction of the decisions to exchange visits with Mr. Reagan, to "expand the political dialogue" and to hold more frequent consultations. He said the Soviet Union was looking to doing more business with American companies if relations improved.

Describing his exchanges with Mr. Reagan in their many hours of private meetings, Mr. Gorbachev said, "Those meetings were frank, sharp, sometimes very sharp."

"Still, it seemed to me, they were productive," the Soviet leader said. "We found and believe that we did have something in common, a starting point for improved relations. And that is the understanding that nuclear war is inadmissible, that it should not be reached, that there is no winner in nuclear war."

Mr. Gorbachev's assessment seemed to betray a desire to put the best possible face on his most important foray into international affairs since taking office eight months ago. It seemed to reflect, too, a political need to give a sense of positive movement in foreign affairs as the Soviet Union prepares for the Communist Party congress opening in late February.

Several times, Mr. Gorbachev began by saying, "I said to the President . . ." or "I tried to tell the President candidly . . ." Mr. Gorbachev said the two men had agreed at the outset sessions to avoid the "banalities" that had marked the presummit maneuvering.

Mr. Gorbachev became animated when he told how he tried to explain to Mr. Reagan that it was wrong to think that imposing an arms race on the Soviet Union would squeeze it economically.

"I said to the President, bear in mind that we are not simpletons," he said. "If the President was committed to that idea, then my task as Soviet leader was to disabuse him of it."

Mr. Gorbachev was equally heated in arguing against the notion that America's advanced technology would give it an edge in shifting to space weapons. The program the Soviet Union would mount in response, he said, "will be effective, though less expensive, and quicker to produce."

Some experts expect to counter the United States' space-based defense program against ballistic missiles by deploying more missiles.

Mr. Gorbachev seemed to disclose a previously unknown Soviet position regarding verification. If the United States were to halt its space-based defense program, he said, the Soviet Union would open its laboratories to inspection, and "this would include international verification."

The United States has often talked about verification as one of the major obstacles to arms agreements with the Soviet Union.

1986

Reagan Exchanges Greetings on TV with Gorbachev
By Bernard Gwertzman

WASHINGTON, JAN. 1—In an unusual television exchange, President Reagan and Mikhail S. Gorbachev extended New Year's greetings today to the Soviet and American peoples. They expressed the hope that the two nations could narrow their differences in 1986.

The substance of the five-minute statements, with voice-over translations, was less significant than the exchange itself.

It was the first time that American and Soviet leaders had directly addressed each other's nation since President Richard M. Nixon visited the Soviet Union in 1972 and Leonid I. Brezhnev the United States in 1973.

The Reagan administration had been urging such televised exchanges, and the Soviet Union agreed on December 20.

Mr. Gorbachev's remarks, in which he wished every American family "good health, peace, and happiness," were carried by ABC, NBC, CBS, and the Cable News Network at 1 P.M. Eastern standard time. Mr. Reagan's statement, in which he said, "Let's work together to make it a year of peace," was carried simultaneously by the Soviet evening television news in Moscow, where it was 9 P.M.

The focal point of Soviet foreign policy remained disarmament. Indeed it seemed that Gorbachev was mounting a virtual peace offensive with offers of disarmament that were themselves disarming to many in the West.

Gorbachev Offers to Scrap A-Arms Within 15 Years

By Serge Schmemann

MOSCOW, JAN. 15 — Mikhail S. Gorbachev proposed a broad timetable today for the elimination of all nuclear arms by the end of the century and announced a three-month extension of the Soviet moratorium on nuclear tests.

But the Soviet leader declared that his disarmament process could start only if the United States joined in renouncing the testing and deployment of what he called "space strike weapons." That is the Soviet reference to President Reagan's research program on space-based defenses.

Mr. Reagan has repeatedly insisted that the space defense program, popularly known as "Star Wars," is not negotiable, and the dispute has blocked substantive movement at the Geneva arms talks. In Washington, Mr. Reagan said he welcomed the Soviet proposal and would study it carefully.

Mr. Gorbachev described his proposal as the most important of several foreign policy decisions made by the Politburo at the start of 1986.

The proposal, read by an announcer on television and published by the press agency Tass, was issued on the eve of the resumption of the Geneva negotiations, and Western diplomats said they saw it in large part as an attempt to seize the public relations initiative in the talks.

The nuclear plan proposed by Mr. Gorbachev consisted of three broad stages that would culminate in 2000 with a "universal accord that such weapons should never again come into being." It called for the Soviet Union and the United States to start the process this year and for other nuclear powers to join later.

The proposal broadly covered all aspects of disarmament and was based mostly on existing Soviet positions. Diplomats said it differed from previous Soviet calls for total nuclear disarmament largely in fixing stages and deadlines for the process.

In his proposals for the elimination of medium-range missiles in Europe, however, Mr. Gorbachev made what Western experts thought could be a significant departure.

Outlining the first stage of his program, Mr. Gorbachev called for the "complete elimination of intermediate-range missiles of the U.S.S.R. and the U.S.A. in the European zone, both ballistic and cruise missiles, as a first step toward ridding the European continent of nuclear weapons."

At the same time, he said, Britain and France would pledge not to enlarge their nuclear arsenals.

The stance appeared to resemble the offer President Reagan made, and the Soviet negotiators rejected, at the Geneva talks on medium-range arms, which collapsed in November 1983 when the Russians walked out. Mr. Reagan proposed in 1981 that the United States would abandon plans to deploy new medium-range missiles in Europe if the Russians dismantled their SS-20 medium-range missiles, a proposal that came to be known as the zero option. Moscow, however, insisted that it should maintain enough SS-20s to counter the 162 nuclear missiles in the British and French arsenals. The talks faltered, the Americans began deploying new missiles, and the Russians walked out.

For all the talk of greater openness and greater freedom, there had been no wholesale guarantees for human rights. Dissidents like Andrei Sakharov were still kept in internal exile while many thousands of less well known figures remained imprisoned because of what they had said, written, thought, or believed. But then one well-known prisoner was released, raising the prospect that others might soon follow.

Mother Sobs with Relief at the News
By Serge Schmemann

MOSCOW, FEB. 11—"Tolya is free, God almighty, Tolya is free!" Anatoly B. Shcharansky's mother exclaimed today, her wrinkled face beaming, wet with tears.

For nine years, the woman, Ida P. Milgrom, had addressed appeals to the authorities at all levels of the Soviet state. A small, slight woman, now 77 years old, she had stood in the cold outside the prison of Chistopol, in the Tatar republic, demanding to see the warden; she had traveled thousands of miles for rare meetings with her son; she had suffered through months with no word from him.

She refused suggestions that she emigrate. She believed she had to remain as long as Anatoly was in prison. Assisted by her older son, Leonid, she struggled to find out what she could of her son's plight, to demand meetings and letters, to complain of his treatment and to appeal for his release. She and Leonid worked, at the same time, to keep the world informed of Anatoly's condition.

More than once over the last nine years there had been rumors that Anatoly Shcharansky was to be released, but Miss Milgrom, who uses her maiden name, always resisted letting her hopes rise too high. Today, too, waiting for news with her other son at the apartment of a friend, she tried to stay calm as she and Leonid awaited word on the exchange.

Leonid took the call from a Western reporter and shouted over to his mother, seated on a couch. Now, after nine years of self-control, the woman threw her head back on the low couch and surrendered to violent, soul-wrenching sobs of joy. Someone handed her a cup of tea, but she spilled it, and it was several minutes before she regained her composure.

Every now and again, as she and Leonid, their arms linked, talked with reporters or took telephone calls from well-wishers, the joy and the sobs would overwhelm her.

"Can you believe it?" she said. "Can you believe it? Tolya is free. Tolya is at liberty. He is breathing; he is free. Is it possible? For so many years the placards read 'Free Shcharansky,' and now Shcharansky is free. Can it be possible?"

Miss Milgrom tried to sort out her own feelings, to explain what she had gone through.

"You know, I always believed he would be set free, but I was afraid I would not live to see it," she said. "It was frightening. I fought with all my power. Until I heard that he was on the bridge I did not believe it. I was afraid to believe; I was afraid that something would happen to block it, a provocation of some sort.

"I would like to thank everyone, President Reagan, Mikhail Sergeyevich Gorbachev, all the people who helped."

Later in the evening, Leonid Shcharansky said that his mother had sent identical telegrams to President Reagan and to Mr. Gorbachev, saying, ACCEPT MY SINCERE THANKS FOR THE GOODWILL AND EFFORTS IN FREEING MY SON ANATOLY SHCHARANSKY.

How did Miss Milgrom explain the decision to release Anatoly?

"I think there has been a liberalization," she said, adding, in apparent allusion to Mr. Gorbachev, "There was a man who realized it was necessary."

Then she said: "I do hope this is a sign of liberalization. I don't want to be the only happy one."

Soon most reporters left, and Miss Milgrom stayed on the couch, talking with friends. To a Western reporter who had often met with her over the years, she seemed to be emerging from under a great sustained effort at self-discipline, from under an all-consuming mission that had dominated every moment of the last nine years of her life.

"For nine years I have never gone to bed without thinking how is Tolya. I never sat down to eat without thinking how is Tolya. His father could not take it; he died on Tolya's birthday, January 20, in 1980. But I survived.

"He was thirty-eight last January 20. When he was arrested, he was twenty-nine. The most creative years of his life he has spent in the most terrible conditions—in prison, in a punishment cell, in an isolation cell, on hunger strikes. It is impossible to believe what this man has survived, what pressures they put on him to betray his friends, to say he is guilty.

"Now I feel calm. He is going home; he is with his wife. Now my only concern is that he regain his health."

Just before Gorbachev was to complete his first year as leader, he presided over the twenty-seventh congress of the Communist Party.

Gorbachev on the Soviet Economy: A Flock of Innovative Ideas
By Serge Schmemann

MOSCOW, FEB. 26—In his marathon keynote speech to the Communist Party congress on Tuesday, Mikhail S. Gorbachev went to great lengths to generate a sense of urgency and excitement over his economic program.

His delivery of the five-and-a-half-hour address in the Palace of Congresses grew more animated when he passed from an exposition of current official ideology to the subject that has dominated his first year in office.

Like a preacher trying to fire a somnolent congregation, Mr. Gorbachev pressed his case before the 5,000 delegates and the nationwide television audience with a blend of fiery rhetoric, tantalizing hints of bold new policies, exhortations, and reprimands.

Ears perked in the hall as he ticked off the buzzwords of the advocates of economic change—market forces, financial incentives, local autonomy, and even a bit of private enterprise.

He said that the present rigid system of government-fixed prices must be made more flexible, that industrial ministries should stop their "petty tutelage" over factories, and that payrolls should be linked to actual sales.

Among the more novel proposals was his call for reviving a "food tax" as a way of easing controls on the marketing of farm produce.

Such a tax was a feature of the New Economic Policy, the period in the 1920s when Lenin gave private enterprise some leeway to revitalize the economy from the ravages of World War I, the Bolshevik Revolution of 1917, and the Civil War. The NEP, as it was known, replaced a period of harsh controls known as War Communism.

In agriculture, the issue was government marketing of the produce grown on what were then still-small private farms. Forcible requisitions under War Communism had alienated the peasants and induced them to shift to subsistence farming, depriving the government of food for the cities.

The food tax, introduced in 1921, was intended to regain the loyalty of the peasants by replacing the requisitions of all surplus produce with a tax. The resulting legalization of market relationships stimulated a recovery of farm output and livestock holdings.

Strict controls were again restored in Stalin's collectivization of agriculture starting in late 1929. The system of compulsory deliveries has since been modified, but Soviet farms are still being assigned procurement quotas.

With the proposed reintroduction of the food tax, as Mr. Gorbachev explained it, collective farms and state farms would be allowed to dispose of their produce as they saw fit after payment of the tax, in effect easing central controls over marketing.

Many of the concepts and phrases used by Mr. Gorbachev in his speech were familiar from the arguments made by Abel G. Aganbegyan, Tatyana I. Zaslavskaya, and other economists concerned with improving the system.

Mr. Gorbachev seemed to be taking their side and to be alluding to past opposition when he said: "Unfortunately, there was a widespread view that any change in the economic mechanism should be regarded as being practically a retreat from the principles of socialism."

Mr. Gorbachev's speech drew different reactions. His supporters were enthusiastic, and an Italian Communist said that if he succeeded in putting his precepts into action, the economy would undergo major change. Diplomats said they found little that augured the sort of basic change that Western economists believe are the key to any real modernization.

The debate reflected a basic difference over what would constitute "revolutionary change." Those less skeptical over Mr. Gorbachev's program said policies that would not be dramatic in the West—letting farmers sell their surplus produce on a freer market, or giving factory managers a say in organizing their production—were heady by Soviet standards.

A suggestion as basic as putting a few routine services in private hands—where they are anyway, albeit illegally—required assurances from Mr. Gorbachev that "socialist economic principles" were not being violated.

Mr. Gorbachev was often vague, and it was probably too soon to expect him to have a detailed blueprint. Diplomats said he might have found it expedient to keep the details of his program vague for now, while signaling his endorsement of the more liberal economic thinkers.

Mr. Gorbachev's specific intentions for the economy were not the only questions raised by his speech.

He opened with an exposition of a Marxist view of the world today, replete with virtuous socialists and devious imperialists. From a leader who had shown little inclination for such exercises in the past, diplomats found it somewhat jarring to hear talk of American "monopolistic totalitarianism" exposing the world to "avalanches of stupefying misinformation."

The likely explanation, diplomats said, is that he felt compelled, before dealing with the problems of the Communist system, to make clear that the capitalist system was worse.

Mr. Gorbachev also left unclear his intentions for the arts. His advocacy of openness in the press had raised hopes among artists and writers that there might be greater leeway for culture.

However, Mr. Gorbachev gave only a brief and ambivalent definition of the tasks of the arts. He said there was no need for "showy verbosity on paper, petty washing of dirty linen, time-serving, and utilitarianism."

"What people demand from the writer is artistic innovation and the truth of life, which has always been the essence of real art," he said. But the question was who would be empowered to decide what was "real art"?

The avoidance of old shibboleths or the breaking of old and not so old taboos, while not quite an everyday occurrence, was no longer limited only to the very brave, the very well protected, or the unbalanced. Still, one speech during the congress was considered widely to have been breathtaking in its candid condemnation of what had been normal behavior within the party. It was delivered by a large white-haired man named Boris Yeltsin, who was chosen to head the party organization in Moscow.

Taking Off the Rose-Colored Glasses in Moscow
By Serge Schmemann

MOSCOW—One of the most talked-about events at the Communist Party congress last week was the speech by Boris N. Yeltsin, the new Moscow party chief.

Mr. Yeltsin spoke for a relatively short time during the period set aside for discussion of the five-and-a-half-hour state-of-the-Soviet Union blockbuster by the Soviet leader, Mikhail S. Gorbachev. But *Pravda* reported that he was interrupted 13 times for applause, and people queued for newspapers carrying the text.

Part of the interest was in Mr. Yeltsin's unusually blunt attacks on the party leadership, an elite once held above public criticism. Why is it, he asked, that "from congress to congress we raise the very same problems"? Why were some beyond criticism? Why was the Central Committee silent about gross corruption in Uzbekistan? Why were top party officials held out as "some sort of miracle workers"?

But the comment that caused the most commotion concerned himself. "Delegates might ask me," he said, " 'why did you not say all this when you addressed the twenty-sixth Party congress?' My answer, my candid answer, is that at that time I apparently lacked the courage and the political experience."

In 1981, at the twenty-sixth congress, Mr. Yeltsin sang the praises of the Central Committee and hailed Leonid I. Brezhnev five times. So had everybody. But it was only Mr. Yeltsin, a rugged engineer, who acknowledged it in public last week. Geidar A. Aliyev, a Politburo member who probably set a record in his 1981 speech by naming Mr. Brezhnev 13 times, dismissed this record Thursday, explaining "He was general secretary; there was nothing unusual about this."

The difference in the attitudes of the two Politburo members underscored one of the main, if subtle, themes of the congress and of the Gorbachev era: the function and limits of official self-criticism and public candor.

Since coming to power less than a year ago, Mr. Gorbachev has called for more openness and candor than is usual. In the weeks before the congress, the press demonstrated an unusual boldness.

But it was Mr. Yeltsin who blamed the Central Committee directly for the problems Mr. Gorbachev had outlined. And Mr. Yeltsin alone touched on the perquisites of the party apparatus, a subject that had become more sensitive since *Pravda* raised it in a series of readers' letters.

"I feel uneasy listening to the indignation at any manifestation of unfairness, current or old," he said. "But it really hurts when people talk openly of special perquisites for leading officials. . . . So it's my opinion that wherever there are unjustified perquisites for officials of any level, they should be eliminated."

Mr. Aliyev defended the special services for the party apparat at his news conference, acknowledging the existence of special shops, clinics, and restaurants for party workers and arguing that most trade unions, professional unions, or large enterprises also had special food outlets, sanatoriums, and clinics, that "one could not say that only the party workers have special facilities or enjoy special rights."

Throughout much of the spring, the Soviet Union and the United States feinted and parried over when and whether to hold a summit meeting. On April 12, Moscow renounced its unilateral ban on nuclear testing, saying continuing American tests threatened its security. On April 16, after U.S. jets attacked Libya, the Soviets canceled a meeting between Eduard A. Shevardnadze and Secretary of State George Shultz, but then five days later Gorbachev said in Bonn that there could still be a summit if the Reagan administration were to alter policies that the Soviets contended were poisoning the international atmosphere.

Then, scarcely a week before the May Day celebrations, the Soviet Union was rocked by a less metaphoric contamination when a nuclear reactor at Chernobyl in the Ukraine went out of control, spewing clouds of radioac-

tive debris over a large area. The event was to become the deadliest nuclear episode of peacetime, eventually leading to the evacuation of entire towns, destruction of farmland, and persistent and abnormal patterns of sickness and death. The political fallout was equally severe, as the government in Moscow, now allegedly committed to greater openness, responded to the disaster by first saying nothing and then very little. The first alarm was sounded by scientists in Sweden who noted the increase in radioactivity.

Nuclear Disaster: How Could It Happen? Soviet Keeps Lid on News Coverage
By Philip Taubman

MOSCOW, APRIL 29—The Soviet government, never forthcoming about domestic disasters, has kept tight control on information about the accident at a nuclear station in the Ukraine.

More than 36 hours after a still-unclear sequence of events that produced the accident at the Chernobyl plant, spreading radioactive debris as far as Scandinavia, government information has consisted of two statements totaling less than 250 words.

While reporting that there had been an accident that left a reactor damaged and two people dead, and forced the evacuation of four population centers, the statements have not explained what happened or how extensive the danger of contamination may be.

News coverage has been limited to the two official statements, which did not mention the spread of radioactive material to Scandinavia.

Izvestia, the government daily, was the only paper Tuesday that printed the government's first, 42-word announcement that there had been an accident. Other papers did not pick up the statement, which was distributed Monday by Tass, the government press agency.

Today, Tass continued to note that there had been many nuclear accidents in the United States and elsewhere.

Two previous Soviet nuclear accidents, for example, though reported in the West, have not been acknowledged by the Soviet Union. They were a chemical reaction in nuclear waste near Kasli, in the Urals, in 1957, and a steam-pipe leak at the Shevchenko breeder plant of Kazakhstan in 1974.

Although Mikhail S. Gorbachev has called for greater openness in Soviet society, stressing the need to be more candid with the public, news about earthquakes, plane crashes, and other disasters has remained minimal.

Nuclear Disaster: What Press Is Saying; "Anti-Soviet Hysteria," Russian Terms Reports

By Felicity Barringer

MOSCOW, MAY 2—A high Soviet official today accused Western journalists of exaggerating the Chernobyl nuclear disaster "to whip up anti-Soviet hysteria."

At the same time, the official press agency, Tass, made public a letter from Mikhail S. Gorbachev to six world leaders criticizing continued American nuclear testing.

Mr. Gorbachev's letter said that the Soviet government reserved the right to resume nuclear tests but that it was "in no hurry" to do so.

The events seemed to indicate a Soviet desire to go on the offensive after five days of harsh worldwide criticism for the Kremlin's refusal to provide detailed information about the disaster at the Chernobyl reactor, about 70 miles from Kiev, which spread a cloud of radioactive debris over much of Europe. After four days of terse official statements on the Chernobyl matter, the Soviet government today offered no new information.

In a speech in West Germany today, Boris N. Yeltsin, a candidate member of the Politburo and the Moscow Communist Party chief, said: "Our ideological opponents do not miss a single opportunity to launch yet one more campaign against the U.S.S.R. The bourgeois propaganda media are concocting many hoaxes around the accident at the Chernobyl atomic power plant."

Citing a West German newspaper report of thousands of deaths from the nuclear reactor accident in the Ukraine, Mr. Yeltsin said, "The purpose of all this is to step up even more the anti-Soviet hysteria in the hope of driving a wedge in the Soviet Union's relations with other countries."

The Russia Syndrome; A Reticent Response to Nuclear Calamity

By Serge Schmemann

MOSCOW—It may be months or years before the world learns exactly what happened at the Soviet Union's Chernobyl nuclear power station and why radiation was spewed over much of Europe. But one thing that emerged with striking clarity in the days after the incident was first reported was the profound difference between the surfeit of speculation, questioning, and information that flooded the West, and the few bare facts divulged in the East.

By week's end, a resident of Kansas City, half a world away, probably knew more about the incident and its potential effects than a resident of Kiev, 70 miles from the damaged plant.

Across the West, ominous talk of meltdowns and gamma rays revived anxieties about nuclear energy. Newspapers and television were filled with reports, sometimes exaggerated. Western tourists, students, and workers were advised by their governments to leave Kiev and were tested for radiation on departure.

In Poland, children were issued iodine pills. In Sweden, milk was tested. In Chicago, wheat futures soared, and nuclear physicists everywhere were sought out by reporters.

In the Soviet Union, by contrast, it took some doing to learn that anything was happening at all. Most reports from Kiev described a city happily preparing for a four-day May Day weekend, unperturbed by the nearby accident that was alarming the West. In Moscow there was even less concern, and those who knew the Western version of events still seemed unworried.

Reporter's Notebook: Bit by Bit, Soviet Gets News
By Serge Schmemann

MOSCOW, MAY 13— "This is the agony of our fatherland. And it will take time for this wound to heal. Chernobyl . . ." These dramatic opening words from Pravda's account today, under the headline THE BATTLE CONTINUES, were a far cry from the brief paragraph in *Izvestia* on April 29 reporting an "accident" at Unit 4 of the Chernobyl nuclear power station.

Two weeks later, the first bits of information have grown into what for the Soviet Union is an unusual torrent of news. The "accident" has turned to "agony," the "damaged reactor" to a narrowly averted "catastrophe."

Early films of Kievans basking in the sun have given way to tales of heroism by workers and helicopter pilots, accounts of the evacuation of 92,000 people, descriptions of exotic measures being contemplated to entomb the damaged reactor, aerial views of the power plant, warnings of health hazards, and the early closing of Kiev schools.

Reports from the Chernobyl area by a special television correspondent, Aleksandr N. Krutov, have become a keenly awaited daily feature on the evening news show. Teams of reporters from national dailies also provide daily reports from the scene.

There are still questions about what exactly happened, why the official reaction was so slow, and how much radioactivity has been emitted.

But steadily, the import of Chernobyl has been driven home to the public. If in the early days, people seemed assured by the bland communiqués, the hushed talk now is whether to buy butter, whether to go south for the summer.

The information has not come hard and fast in the style of the West. The salient facts have often fallen almost casually from epics of valor in a battle against calamity.

Pravda's disclosure of an explosion and fire in the reactor, for example, was threaded through an account of firemen battling 100-foot-high flames while their boots sank in molten tar.

The revelation that 1,100 buses were marshaled for the evacuation was coupled with the assertion that no Kiev driver refused to volunteer, and the fact that 92,000 people were evacuated was couched in an account of the care taken of the refugees.

The measures to contain the damage have been described in terms of a frontline struggle, peopled with fearless helicopter pilots, untiring technicians, selfless scientists. Newspapers have carried accounts of workers from across the country offering assistance.

The fact that a catastrophe had been averted was revealed only when the danger was past.

To some, the slowness in divulging information seemed to contradict Mikhail S. Gorbachev's calls for more candor. Yet his own speeches suggest that what he meant was using facts and information to explain and promote his goals, and in this the coverage of the Chernobyl disaster was following his precepts.

But where was Mr. Gorbachev himself? In the two weeks since the disaster, he has appeared on television to preside over May Day festivities and to greet the visiting Angolan leader. Yet he has avoided any public comment on the Chernobyl disaster. The answer is expected Wednesday, when he will address the nation on television.

Mr. Gorbachev's information policy may have been one reason behind the increased flow of information. Another, it seemed, was the flow of news through Russian-language broadcasts from the West.

Gorbachev, on TV, Defends Handling of Atom Disaster
By Serge Schmemann

MOSCOW, MAY 14—Mikhail S. Gorbachev publicly discussed the Chernobyl disaster for the first time today, telling the Soviet people that the accident had shown the "sinister force" of nuclear energy gone out of control.

Breaking an 18-day silence on the accident, Mr. Gorbachev also accused the West of using the disaster for an "unrestrained anti-Soviet campaign."

In a 25-minute television speech, he defended the handling of the accident, rejecting charges that Moscow had not provided adequate information.

But he also offered a four-point program to hasten exchange of information in accidents like Chernobyl, suggesting at least indirectly that Western criticism had been justified.

Mr. Gorbachev called for a strengthening of the International Atomic Energy Agency, a United Nations body based in Vienna, and for a world conference to discuss an early-warning system on nuclear accidents.

He said he was extending a halt in nuclear tests until August 6, the anniversary of the 1945 bombing of Hiroshima. He renewed his offer to meet President Reagan to discuss a test ban, mentioning Hiroshima as a possible site. The Soviet Union halted its testing last August 6, but the United States has refused to join in or to hold a special summit meeting on the issue.

In Washington, officials affirmed opposition to a test ban and to a special Gorbachev-Reagan meeting. They said the Russians were seeking to divert attention from Chernobyl and were extending the test ban offer for public relations purposes in full knowledge that it would be rejected again. "They seem to have decided that the best defense is a good offense," one official said.

Speaking in somber and sometimes halting cadences, Mr. Gorbachev touched on the themes that have been stressed in Soviet news coverage— the heroism of people, the purported malice of the West, and the need to draw lessons, notably for arms control.

He seemed to affirm that the Soviet Union intended to continue with its ambitious nuclear power program.

"The future of the world economy can hardly be imagined without the development of atomic power," he said, noting that there were more than 370 reactors operating around the world. They include 40 Soviet reactors totaling 28,000 megawatts of capacity.

The "indisputable lesson" of the Chernobyl accident, he said, is the need for science and technology giving priority to "reliability and safety, discipline, order, and organization."

The Soviet leader disclosed that the death toll from the Chernobyl accident had risen to nine—two killed in the original explosion and seven who died later of exposure to radiation. He said that "as of today" 299 people had been hospitalized with radiation disease, 95 more than reported last week.

In defending the handling of information about the disaster, Mr. Gorbachev said it had been reported in the Soviet Union and abroad "as soon as we received reliable initial information."

The first report on the accident, which occurred in the small hours of April 26, was issued on the evening of April 28. The report was issued after Scandinavian countries had detected heightened background radiation, and Sweden had sought an explanation for nuclear fission products apparently emanating from the Soviet Union.

Mr. Gorbachev said it was too early to pass "final judgment" on the causes of the accident, but he supplied some new information on what had occurred.

"As specialists report," he said, "the reactor's power output suddenly surged during a scheduled shutdown of Unit 4. A considerable emission of steam and subsequent reaction resulted in the formation of hydrogen, its explosion, damage to the reactor, and the associated radioactive release."

Mr. Gorbachev made no effort to conceal the scope or gravity of the disaster. He spoke of it as an extraordinary and dangerous misfortune that "painfully affected the Soviet people and caused anxiety among the international public."

"For the first time, we encountered in reality such a sinister force as nuclear energy gone out of control," he said.

He described a national effort, headed in Moscow by Prime Minister Nikolai I. Ryzhkov and at the scene by a government commission, working round the clock to deal with the consequences of the disaster.

"Thanks to the effective measures taken, it is possible now to say that the worst has passed," he said, adding that the level of radiation around the power plant remained at a dangerous level.

He expressed gratitude to foreign countries that had shown "solidarity" with the Soviet people, and he specifically thanked two American doctors who have been working with radiation victims, Robert P. Gale and Paul I. Terasaki.

Mr. Gorbachev's tone changed when he turned to "the way the event at Chernobyl was met by the governments, political figures, and the mass media in certain NATO countries, especially the U.S.A."

"They launched an unrestrained anti-Soviet campaign," he said. "It is difficult to imagine what was said and written those days: 'Thousands of Casualties,' 'Mass Graves of the Dead,' 'Desolate Kiev,' 'the entire land of the Ukraine has been poisoned,' and so on and so forth."

Trying to put the politics of Chernobyl behind him, Gorbachev returned to the question of arms control and the need for a superpower summit. In July at a dinner for France's President François Mitterrand he appealed for Europe to evolve its own views on disarmament independent of Washington. In calling for greater Western European self-reliance, Mr. Gorbachev held out the prospect of a Europe "from the Atlantic to the Urals" ridding itself "of the explosive burden of armaments." He seemed to be trying either to drive a wedge between Washington and its NATO partners or by holding out such a possibility to lure the United States into talks on his terms and with his agenda. As the Soviets toughened their stance on the summit, they seemed to be putting other bargaining chips into play. In Afghanistan, where the Soviets had 120,000 troops, it was announced that Babrak Karmal, the man Moscow had installed in power seven years earlier, would be stepping down. That was followed by Moscow's announced willingness to withdraw six regiments from the force that had not been able to subdue Afghanistan's Muslim fighters.

On August 11, American and Soviet senior arms control officials met in Moscow to plan for a meeting in September between Secretary of State George P. Shultz and Foreign Minister Eduard A. Shevardnadze, which in turn would pave the way for a summit meeting later in the year. Then on August 30, an American correspondent in Moscow was arrested by the K.G.B. as a spy. Minutes before his seizure he had been handed a packet by a man who told him it contained news clippings. Soviet authorities claimed the package held classified documents.

Reagan Writes to Gorbachev About Reporter
By Bernard Gwertzman

WASHINGTON, SEPT. 6—President Reagan has sent a message to Mikhail S. Gorbachev, urging the immediate release of an American reporter held in Moscow on suspicion of espionage, administration officials said today.

Mr. Reagan, in his first direct involvement in the case of Nicholas S. Daniloff, correspondent of the magazine *U.S. News & World Report,* said in the message that he could give personal assurances Mr. Daniloff was not a spy, the officials said.

The President also told Mr. Gorbachev, according to the officials, that Soviet-American relations were too important to be affected by this case.

The message was reported to have been delivered Friday. It was part of a stepped-up American effort that included a public declaration by Secretary of State George P. Shultz on Friday to press for the release of Mr. Daniloff, who was arrested August 30.

The K.G.B., the Soviet intelligence and internal security agency, has accused Mr. Daniloff of espionage and Moscow has rejected American demands for his release. White House and State Department officials said today that if Mr. Daniloff was not freed by Monday, they would begin taking decisions on retaliatory measures. Officials of *U.S. News & World Report* said today that they were grateful to Mr. Reagan for his letter, which they said committed his personal authority to the "cause and innocence" of Mr. Daniloff. "The Soviets are now on the clearest possible notice that Nick is not a spy," said the statement issued on behalf of Mortimer B. Zuckerman, chairman and editor-in-chief, and David Gergen, editor, who is a former high Reagan administration official. . . .

A senior official said the K.G.B. seemed to hope that Mr. Daniloff could be traded for Gennadi F. Zakharov, a Soviet spy suspect held in New York.

Mr. Daniloff told his wife by telephone from prison today that interrogators had made "fuzzy" remarks about a possible exchange, but that in the meantime they were acting as if his case would go to trial.

On Friday, Secretary of State Shultz said the United States ruled out a trade and Mr. Daniloff concurred.

The United States contends the two cases are not equivalent. The Americans say that Mr. Daniloff was set up when an envelope handed him by a Soviet acquaintance turned out to contain secret materials, and that Mr. Zakharov was caught as he was paying for secret documents. . . .

Mr. Shultz is scheduled to meet with Foreign Minister Eduard A. Shevardnadze on September 19 and 20 to discuss, in part, the setting of a date for a meeting between President Reagan and Mikhail S. Gorbachev, the Soviet leader.

"If Daniloff is still in prison by September 19 it is going to be very hard for there to be a very constructive meeting because Daniloff will have to head the agenda," a State Department official said.

Daniloff Out of Jail: Drawn but Jubilant
By Philip Taubman

MOSCOW, SEPT. 12—Moments after his release from Lefortovo Prison this evening, Nicholas S. Daniloff clambered out of a United States embassy car and danced for a moment in the street.

Looking drawn but jubilant, with a stubby growth of beard on his cheeks and chin, Mr. Daniloff held his arms aloft and cheered as Western correspondents pressed around him, shouting and cheering.

Russians, drawn to the scene by the television lights and a phalanx of militiamen who blocked traffic, looked on curiously at the celebration taking place around the Cadillac limousine.

Asked how he felt after spending 14 days in prison on espionage charges, Mr. Daniloff shouted over the uproar, "Terrific, terrific, terrific, terrific!"

Then, turning more somber, he said, "I am not a free man today."

Mr. Daniloff, a correspondent of *U.S. News & World Report,* said that under the conditions of his release he could not leave Moscow while his case remained under investigation.

"I am still obliged to be in touch with the investigator," he said.

As Mr. Daniloff spoke, his wife, Ruth, who served as his spokesman during the 14-day confinement, leaned against the car, smiling at the scene while photographing it.

Under terms worked out by American and Soviet officials in recent days, Mr. Daniloff was released into the custody of the deputy chief of mission of the United States Embassy, Richard E. Combs, Jr., the ranking American diplomat in the absence of Ambassador Arthur A. Hartman.

At the same time, a Soviet physicist held in New York on espionage charges, Gennadi F. Zakharov, was remanded by a federal judge into the custody of the Soviet ambassador in Washington, Yuri V. Dubinin. Mr. Zakharov must remain in the United States pending trial.

As the Daniloff affair played itself out, the spotlight of international attention had focused on the Soviet foreign minister, who like his boss was proving to be a different kind of Soviet official.

Shevardnadze Adds Warmth to Diplomacy
By David K. Shipler

WASHINGTON, SEPT. 20—The man who has been negotiating for the Russians in Washington in the last two days is a novice to foreign affairs and, although a Politburo member, is far from being a top policymaker.

But the official, Eduard A. Shevardnadze, who succeeded Andrei A. Gromyko as foreign minister in the summer of 1985, has also brought a looser style, an easy smile, and a bantering mood to a tense situation between the two superpowers.

Officials and journalists who watched Mr. Gromyko during some of his 28 years as foreign minister credit him with being a fine actor, able to shift from thundering anger to sarcastic ridicule to jovial warmth. But given the trials in Soviet-American relations, it is hard to imagine Mr. Gromyko's allowing even the slightest smile to crack his veneer of austerity on a visit to Washington.

Mr. Shevardnadze, 58 years old, has seemed less calculated, more informal, and more relaxed. He grinned at reporters waiting outside the State Department on Friday as he emerged after a day of meetings with Secretary of State George P. Shultz.

And when he was asked what the Soviet leader, Mikhail S. Gorbachev, had put in a letter to President Reagan, Mr. Shevardnadze smiled warmly and declared, "Oooh, I can't say." He seems to be one of those rare public figures who can refuse so nicely to answer a single question that reporters have trouble feeling annoyed.

But behind the theatrics stands a man with a record of tough, pragmatic social and economic control in his home republic of Soviet Georgia, where he ran the police as minister of internal affairs and then, from 1972 to 1985, served as the Georgian Communist Party secretary.

Georgia, south of the Caucasus Mountains, has its own language, literature, church, culture, and national pride. In its towns and villages a maverick, hot-blooded mood boils up, more reminiscent of the Mediterranean than of the stolid streets of Moscow, from which the Russians exert an uneasy rule over the fiercely independent Georgians.

Georgians have long struggled against Russification, trying to preserve the integrity of their language and culture. In the late 1970s, when new republic constitutions were drafted, thousands of Georgians demonstrated outside the Central Committee offices in Tbilisi, the Georgian capital, to protest the dropping of an article that named Georgian as the republic's official language.

Moscow gave in on the symbol—presumably on Mr. Shevardnadze's recommendation—and reinstated the provision. But the organizers of the demonstration were also quietly arrested and are still in prison, according to Anatoly B. Shcharansky, the recently released Jewish dissident, who said he had met them in a labor camp.

Thus Mr. Shevardnadze showed his ability to compromise and crack down simultaneously, a skill he used with mixed results in his principal assignment as party leader: the suppression of the Georgian penchant for private enterprise, an illegal phenomenon by Soviet statute.

Mr. Shevardnadze did what he could to uproot the small businesses that flourished in Georgia—the entrepreneurs who grew flowers on state land and took them to sell in Moscow, the shoemakers who embezzled state-owned leather and sold their products on the black market, the underground factories that turned out clothing from material that had been pilfered from state supplies.

One result was a spate of arson and bombings in the late 1970s. Although the authorities tried to keep news of the violence quiet, some incidents took place in such public places that word spread rapidly. In one case, bombs at an aircraft factory killed at least one guard. The perpetrators were believed to be either highly organized entrepreneurs who were feeling the pinch of Mr. Shevardnadze's campaign or Georgian nationalists who resented what they saw as growing Russification.

The implications of this background for Mr. Shevardnadze's performance as foreign minister seem fairly clear. He is seen as friendly and tough, conciliatory and stubborn, more loyal to the Soviet national interest than to his own ethnic identity.

This proven loyalty to his superiors in the Communist Party, combined with his relative inexperience in foreign affairs, suggests to American experts on Soviet affairs that in using him as foreign minister, Mr. Gorbachev is seeking to place his own imprint on foreign policy and, perhaps, to diminish the role of the older guard in the Kremlin hierarchy.

American officials who saw Mr. Shevardnadze a year ago, when he made his first trip to Washington, are said to feel that he seems more comfortable with the issues now. But he probably has little, if any, decision-making power and is essentially a messenger in a time of adversity.

Reagan and Gorbachev Agree to Meet Next Week in Iceland; Zakharov, Freed by U.S., Leaves; Soviet to Let 2 Go
By Gerald M. Boyd

WASHINGTON, SEPT. 30—The United States and the Soviet Union announced today that President Reagan and Mikhail S. Gorbachev will meet in Iceland next week.

The announcement came after Gennadi F. Zakharov, a Soviet employee of the United Nations, pleaded no contest to a spying charge in a Brooklyn court and was released. The Soviet Union also agreed to let two dissidents emigrate—Yuri F. Orlov, who has been in Siberian exile, and his wife and fellow dissident, Irina L. Valitova, who lives in Moscow.

The White House referred to the prospective two-day meeting, October 11 and 12 in Reykjavík, Iceland, as preliminary to a regular summit meeting in the United States that was agreed on in Geneva last November. The new summit meeting was supposed to be held this year, but a date has not been set.

The agreement on the Reagan-Gorbachev meeting in Iceland was apparently a key element in the negotiations that led to the release of an American journalist, Nicholas S. Daniloff, and of Mr. Zakharov, both of whom were being held on espionage charges.

As the Americans and Soviets arrived at Reykjavík, it remained unclear as to what subjects would dominate the agenda. The Soviets seemed intent on seeking limits on space weaponry. President Reagan was eager to convince Mr. Gorbachev that any advances in arms control had to be accompanied by Soviet decisions to free emigration, end the repression of dissidents, and pull back even more in its military support for the Afghan regime.

Reagan-Gorbachev Meeting Opens with Plans to Pursue Arms Pact and Rights Issues; Work Units Set Up
By Bernard Weinraub

REYKJAVÍK, ICELAND, OCT. 11—President Reagan and Mikhail S. Gorbachev opened talks here today, and the Soviet leader told Mr. Reagan he would not set a date for a summit meeting in the United States unless prospects for signing a major arms control pact were high, a ranking administration official said tonight.

To meet Mr. Gorbachev's concerns, the United States and the Soviet Union set up two separate working groups, one on arms control and the other on human rights and other issues.

United States officials expressed optimism that the creation of the working groups—and an agreement by Mr. Reagan and Mr. Gorbachev to meet Sunday morning 30 minutes earlier than planned—were hopeful signs in the efforts by both nations to narrow differences and arrange a full summit in the United States later this year or sometime in 1987.

United States officials said the bulk of today's talks between the two leaders focused on arms control, with Mr. Reagan expected to raise human rights and other issues Sunday, the final day of the talks. Officials described the nearly four hours of talks as "businesslike," and said they were marked by friendly exchanges.

Larry Speakes, the White House spokesman, in announcing the working groups, said they would start meeting this evening. "The two leaders thought it was the appropriate way that they should proceed as a result of their discussions held today," Mr. Speakes said.

United States officials said it was too early to make a judgment on progress in the talks, but that the mood was upbeat.

After three days of talks it appeared that the meeting, which had been billed as essentially a preliminary event for a later breakthrough meeting in the United States, was turning into something more substantial. Agreements were being achieved on a variety of issues. But then, just before the finish line, one side or the other, or perhaps both, stumbled.

Gorbachev Talks End in Stalemate as U.S. Rejects Demand to Curb "Star Wars"
By Bernard Gwertzman

REYKJAVÍK, ICELAND, OCT. 12—President Reagan and Mikhail S. Gorbachev ended two days of talks here today with no agreement on arms control and no date for a full-fledged summit meeting in the United States.

While officials said that the two leaders had succeeded in developing tentative understandings on most arms control issues, a possible accord foundered over Soviet insistence that the United States scrap its space-based missile-defense plans.

Secretary of State George P. Shultz said at a news conference, "We are deeply disappointed by this outcome."

It was not immediately clear whether Soviet-American relations would worsen because of the failure to achieve an agreement, or whether the tentative understandings on medium-range and long-range forces and on nuclear testing could be revived even in the absence of an understanding on the missile-defense issue.

The two leaders, after 11 hours of talks and all-night discussions by their experts, displayed frustration and disappointment. Each held the other responsible for the lack of results.

Mr. Reagan, speaking to American forces at the Keflavik Air Base near here before returning home, said, "We came to Iceland to advance the cause of peace and, though we put on the table the most far-reaching arms control proposal in history, the general secretary rejected it."

Mr. Gorbachev, at a news conference, attributed the failure to American intransigence on the plan for a space-based missile defense, known officially as the Strategic Defense Initiative, and popularly as "Star Wars."

The Soviet leader said he had told the President at the end of their meeting: "We missed a historic chance. Never have our positions been so close."

When the Iceland meeting was first arranged, it was expected to set a date for a regular summit meeting in the United States in the coming months, as called for by the two leaders at their first meeting in Geneva last year.

But Secretary of State Shultz said at his news conference after an unscheduled final three-and-a-half-hour session that no date was set.

He said the United States would not pay the price for having Mr. Gorbachev go to the United States if it meant accepting constraints on the missile-defense program.

He said that the tentative package of "extremely important potential agreements," extending into areas other than arms control, failed when Mr. Gorbachev insisted that the 1972 treaty limiting defensive missiles, known as the antiballistic missile treaty, be changed to prevent research, testing, and development of the proposed defenses beyond the laboratory. "As we came more and more down to the final stages," Mr. Shultz said, "it became more and more clear that the Soviet Union's objective was effectively to kill off the Strategic Defense Initiative program, and to do so by seeking a change—described by them as strengthening, but a change in the ABM treaty—that would so constrain research permitted under it that the program would not be able to proceed at all forcefully."

Mr. Gorbachev said, "This has been a failure, and a failure when we were very close to a historic agreement." He said the United States had come to the talks "with empty hands."

President Reagan, in listing the potential understandings, said, "The talks we have just concluded were hard and tough, and yet, I have to say, extremely useful."

Although the emphasis was on arms control, Mr. Shultz said human rights questions had been raised "on a number of occasions and some very significant material was passed to the Soviet Union, which they accepted."

The allusion was to lists of Jews who are set to seek emigration but have been refused visas. Mr. Shultz said that the emigration issue was specifically mentioned in a joint statement that was drafted, but not issued.

Emigration from the Soviet Union in general is heavily restricted, but Jews and some other groups have been permitted to leave in substantial numbers over the last 20 years. The Soviet Union contends that most of those who wanted to leave have done so by now. Jewish groups abroad dispute this. Of all the Soviet-American meetings, this was one of the most unusual. American officials had said that the best they expected was an effort to stimulate the Geneva arms talks and a date for a summit meeting.

In fact, the two sides seemed to rush through every outstanding issue, with the Soviet Union apparently offering a variety of compromises to extract a commitment that would have paralyzed the American missile-defense program.

These potential understandings were reached, but not made final because of the missile-defense issue:

● On medium-range forces, Mr. Gorbachev agreed to a global limit of 100 warheads each, with the Soviet Union deploying its 100 in Asia and the United States its 100 on its own territory, and all Soviet and American medium-range missiles removed from Europe.

● On nuclear testing, the Soviet Union agreed to seek a phased accord, starting with verification of existing treaties and working toward an ultimate reduction of tests.

● On strategic offensive nuclear forces, the two sides agreed to a 50 percent cut in bombers and missile warheads and in the number of missile launchers.

But the talks broke down late in the day, after darkness and cold biting winds swept across Iceland. The issue was how to handle the Soviet demand for continued adherence to the 1972 ABM treaty, which among its provisions bans the deployment of new types of missile defenses.

After consultation with aides, Mr. Reagan proposed a 10-year guaranteed adherence, two and a half years more than he originally suggested. Under the new plan, the two sides would cut their strategic offensive forces by 50 percent over the first five years, with total elimination of all nuclear ballistic missiles after 10 years.

But the Soviet Union insisted on a change in the ABM treaty to ban all but "laboratory" research, testing, and development.

Mr. Gorbachev, according to American officials, asked why there was a need for a missile-defense system if all ballistic missiles were to be eliminated within 10 years.

Mr. Reagan is said to have replied, "For insurance," and made the point that if there were no missiles, the defense program, too, could be curtailed. But this did not satisfy Mr. Gorbachev, the Americans said.

The two days of talks had proceeded as if on a roller coaster. On Saturday, American and Soviet officials were saying that the talks were proceeding well. This morning, Yevgeny P. Velikhov, a vice president of the Soviet Academy of Sciences, said the two sides were close to agreement on a number of issues.

The sense of optimism conveyed by these remarks was seemingly fortified by the longer morning session. Instead of the scheduled two hours, the meeting went on for three and a half hours.

When Mr. Reagan and Mr. Gorbachev came out together, the President said, "We are not through yet." And the two men meet again in the afternoon.

The first indication that the talks were not going to produce a breakthrough occurred when Larry Speakes, the White House spokesman, said that while there had been progress, there were many disagreements. He said the President was "hanging tough."

Mr. Shultz was the first official to address the results of the session, and he seemed eager to strike a middle ground between disappointment at the lack of final result and firmness on the missile-defense issue.

There was uncertainty about exactly what had happened in the final hours. It seemed evident that there was a linkage among the various understandings.

Mr. Shultz said, "Everything that was discussed here was discussed to a degree, you might say, in relation to the other parts."

But Mr. Gorbachev apparently gave no ultimatum that none of the understandings could ultimately be approved unless the missile-defense issue was settled. And Mr. Shultz said the American arms negotiators in Geneva "will be ready to work on these important issues."

Mr. Shultz mentioned four areas in which understandings had been reached on medium-range missiles. They were verification, the issue of short-range tactical missiles, the issue of duration of an accord, and the global ceiling of 100 warheads.

"That is a breathtaking reduction from what now exists," he said. "And those warheads would have been located in the Asian side of the Soviet Union, on the one hand, and in the United States, on the other. So it would have been a very sweeping shift.

"I am not saying that these agreements are not potentially possible, but, as of this moment, they don't have standing other than that we managed to get ourselves to that point."

Gorbachev Terms Reagan Too Timid; U.S. in New Appeal; Russian Is Critical

By Serge Schmemann

MOSCOW, OCT. 14—Mikhail S. Gorbachev said today that President Reagan had proved lacking in courage and political will to take a historic step forward at their Iceland meeting.

But the Soviet leader termed the meeting a "major event" and said he was not shutting the door on the search for arms control.

Mr. Gorbachev offered his assessment in a televised speech, affirming that a Soviet proposal to scale down nuclear arsenals had foundered on Mr. Reagan's adherence to a space-based missile-defense program.

Although Mr. Gorbachev was critical of what he said was Mr. Reagan's dependence on the "military-industrial complex," he said the meeting "was not in vain" and held out hopes for a change of heart in the United States.

"We are realists," he said. "We clearly understand that questions that for many years, even decades, have not found their solution can hardly be resolved at a single sitting.

"We have sufficient experience in doing business with the United States. We know how changeable its political climate is, how strong and influential the opponents of peace are.

"That we are not losing heart and shutting the door—although there are more than enough grounds for that—is only because we are sincerely convinced about the need for fresh efforts in building normal interstate relations in the nuclear age."

Mr. Gorbachev gave a detailed—and at times dramatic—account of the Soviet proposals in Iceland and the bargaining that brought the two sides to the edge of agreement.

"Standing within one or two or three steps of a decision that could become historic for the entire nuclear-technological age, we were unable to take those steps," he said.

"A turn in world history failed to take place, although it was possible. But our conscience is clear. We did all we could. Our partners lacked the breadth of approach, an understanding of the unique character of the moment, and, ultimately, the courage, responsibility, and political determination that are so necessary for resolving vital and complicated world problems. They stuck to their old, time-eroded positions that contradict present-day realities."

The Soviet leader said that, at one point, Mr. Reagan had gone into ideological issues, "showing total ignorance and lack of understanding of what the socialist world is and what is happening in it."

Mr. Gorbachev depicted the missile-defense program known popularly as "Star Wars," as an attempt to impose a new and prohibitively expensive arms race on the Soviet Union.

"The Americans are making two serious mistakes," he said. "One is tactical, that the Soviet Union will eventually come to accept arms limitations because it needs disarmament more than the United States does. This is a profound error, and the sooner they abandon it the better for them, for our relations, for the situation in the world.

"The other error is strategic. The United States wants to hurt us economically through a race in highly expensive space weapons, to undermine Soviet economic and social programs, to foment displeasure among our people with their leadership."

This thinking, he said, is "built on confusion" that can result in nothing positive.

Mr. Gorbachev said that the Soviet proposals in Iceland, "if accepted, would open a new era in human history." The proposals called for a 50 percent cut in strategic arms within five years and the elimination of American and Soviet medium-range missiles from Europe while leaving the French and British national arsenals intact. Mr. Gorbachev said he subsequently offered to eliminate the remaining strategic arms by 1996.

Mr. Gorbachev said Soviet concessions in the package included omitting French and British missiles and American bombers that could reach the Soviet Union, freezing the stocks of short-range missiles, and limiting the number of medium-range Soviet missiles in Asia to 100 warheads while permitting the United States the same strength on its own soil.

The problem arose with the third component of the Soviet offer, which Mr. Gorbachev described as an "integral part" of the package—that the 1972 antiballistic missile treaty be made binding for 10 more years and that this be understood to restrict research and testing on new missile defenses to the laboratory.

The proposal would in effect freeze development and testing of the program, which Mr. Reagan refused to do.

Mr. Gorbachev's argument was that if the two sides embarked on a broad disarmament program, the Russians could not accept the continuation of a program that stood to produce an entirely new type of weapon.

The Soviet Union, which had in different times placed such words as **sputnik** *and* **gulag** *into the global dictionary, was under Gorbachev offering another term.*

Greater "Glasnost" Turns Some Soviet Heads
By Serge Schmemann

MOSCOW—*Glasnost* is one of those Russian words with no direct equivalent in English. It is usually translated as "openness" or "publicity," but both fall short of the broad Russian meaning derived from *glas,* the poetic word for "voice." To embrace *glasnost* is to give voice, to speak out boldly and openly.

Of all the aspects of Mikhail S. Gorbachev's new leadership style, none—with the possible exception of the war on vodka—has had so visible and far-reaching an impact as his call for greater *glasnost* in Soviet life.

"The matter of broadening *glasnost* is a matter of principle for us," the Soviet leader said at the Communist Party congress in February. "And it is a political matter, too. Without *glasnost* there is not, and there cannot be, democratism, the political creativity of the masses and their participation in management."

Conditioned by hard experience to be cautious in taking such calls too literally, Russians reacted slowly at first. The poet Yevgeny Yevtushenko's call for *glasnost* before the Moscow writers' organization in December 1985 was carefully trimmed in the printed version.

Since then, the *glasnost* campaign, prodded regularly by Mr. Gorbachev and his top aides, has steadily gathered momentum, and now new sensations in print, on television, in the theater, or in movies seem to come at dizzying speed.

In recent weeks, literary journals have announced plans to publish long-suppressed works, ranging from those by the Russian-American novelist Vladimir Nabokov to a novel on Stalinist times by Anatoly Rybakov. Special Moscow audiences have been shown *Repentance,* a brilliant film by the Georgian director Tengiz Abuladze on Stalinist terrorism. The Communist Party newspaper in the Moldavian republic sharply criticized the local party chief for padding the books, the first time an official of such stature had been reprimanded publicly.

The statistical yearbook revived the publication of embarrassing figures on grain harvests and child mortality. State television showed an American documentary on Soviet émigrés, including candid talk about why they quit their homeland; and a notoriously strident television correspondent, Vladimir Dunayev, gave an unexpectedly approving report on McDonald's restaurants, suggesting that their cleanliness and efficiency were something the Soviet Union might emulate.

In the field of foreign affairs, Soviet spokesmen seem more visible and aggressive. A platoon of officials followed Mr. Gorbachev to Reykjavík to brief reporters, and in the aftermath of the summit Foreign Ministry officials gave a series of briefings assailing President Reagan's version of events, even taking the unusual step of publicizing statements the President reportedly made to Mr. Gorbachev.

Last week, the Novosti News Agency told American editors that two officials were standing by phones in Moscow to answer questions about Afghanistan. No calls were logged in the first two days, but the officials said they would continue to be available.

According to reliable information, Mr. Gorbachev has done more than give the starting signal for *glasnost*. Members of the Moscow intelligentsia reported that he and some of his top allies—most notably Yegor K. Ligachev, the chief ideologist in the Politburo, and Aleksandr N. Yakovlev, chief of the Central Committee's propaganda department—had personally approved some of the developments, including the publication of Mr. Rybakov's novel and the release of Mr. Abuladze's film.

"Broader *glasnost* is a matter of principle, just as is honest and open criticism of those who deserve it," Mr. Ligachev said in a Revolution Day speech Thursday night. "It is only useful. It contributes to the process of cleansing socialist society of everything that is alien to it."

But if greater openness has become the policy of the new leadership, it is still a policy ordered and defined from on high, channeled through media that remain very much the monopoly of the state.

In a system in which authority flows top to bottom, it is notable that the *glasnost* banner has been carried largely, so far, by major newspapers and cultural institutions with close ties to Mr. Gorbachev's Kremlin. Smaller newspapers often maintain a timid deference before local party authorities. Recently, *Pravda* took the unusual step of reproducing the front page of a Pskov newspaper that had been suppressed by local authorities for criticizing a local exhibition.

In its first months, the campaign demonstrated how creative Soviet society could be, given even a measure of breathing room. People with longer memories compared the times with the eruption of creativity during the "thaw" of Nikita S. Khrushchev's 1960s. Some remembered, too, how abruptly that thaw ended, and how many of the writers who had emerged then ended up in exile or in a labor camp. But the frontiers of the permissible are still expanding day by day, and there are heady feelings in the theaters and living rooms of Moscow.

Another example of glasnost *came when the official media reported an outbreak of ethnic violence, presumably the most serious communal clash in many years.*

Soviet Reports Rioting in City in Central Asia
By Philip Taubman

MOSCOW, DEC. 18—The Soviet Union reported today that there had been an outbreak of anti-Russian rioting in the capital of the Central Asian republic of Kazakhstan.

A report by the official press agency, Tass, said a group of students "incited by nationalistic elements" took to the streets of Alma-Ata Wednesday night and today, burning cars and setting fire to a food store to protest decisions made earlier this week by the republic's Communist Party organization.

On Tuesday the Kazakhstan Party Central Committee ousted its long-time leader, Dinmukhamed Akhmedovich Kunayev, a Kazakh, replacing him with an ethnic Russian, Gennadi V. Kolbin.

The Tass dispatch from Alma-Ata reported that city services were functioning normally, but stopped short of saying that the unrest had been quelled. It did not report any injuries or deaths.

Although the report did not provide a clear picture of the extent of the disturbance or the number of people involved, it said that meetings were organized by the authorities throughout the city to discuss the situation, suggesting serious concern.

Both the rioting and the immediate public report about it, read by an announcer at the end of the prime time evening news broadcast, were viewed as extraordinary developments by Western diplomats.

Ethnic Russians dominate the nation's government and control the central Communist Party machinery. Tensions between the Russians and the Soviet Union's other nationalities, including the Kazakhs, have long smoldered beneath the surface and are considered to be a potential long-term problem for the Soviet Union.

But open rebellion, while periodically rumored, has not been officially confirmed since the 1920s and the period immediately after the formation of the Soviet Union, diplomats said.

The diplomats said they could not recall a previous time when the government publicly reported a civil disturbance. Moscow's traditional reluctance to acknowledge domestic problems has eased somewhat under Mikhail S. Gorbachev, who has repeatedly called for greater openness, *glasnost* in Russian.

Telephone lines from Moscow to Alma-Ata were open this evening, but there was no answer at police headquarters or the offices of *Kazakhstanskaya Pravda,* the republic's main party newspaper. The calls were placed by Western reporters in Moscow after business hours in Alma-Ata, which is three time zones ahead of the Soviet capital.

The Kazakhstan government office in Moscow would not comment on the situation in Alma-Ata.

The republic, with a total population of 16 million, takes its name from the Kazakhs, Turkic-language-speaking Moslems. In the last census, in 1979, the government said Russians represented 40.8 percent of the population, while Kazakhs represented 36 percent. The percentage of Russians is dropping, however; in the 1959 census, Russians represented 42.7 percent of the population and Kazakhs 30 percent.

Local demographers have predicted that because of the higher birthrate among Kazakhs, they will outnumber Russians by 1990. Also, large influxes of non-Kazakhs—such as those in the late nineteenth and early twentieth centuries, in the 1930s in connection with industrialization and collectivization, and in the late 1950s in connection with the virgin lands campaign—have ceased.

Other nationalistic domestic disturbances were widely reported to have taken place in the last 15 years in Georgia and in the Baltic republics, particularly Lithuania and Estonia. Such disturbances were never reported in the press or officially confirmed by the government.

Along with glasnost *came increased attention to the issues of "human rights," particularly as they related to easing emigration and relaxing the repression of dissidents. On December 19, Soviet officials announced that Andrei D. Sakharov, the physicist and human rights campaigner, was free to return to Moscow from Gorky, the city to which he had been banished without trial in 1980.*

Sakharov Says He Plans to Renew Civil Rights Advocacy in Moscow
By Bill Keller

MOSCOW, DEC. 20—Andrei D. Sakharov said today that he planned to continue his advocacy of human rights when he returns to Moscow after nearly seven years of exile.

Reached by telephone in Gorky, the city to which he has been confined since 1980 for his public criticism of Soviet policies, Mr. Sakharov said he had not promised Mikhail S. Gorbachev that he would curtail his activities in exchange for permission to come back to the Soviet capital.

"I am going to live as I lived before my exile, and resume all of my activities," Dr. Sakharov, a 65-year-old physicist, said.

He confirmed that Mr. Gorbachev had telephoned on Tuesday, one day after the authorities had unexpectedly installed a telephone in the physicist's Gorky apartment. The Soviet leader told Dr. Sakharov that he could go back to Moscow and to his work in theoretical physics.

"He told me to return to work for the public good—that is the formula he used," Dr. Sakharov recalled.

Dr. Sakharov's wife, Yelena G. Bonner, who was sentenced to five years of exile in Gorky in 1984 on charges of anti-Soviet activity, will also be permitted to return.

The physicist declined to discuss in detail his conversation with the Soviet leader, calling it "complicated."

When Dr. Sakharov was asked whether he had agreed not to take part in political activities, he said: "Gorbachev never made such demands on me, and I told him the exact opposite."

Dr. Sakharov's continuing fellowship with the dissident community was implicit from the beginning of the interview. Asked at the outset how he was feeling, he said his happiness was tempered by the news of the death of Anatoly T. Marchenko, a dissident who died December 8 in prison.

Soviet officials announced the end of Dr. Sakharov's exile on Friday at a news conference. The announcement was the most dramatic of recent signs that the government was taking a new approach to human rights issues.

The news of his impending return sent a thrill through the dissident community, a group that had been depleted and demoralized by imprisonments, deaths, or deportations. Last May, Dr. Sakharov's stepdaughter said that in a July 1985 letter to Mr. Gorbachev, the physicist volunteered to curtail his activities as a rights campaigner, "apart from the most exceptional cases," if the government ended his exile.

But last February 19, he broke a long silence on human rights issues. In a letter to Mr. Gorbachev, given to Western reporters by dissidents, Dr. Sakharov called for a general amnesty for all those imprisoned or exiled for religious or ideological beliefs.

In the interview today, Dr. Sakharov said he had reminded Mr. Gorbachev of the February letter "about prisoners of conscience" when the two men talked on Tuesday. He declined to report the Soviet leader's reply.

Both Dr. Sakharov and his wife have reportedly been in poor health. The physicist has staged hunger strikes to pressure the authorities to let Miss Bonner travel to the United States for heart surgery.

He said today that his own health was "more or less fine" and that his wife "has gotten no worse," although her heart condition keeps her confined to the apartment in cold weather. In the telephone conversation, his voice was strong and clear, and he answered questions directly and politely.

Dr. Sakharov won the 1975 Nobel Peace Prize for his activism on behalf of human rights. For decades, he has lent his name in support of the civil liberties of religious and ideological dissenters, and has called for changes in Soviet domestic and foreign policies. He has urged Western nations to make improvement of relations with the Soviet Union contingent on internal liberalization.

A theoretical physicist, he was part of the team that developed the Soviet Union's hydrogen bomb in the early 1950s, and reached the pinnacle of scientific prestige.

He was one of the few Soviet citizens who was a three-time winner of the title of Hero of Socialist Labor, awarded for his nuclear weapons research. The awards were canceled when he was exiled to Gorky in 1980. It is not known whether they will be restored.

In 1968 he was removed from secret defense work after circulating an essay titled "Thoughts on Progress, Peaceful Coexistence, and Intellectual Freedom." And on January 22, 1980, after he had denounced the Soviet military intervention in Afghanistan, he was exiled to Gorky, a center of defense industries with a population of 1.4 million that is closed to foreigners.

His contacts with the outside were limited. He had no telephone at home, and had to go to the Gorky post office to receive and make calls.

A friend who spoke with Dr. Sakharov this week said the physicist had been visited by the new president of the Academy of Sciences, Guri I. Marchuk, to discuss his future work in Moscow.

Despite his exile, Dr. Sakharov has remained a member of the academy, which entitles him to a wide array of privileges, such as a summer home, a car, and access to elite stores and services.

"I am going to work at the Physics Institute as I did before," Dr. Sakharov said. "And I will also work on human rights as I did before."

He said that he did not know exactly when he and his wife would make the permanent move back to Moscow, but that they planned to visit in a few days to make arrangements for the relocation.

1987

Soviet Turns a Big Corner; Release of Dissidents More Than a Gesture

By Philip Taubman

MOSCOW, FEB. 11—The Soviet Union has turned a major corner in its handling of human-rights cases with the pardoning of dozens of imprisoned dissidents, Western diplomats and Soviet officials say.

In response to Western demands for freedom of expression and movement, the recent steps have gone beyond token gestures, reducing but not eliminating the human-rights issue as a barrier to East-West relations, the diplomats say.

At the same time, the moves, although still unpublicized in the Soviet Union, have signaled a new tolerance and seem intended to energize Soviet society, particularly intellectuals.

The pardons, like the new freedom in the arts, are considered elements in Mikhail S. Gorbachev's effort to revitalize the public attitudes.

"We cannot hope to succeed," Mr. Gorbachev said last month, "without decisively changing public mentality and remolding popular psychology, thinking, and sentiment."

But that some limits on dissent remain was made clear today as plainclothesmen tangled on a crowded pedestrian mall with 20 protesters demonstrating on behalf of an imprisoned Jewish dissident. The dissident, Iosef Z. Begun, remains in prison because he has reportedly declined to sign a statement requesting a pardon and renouncing illegal activities in the future.

The demonstration, the third this week, was broken up when security agents pushed the protesters onto a side street, tearing down their placards and roughing up Western reporters covering the event.

It has also become clear that Anatoly Koryagin, a dissident psychiatrist who has been offered freedom if he agrees to leave the country, remains incarcerated, also apparently for refusing to sign the required statements.

The Foreign Ministry spokesman, Gennadi I. Gerasimov, said the pardons, granted under two decrees, dated February 2 and last Monday, were part of a review of the Criminal Code being made "so that we may have fewer people behind bars and behind barbed wire."

Diplomats described the pardons and Mr. Gerasimov's comment as an acknowledgment by the government that Soviet citizens had been improperly imprisoned.

Soviet officials said the pardons and related measures, including the return to Moscow of Andrei D. Sakharov, reflected a genuine determination by Mr. Gorbachev to expand the limits of acceptable dissent.

As first word of the pardons spread over the weekend, Dr. Sakharov said: "Objectively, something real is happening. How far it is going to go is a complicated question, but I myself have decided the situation has changed."

Dr. Sakharov, in a move that would have seemed unimaginable six months ago, is scheduled to appear here this weekend at an international conference organized by the government.

The Soviet government has so far not publicized the prisoner releases domestically, apparently waiting for the right moment and format. Georgi A. Arbatov, director of the Institute for United States and Canadian Studies, said in an interview that the Soviet press would announce the pardons soon, together with an explanation for the change in policy.

The handling of the news suggested to diplomats that some members of the leadership might be opposed to the pardons. Mr. Gerasimov said Tuesday that some officials opposed a planned liberalization of the Criminal Code.

"I can say to you that there are comrades who think, the harsher the better," Mr. Gerasimov said.

The Kremlin's increasing emphasis on tolerance was setting off anxiety among Moscow's East bloc allies. There, old reflexes against reform and liberalization were clashing with equally old tendencies to genuflect before Soviet leaders and applaud their directives.

Gorbachev Draws a Mixed Reaction

By Michael T. Kaufman

WARSAW, FEB. 11—Mikhail S. Gorbachev's espousal of greater openness in Soviet society has met a mixed response from his Eastern European allies, from applause in Poland to apparent unease in Czechoslovakia.

In Poland, which with Hungary has the greatest cultural and religious freedom in Eastern Europe, General Wojciech Jaruzelski has echoed most closely the signals of reform and modernization that have characterized Mr. Gorbachev's rule.

But in other countries, where cultural, political, and religious expression is more circumscribed, the official response has tended toward suspicion.

In Czechoslovakia, the Communist Party newspaper, *Rude Pravo,* failed to carry Mr. Gorbachev's recent speeches advocating reform in the Soviet government and party.

At the same time, East Germany has shown little enthusiasm for Mr. Gorbachev's calls for "openness" and "democratization," and has signaled that it does not intend to imitate the Soviet Union. Erich Honecker, the East German leader, has been praising East Germany's own economic and political system but has avoided mentioning Mr. Gorbachev's initiatives.

Czechoslovakia's leaders, who were placed in power when Soviet tanks toppled the liberal Communist regime of Alexander Dubček in 1968, have called in the last few weeks for "weighing any innovations against the experiences of the late 60s."

Like Mr. Honecker, the Czechoslovak leader, Gustáv Husák, has pointed to the relative economic prosperity of his country. The position of both men appears to be that any relaxation of authority and control can unleash social yearnings that lead to conflict.

The very word "reform" has remained a taboo deleted by censors in Czechoslovakia since 1968. Only "change" is permissible, and Czechoslovak observers have suggested that some of the "technical" problems cited by *Rude Pravo* in failing to publish Mr. Gorbachev's speeches may have stemmed from a debate over what to do when the leader of the Soviet Union uses forbidden terms and alludes to forbidden ideas.

Unlike Poland or Hungary, all parts of Czechoslovakia receive Soviet television broadcasts, and according to many Czechoslovaks, the popularity of the Soviet news programs has risen remarkably with viewers watching for much the same reason that so many Poles listen to Western shortwave broadcasts.

In Hungary, the response to Mr. Gorbachev's initiatives was candidly presented this week in a radio address by Matyas Szuros, a Central Committee secretary who had been an ambassador to the Soviet Union. He said the courage shown by the Soviet leadership "commands respect" but should not serve as a model.

Gorbachev Candid About Opposition
By Philip Taubman

MOSCOW, FEB. 25—Mikhail S. Gorbachev, in his most candid acknowledgment of opposition to his policies, sought today to assure critics that "democratization" would not produce disarray in Soviet society.

Addressing a labor union convention, he said: "Greater democratization may prompt some people to ask whether we are not disorganizing society, whether we shall not weaken management and lower the standards for discipline, order, and responsibility."

He answered by saying that "democracy is not the opposite of order . . . democracy is not the opposite of discipline . . . democracy is not the antithesis of responsibility."

The speech, which was later televised, represented Mr. Gorbachev's most extensive public commentary about opposition to his plans and reflected the concern of critics that his policies might produce social unrest.

The critics have not been publicly identified. The view among Western diplomats, reinforced by Soviet officials, is that Mr. Gorbachev commands a clear majority support in the party's Politburo, which makes policy, and in its Secretariat, which carries it out. According to this view, his support thins out in the 307-member Central Committee and down through the bureaucracy.

Mr. Gorbachev, departing from the traditional Soviet practice of revealing little about internal deliberations, said preparations for a Central Committee meeting in January to endorse his program had "proved a difficult matter."

"Suffice it to say that we postponed the meeting three times, for we could not hold it without having a clear idea of the main issues," he said.

At the meeting, Mr. Gorbachev charged the ruling party with stagnation and systematic failures and called for a choice of approved candidates in some elections of party officials and of government bodies. In the past, an election constituted simple approval of a single designated candidate.

The speech today was Mr. Gorbachev's fifth in 10 days, including appearances in Latvia and Estonia. He has often followed key party meetings with bursts of public activity aimed at building popular support.

Fears stirred up by his initiatives, as outlined by Mr. Gorbachev today, include concern that increased openness and expanded liberties may snowball out of control.

"This is an extremely important question, and we must have complete clarity on it," he said. But he concluded that the alternative was stagnation and decline.

"So, it is either democracy or social inertia and conservatism," he said. "Nothing will come of it if we do not fully break the forces of inertia and deceleration, which are dangerous in their ability to draw the country back again into stagnation and dormancy, threatening a freezing up of society and social corrosion."

Mr. Gorbachev told the audience of 5,000 labor union delegates that the Central Committee meeting last month had shown strong support for his program, but he cautioned that the most difficult part lay ahead.

"Up to now we have been mostly preparing for reorganization," he said.

Reviewing his economic initiatives, including programs to give workers more incentive and to reduce centralized management, he said he sensed public impatience for results.

He said the new goals had resulted in a "revolution of expectations."

"Many want a speedy social and material return," he said. "I can judge this from recent meetings with the working people of Latvia and Estonia."

On the basic theme that his program of liberalization would not produce unrest, Mr. Gorbachev made these points:

● "Democracy is not the opposite of order. It is order of a higher degree, based not on implicit obedience and mindless execution of instructions but on full-fledged, active participation by all of society in its affairs."

● "Democracy is not the opposite of discipline. It is a conscious discipline and organization of the working people based on a sense of really being master of the country, on collectivism, and on a solidarity of interests and efforts by all citizens."

● "Democracy is not the antithesis of responsibility. It does not mean absence of control. It does not imply a mentality that anything goes."

Throughout the Soviet Union the Kremlin's cheerleading for economic transformation was not bringing the hoped-for results.

Soviet Economic Improvement Below Expectations

By Philip Taubman

MOSCOW, MARCH 23—Two years after Mikhail S. Gorbachev took power promising a new prosperity, the Soviet economy is sputtering and political pressure for better fiscal and industrial results is building, according to Soviet officials and Western experts.

Moreover, in an apparent departure from the increased openness, national income statistics, a key indicator of overall economic growth, have been modified to give a misleading impression of expansion, according to Western economists.

The failure to revitalize the economy is widely viewed as a liability for the Soviet leader, overshadowing political problems caused by other initiatives like his encouragement of greater openness. Severe winter weather and the introduction of a new quality-control program have disrupted the economy in the first two months of this year, according to Soviet officials.

Especially hard hit was the machinery sector, considered the key to modernization. Machinery output in January and February was 3.6 percent below the level in the first two months of 1986 and 1.5 percent below the goal for the first two months of 1987.

Last year, despite advances in some areas—notably energy and agriculture—economic performance failed to meet expectations. One contributing factor was a slowdown in the growth of retail trade turnover produced by a crackdown on alcohol consumption. The sale of alcoholic beverages plunged 37 percent, depriving the government of an estimated 16 billion rubles ($25 billion) in revenue.

Reflecting a more general problem of misleading economic reporting, a Soviet economist, Aleksei A. Sergeyev, said this month that padding of economic data had inflated industrial output figures by as much as 3 percent.

He told the newspaper *Sovetskaya Rossiya,* "According to information of state monitoring organs, the padding of figures makes up 1.5 to 3 percent of the volume of production."

"In my opinion, it is significantly higher," he added.

A Western European diplomat commented, "Gorbachev has painted himself into a corner in which he must either kiss good-bye to economic reform, manipulate the statistics, or brazen out the changes, giving ammunition to his opponents."

Mr. Gorbachev, acknowledging difficulties, has spoken of a "revolution of expectations" among the Soviet people, who, long burdened with shoddy goods and minimal incentives, are impatient to see the better life he promised.

To achieve the goals he has outlined, Mr. Gorbachev may eventually be forced to adopt the kind of radical measures, including Western business practices, that would be anathema to many established institutions.

His recent public comments about the economy, and those of other leaders like Prime Minister Nikolai I. Ryzhkov and Yegor K. Ligachev, the second-ranking party leader, seemed to have a tone of greater urgency.

Mr. Ligachev, addressing railway officials three days ago, said, "On the whole the situation in the national economy continues to be complicated." He said industrial output in three of the 15 constituent republics, including the Ukraine, had fallen below last year.

The problem has been made worse by the introduction in selected industries of a tough new quality-control program that shut down numerous manufacturing lines in a drive to reduce the production of inferior goods. The program forced production shortfalls at more than 900 enterprises in January, the Tass press agency said this month.

The changed tone of the Soviet leadership was clearly shaking the old prevailing social order in the Soviet Union. The man everyone held responsible was being attacked by some for not going far enough, by others for going too far. Sometimes the criticism was indirect.

Raisa Gorbachev Is the Target of a Clandestine Soviet Video
By Philip Taubman

MOSCOW, APRIL 1—Mikhail S. Gorbachev's wife, Raisa, and her Western wardrobe are the subjects of a critical underground video, according to Muscovites who have seen the film.

The tape, a compilation of film clips of Mrs. Gorbachev buying and wearing fashionable clothing and jewelry, depicts her as an extravagant, vain woman and seems intended to make her an object of scorn.

One viewer said the video showed her signing an American Express card receipt for jewelry. When Mr. Gorbachev visited London in December 1984, before assuming the Soviet leadership, Mrs. Gorbachev reportedly made purchases with an American Express Gold Card.

The origin of the clandestine tape is unknown. Its appearance has troubled Mr. Gorbachev's aides, who believe it may be part of a campaign to undermine confidence in him.

Although video players remain scarce in the Soviet Union compared to the West, the number of owners has increased rapidly and government-run video stores have appeared in major cities. The units, foreign or Soviet, cost more than $1,500 but are distributed across social groups.

The public activities of Mrs. Gorbachev have long stirred debate in a society unaccustomed to having the wife of a Soviet leader play a visible role.

For example, when Prime Minister Margaret Thatcher arrived here on Saturday, Mrs. Gorbachev joined her husband in greeting the British leader in the Kremlin, and a photograph of all three appeared the next day on the front page of *Pravda*.

In what appears to be an intentional effort to provide a new role model for Soviet women, Mrs. Gorbachev has also stepped out from the shadow of her husband to carve out an independent identity as a patron of the arts, literature, and fashion.

The wives of previous Soviet leaders played no official role and were rarely seen in public. Many Russians were uncertain whether Yuri V. Andropov had a wife until she appeared at his funeral in February 1984.

"You are used to seeing women like Mrs. Gorbachev; we are not," an aide to Mr. Gorbachev said this week. "Many people here do not understand what she is doing and find it inappropriate in our society. Without question, she has become an issue, but it would be wrong now to retreat."

The reaction seems to divide along generational lines, with older people irritated by her activities and appearances, while younger people see her as a pioneer in giving women more influence and flair.

But she also serves as a lightning rod for criticism of her husband's policies of greater openness, drawing a hostility that opponents of change cannot direct against Mr. Gorbachev himself.

The underground video focuses on her fashionable wardrobe, including scenes showing her shopping in Parisian boutiques during her husband's visit to France in October 1985.

In addition to such attacks, new voices representing very old Russian attitudes and prejudices were surfacing to add more challenges to Gorbachev's leadership.

Russian Nationalists Test Gorbachev
By Felicity Barringer

MOSCOW, MAY 23—The 400 demonstrators began their evening recently by milling around in a large square by the Kremlin wall, bearing hand-painted signs reading DOWN WITH THE SABOTEURS OF RECONSTRUCTION, WE NEED RECONSTRUCTION, and GIVE STATUS TO THE PATRIOTIC ASSOCIATION PAMYAT.

But instead of moving to disperse the demonstrators, as happens swiftly during most unsanctioned demonstrations, the police ringing the group merely asked the participants to stay out of the way of traffic.

Later, the police kept traffic out of the demonstrators' way while they marched to an apparently impromptu meeting with Boris N. Yeltsin, head of the Moscow Communist Party and one of Mikhail S. Gorbachev's closest allies in the ruling Politburo.

With that widely discussed demonstration on May 6, the Russian nationalist organization Pamyat—meaning "memory"—emerged from the shadowy semilegitimacy of neighborhood meeting halls into the political limelight, putting Mr. Gorbachev's calls for openness and democracy to something of a ticklish and unexpected test.

Pamyat is the first grass-roots organization to invoke the official watchword of *glasnost,* or "openness," in support of a decidedly unofficial political agenda, in which a yearning for a return to traditional Russian values has become inextricably intertwined with a darker nationalism that sees the Russian homeland beset by enemies, chiefly "international Zionism."

"They are Russian fascists," said a Jewish woman familiar with the group.

Among the group's declared enemies are international Zionists and Masons, who, they say, have infiltrated the Soviet bureaucracy and are seeking world domination; "conspirators" who want to destroy Russian national monuments and who have routed the Moscow subway system to "make it easier to blow up government establishments"; and rock musicians who are called purveyors of "satanism."

Now the initial, and uncharacteristically neutral, articles about Pamyat in the controlled newspapers have given way to a chorus of denunciation. It reached a crescendo in the last two days with harsh articles in *Komsomolskaya Pravda,* the newspaper of the Communist Youth League, and the illustrated weekly magazine *Ogonyok.*

But even these denunciations paid the group a glancing tribute by applauding its goals, including fervent support for Mr. Gorbachev's antialcoholism campaign and devotion to Russian history.

Pamyat's message, *Ogonyok* said, is that by abandoning history, "we have inevitably become spiritually poorer, less significant." *Ogonyok* then gave a mocking account of a Pamyat meeting, in which the magazine focused on what it called the group's obsession with "international Zionism and the Masons," and "silly pronouncements" by its leader, Dmitri Vasilyev.

Westerners here say they believe the Soviet journalists have reason to be cautious in their criticism. "I feel that people of the Pamyat strain have some protection in the ruling circles of the Communist Party," a Western diplomat said. "They are really talking about very basic issues that go very deep in their culture and very deep in their history."

The diplomat said Pamyat's demonstrations seemed to be tolerated for now while the Soviet leadership decides what to do about the group.

Another Western diplomat said Soviet leaders "don't want to come down too hard on Pamyat because some of the ideas they espouse are popular and respectable and supported by some of the leadership."

"And they don't want to discredit the whole idea of democratization," the diplomat said. "They want to take this business in their stride—but at the same time discourage it."

During the meeting with Pamyat, Mr. Yeltsin was said to have displayed a placating yet ambivalent attitude toward the group—an attitude characteristic of the evident official discomfort with this unlooked-for by-product of the *glasnost* campaign.

Even before the May 6 demonstration, the group had made its influence felt by letter-writing campaigns to Communist Party and government officials. In one campaign the members inveighed against an anti-Stalinist movie, *Repentance.* In another they attacked *Ogonyok* for removing the symbol of the Order of Lenin from its cover.

Tapes of the group's meetings are passed from hand to hand in Moscow—by supporters who want to hear the latest words from their leaders and by Jews concerned over how anti-Semitic the group's rhetoric has become.

"I think Yeltsin just didn't know who he was dealing with," said a Russian historian, who added that the Pamyat movement, which opposes the demolition of historic buildings and neighborhoods, has gained wide respectability. "But," he added, "the leaders of this group are sick."

A diplomat compared the group to the Black Hundreds, gangs that beat and sometimes killed Jews in the tumultuous months after the unsuccessful 1905 Revolution. "I think that *glasnost* is simply bringing various things to the surface, like Pamyat," he said.

Muscovites familiar with Pamyat say its membership, estimated at more than a thousand, came from fringe elements of a more loosely organized coalition of Russophiles that in the 1970s called itself Rodina, or "motherland," and was championed by a popular Soviet artist, Ilya Glazunov.

Mr. Glazunov, whose canvases glorify old Russian Orthodox churches, Russian saints, and cultural figures like Dostoyevsky and Tchaikovsky, had led a campaign to preserve Moscow's architectural monuments.

Several Muscovites said this week that Pamyat's fervent support for the legacy of Old Russia strikes a chord with many young Muscovites. A woman said, "It's something vivid, in comparison with the sterile, bloodless Marxist analysis they are getting."

Gorbachev's enthusiasm for openness did not wane, and he even took his message to the Warsaw Pact country that had long been ruled by the most repressive of old-style Communist governments.

Gorbachev Speaks to Rumanians on "Openness" to Cool Response
By Henry Kamm

BUCHAREST, RUMANIA, MAY 26—Mikhail S. Gorbachev explained his concepts of openness and restructuring today to a mass rally in the Communist country whose leader is believed to be the least interested in introducing such policies.

The handpicked crowd of 5,000 party faithful, following the example of the Rumanian leader, Nicolae Ceauşescu, listened in silence to the Gorbachev passages alluding to his innovations in Soviet society.

Their lack of response was in sharp contrast to the effusiveness with which the listeners at the rally punctuated Mr. Ceauşescu's speech with rousing ovations.

The Rumanian leader was interrupted by applause 30 times in 45 minutes at the rally. Eighteen times the crowd rose to its feet to applaud rhythmically, shouting the names of the two leaders in unison or such slogans as "Ceauşescu—Peace!" and "Disarmament—Ceauşescu!"

Mr. Gorbachev's words were greeted by applause 16 times, but not once through his long, almost professorial, portion explaining the two concepts to which he has dedicated his leadership.

At one point during this part of the speech, Mr. Ceauşescu pushed aside the Rumanian text he was following and looked at his wristwatch.

While the Rumanian leader, in his speech, appeared to be encouraging outbursts of applause and frequently prolonged them with waves of his hand over his head, Mr. Gorbachev often showed impatience with interruptions, gesturing as if to cut them off.

During his host's speech, as well, the Soviet leader was often the first to stop applauding, cutting short the long waves of ovations that are standard at Mr. Ceauşescu's speeches.

Another source of obstructive criticism that Gorbachev had been facing had come from within the Soviet military. But late in May a 19-year-old West German adventurer named Mathias Rust performed a stunt of aviation that provided Mr. Gorbachev with a pretext to purge at least some of his enemies within the defense establishment. What the young West German did was to fly a small plane over 400 miles of the Soviet territory evading detection by the vaunted security system until he nosed down to land his plane in Red Square, the very heart of the empire.

Soviet Ousts Military Chief and Head of Its Air Defense for Kremlin Plane Incident; Intruder Was Seen

By Philip Taubman

MOSCOW, MAY 30—Defense Minister Sergei L. Sokolov was relieved of his duties today, and the Soviet military was rebuked by the Politburo after a small civilian plane penetrated Soviet airspace Thursday and flew unimpeded 400 miles to Moscow to land beside the Kremlin.

The Politburo, moving swiftly to deal with the incident, also announced at the end of a special meeting that it had dismissed the commander of Soviet air defense forces, Marshal Aleksandr I. Koldunov, "for negligence."

Reporting that Soviet fighter planes twice circled the civilian plane, the Politburo said the air defense command "had shown intolerable unconcern and indecision about cutting short the flight of the violator plane without resorting to combat means."

The Politburo statement said, "This fact attests to serious shortcomings in organizing for the protection of the airspace of the country, a lack of due vigilance and discipline, and major dereliction of duty in the guidance of forces by the U.S.S.R. Defense Ministry."

The announcement about Marshal Sokolov did not mention the flight to Moscow by a 19-year-old West German, Mathias Rust, who took off from Helsinki and entered heavily defended Soviet airspace over Estonia, 100 miles west of Leningrad. The flight was a strong feature in the announcement of the dismissal of Marshal Koldunov.

The rapid developments, announced in a statement by Tass read on the evening television news, represented a stunning public castigation of the military in a country where military failures have usually been dealt with behind the scenes.

The moves were seen by Western diplomats as a dramatic assertion of civilian authority over the military by Mikhail S. Gorbachev and the party leadership.

Marshal Sokolov, a 75-year-old World War II veteran and armored forces specialist, was replaced by General Dmitri T. Yazov, deputy minister of defense for personnel, according to an announcement by the Presidium of the Supreme Soviet, the nominal parliament.

The announcement of Marshal Sokolov's retirement, which was separate from the Politburo announcement, said that the marshal was being relieved in connection with retirement and that General Yazov was replacing him. The marshal was not known as a strong supporter of Mr. Gorbachev and the Soviet leader's policy of restructuring Soviet society.

Although the Sokolov announcement did not mention Mr. Rust's flight, which ended near St. Basil's Cathedral at the edge of Red Square, the incursion was apparently viewed by Mr. Gorbachev and the Politburo as an intolerable breakdown in Soviet defenses.

The Politburo statement announcing the Koldunov dismissal said Mr. Rust's actions were also being investigated by the prosecutor's office.

Western diplomats said there was no question but that the flight had led to the dismissal of Marshal Sokolov. He had gone to East Berlin just this week as Moscow's senior military representative at a Warsaw Pact meeting.

The Soviet Union drew harsh worldwide criticism after one of its jets shot down a Korean Airlines Boeing 747 jetliner on September 1, 1983, killing all 269 people aboard. The airliner had strayed into Soviet airspace on a flight from Anchorage to Tokyo.

Marshal Koldunov has defended the shooting of the Korean airliner by comparing it to the 1960 downing of an American U-2 spy plane.

On Friday, at a Foreign Ministry briefing on Mr. Rust's flight, a ministry spokesman said, in obvious reference to the Korean airliner, "You criticize us for shooting down a plane, and now you criticize us for not shooting down a plane."

The Politburo said that prosecutors were investigating all circumstances related to Mr. Rust's flight, suggesting the possibility of criminal prosecution.

• • •

Since taking power in March 1985 Mr. Gorbachev has moved cautiously but surely to increase civilian control of the military.

The Politburo's quick action today came as Muscovites talked of nothing but Mr. Rust's flight and their amazement that Soviet air defenses and borders, long described by the government as impenetrable, were easily compromised.

The arrival of Mr. Rust's Cessna over the offices, hotels, and apartments of central Moscow, an area closed to air traffic, prompted Russians to look up unbelievingly. "I saw it going low, really low over the Moskva Hotel," one said. "It was absolutely astounding. I couldn't believe it."

As the summer wore on, Gorbachev showed no sign of halting, let alone retreating, in his efforts to press for reform in virtually all sectors of Soviet life, but most importantly in economic practices.

Gorbachev Urges "Radical" Changes to Spur Economy

By Philip Taubman

MOSCOW, JUNE 25—Mikhail S. Gorbachev called today for a partial dismantling of two linchpins of the Soviet system: central control of the economy and subsidized prices.

In an address to a meeting of the Communist Party's Central Committee, the Soviet leader talked openly, for the first time, about likely dislocations in the country's work force, including layoffs, and he recommended the creation of retraining programs.

In the most forceful outline for economic change that he has provided since taking office in early 1985, Mr. Gorbachev asserted that "a radical reorganization of economic management" must be approved by the end of the year and be in place by the end of the decade. The changes, if enacted without having been eviscerated by opponents, would constitute the most extensive restructuring of the economy since Stalin forged the present system in the 1930s with forced socialist industrialization and collectivization of agriculture.

Mr. Gorbachev's 111-page speech, which opened the first day of the Central Committee meeting, set the stage for what is likely to be a struggle within the party and government over the next phase of an economic overhaul outlined by the Soviet leader when he took over after the death of Konstantin U. Chernenko.

"We have entered the most difficult period of restructuring—the period of practical deeds," Mr. Gorbachev said.

The Central Committee meeting was closed, but the speech was made available by the press agency Tass.

Complaining that the pace of restructuring was too slow and that the Communist Party itself has been unresponsive, Mr. Gorbachev rebuked several government officials for mismanagement, including Nikolai V. Talyzin, the head of Gosplan, the State Planning Committee, who is a nonvoting member of the Politburo. Mr. Gorbachev said the reorganization would include elimination of day-to-day management of the economy by powerful and autocratic agencies like the State Planning Committee.

These agencies would instead set overall guidelines for the economy and insure that key institutions, like the military, would receive sufficient resources.

He said the power of central ministries should also be curbed, and some merged into more efficient agencies.

At the same time, Mr. Gorbachev said there must be "a radical reform" of the elaborate controlled and subsidized pricing system, in which prices of more than 200,000 commodities and products are fixed by the government, often at a fraction of true cost and sometimes greatly in excess.

"The whole of our pricing system, including wholesale, purchasing, and retail prices and tariffs, needs to be rebuilt as a package," he said.

Western economists have said that Mr. Gorbachev's willingness to tackle the pricing system and to curtail central control would be crucial tests of how serious he was about rebuilding the economy.

The 12 decrees cited by Mr. Gorbachev, which he said earlier this month did not yet have the endorsement of the Politburo, seem destined to be the battleground for continued debate about the degree and speed of economic change.

Mr. Gorbachev complained about the scarcity or low quality, or both, of consumer goods. "Comrades, we cannot put up with the lag in community and consumer services, with an unsatisfactory situation in passenger transport, communications, tourism, physical training, and sport," he said.

On the question of unemployment, a politically volatile issue, Mr. Gorbachev declared: "Problems of employment under socialism acquire a new dimension. The release of workers in conditions of the socialist economy will not bring about unemployment, with the specter of which both our own opponents of restructuring and Western 'sovietologists' are trying to scare us."

New World for Russians; The Course Is Clear but Some See Perils
By Bill Keller

MOSCOW, JUNE 26—Abel G. Aganbegyan, for years a maverick among Soviet economists, sat before a crowd of reporters tonight and conjured up a strange new world of Soviet socialism in which the omnipotent central planning agencies have withered, unneeded workers are dismissed, good companies are measured by their profits, and bad companies go bankrupt.

Mr. Aganbegyan has spun his fanciful scenarios before, but this time he spoke as the designated explainer of the new Communist Party gospel.

In a startling turn of Soviet policy and politics, the course he described tonight had become Mikhail S. Gorbachev's and the party's.

With his manifesto for loosening the state's grip on Soviet industry and agriculture, Mr. Gorbachev has laid to rest any doubt about whether he sided with the self-styled radicals pushing to quicken the pace and extend the reach of economic change. He is with them.

With the party endorsement of his proposals today, and the promotion of more Gorbachev allies to the ruling Politburo, he also dispelled a growing conventional wisdom among Western analysts that his campaign was flagging, faced by top-level opposition.

Whatever opposition was voiced in the closed party leadership meeting today—Mr. Aganbegyan portrayed the debate as emotional—Mr. Gorbachev weathered it with an air of revived self-confidence.

But while his course is now clear, it is nonetheless dangerous.

Translating his manifesto into action, and actions into an economic revival, will pit him against a more formidable opposition than anything he has faced so far—the inertia created by 50 years of Stalinist central control.

Mr. Gorbachev's far-reaching proposals reveal a process of education—even radicalization—that has surprised many Western analysts.

Beginning with the Communist Party Congress in February 1986, where his comments on the economy struck Western analysts as vague and noncommittal, Mr. Gorbachev has seemed to be getting more and more restless.

He has spent many hours conferring with economists, including Mr. Aganbegyan, known as market-minded reformers. But the Soviet leader has always stopped short of embracing their most far-reaching proposals.

"Every month he's seemed somewhat more radical, somewhat more irritated with the opposition," said Ed A. Hewett, an American specialist on the Soviet economy.

On Thursday, Mr. Gorbachev surveyed his first two years of economic experiments, bureaucracy-shuffling, and exhortations to harder work, and found them wanting. "There are changes," he said. "But they are insignificant and not radical."

Western analysts agreed today that the program outlined this week deserves that term, at least by the standards of Mr. Gorbachev's predecessors.

The program begins with a new law expanding the rights and powers of Soviet companies and farms. By the end of the year, the ruling Politburo, now fattened with Gorbachev allies, is expected to approve supplementary directives this year that will diminish the power of central planning committees and ministries to dictate to industry.

Under the new system, companies would no longer be bound to produce according to the plan handed down from Moscow. The plan would now become a general guideline. Factories would deal with each other on the basis of "wholesale trade"—signing contracts based on negotiated prices rather than prices set at the top.

They would still rely on state contracts for a share of their business, but Mr. Aganbegyan said the share would decline to an average of about 25 percent.

Factories and cooperatives would be encouraged to compete with one another. Mr. Gorbachev also called for a heavy emphasis on private farming, usually family farm plots loosely affiliated with larger state farms.

By 1991, Mr. Gorbachev has called for further changes, including merger and sharp staff cuts at central ministries and further dismantling of the centralized pricing system.

Delicately and sometimes indirectly, Mr. Gorbachev touched several taboos of Soviet thinking, including these:

● Job security, a sacred tenet of Soviet socialism, would become less certain. The new plan permits unneeded or lazy workers to be laid off and unproductive enterprises to be shut down, with elaborate safeguards to find new jobs for the workers. Mr. Aganbegyan said today he would like to see "several thousand" companies closed quickly, but that he expected the first few bankruptcies to be more "symbolic."

● In a society where inflation is officially denied, prices of many things will go up in an attempt to solve shortages of supply. Initially the effect will be on wholesale prices, but Mr. Aganbegyan said that by the early 1990s he expected changes in government subsidies of such political untouchables as meat, bread, dairy products, and housing. He said there would be safeguards for poor families, yet to be worked out.

● Workers will have a chance to get rich, challenging the widespread popular resentment here of sharp disparities in income. Mr. Gorbachev said "no limit" should be set on workers' pay, as long as it is earned.

Soviet and Western analysts agree that putting those measures into effect will be more difficult than anything the Soviet leader has undertaken in the area of cultural liberalization or foreign policy.

First, he faces continued opposition from officials, whose power would be diminished, and from conservatives, who feel the reforms will explode out of control. They may be able to find loopholes in the new laws and directives, or simply ignore them.

Second, Mr. Gorbachev has set an ambitious timetable, demanding, for example, that factory managers dramatically change their method of operations in a matter of months. If this causes mass confusion, Mr. Hewett said, opponents may muster support for a return to more familiar ways.

Third, even a gradual attack on job security or consumer subsidies carries a risk of political backlash.

And finally, many analysts, including some Soviet experts, doubt that Soviet workers, accustomed to minimal demands and basic guarantees of a reasonably comfortable life, will sense the urgency and improve their performance.

The euphoria that accompanied the announcement of the breakthrough on a missile agreement was quickly and, as it turned out, only temporarily dashed when on October 23 Gorbachev told Secretary of State George P. Shultz that he was unprepared to set a date for the final signing of the agreement unless President Reagan showed more flexibility in his insistence on going ahead with testing of space-based missile systems. The following day, after briefing NATO ministers in Brussels, Mr. Shultz attempted to play down the seeming setback for the treaty by saying that it could be signed without a summit meeting between President Reagan and Mr. Gorbachev. Then scarcely a week later plans for the summit were resuscitated.

Gorbachev Agrees to Meet Reagan in Capital on December 7 to Sign a Treaty on Missiles
By David K. Shipler

WASHINGTON, OCT. 30—President Reagan announced today that Mikhail S. Gorbachev had agreed to begin talks in Washington on December 7 and to sign a treaty eliminating their countries' medium- and short-range nuclear missiles.

The announcement ended a week of uncertainty about the Soviet leader's plans to visit the United States.

The announcement was made by Mr. Reagan in the White House press room after a meeting with Soviet Foreign Minister Eduard A. Shevardnadze, who brought a letter, in Russian, from Mr. Gorbachev accepting the long-standing American invitation. Mr. Gorbachev's visit will be the first by a Soviet leader since Leonid I. Brezhnev came to this country in 1973.

President Reagan also said he hoped to travel to Moscow during the first half of 1988 to sign a second accord, if it can be negotiated by then, which would cut long-range strategic nuclear weapons by half.

President Reagan conceded that the prospective treaty to eliminate intermediate-range missiles—those with ranges of 300 to 3,400 miles—required the resolution of technical details "insuring effective verification."

When he was asked whether the work was done, he turned uncertainly toward Secretary Shultz and then said, "No, I don't think we can say that."

"It's not done," Mr. Shultz put in. "But if it doesn't get done, Mr. Shevardnadze and I are going to get kicked in the rear end very hard by our leaders." Mr. Reagan laughed, and Mr. Shevardnadze gave a belated smile as his interpreter whispered the translation in his ear.

As most of the political activity in Moscow was focused on the future, a concerted effort was also being led by reforming elements within the party to fill in some of the blank pages of its own history.

Gorbachev Assails Crimes of Stalin, Lauds Khrushchev
By Philip Taubman

MOSCOW, NOV. 2—Resuming a painful examination of Soviet history that was all but suspended for the last 25 years, Mikhail S. Gorbachev said today that Stalin was guilty of "enormous and unforgivable" crimes and praised two Soviet figures who had been officially repudiated.

Mr. Gorbachev, in a long-awaited speech marking the seventieth anniversary of the Bolshevik Revolution, opened the door on the past more than had been allowed in recent years, but less dramatically than some of his aides had earlier predicted.

Explaining his emphasis on Soviet history, Mr. Gorbachev said the Soviet Union could plot its future only if it faced up to its past, and he linked the lessons of history to the changes he has set in motion.

In the speech, Mr. Gorbachev restored official respectability to Nikita S. Khrushchev, the Soviet leader from 1953 to 1964, and Nikolai I. Bukharin, a revolutionary associate of Lenin who was executed by Stalin in 1938.

But in both cases, the praise was balanced with continued criticism of their records, demonstrating the caution with which Mr. Gorbachev approached the subject. And nothing was done to rehabilitate Leon Trotsky, Grigory Y. Zinoviev, and Lev B. Kamenev, three famous associates of Lenin who ran afoul of Stalin.

None of those cited by Mr. Gorbachev today is still alive, but discussion of Stalin and other figures from the past remains a sensitive political issue, with criticism of Mr. Gorbachev sometimes disguised as praise for Stalin.

But the speech fell short of the unstinting recapitulation of history many anticipated.

Mr. Gorbachev was not as harsh or as detailed in his indictment of Stalin as Khrushchev was in a famous speech in 1956 that opened the way to a recognition of Stalin's abuses of power.

"To remain faithful to historical truth, we have to see both Stalin's incontestable contribution to the struggle for socialism, the gross political errors, and the abuses committed by him and those around him," Mr. Gorbachev said.

"Contrary to the assertions of our ideological opponents, the Stalin personality cult was certainly not inevitable," he added.

Mr. Gorbachev announced that the investigation of Stalin's actions, begun by Khrushchev in the 1950s but cut short in the early 1960s, would be renewed by a special commission appointed by the Politburo last month.

"The process of restoring justice was not seen through to the end and was actually suspended in the middle of the 1960s," he said.

Mr. Gorbachev said continued neglect of Stalin's crimes was unacceptable.

"Many thousands of people inside and outside the party were subjected to wholesale repressive measures," Mr. Gorbachev said. "The guilt of Stalin and his entourage before the party and the people for the wholesale repressive measures and acts of lawlessness is enormous and unforgivable. This is a lesson for all generations."

Western historians generally put the number of Stalin's victims in the millions, and several Soviet scholars noted today that Mr. Gorbachev had failed to state explicitly that thousands of Stalin's perceived enemies in the party were executed.

Mr. Gorbachev also spoke of the Soviet Union's foreign policy before World War II. Noting that it has been said that the 1939 decision to sign the Molotov-Ribbentrop nonaggression pact with Nazi Germany was "not the best," he justified the pact as the country's best defense at the moment against the backdrop of "Western political leaders who were coolly scheming how best to involve socialism in the flames of war and bring about its head-on collision with fascism."

Within the still often opaque politics of Moscow the most dramatic event was the eruption of conflict and differences between Gorbachev and Boris N. Yeltsin, the man who had been his closest ally.

Aide Who Assailed Gorbachev's Pace Ousted in Moscow
By Philip Taubman

MOSCOW, NOV. 11—Boris N. Yeltsin was removed today as head of the Moscow Communist Party organization in the first public dismissal of a senior official who had been promoted by Mikhail S. Gorbachev.

Tass, the Soviet press agency, said Mr. Gorbachev had attended the meeting of the Moscow city party organization at which Mr. Yeltsin was dismissed, but the Soviet leader's own reaction was not made known.

The dismissal stemmed from Mr. Yeltsin's actions at a meeting of the Communist Party's ruling Central Committee on October 21. According to reports of the meeting printed in the Western press, Mr. Yeltsin complained about the slow pace of change and criticized several top officials, including Mr. Gorbachev and Yegor K. Ligachev, the number two party leader.

It was not clear today whether Mr. Gorbachev wanted Mr. Yeltsin removed because of the outburst or felt he had no choice.

Several senior party officials have been removed since Mr. Gorbachev took power in March 1985, including five voting members of the Politburo, but before Mr. Yeltsin's ouster today, no one appointed to a top party post by Mr. Gorbachev had been dislodged.

Tass said Mr. Yeltsin, who is almost certain to lose his position as a nonvoting member of the Politburo, would be replaced in the Moscow post by Lev N. Zaikov, a full member of the Politburo, who is considered to be one of Mr. Gorbachev's allies.

The ouster of Mr. Yeltsin, who had seemed to personify the forces for change set in motion by Mr. Gorbachev, appeared to be at least a momentary victory for those who have resisted a thorough restructuring of Soviet society.

Mr. Ligachev has given the impression from some of his comments that he was wary of Mr. Gorbachev's pace. But Mr. Gorbachev himself, in a major speech on November 2, also criticized those he said were too impatient for change.

Before his remarks on October 21, Mr. Yeltsin appeared to be the quintessential Gorbachev man, a hard-driving manager, an ardent advocate of *glasnost* and restructuring, and an acerbic critic of past party failures and ideological cant. He also seemed to enjoy publicity in the Western manner, allowing himself to be featured last spring in a CBS News documentary on Soviet life under Mr. Gorbachev.

Mr. Gorbachev was reportedly angered by Mr. Yeltsin's outburst at the Central Committee meeting, and may have felt compelled to remove someone who had so openly defied the party leadership. But it is widely assumed by Western diplomats and many Soviet officials that it was Mr. Ligachev who insisted on the ouster.

A good deal of information about the Yeltsin affair has become known to Western reporters in a break in the secrecy that has traditionally hidden frictions in the Kremlin. But many key details remain unknown, including the exact roles Mr. Gorbachev and Mr. Ligachev played in today's decision.

Some Soviet officials have reported that Mr. Ligachev was the primary target of Mr. Yeltsin's attack on October 21, and that the two men engaged in a heated argument before their astonished Central Committee colleagues.

Mr. Ligachev and Mr. Gorbachev have often differed in their public pronouncements, with Mr. Ligachev advocating a more cautious approach to change, particularly in liberalizing the arts, scholarship, and the press. This circumstantial evidence has led most Western analysts to conclude that the two men are rivals, and that Mr. Ligachev has positioned himself to replace Mr. Gorbachev if the Soviet leader stumbles.

The Tass account of today's meeting said, "The plenary meeting relieved Boris Yeltsin of his duties of first secretary and member of the bureau of the Moscow city party committee for major shortcomings in his leadership of the Moscow city party organization."

Tass said the Moscow committee had "fully endorsed" a resolution approved by the Central Committee on October 21 that found Mr. Yeltsin's speech that day to be "politically erroneous." The existence of a resolution condemning Mr. Yeltsin had not been previously reported.

Tass said Mr. Gorbachev addressed today's meeting, which was also attended by Mr. Ligachev, but it did not provide any details about the Soviet leader's remarks.

The Tass announcement, read on the evening television news, was the first report about the Yeltsin affair to be made public in the Soviet Union. A Tass dispatch about it on October 31 was withdrawn by the agency minutes after reaching Soviet newspapers, and comments by several top Soviet officials at news conferences were never reported inside the country.

The rapid removal of Mr. Yeltsin suggested that the climate of openness nurtured by Mr. Gorbachev does not yet extend to outspoken criticism of the party leadership, even by one of its members, and that discipline in party ranks remains an unbreakable code.

Gorbachev Accuses Former Ally of Putting Ambition Above Party
By Philip Taubman

MOSCOW, FRIDAY, NOV. 13—Mikhail S. Gorbachev, backing the removal of a former ally as Moscow party chief, accused him of mismanagement and undisciplined behavior, Tass, the official press agency, reported today.

In a highly unusual public account of internal party deliberations and frictions within the Communist Party hierarchy, Tass described Mr. Gorbachev's criticism at a meeting of the Moscow party organization on Wednesday at which Boris N. Yeltsin was removed as local leader.

According to Tass, Mr. Gorbachev said Mr. Yeltsin had disrupted a key party meeting last month with a "politically immature" speech in which he said that Mr. Gorbachev's economic restructuring plan "was giving virtually nothing to the people."

Tass, in a separate dispatch about the Moscow party meeting, reported what it said was a virtual confession of error by Mr. Yeltsin. According to Tass, Mr. Yeltsin acknowledged making serious mistakes and reiterated his support for Mr. Gorbachev's program of change, known in Russian as *perestroika.*

"I'm guilty before the Moscow city party organization, the Moscow city party committee, before you, and, of course, I am very guilty before Mikhail Sergeyevich Gorbachev," Mr. Yeltsin said, according to Tass.

"One of my most characteristic personal traits, ambition, has manifested itself of late, which was mentioned today," Tass said Mr. Yeltsin said. "I tried to check it, but regrettably, without success."

The Tass account gave Mr. Gorbachev's reconstruction of a meeting of the Communist Party's Central Committee on October 21 at which Mr. Yeltsin criticized the party leadership.

Mr. Gorbachev also told the Moscow party leaders that Mr. Yeltsin, a nonvoting member of the Politburo, had been reprimanded several times by that body for disrupting their meetings by insisting that his personal concerns be considered, Tass said, adding, "Mikhail Gorbachev said that Boris Yeltsin had placed personal ambitions above the interests of the party."

Mr. Yeltsin made it known over the summer that he intended to resign as Moscow party boss, Mr. Gorbachev was quoted as saying, and the Soviet leader told him after returning from vacation at the end of September that the issue should be deferred until after the seventieth anniversary of the revolution, on November 7.

Mr. Gorbachev said that Mr. Yeltsin's effort to raise the issue during the October 21 Central Committee session was a "breach of party ethics."

According to Tass, Mr. Yeltsin had raised questions about the Communist Party's work in bringing changes to Soviet society, "and went as far as to say that restructuring was giving virtually nothing to the people."

For Muscovites, *Pravda* Account of the Yeltsin Ouster Is Riveting Reading
By Francis X. Clines

MOSCOW, NOV. 13—*Pravda* offered Soviet citizens a rare look today at the purging of Boris N. Yeltsin by his peers in the Communist hierarchy.

As they read the two full pages devoted by the Communist Party newspaper to Mr. Yeltsin's political indictment and demise, citizens here alluded to the grimmest period of Stalin's purges. The newspaper account detailed how Mr. Yeltsin's colleagues turned as a pack to destroy him, with the rhetorical edge flashed foremost by Mikhail S. Gorbachev, the Soviet leader.

"What have you come to finally?" Yuri A. Prokofyev, a city government official, asked directly of the accused man at the peak of the group denunciation Wednesday by the Moscow party leadership. "Who is supporting you now?" he demanded.

"His actions should be considered a kick below the belt to *perestroika* and all Muscovites," another party committee official said as the denunciations resonated with the catchword for Mr. Gorbachev's program of national restructuring.

The government stressed the unanimity in the excoriation, including in the *Pravda* excerpts such quotes as this one from A. S. Yeliseyev: "Incidentally, I, as a member of the Moscow party, would separate myself from Boris Nikolayevich in his guilt."

But many readers found that the total lack of defenders only reinforced a heroic image in Mr. Yeltsin's isolation before the hierarchy.

Early this morning outside the *Pravda* office, the black sedans of ranking Soviet officials could be seen waiting for the newspaper, one of the most sensational editions in its history. As candid as the disclosures were, they also shocked many readers for the image presented of the hierarchy turning so on one of its own after he had demanded faster government changes and criticized colleagues at a party meeting in October.

"Many of us become brave afterwards," one party official declared in mid-denunciation, explaining why, if Mr. Yeltsin's flaws were so obvious, no one had bothered to speak until the meeting.

The *Pravda* report was read by some as an attempt to display party unity and justification in ousting Mr. Yeltsin, and to do so in the name of *glasnost*—"openness." It painted a picture of two dozen party officials rising one after another to denounce Mr. Yeltsin for his alleged "big boss syndrome," political adventurism, pretensions of infallibility, impatience, intolerance, mistrust of colleagues, wrathful speech, personal ostentation, immaturity, self-contradiction, lack of ethics, and of calling some party officials "S.O.B.s."

"The dog is down and everyone joins in kicking him," a reader said angrily, looking up from his *Pravda* to echo the view that Mr. Yeltsin's main offense was to test too well Mr. Gorbachev's heralded call for openness.

The Summit; Reagan and Gorbachev Sign Missile Treaty and Vow to Work for Greater Reductions

By David K. Shipler

WASHINGTON, DEC. 8—With fervent calls for a new era of peaceful understanding, President Reagan and Mikhail S. Gorbachev today signed the first treaty reducing the size of their nations' nuclear arsenals.

The President and the Soviet leader, beginning three days of talks aimed at even broader reductions, pledged to build on the accord by striving toward what Mr. Gorbachev called "the more important goal," reducing long-range nuclear weapons.

In their White House conversations, the leaders were said to have reviewed their previous proposals aimed at furthering those negotiations, and they established an arms-control working group of ranking officials to hold parallel sessions.

An immediate mood of warmth was established as the two leaders agreed this morning to call each other by their first names, a White House official said. He quoted the President as telling Mr. Gorbachev, "My first name is Ron."

Mr. Gorbachev answered, "Mine is Mikhail."

"When we're working in private session," Mr. Reagan reportedly said, "we can call each other that."

The new treaty, which provides for the dismantling of all Soviet and American medium- and short-range missiles, establishes the most extensive system of weapons inspection ever negotiated by the two countries, including placing technicians at sensitive sites on each other's territory.

The signing, the fruition of years of negotiation, set the mood for two and a half hours of talks between the leaders. The talks were "very serious, substantive discussions," Secretary of State George P. Shultz said tonight before a formal dinner in the White House.

The visit to Washington by Mr. Gorbachev was the first by a Soviet leader since Leonid I. Brezhnev was here 14 years ago, and it took on immediate drama as Mr. Reagan, who entered office with deep suspicions of the Soviet Union, welcomed Mr. Gorbachev on the south lawn of the White House.

"I have often felt that our people should have been better friends long ago," he told his guest as they stood facing the Washington Monument across an array of full-dress military honor guards. Mr. Gorbachev received a 21-gun salute usually reserved for chiefs of state.

Mr. Gorbachev plunged energetically into a round of talks and public appearances. He met twice with the President, attended a formal dinner at the White House, and met with a group of American public figures and intellectuals at the Soviet embassy.

Prominent Americans Hear Gorbachev's World Vision

By Philip Taubman

WASHINGTON, DEC. 8—Mikhail S. Gorbachev summoned some of the nation's leading cultural, intellectual, and political leaders to the Soviet embassy this afternoon, turned on the television lights, and delivered a two-hour sales pitch for his vision of a new world order.

Working a gathering of prominent Americans with the same fervor and energy that he displays in encounters with groups in the Soviet Union, Mr. Gorbachev told his guests that intellectuals and political leaders, including them and him, were lagging behind the public yearning for peace.

Jutting his fingers into the air to punctuate key points and leaning toward his audience like a lawyer trying to convince a doubting jury, Mr. Gorbachev opened the meeting with a lengthy lecture about the need to rethink the arms race and the years of hostility between the United States and Soviet Union.

"We are all part of one and the same civilization; we are interconnected," Mr. Gorbachev said, repeating a refrain that appears often in his public appearances in the Soviet Union.

The meeting at the embassy, which included leading American actors, writers, scholars, scientists, and former political leaders, was the first in a series of encounters Mr. Gorbachev's aides have organized with prominent Americans during the Soviet leader's visit to Washington. He is scheduled to meet with editors and publishers on Wednesday and to see a group of business leaders on Thursday. Mr. Gorbachev's schedule was arranged mainly by the Soviet embassy, and Reagan administration officials have been more than a little frustrated by their inability to learn whom Mr. Gorbachev is meeting and when and where these sessions are scheduled.

Those at the gathering on Tuesday included Henry A. Kissinger, Paul Newman, Billy Graham, Joyce Carol Oates, John Kenneth Galbraith, Yoko Ono, John Denver, and several leading experts on Soviet affairs.

Showing no signs of fatigue after his long flight from Moscow Monday and a full day of talks with President Reagan at the White House today, Mr. Gorbachev began the kind of exchange he relishes in travels around the Soviet Union. Mr. Gorbachev, like an American politician barnstorming the country, often jumps from his motorcade in provincial cities to talk to crowds of citizens.

Like the sidewalk meetings at home, portions of which are usually taped and broadcast during prime time, the embassy gathering gave Mr. Gorbachev a stage for presenting his views to the American public. The first part of the meeting was broadcast on Cable News Network. The transmission was ended when the network lost its audio link to Mr. Gorbachev's translator.

Describing a number of letters he has received from Americans, Mr. Gorbachev said he detected a desire in both the Soviet Union and United States to open a new era of peaceful relations between East and West.

"I feel something very serious is afoot, something that embraces broad sections of the people, an awareness that we cannot go on as we are," he said.

"We, the representatives of political and intellectual circles, are we not lagging behind what the people have come to realize?"

Apparently realizing that he had spoken longer than his audience expected, Mr. Gorbachev said, "I want to thank you all for having had the patience to listen to my long speech."

He added, "Some of you, though, do write long books."

Before answering questions, Mr. Gorbachev went on to talk about his goals for changing the Soviet Union. "We could not live any longer in the way we had been living." he said. "We tried to take a fresh look at our society and came to the conclusion that the potential of the socialist system was not being utilized to the full."

Brent Scowcroft, a retired Air Force general who served as national security adviser for President Ford, pronounced Mr. Gorbachev's performance "impressive," a description repeated by several of the guests as they left the Soviet embassy.

"The meeting seemed designed to give the impression that we have nothing to fear from them," General Scowcroft said. "He knows how to appeal in a Western style to his audience."

Mr. Gorbachev, like any good politician, picked out a few familiar faces in the audience and offered compliments and banter. Seeing Mr. Galbraith, he made a point of noting his presence and remarked how impressed he had been with his books.

At one point, when he said that the United States and the Soviet Union should rethink their mutual attitude toward each other, he turned to Henry Kissinger and said, "Isn't that right, Dr. Kissinger?"

Mr. Kissinger said his afternoon at the Soviet embassy was "interesting" and Mr. Gorbachev's presentation was better than the questions he received from those in the audience.

The Summit: Reagan and Gorbachev Report Progress on Long-Range Arms; Mute Quarrel over "Star Wars"; Reagan Trip Is Due

By R. W. Apple, Jr.

WASHINGTON, DEC. 10—President Reagan and Mikhail S. Gorbachev concluded their three-day summit conference today with what they described as significant progress toward a treaty limiting strategic weapons. But they failed to conclude major new agreements on Afghanistan or the other key issues that still divide them.

Shielded from a drenching rain by black umbrellas as they stood on the south lawn of the White House, the President said the two could "walk away from our meetings with a sense of accomplishment," and the Soviet general secretary asserted that "a good deal has been accomplished."

Their main achievements, other than the signing of a treaty Tuesday on intermediate-range nuclear missiles, appeared to consist of better personal relations and a decision not to let "Star Wars" stand in the way of negotiating a new strategic missile pact.

"This summit has lit the sky with hope for all people of goodwill," the President said, reflecting the administration's conviction that the sense of goodwill generated here will help to alleviate superpower tensions. At a one-hour-and-50-minute news conference this evening, which ended not long before Mr. Gorbachev boarded his Aeroflot jet for the trip to East Berlin, where he will brief his Warsaw Pact allies, the Soviet leader described his visit to Washington as "a major event in world politics."

It had opened, he said, "a new phase in U.S.-Soviet relations," and because of a "deepening political dialogue" with Mr. Reagan, remaining differences were no longer insurmountable.

The President spoke in a similar vein in a nationally televised summit report tonight, asserting that he and the Soviet leader had shifted the basis of Soviet-American relations. They are "no longer focused only on arms control issues," he said, but "now cover a far broader agenda, one that has, at its root, realism and candor."

"Mr. Gorbachev and I have agreed, in several months in Moscow, to continue what we have achieved in these past three days," the President declared. "I believe there is reason for both hope and optimism."

No date was set for the next meeting, but Marlin Fitzwater, the White House spokesman, said the President would travel to Moscow in the first half of next year, probably in the spring. The two leaders indicated in their communiqué that the meeting would take place whether a strategic arms treaty was ready for signature or not.

On the withdrawal of Soviet troops from Afghanistan, a topic that preoccupied the leaders on Tuesday, no visible progress was made.

The outcome on strategic nuclear weapons was better, American officials reported. The two sides approached agreement on the outline of a treaty that could be signed in Moscow, though they remained sharply divided on the meaning of the 1972 antiballistic missile treaty, the interpretation of which could provide the key to breaking the stalemate over the "Star Wars" program.

Negotiators reached a limited but nonetheless important agreement, arms control officials said, on a limit of 4,900 ballistic missile warheads, a compromise between the previous Soviet figure of 5,100 and the United States demand for 4,800.

In addition, the team headed by Paul H. Nitze and Marshal Sergei F. Akhromeyev decided that for the moment negotiators in Geneva should work around "Star Wars," more formally known as the Strategic Defense Initiative. According to American officials, the negotiators will draft an agreement on strategic arms that would in no way preclude widespread "Star Wars" testing, which the administration has said is permissible under its broad interpretation of the ABM treaty.

The Russians, who oppose such testing, apparently agreed to such an arrangement because the administration has already been prohibited by Congress, through most of the remainder of Mr. Reagan's term, from carrying out any tests except those permitted under the narrow interpretation of the treaty that is favored by Moscow.

This method of skirting the "Star Wars" issue, on which the summit talks in Iceland last year foundered, amounts to an agreement to disagree that should allow for progress on the strategic arms treaty. The Soviet leadership had made it plain before arriving in Washington that it did not want the issue to block progress toward an agreement reducing long-range nuclear arsenals by up to 50 percent.

In his news conference, Mr. Gorbachev acknowledged that there had been little movement on resolving the "Star Wars" issue.

In the last question of the two-hour session, he was asked, "Has your meeting here this week made it any less likely that the arms race will be extended into space?"

He answered: "I don't think so. I can confirm that it remains the goal of the Soviet Union to prevent the extension of the arms race into space. That's all."

One important question that must be settled in Geneva, in addition to limits on specific types of missiles, is how long the two nations would agree not to withdraw from the ABM treaty. The length of that period would determine, in part, when a "Star Wars" system could be deployed.

In the final communiqué, the matter was covered in this veiled language: "The leaders of the two countries also instructed their delegations in Geneva to work out an agreement that would commit the sides to observe the ABM treaty, as signed in 1972, while conducting their research, development, and testing as required, which are permitted by the ABM treaty, and not to withdraw from the ABM treaty for a specified length of time."

The final hours of the meeting, the first between Soviet and American leaders in this country in 14 years, were cloaked in the same sort of mystery and characterized by the same sort of furious last-minute activity that marked the Reykjavík summit conference in October 1986.

Secretary of State George P. Shultz appeared, unannounced, at the Soviet embassy at 8 A.M. for last-minute negotiations. Mr. Gorbachev left for the White House more than an hour late, and then he stunned everyone by leaping from his limousine to shake hands with people standing on the sidewalk along Connecticut Avenue.

But there were no surprise proposals here, as there were at Reykjavík, and the two leaders did not fall here, as they did there, over the hurdle of "Star Wars."

Today, moreover, they smiled at each other, if only intermittently, as they parted; they had departed from Iceland smothered in scowls.

Because both men needed for domestic political reasons to seem to do well, and because both want to encourage prompt Senate ratification of the treaty covering short- and medium-range missiles, they joined in putting the best possible face on things.

Almost up to the time of his departure, Mr. Gorbachev continued his remarkable campaign to sell himself, his policies, and his country to the American people. Besides getting out of his limousine to meet with the crowds along Connecticut Avenue, he talked with 15 high school and college students, whom he urged to learn more about world problems, and met with American business leaders to whom he made a strong pitch for large American investments in joint ventures to develop Soviet natural resources.

While Mr. Shultz was conferring in another part of the embassy with Eduard A. Shevardnadze, the Soviet foreign minister, Mr. Gorbachev joined Vice President Bush and other guests for a breakfast of blinis—thin Russian buckwheat pancakes—and caviar. Mr. Bush said of his host, "This man has a good way about him, yet he's strong and he's tough in negotiations."

The Soviet leader's wife, Raisa, was also active, receiving a group of Armenian-Americans who expressed gratitude for permission granted to Armenians to emigrate from the Soviet Union, and talking with a small group of prominent women at the elaborate Georgetown residence of Pamela Harriman, the widow of W. Averell Harriman, the wartime

American ambassador to Moscow. Mrs. Harriman is a prominent fund-raiser for Democratic candidates.

According to American officials who spoke at a background briefing on the condition that they not be identified, the Soviet Union refused to set a date for the start of their withdrawal from Afghanistan until agreement could be reached on what sort of transitional government would be formed in Kabul after a withdrawal. Mr. Gorbachev reportedly insisted upon a nonaligned regime, while Mr. Reagan wants one elected by the Afghans.

There was also a disagreement, the officials said, about the timing of a cutoff of American aid to the guerrilla forces fighting Soviet troops. "It takes two sides to agree on something, and it just wasn't there," one of the officials involved commented later.

At his news conference, Mr. Gorbachev talked for more than an hour, explaining and analyzing the agreements he reached with Mr. Reagan, before he began answering questions.

He put particular emphasis on the limit of 4,900 missile warheads. The 4,900 figure covers both intercontinental ballistic missiles and sea-based ballistic missiles, which have represented a particular problem because they are fired from naval vessels, whose movements make positive verification very difficult.

The Soviet leader said he agreed with American officials that the Geneva negotiators would have a difficult time between now and June working out the details of the strategic arms treaty. How to count certain categories of weapons, the Americans said, will present particularly thorny questions.

Mr. Gorbachev said United States officials had "displayed interest" in Soviet ideas about reducing conventional forces in Europe, in which the Soviet Union and its allies have considerable superiority. He urged urgent, early negotiations that would "cast aside all altercation" and said they would show "who is in earnest and who is, perhaps, trying to be too sly."

Some elements of the plan on strategic weapons were "resolved," the Soviet leader said, "while the participants in the official farewell ceremony" were waiting on the White House lawn. As a result, publication of the joint statement by the leaders was delayed until late tonight.

Asked at the end of his presentation whether he thought anything he had done here had reduced the chances that the United States would eventually have weapons in space, Mr. Gorbachev's "I don't think so" and his short answer suggested that he felt he had made a major concession to Mr. Reagan in agreeing to put aside the "Star Wars" question, at least for the time being.

On the more general question of how his relationship with Mr. Reagan had changed since their meetings in Geneva and Reykjavík, the Soviet leader replied, "It's more businesslike, we have more of a constructive approach, and I would even venture to say that we trust each other more."

In his televised speech, Mr. Reagan tried to rebut many of the criticisms that have been made of the short- and medium-range missile treaty. Using a map, he argued that removing those missiles would remove a major threat to Europe and Asia, and he also insisted that the verification procedures were more than adequate.

1988

*A*s the new year opened, the Soviet Union was embarked on a zigzag course into what was still largely unknown territory. There were, however, several clear stars by which Gorbachev was steering. In international relations, constant pressure for arms control and improved relations with the West. In domestic politics, a turning from the people and the practices of the past toward something that was still less than democracy. In culture, more open discussion, and in economics, **perestroika.**

Sharp Turn for Russians; Autonomy in Industry to Challenge Worker
By Bill Keller

MOSCOW, JAN. 1—The Soviet Union today entered a critical phase in Mikhail S. Gorbachev's attempt to resuscitate the economy, in which workers will be asked to change their notion of work radically without yet having enjoyed any great rewards from two years of economic experiments and promises.

Under an elaborate set of economic laws and decrees that took effect today, much of the responsibility for Soviet industry is shifted from central planners in Moscow to plant managers and the workers themselves.

The system of economic accountability introduced today is the most dramatic step yet in Mr. Gorbachev's program of economic *perestroika,* or "restructuring." Soviet economists say it is expected to bring a period of wrenching change and economic uncertainty to a society long in love with the predictable.

But Western economists question whether Soviet workers will rise to the challenge if Mr. Gorbachev cannot sweeten the deal by delivering some short-term rewards.

A series of consumer-oriented economic measures, introduced over the last two years in an effort to bring quick improvements in the lives of ordinary citizens, has so far had a limited effect.

Mr. Gorbachev's most ambitious bid for a rapid improvement in the standard of living has been an attempt to rejuvenate agriculture, where a rigid system of state farming has made this country an importer of food.

The program, which has given farmers more independence and the right to sell more goods at market prices, appears to have increased food production.

But much of the harvest rots in the field owing to a lack of storage and processing capacity. Moreover, the extra meat and vegetables that do get to consumers are sold in cooperatives and farmers' markets where food is priced beyond the reach of many ordinary families.

Mr. Gorbachev has called for further changes, including a major campaign to build up storage and food processing and greater use of family farming.

"Agriculture is still an area where he could get the short-term payoff he needs," said a European diplomat specializing in economic affairs. "But so far he hasn't delivered very much."

The Soviet leader's other search for quick results has been an effort to improve the dismal quality of restaurants, taxis, home repair, and other services. A series of new laws beginning in November 1986 encouraged small cooperatives and individuals to compete with the state in offering these services.

The new laws have led to the opening of many new cooperative cafés and an eclectic range of services, ranging from dog grooming and lonely-hearts matchmaking to auto repair and clothing design. The official press agency, Tass, reported this week that 200,000 people were now engaged in either cooperative or individual ventures.

But private enterprise has run up against obstacles set deep in the Soviet system and psychology.

In recent months Soviet newspapers have been filled with stories of cooperatives or would-be entrepreneurs stymied by red tape or by public resentment of their large incomes.

Like the so-called nepmen of the 1920s, who thrived in the more liberal business environment of Lenin's new economic policy, today's entrepreneurs live with the sense that their activities are alien and could be cut short any day.

Yuri Luzhkov, chairman of the Moscow city commission on cooperative and individual labor activities, recently wrote an article in the weekly

Moscow News explaining why cooperative restaurants had failed so far to brighten the lives of ordinary Muscovites.

"There is practically no competition, which is why the cooperatives, not taking much care about the quality of cooking, offer simple meals at a high price and amass huge profits," Mr. Luzhkov said.

Ed A. Hewett, a Brookings Institution economist who specializes in the Soviet economy, said during a recent visit to Moscow that Soviet officials could make a serious impression on public opinion by allowing home-building cooperatives to help relieve the severe shortage of apartments.

Cooperatives are prevented from such an ambitious undertaking by strict limits on their size, their access to bank loans, and their ability to hire labor.

One change that may produce some immediate improvements in the public mood is a relaxation of rules on foreign travel.

The government newspaper, *Izvestia,* reported today that Soviet tourists would now be allowed to travel to East Germany, Czechoslovakia, Poland, Bulgaria, and a number of other Communist-ruled countries without getting visas. They will be allowed to travel as individuals, not just in closely policed tour groups. The move is likely to be quite popular with Russians, who consider Eastern Europe a consumer mecca.

The lack of dramatic results from the economic experiments has engendered skepticism toward the changes that are to sweep through Soviet industry in the coming months.

Soviet citizens have been promised that the new law on decentralized control of industry will improve living standards by rewarding workers based on performance and giving factories more discretion to spend profits.

"The life of everyone will definitely become materially better and spiritually richer," Mr. Gorbachev promised Thursday night in his televised New Year's message. But he reminded the Soviet people that the change would be "not easy and not without pain."

In its barrage of articles leading up to the change, the press has focused on the happy results in factories that had already gone on the new system experimentally, and had used their profits to build worker housing, kindergartens, and other benefits. But the experimenters—about 20 percent of Soviet industry—are primarily enterprises that were profitable to begin with.

Beginning today, the new system applies to enterprises producing 60 percent of Soviet industrial goods, and by 1990 almost all of Soviet industry will be put on a pay-as-you-go basis. One in four enterprises either operates at a loss or with marginal profits, and many of them are expected to face a period of hardship when they have to pay their own way.

The system is being introduced gradually, with safety nets to prevent enterprises from going bankrupt or workers from going jobless.

Even so, the new system entails a measure of risk. If a factory fails to turn a profit, workers' pay can be cut. Superfluous workers may face retraining and relocation. And in 1990 the government is to decide whether to end subsidies on food and housing prices.

"In a sense, Gorbachev is a victim of his own *glasnost,*" a Western diplomat said, referring to the program of more openness. "The press focuses on all the problems in the economy and pushes for changes, and that raises people's expectations. People expect something short-term, and if they don't get it, cynicism may set in before the real reforms get off the ground."

Notes on the Soviet Union; Once More unto the Breach! Ink-Stained Warriors Rush the Citadel Anew
By Bill Keller

MOSCOW, JAN. 27—Sometimes it seems there is a collective instinct here that tells the unorthodox economists, the muckraking journalists, the anti-Stalinist writers, and other warriors of *glasnost* when it is time to gather for another storming of the barricades. Now is such a time.

After an uneasy lull in the closing months of 1987, the new year has brought a renewed assault on the nerves of the censors.

The latest literary event is the publication in the monthly magazine *Oktyabr* of the first installment of Vasily Grossman's immense novel *Life and Fate.* It easily overshadows the long-awaited serialization of Boris Pasternak's *Doctor Zhivago,* which hit the newsstands the other day in a rival periodical, *Novy Mir.*

The publication of *Zhivago* rights a wrong, but the novel is already well known among the intelligentsia and not as highly regarded as Pasternak's poetry. Grossman's epic novel, on the other hand, draws uncomfortable parallels between Nazi and Soviet power, a politically potent theme.

The journalistic sensation of the moment is the astonishing story in *Literaturnaya Gazeta* of Akhmadzhan Adilov, director of a state cotton farm in Soviet Uzbekistan, who built a small empire on millions of rubles in stolen cotton proceeds. Until his arrest in 1984, the newspaper reports, he maintained a small private army, a dozen vacation homes, an underground bunker with its own prison, and a legion of cowering subordinates whom he sometimes tortured in public.

The article is the raciest in a genre portraying corruption during the rule of Leonid I. Brezhnev, now increasingly regarded as the patron of economic stagnation.

Perhaps the newspaper took its signal from the Kremlin's own Brezhnev bashing. Early this month the Communist Party stripped the former party leader's name from a prestigious Moscow district, a city on the Volga River, and a square in Leningrad.

It was the humiliation of another party figure, Boris N. Yeltsin, who was ousted as Moscow party chief in November for excessive zeal in the name of reform, that caused a sharp mood swing in Moscow. Many intellectuals fell to worrying that *glasnost,* or providing the public with information it needs to make the economy work better, was running out of steam.

Now *Krokodil,* a satirical magazine that has lagged behind the more daring publications, has published a piece by the émigré novelist Vasily Aksyonov, a reminiscence of Moscow intellectuals' addiction to American fads in the 1950s. The piece is less daring than the byline. The last time Mr. Aksyonov's name appeared in the Soviet press was last spring, when he co-signed an émigré letter criticizing Soviet policies on human rights and foreign affairs. *Moscow News,* a limited-circulation weekly, published the letter and was promptly chastised for it.

It is not likely that the *glasnost* brigade is emboldened because it senses the opposition crumbling. On the contrary, the voices arguing against permissiveness in the press have also raised their decibel levels. Last week the defense minister, Dmitri T. Yazov, was shown on television chiding writers for undermining respect for the military.

Earlier in the month the chief editor of *Pravda,* the Communist Party newspaper, criticized Mikhail F. Shatrov's new play, *Onward . . . Onward . . . Onward!* a fierce anti-Stalinist work. The *Pravda* editor, who said the play lacked balance and accuracy, made his complaints in a meeting with Mr. Gorbachev himself.

But these comments do not seem to inspire the same degree of fear they once did. A few years ago denunciations by the defense minister or the chief editor of *Pravda* would have been enough to make an editor contemplate the invigorating pleasures of the Siberian winter.

Now the journals that are most sharply criticized tend to rebound with fresh vigor.

Six months ago Yegor K. Ligachev, the second-ranking member of the Politburo and the least favorite Soviet leader among the avant-garde, visited the offices of the daily *Sovetskaya Kultura* to deliver a scolding on the need for stricter Communist standards in the Soviet press. The waves of liberalization, he warned, had washed up "some scum and debris."

Yet one of the first 1988 issues of *Sovetskaya Kultura* featured, side by side, two bold critiques of the disappointing pace of change. Gavriil K. Popov, an economist, outlined shortcomings in the latest phase of economic initiatives, while Yuri N. Afanasyev, a historian, complained of continuing limits on honest discussion of Soviet history.

Moscow News, chastised by Mr. Ligachev last September for pushing the limits, opened the new year with Nikolai Shmelyov's outcry against what he sees as a conservative backlash thwarting economic change.

Ogonyok, the target of the defense minister, has not disappointed its fast-growing list of subscribers, either. Initial issues of the year include articles on violence and homosexuality in a labor camp for juvenile offenders and coverage of the war in Afghanistan.

One sign that editors are still responsive to criticism from the top: the press seems to have called a cease-fire in recent days in its attacks on the new economic-accountability law that took effect in most of Soviet industry January 1. After Mr. Popov and others criticized the much-touted economic changes as too little, Mr. Gorbachev indicated he wanted a little moral support, and the coverage has become more upbeat.

How to explain the seeming reinvigoration of the press?

Some of the new year's eye-openers, especially those in the monthly literary magazines, were planned months ago and say little about the editors' current level of optimism. But the publication of works like Mr. Shatrov's play seems to open new territory into which the other journals follow in a rush.

Another factor may be the budding commercial consciousness of publications that are now expected to pull their own weight financially. Editors have discovered that sensational articles are good for circulation.

It may be that editors and writers have sized up the mixed signals from the top and decided the conservative backlash was not as menacing as they thought.

Another theory is that the more adventuresome editors have been quietly encouraged by those in the leadership who feel the need for an occasional shot of adrenaline to keep alive a sense of forward motion.

The basic idea behind Mr. Gorbachev's liberalization of culture and the press is that it will stimulate an outpouring of public energy and initiative. He needs such a spur now, more than ever, as the country slogs into the bewildering swamp of the new economic program.

Mr. Gorbachev's basic thesis seems to be that without *glasnost* the whole process of change stalls. Perhaps the warriors of *glasnost* are kicking again because they know the reverse is also true—if Mr. Gorbachev's economic and political program fails, the new openness could be the first casualty.

In terms of international goals, the Soviet Union was continuing to offer what appeared to be tantalizing concessions. Early in February, Gorba-

chev announced that he could envision ordering the start of a withdrawal of Soviet troops from Afghanistan in three months if ongoing Afghan peace talks in Geneva continued to move toward agreement. Later in the month Secretary of State George P. Shultz, while visiting Moscow, said the United States and the Soviet Union were in essential agreement on terms for ending the Afghan War. "I don't have the slightest doubt that the Soviet Union has decided that it wants to leave Afghanistan. The question is how," Mr. Shultz said. During the secretary of state's visit he also announced that progress had been made in two days of negotiations on a treaty to reduce long-range nuclear weapons, raising some optimistic speculation that such a pact might be ready for signing when President Reagan was to visit the Soviet Union in the spring.

Meanwhile, on the domestic front, the declarations and pronouncements of new departures were setting off reverberating, and not necessarily envisioned, responses far from Moscow. Midway through February demonstrations erupted in the south that pitted the rival claims of nationalistic Armenians against nationalistic Azerbaijanis. Like earlier protests by Lithuanians and Estonians, the outburst was seen by some in Moscow as both a portent of spreading troubles and a direct consequence of the Kremlin's policy of loosening reins. It seemed to suggest that among the first things that a people did with the freedom they gained was to proclaim their particular identity by stressing their differences with their immediate neighbors.

Gorbachev Urges Armenians to End Nationalist Furor
By Philip Taubman

MOSCOW, FEB. 26—Mikhail S. Gorbachev, faced with one of his most difficult challenges since taking office, called on Armenians today to end nationalist protests that have disrupted two Soviet southern republics.

"I call on you to display civic maturity and restraint, return to normal life and work, and observe social order," the Soviet leader said in remarks that were read over television at midday in the Azerbaijani and Armenian republics by Politburo colleagues sent to the area to help restore order.

"The hour for reason and sober decision has struck," Mr. Gorbachev said.

Mr. Gorbachev's appeal signaled that the disturbances have turned into perhaps the most serious domestic crisis the party leadership in Moscow has faced since Mr. Gorbachev took office in March 1985, rivaled only by the Chernobyl nuclear disaster of 1986.

Mr. Gorbachev's intervention came as tens of thousands of Armenians reportedly marched again through the Soviet Armenian capital, Yerevan, and the Armenian Communist Party organization appeared to challenge Moscow's leadership by calling for reconsideration of the issues that have fueled the protests.

"I must say frankly that the Soviet Communist Party Central Committee has been disturbed by this turn of events," Mr. Gorbachev said of the unrest. "It is fraught with serious consequences."

The demonstrations center on demands that the Nagorno-Karabakh Autonomous Region, a predominantly Armenian area within Azerbaijan, be incorporated into Armenia. Most Armenians are Christian, most Azerbaijanis Moslem.

The demonstrations began in Nagorno-Karabakh two weeks ago and spread to Yerevan a week ago.

The Communist Party Central Committee last week rejected the unification demands. The Armenian party Central Committee, at a special meeting today, petitioned Moscow to set up a commission to reconsider the status of Nagorno-Karabakh, according to Armenian officials.

Government reports today about the unrest were largely uninformative. But phone connections from Moscow to Yerevan were restored, and Western reporters in Moscow were told in many calls to newspapers and government offices in Yerevan that large crowds continued to gather in the city after Mr. Gorbachev's appeal.

The Soviet government, which had banned travel by Western reporters to Armenia and Azerbaijan, today added the neighboring republic of Georgia to the list of prohibited destinations.

The press agency Tass reported today that Mr. Gorbachev had called for the restoration of order but did not make public the text of his remarks.

The text was made available in London by a British Broadcasting Corporation service that monitors television and radio broadcasts in the Soviet Union.

It was read over Azerbaijani television by Georgi P. Razumovsky and in an Armenian broadcast by Vladimir I. Dolgikh, both nonvoting members of the Politburo.

The crisis poses acute political problems for Mr. Gorbachev as he tries to steer a middle course between those who want faster change in the Soviet Union and those who fear his programs will produce a breakdown in order.

He can ill afford to let the unrest continue but would also be damaged if he used force to suppress it.

His programs of change have come under attack by conservatives who have warned that increased openness and democracy would lead to the kind of disorder that has shaken Armenia and Azerbaijan.

Mr. Gorbachev, trying to blunt the criticism, has said in almost every major speech in the last year that his policies would not cause order to collapse.

If the protests continue, Mr. Gorbachev will face growing pressure to stop them, with the use of military force if necessary.

The party has never shown much tolerance for political unrest, and would almost certainly consider the continuation of the Armenian protests an unacceptable precedent.

A failure to end the unrest would leave Mr. Gorbachev vulnerable to charges that he is soft on disorder, a fatal label for a Soviet leader.

In his remarks today, Mr. Gorbachev made clear that he has little flexibility in dealing with the protests.

"We do not wish to evade a frank, sincere discussion of various ideas and proposals," he said. "But this must be done calmly, within the framework of the democratic process and legality, without allowing even the slightest damage to the internationalist cohesion of our peoples."

The Soviet Union is composed of more than 100 ethnic groups united under Soviet rule in the early 1920s, in some cases by force. Many have long agitated for greater autonomy.

The Armenian protests are the latest of nationalist demonstrations around the Soviet Union that have alarmed party leaders in Moscow. Last week, before the Armenian activities stepped up, Mr. Gorbachev called for a Central Committee meeting devoted to nationalities policy, which he described as "the most fundamental, vital issue of our society."

He reminded Armenians and Azerbaijanis of this plan today but did not say specifically that the Central Committee would again consider the status of Nagorno-Karabakh.

The use of force to subdue the demonstrators would also carry risks. An attempt to crush the protests would likely enflame the nationalist sentiments in Armenia and turn them much more sharply against Moscow. So far the demonstrations, while calling for a change in policy in Moscow, have not been notably anti-Soviet.

A crackdown would also damage Mr. Gorbachev's standing at home and abroad as a leader who has sought to make the Soviet system more efficient and humane.

One characteristic of Gorbachev's economic restructuring was its reluctance to forgo the dialectic fox-trot of two steps forward, one back, for some real jitterbugging. For instance, before any real capital was accumulated in private hands, a leveling progressive tax for privately generated incomes was unveiled. The message seemed to be that though private incentives were necessary to generate economic growth, they ought not be allowed to produce the kind of wealth that could stimulate envy.

Soviet Will Tax Private Incomes on Scaled Basis

By Bill Keller

MOSCOW, MARCH 8—The Soviet Union is preparing to introduce a progressive income tax on individuals to curb the growing wealth of private business ventures, Mikhail S. Gorbachev announced in remarks published today.

The Soviet leader, in comments to workers at a Moscow ball-bearing factory on Friday, complained that some of the new private cooperatives that have grown up in the last year have exploited shortages of goods and services to enrich themselves.

"It is understood that we need honest work and initiative, but not the kind in evidence at some cooperatives, which take advantage of shortages and engage in open money grubbing," Mr. Gorbachev said, according to a transcript of his comments published today in the Communist Party newspaper *Pravda*.

"I can report in this regard that a progressive income tax will be introduced," he said. "I think it will be fair."

The Soviet leader's remarks appeared intended to allay widespread public fears that the introduction of private businesses would permit a class of wealthy entrepreneurs.

The deeply ingrained resentment of inequality has been a serious obstacle that has prevented cooperatives from expanding as rapidly as Soviet economists had hoped. Many would-be entrepreneurs seem leery of opening new businesses for fear that a public backlash will force the state to shut them.

Mr. Gorbachev provided no details of how deeply the new tax would hit the incomes of private business people. Members of private cooperatives are now taxed on their profits at the same flat rate as ordinary workers, about 13 percent.

The promise of a new tax code coincides with the publication on Sunday of a law that the authorities say will significantly expand the creation of private cooperatives.

The law gives cooperative ventures a wide range of new powers, including the right to hire workers laid off by state companies, to engage in foreign trade, to file lawsuits, and to organize joint ventures with state enterprises.

The law does not spell out what types of private businesses are banned, although some activities, like publishing, were outlawed earlier.

In addition to the planned national progressive tax on individuals, cooperatives will be subject to local taxes at an unspecified flat rate, a provision apparently intended to make local authorities lower their resistance to private enterprise.

"While the state sector will maintain its leading role, this movement should help saturate the market with goods and increase the range and availability of consumer services," *Pravda* said.

Mr. Gorbachev and his economic advisers see cooperative ventures as a key to winning popular support for broader economic changes. The idea is that these small partnerships will provide a wide range of consumer goods and services that the state monopolies have failed to produce.

According to official estimates, more than 9,000 cooperatives employing 150,000 people have begun under a series of new laws introduced since the autumn of 1986, including restaurants, repair services, clothing shops, and hairdressers.

But the Soviet press has carried many disheartening reports of cooperatives stifled by red tape or inhibited by fear of becoming conspicuously wealthy.

One recent report described a cooperative in Kiev that found great success making shopping bags. Alarmed at their own success, the cooperative members began giving huge donations to the Soviet Peace Fund, a state organization that promotes Soviet disarmament policies, to keep their income from provoking the ire of local officials.

Going Co-op: At the Soviet Economic Frontier
By Bill Keller

ZAGORSK, U.S.S.R., MARCH 21—On a rutted back road of this Russian town, two building supply companies have coexisted for years. Both offered prices fixed by the state, limited selection, indifferent service. Who cared? The state made sure everyone was paid.

But this year Vyacheslev V. Mogilevtsev pulled a fast one. With a little creative reading of new economic laws, he transformed his losing factory into a worker-run cooperative producing parquet flooring and cinder blocks.

He said good-bye to state subsidies, laid off a third of the work force, and turned his thoughts to something new called marketing.

"We'll deliver," the parquet mogul declared. "We'll install. Our construction brigade will even build you a summer home." Casting a sneer in the direction of his rival, he added, "Service—I think that's where we will beat them."

Mr. Mogilevtsev is evidence of the latest Soviet assault on the traditional boundaries of the state-run economy, an attempt to push private and semiprivate businesses into the dreary frontier of Soviet industry.

Soviet economic planners, frustrated about the prospects of reviving the sleepy industrial sector, are turning to private cooperatives—smaller, more independent of state regulation, and profit-minded—to deliver a jolt of competition. More than 14,000 cooperatives have been created by entrepreneurs, attracted by the independence and the prospect of shared profits. But because of long-standing restrictions on membership and capital assets, most are restaurants and other small service ventures.

Mr. Gorbachev wants this to change. A draft law published earlier this month will extend a remarkable array of new rights to "cooperators." A cooperative will be allowed to employ full-time labor and have a freer hand in dismissing workers, engage in foreign trade, own and expand capital assets, and enter joint ventures with state firms.

The law encourages cooperatives and collective farms to compete directly with lethargic state companies in light industry and consumer goods, food processing, and construction.

Soviet leaders have also announced that on April 1 they will introduce a progressive income tax on cooperative businesses, intended to induce cooperatives to pump their profits into expanded production rather than hefty wages for the members.

Some of these notions are being tested now in Zagorsk, 40 miles northwest of Moscow, a town better known as the spiritual center of the Russian Orthodox Church.

Mr. Mogilevtsev's venture, about a mile from the fortified monastery of Trinity-St. Sergius, where Russian Orthodox priests are trained, is an odd hybrid—partly independent, partly still wedded to the old state system.

The idea came to him last year, Mr. Mogilevtsev said, as he was reading another new law that requires Soviet industries to become autonomous and self-financing. The law, now in force in 60 percent of Soviet industry, will affect the heavily subsidized construction sector next year.

But Mr. Mogilevtsev calculated that his company could never become profitable as long as prices on his products were set artificially low by the state. State price-fixing is not destined to be eliminated for another two or three years.

So with the blessing of his superiors in the Moscow region building materials administration, he and his co-workers liquidated the old state factory on February 1, reorganized as the Beryozka, or "birch," cooperative, and signed a lease for the premises and equipment.

There is a catch. The cooperative agreed to continue filling the standing orders of its old state customers at the same unprofitable prices, and to forgo subsidies.

Whatever new customers the enterprise can drum up will pay higher prices. The prices are still regulated—they cannot be more than 30 percent above production costs—but they are high enough, Mr. Mogilevtsev says, to transform the venture into a profitable concern.

The co-op has found no shortage of buyers—nearby factories building housing for workers, private entrepreneurs engaged in home repair, even people planning to rebuild their country cottages.

Private enterprise already accounts for 40 percent of his output, Mr. Mogilevtsev said, and he has ambitious plans for expansion, adding more parquet, a wider range of lumber products, and construction services.

This week he placed an advertisement in the local newspaper offering to build garages, summer cottages, or private homes on contract. Beryozka will also be the general contractor on a local apartment project.

"When we are richer," he said grandly, "we shall think of merger."

A few mud puddles away, the manager of the neighboring Zagorsk Building Materials Shop No. 1, Pyotr K. Bondar, said that his business was fine and that he trusted the state to keep it that way. "We have vast reserves, and we can always sell something different," Mr. Bondar said. "There cannot be any thought of competition in the way you know it."

The 160 members and employees of Beryozka take home 250 rubles a month, or about $415, more than they made as a state factory. They hope their year-end profit sharing will be 3,000 rubles each.

The smell of fresh-cut lumber and the whine of buzz saws fill the workshop. Squares of parquet flooring are trimmed and glued at a pace that violates the desultory norms of Soviet workplace behavior.

At one assembly line, when a conveyor belt fell behind the pace of the workers, a woman left her workbench to fetch a load of fir planks herself rather than wait for the machine to deliver it.

Like many cooperative directors, Mr. Mogilevtsev is cursed by state distribution of raw materials.

The state delivers him enough birch and fir logs and cement to satisfy his state orders, but for the rest of his production he must wheel and deal, scrimp and recycle, and sometimes buy retail.

After years of finding shortcuts through the industrial bureaucracy, however, Mr. Mogilevtsev is adept at barter. This week his mind was on an article about the director of a bus factory near Riga, in Latvia, a like-minded enterpriser. Perhaps, he mused aloud, he should phone the fellow and offer to swap some parquet for a few work buses.

Independence has given the director concerns he did not have before. The new progressive income tax worries him: will it mean he has to raise prices? Then there is the new draft law on cooperatives, which he is searching for loopholes and shortcomings.

And each week delegations of Soviet future entrepreneurs pull up at the Beryozka gate, like fresh MBAs to Lee Iacocca, for instruction in the art of profit.

He tells them he has seen the future, and it pays.

Gorbachev and Afghan Leader Say Way Seems Clear to Start Soviet Troop Pullout by May 15
By Philip Taubman

MOSCOW, APRIL 7—The Soviet Union and Afghanistan said today that they believed the last barriers to a negotiated settlement of the war in Afghanistan had been eliminated.

The two governments indicated, but did not explicitly confirm, that they had accepted an American formula breaking the last remaining deadlock at the Geneva talks aimed at ending the eight-year-old war.

The compromise would permit Washington to continue providing military aid to the Afghan guerrillas during a withdrawal of Soviet forces at a level commensurate with the aid Moscow gives to the Afghan government.

Western diplomats here said the announcement appeared to clear the way for quick completion of the Geneva talks, with the signing of an agreement likely before the end of next week.

In Washington, Reagan administration officials voiced cautious optimism that a settlement would soon be formally concluded and lead to a Soviet withdrawal. But they also said they were reserving final judgment until the United States received a formal response from the Soviet Union and reviewed the detailed Geneva accords.

In a joint statement issued after a meeting today, Mikhail S. Gorbachev and the Afghan leader, Najibullah, said the Soviet Union would begin withdrawing its troops on May 15 if the Geneva accords were completed within the next few days.

The departure date, originally set by Moscow for early February but postponed as the negotiations bogged down, suggested that Mr. Gorbachev wanted to start bringing Soviet soldiers home before President Reagan's visit to Moscow in late May.

Mr. Gorbachev and Mr. Najibullah met in the Soviet Central Asian city of Tashkent, 190 miles north of the Afghan border.

Mr. Gorbachev later told workers at two collective farms near Tashkent: "There is a certainty that an agreement will be signed on a political settlement. I think that Pakistan and Afghanistan will come to an agreement. And we with the Americans will agree to be guarantors, I think."

Accord Completed on Soviet Pullout
By Paul Lewis

GENEVA, APRIL 8—Full agreement has been reached on a treaty under which the Soviet Union will withdraw its 115,000 soldiers from Afghanistan, the United Nations mediator announced today.

After nearly six years of negotiation, an accord was achieved on a four-part treaty that also provides for the safe return of Afghan refugees and the creation of a neutral and nonaligned Afghan state guaranteed by the United States and the Soviet Union.

In addition, Pakistan and Afghanistan promise to cease all interference in each other's internal affairs. A small United Nations military observer team will be sent to Afghanistan to monitor compliance with the treaty, which is to be signed next week.

"The documents are now finalized and open for signature," the mediator, Under Secretary General Diego Cordovez, said at a news conference here. Officially, the treaty will be signed by Afghanistan and Pakistan, which represents the Afghan insurgents. But, in addition, the United States and the Soviet Union will sign the document as "guarantors."

The agreement today between Afghanistan and Pakistan is meant to end a civil war that has cost at least one million Afghan lives and left five million homeless.

The United States–sponsored pact on the Soviet withdrawal from Afghanistan is a historic development, diplomats here say, because it is the first time Moscow has voluntarily abandoned territory conquered by its army since it withdrew from Austria after World War II in 1955.

News of a new Politburo battle emerged.

Soviet Politburo Is Said to Demote the No. 2 Leader
By Philip Taubman

MOSCOW, APRIL 21—The Politburo, meeting in special session this week, approved steps that all but removed Yegor K. Ligachev as the party's number two leader, Soviet officials said today.

In further indications that a major political confrontation has unfolded in the Kremlin in recent weeks, the Politburo's actions reportedly included removing Mr. Ligachev as the party's senior arbiter of ideological issues.

Some officials said the head of the K.G.B., Viktor M. Chebrikov, had defended Mr. Ligachev at the meeting, raising questions about Mr. Chebrikov's loyalty to Mikhail S. Gorbachev.

With Mr. Gorbachev and Prime Minister Nikolai I. Ryzhkov pressing the attack in what was described as a heated discussion, the Politburo reportedly voted at the special session Tuesday to reduce Mr. Ligachev's powers and ordered him to take a two-month vacation.

It was reported Wednesday that as a result of the session, Mr. Ligachev had been forced to give up his role as a key supervisor of the Soviet press and television, at least temporarily, and to take a vacation.

On the basis of the details that emerged today, Mr. Gorbachev appears to have made a breakthrough in his consolidation of power by confronting and neutralizing Mr. Ligachev, his chief rival in the Communist Party leadership.

The clash between the two men, probably the most important political confrontation in the party leadership since Mr. Gorbachev assumed power three years ago, has left the Soviet leader and his Kremlin allies firmly in command of ideological, propaganda, and personnel matters. Mr. Ligachev has played a key role in all three.

Although many details are unclear, it appears that unconfirmed reports in recent days of a major confrontation were generally accurate. Soviet officials said today that the clash came to a climax at the Politburo meeting Tuesday. The officials said Mr. Ligachev, supported by Mr. Chebrikov, had denied charges that he had tried to undermine Mr. Gorbachev's policies.

The Politburo decisions would appear to remove Mr. Ligachev from the scene during the weeks leading up to a pivotal party meeting scheduled to begin in late June. If Mr. Gorbachev can control the selection of delegates, which is considered more likely in Mr. Ligachev's absence, he could gain a much-needed boost for his programs.

There were several different reports about the specific actions approved by the Politburo Tuesday. Some said Mr. Ligachev, along with being stripped of his position as the party's senior ideologist, also lost his role as a key supervisor of propaganda activities, including the press and television.

Although these reports could not be officially confirmed, they came from officials with access to information about top party deliberations. Despite Mr. Gorbachev's efforts to make public more information about government and party decisions, the deliberations of the Politburo and other top party bodies remain largely secret.

Mr. Ligachev openly advocated a more cautious approach to change in the last three years, but before the recent developments the differences between him and Mr. Gorbachev appeared to be manageable. That apparently changed last month with publication of an article in the newspaper *Sovetskaya Rossiya* that directly challenged Mr. Gorbachev's policies.

After receiving reports that Mr. Ligachev had endorsed the article and helped steer it into print, Mr. Gorbachev reportedly moved to limit his power. Many Westerners who have watched the relationship between the two men since they rose to power in 1985 have assumed that a showdown was likely but did not expect it so soon.

"Mr. Gorbachev saw an opportunity and grabbed it," a Western diplomat said this week.

The March 13 article in *Sovetskaya Rossiya,* ostensibly by a Leningrad teacher, criticized Mr. Gorbachev's policies as too liberal and defended Stalin's leadership. On April 5, *Pravda,* the main party newspaper, denounced the article in a full-page editorial.

In the three weeks that the *Sovetskaya Rossiya* article went unanswered, many Russians concluded that Mr. Gorbachev's programs had been reversed and that his opponents had seized control of the party.

Mr. Gorbachev reportedly was particularly angered when told that Mr. Ligachev had endorsed the *Sovetskaya Rossiya* article at a meeting of newspaper editors on March 14, while Mr. Gorbachev was in Yugoslavia.

"This was considered an act of defiance and insubordination," a party official said this week.

Beset by critics who were attacking him on virtually all fronts, Gorbachev cast his nets ever wider.

Gorbachev Sees Church Leaders, Vows Tolerance
By Bill Keller

MOSCOW, APRIL 29—In a highly unusual Kremlin meeting with the hierarchy of the Russian Orthodox Church, Mikhail S. Gorbachev called today for a more tolerant attitude toward religion in the interest of national unity.

The Soviet leader condemned past antireligious repression and promised that a law being prepared on freedom of conscience would give believers broader protection to practice their faith.

The meeting, held in St. Catherine's Palace, is believed by some to be the first publicized reception for religious leaders in the Kremlin in more than 40 years, and part of it was shown tonight at the beginning of the main television news program. It was taken by some believers as an important signal of a more positive climate for the faithful.

According to official Soviet estimates, 40 million of the country's 280 million people consider themselves believers. Western specialists believe the total to be more than twice that, the majority of them Russian Orthodox.

Welcoming the 77-year-old church primate, Patriarch Pimen, and other members of the ruling church synod, Mr. Gorbachev said: "Believers are Soviet people, workers, patriots, and they have the full right to express their conviction with dignity. *Perestroika* and democratization concern them, too—in full measure and without any restrictions."

Mr. Gorbachev's words, and the sight of his smiling reception of the church leaders on national television, underscored his intention to enlist religious believers in his program of social and economic change, which he calls *perestroika,* or "restructuring."

In a statement read on the news, the Soviet leader called for an official policy toward religion that assures the right of the church to "carry out its activity without any outside interference."

"A new law on the freedom of conscience, now being drafted, will reflect the interests of religious organizations as well," Mr. Gorbachev said. "These are all tangible results of new approaches to state-church relations under conditions of *perestroika* and democratization of Soviet society."

He took note of "our differences in world outlook," but said a new attitude toward the church was important for strengthening national unity during a period of change.

Many believers have expressed hope that Mr. Gorbachev would use the 1,000-year anniversary of Christianity in Russia this summer to lift some official limits on religious practice. The meeting today was reportedly held at the request of religious leaders in connection with the anniversary.

Others remain skeptical about the chance of significant changes in the system of state controls, which requires churches to register with the state and sharply restricts religious teaching, charitable work, and proselytizing. About 200 believers remain in prisons and labor camps for violations connected with the practice of their faith, Western human rights groups say.

Acknowledged believers are banned from the Communist Party, and their choice of careers is in effect limited. Baptisms, church marriages, and funerals are often conducted in secret, for fear that discovery will result in official retribution.

Church officials have said that a state commission is reviewing the highly restrictive 1929 laws on religion. The commission is believed to be considering amendments to allow some religious teaching and permit the church to engage in charitable work.

Mr. Gorbachev has talked with church leaders at ceremonial occasions and has included them in visible posts on committees that promote Soviet disarmament proposals, but he previously had little to say about religious rights.

Calling the religious persecutions that began under Stalin in the 1930s a "departure from socialist principles," the Soviet leader said: "Mistakes made with regard to the church and believers in the 1930s and the years that followed are being rectified."

He did not specifically acknowledge any current complaints of believers.

"The attitude to the church, to the believers, should be determined by the interests of strengthening the unity of all working people, of the entire nation," he said.

The Reverend Gleb Yakunin, a campaigner for religious freedom who was freed from Siberian exile and allowed to resume his priestly duties last year, said tonight that Mr. Gorbachev's meeting was "a symbol of a change of policy," adding, "It is very important."

Church leaders have traditionally been invited to the Kremlin on the annual observance in November of the Bolshevik Revolution and for funerals of Soviet leaders, but standard histories of the church indicate that Mr. Gorbachev is the first to hold such a special meeting since Stalin did so during World War II.

According to the histories, the only precedent for today's meeting was when Stalin summoned three senior prelates to a meeting on September 4, 1943, at which he restored the church to good standing and encouraged its support for the war effort.

The pell-mell rush to more glasnost *slowed, stalled, and then seemed to go backward. Was this a merely tactical retreat, or did it signal a more fundamental shift of direction? Clearly what was at stake was timing as two major events loomed on the horizon for Gorbachev. The first of these was the summit meeting with President Reagan, and then just after that there would be a critical party meeting where the Soviet leader would seek to remove and limit some of the party's long-established prerogatives. As he navigated his way past the two events, he had to parry different sets of critics.*

Soviet Closes a Magazine Extolling Openness
By Bill Keller

MOSCOW, MAY 18—The editor of the independent magazine *Glasnost* said today that the authorities had confiscated his printing equipment and destroyed his files and manuscripts, leaving the future of the best-known Soviet dissident journal in doubt.

The editor, Sergei I. Grigoryants, who was released Monday from a week in jail, said tonight that he had also received indirect reports that the Soviet prosecutor was preparing to charge him with defaming the Soviet state, a crime that carries up to three years in prison or internal exile. The dissident editor, who has grown increasingly disillusioned about the prospects for change, charged that the crackdown on his magazine and other recent police moves against dissent were a deliberate presummit message to President Reagan from Soviet police and the K.G.B. that they, not Mikhail S. Gorbachev's liberal supporters, still control the rights environment here.

The crackdown on *Glasnost* magazine—named after Mr. Gorbachev's favorite catchword for greater official tolerance of public expression—was a major setback for an unofficial publication that has become, in a little

more than 10 months, the largest and most influential of the new generation of dissident literature.

The journal of dissident news and opinion is issued twice a month in
editions of about 200 copies, and articles are widely reprinted in other
independent magazines around the country and published in translations
abroad.

Mr. Grigoryants said that while he was imprisoned the police and
plainclothesmen had ransacked the house outside Moscow that he used
as his editorial office, leaving him without equipment to continue publication.

Speaking to reporters today at his apartment in Moscow, Mr. Grigoryants said he was barred from the house Tuesday by a cordon of police
and plainclothesmen, but had managed to inspect it through the open
windows.

Mr. Grigoryants said officials in the Ramensky district had told him
to file documents proving that the house and the equipment belonged to
him, a process that he said the authorities could easily stretch out for a
year or more.

Mr. Grigoryants has spent more than eight years in prisons and labor
camps, including a term for "anti-Soviet agitation and propaganda" for
his work on an earlier underground bulletin. He was one of scores of
political prisoners set free early last year under a mass pardon.

Pieces to a Soviet Puzzle; Why the Selective Tolerance of Dissent?
At a Vital Time, Some of It Aids Gorbachev
By Bill Keller

MOSCOW, MAY 19—Americans who are puzzled these days by the
apparent contradictions of Mikhail S. Gorbachev's Soviet Union might
try to look at it the way many Soviet intellectuals do, as a country in the
grip of an all-consuming political contest.

In the press and in popular discussion, the struggle overshadows President Reagan's visit here in 10 days and even the current withdrawal of
Soviet troops from Afghanistan.

Attention is focused on an extraordinary Communist Party conference
that begins four weeks after Mr. Reagan returns home, and the ultimate
issue is the course of the Soviet Union.

Mr. Gorbachev's strategy helps explain such questions as why one
dissident is welcomed in from the cold while another is sent to jail, why
George Orwell but not Aleksandr Solzhenitsyn is published now, why
Pravda can call for limits on the powers of the Communist Party but a
ragtag band of political amateurs that proclaims itself an opposition party
encounters the fierce indignation of the police and press.

If the party meeting in late June goes as planned, Mr. Gorbachev will begin a new assault on the stubborn political machine perfected by Stalin.

Mr. Gorbachev's opponents are all those who feel threatened by the Soviet leader, especially the entrenched party apparatus that sees its personal power endangered, and ideological conservatives who fear that Communism is being undermined.

The contest is being played out partly in the Soviet equivalent of smoke-filled rooms, where party leaders are trying to manipulate the selection of delegates for the party conference as a way to guarantee the outcome.

But there is also an important public component as Mr. Gorbachev tries to create a bandwagon effect for his program.

For the Soviet leader, the major political tool is *glasnost,* the catchword for his policy of permitting previously banned ideas into print.

Glasnost rallies the intellectuals, who generally revere Mr. Gorbachev and who chart the pace of change by the vigor of debate. Mr. Gorbachev, it is safe to assume, also hopes *glasnost* will intimidate opponents, recruit new supporters, and persuade doubters that his juggernaut is unstoppable.

The first job of *glasnost* is to discredit Stalin's legacy and dispel the popular nostalgia for Stalin that is still widespread among the older generation.

The coming publication in *Novy Mir* of *Nineteen Eighty-four,* George Orwell's parable of tyranny—long suppressed here because the totalitarian state imagined by Orwell too closely resembled the one devised by Stalin—is astonishing to the West. But in the thick of the political contest, the publication is greeted as a natural evolution in the exorcism of Stalin's legacy.

Historical analysis has also pushed steadily deeper into cherished myths regarding Stalin. Last month a historian published a searing analysis of party history, asserting that Stalin "created the ideal totalitarian state," and that many of its features live on.

Glasnost has also enabled Mr. Gorbachev to target new constituencies. His recent televised appeal for greater tolerance for religion, for example, seemed clearly aimed at luring millions of churchgoers onto his bandwagon.

But *glasnost,* so far, stops at the edge of the political contest.

Much of the jockeying over how much openness should be allowed to whom was byplay intended to galvanize and smoke out forces for the upcoming party meeting.

Soviet Moves to Curtail Communist Party's Power

By Philip Taubman

MOSCOW, MAY 26—The Communist Party Central Committee has approved proposals made public today that would curtail the power of the party and limit the term of party and government officials, in most cases, to 10 years.

The proposals, sponsored by Mikhail S. Gorbachev, would expand the authority of popularly elected legislatures and make them more democratic by requiring competitive elections by secret ballot. Similar procedures would govern the election of party officials.

In addition, the Central Committee endorsed plans to overhaul the judicial system by increasing the rights of defendants and the independence of judges.

The proposals, approved at a Central Committee meeting Monday, were made public today by the press agency Tass. The Central Committee said the proposals were the answer to the central question that has developed after three difficult years of trying to revitalize the Soviet Union: "What needs to be done to remove the obstacles, to give a new and powerful impulse to the revolutionary process of renewal, to make it irreversible?"

The broad changes, if put into practice, would leave the party as the ultimate source of authority and policy, but would reduce its ubiquitous involvement in the day-to-day management of government and economic institutions and almost every aspect of Soviet life.

Given Mr. Gorbachev's often-stated allegiance to the principles of Communist governance, including the leading role of the party, the package of revisions seems as far as the leadership is likely to go for now in reordering the political system.

Like other changes suggested by Mr. Gorbachev in the last three years, the measures approved this week are likely to encounter resistance as they are instituted, and there is no guarantee they will in the end have the impact intended.

An initial call for changes in the election of party and government officials was made by Mr. Gorbachev and approved by the Central Committee in January 1987, but so far there has been only limited use.

The measures approved Monday, called theses, will serve as the main subject for discussion at a special party meeting in late June. The meeting was called by Mr. Gorbachev to muster renewed support for his programs and extend his campaign for change into new areas.

The gathering, called a party conference, is likely to approve the Gorbachev proposals now that they have been blessed by the Central Committee. The committee, which numbers more than 300 members at full strength, is the top policy-making body.

But before the party congress was to open, Gorbachev had to contend with and dispose of the summit visit of President Reagan. Though the Kremlin leaders were regarding the visit—the first by an American president in 14 years—as important, they were preoccupied with preparations for the party gathering that was to follow. Moreover, no one on either side was expecting any major breakthrough on arms comparable to what was achieved at the last meeting. Instead, the Soviets were assuming that President Reagan would be concentrating on issues they would find embarrassing. The assumption was borne out when President Reagan's spokesman, Marlin Fitzwater, made clear during a stopover in Helsinki, that Mr. Reagan was eager to reorient the objective of the meeting away from the single issue of arms control toward human rights. In Finland, the President challenged Mr. Gorbachev to improve the Soviet record in this area by helping to reunite divided families, increasing and accelerating the pace of emigration, ending suppression of religion, and releasing political prisoners. He called human rights, "agenda item number one."

Reagan Presses Gorbachev on Church and Civil Rights; "Sermonizing" Annoys Hosts
By Philip Taubman

MOSCOW, MAY 30—President Reagan and Mikhail S. Gorbachev publicly clashed over human rights issues today as the President, quoting Aleksandr Solzhenitsyn, appealed for increased civil and religious liberties in the Soviet Union.

Despite the sharpening debate between the two men on human rights here, the United States and Soviet Union reported making modest progress on some arms control questions and that two minor arms accords would probably be signed Tuesday. One deals with verifying nuclear tests and the other with advance notification of ballistic missile tests. In addition, several accords on exchanges and other bilateral matters will be signed on Tuesday.

From the gilded halls of the Kremlin to the white-walled compound of the Danilov Monastery, Mr. Reagan used his first visit to the Soviet Union and his fourth meeting with Mr. Gorbachev to campaign for greater freedom. Mr. Gorbachev, in a clear response to his guest's remarks on human rights, said at a nationally televised Kremlin dinner this evening that contacts between Americans and Soviet citizens should be improved without lecturing one another.

Standing before a wall of frescoes in the Kremlin's Faceted Chamber, Mr. Gorbachev said that the Soviet Union favored widening exchanges but that "this should be done without interfering in domestic affairs, without sermonizing or imposing one's views and ways, without turning family or personal problems into a pretext for confrontation between states."

Mr. Reagan's comments here are the most sustained criticism of internal Soviet policies by a foreign visitor since Mr. Gorbachev assumed power in March 1985, and raised potentially sensitive political problems for the Soviet leader as he faces an important Communist Party meeting next month.

Spokesmen for both sides said arms control issues were the main topics during a meeting in St. Catherine's Hall this morning between the large Soviet and American delegations.

They said the two sides had agreed on some verification measures for two types of strategic weapons, mobile land-based missiles and cruise missiles fired from bombers.

But they said other problems still blocked a long-range missile accord, which both leaders have said they hope to achieve before Mr. Reagan leaves office next January.

Mr. Gorbachev, obviously irritated with Mr. Reagan's emphasis on human rights, responded caustically several times and seemed eager to focus on other issues, particularly arms control.

Mr. Gorbachev's remarks about "sermonizing" were apparently made in response to a meeting earlier in the day between Mr. Reagan and a group of dissidents at Spaso House, the residence of the American ambassador.

At the meeting, described by the White House as a gathering of "selected Soviet citizens," Mr. Reagan said Moscow has made progress on human rights in recent years but still falls short of acceptable international standards for freedom of religion, speech, and travel.

Many of those in attendance were Soviet Jews who have been denied permission to emigrate to the West.

During a morning visit to the Danilov Monastery, Mr. Reagan said, "We pray that the return of this monastery signals a willingness to return to believers the thousands of other houses of worship which are now closed, boarded up, or used for secular purposes."

The monastery, an ancient center of the Russian Orthodox Church that had been turned into a factory, was only recently returned by the government to control of clerics.

Addressing a group of monks and church leaders who were dressed in the traditional black robes and cylindrical caps of the church, Mr. Reagan used the words of Mr. Solzhenitsyn as he called for a renewal of religious faith in the Soviet Union.

" 'When you travel the byroads of central Russia, you begin to understand the secret of the pacifying Russian countryside,' " Mr. Reagan read from Mr. Solzhenitsyn.

" 'It is the churches. They lift their bell towers—graceful, shapely, all different—high over mundane timber and thatch.' "

Mr. Solzhenitsyn, the winner of the 1970 Nobel Prize in Literature who was forced into exile in 1974, is one of the few contemporary Russian writers whose works remain banned in the Soviet Union. He now lives in Vermont.

After looking at icons, Mr. Reagan said, "Like that of the saints and martyrs depicted in these icons, the faith of your people has been tested and tempered in the crucible of hardship."

Moscow Summit: Gorbachev Voices Irritation at Slow Pace of Missile Talks; Reagan Impresses Soviet Elite; Statement Is Due
By Philip Taubman

MOSCOW, MAY 31—On the third day of President Reagan's visit to Moscow, Mikhail S. Gorbachev expressed exasperation today with the absence of progress in removing key obstacles to a treaty reducing strategic nuclear weapons.

But Mr. Gorbachev's frustration was overshadowed by a bravura performance by President Reagan, who seemed to capture the imagination of Moscow's intelligentsia with a series of speeches and public appearances that celebrated Russia's literary heritage and rallied Soviet citizens to support change in their country.

The performance established common ground between Mr. Reagan and Mr. Gorbachev on the need for renewal in the Soviet Union.

Mr. Reagan, turning away from the emphasis on human rights that marked his first two days in Moscow, called on Russians to support and extend Mr. Gorbachev's program of economic and social change.

Mr. Gorbachev's unhappiness with the pace of the arms negotiations was evident this morning when he met with Mr. Reagan in his private office in the Council of Ministers building in the Kremlin.

"Maybe now is again a time to bang our fists on the table," he told Mr. Reagan, according to reporters who attended the beginning of the meeting. He was referring to their joint effort in Geneva in 1985 to clear away problems.

American officials said the limited substantive gains of the summit meeting this week, the fourth between Mr. Reagan and Mr. Gorbachev, would be outlined in a joint statement on Wednesday. The statement was being prepared this evening.

Gorbachev Criticizes Reagan, Seeing "Missed Opportunities," but Calls Visit a "Major Event"; Summit Talks End
By Philip Taubman

MOSCOW, JUNE 1—Mikhail S. Gorbachev complained today that his fourth and probably final summit meeting with President Reagan was filled with "missed opportunities" and impeded by contradictions in American policy.

But in a concluding two-hour news conference he balanced his criticism of Mr. Reagan by calling the President's visit to Moscow this week a "major event" that moved relations "maybe one rung or two up the ladder."

In a joint statement that recorded modest progress on a number of issues, the two sides expressed hope that the dialogue established by Mr. Reagan and Mr. Gorbachev in their four summit meetings since 1985 would endure, despite "real differences of history, tradition, and ideology."

This week's talks, which officially end Thursday morning with Mr. Reagan's departure for London, seem likely to be remembered less for any particular achievements than for the symbolic spectacle of an American president in the Soviet capital proselytizing for change and expanded liberties.

After the tentative nature of the Geneva summit meeting in 1985, the volatility in Reykjavík, Iceland, in 1986, and the substantive accomplishments in Washington last December, the Moscow summit meeting seems to reflect a sense that the two men have all but exhausted the potential for advancing relations in the waning months of the Reagan administration.

In separate news conferences, the two leaders said they were pleased with the gains recorded this week, but Mr. Gorbachev devoted a good portion of his remarks to criticism of Mr. Reagan, suggesting considerable frustration and irritation with the President.

Mr. Gorbachev's exasperation seemed to stem less from an absence of progress on central arms-control issues—the chance for that had never appeared great—than from Mr. Reagan's concentration on human rights issues and the President's refusal to endorse the general guidelines for Soviet-American relations proposed by the Soviet leader. The general guidelines included in the final joint statement were written by the Americans.

The Soviet leader also accused the American negotiators of trying to dodge issues on conventional arms, and he complained about unfavorable trade treatment.

Although he did not say as much, Mr. Gorbachev left the impression in his news conference that he had lost patience with Mr. Reagan and was ready to turn his attention to the President who will take office in January.

Mr. Reagan, who on Tuesday said he no longer thought the Soviet Union was "an evil empire," added today, "I think there is quite a difference today in the leadership and the relationship between our two countries."

The Soviet press has almost gleefully reported Mr. Reagan's retraction of the "evil empire" description.

One American official said that the two sides had found "important common ground on some aspects of the search for a Namibia-Angola settlement."

The summit over, full attention was being focused on the party meeting both by those who were hoping to change old party structures and practices and those who were intent on keeping things as unchanged as possible.

Local Leaders Rebuff Backers of Gorbachev
By Philip Taubman

MOSCOW, JUNE 8—Local Communist Party organizations across the Soviet Union, resisting the wishes of Mikhail S. Gorbachev, appear to have picked delegates to a key party meeting later this month mostly from their own orthodox leadership ranks.

The selection provoked a series of highly unusual public protests around the country before it ended Friday, as citizens and rank-and-file party members, supported by a number of newspapers, condemned the process as undemocratic and demanded reconsideration of rejected candidates. The protests have coincided with a tumult of debate and preconference suggestions in the official press, many with no evident official blessing, on the future of the country.

The press agency Tass, in a review of the delegate selection process, said Friday, "Certain difficulties developed in a number of party organizations."

The choice of delegates apparently leaves Mr. Gorbachev without the major infusion of new faces he hoped would help generate enthusiastic support for his programs, but does not necessarily threaten his control of the meeting, which is scheduled to begin in Moscow on June 28.

Party officials in the capital remain confident that Mr. Gorbachev can steer the meeting in the direction he wants, which is to renew his mandate for change, and that he can count on traditional deference to his position as leader of the Communist Party to prevent any unpleasant surprises.

A complete list of the 5,000 delegates has not been published, but a partial roster and Soviet press coverage show that some of Mr. Gorbachev's most prominent supporters were not selected and that others were added at the last moment after the intervention of the Soviet leader and his top aides.

Among those chosen as delegates who are identified with Mr. Gorbachev were Leonid I. Abalkin, an economist; Yuri N. Afanasyev, a historian; Grigory Y. Baklanov, the editor of the journal *Znamia;* Yegor V. Yakovlev, the editor of the newspaper *Moscow News;* Vitaly A. Korotich, editor of the magazine *Ogonyok;* and Elem G. Klimov, head of the filmmakers' union.

Those closely identified with Mr. Gorbachev and not selected included Tatyana I. Zaslavskaya, Nikolai P. Shmelev, and Gavriil K. Popov, all economists; and Aleksandr I. Gelman and Mikhail F. Shatrov, both playwrights.

Boris N. Yeltsin, who was removed from his post as Moscow Communist Party leader in November after complaining that change was not proceeding fast enough, was also chosen as a delegate, Reuters reported. The news agency quoted Gennadi I. Gerasimov, the Foreign Ministry spokesman, as saying Mr. Yeltsin had been chosen from the Karelian Autonomous Republic on the Finnish border. He said he did not know whether Mr. Yeltsin had any connection with Karelia, but added that geographical links were not required for election to the conference.

Aleksandr Y. Bovin, a political analyst for the government newspaper *Izvestia,* reflected widespread disappointment with the selection process when he wrote in Sunday's paper, "Frankly speaking, I and everyone I talk to feels we have been cheated."

"The party apparatus," he wrote, "has taken the preparation for the conference in its skilled hands, and, with minor exceptions, it smashed the young seedlings of party democracy. As before, the lists of candidates went from top down."

The selection process, which unfolded over the last month in more than 4,900 party meetings, reflected the struggle between the party's Old Guard and Mr. Gorbachev's followers over the country's political and economic systems. As an experiment in democracy, the selection was clearly flawed, with party organizations unwilling to relinquish their power.

This month's meeting, called a party conference, is the first gathering of its kind since 1941. Party business is normally transacted at weekly meetings of the Politburo, semiannual sessions of the Central Committee, and quadrennial congresses.

Mr. Gorbachev last year proposed the conference in hopes that it would give impetus to his efforts for change.

Last month the Central Committee approved Mr. Gorbachev's proposals that would curtail the power of the party, increase the authority of popularly elected legislatures, revise the legal code, and set fixed terms for party and government officials. The key question about the conference is how detailed a plan it will approve to carry out the broad proposals.

Mr. Gorbachev's campaign to revitalize the economy and reshape elements of the political system has often won the approval of the party leadership in the last three years only to be frustrated by the government and party apparatus.

Beginning at the smallest party cells in factories, laboratories, farms, universities, and other diverse enterprises, the 20 million party members were supposed to nominate and vote for candidates. Those approved would then be passed up to the next level for consideration, with final selection made by primary party organizations.

But many of the candidates supported at lower levels—often teachers, writers, and scientists known to favor radical change—were discarded by higher party bodies to make way for more conventional delegates, frequently veteran officials.

Moscow News, a weekly that has championed change, has reported that when party leaders tried to dictate the choice of candidates at the Volzhsky automobile factory in Kuibyshev, an industrial center southeast of Moscow, party members rebelled.

While the party struggled with formulas for change in Moscow, in the tiny Baltic Republic of Estonia, a crack was opened in the Communist monopoly on political activity.

Setting Precedent, Estonia Allows a Non-Communist Front to Form
By Bill Keller

MOSCOW, JUNE 20—Authorities in the republic of Estonia, in an important precedent for other regions of the Soviet Union, have permitted the creation of the first large-scale political group outside the Communist Party.

According to Estonian press accounts and interviews, the new People's Front of Estonia has mushroomed to 40,000 members in less than two months, embracing a platform that combines ardent support for Mikhail S. Gorbachev with calls for greater political and economic independence for Estonia.

Last Friday, the front demonstrated its popular appeal by gathering more than 100,000 people, including the second-ranking Communist Party official in Estonia, for an emotional rally on the festival grounds in Tallinn, the Estonian capital.

Organizers say they plan to nominate candidates for local and national elections, to lobby for changes in the law, and to promote referendums.

What has happened in Estonia appears to be a trial run for the creation of similar fronts that would serve as a pro-Gorbachev lobby against the entrenched Communist Party apparatus.

Communist Party leaders may also hope that they can use such fronts to assert a degree of control over nationalist sentiments that have presented an unnerving challenge to Moscow in the Baltic republics, in Soviet Central Asia, and recently in the Caucasus Mountain republics of Armenia and Azerbaijan.

Organizers of the People's Front say they intend to maintain their independence by banning Communist Party and government officials from holding leading positions in the front.

Most top leaders of the front are Communist Party members who are considered strong advocates of political and economic change.

The agenda of the People's Front, published earlier this month in the newspaper *Sovetskaya Estoniya,* said participation is open to anyone who supports Mr. Gorbachev's program of *perestroika,* or reducing rigidity in the Soviet system, and who disavows "Stalinist, conservative viewpoints."

Similar fronts are being organized in Moscow, Leningrad, Kiev, and Yaroslavl, and in the republic of Lithuania, according to Soviet press reports and to members of political clubs.

Last month, Tatyana I. Zaslavskaya, a sociologist who is regarded as an influential consultant to Mr. Gorbachev on economic and social problems, called for the creation of popular fronts across the nation as a counterforce to government and party bureaucrats.

Unofficial political clubs have sprung up in cities across the country, but none have succeeded in developing such a mass following or winning such support from local officials.

Estonia has often been in the forefront of economic and political experimentation. The republic's 1.5 million people have the highest per capita income in the country and have taken more readily than other regions to Mr. Gorbachev's calls for private enterprise and more freewheeling debate.

The republic has been a center of nationalist feelings, stirred by nostalgia for the period from 1918 to 1940, when Estonia was independent, and by resentment of Russian dominance.

In Heady Moscow, Political Ferment

By Bill Keller

MOSCOW, JUNE 25—A delegate arriving in Moscow today from the provinces for the Communist Party's national conference next week might well have thought that the Soviet capital had become detached from reality.

At a crowded central square in Moscow, demonstrators demanding a multiparty political system brawled with the police in front of thousands of agitated bystanders.

As more than 200 uniformed police tried to control the crowd, onlookers shouted "Fascist! Fascist!" at the police and tried to protect protesters from arrest.

A mile away, outside Dynamo Stadium, Andrei D. Sakharov joined with an unusual alliance of former political prisoners and establishment figures to demand that the country build a monument honoring Stalin's victims.

The rally, organized by a group that has gathered more than 30,000 signatures on a petition to be presented to the party conference, was held with an official blessing.

Elsewhere in the center of the city, an alliance of unofficial political clubs gathered on the street to pronounce themselves a new "People's Front." They waved portraits of Lenin and Mikhail S. Gorbachev.

As if this were not enough to disorient a delegate from the provinces, an official publisher has begun distributing 50,000 copies of a new book in which proponents of change, including Mr. Sakharov, prescribe sweeping revisions in almost every aspect of Soviet policy.

The unusually frank book, *There Is No Alternative,* is being distributed to all 5,000 conference delegates as a thought-provoking menu of proposals for change.

Mr. Sakharov, in his chapter of the book, calls for a thorough investigation of the K.G.B. and alludes to the 1968 Soviet invasion of Czechoslovakia, a subject still off-limits to criticism in the official press.

"Another attempt at *perestroika* within the socialist camp was suppressed by tanks in 1968," he wrote, using Mr. Gorbachev's term for restructuring Soviet society and the economy.

Moscow today was a dizzying display of a country shaken by new political forces, and straining to find a balance between tolerance and control.

The awkwardness of the balancing act was especially dramatic at the square in front of the *Izvestia* newspaper building, where a few dozen members of a self-styled opposition party, the Democratic Union, set off more than an hour of confusion.

Lately on Saturdays the square has become a gathering point for political activists of different views, from independent Communists and Western-style democrats to Hare Krishnas and members of the Russian nationalist society Pamyat ("memory").

Moscow police have generally tolerated the gatherings while trying to exclude those whose slogans are considered "provocative."

Today's protests were in defiance of a ban on demonstrations in the city center that has been imposed to prevent public disruptions during the party conference, which convenes Tuesday.

When members of the Democratic Union held up signs calling for a multiparty system and an end to "political repression," young men clearly working in league with the police dashed in and tore the signs away.

The uniformed police linked arms and moved in with bullhorns in an effort to clear the square, but bystanders sided with the demonstrators, and scuffles broke out.

At one point hundreds of onlookers took up a resounding chant of "Freedom! Freedom!" while protesters were pulled off to waiting police vans.

Some of the young policemen looked terrified as the crowd surged against their lines.

Across the square, another group of demonstrators, representing several unofficial political clubs, announced the creation of a People's Front that hopes to serve as an alternative political force outside the Communist Party.

Annoyed by the turmoil at the other end of the square, they finally carried their banners to another street corner, where they were allowed to finish their speeches without police interference.

In the middle of the square, Police Col. Girogi V. Postayuk was surrounded by derisive citizens demanding to know why the demonstrations were not permitted.

"They are not permitted in this place, temporarily, during the party conference," the colonel explained defensively. "You should have gone to the demonstration at Dynamo."

The gathering outside Dynamo Stadium was Mr. Sakharov's first street rally since the 1970s, and it brought him together with an extraordinary alliance of figures inside and outside the official establishment.

Speakers who addressed the crowd of several hundred included Elem G. Klimov, the filmmaker who is the head of the official cinematographers' union; Yuri N. Afanasyev, the historian; Lev Timofeyev, the dissident editor; and Vitaly A. Korotich, the editor of the popular weekly magazine *Ogonyok*.

"This was our first real political meeting in Moscow," the writer Yuri

Karyakin told reporters after the gathering. "You may think it was semiliterate, but it was a beginning and it was important that there were many young people there."

Speeding Up the Changes
By Bill Keller

MOSCOW, JUNE 28—The transfer of power was Mikhail S. Gorbachev's theme today as he opened a national conference of the Communist Party, but it was clear from the text that a major motivating force was his disappointment with the economy.

Woven into his call for remaking the Soviet political system was Mr. Gorbachev's most candid admission to date that his economic program has failed to break the stranglehold of central government ministries and to raise his people's standard of living.

As a result, the speech moved the Soviet leader decisively into the camp of his more radical economic advisers, who have complained for months that the economic changes of the last two years were too few and too slow.

Mr. Gorbachev's call for a shift of political power from the Communist Party to elected government bodies, and from Moscow to localities, was accompanied by new proposals to lift controls on farming, industry, and private business and to give more freedom to the marketplace.

The Soviet leader said that his earlier economic proposals had been too timid and shortsighted and that they had become tangled in bureaucratic resistance and in a shortage of public initiative.

"We must analyze not only the successes but also the mistakes and the lessons to be drawn from our activity," Mr. Gorbachev said, referring to his program of restructuring and reducing rigidity in the Soviet system. "We must be self-critical and admit that we could have accomplished far more than we have in these three years in the main *perestroika* areas."

"There was a lot we simply did not know and did not see until now," Mr. Gorbachev said. "The neglect in various fields of the economy turned out to be more serious than we had initially thought." Mr. Gorbachev also warned, apparently for the first time, that the Soviet Union faced a problem familiar to the West: a budget deficit that has created a danger of inflation.

Mr. Gorbachev said one major mistake had been to allow the traditional practices of price setting and government distribution of supplies to continue. These, he said, had turned out to be major roadblocks to economic revival. Discarding his earlier plan to maintain the system until the next decade, he declared that before 1990, companies must begin competing in the marketplace for energy and raw materials.

Mr. Gorbachev also hinted strongly that he no longer planned to wait two years before raising prices on consumer goods like meat and milk. The Soviet leader last year backed away from price hikes on consumer goods because of strong popular resistance.

"It is absolutely necessary, therefore, to resolve this problem, no matter how difficult it may be and no matter what doubts and fears it may create at first glance," he said.

The Soviet leader promised that money taken from consumers in the form of higher prices would be returned in some form of compensation.

In a proposal with important political and economic ramifications, the Soviet leader said local governments should be allowed to tax the earnings of companies in their jurisdictions.

This move, he suggested, would strengthen the financial clout of the local governments, which now take their budgets from Moscow, and would make producers more sensitive to customers in their immediate areas.

In another move that has been urged by many of his economic advisers, Mr. Gorbachev promised strict new limits on the power of government ministries to dominate factories by issuing state orders for products.

He said this power had essentially become a back-door way of running the economy from Moscow instead of letting consumer demand drive industry.

"What is most intolerable is that enterprises are being compelled by means of state orders to manufacture goods that are not in demand, compelled for the simple reason that they want to attain the notorious 'gross output' targets," Mr. Gorbachev said.

"Oh, how many faithful servants we have of 'gross output'!" he declared.

He said the emphasis on churning out more goods, regardless of who wants them, must give way to use of market forces and an emphasis on quality. He said industrial managers have been reluctant to use their new authority to reward better workers with higher pay, because in Soviet society inequalities in pay have been seen as unfair.

"Enterprises that have been given the right to reward their more efficient workers and cut down the incomes of those who are lazy, wasteful, and idle are using it too timidly for fear of offending anyone," Mr. Gorbachev said.

He renewed his appeal for greater use of small-scale farming as the solution to the country's critical food shortage.

In discussing the country's economic straits, Mr. Gorbachev touched on a problem long acknowledged but rarely discussed in public.

"For many years, state budget expenditures grew more rapidly than the revenue," he said.

A Soviet President? Gorbachev Offers Some New Politics and Few Doubt He Intends to Lead

By Bill Keller

MOSCOW, JUNE 29—Mikhail S. Gorbachev, the Soviet leader, has offered his people the design for a prodigious new political contraption, and few doubt that he intends to be its driver.

The proposal he outlined Tuesday in his opening speech to a national Communist Party conference is a blueprint for a new Soviet government, headed by a president—almost certainly President Gorbachev—who would hold real power over domestic and foreign policy.

Nor is there much mystery about what he is up to.

Mr. Gorbachev evidently hopes to free himself from the constraints imposed by his more conservative colleagues in the Communist Party leadership and by the balky party bureaucracy, who are widely accused of hampering the economic and social restructuring Mr. Gorbachev calls *perestroika.*

But as with his jerry-built economic machine, which is now faltering from early design flaws and an unexpectedly rough road, the question is whether Mr. Gorbachev can fully control what he has set in motion.

Mr. Gorbachev's design for a new government is an elaborate balancing act between party control and popular democracy.

He proposed a huge new superlegislature, called the Congress of People's Deputies, composed of 1,500 delegates elected in districts nationwide, with 750 additional seats allotted to Communist Party committees, trade unions, artistic organizations, and others.

This congress would in turn select a standing legislature of 400 to 450 members, and a president to oversee it.

Mr. Gorbachev, who is general secretary of the party, has not said he wants the new post of president, and his close Politburo ally and propaganda chief, Aleksandr N. Yakovlev, was coy on the subject.

"I do not favor prophecies of any sort," he said at a news conference on Tuesday. "We will wait and see."

But no one watching Mr. Gorbachev dominate today's proceedings, or listening to the rapturous tributes of some delegates, harbored serious doubts.

"I am for giving this general secretary full presidential powers," said Yuri D. Chernichenko, an official of the Soviet writers' union and a delegate, stressing the word "this" and seeming rather baffled that anyone would bother to ask.

Mr. Gorbachev's personal stature was evident in the thunderous applause when Mikhail A. Ulyanov, a delegate who is the captivating actor best known for his portrayal of Lenin, pleaded for just one exception to a strict 10-year limit on official service. Mr. Gorbachev alone, he said, should have 15 years.

"It's a social revolution going on, and we should not change horses in midstream," he declared.

By assuming the role of president, Mr. Gorbachev would be able to claim a mandate not only from the party but from the society at large.

The added authority would, perhaps, make it easier for him to present his programs without first whittling them to fit the consensus view in the party's ruling Politburo.

As president, he would also stand astride a newly fortified network of elected people's councils. These bodies, known as soviets, are supposed to be transformed from puppets of the Communist Party into genuine law-making and administrative powers, accountable to the public and armed with the money to back up their authority.

Mr. Gorbachev has clearly calculated that the soviets would supplant the entrenched party apparatus that now rules Soviet life down to the shop floor. He counts on the soviets being more responsive to his calls for cutting red tape and rewarding local creativity.

Approval of Mr. Gorbachev's plan at the party conference looked so certain that delegates spent little time today addressing the substance of his grand scheme. Only two relatively peripheral issues prompted any controversy: the question of whether officials should be limited to 10 years or 15, and the role of local party bosses in the soviets.

Mr. Gorbachev, probably in a concession to those who fear too much dilution of the party's power, suggested that local party leaders automatically be nominated to head the local government councils.

But the Soviet leader has seen that it is easier to win general approval for grand ideas than to make them work.

In his speech Tuesday, Mr. Gorbachev acknowledged that his economic plan was badly bogged down. He admitted that his original proposals to free industry and farming from central control were too timid. The programs have become entangled in bureaucratic resistance and a lack of initiative bred by 70 years of orders from the top.

The political restructuring he proposed is in large measure an attempt to kick the economic program to life.

Yet remaking a government is an ambitious project, one likely to take years. First there will be studies to flesh out the details of a plan that is full of blank spots. Then there are laws to be enacted, constitutional amendments to be approved, new electoral procedures to be invented, and elections to be organized.

Major philosophical questions have still been left unresolved, including what role will be allowed for political organizations outside the Communist Party in promoting candidates for office.

During this time Mr. Gorbachev will be simultaneously preoccupied with tinkering his economic program back to life and trying to solve the food shortages that have become the most acute public grievance he faces, not to mention conducting his foreign policy.

As with his economic program, he can expect to face resistance and bureaucratic subterfuge, if not outright political opposition.

Many of his supporters say they wonder how soon the public will lose patience with persistent food shortages. And the next phase of his economic program includes some measures that will tax his popularity, especially his vow to end the system of subsidized prices.

Not for the first time, Mr. Gorbachev is charging ahead on a risky course, trusting in his own ability to make the necessary adjustments as he goes.

For Soviet citizens, the inauguration of President Gorbachev would be a reminder of how much their country's near future still rests on the shoulders of one man.

Sweeping Political Revision of Soviet System Approved in Stormy Meeting of Party
By Philip Taubman

MOSCOW, JULY 1—Delegates to a Communist Party conference today approved a major overhaul of the Soviet political system in a stormy final session that included the first openly divided votes since the early years of the Soviet state.

The conference, generally following the blueprint of Mikhail S. Gorbachev, endorsed a package of seven resolutions. The resolutions mandated a partial transfer of power from the party to popularly elected legislatures and an end to party interference in the day-to-day management of almost every aspect of Soviet life, and they set a maximum of two five-year terms for elected party and government officials.

In addition, the conference approved plans to establish a new, powerful post of president, an official who would oversee domestic and foreign policy. The position would be filled by the party leader, currently Mr. Gorbachev. The presidency is now a ceremonial position. Party leaders say they expect the changes to be enacted into law next year.

The conference also approved plans to build a monument to the victims of Stalin's tyranny.

The unexpectedly contentious concluding debates, which apparently caught party leaders by surprise, included several arguments between Mr.

Gorbachev and individual delegates as well as repeated demands that specific proposals be amended and put to a vote. The freewheeling finale forced a six-hour delay in the nationally televised broadcast of Mr. Gorbachev's closing speech.

The day's tumultuous events capped the most unfettered political gathering that the Soviet Union has seen since Stalin consolidated his control of the party in the late 1920s.

"This Palace of Congresses has not known such discussions, comrades, and, I think, we will not err from the truth by saying that nothing of the kind has occurred in this country for nearly six decades," Mr. Gorbachev told the delegates in his closing speech.

The limited terms for elected officials, which would cover the office of general secretary of the Communist Party, the post held by Mr. Gorbachev, would not be retroactive to the time that current officeholders assumed their jobs.

The resolutions themselves were not published today, leaving unclear which proposals were approved and what revisions were made in the numerous recommendations submitted by Mr. Gorbachev and the Central Committee on Tuesday, the opening day of the conference.

"A major event in the history of our party has taken place," Mr. Gorbachev told the delegates in his final appearance this evening, near midnight, moments before the assembled party members stood to sing the Communist anthem, the "Internationale," the closing act of the gathering.

Earlier in the day, the delegates sat transfixed as Boris N. Yeltsin and Yegor K. Ligachev brought their bitter rivalry into the open in separate, emotional appearances in which they attacked each other.

Mr. Yeltsin lost his job as Moscow party boss last year after he questioned the results of Mr. Gorbachev's economic program and criticized Mr. Ligachev at a Central Committee meeting. Mr. Ligachev, the party's number two leader and a favorite of conservatives, rejected Mr. Yeltsin's appeal today for political redemption.

Although the concrete effect of the conference on the political system remains to be seen—and will depend on how the resolutions are put into operation—the meeting clearly altered the political climate.

More than any event since Mr. Gorbachev took office in March 1985, the conference shattered the stifling political customs of the Soviet system, making candor, pointed debate, even public confrontation between party leaders acceptable.

The 4,991 delegates themselves seemed to undergo a transformation as the debate progressed during the week in the Kremlin hall, discarding their jackets, leaning forward in their seats, applauding, shouting out questions and criticism as they were swept up in the heady atmosphere of openness and unbridled discourse.

In other developments, one delegate criticized the Soviet intervention in Afghanistan, another faulted the degradation of the environment, and others discussed the crimes of Stalin, the shortages of food and consumer goods.

Georgi P. Razumovsky, a nonvoting member of the ruling Politburo, told reporters late tonight that the process of remaking the political system would begin in two months with new elections of party officials, including a choice of candidates and secret balloting. He did not specify whether this would apply to Mr. Gorbachev.

Mr. Razumovsky said the necessary legal and constitutional changes were to be considered at a session of the national legislature in November. The legislature has the power to change the constitution.

A new supreme national legislature, called the Congress of People's Deputies, would be elected next April, and new local governments would be elected the following fall.

The Congress would in turn appoint a standing legislature and the president, or chairman, who would assume the powers of head of state, directing foreign and domestic policy, heading the defense council, and representing the country abroad. Mr. Gorbachev, in his speech on Tuesday, described this person as "president," but Mr. Razumovsky said the conference favored the term "chairman."

Mr. Razumovsky said the elections next year would feature "broad-based competition," including candidates promoted by groups outside the party. He did not make clear whether a choice of candidates for each seat would be required, or what limits would be imposed on nonparty groups nominating candidates.

Local government councils, called soviets, would be given broad new independent authority, including budgets derived from taxing local businesses, and their own permanent staffs.

The most contentious issue at the conference was the precise division of power between the party and the redesigned soviets, which operate at local, republic, and national levels.

The conference decided that the party leader at each level should automatically be nominated to head the corresponding government body. The soviet could accept or reject him, by secret ballot.

Opponents led by Roald Sagdevev, director of the Space Research Institute, contended that this contradicted the goal of removing the party from day-to-day government, and demanded a separate vote on the question. Mr. Razumovsky said 209 delegates voted against it.

Defenders said the combination of the two posts was important to add clout to the soviets, and would also serve as a vote of confidence on the local party leader.

Mr. Razumovsky said that, aside from the party leader, other top party officials would be excluded from membership in the soviets. It is now common to hold party and government jobs simultaneously.

Conference Lifts Veil on Personalities and Intrigues
By Bill Keller

MOSCOW, JULY 2—The Communist Party conference that ended Friday has given the world an engrossing look into the heart of the party that rules the Soviet Union.

Personalities that have been vague stereotypes, especially the enigmatic party number two, Yegor K. Ligachev, came to life as full-blooded characters in a complex drama.

Political vendettas and intrigues, rifts of generation, status, and philosophy, long obscured behind the traditional mask of collective power, were played out in public, on television.

Even Mikhail S. Gorbachev, the Soviet leader who seemed so familiar, was on display in a new and subtler light, as a master of political balance, a man of overpowering self-confidence and sometimes chilling arrogance.

The four days of freewheeling debate revealed, among other things, the wide gap between the Moscow intellectuals—scholars, journalists, and cultural figures who provide much of what the West knows about the Soviet Union—and the provincial party representatives.

The big-city intelligentsia may be preoccupied with history, freedom, and reform, but the delegates from the provinces wanted to talk about empty stores, dirty rivers, hospitals without hot water, and factories with deteriorating assembly lines.

For Kremlin watchers from the West, and for the nine out of 10 Soviet adults who are not members of this secretive priesthood of power that rules their lives, the conference was the most intimate look they have had at some of the party's leading figures and their working dynamics.

One remark alone, an aside by Mr. Ligachev, provided a telling glimpse of how Mr. Gorbachev got where he is, and what debts he owes.

In a riveting, unusually personal speech to delegates Friday night, Mr. Ligachev confirmed what had been speculation—that Mr. Gorbachev's selection as party leader in March 1985 was a close call.

He said that among those who engineered Mr. Gorbachev's choice were three bulwarks of the orthodox establishment: the K.G.B. chief, Viktor M. Chebrikov; the party disciplinarian, Mikhail S. Solomentsev; and President Andrei A. Gromyko.

"Destiny placed me at the center of these events, therefore I am able to judge," Mr. Ligachev told the delegates. "Completely different decisions could have been made. Quite different people could be sitting on this podium, and this conference might not be taking place at all."

The remark was at once a rebuff to the daring delegates who, on Thursday, had called for Mr. Solomentsev and Mr. Gromyko to be removed because of their association with the past, and a broader reassurance to those older Communists who fear being left behind in Mr. Gorbachev's determined forward march.

At the same time, it was a deft reminder that Mr. Gorbachev serves at the sufferance of the party elite, including Mr. Ligachev.

Mr. Ligachev is often portrayed by Moscow intellectuals as the Darth Vader of *perestroika,* a sinister, even Stalinist conservative engaged in a relentless rivalry with Mr. Gorbachev.

This may be, but it was also clear watching Mr. Ligachev captivate the party faithful that he is a man of formidable stature who brings to the leadership coalition an important constituency.

Mr. Ligachev speaks the language of the party faithful, the provincial bosses and veterans of the Great Patriotic War, and all those who feel that *glasnost* has gone overboard in blackening their history.

On the stage of the Palace of Congresses, he was a weighty presence, an unexpectedly earthy orator and a figure of integrity.

If Mr. Gorbachev is the voice of change and individual responsibility, Mr. Ligachev is his complement, the voice of patriotic duty and discipline, the scourge of self-pity and negativism.

He himself had lost family members to Stalin's terror, he said—"I didn't want to talk about it, but since this is like a confession I'll tell you"—but this did not undermine his faith in Communism, or turn him into a whiner.

"In the years of stagnation I lived and worked in Siberia—a severe but wonderful land," he continued, using the current code for the lethargic 18-year rule of Leonid I. Brezhnev. "I am often asked what I did during this time and I answer proudly—I was building socialism. There are millions like me."

His philosophy, he said, is circumspection: "Policy-making is not as easy as slurping down cabbage soup. Caution should be combined with decisiveness. As the saying goes, before going into the room, make sure you can get out again."

Mr. Ligachev's foil of the moment was Boris N. Yeltsin, the former Moscow party chief who spun out of the leadership orbit last fall in a bitter feud with Mr. Ligachev.

Mr. Yeltsin, now a top deputy in the Construction Ministry, began his remarks with some of the fiery language that had made him a hero to enthusiasts of *glasnost.* He excoriated members of Brezhnev's Politburo for failing to resist the former leader's programs.

"Today it turns out that the only one guilty in the stagnation was Brezhnev," Mr. Yeltsin said. "But where were they who for ten, fifteen, twenty years, now as well as then, were on the Politburo? Each time they voted in favor of various programs."

He called for abolishing elite privileges—other party leaders denied they existed—for mandatory retirement at age 65, and for top officials to appear regularly before the public.

He said the strategy of *perestroika* had not been fully thought through, and the party conference itself was poorly prepared.

But Mr. Yeltsin seemed to disintegrate before the television cameras. His voice turned hoarse as he pleaded pathetically for "political rehabilitation."

He looked tired and sickened by the pressure of his disgrace, by his disbelief that the party could spurn a man who believed in it so strongly. By the end of the night he had heard his plea for dignity rejected by the crowd and by Mr. Gorbachev.

The Gorbachev on display this week was a somewhat different figure from the man of daring, imaginative leaps and chronic impatience now so well known. This week it was Mr. Gorbachev the master politician.

Leaning forward from his seat behind the lectern, he interrupted speakers to inject a thought or challenge a point. Moments that must have shocked his peers on the podium—the attack on Mr. Gromyko, the dramatic charge by the editor Vitaly Korotich that four delegates present were suspected of corruption, the collapse of Mr. Yeltsin—he handled with poise and equanimity.

Presiding over the conference, Mr. Gorbachev seemed to be trying to hold together the centrifugal forces of the party by the strength of his own personality.

The congress was hardly over before challenges to central authority were mounting, most notably in the Baltics.

Estonia Nationalists Begin to Challenge Moscow Dominance
By Philip Taubman

TALLINN, U.S.S.R.—Last fall, the premier of the Soviet republic of Estonia, Bruno E. Saul, ridiculed a proposal for sharply curtailing economic ties with Moscow.

This spring, he endorsed the suggestion after thousands of citizens demonstrated in favor of the idea.

In June the republic's K.G.B. chief, Karl Y. Kortelainen, challenged the appearance in public of the blue-white-and-black flag that was the emblem of Estonia in two decades of independence between the world wars.

Moments later, a senior Communist Party leader told him, within earshot of Estonian journalists, that the ban against use of the flag, which went into effect when the Soviet Union annexed Estonia in 1940, was being lifted.

Mr. Saul and Mr. Kortelainen are just two of hundreds of officials suddenly feeling the effect of a grass-roots political movement that is challenging the established order in Estonia, including the primacy of the Communist Party and the supremacy of Moscow.

The movement, called the People's Front of Estonia, is the leading edge of a resurgence of nationalist activity in Estonia, and the nearby Soviet republics of Latvia and Lithuania, that in recent weeks has brought demands for political, economic, and cultural autonomy from the fringe to the mainstream of political action.

The activity in the Baltic states is taking place at a time of high stress in another part of the Soviet Union, the southern Caucasus region, where the republics of Armenia and Azerbaijan have been at odds over the Nagorno-Karabakh Autonomous Region. Armenians are the largest ethnic group in that autonomous region, which is part of Azerbaijan. On Monday, the Soviet government rejected calls from the region and from Armenia that it be transferred to Armenian control. The Baltics and the Armenian-Azerbaijan tensions represent different strains of the Soviet nationalities problem. But both are serious for Mikhail S. Gorbachev because both involve forces pulling apart the union, the Baltics tugging directly against the center, Armenia and Azerbaijan against one another.

Acting in the name of Mr. Gorbachev's campaign to reshape the country, the Estonian front has forged an imperfect but powerful form of participatory democracy that has thrown officials on the defensive.

"Gorbachev is our angel," said Andres Raid, an Estonian television producer. "We can do many things in his name that we could not hope to do before."

Unlike previous nationalist agitation, which was usually quickly subdued by the authorities, the new activity is not limited to a small band of dissidents or a blatantly separatist agenda. The target is the entire authoritarian system, including the rule Moscow has exercised since annexing the three republics in 1940.

"We've come to the moment when it is impossible to continue on in the old ways," said Tiit Made, an economist, who established an environmental-protection lobby similar to the front.

Mr. Made, whose proposals for economic autonomy helped launch the front, said: "We are pushing for democracy, for the right to manage our own affairs, to make our leaders responsive to the people, to preserve our national culture and environment. I think we've started something major in Estonia."

A similar front has been formed in Lithuania, and one is being established in Latvia.

Soviet Leader's Burden; Behind Opposition to Gorbachev's Policies Is an Economy That Refuses to Spruce Up
By Bill Keller

MOSCOW, JULY 31—The euphoria of attempts by Mikhail S. Gorbachev to revive Soviet society, the intoxicating swirl of political debate and cultural experimentation, seem each month more in danger from the mundane miseries of the unyielding Soviet economy.

The mounting sense of urgency about how his people live has driven the Soviet leader to propose new measures that would expand private control of state-owned farms and factories.

The proposals, which include a Chinese-style farm leasing program and the transfer of failing factories to private entrepreneurs are the latest refinements in a drive for economic revival that has so far produced isolated success stories without raising the general standard of living.

They are another reminder of the monkey on Mr. Gorbachev's back.

By almost any measure, the economy has proven to be Mr. Gorbachev's most intractable problem. The supplies and quality of food, housing, and basic consumer goods have not improved, and many believe they have worsened.

Private cafés and services, one of Mr. Gorbachev's most promising initiatives, are so few that they charge prices beyond the reach of most families.

The wooing of foreign ventures to the Soviet Union has so far consisted either of gimmicks—like the introduction of high-priced American pizza and ice cream to Moscow—or serious joint production projects that are not expected to bring goods to the stores for at least a year.

In Soviet magazines and newspapers, economic theorists who have been his most ardent supporters have been urging Mr. Gorbachev to venture more boldly in the direction of free markets, private enterprise, and consumer choice—and the Soviet leader seems to be listening.

For example, in an article published in the journal *Argumenti i Fakti* earlier this month, Leonid I. Abalkin, director of the Institute of Economics of the Soviet Academy of Sciences, said: "The country's economy is now going through a very difficult time. The situation has not been this bad in many years."

For the first time, Mr. Gorbachev and his allies seem willing to throw out half-measures adopted in the early days of his economic program, and to publicly reject proposals that might have looked fine a year ago.

On Friday the Presidium of the Supreme Soviet, in a rare reversal, formally suspended a four-month-old tax law after private entrepreneurs said its high tax rates, up to 90 percent, would stifle the creation of new businesses. Efforts to devise a new law have bogged down in debate over how to avoid snuffing out the tiny private sector.

A week earlier, a new draft law on industrial quality control was rejected on grounds that it relied too much on orders from Moscow, not enough on the customers.

With each speech, Mr. Gorbachev himself seems more attuned to the popular disenchantment with the grim Soviet economic reality, and more impatient with the stubborn refusal of his system to work better.

Friday, in remarks to a meeting of the Communist Party Central Committee that was dominated by discussion of the electoral system, Mr. Gorbachev devoted more time to economic problems than to the political structure.

At one point Mr. Gorbachev, sounding like a frantic Soviet housewife, deplored the exhausting, degrading hours ordinary Soviet shoppers must spend waiting in lines to buy food.

"How can we tolerate this?" he demanded.

Opposition to government policies was surfacing even within the Kremlin. Further removed from the seat of centralized power, more disatisfaction was being registered on a wide array of issues.

Gorbachev Deputy Criticizes Policy
By Bill Keller

MOSCOW, AUG. 6—In a clear challenge to the current direction of Mikhail S. Gorbachev's foreign policy, the second-ranking Kremlin leader, Yegor K. Ligachev, has publicly disagreed with Foreign Minister Eduard A. Shevardnadze on a key point of Communist ideology.

Mr. Ligachev said that Soviet foreign relations must be guided primarily by the model of a class struggle against capitalism and asserted that too much talk of peaceful cooperation with capitalist countries "only confuses the minds of the Soviet people and our friends abroad."

Mr. Ligachev, speaking at a meeting of Communist Party members in Gorky on Friday, appeared to be deliberately rebuking Mr. Shevardnadze, one of Mr. Gorbachev's closest confidants in the Politburo.

Mr. Shevardnadze told a conference of foreign policy specialists 10 days ago that peaceful coexistence, aimed at overcoming the dangers of nuclear war, ecological disaster, and poverty, must take precedence over the struggle against capitalism.

"The struggle between two opposing systems is no longer a determining tendency of the present era," Mr. Shevardnadze said, in excerpts of his speech reported by the Tass press agency.

Mr. Ligachev appeared to be signaling displeasure with the general tone of foreign policy that Mr. Gorbachev calls his "new thinking."

In the last two years, Mr. Gorbachev has steered away from the ritual courtship of Communist revolutionary movements and cultivated friendships with influential capitalist countries such as India, Mexico, Brazil, Argentina, Saudi Arabia, and Kuwait.

Mr. Ligachev has often taken a more orthodox, hard-line approach to domestic issues than his colleagues in the ruling Politburo, warning against what he sees as excesses in the press, the blackening of Soviet history, and permissiveness toward public dissent.

The critical examination of the Soviet past was accelerating.

Czech Invasion Wrong, Soviet Journalists Say
By Esther B. Fein

MOSCOW, AUG. 24—A group of Soviet journalists strongly suggested in an article published here today that the Soviet-led invasion of Czechoslovakia in August 1968 was a mistake.

In the toughest public criticism yet of the Soviet Union's handling of the period of political liberalization known as Prague Spring, six Soviet correspondents who all worked in Czechoslovakia at the time said in a round-table discussion published by the weekly paper *Moscow News* that history had proven the results of the invasion to be disastrous.

"There should be no dangerous illusions that the political problems of another nation can be solved by military force," said Mikhail Polyakov, who worked in Czechoslovakia for the magazine *World Marxist Review.* "History doesn't forgive false steps." His colleague on the magazine, Vladimir Lukin, said no situation justified the decision by any Communist country to invade another, or to "arrogate the right to decide for the others."

"Respect for this principle is the most reliable guarantee that the events of 1968—from which those involved learned the most serious lesson—can never be repeated in our time," Mr. Lukin said.

Soviet officials have long maintained that the decision to send Warsaw Pact troops into Prague to crush Alexander Dubček's reformist leadership was necessary to protect Czechoslovakia from internal and Western enemies.

Armenian Capital Is Roused by Calls for New Freedoms
By Bill Keller

YEREVAN, U.S.S.R., SEPT. 4—Two nights ago, more than 100,000 Armenians, defying an official ban and a heavy police cordon, streamed into the square in front of this city's imposing stone opera house for a town meeting.

The vast crowd in the southern republic's capital was reminiscent of those in the heady days last February when Armenians began their campaign to claim the territory of Nagorno-Karabakh, ruled by Azerbaijan. But there are two important differences.

The placards displaying the face of Mikhail S. Gorbachev and his slogans of change have disappeared, replaced by an outspoken disenchantment with the Kremlin chief.

And the campaign for Nagorno-Karabakh has grown into something bigger. The movement began as a campaign for the return of the small region, an enclave with a mostly Armenian population that is surrounded and governed by Azerbaijan, yet claimed by both Soviet republics for cultural and historical reasons. But the campaign has become a broad and ambitious political movement that appears to be headed for a direct confrontation with the Communist Party.

Recent developments in Armenia have gone unreported in the Soviet press, which now portrays Yerevan as a city back to normal.

But a visit by this correspondent to the Armenian capital, the first since officials lifted a six-month ban on travel here by Western reporters, tells another story.

It is true that the general strikes that periodically paralyzed Yerevan earlier this year have ended, but no one seems to doubt that they will return. The uniformed troops that once patrolled the city, sometimes carrying automatic rifles and truncheons, are not in sight, but there is evidence that those same soldiers now walk the streets disguised in police uniforms.

And the mass demonstrations that first drew the world's attention to this region are now a weekly event, with a new sense of political purpose.

At the rally on Friday, the 11-member Karabakh Committee, a group of intellectuals recognized by many Armenians as their de facto leaders, read the detailed manifesto of the new Armenian National Movement. The committee described the group's plan to press its demands through electoral politics, backed by the threat of civil disobedience.

"We are very serious about this," said Ambartsum Galstyan, an ethnographer and a member of the Karabakh Committee, in an interview today at an outdoor café. "They gave us a little bit of liberalization, but we are now well beyond that."

The beginning of a national movement resembles the people's fronts that have been organized recently in the Baltic republics to promote greater economic, political, and cultural independence. Many of the goals of the Armenian group are similar, including a measure of Armenian economic sovereignty and priority for the Armenian language in schools and in public affairs.

But in Armenia, the relationship between the new movement and the officials of the Communist Party has been tense.

At the Opera Square on Friday, a member of the Karabakh Committee demanded that the second-ranking party official in the republic, a Russian, be dismissed because of insensitivity to Armenians.

In turn, committee members have been attacked in the local press as extremists.

The authorities have not broken up the mass demonstrations that take place each Friday night, but the latest gathering was reportedly surrounded by thousands of men in police uniforms.

Karabakh Committee members said the police onlookers were in fact Russian soldiers wearing militia uniforms. The troops were reportedly called in because the local authorities did not trust the native police force to take action.

That assertion appeared to have substance. Near the Dinamo Sports Hall, busloads of non-Armenian men in police outfits came and went today from a camp guarded by uniformed army personnel.

The goals laid out in the new Armenian manifesto stopped short of the call for complete Armenian independence advocated by some student firebrands, but the goals are enough to cause concern in the Kremlin.

The Armenians insist on veto power over all federal projects built in the republic, a demand intended to stop a new chemical plant and a nuclear power station.

Other demands include the freedom to fly the flag used during Armenia's brief independence, from 1918 until 1920, when the Armenian Republic came under Soviet rule; the right to open consulates in countries with large Armenian populations; and the creation of an Armenian army detachment so that young men from the republic can perform their military service on home soil, using their own language.

Unification of Armenia with Nagorno-Karabakh, rejected by the Soviet government in July, is still regarded as an overriding goal. Karabakh Committee members said they have gathered more than 400,000 signatures on a petition demanding that the Armenian legislature defy Moscow by unilaterally declaring the disputed territory part of Armenia.

The legislature is scheduled to meet in October, and committee members say they may call a general strike to dramatize their demand.

"We plan to do everything according to the Soviet constitution," said Babken Ararktyan, a member of the Karabakh Committee and the head of the mathematics department at the University of Yerevan. "Our constitution says nothing that prohibits strikes."

The committee has also begun organizing for next year's legislative elections, which Moscow has promised will, for the first time, be open to a wide range of competing candidates.

"If we can elect even a few dozen deputies out of the three hundred forty in the Armenian legislature, that will be enough to force authorities to take up our issues," Mr. Ararktyan said. Judging from interviews in Yerevan and in nearby Echmiadzin, the seat of the Armenian Orthodox Church, the committee has broad public support and respect, not only among intellectuals and students but among ordinary working families and even Communist Party members.

The committee's weekly town meetings draw 100,000 to 200,000 of Yerevan's 1.1 million residents, participants say.

Armenians say that while Mr. Gorbachev's promises of greater democracy and openness originally gave heart to their efforts, the public turned sharply against the Soviet leader after two events in July.

One event was a clash between Soviet troops and Armenian strikers at Yerevan's Zvartnots Airport. A 22-year-old Armenian was killed during the chaos, and dozens of people were injured. This was followed on July 18 by Moscow's decision to leave Nagorno-Karabakh under Azerbaijani jurisdiction.

On Opera Square, where a few hundred people assemble each evening to debate current events, the mention of the Soviet leader's name sets off a hostile murmur.

"He's a scorpion," said one young man Saturday night.

"Gorbachev killed our trust," shouted an older man at the same meeting.

Other Armenians are somewhat more sympathetic to Mr. Gorbachev, pointing out that he feared an uprising in Azerbaijan if he yielded to the Armenian demands, and that conservatives in the Kremlin might seize on any concession as a sign of weakness.

But the sense of disappointment is deep and freely expressed.

"*Glasnost, perestroika,* since July 5 we don't use those words," said Mr. Galstyan. "After all that's happened, those words are discredited here."

5 Soviet Leaders Lose Posts; Shake-up Viewed as Giving Gorbachev Stronger Hand

By Philip Taubman

MOSCOW, SEPT. 30—In a major Kremlin shake-up that appears to strengthen the position of Mikhail S. Gorbachev as party leader, the Communist Party Central Committee dismissed three veteran members of the Politburo today.

The committee approved the retirement of Andrei A. Gromyko, who is the nation's titular President, from the Politburo, and ousted Anatoly F. Dobrynin, who had long served as Soviet ambassador to the United States, from the post of Central Committee secretary.

Two important figures who have questioned Mr. Gorbachev's policies, Yegor K. Ligachev, the number two party leader, and Viktor M. Chebrikov, the head of the K.G.B. intelligence and security agency, retained their Politburo posts but were given new party responsibilities in the reorganization that may diminish their influence.

Mr. Ligachev, the party ideologist, was replaced by Vadim A. Medvedev, 59 years old. Mikhail S. Solomentsev, 74, among the Politburo's senior figures, was also removed, The moves, which took place during an extraordinary one-hour meeting of the Communist Party's 300-member Central Committee, were accompanied by a sweeping reorganization of the party apparatus and the elevation to the Politburo of four new members. The results seemed to diplomats to reflect the most significant enhancement of Mr. Gorbachev's power since he took over as party general secretary in March 1985.

But there was uncertainty why Mr. Gorbachev seemed to move so quickly to carry out a reorganization that had been promised since a special conference of the Communist Party in June.

The departure from the Politburo of Mr. Gromyko opened the way for Mr. Gorbachev to be elected president when the national legislature, the Supreme Soviet, meets on Saturday.

One change that Mr. Gorbachev called for in June was an enlargement of the powers of the president, who now operates very much as a figurehead. He said he would like the president to become the foreign policy and military leader of the country.

An unexpected casualty of today's meeting was Mr. Dobrynin, who was relieved of a post that made him the senior foreign policy adviser to Mr. Gorbachev. His departure was all the more surprising because he had been thought to be a Gorbachev ally.

Mr. Medvedev, who was named a full member of the Politburo today and is now to be responsible for ideology, told a news conference that Mr.

Dobrynin, who is 68, "requested to retire for reasons of age and health. There is nothing else to it."

Mr. Solomentsev had been a full member of the Politburo since 1983 and directed the powerful party control committee, which investigated and disciplined party members for wrongdoing.

Mr. Ligachev, who had reportedly been unhappy with Mr. Gorbachev's policies of openness, was put in charge of a new commission overseeing agriculture, an area of chronic difficulty in Soviet life. And Mr. Chebrikov, who is to head a party commission dealing with legal matters, is expected to give up his K.G.B. post on Saturday.

The decisions today left Mr. Gorbachev with a younger Politburo more firmly under his control, and with a revamped party apparatus, including six powerful new Central Committee commissions, to help carry out his programs.

Mr. Ligachev, who has frequently expressed doubts about the cultural liberalization under Mr. Gorbachev, was named as head of a newly established commission on agriculture.

This appears to reduce his role in setting ideological and foreign policy, where he has been active and sometimes out of alignment with Mr. Gorbachev. At the same time, the appointment gives Mr. Gorbachev the advantage of Mr. Ligachev's strong leadership in a critical, chronically weak sector of the economy.

A key decision will be selection of a replacement for Mr. Gromyko, who is 79, as head of state, or formally chairman of the Presidium of the Supreme Soviet.

Mr. Gromyko, who has served in ranking positions for nearly 50 years, including 28 years as foreign minister, gave up his Politburo post today. His retirement as head of state will become effective on Saturday. Mr. Gorbachev is considered the leading candidate to succeed Mr. Gromyko. A number of his predecessors as party leader served simultaneously as head of state.

Gorbachev Named Soviet President; New Man at K.G.B.
By Philip Taubman

MOSCOW, OCT. 1—Mikhail S. Gorbachev consolidated his leadership of the Soviet Union today by taking over the presidency of the country to match his role as head of the Communist Party.

Completing the major realignment of the party and government of the last two days, several top government officials were replaced, and Vladimir A. Kryuchkov, a longtime K.G.B. official, was named to head that security and intelligence agency.

On Friday, the party Central Committee dismissed three veteran members—and accepted the retirement of President Andrei A. Gromyko—from the ruling Politburo. Anatoly F. Dobrynin, who had long served as the Soviet ambassador to the United States, was also ousted from his post as Central Committee secretary. The three dismissed members of the Politburo were Mikhail S. Solomentsev, Pyotr N. Demichev, and Vladimir I. Dolgikh.

There had also been speculation that Yegor K. Ligachev, the number two party leader and a man who has often questioned Mr. Gorbachev's policies, had lost influence.

Mr. Ligachev was named Friday to head a party commission on agriculture. The move suggested that he would wield less influence on ideological and foreign-policy issues.

But the leadership lineup at today's meeting did not support that speculation. Mr. Ligachev appeared today in his customary position at the front rank of the Politburo, seated on the podium in the same row as Mr. Gorbachev, Mr. Gromyko, and Nikolai I. Ryzhkov, the prime minister.

Although Leonid I. Brezhnev had been both the general secretary of the party and president, there was more significance to Mr. Gorbachev's assuming both roles because he has already said that he intends to invest the presidency with much more power than in the past, as part of a policy of making the government function more independently of the party. These changes have yet to be put into effect and are expected to be high on Mr. Gorbachev's agenda.

The formal election of Mr. Gorbachev as president, known officially here as chairman of the Presidium of the Supreme Soviet, took place in the time-honored Soviet style of virtually no debate, with the members of the Soviet parliament voting unanimously. The liveliness and debate that marked last summer's special Communist Party conference, which had outlined the changes now taking place, were noticeably absent today.

Following up the extraordinary meeting of the Communist Party Central Committee on Friday, the Supreme Soviet voted to have Mr. Gorbachev succeed Mr. Gromyko as president. Mr. Gromyko, who is 79 years old, spoke briefly to ask the Supreme Soviet to accept his retirement, noting that on Friday he had also quit the Politburo, the inner core of the Communist Party.

The legislature, following the recommendation of the Central Committee, named Mr. Kryuchkov as chairman of the K.G.B., the agency officially known as the Committee for State Security.

Mr. Kryuchkov, a deputy chairman of the K.G.B. since 1978, succeeded Viktor M. Chebrikov, who directed the agency for the last six years. Mr. Chebrikov, a full member of the Politburo, was appointed a party secretary on Friday and named to head a new Central Committee commission on legal policy.

Mr. Kryuchkov is apparently the man who has supervised the handling of Edward Lee Howard, the C.I.A. agent who defected here several years ago.

David Wise, in his book about the Howard case, *The Spy Who Got Away,* reports that Mr. Kryuchkov personally supervised the handling of Mr. Howard.

Mr. Wise reports that Mr. Kryuchkov is chief of the K.G.B.'s first chief directorate, in charge of all foreign operations. Mr. Wise says that Mr. Kryuchkov was a third secretary in Budapest in 1956 when Yuri V. Andropov was ambassador and when the Soviets crushed the Hungarian revolt. Mr. Wise reports that Mr. Andropov brought Mr. Kryuchkov back to Moscow with him when he became K.G.B. chief in 1967.

The election of Mr. Gorbachev, which was expected after Friday's announcement that Mr. Gromyko was retiring after 49 years of government service, leaves Mr. Gorbachev as both head of the Communist Party and head of state, reinforcing his position as the dominant figure in the leadership.

Although much remains unknown about this week's developments, including the reason that Mr. Gorbachev moved with almost no warning to convene the Central Committee, there seemed little question that he achieved an important breakthrough in consolidating power.

Along with approving the retirement of Mr. Gromyko, the Central Committee dismissed three other veteran members of the Politburo, appointed four new members, and endorsed a sweeping reorganization of the party apparatus.

In his acceptance speech, Mr. Gorbachev gave a hint of one reason for the shake-up. "*Perestroika* and the renewal of our society have entered a new stage," he said.

"Stormy discussions and meetings and analyses of the mistakes of the past are no longer enough. We need practical headway and real improvement of the state of affairs in all fields of our work, especially where the people's living standards are concerned."

"The working people," he added, "are not satisfied with the way our government and economic bodies, public organizations, and many party committees work."

Meanwhile, proclamations issued at another gathering in the tiny Baltic republic of Estonia suggested that Communists there were looking for ways to harness or exploit nationalist sentiments flowering under glasnost.

The Estonians Say, Let Us Be Estonian

By Bill Keller

TALLINN, U.S.S.R., OCT. 1—While Mikhail S. Gorbachev was busy in Moscow shaking up the high command of his social revolution, the residents of the tiny republic of Estonia today advanced the front line.

Here in the cavernous auditorium of the Lenin Palace of Culture, the Communist Party gave its blessing to a mass political movement that it does not control—at least not yet.

The occasion was the first congress of the Popular Front of Estonia, an independent force that is perhaps the most interesting experiment in political pluralism ever tolerated in the Soviet Union.

This weekend the group, which claims nearly 60,000 active participants and many more sympathizers, is expected to formally endorse a program of Estonian economic and political independence that, not long ago, would have been grounds for arrest.

The platform calls for Estonia to adopt a capitalist-style economy in which free-market incentives would go far beyond the economic changes now being offered by Mr. Gorbachev. It also calls for a measure of home rule that would render Estonia almost immune from Moscow's economic and political directives.

Today, Vaino Valas, head of the Estonian Communist Party, fresh from a meeting with Mr. Gorbachev in Moscow, invited the Popular Front to put up its own candidates for election and to promote ideas that may differ from the Communist agenda.

"Whether we like it or not, we have become a center for experimentation," Mr. Valas said, addressing the delegates as "comrades and like-minded people."

Some of the 3,000 delegates professed indifference to the party upheavals in Moscow. "That is politics," scoffed a schoolteacher from Tartu. "This is history!"

But the prevailing view was that by strengthening his position as party leader, Mr. Gorbachev had also made it easier to continue this experiment.

The Popular Front was founded in April, arising in part from local resentment of factories built in the republic, on Moscow's orders, that Estonians fear are damaging the environment.

The movement has become a model for similar groups in other republics, such as Latvia and Lithuania, and in major cities, such as Moscow and Leningrad.

The program that the congress is expected to adopt calls for giving elected Estonian officials almost complete autonomy in running the republic, except for national defense and diplomacy.

Even in those areas, the front demands new prerogatives, including creation of an Estonian army unit, the freedom to conduct foreign trade relations and independent relations with international organizations such as the United Nations.

The group calls for amending the Soviet constitution to make Estonian the only official language of the republic; it is now used officially only in conjunction with Russian.

Other demands include the power to stop immigration of non-Estonians and to encourage some of the Russian minority to leave, and local control over school curriculums and the press and television.

Leaders of the front deny that the movement is a political party (the Soviet constitution permits only the Communist Party) or that their ultimate goal is secession.

"Naturally, independent Estonia is the aim of each Estonian," said Ulo Kaevats, a member of the front's organizing committee. "As politicians, we see the realization of this idea in the transformation of the Soviet Union from a federation into a union of independent republics."

If this transition proves unsatisfactory, he added, "the issue of whether to remain in the union or secede from it must be decided democratically."

The front's membership, however, includes many avowed separatists. One of the delegates was Mart Niklus, an entomologist only recently released from prison, where he was serving a sentence for advocating independence. Like Latvia and Lithuania, Estonia enjoyed a period of independence between the world wars.

The key question in the Palace of Culture today was the relationship between the Popular Front and the Communist Party.

Party officials here have clearly decided they can use this movement to awaken citizens who long ago lost interest in the political life that was dictated by Moscow, and enlist them in a revival of the economy.

The front's program has been printed in the official press and publicized on television, and local officials turned over the modern Palace of Culture with rare efficiency. There are simultaneous translations into Russian and English, a sophisticated press center, and daily news bulletins.

About one fourth of the active members of the front, including a high percentage of its leaders, are Communist Party members, and some of the Communists express the concern that the demands of the front's more extreme wing will eventually provoke a crackdown by Moscow.

Russians and other non-Estonians here have organized a counter movement to combat the front's proposals for making Estonian the only official language, for limiting non-Estonian immigration, and for restricting citizenship rights in the republic to those who can demonstrate a knowledge of Estonian language and culture.

With internal challenges to Soviet units and security increasing, Gorbachev met with an old foreign adversary.

Gorbachev Hails Kohl in Moscow, Saying the "Ice Has Been Broken"

By Felicity Barringer

MOSCOW, OCT. 24—Chancellor Helmut Kohl of West Germany arrived here today, and his first talks with Mikhail S. Gorbachev set a promising tone for the four-day visit, which both sides hope will finally take the chill out of Soviet-West German relations.

"The ice has been broken," Mr. Gorbachev, the Soviet leader, said after the opening meeting with the West German leader.

At a Kremlin dinner in honor of Mr. Kohl, Mr. Gorbachev said, "The role of our two countries in the overall complex of big politics is indispensable."

"I state with satisfaction that the summit meeting is being dominated by the search for a reliable route leading to a new stage in relations," Mr. Gorbachev added, according to the official Soviet press agency, Tass.

Mr. Kohl's speech was a mixture of optimistic appraisals of the new possibilities in the East-West dialogue and firm reminders that the most difficult issues in the German-Soviet relationship are still military: Warsaw Pact superiority in short-range nuclear missiles aimed at West German targets and in conventional troops ranged along the German border.

"The great superiority of the Warsaw Pact in terms of short-range nuclear weapons remains a source of great concern to us and our allies," Mr. Kohl said in his speech at the state dinner tonight, according to Tass. "I repeat my appeal to the Soviet Union to dispense with part of these weapons."

Then, saying that "the main obstacle to European security is the serious conventional imbalance," Mr. Kohl urged that negotiations on the existing level of conventional forces in Europe begin "as soon as possible."

The aims of these talks, Mr. Kohl said, should be "to secure a stable balance of power at a lower level and to create a situation in Europe in which neither side has the capability for launching surprise attack and for initiating large-scale offensive action."

Mr. Kohl also renewed his call for an East-West understanding that would lead to a reunited Germany.

But the West German leader referred in a positive spirit to the improved lot of the two million ethnic Germans in the Soviet Union, though he called on Moscow to make further efforts to eliminate the cultural and religious restrictions placed on these Germans, whose ancestors came to Russia more than 200 years ago.

Key aides in Mr. Kohl's entourage, including top West German diplomatic, military, economic, and cultural figures, all took part in meetings today, indicating that in their depth and breadth the Kohl-Gorbachev talks would parallel those at the Reagan-Gorbachev summit meeting in May and June.

Mr. Kohl prompted deep Soviet hostility in 1983 when he permitted the deployment of Pershing medium-range nuclear missiles on West German soil, and evoked a more personal sense of bitterness here two years ago when he compared Mr. Gorbachev's public relations efforts to those of the Nazi propagandist Goebbels.

That anger appeared to have faded, however, judging from Mr. Gorbachev's evening speech, in which he stressed the Soviet Union's European heritage.

"We Europeans should, at last, behave in accordance with the logic of the new times: not to get ready for war, not to intimidate one another, not to compete in perfecting weaponry, and not simply to try to prevent war, but to learn to make peace," he said.

Among the economic agreements signed in connection with the talks was one that would allow West German companies to work with the Soviet state atomic energy committee on projects to design and build reactors for nuclear power stations.

Other agreements were concluded on the joint manufacture of medical and agricultural equipment.

Economic discussions are at the top of Mr. Kohl's agenda here, in part because there is so much room for improvement in this area: trade between the Soviet Union and West Germany stands at about $7 billion this year, half of what it was three years ago.

But while the strategic and trade issues facing the two men, both tractable and intractable, were in the forefront of the extensive coverage the visit received on Soviet television tonight, the speeches of the two leaders at the state dinner also touched on a less tangible and more painful issue: the bitter memories of a war in which most of the Soviet Union's western half was ravaged by the Nazis.

The horrors of World War II, in which the Soviet Union estimates it lost 20 million people, are an omnipresent part of the Soviet consciousness.

"We Germans realize how much distress and suffering was inflicted on individuals, on families, in your country, and how much destruction was caused in this country, how much trust was lost," Mr. Kohl said.

Gorbachev's Plan to Realign Power Voted by Soviets

By Philip Taubman

MOSCOW, DEC. 1—The Soviet legislature today approved the first phase of Mikhail S. Gorbachev's plan to redesign the political system, enacting into law a partial transfer of power from the Communist Party to popularly elected legislative bodies.

The reorganization plan, presented in June, creates a powerful new post of state president, establishes a new national legislature with broad authority, limits terms of office for government officials to 10 years, requires competitive elections, and strengthens the independence of judges.

The changes have inspired considerable opposition, especially among those who fear that the changes will give Mr. Gorbachev a dangerous monopoly of power, and among minority national groups that see in the new laws an infringement of local autonomy.

In a small but rare display of defiance for the docile legislature, five deputies out of 1,500 in the Supreme Soviet voted against some provisions, and 27 abstained, all from the Baltic region, where elements of the plan are widely seen as limiting local rights.

Mr. Gorbachev said today's approval was a milestone in his effort to reshape the country, particularly his campaign to increase democracy in the hope of enhancing a restructuring of the economy.

The new laws "open a new chapter in the development of Soviet statehood on the basis of democratization and popular self-government," Mr. Gorbachev told the legislature as it concluded a three-day session, its last as now constituted. He said today's action would clear the way for further changes responding to demands for expanded power for individual republics and for local governments.

If instituted in full, something that is far from certain, the package of changes could produce the most extensive realignment of power since Stalin forged the current system almost 60 years ago.

But like many of Mr. Gorbachev's other initiatives, which have foundered in the transfer from theory to practice, the impact and effectiveness of the political changes will ultimately depend not on their enshrinement as law but on how they are carried out.

The impact, above all, will be determined by the willingness of the party, including Mr. Gorbachev, to relinquish some of the absolute power it wields over every aspect of Soviet life. The approval of the Supreme Soviet, although never in doubt, nevertheless culminates a two-year process that has brought the changes from Mr. Gorbachev's drawing board through the crucible of debate and modification to inclusion by today's vote in the Soviet constitution and legal code.

It gives Mr. Gorbachev a sense of forward motion just days before he departs on an important foreign trip that will include a meeting with President Reagan and President-elect Bush in New York next week, as well as stops in Havana and London.

Those who take Mr. Gorbachev at his word say he is using the reorganization as a way to make the country more democratic, and to maneuver around a recalcitrant party by placing increased power in legislative bodies that may be more responsive to his efforts to change the country.

Those who doubt Mr. Gorbachev's intentions question whether the changes, in the end, will amount to anything more than a cosmetic alteration that creates an appearance of increased democracy while leaving power primarily in the hands of the party.

Approval of the Gorbachev plan itself was handled in the traditional way, with the decisive vote of approval cast on Monday by the party Central Committee, leaving the Supreme Soviet with the largely ceremonial job of enacting the program into law.

The legislative session was punctuated by several moments of genuine debate, including a last-second appeal today by Dzemma Skulme, a legislator from Latvia, to consider amending the plan to give republics greater say.

The appeal was rejected, with support coming from only 23 deputies representing the Baltic republics of Latvia, Lithuania, and Estonia. Many of the same deputies accounted for the handful of abstentions and votes against some provisions of the Gorbachev plan.

Several provisions in the plan have provoked opposition in some of the country's 15 constituent republics because the laws would appear to concentrate power in Moscow, rather than dispersing it around the country, as Mr. Gorbachev has promised to do.

In the most direct challenge, Estonia last month amended the republic's constitution, asserting the right to reject Soviet laws that appear to infringe on local autonomy.

The action, declared invalid last week by the Soviet government, was a reaction to provisions in the Gorbachev plan that would give a new national legislature power to set economic and social policy for the whole country and to overrule decisions made by republic legislatures.

The changes approved today would enhance Mr. Gorbachev's power, since he is likely to fill the new post of president, while retaining his job as general secretary of the party.

Andrei D. Sakharov, the physicist and human rights campaigner, reflecting a view held by many intellectuals, has warned that the new governmental system, while perhaps benign as long as Mr. Gorbachev remains in office, represents a dangerous concentration of power that could be abused.

"Today it will be Gorbachev," Dr. Sakarhov said last month. "Tomorrow it may be somebody else, and there are no guarantees—we must be frank about this—no guarantees."

Among other duties, the President will serve as chairman of the Defense Council, the country's highest national security body. The post has been traditionally filled by the party leader. Mr. Gorbachev is expected to become the first occupant of the new job.

Fresh from his political maneuvers at home, Gorbachev headed for New York and the United Nations. The city, often blasé in its response to the famous and powerful, reacted enthusiastically as people lined the streets to catch a glimpse of the Soviet leader. At the U.N. he boldly raised the previous bid on troop reduction, winning wide credit. But as he was preparing to accept the plaudits and take one more victory lap around Manhattan, another one of those spasms of bad luck struck in the form of a powerful earthquake in Armenia.

Gorbachev Pledges Major Troop Cutback, Then Ends Trip, Citing Vast Soviet Quake
By Bill Keller

NEW YORK, DEC. 8—In an audacious bid to seize the initiative in East-West relations, Mikhail S. Gorbachev announced at the United Nations yesterday that the Soviet Union would sharply cut its military forces.

Just hours later, Soviet officials said Mr. Gorbachev was being forced to cut short his visit to the United States to return home this morning and lead rescue efforts after a severe earthquake centered in Soviet Armenia yesterday.

At a midnight news conference in New York, Foreign Minister Eduard A. Shevardnadze said thousands of people had died in the quake. Mr. Shevardnadze said Mr. Gorbachev would proceed from Moscow to the Armenian capital of Yerevan to supervise rescue efforts by the military and medical teams.

The announcement meant the cancellation of the rest of Soviet leader's trip, which was to have included stops in Cuba and Britain. Mr. Gorbachev had planned to leave the United States tomorrow.

In his address to the General Assembly yesterday morning, Mr. Gorbachev announced that over the next two years, his country would reduce its military forces by 500,000 men and 10,000 tanks, removing about half of its tanks in Eastern Europe and bringing home "a major portion" of its forces in Mongolia, on the Chinese border.

The cuts amount to about 10 percent of the total Soviet troop strength and more than a quarter of the Soviet army's tanks in Europe.

Mr. Gorbachev later had a luncheon meeting with President Reagan and President-elect Bush. For Mr. Reagan, it was his fifth and probably last encounter with the Soviet leader.

Asked whether the abrupt return home might have been motivated by a domestic political crisis rather than the quake, Mr. Shevardnadze fixed the questioner with an icy look and replied, "I'm sorry to say this, but that is not a serious question."

Mr. Gorbachev's sudden return follows not only a severe earthquake but violent ethnic unrest in the same Caucasus Mountain region as well.

In his speech to the United Nations, Mr. Gorbachev said the Soviet military cuts would be "unilateral," although he later told reporters, "We do hope that the U.S. and the Europeans will also take some steps."

All Soviet divisions remaining in Eastern Europe would be reorganized, he said, becoming "clearly defensive."

As Mr. Gorbachev made his announcement, the Soviet Foreign Ministry spokesman, Gennadi I. Gerasimov, said Sergei F. Akhromeyev, the chief of staff of the Soviet armed forces, had retired for health reasons.

As recently as July, Marshal Akhromeyev appeared to reject Soviet troop cuts without reciprocal reductions by NATO. But the marshal had been a seemingly enthusiastic supporter of Mr. Gorbachev's arms-control initiatives, including last year's treaty abolishing medium-range nuclear weapons, and Soviet officials denied that his departure reflected unhappiness in the military over the cutbacks.

Soviet officials had said earlier that there was no need to cut short Mr. Gorbachev's visit because of the earthquake. But Mr. Shevardnadze said that as more information trickled in about the extent of the devastation, it became clear that "we have to go back."

"If we did not go back, that would be immoral, that would be incomprehensible in this situation," said the weary and saddened foreign minister, whose home republic of Georgia was also damaged by the quake.

B. J. Cooper, a White House spokesman, said Yuri V. Dubinin, the Soviet ambassador to the United States, called Lieut. Gen. Colin L. Powell, the White House national security adviser, at 11:30 last night to inform him of Mr. Gorbachev's plan to leave early.

Mr. Cooper said President Reagan was then notified. The earthquake was cited as the reason for the move, and "we have no reason to believe otherwise," the spokesman said.

Mr. Gorbachev, whose speech dominated a hectic day of superpower diplomacy, also outlined a new plan for a settlement in Afghanistan, including a January 1 cease-fire policed by United Natiions peacekeeping forces, negotiations to form a new government, and a cutoff of all military aid to the warring factions.

Moscow earlier this year rejected an American offer to end United

States support for the guerrillas if the Soviet Union stopped sending arms to the Kabul regime. The reversal yesterday reflected mounting concern in Moscow that Afghanistan could deteriorate into bloody chaos soon after the last Soviet troops withdraw, as they are scheduled to do by February 15.

The Soviet leader also used his first appearance in the United Nations to make one of his strongest commitments to broadening civil rights in his country. He promised that new laws would be enacted in 1989 guaranteeing freedom of expression and assembly and prohibiting "any form of persecution" for political or religious beliefs.

He offered to submit to verdicts of the International Court of Justice in interpreting international human-rights agreements. He promised that would-be Soviet émigrés who have been denied exit visas on the ground that they once had access to government secrets would be allowed to leave after a uniform but unspecified waiting period.

"This removes from the agenda that problem of the so-called refuseniks," he said.

After his speech, the Soviet leader took a ferry to Governors Island in New York Harbor, where he joined Mr. Reagan and Mr. Bush for a two-and-a-half-hour meeting that dramatized the steady warming trend in Soviet-American relations.

Secretary of State George P. Shultz, meeting reporters in the afternoon, said the lunch had been a cordial and informal session that moved from light banter about the healthfulness of horseback riding to exchanges on arms control, human rights, and regional conflicts.

At one point, Mr. Reagan interrupted the meal of wild-mushroom ravioli, veal with smoked quail, and lobster sausage, to propose what the White House spokesman Marlin Fitzwater called an informal and spontaneous toast: "I'd like to raise a toast to what we have accomplished, what we together have accomplished, and what you and the Vice President after January 20 will accomplish together."

Both leaders seemed intent on making the occasion harmonious.

Although American officials had worried that the Soviet leader would put the United States on the defensive with a predominantly propagandistic arms-control gesture, President Reagan shook off a question about ulterior motives, saying, "I think he's sincerely dealing with the problems that he has in his own country."

Mr. Gorbachev also seemed attuned to concerns that his speech was intended to put the Americans on the spot. He told reporters the speech was "an invitation to work together."

"If we score any points, we can do it only together," he said. "If we try to score points alone, nothing good will happen."

Mr. Gorbachev laced his morning speech with warm praise of President Reagan and Mr. Shultz, although he condemned Mr. Shultz's decision to deny a visa to Yasir Arafat, the Palestine Liberation Organization leader, for a United Nations session.

"The next U.S. administration headed by President-elect George Bush will find in us a partner who is ready—without long pauses or backtracking—to continue the dialogue in a spirit of realism, openness, and goodwill, with a willingness to achieve concrete results," he said.

The three men chatted for half an hour privately before lunch, and afterward rode together to a specially constructed platform, where they posed together before a breathtaking backdrop of the Statue of Liberty.

At a reception in Mr. Gorbachev's honor at the United Nations last night, Secretary General Javier Perez de Cuellar called Mr. Gorbachev's speech to the General Assembly "remarkable for its vision and far-reaching ideas."

Among the guests at the reception were former President Richard M. Nixon, former Secretary of State Henry A. Kissinger, the industrialist Armand Hammer, the banker David Rockefeller, Mayor Koch, the publisher Malcolm Forbes, Yoko Ono, and Prince Bandar, the Saudi ambassador to the United States.

Mr. Gorbachev's announcement of the military cutbacks was the first major troop reduction the Soviets have announced since Nikita S. Khrushchev demobilized two million men after the Korean War, earning the bitter opposition of his military.

Asked yesterday if Kremlin hard-liners opposed the cuts, Mr. Gorbachev replied emphatically: "*Nyet! Nyet! Nyet! Nyet!*" Mr. Gorbachev said that by 1991 the Soviet Union would withdraw six tank divisions from East Germany, Czechoslovakia, and Hungary, along with assault landing and river-crossing units that would be the leading forces in a European offensive.

He said the remaining forces would be reorganized in a clearly defensive posture.

At a news conference later, Mr. Gerasimov said, "We are finally doing away with that endlessly repeated myth of the Soviet threat, the Warsaw Pact threat, of an attack on Europe."

Mr. Gorbachev said the Soviet Union was making the unconditional cutbacks to prove a commitment to "demilitarizing international relations" and to break a stalemate in negotiations to reduce conventional weapons.

For Mr. Gorbachev, a clear underlying motive was to reduce the military drain on his deeply troubled domestic economy.

That desire was reflected in his United Nations speech when he promised that next year the Soviet Union would convert two or three weapons plants to civilian use. He called on other major powers to offer similar conversion plans.

"By this action, and by all our activities in favor of demilitarizing international relations, we wish to draw the attention of the international community to yet another pressing problem—the problem of transition from the economy of armaments to an economy of disarmament," he said.

The West also faces budgetary pressures to reduce its military commitments, and Mr. Gorbachev's initiative will certainly increase political pressure on the NATO countries to follow

Once again, the cheers abroad quickly gave way to anger and complaints at home.

Amid the Rubble, Armenians Express Rage at Gorbachev
By Bill Keller

MOSCOW, DEC. 11—In the midst of a huge international earthquake-rescue effort, the ethnic grievances of Soviet Armenians burst out anew today.

Armenian protesters, mistrusting Moscow's handling of salvage efforts, clashed with army troops, and Mikhail S. Gorbachev lashed out at protest leaders for failing to set aside their political dispute at a time of national disaster.

"To behave like this at such a time—what sort of morals do these people have?" the Soviet leader asked angrily in an interview on the main evening television news program.

The relief effort was dealt another blow today when a Soviet military transport plane crashed on approach to Leninakan, among the Armenian cities hit hardest by the quake. Tass, the official press agency, said the crash killed 78 people, all military personnel.

Yevgeny P. Chazov, the Soviet health minister, said in an interview at a makeshift command post in Yerevan, the Armenian capital, that 50,000 to 70,000 people had died in the earthquake. The government said Saturday that the disaster left about 45,000 dead, 12,000 injured, and 500,000 homeless.

Mr. Gorbachev, who toured the devastation in Leninakan, Kirovakan, and Spitak to inspect rescue activities, said he was astonished to be confronted at each stop by people who wanted to debate the status of the Nagorno-Karabakh region, the mountainous sliver of land claimed by both Armenia and neighboring Azerbaijan.

Many Armenians, he said, asked suspiciously whether Armenian children orphaned by the earthquake would be sent to the Russian republic and never returned. Others demanded to know why Moscow had not predicted the quake.

Armenia Opens to Show Capital Under Tight Lid
By Bill Keller

YEREVAN, U.S.S.R., DEC. 20—At Yerevan University and at the Polytechnical Institute, where passions have run high during this year of Armenian self-assertion, soldiers with automatic rifles take attendance each morning.

Army tanks and armored personnel carriers straddle entrances to city squares that earlier this year teemed with tens of thousands of demonstrators. After midnight, armed soldiers stop any car not bearing a pass from the Ministry of Defense.

In the last week and a half, the authorities have methodically arrested many nationalist leaders, including a member of the Armenian legislature, and others have gone into hiding, emerging occasionally to give defiant interviews to Western reporters.

The authorities do not call it martial law, but the capital of Armenia has all the outward markings of a city under military rule.

The Soviet press briefly reported the imposition of military discipline after ethnic unrest broke out in the city last month. But the sense of occupation has been conveyed far more dramatically in the past two weeks, as Armenia has been opened to crowds of outsiders, both Soviet and foreign, in the relief effort mounted since the devastating earthquake north of here on December 7.

For many of the visiting relief workers, journalists, doctors, and diplomats, the emergency measures are a visible admission of defeat for Mikhail S. Gorbachev, the Soviet leader, who has professed the goal of liberalizing Soviet society.

"This is *glasnost* and democracy?" a Moscow psychologist murmured the other day, as the taxi carrying him to a children's hospital pulled alongside a towering tank. His face and tone of voice registered shock and dismay.

Military officials at the army headquarters, which overlooks Yerevan from a hill in the north of the city, said they do not know when the troops will be withdrawn.

"When all the industrial enterprises are working at 100 percent, when all the students are showing up for classes, when it is felt that the safety of Soviet citizens in Yerevan is secure, then this will end," said Col. Mikhail M. Sorokin, a member of the Yerevan army command staff. He declined to be interviewed on the military's role in the city.

The Soviet authorities describe the state of emergency as regrettably necessary to contain nationalist passions that raged out of control, claiming scores of lives in the neighboring republics of Armenia and Azerbaijan.

Since February, the dispute between the two republics over possession of Nagorno-Karabakh, a region of Azerbaijan with an Armenian majority, has grown into the Kremlin's most intractable domestic political crisis.

What began with street demonstrations and petitions grew into widespread civil disobedience as the Kremlin refused to comply with Armenian demands. Meanwhile, the dispute fed a volatile, historically rooted bitterness between the Christian Armenians and the predominantly Muslim Azerbaijanis.

Mr. Gorbachev initially responded with appeals for calm and compromise, but his patience steadily wore thin as the Armenians kept up a campaign of public protest and novel maneuvers in the largely sympathetic Armenian legislature.

Armenians generally believe that Mr. Gorbachev seized on the earthquake as a pretext to begin a concerted assault on nationalist organizers.

On December 10, the police raided the Yerevan writers' union building and arrested several members of the Karabakh Committee, the unofficial leadership of the campaign to claim Nagorno-Karabakh. The authorities asserted that the arrested Armenians had tried to disrupt relief efforts by organizing demonstrations and spreading rumors.

Friends and relatives of the arrested men deny the charges, contending that the committee was simply trying to organize its own, alternative relief effort because so many Armenians did not trust Moscow to deliver donated goods.

Demonstrators demanding the release of the nationalist leaders clashed with the police in the streets of Yerevan the next day.

Mr. Gorbachev, who had flown to the region to inspect the quake damage, furiously denounced the protest leaders for failing to set aside their political campaign at a time of tragedy.

With public attention focused on the earthquake, the arrests have continued. Seven of the 11 committee members are in custody, serving 30-day sentences that family members and friends predict will be extended as long as it suits official convenience.

Khachik Stamboltsyan, a popular nationalist who defeated the Armenian interior minister in a highly unusual write-in campaign for a vacant seat in the legislature, is also in custody, as is Igor Muradyan, a former Karabakh Committee member who helped begin the Armenian campaign.

The Soviet press has reinforced the campaign with fierce, daily attacks on the Armenian protest leaders, portraying them as extremists and political demagogues.

"They've seized the moment to eradicate the Armenian national movement," said Rafael Popoyan, a literary critic and nationalist sympathizer, voicing a view that seems to be widely shared in Yerevan.

The mood in Yerevan has changed markedly since September, when the authorities briefly lifted a ban on travel to the republic by foreign reporters.

The virtually nonstop, open-air political discussions that raged outside the city's neoclassical opera house have ended. The square beside the opera house is now ringed by tanks and troops, who wear bulletproof vests at nightfall.

Soldiers step in quickly to break up any public gathering. No longer are there tables where signatures are gathered in support of Armenian causes, or banners strung with slogans of Armenian self-determination.

Yerevan residents said the Armenian-language newspapers, which once walked the borderline by printing articles sympathetic to the nationalists, now write almost nothing at all on the issue, although they have added to their regular features a column written by the military commander of the city.

The army, which has given foreign reporters nearly free rein in the quake zone, prohibits photographs of tanks and troops in Yerevan.

1989

*A*s it turned out, this was the year that Communism collapsed in Eastern Europe, but in the first months there were few portents of the remarkable changes to come. In Washington, the Bush administration replaced the Reagan administration. In Warsaw, the beleaguered Communists were preparing to talk with the Solidarity opposition they had imprisoned and sought to squelch. In Moscow, the political atmosphere remained stormy, and the economic prospects were poor.

Soviets' Harvest Worst in 3 Years
By Craig R. Whitney

MOSCOW, JAN. 16—The Soviet Union's grain harvest last year fell 40 million tons short of the target of 235 million tons, according to preliminary estimates, a Soviet official said today.

That would be the worst harvest in three years and lower than had been anticipated by American experts. In September, the Agriculture Department estimated that the total would be closer to 205 million tons. More recently it downgraded the estimate to 200 million tons.

An American embassy official said dry weather had affected the Soviet harvest just as it had hurt the American and Canadian harvests last summer. Moscow is likely to make up the shortfall by buying grain, mainly for livestock, on Western markets, he said.

Some grain traders in the United States said Moscow's grain imports could reach near-record levels this year. They said 45 million to 50 million tons might be imported, compared with 32 million last year and a record 55.5 million tons in 1985. At a news conference here today, Stepan Sitaryan, first deputy chairman of the state planning committee, put the preliminary harvest estimate at 195 million tons. That is about 17 percent below the official target.

A major sign of waning Soviet power was the pullback of forces from Afghanistan.

Getting Out with Honor; Soviets Focus on Task of Afghan Pullout as a Pact Fades and Analysis Is Deferred
By Bill Keller

MOSCOW, FEB. 2—As the last Soviet troops muster in Kabul for their convoy home from Afghanistan, the Kremlin has already turned its attention to a desperate salvage operation aimed at snatching as much honor as possible from the jaws of retreat.

With the hope of a last-ditch political settlement all but dissolved, and the search for any long-term lessons postponed to the future, Soviet officials have focused their diplomatic and military efforts on a set of more immediate goals.

"The main object of all this activity," a Western diplomat said, answering the question of what Moscow wants, "is to prevent the Soviet Union from being humiliated."

What Moscow seems to want, first, is to get out without further indignities, avoiding heavy casualties as the final Soviet convoy moves north in the next few days.

The mood in Moscow in the closing days of this nine-year misadventure is neither celebration nor defeat, but fatigue.

The Soviet public, having long since breathed its relief over the withdrawal and disinclined to dwell on the possible collapse of the Afghan regime, now seems eager to put the whole affair behind it.

"We are leaving as we arrived: neither victorious nor vanquished," Vladimir Bavin, who served with the Soviet Army in Afghanistan from 1984 to 1986, said in an interview this week at a club for war veterans. "So I don't think there will be a national holiday on February fifteenth."

Near Departure, Russians Expect Worst for Kabul
By Bill Keller

MOSCOW, FEB. 14—In the final hours of the Soviet military withdrawal from Afghanistan, the Soviet Union seemed braced today for a rapid deterioration of the military situation it is leaving behind.

A Soviet newspaper said that some Afghan army units had begun looting the strongholds left in their control and then abandoning them to the guerrillas.

And a Soviet Foreign Ministry spokesman said 30,000 guerrillas had massed around Kabul, the Afghan capital, and 15,000 more around the eastern city of Jalalabad, preparing for a quick offensive as the Russians leave the country.

Reuters reported from Kabul that the last Soviet troops guarding the capital's airport flew home tonight, a few hours after guerrillas resumed rocket attacks on the city.

The Foreign Ministry repeated that the last Soviet soldier would leave Afghanistan on Wednesday, the deadline set in the Geneva agreement last April on which the withdrawal is based.

Lieut. Gen. Boris V. Gromov, commander of Soviet forces in Afghanistan, told reporters earlier that he would be the last to leave, crossing the Amu Darya River to the city of Termez in Soviet Uzbekistan.

The Foreign Ministry flew a small group of television and news-agency reporters to the scene today to record the event.

Mikhail S. Gorbachev appeared today after a three-week absence from public view. However, in televised remarks to a group of industrial workers, he did not mention Afghanistan—suggesting that he is as eager as the public to relegate the nine-year war to the past.

Western diplomats had said Mr. Gorbachev was believed to be on vacation, but they also said his absence seemed conveniently timed to avoid comment until the withdrawal is safely completed and the Kremlin sees how well the Afghan government of President Najibullah begins to fare on its own.

Maj. Pavel Pinchanov, a battalion commander, expressed bitterness about the lack of spirit among the Afghan allies.

"We left the Afghan soldiers warm, well-swept barracks with neatly made beds, refrigerators stocked with food, air conditioners, televisions," he told *Trud*.

"Soviet soldiers are selfless and sincere," he went on. "But I am not sure, did we need this war? Have our many victims been justified?"

The war has cost the Soviet Union nearly 15,000 lives, and left the public weary.

More than 600,000 soldiers are estimated to have served in Afghanistan since Moscow sent troops to Afghanistan in December 1979 to prop up a shaky Marxist ally. At the high point of Soviet involvement, Western intelligence agencies have estimated, there were 115,000 Soviet troops in the country; Moscow says that when large-scale withdrawals began last May, there were 100,300 Soviet troops in Afghanistan.

The Soviet troops' homecoming has contributed to domestic problems of health care, crime, drug use, and unemployment, some of the aspects of the war that have evoked comparisons to America's experience in Vietnam.

Though in its early infancy the new political culture was developing quickly. Boris N. Yeltsin quit his job in the Construction Ministry to campaign for a key Moscow seat in the Congress of Deputies.

Full of Fight, Yeltsin Feels He's the One
By Esther B. Fein

MOSCOW, FEB. 22—Boris N. Yeltsin leaned into the microphone at the elegant Hall of Columns and bellowed his determination to battle the almighty bureaucrats: "I am physically fit and ready to fight."

Early today, Mr. Yeltsin, who was demoted from his job as Moscow Communist Party leader a year and a half ago, got a new chance at political pugilism. He won a spot on the ballot for the capital's only at-large seat in the new national Congress of Deputies, which will be voted on by Moscow residents.

Mr. Yeltsin, whose reputation as a "give 'em hell" populist soared after he was demoted, will face a quintessential insider: the director of the factory that makes limousines for the party elite. The race is sure to be one of the most closely watched and symbolically rich contests of the March 26 election.

The nominating process for the new Congress ended today, beginning a month-long general-election campaign, the first in Soviet history in which most of the races will be contested. The election is the critical stage in what Mikhail S. Gorbachev has called a major realignment of power toward greater democracy.

Some see the election as a chance to promote reform. But Mr. Yeltsin, a burly man with a wave of white hair and a lip that often seems curled on the verge of a defiant sneer, sees it as a vehicle of bitter popular discontent.

Winning the nomination—Mr. Yeltsin was backed by a majority of the 875 electors who chose candidates for Moscow's single at-large seat—was a personal triumph for Mr. Yeltsin, who was publicly rebuked and ousted from the Politburo for sparring too roughly with the leadership.

Mr. Yeltsin appealed for rehabilitation at the nineteenth party conference, which was televised nationally. Flatly turned away by the party hierarchy, he said he saw this election as a second chance.

Though he was selected to run in at least 13 precincts, Mr. Yeltsin acknowledged in an interview before the nominating vote that the at-large Moscow seat was the one that he most coveted.

"This would mean a certain rehabilitation for me," said Mr. Yeltsin, now a high official in the Construction Ministry. "I want to be chosen from here more than from anywhere else."

Contenders for the city-wide nomination at one time included candidates as diverse as Andrei D. Sakharov, the human-rights advocate and physicist, and Vitaly I. Vorotnikov, the leader of the Russian republic and one of the 12 leaders of the ruling Communist Party.

Dr. Sakharov, rebuffed by the Academy of Scientists as a candidate for one of its guaranteed seats, decided to drop out of all other races to protest the academy's unpopular decision. Mr. Vorotnikov bowed out to run for a safer seat in the city of Voronezh.

The list of candidates was whittled to 10, including an astronaut, a famous folk singer, and a school principal.

When the vote was counted nearly 14 hours after the meeting began, two people had secured a majority of the 875 votes and the right to be on the ballot: Mr. Yeltsin, with 532 votes, and Yevgeny A. Brakov, the director of the Zil auto factory, with 577 votes.

As spring approached the talks between the government and Solidarity in Poland yielded a formula that would enable the anti-Communist opposition there to contest 40 percent of parliamentary seats. In the Soviet Union, no single social opposition force comparable to Solidarity had emerged, and the driving force for change and reform lay at the top. Still, that top, in the person of Gorbachev, had so changed the political rules that in many parts of the vast country organizations were forming to seek even more than the leader was willing to give. With the approach of elections to the Congress of People's Deputies, the intensity and scale of political activity were growing.

Ukraine Intellectuals Lead Challenge to Communists
By Bill Keller

LVOV, U.S.S.R.—Ukrainians by the millions turned on their television sets the other night to witness a wondrous sight, a popular Ukrainian literary critic in fiery debate with a senior ideologist from the republic's Communist Party.

The issue was a recent move by the Ukrainian Writers' Union to organize an independent political movement similar to the popular fronts that have attracted mass support in the Baltic republics.

Viewers rendered a split decision on who prevailed in the televised confrontation, but the event signified an important awakening here in the Soviet Union's second-largest republic: after a period of deceptive quiet, the Ukraine's intellectual establishment has ventured into open conflict with the Communist Party, and Ukrainian nationalism—or patriotism, as its adherents prefer—is becoming respectable.

Nationalism in the Ukraine, which is the Soviet Union's breadbasket and industrial engine, is surely high on Mikhail S. Gorbachev's list of nightmares as Soviet leader.

"Here we're not talking about 1.5 million people, as in Estonia, but 50 million, a nation the size of France or Italy," noted Bogdan N. Gorin, a leader of the Ukrainian Helsinki Association, a dissident human-rights group. "We think the question of the Soviet Union, whether it survives or not, will be resolved not in Estonia, but in the Ukraine."

Many in the republic believe that is a major reason the Soviet leader made a hastily arranged five-day tour of the republic in late February.

A trip through the Ukraine in Mr. Gorbachev's footsteps—from Kiev, the capital, to the cultural center of Lvov in the west, to the industrial city of Donetsk in the east—found that rivulets of discontent have begun running together into a rising stream.

From the hearty welcome of a Kiev taxicab driver who proudly introduced himself as "a Ukrainian, and a nationalist," to the carefully worded calls for greater autonomy embodied in the platforms of seemingly establishment candidates in the current election campaign, a visitor finds the caution and intimidation that prevailed here a year ago beginning to dissipate.

In just the last few months, movements for environmental protection, for promotion of Ukrainian language, for the honoring of Stalin's victims, and for the legalization of the outlawed Uniate Catholic Church have all shown signs of vigor. All seem likely to align themselves with the writers' new Popular Movement in Support of Perestroika, called "Ruk" in Ukrainian, which advocates greater political and economic autonomy from Moscow.

Spreading from Lvov, the center of ferment, to the more establishment intellectual circles of Kiev, those movements are being drawn together now by several factors, including the example of the Baltic republics, the sense that Vladimir V. Shcherbitsky, the Ukrainian party strongman, is slipping from power, and an election campaign that has encouraged people to come out and defend themselves.

The Ukrainian authorities must also be concerned about recent signs of cooperation between the outlawed Uniate Catholics and Ukrainian Orthodox believers.

Uniate refers to members of Eastern Christian Churches in union with the Roman Catholic Church but with their own rite.

Both groups have strong grievances. The Uniates, banned for nationalist tendencies, want legalization and the return of former Catholic churches that have been handed over to the Russian Orthodox Patriarchate in Moscow.

Ukrainian Orthodox believers want the right to hold services in their language, and some favor creation of a separate orthodox denomination independent from Moscow.

On February 26 a crowd estimated by organizers at 25,000 people thronged outside the Uspenski Cathedral here for a requiem service on the one hundred twenty-eighth anniversary of the death of the poet Shevchenko. The service was led jointly by the Rev. Mykhailo Neiskoguz, a renegade priest of the Orthodox Church, and the Rev. Mykhailo Voloshyn of the Ukrainian Catholic Church, a demonstration of solidarity that reportedly left many in the crowd weeping with joy.

The most important recent development is creation of "Ruk," the popular movement that promises to unite the various strains of Ukrainian patriotism, religious and cultural, dissident and establishment, under a flag of greater independence for the republic.

The group's draft platform, made available by Ivan F. Drach, is a more cautiously worded version of the national front declarations that have rallied mass support in the Baltics.

It calls for Ukrainians to control their natural resources and industry, for religious and political diversity, for a halt to Russification—which the platform describes as "the raising of little Ivans who don't remember who their kin are."

The group demands the right to submit draft laws, sponsor candidates in the elections, and put up questions for popular referendum.

Ruk does not favor secession from the union—even the more radical Helsinki Association stops short of that—and it is careful to present itself as a supporter of Mr. Gorbachev's economic and political policies rather than as a political alternative.

Unlike the Baltic popular fronts, the Ruk platform diplomatically "acknowledges the leading role of the Communist Party."

Lithuanian Nationalists: A Fine and Fragile Line
By Bill Keller

VILNIUS, U.S.S.R., MARCH 9—Ignoring damp snowflakes, Lithuanians by the thousands filed into the sylvan amphitheater of a Vilnius park the other day for an election rally.

They cheered the candidates of the popular movement called Sajudis, whistled their collective disdain for the Communist Party, listened stoically as their leaders appealed for calm in the face of official resistance, and then lifted perhaps 15,000 voices in the Sajudis oath: "Our goal is a free Lithuania!"

A few weeks ago these were words of nostalgia and bravado. But in the heat of an uninhited Soviet election campaign, the notion of "free Lithuania"—free, that is, of the Soviet Union—has become a live and explosive issue.

In February, Sajudis, now a commanding political presence in this republic of 3.7 million people, took a daring step by announcing that its ultimate goal is to restore "an independent and neutral Lithuanian state in a demilitarized zone," like the nation that existed here between the two world wars, until the Soviet Union annexed the Baltic states in 1940.

The group had earlier called for a form of home rule, but stopped short of endorsing independence. But with the new declaration, including the statement that Lithuania had been "occupied" by the Red Army against its will, Sajudis portrayed itself as a lineal descendant of the partisans who waged armed resistance against Soviet power until 1953.

The declaration made Sajudis the first of the Baltic popular fronts to explicitly chart a separatist course, although similar groups in Estonia and Latvia include factions that favor full independence.

The group's leaders say their declaration was a statement of principle, not a short-term program. But some Sajudis members who are running for office in the election on March 26 are quite prepared to push for secession almost immediately.

The Lithuanian Communist Party leader, Algirdas Brazauskas, who had been nervously tolerant of the nationalist group, was called to Moscow for consultations last month, and returned with a new, firm set to his square jaw.

The party promptly announced new limits on Sajudis' independent press, purged several party and government officials considered sympathetic to the movement, and warned of a possible state of emergency if the separatist calls did not subside.

"We have told Sajudis that together we can approach that red line, but we, the official leadership, cannot cross it," Mr. Brazauskas said in an interview, adding that he "cannot imagine the consequences" if Sajudis pushes for secession.

"On the other side of the line, we can no longer remain friends or support their ideas," he said. "You can criticize us, you can mistrust us—whatever. But we won't cross that line." What makes the debate especially pointed is the prospect that, thanks to the Soviet Union's first competitive elections, Sajudis is likely soon to acquire real power in the Lithuanian government.

The organization is backing candidates for 39 of Lithuania's 42 seats in a new national congress to be elected on March 26, and even party officials concede that the movement stands a good chance of winning most of them. The popular fronts in Latvia and Estonia are also backing candidates, but have not organized such complete slates.

While Sajudis is optimistic about its election prospects, such a triumph would have a largely symbolic effect, rather than any immediate consequences for the Lithuanian government. The 2,250 members of the new national Congress of Deputies, which is to be the nation's supreme governing body, will appoint a standing legislature and a president from among their number.

More important, Sajudis expects to win control of the republic's legislature in the next round of local elections. Already, Sajudis has gone up against the party in three special elections to fill vacant seats in the Lithuanian legislature and won all of them handily.

Alarmed that Sajudis members might use a majority in the legislature to formally declare Lithuanian independence, the Communist Party is now pressing to have the local legislative elections postponed from next fall until at least the following spring.

While in the buildup to the elections the emphasis was on "democratizing" politics, Gorbachev continued to press for basic economic changes, in this case dealing with the chronic problems of growing food and getting it to consumers.

Gorbachev Urges New Farm Policy and Freer Market
By Bill Keller

MOSCOW, MARCH 15—Mikhail S. Gorbachev called today for a radical reversal of the Soviet Union's 60-year history of centralized farming, including the immediate dismantling of the state agricultural bureaucracy and the gradual introduction of free markets.

The Soviet leader's proposed "new agrarian policy," outlined at the opening of a critical party meeting on the nation's food crisis, would give different areas wide latitude to choose among various types of collective and private agriculture.

Mr. Gorbachev called for new legal guarantees to allay the anxiety of private farmers and other experimenters, a new system of cooperative banks and stock markets to finance them, and more flexible prices to reward those who succeed.

After a transition period, he said, farmers must be given "complete freedom" to choose ways of marketing their products. Farmers now in most cases deliver their goods to the state at fixed prices to fulfill quotas set in Moscow.

Acknowledging that his previous efforts to revive Soviet farming had failed because they did not go far enough, Mr. Gorbachev said, "the essence of economic change in the countryside should be in granting farmers broad opportunities for displaying independence, enterprise, and initiative."

Once the Communist Party's top official for agriculture, Mr. Gorbachev leads a country in which nearly half the 50,000 farms operate at a loss or barely break even, requiring annual subsidies amounting to billions of dollars. As much as one third of Soviet produce rots before it reaches markets; vast amounts of grain, meat, sugar, and butter are imported to meet domestic shortages.

Mr. Gorbachev said his new farm program had the approval of the ruling 12-member Communist Party Politburo and the government's Council of Ministers, the rough equivalent of a cabinet. But his package of proposed laws and directives, which touch on explosive issues of Communist ideology and entrenched interests, may face resistance during debate Thursday in the 300-member Central Committee.

And the changes may encounter further resistance as they are carried out, both from farm managers reluctant to give up power and from farmers comfortable with the current, undemanding system.

Underscoring the importance that Mr. Gorbachev is placing on a resurgence in farming, the Central Committee gathering was televised tonight, the first time in history that cameras have been allowed into that inner sanctum.

The Central Committee also formally elected the 100 candidates it nominated in January to fill the party's 100 guaranteed seats in a new national legislature. The candidates, including Mr. Gorbachev, were all unanimously approved except for Yegor K. Ligachev, the conservative Politburo member formally in charge of agriculture, whose candidacy also received one abstention.

Mr. Ligachev had cast himself as the defender of the status quo in a series of speeches over the last six weeks, arguing that the main thrust of a new policy should be bolstering the big state farms with infusions of money.

Tonight, Mr. Gorbachev condemned this argument, saying that decades of investment had produced marginal results.

"Analysis of history and the experience of the past few years of *perestroika* offer compelling evidence that if we opt for this as the mainstay of agrarian policy, we shall make a serious mistake," he warned.

While Mr. Ligachev has argued against the breakup of unprofitable state and collective farms, saying this would violate the Communist notion of social justice, Mr. Gorbachev said that the worst of these enterprises must be turned over to new owners "without delay."

"Among the enterprises that lag behind, some have lost prospects for independent development," the Soviet leader said. "Radical measures are called for in such cases."

State and collective farms that are not chronic losers should be "radically restructured" into amalgamations of relatively independent units joined by lease agreements, Mr. Gorbachev said.

He emphasized that leaseholders in these new farms would be given real power. Many state farms now claim to be operating on a lease basis, when in fact they use a system of "lease contracts" that gives the farmers little freedom. Mr. Gorbachev denounced such ruses.

Families or groups of farmers who chose private farming must be given equal legal and financial footing to compete with the big state farms, the Soviet leader said.

Mr. Gorbachev has said in the past that the law should allow 50-year leases to give farmers a sense of stability, and others have argued that farmers should also be permitted to bequeath the land to their children. Today, the Soviet leader did not spell out the terms of the law he wants.

As expected, Mr. Gorbachev called for dismantling the vast ministry called Gosagroprom, the creation of which in November 1985 was Mr. Gorbachev's first major economic initiative as national leader. A merger of several agriculture and food-processing ministries, it was envisioned as a streamlining but quickly became a bureaucratic impediment.

Mr. Gorbachev called for quick enactment of a law assuring farmers the right to sell their surpluses directly to processing plants, consumer cooperatives, farm markets, or restaurants. Farmers have been promised this right in the past, but in practice the state requisitions most of their products.

The proposed agricultural policy includes an increase next January in prices paid to farmers and somewhat greater flexibility to negotiate the prices of what they sell.

"In general, comrades, we are for cost-accounting relations with leaseholders to be based on complete freedom to choose ways of marketing products," Mr. Gorbachev said. "We shall inevitably come to this, sooner or later."

He said free markets could not be introduced before a major relaxation of price controls, which is still several years away.

The Soviet leader said that for the next two or three years, state-controlled retail prices on staples like bread, meat, and dairy products would not change.

He sounded tonight like a man wiser in the ways of bureaucratic resistance, repeatedly taking note of how his past economic proposals had been thwarted, and suggesting that the laws he was proposing include safeguards against such trickery.

For example, Mr. Gorbachev said that during the transition period until free markets are introduced, farmers would still sell much of their produce to the government for distribution. But he insisted these state orders not turn into a new, permanent form of command from Moscow—as they have in many other Soviet industries that have purportedly been given greater economic liberty.

While only a portion of the seats was openly contested, the election for the new Congress marked the freest poll that any voter could remember.

Soviet Voters Deal Humiliating Blow to Party Officials
By Bill Keller

MOSCOW, MARCH 27—The Soviet electorate has dealt a mortifying rebuke to the high and mighty in elections for a new national Congress, including stunning upsets of a Politburo member and several other senior Communist Party officials who ran without opposition.

Results piling up today from the freest nationwide elections since 1917 showed that the mayor and the second-ranking Communist official of Moscow, the Communist Party leader in Leningrad, the commander of the Northern Fleet, the President and Premier of Lithuania, the Estonian K.G.B. chief, the commander of Soviet troops in East Germany, and other prominent officials were defeated by candidates promising more rapid change.

The elections on Sunday, for the new and theoretically powerful Congress of People's Deputies, swept in a substantial minority of independent candidates, planting the seeds of the first national opposition since the time of Lenin.

The results were not a rejection of the Communist Party as such—many of the winners viewed as champions of change were Communists—but they were a disavowal of party members seen as unenthusiastic about the program of economic and political revival undertaken by Mikhail S. Gorbachev, the Soviet leader.

The popular sentiment against the Old Guard was so strong that in Leningrad, Yuri F. Solovyev, the regional Communist Party leader and a nonvoting member of the ruling Politburo, was reportedly defeated even though he was the only candidate on the ballot. This came about, as Leningrad radio and television journalists explained it, because enough voters crossed Mr. Solovyev's name off the ballots to deny him the required majority, forcing a new election.

The same humiliation befell both the Communist Party leader, Konstantin I. Masik, and the mayor, Valentin A. Zgursky, in Kiev, the third-largest Soviet city, and Yakov P. Pogrebnyak, head of the Lvov regional committee in the western Ukraine, as well as other Ukrainian officials, according to the official press agency, Tass.

Even in the Siberian city of Tomsk, not known as a hotbed of unrest, a majority of voters crossed out the name of the unopposed party leader, Vadim I. Zorkaltsev, a protégé of the Politburo member Yegor K. Ligachev, the government newspaper, *Izvestia,* said tonight.

None of these officials will lose the job he already holds, but the defeat nonetheless stands as a vote of no confidence by the public.

Mr. Gorbachev has said several times that the party would take into account poor showings in elections when considering the future of Communist officials, warning that those rejected or heavily opposed by the public cannot count on keeping their party posts indefinitely.

Aside from Mr. Solovyev, three other Politburo members, including the Ukrainian party leader, Vladimir V. Shcherbitsky, ran in uncontested elections, but the results of those races were not available.

Boris N. Yeltsin, the deposed city party chief, won with a landslide of 89 percent over a candidate backed by the local party machine, Yevgeny A. Brakov, the director of the Zil limousine factory.

Where ethnic consciousness was the issue, it proved a compelling political force.

The victors included most of the candidates who campaigned for greater autonomy in the Baltic republics of Lithuania, Latvia, and Estonia, including some candidates who favor the secession of their republics from the Soviet Union.

The Lithuanian movement Sajudis claimed victories for 32 of the republic's 42 seats, with eight others forced into runoffs.

Sajudis (pronounced SAH-you-dis) withdrew its challenges to the number 1 and number 2 Lithuanian party leaders, who are regarded as relatively sympathetic to the demands for greater independence, but at least six other top Lithuanian officials fell to Sajudis.

The Latvian Communist leader, Jan Vagris, withstood a nationalist challenge with a bare 51 percent against a candidate from a fringe group, the National Independence Movement. Supporters of the independence candidate asserted that the margin of victory came from navy ballots collected in the Baltic fleet, based in Riga.

There was also a kindling of regional consciousness in tiny Moldavia, where six radicals from the writers' union were all elected, and a major establishment figure, the ideologist Aleksandr Zhuchenko, chief of the Soviet Academy of Sciences, was beaten.

In the Ukraine, Ivan F. Drach, a poet and organizer of a popular front group, placed second in a field of seven candidates, but Ukrainian nationalists consoled themselves that the winner, a Kiev surgeon, had strongly endorsed the Popular Front.

One of the most startling upsets came in the northern Russian city of Yaroslavl, where Gen. Boris V. Snetkov, commander of Soviet forces in East Germany, lost to a lieutenant colonel who called for "radical reform" of the military, including abolition of the draft.

The military commanders of Moscow and Leningrad and the commander of the Northern Fleet in Murmansk all fell to civilian challengers.

It was impossible to tell from the partial results trickling in today how large an independent bloc—or how potentially united—would emerge in the new congress.

Election officials do not expect a full list of deputies to be published until April 5, and that will not include several races where runoffs or new elections are required.

Voters in many of the 1,500 districts that voted Sunday were offered only a single candidate, and many more faced a choice between two candidates similarly unthreatening to the status quo.

"The main thing is not the quantity of independent deputies, but the fact itself," said Roy A. Medvedev, a Marxist historian restored to official favor less than a year ago. Mr. Medvedev came in first among six candidates in a Moscow district and faces a runoff on April 9.

The winners in Moscow's 27 election districts include a number of potential members of an informal independent bloc. Mr. Yeltsin told Reuters today that he was examining the election returns from different regions in search of possible allies in the new Congress.

Whatever quasi opposition emerges when all the votes are counted will presumably be fractious, and will surely be outnumbered by candidates beholden to the Communist Party.

The four-month-old constitutional amendments under which the elections were conducted gave the party an extra margin of security by reserving 750 places of 2,250 for mainstream official groups, including the party itself.

Moreover, the party will have another opportunity to filter out potential opponents when its 2,250 members pick 542 of themselves for a standing legislature, where most of the lawmaking is to take place.

The more independent candidates have, almost without exception, pledged their loyalty to Mr. Gorbachev and his program of political and economic change.

The Soviet leader may thus use his new parliament—which he is expected to head from the newly enhanced post of president—to push his program faster than hard-liners in the party would like.

But Mr. Gorbachev may also find that a free-thinking legislature will make his life more difficult, with some nationalist deputies threatening to bolt from the Soviet Union and reformers impatient for more radical change than even he wants.

The best known of the victorious candidates in Sunday's elections, Mr. Yeltsin, fell from Mr. Gorbachev's favor because he became impatient with change, and Mr. Gorbachev on election day pointedly warned against "great leaps."

Though the political changes were for the most part homegrown, there was a growing awareness within the Soviet Union of how Communist power, inspired by Moscow, was in retreat around the world.

Isvestia Reports Poland's Changes in Detail and Straightforwardly
By Francis X. Clines

MOSCOW, APRIL 6—Soviet newspaper readers were presented today with a long and straightforward account of the Polish government's sweeping political initiatives, including news of a crucial innovation notably absent here: the establishment of a formal opposition.

A dispatch from Warsaw in *Izvestia,* the Soviet government newspaper, dwelt in detail on the changes and significance of the Polish program, declaring: "Thus, the participation of the opposition in the official political life of the country has become a fact. This inarguably has become the primary change that has taken place in society in recent months."

Izvestia reported that the opposition was taking on greater responsibilities and a "psychologically quite difficult" role. "Its representatives will take their place in parliament, where, incidentally, the Polish Communist Party will not have a majority," the article said in a rather casual tone, in contrast to the Soviet press tradition of defending the Communist power monopoly at all turns.

In the current period of elections for the new Soviet Congress, various independent candidates have questioned whether the issue of introducing opposition politics might someday have to be considered in this country. But Mikhail S. Gorbachev has dismissed the multiparty idea as "rubbish," insisting there is ferment enough in the ruling Communist Party to carry out the political and economic changes he is seeking.

The article on page 5 of *Izvestia* made no comparisons with the Gorbachev program, but it declared that the Polish changes were particularly significant for "putting to rest the myth that socialism cannot be subject to renewal."

The *Izvestia* report may have been foreshadowed last month when the Soviet press broke an eight-year taboo and printed a long, favorable profile and interview with Lech Walesa, the Polish labor leader. Before that article in *New Times*, a current events weekly, Mr. Walesa had been regularly excoriated in the Soviet press. Western diplomats have been watching for additional signs of the Kremlin's growing flexibility in its attitudes toward Eastern Europe.

Soviet Upstarts Form a Coalition
By Bill Keller

MOSCOW, APRIL 22—Scores of political upstarts who triumphed in last month's elections have begun to join forces in what promises to be the first independent bloc in the Soviet government since Lenin's time.

Newly elected deputies who gathered today in Moscow predicted that the bloc—tentatively called the March Coalition in honor of the March 26 elections that made it possible—could number from 200 to 400 members, enough to give the more divided Communist regulars a significant challenge in the new Congress of Deputies that convenes next month.

Moving quickly from the intoxication of victory to the crucial drudgery of government, like-minded deputies in Moscow, the Baltic republics, and elsewhere have begun forming committees, establishing links, and drafting plans to increase their leverage in the new Congress.

"We may have only ten or fifteen percent of the Congress," said Marju Lauristin, an Estonian deputy who came to Moscow today to cultivate the new coalition. "But it is a minority made up of real leaders."

The independents have shown a flair for using their new official status to generate attention and shape public opinion.

Earlier this week a group of new deputies traveled to Georgia—like American congressmen on a fact-finding mission—to investigate the clash earlier this month between troops and nationalist protesters. Their conclusion that troops attacked the demonstrators with little or no provocation was given wide coverage in the more aggressive Soviet newspapers.

The Soviet legislature has had no organized rival to the Communist Party since 1918, when Lenin expelled competing parties from the government.

The independent deputies, who describe themselves as progressive or democratic, share a common platform calling for democracy, civil rights, a free press, relaxation of state controls on the economy, and greater autonomy for minority republics.

They consider themselves the true supporters of Mikhail S. Gorbachev, although their prescriptions often go beyond what he has explicitly endorsed.

The newly elected deputies are careful to say they do not want to form an opposition party, which is prohibited by the constitution in any case. And many if not most of the new bloc are Communist Party members, albeit Communists who say that reform is more important than party unity.

The fledgling bloc already seems to have the jump on the Communist Party in organizing its strategy and setting its priorities. The Communist Party's 300-member Central Committee is expected to meet next Tuesday, where its planning for the Congress is likely to be distracted by the plaints of many party regulars who suffered repudiation at the polls.

At the meeting today, sponsored by an intellectuals' discussion club called the Moscow Tribune, about 15 deputies described their strategies. Among the top priorities of the independent deputies are these:

● Organization and working rules in the new Congress that will protect the minority's foothold. The deputies want to make sure independents are not left by the wayside when the 2,250-member Congress picks 542 of its members for the standing legislature.

● Electoral reforms to assure that candidates outside the party apparatus will have a better chance in future elections, including the critical races for local and republican governments planned for later this year.

● Revoking or amending recent decrees that limit freedom of speech and protest, and enlarging the liberties of the press.

Most of the deputies have ambitious legislative platforms, including proposals to relax central controls over the smaller republics and decentralize the economy, but those who spoke today said their first aim must be to make sure their voices are not drowned out.

"If we cannot maintain the level of political interest we achieved during the elections, then a significant part of our success will be wiped out," the historian Yuri N. Afanasyev warned his fellow deputies.

The economist Gavriil K. Popov, speaking for a group of about 25 Moscow deputies, laid out a number of proposals to prevent manipulation of the new Congress by the Communist Party apparatus, including the creation of a sort of Soviet C-Span, a television channel devoted to live coverage of the Congress.

To assure more uninhibited coverage, he suggested that the Congress itself elect the editor of *Izvestia,* the government newspaper, and the head of the congressional television channel.

He also proposed that all deputies who are party members be registered as part of a special congressional party chapter to liberate them from the directives of their local party bosses.

Galina V. Starovoitova, a sociologist who is a candidate in a special election in Armenia, said an analysis of the election results suggested that about 20 percent of the deputies appear to be potential allies, about 30 percent are wed to the Communist Party apparatus, and the remaining 50 percent will be the battleground of opinion and power.

Kremlin Approves a Sweeping Purge of Its "Dead Souls"
By Bill Keller

MOSCOW, APRIL 25—The Communist Party approved a sweeping purge of political holdovers from its top leadership today, as well as the promotion of two dozen junior leaders to the party's all-important Central Committee.

The removal of 110 inactive party officials—74 of whom had full voting rights in the 301-member committee, and 36 of whom were nonvoting members or members of the party auditing commission—seemed to rid Mikhail S. Gorbachev of a bloc regarded by his aides as a significant drag on his program of change and an impediment to the promotion of his supporters.

Twenty-four nonvoting members of the Central Committee were promoted to full membership in the Central Committee, meaning that the committee, which is charged with overall policy making, will be smaller, decreasing in size from 301 to 251.

Vadim A. Medvedev, the chief Communist Party ideologist, who held a news conference tonight to announce the changes, said that voters in the elections last month had given the leadership a mandate to speed the pace of change.

"They spoke out again against conservative tendencies, against the preservation of administration by command, for renewal, for democracy, for *glasnost,* for economic reform," Mr. Medvedev said.

In a brief speech to the party gathering, Mr. Gorbachev said the 110 officials, a few of them holdovers from the time of Stalin, had all signed a letter withdrawing voluntarily. The group included some prominent names, among them Andrei A. Gromyko, the former president, and Nikolai A. Tikhonov, a former prime minister.

Evidently in exchange for their cooperation, the retirees were allowed to leave with effusive praise for their service and without criticism.

The removed officials—popularly referred to as "dead souls," after the Gogol novel—were Central Committee members who had largely been retired from their active party jobs because of old age, ill health, or a fall from favor.

Mr. Medvedev also said in response to a question that he is not opposed to a national debate of the idea of a multiparty political system, although he is personally opposed to permitting opposition parties. He thus took a more moderate position on the issue than Mr. Gorbachev, who has described talk of a multiparty system as "rubbish."

He noted that today's turnover in the leadership leaves a large number of new, Gorbachev-era leaders outside the Central Committee.

Seven of the 14 republic party chiefs—the leaders of Georgia, Armenia, Azerbaijan, Uzbekistan, and the Baltic republics of Lithuania, Latvia, and Estonia—and more than half of the regional party leaders are not even junior members of the body that must approve each shift in the party line.

While the proponents of greater changes were organizing to pressure Gorbachev, the party's fading Old Guard was voicing disgust and sounding alarms and signaling that it was not prepared to go gently.

Russian Party Officials Rage at Changes Under Gorbachev
By Bill Keller

MOSCOW, APRIL 27—The Communist Party newspaper *Pravda* today published a startling outpouring of anger and frustration from senior party officials distressed by the currents of change and contention Mikhail S. Gorbachev has let loose in the country.

In speeches at the party's Central Committee meeting Tuesday, an array of regional leaders blamed Moscow—and implicitly Mr. Gorbachev—for mismanaging the economy, for undermining the authority of the party and the military, and for tolerating nationalist fevers in the country and unorthodox ideas within the party.

One speaker, Vladimir I. Melnikov of Komi, recounted the shortages of basic consumer goods and then said: "And people understand that many of these problems cannot already simply be attributed to the legacy of the stagnation period. We are duty-bound to admit that many mistakes and miscalculations have been made in the years of *perestroika,* too."

Several of the speakers were local party leaders rejected by voters in last month's elections. Others were political holdovers who on Tuesday were forced into retirement in a purge of the policy-making Central Committee.

While the anguished voices probably spoke for many party regulars, the critics appear at the moment to be a relatively powerless clique in the party—hobbled by Mr. Gorbachev's consolidation of power and discredited by their own failure in the election.

The targets of the party officials' outrage ranged from the growth of private enterprise to a proposal by a prominent theater director to remove Lenin's glass-encased body from his mausoleum on Red Square and bury it.

Valery T. Saikin, the mayor of Moscow and an election casualty, gave a law-and-order speech that complained of undue attention to the rights of criminals and prisoners.

In a sideswipe at Mr. Gorbachev's gospel that in world affairs "universal human values" must take priority over the class struggle against capitalism, the Moscow mayor added, "It's strange, but under the guise of the priority of the universal values, mindless imitation is taking place—imitating on our socialist ground, in our socialist reality, everything that is considered novel, for the single reason that this novelty is borrowed from across our western or eastern borders."

Publication of the speeches in five full pages of the party newspaper laid bare a deep rift in the Communist Party, brought into the open by the repudiation of many party officials in the elections March 26.

Mr. Gorbachev, in his closing remarks at the meeting, conceded that the party's candidates had been hurt by the intractable economic crisis and other discontents, but he said some regional party officials shared the blame.

He seemed to dismiss his more vociferous critics with gentle mockery. "Some of our party committees have found themselves in the position of that commander whose regiment or division has launched an offensive, while he himself is still stuck in his trench," he said.

The wails of the indignant party officials focused on the press, independent political groups, private entrepreneurs, and government bureaucrats. But underlying the speeches was an unmistakable sense that Mr. Gorbachev had betrayed the party regulars.

Mr. Melnikov suggested that Mr. Gorbachev was out of touch with problems in the country because his aides were "clearly guarding the general secretary from the severity of the situation." Several officials complained that liberalization was getting out of hand, a criticism often heard in letters to the press but rarely from the lips of senior party officials.

Yuri F. Solovyev, party chief of the Leningrad region and a nonvoting member of the ruling Politburo, said: "It is no secret that things have gotten to the point where we have people with party membership cards openly speaking against the Communist Party of the Soviet Union, against its vanguard role in society, calling for transforming the party of action into a party of discussion clubs.

"On that fundamental question the position of our Central Committee should be clear, precise, and public."

Mr. Solovyev was one of six top Leningrad party figures who lost in the elections. Mr. Solovyev ran unopposed but was rejected by voters who crossed his name off the ballot.

Ratmir S. Bobovikov, the party chief of the Vladimir region, criticized two of Mr. Gorbachev's Politburo allies by name—Aleksandr N. Yakovlev and Vadim A. Medvedev—for not going out to protest rallies and rebuffing the demonstrators. "They would not have to go very far," he added ironically. "Everyone knows that in Moscow there's no shortage of rallies."

Mr. Bobovikov was passed over on Tuesday when 24 nonvoting members of the Central Committee were promoted to full status.

Most of the 20 speeches were laced with at least some criticism of lax political discipline and economic failings under Mr. Gorbachev's program.

Mr. Bobovikov, one of the harshest, suggested that any program as popular in the West as Mr. Gorbachev's *perestroika* must be regarded with suspicion. "The elated tone of the articles in our press about how bourgeois leaders praise *perestroika* also causes natural questions in people," he said, "because they remember well Lenin's testament: think carefully any time your class enemy praises you."

Confronted at home by momentous economic problems and an inflamed politics of discontent, Gorbachev turned again to foreign policy as if to demonstrate that it was he who stirred the pot and kept it simmering. In April he had paid a visit to Cuba where he had hugged Fidel Castro in what seemed to be a perfunctory embrace. He stopped off in London and announced that the Soviet Union would no longer produce uranium for weapons since it had sufficient stockpiles. He was getting ready to travel to China to pave over the chasm that had long separated the two Communist behemoths. But before that, he again resorted to his tactic of staggering his opponent with what seemed to be an unexpected concession, he threw another disarmament bid into the already sizable pot.

Gorbachev Hands a Surprised Baker an Arms Proposal
By Thomas L. Friedman

BRUSSELS, MAY 11—Mikhail S. Gorbachev told Secretary of State James A. Baker 3d today that Moscow plans a small cut in its nuclear arsenal in Europe by the end of the year, State Department officials said.

At a meeting in the Kremlin, Mr. Gorbachev also disclosed specific proposals for reductions in conventional arms in Europe and called on Mr. Baker to let the North Atlantic Treaty Organization begin immediate negotiations with the Soviet-led Warsaw Pact for mutual reductions in short-range nuclear weapons in Europe.

Mr. Baker rejected the call for talks, which seemed intended to upstage Mr. Baker on his first visit to the Soviet Union.

Aides to Mr. Baker said they were somewhat surprised by Mr. Gorbachev's heavy emphasis on arms-control issues. The Baker team had wanted to focus on other issues, like regional conflicts and terrorism.

Mr. Baker told reporters on his plane from Moscow to Brussels, where he flew to brief the NATO allies on Friday, that he welcomed the planned Soviet reduction, which he said would be a "good step, but a very small step."

Mr. Gorbachev said he would cut 500 weapons from the Warsaw Pact arsenal of roughly 10,000 nuclear bombs and short-range warheads and artillery shells. NATO has about 4,000 short-range nuclear weapons in Europe, and Washington considers these essential to a stable balance of power on the continent. Such weapons have a range of up to 300 miles.

An administration official said that when Mr. Gorbachev told Mr. Baker during their talks that his move was not politically motivated, the Secretary of State shot back, "It certainly is."

The Soviet leader's initiative can only widen the rift between two groups of NATO members: those who agree with West Germany's call for Washington to negotiate with Moscow on short-range nuclear arms, and Britain and the United States, who staunchly oppose such a move.

In a news conference after Mr. Baker's two-day visit to Moscow, his host, Foreign Minister Eduard A. Shevardnadze, called the Bush administration's position on short-range nuclear weapons "very negative," adding, "This concerns us seriously."

Mr. Gorbachev also used his first encounter with a senior Bush administration official to disclose the specific, large reductions in nonnuclear weapons that the Kremlin intends to submit to the NATO–Warsaw Pact conventional arms talks, which opened in Vienna on March 6.

Up to now, the Soviet proposal at the talks has been confined to a general call for both sides to reduce their armies to levels 10 to 15 percent below the current NATO level—which, given the Warsaw Pact's current superiority over NATO, would involve a major reduction by the East bloc.

In his meeting with Mr. Baker, which lasted three and a half hours, Mr. Gorbachev put some numbers behind those percentages, State Department officials said. He told the American delegation that the Warsaw Pact was prepared to withdraw from Europe or retire 40,000 tanks of the alliance total, which Moscow says is 59,470; 47,000 artillery pieces of the alliance total, which Moscow puts at 71,560; and 42,000 armored vehicles of a total put by Moscow at 70,330.

The Soviet leader also said the Warsaw Pact was ready to withdraw 1 million troops from Europe, out of an alliance total that Moscow has put at about 3.6 million.

At the same time, he told Mr. Baker that he would demand a 55 percent reduction in NATO's attack aircraft in Europe; a cut of 1 million troops; and smaller cuts in tanks, artillery, and armored vehicles so that by 1997 both sides would reach the following equal levels on the continent:

1,350,000 troops, 1,500 strike aircraft, 1,700 helicopters, 20,000 tanks, 24,000 artillery pieces, and 28,000 armored personnel carriers.

When a senior administration official traveling with Mr. Baker was asked if Mr. Gorbachev was keeping them off balance, he shook his head and smiled, saying, "Yes, he's extraordinary."

"We expected something from him, but I can't say it was exactly this," the official said.

Gorbachev Visits Beijing for Start of Summit Talks
By Bill Keller

BEIJING, MONDAY, MAY 15—Mikhail S. Gorbachev arrived in Beijing today to seal the reconciliation of the two largest Communist nations when both are struggling through profound economic and political changes.

The Soviet leader's visit was almost immediately disrupted by China's internal unrest. Officials hastily relocated a welcoming ceremony that had been planned for Tiananmen Square because thousands of student demonstrators and several thousand hunger strikers camped out in the square refused to end their vigil for greater democracy. Mr. Gorbachev was instead met at the airport by President Yang Shangkun and Foreign Minister Qian Qichen.

The four-day visit by the Soviet chief, the first Soviet-Chinese summit meeting since Nikita S. Khrushchev came here in 1959, confirms the return to normality of a relationship marked for the last 30 years by ideological rifts, military confrontation, and intense rivalry for influence across Asia.

Between state banquets and the requisite pose atop the Great Wall, Mr. Gorbachev and the Chinese leaders are to discuss the remaining irritants in their relationship, especially the political future of Cambodia, where the Soviet-backed government of Hun Sen is opposed by a China-supported rebel alliance that includes the Khmer Rouge.

Mr. Gorbachev's visit coincides with a domestic political upheaval that his presence cannot help influencing, however inadvertently.

For the last month, students have taken to the streets of Chinese cities demanding greater democracy, and the Chinese leadership has been divided over how to cope with a movement that seems to have wide public support.

Many of the students see in Mr. Gorbachev a vigorous symbol of political liberalization and regard his visit as an implicit rebuke to the aging leadership of China.

Gorbachev Meets Deng in Beijing; Protest Goes On

By Nicholas D. Kristof

BEIJING, TUESDAY, MAY 16—Deng Xiaoping and Mikhail S. Gorbachev shook hands today to signal the formal end of three decades of hostility between China and the Soviet Union.

The two leaders then met for two and a half hours. Afterward, Mr. Deng was the host at a banquet for the Soviet President.

The 84-year-old Mr. Deng, whose frailty and stumbling speech contrasted with the strength and vigor of the 58-year-old Mr. Gorbachev, said as they met that several years ago he had noted a new mood in the Soviet Union and had hoped for the summit meeting. Mr. Deng added that he believed the new Soviet outlook held the potential to help resolve what he described as the central problem in international affairs, the Soviet-American relationship.

"For a long time, cold war and confrontation have made the international situation tense," Mr. Deng, the foremost Chinese leader, said. "This leads nowhere."

The summit meeting, the first between the two countries since 1959, is described by both sides as marking the beginning of normalization of relations. However, the domestic atmosphere in Beijing was decidedly abnormal because of continuing protests.

In a major loss of face for the Chinese leadership, Monday's itinerary had to be repeatedly adjusted to avoid 150,000 students and spectators who took over Tiananmen Square. While Mr. Gorbachev did not directly refer to the student demonstrations in his meeting on Monday with President Yang Shangkun, the entire day seemed to be an exotic dance in which the Chinese side tried to shield Mr. Gorbachev from the protesters.

The demonstrations were doubly embarrassing for the Chinese leaders because of the obvious enthusiasm that many of the protesters felt for Mr. Gorbachev. Several had prepared banners in Russian hailing him as a great reformer, and a crowd of workers and bicyclists applauded when he drove past them on his way to the Great Hall of the People.

Mr. Gorbachev was to lay a wreath at a monument in the center of the square, but because of the crowds of protesters occupying the area, the Chinese government canceled the event this morning.

Because of the demonstrations, the Chinese government held its welcoming ceremony for Mr. Gorbachev at the airport, instead of on the edge of the square where the students gathered. Officials then had to drive Mr. Gorbachev by a back road to his guest house when students blocked the avenue that had been decked with Soviet and Chinese flags in preparation for Mr. Gorbachev's entry.

Later, the Chinese postponed the discussions between Mr. Gorbachev and President Yang by two hours, and then changed the site of his arrival at the Great Hall of the People from the main entrance first to a side door and then to a back door.

Mr. Gorbachev and his spokesman were careful on Monday to avoid any criticism of their hosts. But Mr. Gorbachev made comments that seemed to be aimed at the demonstrators and were likely to resonate among them.

"We have gotten smarter, and the next generation will be smarter yet," he said during his meeting with Mr. Yang. He then called for "a sensible balance between the generations—the energy of the young people speaking out against conservatism and the wisdom of the older generation."

On May 17, just before he headed for home, Gorbachev had some cautious praise for the students, saying their uprising was part of a painful but healthy worldwide upheaval in Communist countries. The Chinese protest, meanwhile, kept mounting until June 4 when tanks and troops began firing on the crowds.

In the Soviet Union, upheavals were taking place less in the street than in the newly forming institutions of government. There open attacks on living leaders and at times their close relatives were being closely watched by a surprised public following it all on television.

Feuding Sets Tone in Soviet Congress
By Bill Keller

MOSCOW, MAY 26—The Soviet Union today struggled to give birth to a new kind of government in a process that laid bare bitter divisions of class, geography, nationality, and outlook.

After a day of haggling, the Congress of People's Deputies adjourned late tonight to a voting chamber with fine-print ballots listing 600 names, from which they were to select a 542-member standing legislature called the Supreme Soviet.

In a move that some members said would tend to make the new legislature more staid, the Congress refused to exclude full-time Communist Party and government officials from sitting in the legislature.

Self-styled progressives in the 2,250-member Congress had pressed for a rule requiring legislators to give up other jobs. They said that would make the parliament more professional and independent of the Communist Party apparatus.

The proposal mustered 636 votes despite the opposition of President Mikhail S. Gorbachev, one of several signs that the Congress, which held its inaugural session on Thursday, was growing steadily more self-confident. In a country where unanimity has been the political norm, the clash of ideas, televised live from beginning to end, is a crash course in self-government.

An even more sizable minority, 831 members, voted this morning to suspend a law limiting demonstrations after some asserted that the police had broken up a gathering of citizens trying to meet with deputies Thursday night.

The Moscow City Council later agreed to open up an area near Luzhniki Sports Stadium for unrestricted public assembly while the Congress is in session.

After an extraordinary televised cross-examination by the members on Thursday, Mr. Gorbachev was elected president by the Congress, the supreme governing body and the first Soviet assembly in more than 70 years whose members were mostly chosen in competitive elections.

Today the Congress turned to what many consider its most critical task, selecting a parliament to govern a country that, for most of its history has been united primarily by the brute power of the Communist Party.

The exercise quickly became a lesson in the powerful stresses set free by the loosening of the autocracy: the hostility of the Soviet provinces toward Moscow, the cultural gap between workers and intellectuals, the aloofness of the Baltic republics, the animosities and grievances of ethnic minorities.

Raisa Gorbachev Hits Back: "The Women Are All for Me"
By Bill Keller

MOSCOW, MAY 26—For a woman who the night before had been likened unflatteringly to Napoleon's Empress Josephine on nationwide television, Raisa Maksimovna Gorbachev was showing no signs of post-*glasnost* depression this morning.

Encountered as she swept through the marble foyer of the Kremlin Palace of Congresses, where reporters have been given license to roam amid the deputies during breaks from their parliamentary free-for-all, the Soviet first lady paused to assure a couple of Americans that, no, she did not feel unloved by her countrymen. Well, at least by her countrywomen. "It's the men," she said with a sigh. "But the women are all for me." To prove her point, she steered the bemused foreigners over to a cluster of deputies—in this case women.

"Just look. Here's a woman. Hello! Hello, my dears. Let's answer together. This is the American press. And they just came up to me and asked me, 'How do you feel about the fact that one man deputy came up yesterday and went to battle against you?'"

Mrs. Gorbachev, stylish, visible, and reputedly influential in a country where official wives are traditionally dowdy and silent, has surely helped civilize the image of Soviet leadership abroad. But at home her manner and wardrobe are the stuff of rude jokes.

The kitchen-table criticism became the stuff of prime-time television on Thursday night when a deputy from Kharkov used his minute on the podium to scold her husband, Mikhail S. Gorbachev, for imperial tendencies.

Napoleon was tempted into tyranny by "sycophants and his wife," the deputy asserted. "I think you too are incapable of avoiding the adulation and influence of your wife."

This morning the women around Mrs. Gorbachev voiced their disapproval in chorus.

"All women are for you!" one exclaimed. "Write this down," the first lady instructed the press.

"That's right," chimed in another. "That's exactly how the spouse, the wife of the general secretary, should be, like Raisa Maksimovna, with her intellect, with her schooling, with her charm. And we're proud of her."

"We finally have someone to show off abroad," the chorus continued. "At last! At last! Someone to show off."

"Write that down, if you're not ashamed," Mrs. Gorbachev repeated, glowing with triumph. "I always knew that women were with me. I know it's only men who say that. We're ashamed for men."

Just then a man poked his head into the chorus to interject: "Here's a big thank-you from the men. From all men. Good for you, you're a great, hardworking gal." The first lady flushed happily. "Thank you, thank you," she said and turned to the foreigners to dictate an amendment: "Write down that not all men are alike."

Soviet Dissenters Denied Major Role in New Parliament
By Bill Keller

MOSCOW, MAY 27—Advocates of more radical change in the Soviet Union suffered a bitter defeat today when many of the most outspoken political insurgents were denied seats in the country's new legislature.

Among those rejected in the secret ballot by the Congress of People's Deputies was Boris N. Yeltsin, the ousted Moscow Communist Party chief and hero of a populist uprising, who apparently fell victim to a shrewd tactical ploy.

Others who were scratched from lists for the 542-member Supreme Soviet, which is to be the standing lawmaking body in a revamped Soviet government, included an array of Moscow intellectuals regarded as champions of Western-style political and economic pluralism.

"We have created a Stalinist-Brezhnevite Supreme Soviet," charged the historian Yuri N. Afanasyev, in an angry speech that opened the stormy third day of the televised Congress. He attributed the outcome to "an aggressively obedient majority" subservient to the conservative apparatus of the Communist Party.

"The apparatus has undoubtedly won a victory here," added Gavriil K. Popov, one of the Moscow insurgents who was rejected in the election.

But the outcome also reflected a backlash against Moscow intellectuals, who are regarded in many parts of the Soviet Union as arrogant, impatient, and iconoclastic.

"I don't understand why we have to behave like pirates who, having seized the ship of state and torn it asunder, want to sail the stormy seas on its debris," said Yevgeny M. Meshalkin, a Siberian deputy.

Moscow Maverick, in Shift, Is Seated in Supreme Soviet
By Bill Keller

MOSCOW, MAY 29—In the face of mounting public indignation, the four-day-old Soviet Congress reversed itself today and voted to give Boris N. Yeltsin, the maverick Communist, a seat in a new legislature.

The election of Mr. Yeltsin, made possible when a legislator agreed to sacrifice his seat, was the most dramatic of several indications that the 2,250-member Congress of People's Deputies was feeling the impact of public opinion, stirred by live television broadcasts of its every move.

Although 964 members voted against seating Mr. Yeltsin in the 542-member legislature in a secret ballot early Saturday morning, no one publicly opposed the change of course today.

The Congress, the first in seven decades chosen mostly by competitive elections, is to rule on important issues and set general policy. It elects from its ranks the smaller organization, the Supreme Soviet, which is to be the standing lawmaking body and is to meet for two sessions a year.

The Congress also approved President Mikhail S. Gorbachev's choice as vice president, Anatoly I. Lukyanov, a 59-year-old lawyer and nonvoting member of the Communist Party's ruling Politburo. In the event of Mr. Gorbachev's death, Mr. Lukyanov would fulfill the duties of president until a special session of the Congress could choose a successor.

But it was clear that the Soviet tradition of faceless, collective rule was giving way to a new standard of personal accountability. Before giving overwhelming approval to Mr. Lukyanov, a friend of Mr. Gorbachev since university days and most recently his chief legal adviser, members subjected him to intense questioning. The topics ranged from his role in several controversial laws and government decrees to his activities as a

Kremlin legal adviser during political upheavals in Hungary, Czechoslovakia, and Poland.

Pressed, Mr. Lukyanov said he had personally supported a decree last month that provided up to three years in prison for statements "insulting or discrediting" the government, but he said that on further consideration he believed the decree should be revised.

One questioner asked why Mr. Lukyanov, as a senior legal official, should not be held responsible for the dramatic rise in crime, and two federal prosecutors suggested he had helped obstruct their investigations into high-level corruption.

Mr. Gorbachev underwent a similar questioning last week before the Congress elected him president.

The mute reverence for authority customary in official gatherings has also disappeared. Today Mr. Gorbachev was accused of exerting too much influence by signaling his opinion before votes were cast. Members also urged that Politburo members be obliged to leave their special seats in a raised loge and sit among the other deputies.

In a secret ballot that stretched into the early hours of Saturday morning, the Congress eliminated from the legislative ranks Mr. Yeltsin and a number of Moscow deputies who have been outspoken proponents of far-reaching political and economic change.

The exclusion of Mr. Yeltsin, who won the election to represent the city of Moscow in a landslide, was a satisfying victory for Communist Party regulars who have been the butt of his attacks on the establishment.

But the Congress quickly felt the sting of public anger. Thousands of Muscovites rallied in protest at the outcome, and many deputies said today that they had received phone calls and telegrams from constituents upset at the treatment of the radical insurgents.

Georgy K. Shakhnazarov, a top Gorbachev aide, said in an interview today that the President himself had been distressed at Mr. Yeltsin's exclusion but saw no way around it.

But this evening Aleksei I. Kazannik, a university law lecturer from Omsk, unexpectedly announced that he would forfeit his seat in the legislature if the Congress would give it to Mr. Yeltsin.

"If I were a regional party secretary, I would not be making such a decision," Mr. Kazannik told the stunned Congress. "I would go quietly home and lock myself away from the people. But as for me, I would have been ashamed to face my voters."

Mr. Gorbachev quickly gave his blessing to a legal procedure that enabled Mr. Kazannik to surrender his seat to Mr. Yeltsin.

Tonight Mr. Yeltsin's walk from the Kremlin up Gorky Street toward his apartment turned into a triumphal procession. Hundreds of Muscovites flocked around him, pumping his hand and handing up babies to be kissed.

Mr. Yeltsin said the decision to admit him was a reaction to an outpouring of anger.

"I think it shows the growth of the level of democratization in the Congress itself," he said. "Step by step, from the first day, people have begun to figure out the atmosphere."

Mr. Yeltsin said he had recently had a 90-minute talk about his future with Mr. Gorbachev.

"I think we have had a rapprochement," he said of Mr. Gorbachev, according to Reuters. "We have always had good, normal relations, maybe with the exception of a year ago when some members of the leadership helped relations grow colder.

"I think there is a warming, without a doubt. I always supported the strategic line of Comrade Gorbachev, and moreover I fought for it."

No rescue seemed in sight for the Moscow radicals who fell victim in the vote Saturday, but in speeches today it was evident that they had also benefited from a show of public support.

Where on Saturday many deputies were openly scornful of the Moscow group, today the Muscovites were repeatedly praised for their boldness. Some deputies, citing telegrams from constituents, said the Muscovites' speeches had struck a popular chord in the country.

Soviet TV's Biggest Hit: 200 Million Watch Political Drama
By Francis X. Clines

MOSCOW, MAY 30—Olvar V. Kakuchaya chain-smoked his way through another day as the nation's chief of broadcast news, wondering if there will ever be a letup in what is now the biggest television hit in Soviet history, the daily eight hours of live coverage of the new Congress of People's Deputies.

Mr. Kakuchaya goes back 30 years in Soviet broadcasting, when he had to first write out the proper answers for government ministers to read while he "interviewed" them for radio news.

In contrast to the wooden, fearful ministers of old, members of the new Congress, prodded by the live television coverage, have begun reserving speaking time days in advance in their sudden discovery of the new electronic rostrum.

"The list is up to 400 and still growing," said the obviously amazed news czar. "Something is really turning over in our national consciousness. The deputies are realizing the people are watching them, the voters can see them live, and the level of discussion is rising. There's never been anything like this—people watching how the leadership is changing."

This afternoon state television demographic researchers told Mr. Kakuchaya that the live coverage had hit a new peak of mass interest, 200 million viewers across 12 time zones. This is a leap of 25 percent over any previous audience for a show that viewers find remarkable not only for its unpredictable political content but also for the subtle revelations of relatively fearless camera work in the hall.

Eight cameras have been zooming in on deputies as they make angry charges of scandal, on their pained targets as they sit tight-lipped in the hall, on some of the old stony-faced party hard-liners looking incredulous at the scene, on the new generation of younger politicians confidently rising to confront their elders.

Laughter at a colleague's ineptitude, badly disguised sneers, sudden hubbub, and the sheer self-discovery of the legislators caught in this new age of competitive electioneering have been crosscut handsomely while the people watch, all night long in the reaches of Siberia and the Far East.

In contrast to coverage of Western legislatures that have banned or tightly restricted the television eye in their presence, the Soviet show is kaleidoscopically free in the hands of the director, Kaleriya V. Kislova, who works in a van parked on the Kremlin grounds outside the Palace of Congresses.

Miss Kislova, one of the hidden legion of women who dominate state television directing, is obviously making up for lost decades as she has cameras poke about the room. Today, she lingered long on Col. Gen. Igor N. Rodionov, who was in charge of the troops that killed 20 civil demonstrators in Tbilisi last month.

As a member of the Congress, the general was summoned to speak and he did so hesitantly, defensively. The screen showed the eyes of critical fellow deputies growing furious in the audience as he contended that the dead, mostly women, were to blame. He said, "These people were . . ." and did not finish the characterization as Miss Kislova's camera zoomed slowly on his frowning, tight-lipped anger.

Such scenes are a crash course in the power of television as much as democracy for this candor-starved nation. They drive Muscovites down to Pushkin Square after the daily show for more of their own avid midnight discussion groups.

Gray-haired couples, students, passing loners, and lingering spooners create their own live show for an extra fix of polemics in informal hives ostensibly outlawed but tolerated lately by bemused policemen. "Did you see it when . . ." begins a typical conversational overture in the night buzz, the scene heady with human curiosity.

"Thirty years ago I knew exactly what was supposed to happen," Mr. Kakuchaya said, smiling at the power of live television. "Now it's a world full of surprises," he said, adding that aside from the basic decision to televise the Congress live, he has received no orders from the Kremlin about camera content and angles.

Mr. Kakuchaya, first deputy for news of the state broadcasting monopoly, conceded he is not so liberated that he will not seek a correction should Mr. Gorbachev commit a serious gaffe on a taped news report. But he said this is a rarity. "Unofficially, we hear he approves of the Congress TV," he said. "We'd certainly know if he didn't." With a grandfatherly, shrewd twinkle, he indulged in now safe recollections of how the Kremlin television technicians had to doctor videotape to correct the many speaking mistakes of Leonid I. Brezhnev, the Soviet leader now lampooned as the antithesis of *glasnost.*

Mr. Kakuchaya also tells back-stabbing tales worthy of Western networking, like one about a party spy who went around collecting scraps of outtakes from Nikita S. Khrushchev's long television harangues in order to challenge a director's patriotism.

"I think there's no going back from this," he said, watching the Congress plunge into its afternoon session. "I have the feeling that everyone will want the floor," he continued, mock-anxious at the unpredictable implications of the tube.

He said the safe television rules of the old days were reversing at a rate "impossible to describe."

"Now if we don't put the politicians on the screen they will be complaining," he said, watching his hit show.

Yeltsin, Gorbachev's Wily Goad, Hints of Some Future Ambitions
By Bill Keller

MOSCOW, JUNE 8—Each evening after the Congress of People's Deputies adjourns from another day of parliamentary combat, the wavy white hair of Boris N. Yeltsin looms above a reverent crowd in the lobby of the Kremlin Palace of Congresses.

Reporters have already begun to weary of him, but deputies from across the country still cluster around, soliciting his views on the debate, thrusting upon him letters from their voters, sizing up the man who seems to be gravitating toward the front of a political opposition.

"I think Comrade Gorbachev is a little nervous about me," Mr. Yeltsin said the other day during a stroll through the cool refuge of the Kremlin gardens. "Yes, unfortunately I think he has the idea I want his job."

The 58-year-old Mr. Yeltsin says he has no designs on Mikhail S. Gorbachev's positions as president and Communist Party leader—"now," he adds, smiling enigmatically. But he is openly critical of Mr. Gorbachev for a program of "half-measures that give us no results," for an accumulation of power that leans ominously toward "dictatorship," and for being too detached from the people.

Last week he called for an annual referendum on Mr. Gorbachev's performance as president. The speech prompted Mr. Gorbachev to call in Mr. Yeltsin for a gentle scolding on party loyalty.

"If we had such a referendum, I think he would win," he said. "But I'm not so sure he would win a year from now. People are losing faith in *perestroika,* and if there are no changes in the next year, people will feel differently about Gorbachev."

He happily rattles off the names of half a dozen men he thinks should be dismissed from the 12-man ruling Politburo: his nemesis, the ranking conservative, Yegor K. Ligachev, "of course"; Viktor M. Chebrikov, the former K.G.B. chief; the Ukrainian party boss, Vladimir V. Shcherbitsky; the party ideologist, Vadim A. Medvedev; the Russian Federation president, Vitaly I. Vorotnikov; and Lev N. Zaikov, the longtime defense industry chief who replaced Mr. Yeltsin as Moscow city party boss. "Their time is past," he said.

Mr. Yeltsin's platform is essentially Gorbachevism with a populist spin: attacks on the privileges of the elite, calls for tough law enforcement. But he goes beyond Mr. Gorbachev in several areas, advocating "something close to" private ownership of farmland, direct election of the president, a wide discussion of permitting alternative political parties, and constitutional amendments to give the elected government clear supremacy over the Communist Party.

Soviet Congress Ends with One Last Spat
By Bill Keller

MOSCOW, JUNE 9—The National Congress of People's Deputies ended its marathon thirteen-day debut tonight with Andrei D. Sakharov raging at the restless assembly that they had failed in their main task: to wrest control from the Communist Party elite.

As the crowd tried to shout him down and an irritated President Mikhail S. Gorbachev fingered the time-limit buzzer, the human-rights advocate labored on defiantly through his indictment of the newborn Congress until Mr. Gorbachev switched off the microphone and tried to salvage an upbeat adjournment.

Warning that the country was faced with economic catastrophe and explosive ethnic conflicts, Dr. Sakharov said the solution depended on turning real power over to local governments.

"If the Congress of People's Deputies fails to take power into its hands here, there is not the slightest chance that the soviets in the republics, the provinces, the districts, and the villages will be able to do so," he said.

He called for canceling the Communist Party's constitutional monopoly on power, direct election of the president and other top officials, limiting the K.G.B. to protecting the country against foreign threats, creating a smaller, professional army, and transforming the centralized country into a federation of more autonomous republics.

When Mr. Gorbachev implored him to "respect the Congress" and be seated, Dr. Sakharov stood his ground.

"I respect humanity," he declared. "I have a mandate that goes beyond the limits of this Congress."

His last words before the microphone went dead were a plea to recall the Soviet ambassador from China in protest of the army's bloody put-down of prodemocracy demonstrations there.

Mr. Gorbachev, who has made a point of giving Dr. Sakharov the floor often, seemed in the end to have lost patience with him.

"I reject the attempts of Deputy Sakharov to disparage the role of the Congress and its milestone significance in the history of our country," he said, before the Congress stood for the closing national anthem.

Gorbachev, in Bonn, Sees Postwar Hostility Ending
By Serge Schmemann

BONN, JUNE 12—Arriving for his first state visit to West Germany, a nation that has come to hold him in unusually high esteem, President Mikhail S. Gorbachev declared today that "we are drawing the line under the postwar period."

Along with these words of reconciliation to the West Germans, the Soviet leader also welcomed President Bush's proposals to reduce conventional forces in Europe, saying these could bring agreement at the negotiations in Vienna "considerably sooner."

The two messages were certain to be heartily received by the West Germans, who have been shown in public-opinion polls to be the most enthusiastic of Western nations about Mr. Gorbachev and his initiatives, and the most anxious to reduce the large arsenals in their country and in East Germany.

As Mr. Gorbachev began his landmark visit to West Germany, the United States signed an agreement with the Soviet Union that is meant to avoid or to limit accidental military encounters before they grow into critical confrontations. At a banquet in a palace in the suburb of Bad Godesberg, Mr. Gorbachev reminded Chancellor Helmut Kohl that during the West German's visit to Moscow last October, they had pledged to give their relations a "qualitatively new character."

"Today we can already declare that we have begun to turn the first leaves in the 'new chapter' of our mutual relations," Mr. Gorbachev said in comments televised throughout West Germany and easily seen in most of East Germany.

"We are drawing the line under the postwar period. And this, in our view, will allow each of our countries to take another, decisive step toward one another."

After dinner, Mr. Gorbachev plunged briefly into a large crowd of admirers who had gathered outside the palace, creating a scene of excited chaos.

"I think Gorbachev is one of the very best statesmen in the world right now," Wilhelm Trimborn, a 59-year-old insurance salesman, said in what seemed a typical comment.

The significance of Mr. Gorbachev's visit to West Germany was underscored by a poll commissioned on the eve of his arrival by the ZDF television network. A record 90 percent of the respondents declared "yes" when asked whether Mr. Gorbachev was a man they could trust.

No other leader has ever achieved such a rating, not even John F. Kennedy or Charles de Gaulle. Mr. Bush received a rating of 58 percent, and Mr. Kohl, 50 percent.

A Gorbachev Hint for Berlin Wall
By Serge Schmemann

BONN, JUNE 15—Wrapping up a triumphant visit to West Germany, President Mikhail S. Gorbachev said today that the Berlin wall was not necessarily permanent, but would be taken down only when conditions that created it fell away.

Though Mr. Gorbachev's visit produced no concessions on Berlin's status, his willingness to address the emotionally charged issue in practical terms was taken by West Germans as evidence of the "new chapter" that the Soviet leader proclaimed in Soviet–West German relations.

"The wall was raised in a concrete situation and was not dictated only by evil intentions," he said at his concluding news conference. East Germany "decided this as its sovereign right, and the wall can disappear when those conditions that created it fall away," he continued. "I don't see a major problem here."

He did not elaborate, and the reference to "conditions" had an echo of the hard-line stand taken by Erich Honecker, the 76-year-old leader of East Germany. But in the past, any talk of the wall was either stonily ignored by the Russians or assailed as "revanchism."

Hans Klein, the West German government spokesman, called Mr. Gorbachev's comment on the wall "extremely positive," reflecting a consistent effort by the Germans to frame all facets of the visit in the best possible light. Mr. Klein said Berlin had been discussed at some length in the three meetings between Mr. Gorbachev and Chancellor Helmut Kohl, but he declined to give any details.

Mr. Gorbachev also did not rule out a resolution of the division of Germany, though he spoke only in broad terms. "Time itself must determine this," he said. "The current situation in Europe was created at a specific time by specific realities, and we are bound by this situation. But we hope that time will resolve this."

In addition to the ongoing nationalistic ferment under way in many parts of the Soviet Union, Gorbachev was faced with mounting labor unrest.

Siberia Mine Strike Affects 100,000 and Is Spreading
By Francis X. Clines

MOSCOW, JULY 16—The western Siberian coal mines were at a virtual standstill today with about 100,000 strikers demanding further economic and political concessions in the worst wave of labor unrest yet to confront President Mikhail S. Gorbachev.

Only minimal operations were reported at a few collieries in the Kuznetsk Basin mines, the country's second-richest coal region, as the severity of the unusual seven-day-old wildcat strike was made clearer in Soviet news reports.

Workers in related industries were joining in the widespread stoppage, according to dispatches from the isolated Siberian fields, where miners have been organizing rallies and confronting political leaders in cities and towns.

Last Monday, the miners began refusing to descend into the pits unless the government made concessions on more than 40 grievances ranging from food shortages in the local stores to the double standard by which Communist Party officials receive greater economic benefits.

Hard-pressed government ministers sent to the region have been making various promises of improvement. But their efforts have thus far failed to stem the labor stoppage, the first in the region's history, according to strike leaders who report nonviolent solidarity in a dozen principal communities of the Siberian fields.

Some of Siberia's Miners Return; Gorbachev Calls Strike a Crisis
By Francis X. Clines

NOVOKUZNETSK, U.S.S.R., JULY 19—After decades of grimy subservience, some of the striking miners of the vast Siberian coal region began pronouncing themselves victorious today in a wildcat strike that has paralyzed the mines and brought unexpected economic and industrial concessions from the government.

Tens of thousands of strikers in widespread parts of the Soviet coal-fields still militantly negotiated grievances today. But the first large groups of miners also voted to return to the pits on the midnight shift tonight in parts of the Siberian heartland where the strike began nine days ago.

In an unexpected speech today before the Supreme Soviet in Moscow, President Mikhail S. Gorbachev described the walkout in Siberia and in key parts of the Ukrainian coal region as a "very acute" crisis, underlining the notion that no clear end lay firmly in sight for the most critical labor challenge in his four years in power.

"The situation is fraught with dangerous political and economic conse-quences," Mr. Gorbachev said, adding that there were reports that rail-way workers were being encouraged to join in the work stoppage.

Here in western Siberia, miners were pleased that the strike committee had signed a document that was said to guarantee from the government an array of night-shift pay increases and precisely designated quantities of foods, medical supplies, road improvements, and other consumer needs considered in critically short supply.

"That may sound wild to you," Andrei M. Mikhailchenko, a 27-year-old miner, commented to an outsider, "but such a signed promise from the government is very important."

The work stoppage by upward of 150,000 miners has provided one of the more dramatic demonstrations of how decisively Soviet workers are shedding their timidity under the new freedom of expression invoked by Mr. Gorbachev. Strikes were rare, but a dozen of them have been reported this year, none so serious or as long as here.

It was only 15 years ago that a Ukrainian coal miner who tried to organize a protest, Aleksei Nikitin, was arrested and put under enforced psychiatric treatment. Communist theory held that labor strikes were unnecessary in a "workers' paradise," and various pressures were used to snuff protests.

Now, the Soviet President has proposed formal recognition of the right to strike, and a draft law is before the new legislature. Mr. Gorbachev is also intent on reviving a national economy significantly rooted in the heavy industries fed by the coal mines.

Soviet reports said tonight that the strike situation remained critical, with tens of thousands still striking here in the Kuznetsk Basin, the nation's second-richest coal region, and more walking out in the Donets Basin in the Ukraine, the prime coal center, where the strike has spread from 30 to 70 fields.

Amid Rising Alarm, Gorbachev Urges a Purge in Party

By Bill Keller

MOSCOW, JULY 21—With Kremlin leaders openly alarmed that the Communist Party is losing control over events in the country, President Mikhail S. Gorbachev has called for a sweeping purge of the party ranks from the shop floor to the ruling Politburo, according to a transcript made public today.

As wildcat strikes and nationalist violence broke out across their domain, besieged party leaders met to share their fears that the party's prestige is plummeting and that the pace of political change is beyond the party's ability to keep up, according to the transcript of the Tuesday meeting, which was published in *Pravda.*

Mr. Gorbachev, the party leader, joined in the chorus of self-doubt, and demanded an urgent "renewal" of the party's leadership ranks—an unmistakable call for replacement of conservatives at all levels with officials more attuned to the public mood.

"The cadres need renewal, an influx of fresh forces," he said. "And they need to be renewed at the level of the work collective, district, city, region, territory, republic, Central Committee, and Politburo. This concerns everyone. Everywhere, at every level, overdue cadre issues must be resolved in a timely fashion."

As if to confirm the party's dwindling stature, official television tonight broadcast an appeal to striking coal miners by Boris N. Yeltsin, a maverick Communist who made clear that he was speaking not for the party but for an independent, radical faction in the new national legislature.

The transcript of the Tuesday party meeting read like the dispirited locker-room talk of a team on a losing streak, in which everything from the playbook to the front office to the farm club system comes in for bitter recriminations.

But Mr. Gorbachev cautioned his comrades against panic in the face of the surrounding turmoil.

"If *perestroika* is a revolution—and we agreed that it is—and if it means profound changes in attitudes toward property, the status of the individual, the basics of the political system, and the spiritual realm, and if it transforms the people into a real force of change in society, then how can all of this take place quietly and smoothly?" he said.

Unless the party adjusts to the upheavals in society, Mr. Gorbachev said, other political forces will seize the initiative.

"This is already happening," he said. "How is it that a party organization numbering many thousands of Communists and having its own newspapers, its own professional cadres—having everything—suddenly begins to lose the initiative?"

The most surprising outburst of dismay at the meeting came from Prime Minister Nikolai I. Ryzhkov, who warned that despite a built-in majority the party was losing its grip in the increasingly independent new legislature, which has been ceded legal and budgetary power over the government.

"If the party does not find a way out of this situation, then it may lose its influence over the state government," said Mr. Ryzhkov, who has seen several of his nominees for major government posts rejected by the legislators.

He said it was now clear—contrary to what Mr. Gorbachev has insisted—that the elections in March were a crushing defeat for the party.

While it is true that 85 percent of the newly elected deputies are Communists, Mr. Ryzhkov said, many of them are doubtful Communists who show no inclination to defend the party when its authority is attacked.

The Soviet press has recently published articles noting the party's dwindling recruitment of new members and letters bemoaning the loss of public respect, but for Soviet readers it was surely a revelation to see how thoroughly this angst has penetrated the leadership.

The summer of 1989 saw a quickening in the tempo of historic events in Eastern Europe. In Hungary the body of Imre Nagy, the man who led the uprising against Soviet domination, was moved from the unmarked grave where it has lain since his execution to a place of honor as 100,000 mourners watched. In Poland, where a Solidarity slate swept to victory in parliamentary elections, General Jaruzelski appointed Tadeusz Mazowiecki, an anti-Communist Solidarity adviser and a devout Catholic to be prime minister. In Moscow, the Polish events were greeted with calm. "This is entirely a matter to be decided by Poland," said Yevgeny M. Primakov, a senior Gorbachev aide. But if the nationalistic passions that drove events in Warsaw were treated with indifference by Moscow, what of similar yearnings in the Baltic republics and in the south tier of the Soviet Union where the brush fires of nationalism were getting hotter?

Moscow Condemns Nationalist "Virus" in 3 Baltic Lands
By Esther B. Fein

MOSCOW, AUG. 26—In its strongest response yet to the growing calls for independence in the Baltic republics, the Communist Party today condemned nationalist movements in Estonia, Latvia, and Lithuania and declared that the agitation had caused alarm and hysteria and raised the prospect of "civil conflict."

Saying that "things have gone far," the Central Committee of the

Communist Party warned the restive republics that if the situation continued, their "very existence could wind up in question."

The "virus of nationalism" in the Baltics affects "the vital interests of the entire Soviet people," the statement said, and if it continues, there will be "a real threat of a civil conflict and mass street clashes which will involve grave consequences."

"The situation that has emerged demands a profound awareness, a realistic and serious appraisal, and decisive, urgent measures to purge the process of *perestroika* in the Baltics of extremism, of destructive, harmful tendencies," the party leadership said.

The Central Committee statement, issued tonight and read in the opening 19 minutes of the main evening news program, *Vremya,* did not specify what urgent actions were being considered or whether such moves were already under way.

Ever since government troops attacked and killed nationalist demonstrators in Soviet Georgia in April, people in the Baltics have feared that similar measures might be used against them if the Kremlin objected to their demands and methods.

President Mikhail S. Gorbachev is reported to be on vacation, and it was not known whether he initiated or supported today's hard-line statement.

The warning comes several days after mass demonstrations were held in the three Baltic republics, commemorating the fiftieth anniversary of the Stalin-Hitler pact that led to their annexation by the Soviet Union.

Over a million people were reported to have taken part on Wednesday in a 400-mile human chain linking Estonia, Latvia, and Lithuania in a symbol of solidarity and a call for a restoration of their "independent statehood."

Those demonstrations, the party leadership said, were trying "to incite the peoples of the Baltic republics to secede from the Soviet Union."

The Soviet constitution guarantees the right of any republic to secede from the Soviet Union, but this has long been considered a symbolic right and one that would be vehemently resisted by Moscow.

The statement said that leaders of the republics were to blame for failing "to contain the process" and that some Communist Party leaders "lost heart" and "began to play up to nationalist sentiments."

The statement also strongly condemned a report issued this week by a Lithuanian parliament commission, which declared that Moscow had illegally occupied and annexed the Baltic republics in 1940. The commission was the first official body to directly challenge the legitimacy of Soviet rule in Estonia, Latvia, and Lithuania.

The party leadership in Moscow said the Lithuanian action was "directly linked with the separatist line which has been pursued in the past months with growing persistence and aggressiveness by certain forces in Lithuania, Latvia, and Estonia."

Turkic Republics Press Soviets to Loosen Reins
By Bill Keller

BAKU, U.S.S.R., AUG. 26—While world attention is focused on the Baltic republics' steady independence march, a strange thing is happening along President Mikhail S. Gorbachev's southern flank.

In the republics that stretch from the Caucasus Mountains to the central Asian steppes, Turkic peoples are also beginning to channel their grievances into mass political movements under the banners of democracy and sovereignty.

"We want what the Baltics want, an end to colonialism and the freedom to run our own affairs," said Ekhtibar Mamedov, a Baku historian and a leader of the new Azerbaijani Popular Front, which has shown unexpected public support by holding mass demonstrations and a large-scale protest strike in the city's factories. (On Saturday a crowd estimated by local journalists at tens of thousands gathered in central Baku, chanting for a general strike starting Monday to press the popular front's demands and for the ouster of the Azerbaijani Communist Party boss, Abdulrakhman K. Vezirov, who has refused to legalize the popular front.)

Although the republics of the south are predominantly Muslim, the movements take pains to avoid any identification with religion, asserting that the threat of Islamic fundamentalism is a myth Soviet authorities use to keep their Muslim subjects in check.

They have focused instead on unhappiness with unresponsive and corrupt local governments, resentment of economic exploitation by Moscow, alarm about a tortured environment, and rising cultural awareness.

Leaders of the groups say their movements were invigorated this spring and summer by televised proceedings of the new Soviet parliament, which gave Turkic peoples a chance to compare their own, machine-elected deputies with the more aggressively independent political figures elected from the Baltics, Moscow, and other regions.

"The deputies from Azerbaijan and central Asia were just tools of the party leadership," said Arif Aliyev, one of several young journalists aligned with the popular front. "Everything proposed from the top, they approved. Everything approved by the radical deputies from the Baltics, Moscow, or Leningrad, they blocked."

"The Congress showed people who was who, and what was possible," agreed Muhamed Salikh, a poet who is active in Uzbekistan's popular movement, called Birlik, or "unity."

Although the southern Soviet Union has experienced bloody outbreaks of ethnic conflict—most notably Azerbaijan's clash with neighboring Armenia over the disputed territory of Nagorno-Karabakh, murderous Uzbek assaults on the Meskhetian minority, and economic riots in Kazakhstan—the Turkic republics have lagged far behind in the formation of organized political movements.

Local leaders attribute that to a lack of political sophistication and the feudal domination of local Communist Party bosses.

In Uzbekistan, the political movement has been stimulated by the rural poverty and environmental degradation associated with the republic's role as Russia's cotton-growing colony.

In Kazakhstan, alarm about contamination from the republic's vast nuclear-weapons testing range at Semipalatinsk and anger about the importation of non-Kazakh laborers have become focal points for unofficial political movements.

In Azerbaijan, where the mass movement appears to have made the most headway, the crowds have been galvanized by the battle with neighboring Armenia over custody of Nagorno-Karabakh, a semiautonomous region of Azerbaijan with a predominantly Armenian population.

The popular front has capitalized on public dissatisfaction with the republic's party leaders, who in January acceded to a compromise putting the contested territory under Moscow's administration. The first demand in the front's manifesto is for restoration of full Azerbaijani control over Nagorno-Karabakh.

Thus, while the popular front is led by Baku intellectuals, it has won particularly emotional support among Azerbaijani refugees, estimated at 160,000, who fled Armenia in 18 months of sporadic hostilities over Nagorno-Karabakh.

"We're fed up with Gorbachev, fed up with the Communist Party," said the 55-year-old Abdulazim Khudaverdiev, interviewed at a refugee settlement in Shusha, in the Azerbaijani sector of Nagorno-Karabakh. "With the popular front, we'll solve our own problems."

Exploiting the Nagorno-Karabakh issue is a sensitive problem for popular front organizers, who recognize that the territorial dispute is their most potent issue for organizing mass support, but who want to broaden the agenda beyond the dangerous passions of interethnic conflict.

"Nagorno-Karabakh is not this republic's real problem," said Mr. Aliyev. "The real issues are political and economic sovereignty, human rights, the ecology. But the question of Nagorno-Karabakh is so dangerous and so intense that it blocks the solution of all other problems."

The popular front has also demanded that Azerbaijan's indigenous wealth, especially the oil wells and refineries along the Caspian Sea, be used to benefit Azerbaijan rather than siphoned off to Moscow.

Front leaders insist that Azerbaijan, with its petroleum, cotton, fruits and vegetables, and Caspian ports, has the ability to be self-sufficient, and they dangle the long-range threat of secession if they are not appeased.

Defiantly, some front leaders wear on their lapels the blue-red-and-green flag of independent Azerbaijan, which was governed by the Social Democratic Muslim Party from 1918 until the Red Army conquered it in 1920.

While Uzbekistan and Kazakhstan have new Communist Party leaders regarded as more sympathetic to unofficial movements, the Azerbaijani Communist leader, Mr. Vezirov, has refused to legalize the popular front here.

"They talk of political sovereignty, but what does that mean when you live in a federation?" said Azad K. Sharifov, director of the official press agency Azerinform and a member of the Azerbaijani legislature. "It's just a slogan."

Mr. Sharifov asserted that the front used strong-arm tactics to enlist shopkeepers and bus drivers in a recent two-day work stoppage, and that its demonstrations attract hooligans.

But Mr. Sharifov said he believed authorities may soon recognize the front. Already Mr. Vezirov has met several times with the group's leaders.

Tuesday night, in a televised address to the republic, the party leader vowed to cooperate with "informal organizations" and repeatedly called for Azerbaijani sovereignty, though he clearly did not mean the kind of political autonomy the front demands.

While popular front leaders support the reopening of mosques closed under earlier Soviet regimes and acknowledge the binding force of Islamic tradition across the Soviet south, they have carefully avoided making their appeal religious.

They heatedly disavow any attraction to neighboring Iran. Azerbaijani Muslims, like those in Iran, are predominantly Shiite, while the rest of Soviet central Asia mostly adheres to the Sunni sect, but many say that superficial similarity is overridden by the poor living conditions of the large Azerbaijani population living under Iranian rule.

When President Hashemi Rafsanjani of Iran visited Baku in June and prayed at the city's Taza-Pir Mosque, local residents said, the event stirred little excitement.

The intellectuals who lead the Azerbaijani Popular Front say they identify not with Islamic Iran, but with secular Turkey. Except for Tadzhikistan, where the population is of Persian origin, all the republics of central Asia share Turkic roots.

Mr. Mamedov said Soviet authorities had deliberately raised the specter of Islamic fundamentalism to isolate the southern republics from the sympathy of the country's Christian majority and the West.

"They're not afraid of Islam," Mr. Mamedov said. "They're afraid of losing control of their colonies."

Latvians to Seek a "Special Status" Within the U.S.S.R.
By Esther B. Fein

RIGA, U.S.S.R., AUG. 31—Defying a warning from the Kremlin to curb separatist and nationalist calls in the Baltic republics, the leadership of the largest political movement in Latvia said today that it would demand that Moscow grant the republic "special status" within the Soviet Union.

The president of the Latvian Popular Front, Dainis Ivans, said in an interview that the nationalist group's leadership today completed the draft of a program calling for "full economic and political independence" for Latvia within the Soviet Union, as a "state of transition to complete independent statehood."

In another restive Soviet region, the Moldavian legislature established Moldavian as the official language despite warnings by Russian-speaking residents of the republic that the law would increase ethnic tension.

Leaders of the popular fronts of Latvia and Estonia and of the Lithuanian movement Sajudis met here today and issued a joint statement that condemned last weekend's harsh warning from the Communist Party Central Committee in Moscow against carrying the independence movements too far. Sajudis and the popular fronts are political organizations outside the Communist Party that have won support from many party members. They have become vehicles for nationalist sentiment in the Baltic republics.

"There has been no such sinister and dangerous document for the cause of democracy since the death of Stalin and the events in Czechoslovakia in 1968," the three movements said in the statement, according to Reuters.

They said the authors of the Central Committee statement—which was approved by the ruling Politburo, including its leader, President Mikhail S. Gorbachev—"looked like younger brothers" of the authors of the Nazi-Soviet pact of 1939. The pact gave Moscow spheres of influence in the Baltic republics, which had been independent between the two world wars.

The meeting here today also drafted letters to the Soviet people, Mr.

Gorbachev, and the United Nations to present their demands for political self-determination and to tell people that they are not seeking unrest in Soviet society.

The summer was ending. In Eastern Europe the annual migration of vacationers was about to change the political map of a divided continent. For years East Germans and West Germans had gathered by the shores of Lake Balaton in Hungary only to return to their respective countries at the end of the holidays. In keeping with Warsaw Pact solidarity the Hungarian border guards made sure that no East German went to West Germany. But now that Communist solidarity had crumbled, thousands of East Germans were receiving friendly winks and good wishes from the Hungarians as they crossed over to Austria and then to Germany. For East Germans, a new way to the West had been found, one that was far less dangerous than trying to sneak past the dogs and the East German guards who had orders to shoot to kill.

Vacations were also ending in the Soviet Union. Mikhail Gorbachev returned from his own holiday to find that the pile of difficult problems he had left behind had grown thicker in his absence.

Gorbachev Says Internal Enemies Endanger Change
By Bill Keller

MOSCOW, SEPT. 9—President Mikhail S. Gorbachev said tonight that his program of change was endangered by internal enemies who have whipped up public alarm and disorder.

In his first appearance after a monthlong vacation during which the country has been rattled by ethnic unrest and economic anxiety, the Soviet leader condemned the protest strikes that have spread through several republics, and asserted that conservatives and radicals were trying to push the country to the brink of instability.

"In this multivoice choir, we can hear threats of approaching chaos and talk of a threatened coup, and even of civil war," Mr. Gorbachev said. "It is a fact that some people would like to create in this society an atmosphere of alarm, a feeling that there is no way out, a feeling of uncertainty."

"We should not fall for this," he said. "We should not halt in our tracks, but continue along the road of planned change."

Somber in tone, the televised 25-minute address was evidently intended as a warning to nationalist movements challenging the Communist Party's authority and to conservatives who hope for a reassertion of central authority.

Mr. Gorbachev appeared to have meant his comments in part as a rebuttal to the senior party conservatives Viktor M. Chebrikov and Yegor K. Ligachev, two Politburo members who have issued dire warnings in the last two weeks about the dangers of nationalist disorder.

Gorbachev Ousts 5 from Politburo in Party Shake-up
By Francis X. Clines

MOSCOW, SEPT. 20—President Mikhail S. Gorbachev carried out a major purge of the Communist Party leadership today, in a strong demonstration of his concern that the party is losing initiative in the face of wide social upheaval in the Soviet Union.

In a brief statement this evening at the end of a two-day closed session of the party Central Committee, the Kremlin announced without comment a handful of changes in the party's Politburo and Secretariat, the largest shake-up thus far in the Soviet leader's four and a half years of power.

In engineering these major changes in the party hierarchy, Mr. Gorbachev made good on a two-month-old warning that a purge might be necessary because the party was losing ground in facing the struggle with ethnic unrest, a floundering economy, and a wave of doubt about the party's own future.

The chief victims of the purge, which strengthened Mr. Gorbachev's dominance in both the party and the government, were three of the 12 voting members of the Politburo, including some but not all of the hardliners in the party leadership. Yegor K. Ligachev, who is believed to be the Soviet President's leading critic on the Politburo, was apparently untouched by the shake-up.

Perhaps the most prominent of the men dismissed today was Vladimir V. Shcherbitsky, the longtime Ukrainian party chief who had spent nearly a quarter century on the Politburo, the policy-making body of the party.

Also removed were Viktor M. Chebrikov, the former K.G.B. police chief, who, like Mr. Shcherbitsky, had been one of the powers in the party's hard-line faction, and Viktor P. Nikonov, the nation's secretary for agriculture. He was appointed to that post by Mr. Gorbachev three years ago, but popular dissatisfaction with the party's handling of the troubled consumer economy has only grown in the interim.

Mr. Gorbachev, acting through the Central Committee, chose to fill two of the Politburo voting seats with Vladimir A. Kryuchkov, the K.G.B. chief who has lately become one of the most prominent Kremlin officials with his campaign to improve the K.G.B.'s reputation, and Yuri D. Maslyukov, for the last year chairman of Gosplan, the state planning body for the economy, an appointment also apparently made with an eye to soothing consumer frustration.

Mr. Shcherbitsky is the last Politburo holdover—besides Mr. Gorbachev himself—from the now-discredited era of Leonid I. Brezhnev, the Soviet leader regularly blamed by Mr. Gorbachev for the economic, political, and social problems that increasingly dog his leadership.

Mr. Shcherbitsky's removal, while regularly rumored in the Gorbachev era, was unusual in its form. Normally, he would have first been ousted as Ukrainian party chairman before being removed from the national Politburo.

But Mr. Gorbachev apparently chose to act first in Moscow, thus encouraging speculation that he sought to avoid a possible rebuff from the Ukrainian Central Committee, controlled by Mr. Shcherbitsky.

Ukraine Removes Its Party Leader
By Bill Keller

MOSCOW, SEPT. 28—The Communist Party in the Ukraine today ended the 17-year-rule of its party boss, whose firm control of the second-largest Soviet republic had been shaken by rising nationalism and coal miners' unrest.

The ousted official, Vladimir V. Shcherbitsky, was replaced by his deputy, Vladimir A. Ivashko, who is regarded as a cautious political pragmatist, and who recently called for sterner measures to suppress nationalist movements.

Mikhail S. Gorbachev, the President of the Soviet Union and the nation's party leader, flew to Kiev to oversee the transfer of power.

Mr. Gorbachev's speech to the Ukrainian Communist Party Central Committee, broadcast tonight on national television, resembled a precampaign pep talk in which he flatly rejected the idea that the party would either surrender political leadership or deviate into capitalism.

"There are attempts to charge that the party is straying from the Marxist-Leninist path, and that this is what brings the country to chaos," he said. "This is slander." But he also called for the party to forsake "the old, forcible methods" and to work in harmony with other political forces.

Mr. Shcherbitsky's departure was foreordained last week when he was removed from the ruling Soviet party Politburo, where he had served for 26 years. Except for Mr. Gorbachev and Foreign Minister Eduard A. Shevardnadze, he was the last Politburo holdover from the period of Leonid I. Brezhnev, the now-discredited leader who died in 1982.

Despite his reputed coolness toward the liberalizations Mr. Gorbachev has fostered, Mr. Shcherbitsky clung to power largely because his party machine kept tight control over the great mineral, industrial, and agricultural heartland of the Ukraine and its 52 million people.

But in the past year, sparks of nationalist discontent have begun to catch fire.

A Ukrainian popular front group has organized, calling for the ouster of Mr. Shcherbitsky, the revival of Ukrainian language and culture, and greater economic and political autonomy.

Movements for greater independence have not coalesced as quickly in the Ukraine as they have in the Baltic republics. They have been hampered by a lack of political sophistication and by a cultural divide between the heavily Ukrainian west and the eastern part of the republic, where the population is heavily Russified.

But Moscow takes any sign of instability in the Ukraine seriously.

One of the worst blows to Mr. Shcherbitsky's prestige came in the election of a new Soviet parliament last March, when, despite poorly disguised attempts to manipulate the outcome, several senior Ukrainian party figures were beaten by political upstarts.

A coal strike that paralyzed Ukrainian mines in July further demonstrated Mr. Shcherbitsky's slipping control, especially when the strike committees began to organize into permanent political committees.

For perhaps the first time since he ascended to power, Gorbachev was not at the center of world events. The changes and challenges in the Soviet Union, profound and critical as they were to the peace of the world, were overshadowed by the rapid, unexpected, and revolutionary developments raging through the Communist countries of Eastern Europe. The loosening of Moscow's grip on these countries during the Gorbachev years had contributed to the weakening of their rulers. Would Moscow now reverse those policies of tolerance and seek to crush the new movements with military might as it did in Budapest in 1956 or in Prague in 1968? Could Moscow sustain Gorbachev's reforms and maintain any hope of gaining the goodwill of a rich and generous West if it reverted to the practices of the past? Also, did the Soviets have sufficient military strength to simultaneously defend Communism everywhere it was being challenged—Poland, Czechoslovakia, Hungary, East Germany, and pretty soon in Bulgaria and even Rumania—while also keeping the lid on nationalist passions in the Baltics and the Caucasus?

As marchers in Eastern Europe were chanting his name and citing his example in demanding greater freedom, Gorbachev seemed to be straddling the issues. He was for change and reform, but he was also for Communism and Communists.

Gorbachev Lends Honecker a Hand
By Serge Schmemann

EAST BERLIN, OCT. 6—President Mikhail S. Gorbachev of the Soviet Union arrived in East Berlin today to offer the East German Communists a measured show of solidarity and to declare that Moscow would not interfere in East Germany's problems.

In a line that won a particularly loud burst of applause from an elite congregation gathered in the glittering Palace of the Republic for a special meeting on the eve of East Germany's fortieth anniversary, Mr. Gorbachev declared: "First I should tell our Western partners that matters relating to the German Democratic Republic are decided not in Moscow, but in Berlin."

Without referring directly to the exodus that has cost East Germany 45,000 citizens and enormous humiliation this summer, Mr. Gorbachev acknowledged that East Germany had problems "that demanded solutions," and that these were related to the modernization and renewal sweeping much of the Communist world.

But the Soviet leader said he had full confidence that the East German Communists would themselves find solutions, "in cooperation with all powers of society."

After the gala meeting, Mr. Gorbachev stood late into the night shoulder to shoulder with Erich Honecker, the East German leader, reviewing a torchlight parade of 100,000 members of the Free German Youth, the German Communist youth organization.

The image of the two leaders side by side, smiling and waving to a flood of loyal German youths flowing down the grand Unter den Linden boulevard under a thicket of flags and torches, was shown constantly on East German television.

It appeared to be what Mr. Gorbachev had come for, to demonstrate to East German Communists that he would not abandon them in a period of crisis, while at the same time suggesting that the problem demanded a new approach.

On October 18, the East German Communist party removed Mr. Honecker and replaced him with his younger deputy, Egon Krenz. The protests demanding more change did not stop. Gorbachev replaced the old Brezhnev doctrine that sanctioned "fraternal assistance" to socialist states with what his aide called "the Sinatra doctrine."

Gorbachev, in Finland, Disavows Any Right of Regional Intervention

By Bill Keller

HELSINKI, FINLAND, OCT. 25—President Mikhail S. Gorbachev declared today that the Soviet Union has no moral or political right to interfere in the affairs of its East European neighbors, and held up neutral Finland as a model of stability in stormy Europe.

His spokesman embroidered the theme jokingly, saying that Moscow had adopted "the Sinatra doctrine" in Eastern Europe. "You know the Frank Sinatra song, 'I Did It My Way'?" said Gennadi I. Gerasimov to reporters. "Hungary and Poland are doing it their way."

"I think the Brezhnev doctrine is dead," he added, using the Western term for the previous Soviet policy of armed intervention to prevent changes in the Communist governments of the Warsaw Pact. In talks with Finland's president, Mauno Koivisto, at the beginning of a three-day state visit, Mr. Gorbachev was reported to have said that the current political upheavals in the East bloc must be allowed to run their course.

Mr. Gorbachev has repeatedly pledged a policy of noninterference, but his emphasis on the point—and his lauding of the Finnish example—were striking in a week when Hungary was joining Poland in a retreat from orthodox Communist rule, and East Germany was boiling with demands for political liberty.

"The events that are now taking place in the countries of Eastern Europe concern the countries and people of that region," the Soviet leader told the Finnish President, according to Mr. Gerasimov, whose formal position is that of spokesman for the Soviet Foreign Ministry. "We have no right, moral or political right, to interfere in events happening there. We assume others will not interfere either."

Finland, once an autonomous part of czarist Russia, gained its independence in 1917. It was invaded by the Soviet Union late in 1939, after the formal outbreak of World War II, and was forced to cede some territory to the Russians. The Karelian Autonomous Republic, which borders on Finland, is largely populated by Finnish speakers.

Today, as Mr. Gorbachev moved through largely friendly crowds, there were some cries of "Give us back Karelia," but no indication that he heard them.

Mr. Gerasimov, who served for many years as a correspondent for the Soviet news-feature agency Novosti in New York, has used the "Sinatra doctrine" expression before to explain the willingness of the Soviet Union to allow its allies to follow different political lines.

Mr. Gerasimov declined a direct answer when asked how Moscow would respond if its allies wanted to move toward neutrality. He noted that Hungary and Poland still have obligations as members of military and economic alliances with the Soviet Union.

"We may witness a change of government in Warsaw or Budapest, but international obligations do not necessarily go away with a change of government," Mr. Gerasimov said.

He added that Moscow has long proposed a mutual breakup of both the North Atlantic Treaty Organization and the Warsaw Pact, but he did not say how the Kremlin would react if the Warsaw Pact showed signs of breaking up on its own.

Still, Mr. Gorbachev's remarks today seemed to suggest that Moscow is open to more fundamental changes in its relations with East bloc allies.

In mid-October rallies and protests, some involving as many as 500,000 people, took place almost daily in East German cities. Thousands of East Germans thronged the West German embassy in Prague and were eventually given free passage through East Germany to West Germany. As the pressure continued, the besieged East German government offered a draft law on November 6 that every citizen had the right to travel abroad or emigrate. The next day the East German cabinet resigned. On November 9 the East Germans agreed to open the border with West Germany, leading to a jubilant mass breaching of the suddenly porous wall. On November 10, Todor I. Zhivkov, the Communist Party chief who had led his country for 35 years, resigned.

Making Policy of the Inevitable, Gorbachev Accepts Wide Change
By Bill Keller

MOSCOW, NOV. 11—Any doubt that Mikhail S. Gorbachev is prepared for a fundamentally new order in Eastern Europe has been largely erased this week, as Soviet officials calmly applaud the crowds pouring through the newly perforated Iron Curtain.

The changes in East Germany, following those in Hungary, Poland, and the Soviet Union itself—and perhaps to be followed by a liberalization in Bulgaria—are taking place with an alacrity that surprises Soviet officials almost as much as it does the West, and jangles nerves in both the East and the West.

Just how much the Soviet leadership is prepared to tolerate is still a question. But it is already clear that the limits are looser than most Westerners assumed even a few months ago.

President Gorbachev has already sent President Bush a message supporting the changes taking place in East Germany, and in it he expressed hope that the situation would remain "calm and peaceful," the White House spokesman said today.

Zbigniew K. Brzezinski, the former United States national security adviser, had a preview of the looser limits two weeks ago when he appeared before Mikhail S. Gorbachev's foreign policy establishment here and offered a sweeping prescription for the dismantling of Soviet power in Eastern Europe.

Addressing 500 Soviet diplomats and academics, Mr. Brzezinski said the socialist countries would have to transform themselves from Communist dictatorships to pluralist democracies. The two Germanys must be united, perhaps in a loose confederation at first. The "neo-Stalinist regime" in Czechoslovakia would fall within a year or two, he predicted.

The response to the speech was so warm that an American embassy official promptly drafted a cablegram to Washington reporting on the "extraordinary" event.

Not only did the crowd agree with almost everything Mr. Brzezinski said, the diplomat reported, but afterward some listeners said that Mr. Brzezinski's speech was "actually mild in comparison to the current tenor of debate in party and academic circles, and that most of the ideas he mentioned had adherents in the party and government structure."

Soviet officials and Westerners who follow these issues closely cite several reasons why Mr. Gorbachev has embraced changes that previous Soviet regimes would have brutally repressed.

First, the Soviet Union has drastically redefined its security interests, recognizing that halting its own economic decline is more important to the ultimate survival of Soviet power than enforcing an unpopular Communist gospel.

To some extent, Mr. Gorbachev is making a policy of the inevitable.

He realizes that even if he wanted to stop the transformations of Eastern Europe, he could not do so without endangering his support at home and abroad. Better to claim the initiative, winning admiration in his own bloc and credibility in the West.

The opening of the Berlin wall, the Communist Party newspaper *Pravda* commented today, shows that "the new political thinking is blazing a trail" and that East Germany is moving toward creation of a "common European home."

Soviet television tonight, in an understated report that showed happy reunions in the West and workers taking jackhammers to the wall, stressed that this was the initiative of the German Communists. Most of the East Germans who took the chance to inspect West Berlin, the Soviet accounts noted, lined up later to go home again.

Mr. Gorbachev seems convinced that Western Europe is not likely to take strategic advantage of the situation, in part because the West now has a stake in Mr. Gorbachev. He will surely try to bolster his confidence in Western intentions in his meeting with President Bush next month.

Because the West worries about the stability of the continent no less than the East does, Mr. Gorbachev is likely to find willing partners for new types of political and economic cooperation to prevent events from swerving out of control.

Most of Moscow's satellites had become economic cripples, and Mr. Gorbachev is well aware that without integration into Western markets they will remain a drain on his own budget.

The Soviet leader has not just endured the retreat of his allies from Communism, he has promoted it by both his words and example.

"Freedom of choice is a universal principle which allows no exception," he said in his speech last December to the United Nations General Assembly. And in Finland two weeks ago, he said the Soviet Union had no moral or political right to meddle in its neighbors' affairs.

"The Brezhnev doctrine is dead," added Gennadi I. Gerasimov, the Foreign Ministry spokesman, referring to the Western term for Leonid I. Brezhnev's determination to preserve the postwar order in Europe, with force if necessary.

The Kremlin has remained serene through the rise of a Polish government led by non-Communists, and through the abrupt disintegration of the Hungarian Communist Party.

In East Germany, Mr. Gorbachev was at least the catalyst for the departure of Erich Honecker, the aging party leader, and almost certainly counseled the initiatives of his successor, Egon Krenz, who hastened to Moscow within days of his ascent.

No one knows just what Mr. Gorbachev said to Mr. Krenz during their three-hour meeting on November 1, but the East German leader emerged from the encounter sounding like a disciple, and there is little doubt the decision to open the borders had the Soviet leader's blessing in advance.

East Germany, where the Soviet Union keeps 380,000 troops stationed, presents the trickiest test to date of Mr. Gorbachev's hands-off policy.

In a recent interview, Georgy K. Shakhnazarov, Mr. Gorbachev's longtime adviser on Eastern Europe, acknowledged the Soviet stake there.

"One of our concerns is that the situation in the German Democratic Republic is normalized," he said. "They have a very strong foundation; the economic foundations are sound. They have to solve certain tasks— make more information available, establish dialogue between the leadership and the people. Certain reforms will take place, and that in no way excludes cooperation between the two German states."

Asked about reunification of the two Germanys, Mr. Shakhnazarov said it was not "on the agenda now," but added, "I don't think anyone would dare to predict whether it's going to happen, when or in what way."

The opening of the border between the Germanys is likely to make the West look more seriously at Mr. Gorbachev's proposals for a broader disengagement of East and West in Europe. He has repeatedly proposed negotiating an end to the two military blocs, the North Atlantic Treaty Organization and the Warsaw Pact, as well as conventional arms agreements that would involve a drastic rollback of military front lines.

"Both East and West realize that all events should be taken as a complex," Mr. Shakhnazarov said, when asked about the prospect of pulling back Soviet troops from Eastern Europe.

"The troops will be withdrawn, but it will be done within the framework of the all-European process," he said. "From the standpoint of mutual confidence and stability, it would be much better for everyone if it happens on the basis of common consent, with participation of both alliances."

In this, Mr. Gorbachev may be willing to go further than many in the West think is wise.

Marxism Will Revive, Gorbachev Insists
By Bill Keller

MOSCOW, Nov. 26—Faced with a growing clamor from Communist Party conservatives, President Mikhail S. Gorbachev published a manifesto today insisting that Marxism will be revived in the Soviet Union, and under the leadership of the Communist Party.

With Communist governments in headlong retreat throughout Eastern Europe, the document, spread across two full pages of *Pravda,* was apparently intended to reassure the party faithful at this uneasy juncture that Communism is not collapsing, at least not here.

"Today we face the difficult challenge of reviving the authority of Marxist thought, the Marxist approach to reality," he wrote, and asserted that "at this complex stage" the party must keep its monopoly on political power.

Mr. Gorbachev described his goal as "humane socialism," a clear echo of the "socialism with a human face" promoted by the Communist liberalizers of the Prague Spring in Czechoslovakia in 1968.

Mr. Gorbachev's manifesto—essentially his revisionist view of Marxism—seemed intended to counter conservatives, who have recently shown signs of trying to consolidate their forces against what they view as heresies in the party.

Tonight, the central television showed excerpts from a rally sponsored last week by Leningrad party leaders in which the crowd poured out their anger at the Politburo and legislature for tolerating a drift toward capitalism.

As the crowd waved banners denouncing private businessmen as "crooks" and warning Mr. Gorbachev, "Mikhail Sergeyevich, pay attention to the party," speakers bitterly lamented the party's loss of authority.

"Maybe we're in this situation because of the cold-bloodedness and absence of emotions that prevail in our Politburo," yelled one speaker.

The Politburo has had its chance, shouted another, "now let us steer."

Aleksandr N. Yakovlev, a Politburo member who is Mr. Gorbachev's senior ally in rethinking Communism, appeared to have the Leningrad gathering in mind when he told a Soviet television interviewer tonight that the country must guard against "these dangerous conservatives."

"When they say, 'let us steer,' sometimes I wonder if they're really saying, 'let us shoot,' " Mr. Yakovlev said.

In addition to the restive party regulars, Mr. Gorbachev has recently witnessed the growing influence of new "worker fronts." These groups, backed by party and trade union functionaries, are demanding protection against the economic insecurity certain to come with moves toward a market economy.

Responding to this new lobby, the Soviet legislature last week approved a freeze on the prices of soap, nylons, cigarettes, and other consumer goods.

Mr. Gorbachev's article in the party newspaper was presented as "a synthesis and development" of several recent speeches, and was aimed at emphasizing his program's Marxist-Leninist roots and working-class orientation.

He said, however, that Lenin might have been wrong about one central point of his philosophy, that there can be no intermediate phase between capitalism and socialism.

This was Mr. Gorbachev's most explicit suggestion that the "new socialism" he has in mind for the Soviet Union will be a hybrid, incorporating aspects of capitalism.

Such speeches have little appeal to those who favor more far-reaching changes and who chafe at Mr. Gorbachev's caution. But the Soviet leader seems to feel a need to shore up his defenses against the conservatives as he heads off on visits to Italy and the Vatican and prepares for his Malta meeting next weekend with President Bush.

The article appeared as the Polish Prime Minister, Tadeusz Mazowiecki, the first non-Communist to lead a government in the Soviet bloc, was leaving Moscow after a remarkably warm reception, and as the Communist Party in Czechoslovakia was wobbling under public pressure.

Often criticized for falsely raising public expectations of quick results, Mr. Gorbachev today conceded that the remaking of socialism "is a process that will stretch beyond the decade into the twenty-first century."

Once again Gorbachev headed into a summit to consolidate the changing posture of the Soviet Union. This time he was to meet President Bush in Malta. On the way he stopped in Rome and met the Pope, whose selection as head of the Catholic church had helped inspire the decline of Communist power, first in his native Poland and then beyond.

The Kremlin and the Vatican; Gorbachev Visits Pope at Vatican; Ties Are Forged
By Clyde Haberman

ROME, DEC. 1—With an agreement to begin official relations and a pledge of expanded religious freedom for Soviet citizens, President Mikhail S. Gorbachev joined hands today with Pope John Paul II.

Seven decades of spiritual and philosophical conflict came to a symbolic end as the two talked for more than an hour in the heart of Vatican City, the first encounter between a Soviet Communist leader and a pope.

Both men agreed in principle to establish diplomatic ties, and Mr. Gorbachev invited the Pope to make a return visit to the Soviet Union.

The Pope's reply to the invitation was noncommittal. It appeared that before saying yes, he intended to keep on pressing Moscow to restore religious liberties to Soviet Catholics. According to a spokesman, the Pope "cordially thanked" his guest, and said he hoped that "developments would make it possible for him to accept."

Much will apparently depend on what happens to the four million to five million Eastern Rite Catholics in the Ukraine, where the Polish-born Pope has a special interest. Much of the western Ukraine was once part of Poland, until it was incorporated into the Soviet Union after World War II.

The Ukrainian Catholic Church was driven underground by Stalin in 1946. It was forcibly dissolved, and its parishes were closed or merged into the Russian Orthodox Church. Centered in the western Ukraine, the Ukrainian Catholics follow the Eastern liturgy but profess allegiance to the Pope.

The Pope has insisted repeatedly that the Ukrainian Catholic Church be made legal again, and he got an important start toward that goal when Mr. Gorbachev promised him today that a new law guaranteeing freedom of conscience would soon be enacted.

In turn, the Soviet leader won something he had come for: legitimacy from the leader of the world's 900 million Roman Catholics. It came in the form of a papal blessing for his plans to restructure Soviet political and economic life. John Paul said the Holy See "wishes you success and declares itself ready to support every initiative that will better protect and integrate the rights and duties of individuals and peoples."

But the Pope's main concern was religious liberty, and he stuck to that point tenaciously, reminding Mr. Gorbachev that Moscow had signed international treaties guaranteeing freedom of worship. "I express the fervent hope," he said, that Catholics in the Ukraine, the Baltic republics, and Armenia will be able "to practice freely their religious life."

In his brief remarks, the Soviet leader said all believers "have a right to satisfy their spiritual needs." On Thursday, he told Italian leaders that his country had made the mistake of treating religion in "a simplistic manner."

Developments such as these, the Pope said to him today, "lead us to hope that the situation will change."

Indeed, in the Ukranian city of Lvov, the layman who leads the Ukrainian Catholic Church reported that a major shift had already occurred. The leader, Ivan Hel, said that Ukraine officials had announced that the church could register like any other accepted religious organization.

Beyond the immediate agendas of each leader, the meeting today in the ceremonial library of the Vatican's Apostolic Palace contained a symbolism of almost epic proportions.

At an earlier time, Stalin had scornfully asked how many divisions the Pope had. Now, a successor intent on undoing Stalin's legacy has crossed St. Peter's Square in open recognition that he must reckon with the Vatican as a moral and political force.

Certainly, the significance was not lost on either of the participants, who have many points in common. Both are Slavs. Both say spiritual values must go hand in hand with material gains. Both talk of a Europe unified by a common civilization despite political diversity. And both can maintain, in different ways, that their separate visions helped trigger the tumultuous changes under way across the continent.

The two symbol-conscious men were also aware of the power of photographs and televised images showing them clasping hands and appearing in the relaxed company of each other.

"A truly extraordinary event has taken place," said the Communist leader, who was baptized as a boy in the Russian Orthodox Church. "It has become possible due to the profound changes that are sweeping many countries and nations. What is more, we can expect it to help assure their positive continuation."

"Our meeting today," the Pope said, "will hardly fail to have a powerful impact on world opinion." Not only is it something new and unusual, "It will also be interpreted as singularly meaningful, a sign of the times that have slowly matured, a sign that is rich in promise," he said.

For the Vatican, the Gorbachev visit crowned a year of dramatically improved relations with the Eastern bloc.

The church has been permitted to make long-prohibited ecclesiastical appointments in Czechoslovakia and in the Soviet republics of Lithuania and Byelorussia. Four months ago, it established diplomatic relations with Poland, its first with a Warsaw Pact nation. Last week, Hungary announced that it was ready to follow suit.

But full Vatican relations with the Kremlin are expected to take considerably more time. Even so, it was a giant stride today when Mr. Gorbachev said, "We have reached agreement in principle to give official status to our interstate relations."

Asked later if this was a move toward full diplomatic relations, the chief Vatican spokesman, Dr. Joaquin Navarro-Valls, said it was.

While the meeting today was friendly—punctuated with smiles and occasional laughs—the two leaders did not show true warmth in public. Still, the special nature of the occasion shone through, even in small gestures.

Mr. Gorbachev called the Pope "Holy Father." For his part, John Paul varied his routine in a significant way.

Normally, he greets visitors at the door of his library, which is on the second floor of the Apostolic Palace, one floor below his private apartment. To show his esteem for this guest, he came out several dozen yards from the library, to the throne room.

Then they entered the library, sitting on either side of a wooden desk during a 70-minute conversation. For the first five minutes, according to Dr. Navarro, they were alone, speaking in Russian. But then they brought in interpreters, with Mr. Gorbachev continuing in Russian and the Pope alternating between Polish and Italian.

While the two men talked, Mr. Gorbachev's wife, Raisa, toured the Sistine Chapel and the Raphael rooms of the Vatican Museum. Then she returned to meet the Pope, raising eyebrows by turning out in a bright red suit. It is customary for women to wear black at private papal audiences. But if the Vatican was displeased, it kept its feelings to itself.

In an exchange of gifts, John Paul presented Mr. Gorbachev a reproduction of an early Christian mosaic showing Christ on St. Peter's tomb, and gave Mrs. Gorbachev rosary beads of gold and mother-of-pearl. In return, he received two fourteenth-century psalmbooks from Kiev.

Just before this exchange, Dr. Navarro said, the Soviet leader told the Pope, "Holy Father, we are aware that we are dealing with the highest religious authority in the world but also someone who is a Slav."

"Yes, I'm the first Slav pope," John Paul reportedly replied, adding, "I'm sure that Providence paved the way for this meeting."

Amid the storm-tossed setting of the summit, everything seemed warm and cozy.

Bush and Gorbachev Proclaim a New Era for U.S.-Soviet Ties; Agree on Arms and Trade Aims
By Andrew Rosenthal

VALLETTA, MALTA, DEC. 3—President Bush and President Mikhail S. Gorbachev ended their first summit meeting today with an extraordinary public affirmation of the new relationship between their countries.

Mr. Gorbachev said he and Mr. Bush agreed that "the characteristics of the cold war should be abandoned."

"The arms race, mistrust, psychological and ideological struggle, all those should be things of the past," he said.

Mr. Bush said: "With reform under way in the Soviet Union, we stand at the threshold of a brand-new era of U.S.-Soviet relations. It is within our grasp to contribute each in our own way to overcoming the division of Europe and ending the military confrontation there."

In the most substantial agreements reached at the meeting, the two leaders said they would strive to conclude treaties on long-range nuclear weapons and conventional arms in 1990. They also agreed to hold another summit meeting in June in the United States.

But the significance of the first summit meeting between the leaders seemed to lie more in the tone than the substance.

They ended their rain-soaked two-day meeting with the first joint news conference by Soviet and American leaders.

There had been some annoyance aboard Mr. Gorbachev's ship, the *Maxim Gorky,* on Saturday night when Mr. Bush canceled an afternoon session and a dinner because of a gale. The tension lingered in the background today, but it melted under the television lights in a 65-minute display of cordiality that ended with Mr. Bush reaching over to grasp Mr. Gorbachev's right forearm. The news conference was remarkable for its lack of conflict over issues that have long divided East and West, including arms control, the Middle East, and economic relations.

For all the cordiality, the meeting did not produce any new treaties or specific agreements, or even a joint statement.

After eight hours of intimate discussions, the two leaders were still far apart on the issue of sea-based nuclear cruise missiles, a major point of disagreement on a strategic arms treaty. They remained at odds on Central America, and administration officials said Mr. Gorbachev did not give a definitive answer to Mr. Bush's proposals on an agreement reducing chemical weapons.

But Mr. Gorbachev, clearly pleased that Mr. Bush had shown some initiative on economic issues, registered approval on most of the proposals offered by Mr. Bush on Saturday, and the two leaders expressed broad optimism about the course of their relations.

Although they said they did not reach any specific accord on how to deal with the unraveling political power structure in Eastern Europe, Mr. Bush and Mr. Gorbachev seemed optimistic even about that problem.

"We searched for the answer to the question of where do we stand now," Mr. Gorbachev said. "We stated, both of us, that the world leaves one epoch of cold war and enters another epoch."

The two leaders did not dwell on Eastern Europe at length in their news conference, and American officials said the subject did not take up as much of the summit talks as they had expected. In response to a question about the two Germanys, Mr. Bush adopted what had long been the Soviet position. He said the conference on European security that began in Helsinki "spells out a concept of permanent borders."

Mr. Gorbachev said, "any artificial acceleration" of the unification process would make it more difficult to carry through the changes taking place in Eastern Europe.

At times, the cautious Mr. Bush seemed to make an effort to show that all was not settled between the two nations. Even then, the statements from both sides were far more mild than the political oratory that has characterized the Soviet-American relationship for much of the last four decades.

Mr. Bush said his conversation with Mr. Gorbachev stayed cordial even on human rights. "I remember a time when I first met Mr. Gorbachev and we talked about human rights and he became visibly agitated with me for raising it," Mr. Bush said.

"And I think there's been a great evolution in his thinking on that question, and certainly on his relations with the United States, just as there has been an evolution in my thinking," Mr. Bush said, noting that he had once opposed holding the very type of meeting he had with Mr. Gorbachev here.

Indeed, when it came to what American officials said was the most troublesome policy dispute between the two leaders during the shipboard meeting—American charges that Nicaragua is sending arms to the leftist rebels in El Salvador—Mr. Gorbachev said, "We understand the concerns of the United States."

On Saturday, Mr. Bush outlined 18 proposals to Mr. Gorbachev that ranged from nuclear arms control to educational exchanges. A senior American official who sat in on the talks said Mr. Gorbachev responded positively to almost all of them.

The notable exceptions, he said, were Mr. Bush's proposal that the two nations negotiate and sign an agreement in 1990 limiting their chemical arsenals to 20 percent of the present American level and that they call jointly for the holding of the 2004 Olympic Games on both sides of Berlin.

The official said that Mr. Gorbachev did not give Mr. Bush a clear no on those points but rather did not register the approval that he offered on the other issues.

Mr. Bush called trade "one of the most fruitful parts of our discussion" and said he would "like to have a climate in which American businessmen can help with what Chairman Gorbachev is trying to do in terms of reform and *glasnost.*"

The Malta summit marked the clearest expression of what until then had been a somewhat muted aspect of Gorbachev's strategy for change, namely that economic aid, probably massive aid, would be needed from the West to help underwrite the transformation of the Soviet economy and subsidize some of the cost of maintaining social stability during the process of renovation.

Bush Says Soviets Merit West's Help to Foster Reform
By Alan Riding

BRUSSELS, DEC. 4—President Bush said today that the West should help out President Mikhail S. Gorbachev to show support for the changes taking place in Eastern Europe and the Soviet Union.

At a news conference after meeting the other leaders of the 16-nation North Atlantic Treaty Organization, Mr. Bush provided new insights into why he offered economic concessions to the Soviet leader during their two-day weekend meeting in Malta.

Asked why he was now more supportive of Mr. Gorbachev than he had been earlier in the year, Mr. Bush said his "new thinking" was based on admiration for "the way in which Mr. Gorbachev has handled the changes in Eastern Europe," and for his willingness to go along with arms control reductions in which Soviet forces are cut deeper than Western forces.

"When I hear him talk about peaceful change and the right of countries to choose—countries in the Warsaw Pact to choose—that deserves new thinking," Mr. Bush said of the Soviet leader. "And so I approach this, and I think, in step with our allies, with a certain respect for what he's doing, and thus we want to try to meet him on some of the areas where he needs help. I'm thinking of a few suggestions I had in the economic area."

Soviet analysts barely mentioned Mr. Bush's offer of economic cooperation, in part because Moscow is wary of seeming to grovel for Western aid, and in part because it does not want to encourage the popular feeling there that the West can bail out the floundering Soviet economy.

But as Soviet bridge-building efforts to the West were succeeding, at home matters continued to fray.

Communist Party Begins to Splinter Under Gorbachev
By Bill Keller

MOSCOW, DEC. 5—While President Mikhail S. Gorbachev has been applying his diplomatic skills to the stability of Europe, his own Communist Party is beginning to splinter along ethnic and ideological lines.

Amid increasingly plaintive Kremlin appeals for unity, members of the party have begun challenging the dominance of the party in Soviet society, following the example of Poland, Hungary, Czechoslovakia, and East Germany.

Although Mr. Gorbachev has promised that the Communist Party will usher in a period of political pluralism, there are several signs that this time is arriving faster than he expected.

For example, leaders of the vital Leningrad party organization, humiliated by the defeat of their candidates in elections last March, seem to be preparing their own platform, sharply at odds with Mr. Gorbachev's program of social and economic change.

And although Kremlin officials have denounced attempts to "federalize" the party, Communists in the republic of Latvia, following the defiant lead of neighboring Lithuania, have declared their intention of creating a breakaway party independent of Moscow.

In Lithuania, the Communists are openly challenged by a strong popular front, a new social democratic party, and other rivals. This may lead to the Baltic republic becoming the first to formally repudiate the party's special status, at a session of its parliament on Wednesday, journalists in Lithuania say.

Opponents of the party's dominant status hope to force a decision on the issue when the Soviet Union's 2,250-member Congress of People's Deputies convenes in Moscow next week. They call for repealing Article 6 of the Soviet constitution, which establishes the Communist Party as "the leading and guiding force of Soviet society and the nucleus of its political system, of all state organizations and public organizations."

Lithuania Legalizes Rival Parties, Removing Communists' Monopoly
By Esther B. Fein

MOSCOW, DEC. 7—Lithuania became the first Soviet republic to abolish the Communist Party's guaranteed monopoly on power when its parliament voted overwhelmingly today to legalize rival political parties.

Rejecting repeated Kremlin pleas and warnings to curb its political defiance, the Lithuanian parliament changed the republic's constitution to abolish the guarantee of power for the Communist Party.

With the vote of 243 to 1 with 39 abstentions, Lithuania, one of 15 Soviet republics, joined the majority of Eastern bloc nations in legalizing a multiparty system.

In neighboring Estonia, the Central Committee of the Communist Party agreed at a meeting today that Article 6 of the republic's constitution, which guarantees the Communist Party's preeminence, should be annulled, setting the stage for a similar constitutional amendment in that republic.

Both decisions today are clear signs that the tensions tearing at the former strongholds of Communist power elsewhere in Eastern Europe are growing in the Soviet Union itself.

The actions are sure to anger President Mikhail S. Gorbachev, who while not interfering with such moves by the Soviet Union's East European allies, has said the Communist Party is the only force capable of seeing the country through its current economic and political crises.

On December 13, as the Congress of People's Deputies began its session, the government defended its economic policies in the face of robust criticism. On the second day, as Gorbachev spoke, Andrei D. Sakharov tried from his seat in the sixth row to prod the President into an acceptance of democratic practices only to be shouted down. "I am very tired," said the physicist whose release from exile in Gorki two years earlier had with one stroke gained international credibility for Gorbachev's proclaimed new course. On Friday, the third day of the conference, Sakharov was dead at the age of 68.

Government That Exiled Him Hurries to Mourn Sakharov
By Francis X. Clines

MOSCOW, DEC. 15—The Soviet government, which once exiled Andrei D. Sakharov for being a human rights champion, today embraced him in death. President Mikhail S. Gorbachev mourned the national loss of "a man of conviction and sincerity."

The government moved swiftly to seek a state funeral and marshal

Politburo tributes for the tart-tongued humanist who died on Thursday night, only hours after delivering another denunciation of the Communist monopoly of the nation.

But the Sakharov family was reported working on other plans for the burial of the 68-year-old Nobel laureate and deputy to the new national legislature who collapsed from a heart attack and died alone in his study.

The sudden news swept this hard-pressed nation with much of the political and emotional power that Dr. Sakharov wielded in two decades of singular criticism of the Kremlin.

Many Soviet citizens felt that with this death, President Gorbachev had lost a badly needed, greatly respected moral goad. And Dr. Sakharov's nation had lost another embattled individualist who demonstrated the virtue of resisting the regime at personal risk in the service of others' freedom.

"As long as he was alive, we all felt safe," said a woman who stood mourning on the street below his apartment, her face wet with tears and snow.

"*Uzhasna,*" she muttered in Russian: "terrible."

No less lamentable than the death of the physically frail, spiritually relentless man were the political ironies that ensued before the eyes of Muscovites: guards of the K.G.B., who once kept Dr. Sakharov at bay in his apartment, cleared a path to his front door this afternoon so a quickly assembled government funeral commission could express sad-faced grief to his widow, Yelena G. Bonner.

Tass, the government press agency, which once denounced Dr. Sakharov as a traitor deserving his six years of internal exile in Gorky, issued warm posthumous descriptions of him as a civil rights battler and even offered videotapes of his final days for sale to foreign correspondents at $1,500.

Dr. Sakharov's death was the opening story on the evening television news program, *Vremya.* The account focused briefly on the moment of silence observed in the Congress rather than on a detailed biography of Dr. Sakharov and his long history of resisting the Kremlin. *Izvestia,* the government newspaper, had no mention in its evening edition.

Zglyad, the alternative Friday television program of current events, now the most popular in the nation, devoted considerable time and sympathy to Dr. Sakharov in the recollective style reminiscent of American television's treatment of the assassination of Senator Robert F. Kennedy and the Reverend Dr. Martin Luther King, Jr. Most poignant was a moment when Dr. Sakharov's widow paused in mid-interview as it dawned on her what she was discussing.

"My God," she said, her eyes welling with tears. "My God."

"They did all they could to kill him," lamented Boris Fayants, one of the many ordinary Soviet citizens who seemed clearly to feel that Soviet political life, with its fresh seeds of hope born when President Gorbachev ended Dr. Sakharov's exile, had been drastically altered by the death.

"For us, it was wonderful to see him elected to the Congress, but for him it was a terrible mistake," Mr. Fayants, a mathematician, said, grasping at his own heart.

Mr. Gorbachev said, "This is a big loss," choosing to comment not from the Congress rostrum but in a corridor outside in a brief interview with reporters. "This was not some sort of a political intriguer, but a person who had his own ideas, his own convictions, which he expressed openly and directly."

The death of Dr. Sakharov, a physicist who evolved from designing the Soviet hydrogen bomb to leading the nation's antiwar movement, deprives the Soviet leader of a badly needed force for credibility.

Mr. Gorbachev was obviously peeved at times to see Dr. Sakharov arise regularly from his sixth-row congressional seat to deliver sharp-toned blasts at Gorbachev programs. But the President seemed far more mindful of the fact that he gained credit for having invited such political change and goading in the first place.

It was credit from the outside world more than the members of the Communist majority in Congress. After Dr. Sakharov's death, they all had to stand for a moment of silence in his memory this morning.

Sakharov associates complained that the funeral commission included prominent party officials who did nothing to help him a decade ago when the government ostracized him for refusing to cease his criticism of the Soviet combat role in Afghanistan, and he was exiled to Gorky.

Dr. Sakharov died in the midst of a campaign to demonstrate to the nation the value of opposition voices in the one-party legislature. The stilling of his own special voice now makes this point most dramatically but raises questions of how the nebulous early opposition caucus he helped found, the Interregional Group, will carry on without him.

Both the opposition and Mr. Gorbachev seemed to benefit from Dr. Sakharov's treks to the rostrum. The last public exchange of the two men on Tuesday was typical. Legislators groaned as Dr. Sakharov came up to speak. Mr. Gorbachev had been busy brushing aside other speakers, but not Andrei Dmitrivich.

In one sentence, squinting and craggy voiced, Dr. Sakharov ripped into the government's failure to move toward its promises on land reform. In the next, he turned toward Mr. Gorbachev wielding a sheaf of telegrams like a fiery sword, speaking for citizens demanding that Congress repeal the Communist Party's power monopoly.

"That's all," Mr. Gorbachev snapped, growing short with the man he freed from exile. Dr. Sakharov retreated from the uncertain new legislature for the last time looking unsurprised and unsatisfied, as if he harbored every intent of complaining another day.

As the momentous year was drawing to a close, it was still the events in Eastern Europe that were dominating the news. The leaders of East and West Germany were meeting for the first time. The Brandenburg Gate in Berlin was opened, and there was free movement across the long-barricaded border for all Germans. In Czechoslovakia, the so-called velvet revolution was prevailing, as once jailed dissidents led by the playwright Vaclav Havel were establishing a party and a government to replace the Communists. Similarly in Hungary, Poland, and Bulgaria the old Communists were either out of power entirely or hanging on to some posts by their fingernails. In East Germany whatever government came and went was proving irrelevant as the country was fading away entirely to meld with its richer, bigger German neighbor. Basically, with the approach of 1990, Communists were in control in Albania and Yugoslavia, both of which were idiosyncratically anti-Soviet, and in Moscow. There the Soviet Communist system was dominant and entrenched, and no one was seriously predicting its rapid disintegration. The Soviet state, after all, was a superpower. But at the edges of that state, particularly in the non-Slavic Baltic states, challenges to Moscow were growing bolder.

Communist Party in Lithuania Parts with Soviet Rule
By Esther B. Fein

VILNIUS, U.S.S.R., DEC. 20—The Communist Party of Lithuania voted overwhelmingly today to break away from the leadership in Moscow, becoming the first local party organization in the history of the Soviet Union to defy the Kremlin by declaring independence.

The party immediately declared that a primary goal was the creation of "an independent democratic Lithuanian state."

The Lithuanian party leader, Algirdas Brazauskas, hailed the decision and said, "I hope and wish our party will always be resolute, rejuvenated, and ready for new battles."

The newly independent party's first battle is likely to be with the Communist Party leadership in Moscow, which has repeatedly warned the Lithuanian organization against making such a dramatic move. Mr. Brazauskas himself has been personally rebuked on many occasions by President Mikhail S. Gorbachev for supporting calls for Lithuania's independence from the Soviet Union.

But Mr. Brazauskas and the other delegates to the Lithuanian Communist Party conference here in the capital of the republic resisted the pressure and voted for the bold separation. And it is unclear what kind of action the Kremlin could take against a party organization that has disavowed Moscow's authority.

The parliament in Vilnius rejected Kremlin appeals earlier this month and voted to abolish the Communist Party's constitutionally guaranteed monopoly on power in the republic. Both defiant Lithuanian actions are likely to be repeated in the near future by other republics where resistance to Moscow's control is strong, including the neighboring Baltic republics of Latvia and Estonia, and Armenia and Georgia.

Mr. Gorbachev has tolerated decisions by Eastern European allies to break the Communist hold on power. But while he struggles to advance his program of economic and political changes in the Soviet Union, he has firmly resisted similar tendencies at home.

The Kremlin did not have an immediate comment on today's vote.

Speaking before today's vote, Riamondas Kasauskas, a writer, reminded the delegates that Mr. Gorbachev had said of the changes in Eastern Europe, "Every nation has the right to choose its own way to develop its social structure."

"All European nations includes us," Mr. Kasauskas said. "We're no worse than anyone else in Eastern Europe."

The conference delegates could have chosen a less drastic split, by deciding to become an independent party "within a rejuvenated Communist Party of the Soviet Union," but they rejected that alternative.

One delegate described the choice as voting to be "an independent goldfish in the body of a whale."

In the balloting, 855 delegates voted to become "an independent Communist Party of Lithuania with its own statutes and programs," 160 voted to be independent within a renewed Soviet structure, and 12 abstained.

When the results were read, the delegates sitting in the Vilnius Opera and Ballet Theater rose to their feet in thunderous applause and began singing the Lithuanian national anthem, which until recently had been considered a subversive act punishable by law.

On December 25, Nicolae Ceauşescu, Rumania's dictator, and his wife were executed by a firing squad from the army he had commanded for 24 years. He had been Europe's last Stalinist leader.

1990

I f the pace of disintegration in Moscow was not quite like what had just been experienced in Rumania, there was still an unmistakable sense of unraveling.

Gorbachev Urges Lithuania to Stay with Soviet Union
By Esther B. Fein

VILNIUS, U.S.S.R., JAN. 11—President Mikhail S. Gorbachev implored Lithuanians today to remain within the Soviet Union, warning that secession would mean economic calamity for this tiny republic, while weakening Soviet security and endangering his own position and program.

But Yuri D. Maslyukov, a fellow Politburo member who joined Mr. Gorbachev as he started a three-day mission to stem the tide of separatism here, told factory workers that Lithuanians have a legal right to secede by popular referendum and that a law to specify the steps for making and implementing such decisions was being drafted in the Soviet parliament.

For his part, Mr. Gorbachev noted that he would accept such a law but he sought to persuade Lithuanians that the procedures covering a secession would be costly and far from simple, involving negotiations on defense, trade, communications, and possible compensation for federal investments.

Mr. Maslyukov's views on the right to secession constituted the first explicit acknowledgment by a top Kremlin leader that a republic has the right to withdraw from the Union of Soviet Socialist Republics. Mr. Maslyukov, head of the state planning commission, said, "Our position is that leaving the Soviet Union is possible.

"It is only natural that Lithuanians have the right to decide their fate—to be within the Soviet Union or to leave the Soviet Union," he told workers at a factory on Wednesday, according to an account published tonight in the government newspaper, *Izvestia.*

This afternoon, a quarter of a million of the republic's 3.5 million people jammed into Cathedral Square here to hear nationalist and local Communist Party leaders reaffirm calls for a reconstituted independent Lithuania as they brushed aside the appeal for national unity that Mr. Gorbachev had made earlier in remarkable encounters with nationalist-minded people on the streets of Vilnius.

In one spontaneous meeting before the big rally, Mr. Gorbachev used a pleading tone as he said that Lithuanian separation would spell the end of his economic and political changes in the Soviet Union, and strongly suggested it could threaten his position.

"We have embarked on this path, and I am the one who chose it," he said. "My personal fate is linked to this choice. The two states must live together."

The demonstration drew huge masses of people who spilled beyond the central square into nearby streets and onto the knoll behind the grand cathedral. The crowds waved placards demanding "complete independence" and rejecting Mr. Gorbachev's promise of greater freedom within a restructured Soviet federation.

But Mr. Gorbachev warned that if "someone" succeeded in turning Moscow and Lithuania against each other, "There will be a tragedy."

The Soviet President warned repeatedly that any republic's decision to secede would reverberate throughout the union, including Russia, where the Baltic independence movement has already given impetus to conservative Russian nationalists.

"You think it's all so simple?" he said to people at Lenin Square. "If even the slightest suppression occurs, or a misunderstanding, say, in Estonia or Moldavia, it spills over to the rest of the country."

Siberia; Miners Threaten New Soviet Strike
By Francis X. Clines

NOVOKUZNETSK, U.S.S.R., JAN. 13—The Siberian miners who started a nationwide coal strike last summer say they are likely to resume their walkout, in defiance of a government ban, because life remains miserable for their families despite the Kremlin's promise of improvements within six months.

"I speak for all here when I say the politicians are not to be trusted, and we want our demands to be met," said Boris N. Goryev, pausing with his begrimed crew far down below the frigid whiteness of Siberia where they man a snaggle-toothed combine machine that chews away at the labyrinthine blackness.

A midwinter resumption of the strike would greatly compound the problems of President Mikhail S. Gorbachev, who is being forced to juggle such assorted crises as separatist pressures on the nation's borders, renewed ethnic violence in the south, widespread anger over consumer shortages, and turmoil in the Communist Party over its power to continue governing.

"We have a government by patchwork," said Vladimir E. Petrov, a member of the citywide workers' committee organized in last summer's miners' strike, which paralyzed the industry.

"One day they attend to Lithuania; the next day it's the Armenians; tomorrow it will be somewhere else," he said, demanding to know what happened to the government's heralded strike-ending "compact" with the miners to permit them to try such revolutionary experiments as management by workers and free-enterprise mining for foreign profits.

Instead of self-management and hard-currency foreign profits that the miners need to upgrade their life, the six-month deadline of the strike settlement finds the mines still tightly controlled by the government, with labor working under the decades-old quota system rather than for the individual profit-sharing that the miners thought they had negotiated last summer. Central government officials are due to visit the miners again next week, but the workers say they know what to expect.

"The same thing we saw in the Congress of People's Deputies on television last month: talk, talk, and more talk," one miner said.

Soviet Azerbaijan in Ethnic Turmoil
By Bill Keller

MOSCOW, JAN. 14—The southern Soviet republic of Azerbaijan has erupted in civil violence, leaving at least 25 people killed in the capital city, Baku, and several towns in disarray, official reports and residents reached by telephone said today.

Witnesses said Azerbaijani mobs broke away from a huge rally in Baku on Saturday night and rampaged through the streets, using mimeographed address lists to find the homes of Armenians and drive them outside.

Gangs continued to roam the Armenian quarter today, committing what the official press agency, Tass, described as atrocities and pogroms despite the presence of a division of Interior Ministry troops flown in to control the violence.

In one rural district of the republic, the entire Communist Party leadership has reportedly been held hostage for five days. In another area, heavily armed vigilantes were said to have attacked a military patrol and stolen its armored vehicles. Two cities along the Caspian Sea were reported to be under nationalist control after officials and the police essentially abdicated.

President Mikhail S. Gorbachev, who just returned to Moscow from Lithuania, where he tried without apparent success to head off a peaceful secession campaign, sent delegations of senior government and Communist Party officials to Azerbaijan and neighboring Armenia.

The two nationalist crises—the deliberate, ballot-box independence campaign in the Baltic region and the eruptions of ethnic hatred in the Caucasus Mountains—could hardly be more different, but both contribute to the impression of events spinning out of Mr. Gorbachev's control.

The central issue in the Caucasus is the status of Nagorno-Karabakh, a mountainous region of western Azerbaijan where the Armenian majority demands to be annexed to Armenia.

The central television tonight portrayed Nagorno-Karabakh and the area around it as verging on civil war, with armed crowds of both ethnic groups converging on the area and federal peacekeeping troops under frequent attack.

Troops Seek to Calm Azerbaijan; Soviets Debate Cause of Violence
By Bill Keller

MOSCOW, JAN. 17—Soviet troops tried to impose martial law in Azerbaijan today as the country began to debate the causes of a bloodbath that seemed both unthinkable and inevitable.

Sketchy initial reports from the combat zone said army and Interior Ministry troops were being hampered by roadblocks in the hilly countryside of western Azerbaijan.

The clashes between Azerbaijanis and Armenians have claimed more than 60 lives, most of them Armenians killed by mobs in Baku, the capital of Azerbaijan.

The authorities in Moscow underscored their determination to stop the fighting by announcing tonight on television that army, Interior Ministry, and K.G.B. troops had been cleared to shoot to defend themselves or to protect official arms caches.

The television announcement said troops had employed "maximum restraint" even though several members of the Interior Ministry force had been killed, but "the situation has become intolerable."

Azerbaijan has been closed to foreign reporters since the first signs of unrest early this month. The Foreign Ministry today also banned travel to Armenia, where angry citizens were reported preparing for civil war.

Soviet Troops Bogged Down by Azerbaijanis' Blockades of Railroads and Airfields
By Bill Keller

MOSCOW, JAN. 18—Soviet troops were apparently bogged down by widespread obstruction today, including airfield and railroad blockades, sabotage, hostage taking, and civil disobedience, as they tried to control the violence in Azerbaijan.

The official press agency, Tass, said the situation had deteriorated in the last 24 hours as Azerbaijani militants ignored appeals for order from army and Interior Ministry troops sent to enforce emergency measures.

Defense Minister Dmitri T. Yazov said in a radio interview that army reserves had been mobilized for the operation, and he hinted that many of them were not enthusiastic about being sent to quell domestic disorders.

None of the government's sometimes-contradictory accounts of events in the region could be reliably confirmed. . . . The government has reported that more than 60 people have been killed in the fighting, although that number, too, could not be checked.

Russians; Cry of "Won't Give My Son!" and Soviets End the Call-up
By Bill Keller

MOSCOW, JAN. 19—The Kremlin abandoned its emergency mobilization of army reserves today after an outpouring of protests from Russian parents unwilling to let their sons police the fighting in Azerbaijan.

Moscow said tonight that all the young reservists conscripted for the special duty would be released within five days, and that the government would rely on army and Interior Ministry regulars in its so far unsuccessful attempt to regain control of the republic from Azerbaijani militants.

The public resistance to the call-up was given remarkably sympathetic coverage in the Soviet press, with a commentator on central television questioning whether the authorities "have forgotten that this is peacetime."

A mother at a meeting in Stavropol, the southern Russian city best known as the birthplace of President Mikhail S. Gorbachev, cried: "We don't want the people of those republics to call us occupiers. We don't need a second Afghanistan."

Although by all accounts Mr. Gorbachev's decision to declare a state of emergency and send troops has widespread support from a country weary of ethnic violence, the fruitless, 10-year Soviet military intervention in Afghanistan has erased much of the glory of military service.

For many Soviet citizens, the television coverage from Azerbaijan in recent days has had a haunting resemblance to film of that war, with footage of skirmishes in a biblical-looking landscape and somber reports of troops encountering resistance from well-armed guerrillas.

"I won't give my son!" shouted another woman, during a Stavropol protest shown on television tonight. "I won't! I won't give my son for this! We endure and endure and endure! How long will we have to endure? Why do they take them at night?"

Similar protests and frantic phone calls to newspapers were reported in other cities in the Russian republic, in the northern Caucasus Mountains, just north of the fighting.

The storm of protest—and the authorities' quick response—underscored the depth of what some Soviet commentators call "Afghanistan syndrome," a mood of isolationism driven in large part by the now officially condemned war, which cost more than 15,000 Soviet lives and left a legacy of bruised lives, drug abuse, and cynicism.

This attitude may be one reason Moscow waited until the situation in Azerbaijan had clearly raged out of control before moving in additional troops and giving them clearance to fire on militants.

President Mikhail S. Gorbachev acknowledged the unpopularity of the call-up in remarks this morning at the Kremlin to a conference of workers and farmers.

"A partial mobilization of reservists has been declared in the northern Caucasus to give help quickly, but that gave rise to discontent among the population," Mr. Gorbachev said.

One source of indignation was that the government did not publicly disclose the reserve call-up until it was well under way.

Defense Minister Dmitri T. Yazov disclosed the mobilization in an early-morning radio interview Thursday, after numerous calls from parents and wives demanding an explanation.

The drafting of reservists primarily from Russian cities suggested that the sudden draft may have been necessary because the standing army was short of men of Slavic descent.

One official account last year said that 37 percent of the army's conscripts come from minority groups in the south, many of whom might feel sympathies for one side or the other in this domestic combat.

The army has not disclosed how many young men it called up for the first move into Azerbaijan.

About 5,000 soldiers, along with 6,000 interior troops, were reported in the first wave ordered in Tuesday to supplement those already stationed there during many months of tension.

Soviet television tonight showed Communist Party officials in Stavropol trying to reassure a rally of parents that the reservists would be doing guard duty in Armenia—protecting arms caches and railroads—not fighting militants in Azerbaijan. But the parents appeared disbelieving.

"If we judge by the bitter tears," the television commentator concluded, "I think the military registration and enlistment offices have forgotten that this is peacetime."

Later in the broadcast a district army commandant appeared at General Yazov's instructions and declared that the short-lived mobilization "permitted the fulfillment of urgent tasks" and was being ended.

"The conscripted reservists will be returned home during the next five days as they will be replaced by cadre subdivisions of the Interior Ministry, the Defense Ministry, the K.G.B., and forces of order," he said. "Reservists called up and currently at the registration points will not be sent to the trans-Caucasus."

Soviet Military Takes Control of Baku; Scores of Azerbaijanis Killed; Coup Averted, Gorbachev Says
By Bill Keller

MOSCOW, JAN. 20—Soviet troops claimed control of the Azerbaijani capital of Baku today and began settling in for a probable long-term occupation after a night of urban conflict that left scores of civilians and several soldiers dead.

The military commandant in the stunned Caspian Sea port said 60 people had died as columns of tanks and soldiers crashed through the barricades erected by Azerbaijani insurgents and suppressed scattered resistance.

Baku residents reached by telephone, citing estimates by local health officials and hospitals, gave death tolls ranging up to several hundred.

Several witnesses described army and Interior Ministry soldiers blazing their way through the city before dawn, firing into apartment balconies and at bystanders who rushed from their apartments out of curiosity.

The taking of Baku climaxed a week of turmoil that began when deadly anti-Armenian riots broke out in the city on January 13.

President Mikhail S. Gorbachev, who signed the order that launched the midnight assault on the city, appeared on television tonight and said the military intervention had been taken to prevent an attempted coup by the Azerbaijani Popular Front.

"There were growing calls for a seizure of power by force," Mr. Gorbachev said.

Despite a reported heavy martial presence in the city, popular front leaders rallied supporters this morning for a demonstration in front of the

Communist Party headquarters in Baku and vowed to defy the military
with a campaign of strikes and civil disobedience.

"We will fight until we win," said Uussef Samadoglu, a poet and
popular front leader. "The goal is to drive out the army, liquidate the
Azerbaijani Communist Party, establish a democratic parliament."

The Communist Party of Azerbaijan today dismissed the party chief,
Abdulrakhman K. Vezirov, who had bowed to popular front strikes and
demonstrations by legalizing the group and ceding it large influence in the
republic's internal affairs.

Apparently in response to the taking of Baku, the Azerbaijani province
of Nakhichevan declared its independence from the Soviet Union and
called on Turkey, Iran, and the United Nations to come to its help, the
Iranian press agency Irna said. The report was confirmed by a local
journalist in an interview with Reuters.

Nakhichevan, which is on the border with Turkey and Iran and completely cut off from the rest of Azerbaijan by the hostile Armenian republic, is a popular front stronghold where crowds last month tore down
fences and guard posts to open the border with Iran, where millions of
ethnic Azeris live.

"If true, that would be a serious violation of the constitution" and
legally invalid, said Deputy Foreign Minister Aleksandr A. Bessmertnykh when asked about the secession at a hastily arranged press briefing
this morning.

No one interviewed today in Moscow or Azerbaijan believed Mr. Gorbachev would have a quick or easy time pacifying Azerbaijan, a republic
the size of eight Lebanons now largely obsessed by its centuries-old
conflict with neighboring Armenia.

"We now have an internal Afghanistan," a Communist Party official
said today, anticipating a long-term occupation that he feared would
quickly wear on the patience of the Soviet public.

The President of Azerbaijan, Elmira Kafarova, went on Baku radio this
morning to condemn the introduction of troops into the city in a broadcast monitored by the British Broadcasting Corporation.

The ancient enmity between the Islamic Azerbaijanis and the Christian
Armenians has flared for the last two years as the two peoples vied for
control of the Nagorno-Karabakh region, a predominantly Armenian
enclave completely enclosed in Azerbaijani territory.

Baku had become increasingly volatile as the city absorbed tens of
thousands of embittered Azerbaijani refugees driven from Armenia during the period of tension. These refugees gave the popular front a street
power that cowed local Communist officials but that the front's intellectual leaders could not fully control.

Mr. Bessmertnykh, the deputy foreign minister, said troops moved in only after it became clear that militants threatened to take control of the republic.

"A headquarters was established whose purpose was in essence to remove the legal authorities from power, and to take power themselves," Mr. Bessmertnykh said.

"There were attempts to take over the television and radio stations, and to paralyze the functions of party, state, and Soviet bodies," he said. "In the city of Baku, teams of commandos had started erecting barricades, blocking lines of communications."

The authorities in Moscow provided no information about the scale of the storming of Baku and showed no television footage from the city except a glimpse of some tanks and army trucks and a scene of today's protest rally.

Moscow Arrests Azerbaijan Rebels
By Bill Keller

MOSCOW, JAN. 24—Soviet troops arrested dozens of insurgents and outlawed "illegally functioning organizations" in defiant Azerbaijan today in a selective crackdown aimed at consolidating the Kremlin's hold on the republic, the authorities and residents said.

The authorities also broke a blockade of Baku harbor, dispersing the obstructing Azerbaijani merchant ships with what one witness described as a 40-minute bombardment by warships, tanks, and artillery.

Residents of Baku, the Azerbaijani capital, said a general strike had brought the city's industries, including its offshore drilling rigs and critical oil equipment factories, to a standstill, despite a military order to return to work.

The official press agency, Tass, said the military reported that it had evacuated about 12,000 members of the families of army, K.G.B., and interior troops in the face of attacks and threats that, officials claimed, were assuming an increasingly anti-Russian character.

"Events are taking on the shape of a guerrilla war," the government newspaper, *Izvestia,* said tonight. "People drive around the city on motorcycles at night, attacking military foot patrols and then vanishing. Cans of gasoline are thrown onto armored personnel carriers that are transporting the army."

The newspaper said the capital "is literally shattered by terrible rumors" that people of Russian heritage are being singled out for attack in vengeance for killing of Azerbaijanis when tanks crashed into the city early Saturday morning after days of conflict with neighboring Armenia turned into separatist turmoil.

Like an adept boxer against the ropes, Gorbachev managed to land some counterpunches and hang on. Delegations of Azerbaijanis and Armenians participated in peace talks in Latvia, which defused the situation in the south and simultaneously gave a boost to Baltic nationalism. Then Gorbachev pointedly said that pressure was building for German reunification, which the West Germans took to mean that Moscow was signaling that under the right terms it might accept a single German state. Finally, as he faced a critical party congress Gorbachev's close advisers were saying, equally pointedly, that the leader was willing to accept real political pluralism, allowing the party to lose its old monopoly and create new institutions of government.

Gorbachev as Houdini
By Bill Keller

MOSCOW, FEB. 4—Less than a month ago, President Mikhail S. Gorbachev was facing the rebellious Lithuanians, and conspicuously failing to dampen their longing for independence from the Soviet empire.

Two weeks ago he was sending the army to Azerbaijan to shore up the hollow shell of Communist power in that bloodied republic.

Now Mr. Gorbachev, the Houdini of politicians, is back on the stage, ready for his next act. He has slipped out of those two perilously tight spots and again confounded the credulous spectators who believe, each time the master is wrapped in chains and dropped into the river, that they are witnessing his final stunt.

On Monday, the Soviet leader heads into a showdown on the future course of the Soviet Communist Party, an event that has already distracted public attention from the crises on the empire's periphery.

If he prevails, many believe Mr. Gorbachev will then be ready to begin his ultimate escape: jumping free of his place atop the Communist Party before that institution falls of its own dying weight.

Mr. Gorbachev's overall strategy seems reasonably clear. He wants to tame the Communist Party by neutralizing what remains of the Old Guard and modernizing its program, and simultaneously build up the presidency and elected legislature as stable power centers.

Then, many Gorbachev supporters predict, he will hand over his job of party chief to someone trustworthy, and turn his full attention to the presidency.

"As a Communist, Gorbachev would of course like the party to retain its leading role," a Soviet journalist said recently. "As a patriot, he wants the country to survive even if the party does not."

When he stands up Monday morning before a meeting of the party's fractured governing body, the Central Committee, to deliver his draft program for the party's future, Mr. Gorbachev will be at a critical juncture in this transfer of power.

His party is fast losing its authority before the newer, more democratic government institutions have taken control.

Judging by early disclosures from the party's liberal faction, Mr. Gorbachev is prepared to push through several changes that the hard-liners have long resisted.

A working draft of his proposed platform would give the party's blessing to abolishing Article 6 of the Soviet constitution, which guarantees the party's monopoly. It would accept the impending reality of rival parties and open a dialogue with informal political groups.

The draft would end the party's categorical objection to private ownership of land and industry, a prohibition that has limited economic experiments to small-scale ventures.

It would relax the central control of ideology, which has made insurgents out of many alienated young party members, and would open the party itself to greater internal diversity of opinion.

Mr. Gorbachev is also under pressure to move up the date of a nationwide party congress, now scheduled for October, which would have the final word on the new party platform and would also give Mr. Gorbachev his first opportunity to induct new members into the Central Committee.

Despite the disorders that have occurred on Mr. Gorbachev's watch, few party members believe the hard-liners have a rival capable of replacing him.

He has enhanced his security by an instinct for the middle, trying to appease those who crave democracy and free markets while accommodating the resistance imbedded deep in the country's ruling structure and in the psychology of its people.

But it is increasingly clear that Mr. Gorbachev's penchant for compromise has cost him.

100,000 at Rally in Moscow Urge Democratic Changes; Crucial Party Talks Today

By Francis X. Clines

MOSCOW, FEB. 4—Throngs of Soviet citizens demonstrated their hunger for democracy today by parading 100,000 strong to the Kremlin walls to demand that the Communist Party surrender its monopoly of power over the life of this troubled nation.

Delighting in its bold cry for the political pluralism that has swept the Soviet satellites of Eastern Europe, the crowd shouted "Resign! Resign!" in chants aimed at the party's governing Central Committee.

The six-hour parade and rally in the heart of the city, the biggest unofficial demonstration in Moscow in more than 60 years, comes on the eve of a critical meeting of the Central Committee. President Mikhail S. Gorbachev is expected to use the session to take up a risky effort to persuade the entrenched party apparatus to give up its monopoly on power.

"We started the revolutionary events in Eastern Europe, and now they are finally having a reverse effect on us," exulted Solomon Dubovsky, a 67-year-old fuel engineer, happy to march and to proclaim an end to the Soviet public's widely admitted political passivity in the streets.

"Something in my soul exploded and I got up from my soft chair—we all got up from our soft chairs—because this plenum tomorrow is our last hope to bring about change," he said as he marched with the crowd. "It's a pity it took us all so long to come out because we are so passive. But today, here, we can see a historic moment."

Soviet Leaders Agree to Surrender Communist Party Monopoly on Power
By Francis X. Clines

MOSCOW, FEB. 7—The Communist Party leadership agreed today to surrender its historic monopoly of power in the Soviet Union and accept a program that recommends the creation of a Western-style presidency and cabinet system of government.

The Soviet party's governing Central Committee ended a contentious three-day meeting with a strong endorsement of President Mikhail S. Gorbachev's latest prescription for dealing with the badly ailing party and nation, including unspecified additional executive powers for the President.

Central Committee leaders, summarizing what they conceded was a storm of questions, doubts, and complaints, said the hierarchy had finally agreed to end more than seven decades of party dictatorship by accepting the possibility of political pluralism and by making "no claim for any particular role to be encoded in the constitution" for the Communists.

"Society itself will decide whether it wishes to adopt our politics," said Aleksandr N. Yakovlev, the Politburo member and Gorbachev confidant who is a leading architect of the latest Kremlin proposals to deal with the unrest that has pushed world Communism into retreat and reform.

Central Committee members repeatedly stressed that they were only recommending, not dictating, changes for possible enactment by the national parliament, thereby underlining their own shrinking role in the state's executive affairs.

These proposals would thus continue Mr. Gorbachev's attempt to channel power from the party to the government. They would, if enacted, enhance his role as president, but how fully competitive party or presidential rivals might arise, if ever, was in no way clear from the early proposal sketched after the meeting.

The 250-member committee also acceded to the view of the Gorbachev leadership that no immediate sanctions be attempted against the Lithuanian Communist Party, which has declared independence from the Soviet party in a pioneer attempt to force political pluralism onto the land.

Instead, the committee members opted for a conciliatory approach, urging the Lithuanian insurgents to reconsider their action in the face of "top to bottom" changes that are promised for the critical party congress, to be held this summer.

The meeting also appeared to hedge on a crucial economic issue and reject proposals from some of the more radical delegates for a clear repeal of the party's standing opposition to private property.

Mr. Gorbachev once again displayed whip-hand success with the badly demoralized and increasingly unpopular party, but the meeting ended today with no purge of Mr. Gorbachev's remaining critics from the hierarchy.

Amid the party's general anxiety, these hard-liners were warning that there was no guarantee of success in Mr. Gorbachev's rapid-fire attempts to ignite national renewal. But despite all the anger and contention at the meeting, Mr. Yakovlev portrayed the Central Committee's solid center majority as being firmly with Mr. Gorbachev.

Some speakers warned that chaos and anarchy awaited the nation should the party fight the peoples' wish for pluralism. "Either we prove able to lead a rapid but controlled process of transformation or it will become an uncontrolled deluge," Vadim A. Medvedev, the party's ideology chief, told the meeting.

"It was not just a series of friendly embraces," Mr. Yakovlev said of the meeting at which the party leaders conceded that they had best retreat from their guaranteed power monopoly, seized by the Bolsheviks seven decades ago and first encoded in the constitution of 1936.

"It would be very strange if after seventy years of silence all of us would begin talking in a single voice," he said of the impassioned session.

Party Maps Plan to Give Gorbachev Broader Powers
By Bill Keller

MOSCOW, FEB. 8—The Communist Party leadership has mapped out a strategy to endow Mikhail S. Gorbachev with broad new presidential powers, probably without forcing him to undergo a popular election, party officials said today.

One day after the party's governing Central Committee agreed to forfeit the Communist legal monopoly, officials said the moves to consolidate Mr. Gorbachev's government powers could be enacted by a special parliamentary session in a matter of months.

In a draft Communist platform approved on Wednesday that opened the way for multiparty politics, the party leadership called for establishing something resembling a Western-style presidential government with a strong executive and separation of powers.

Ivan T. Frolov, editor in chief of *Pravda* and a Gorbachev confidant, indicated today that the party hopes to have Mr. Gorbachev named to the enhanced post without facing a general election. But that idea is likely to face resistance from some legislators who already worry about too much power being concentrated in the hands of one unelected man.

While party leaders touted the Central Committee meeting as a big advance for Mr. Gorbachev's *perestroika* program, insurgents in the Communist Party said today that the new platform did not go far enough toward democracy. They said that a formal split of the party seemed unavoidable.

Members of one party faction, including Yuri N. Afanasyev, the historian, announced plans to meet this weekend to consider whether to break off and form their own party or to focus their energies on a Communist Party congress scheduled for the summer.

Critics said the platform was too vague about the legalization of new political parties, that it failed to assure the removal of party domination of the army and the police, and that it fell short of opening the party to internal, grass-roots democracy.

Boris N. Yeltsin, the unorthodox Communist who cast the only vote against the platform in the 249-member Central Committee, told the Associated Press today that the platform was "a half-step forward" that would relieve tension until the summer congress.

But he said he would favor the creation of a breakaway party if the congress failed to expel hard-liners and adopt a more far-reaching program.

Weighed down by domestic politics, Gorbachev was also quick to seize a critical role in determining the shape of a new Europe.

Kohl Says Moscow Agrees Unity Issue
By Craig R. Whitney

MOSCOW, FEB. 10—Chancellor Helmut Kohl of West Germany said today that he and President Mikhail S. Gorbachev of the Soviet Union had agreed that it was "the right of the German people alone to decide whether to live together in one state."

But Mr. Gorbachev's comments on German self-determination were not unqualified. After three hours of talks with Mr. Gorbachev in the Kremlin, Mr. Kohl quoted him as saying the Germans should take the security interests of "our neighbors, friends, and partners in Europe and the world" into account.

Soviet officials said foremost among their concerns was that German unification not put the postwar European boundaries in question. That left open the possibility of extended discussions to insure that the various interests are taken into account.

"General Secretary Gorbachev assured me unmistakably that the Soviet Union would respect the right of the German people to decide to live in one state, and that it is a matter for the Germans to determine the time and the method," Mr. Kohl said at a late-night news conference.

"The German question can be solved only on the basis of reality," he said. "That is, it must be embedded in the architecture of all Europe. We must take into account the legitimate interests of our neighbors, friends, and partners in Europe and the world."

Today's comments suggested that Moscow has now agreed to let talks on German reunification go ahead. A plan for unification is to be considered at a 35-nation East-West summit meeting this fall.

Shortly after the Berlin wall was opened on November 9, Mr. Gorbachev said the question of German reunification was "not on the agenda." Since then, the accelerating collapse of authority in East Germany has apparently forced Soviet leaders to revise their view and accept reunification as something they must quickly help to shape.

Last week, Mr. Gorbachev first indicated acceptance of the idea by endorsing the plan of the East German Prime Minister, Hans Modrow, who called for a unified, demilitarized, neutral state to be achieved in stages.

Mr. Kohl and his Foreign Minister, Hans-Dietrich Genscher, said that they expected an accelerated round of consultations between East and West Germany, and between the two Germanys and their allies, from now until next fall, when the 35-nation summit meeting of the Conference of Security and Cooperation in Europe can discuss the question of German unity.

Gennadi I. Gerasimov, the Soviet Foreign Ministry spokesman, said that in the talks "various frameworks were considered for possible reunification," but he did not indicate if the Soviets had agreed to any one of them.

"President Gorbachev and Chancellor Kohl reached understanding on the point that the future of Germany is not only the business of Germany," he said, "but also that of its neighbors." He said the people of Europe "should have a guarantee that no threat of war will emanate from German soil."

With unification taking shape more rapidly than anyone predicted, the main Soviet concerns are security and the inviolability of the postwar European borders.

"This is the question of questions," the Soviet Foreign Minister, Eduard A. Shevardnadze, said earlier this morning.

Moscow Accepts U.S. Advantage of 30,000 Soldiers Across Europe
By Thomas L. Friedman

OTTAWA, FEB. 13—The Soviet Union abandoned its demand for equal American and Soviet troop levels in Europe today and accepted President Bush's proposal that the United States be allowed to maintain a 30,000-soldier advantage.

The Soviet concession came four days after President Mikhail S. Gorbachev told Secretary of State James A. Baker 3d during talks in Moscow that he would not accept a troop proposal by President Bush. Mr. Bush's plan called for the superpowers to reduce their troops in Central Europe to 195,000 each, but urged that the United States be allowed to maintain an additional 30,000 men on the periphery of Europe, in England, Portugal, Spain, Greece, and Turkey.

The Soviet decision to back down was delivered to Mr. Baker late this afternoon in talks with Foreign Minister Eduard A. Shevardnadze. Both were in Ottawa for NATO and Warsaw Pact negotiations on an "open skies" treaty, which would allow Eastern and Western countries to conduct surveillance flights over each other's territory.

In announcing the troop accord, the Canadian State Secretary for External Affairs, Joe Clark, who is officiating at the talks, said, "the agreement on manpower overcomes one of the most important obstacles" to a treaty reducing conventional forces in Europe "and provides additional impetus to reach an agreement this year."

The Soviet concession was as important politically as it was militarily. Arms control agreements are usually based on parity, be it in troops, tanks, aircraft, or nuclear weapons. But on the troop question, President Bush deliberately outlined his proposal, included in his State of the Union Message on January 31, to give the United States a slight advantage. That was intended to underscore the American view that while the Soviet forces in Europe are there by occupation, the American troops are there by invitation.

The fact that the Soviets have accepted an asymmetrical arrangement is a virtual admission that their forces are an army of occupation.

The decision also amounts to a tacit acceptance that with all the changes in Eastern Europe in the last year, Moscow simply cannot maintain equal levels with the Americans, even if it wants to. Poland, Hungary, and Czechoslovakia have already asked the Soviets to remove their forces, roughly 560,000 men in all of Eastern Europe.

The largest share of Soviet troops, about 350,000 men, are based in East Germany. With East and West Germany moving closer to unification, as agreed here today, Moscow apparently recognized that in the coming years its troop presence there may be in jeopardy.

Some analysts believe that Mr. Gorbachev may have decided that it would look better for him to cover his inevitable troop withdrawals from Europe with an apparently orderly agreement with the United States, rather than be forced into a series of unilateral pullbacks that would only make him look weak at home.

Inside the Soviet Union, issues of self-determination were still simmering.

Once-Docile Azerbaijani City Bridles Under the Kremlin's Grip
By Bill Keller

BAKU, U.S.S.R., FEB. 16—Four weeks after troops swarmed into this seaside city to suppress a nationalist uprising, the most popular excursion for classes at local schools is the hilltop park where the city has buried its dead.

Each day the schoolchildren come by the busload from around the Republic of Azerbaijan to study the row of graves heaped with red carnations, to honor those who died under Soviet tanks and gunfire, and to absorb new lessons about their country.

"The soldiers came and killed them," said Ali, a 10-year-old boy from School No. 27 in the nearby industrial center of Sumgait. "They wanted our Azerbaijanis to die. Because they said we were savages."

"Gorbachev is to blame," added his 13-year-old schoolmate, a soft-spoken girl named Rukhangiz. Teachers and children murmured their agreement. As if reciting a lesson, she added: "It will not happen again. The blood of the victims will not remain on the earth. Those who did it will pay for it."

The acute mourning is over and a veneer of normalcy prevails in Baku, which was reopened to foreign reporters two weeks ago for the first time since mid-January. Stores are open. Buses are running. The soldiers who occupy the city keep a low profile.

But since the taking of Baku, a resentful loathing of Moscow and of President Mikhail S. Gorbachev has penetrated the culture of Azerbaijan, completing the alienation of this once docile colony.

"I do not believe in the party any longer," declared Niyar Nezarova, 16 years old, the leader of her eleventh-grade Communist youth league at Baku School No. 83.

"Nobody does," her classmates say, chiming in.

"The party cannot lead our people," the girl continued, her light brown eyes blazing with the fervor of a convert. "The party led us to this tragedy."

An inattentive tourist could travel through Baku without realizing it is a city under armed occupation, a city recently visited by great violence.

In daylight the 17,000 troops assigned to enforce the state of emergency keep largely to the outskirts or to their temporary barracks in high schools and sporting clubs.

Four armored personnel carriers hold the corners of Freedom Square, formerly Lenin Square, where tens of thousands used to meet in protests organized by the Popular Front of Azerbaijan.

Five-man foot patrols armed with automatic rifles are seen occasionally in the central residential neighborhoods. Troops have secured strategic buildings like the television studio, power plant, and party headquarters.

Lieut. Gen. Vladimir S. Dubinyak, the military commandant of Baku, said his early optimism about removing the troops by mid-February has given way to a gloomier outlook. He now indicates that the troops will not leave until a "normal working rhythm" has been restored, meaning some easing of the strikes that have paralyzed much of the city's industry.

Newspapers, except for those published by the popular front, have resumed publication.

Television broadcasts have been restored after a long blackout brought by a mysterious explosion at the central transmitting station.

The local programming ends each night with a uniformed colonel of the Interior Ministry reading the day's report of incidents, along with the commandant's appeal for order.

Black flags are draped from some buildings, and some cars fly black strips of cloth from their antennas. Red carnations carpet the places where bodies were found after the sun came up January 20.

The Armenian Orthodox Church, whose congregation has been depleted over the past two years by an emigration based on fear, is now a charred ruin. A neighbor said firefighters and the police watched without intervening as vandals destroyed the building at the beginning of the year.

The walls are daubed with profanities directed at Mr. Gorbachev and

Russian soldiers. By the back and side doors someone has painted the words "Pay Toilet."

Baku has developed a whole set of social rituals around the "January events."

Photographs circulate in the city, reinforcing the sense of grievance. They show the bullet-riddled bodies of bare-chested Azerbaijani men laid out on a hospital floor, an ambulance crushed by tanks, a bus strafed by machine-gun fire.

In his apartment in the city center, one middle-class resident flipped through a stack of videotapes, offering a visitor a choice of carnage, interviews with anguished witnesses, or highlights from the Azerbaijani parliament during the months of political confrontation between the popular front and the Communist Party.

Every day thousands of people stream past the hilltop grave site. Women press handkerchiefs to their faces, and an occasional wail interrupts the Islamic prayers for the dead from a public address system.

Last Tuesday the seventy-seventh body was buried in the park, an Azerbaijani man who had been shot through the throat and lingered in a hospital for 26 days. The official death count has crept up to 142, including 35 servicemen.

A self-appointed burial committee directs traffic and maintains authority in the style of vigilantes. An Azerbaijani who accompanied a foreign reporter to the spot was stopped and interrogated, suspected as a K.G.B. agent.

"Please notice that we have not only Azerbaijanis buried here, but Russians, Jews, Tatars," said Gudrat Adbulsalim-Zadeh, an economist and chairman of the committee. "Gorbachev talks about Islamic fundamentalists. What nonsense. If we were Islamic fundamentalists, would we allow our dead to be buried alongside Jews and Russian Orthodox?"

Despite visits from high-ranking industrial officials from Moscow and the arrests of strike organizers, much of the city's industry has been stopped for a month.

At the Montin oil-drilling equipment factory, in the smokestack region of Baku aptly named Chorny Gorod—"Black City"—the 1,200 workers walked off the job January 17 when troops began to take positions outside the city.

Counting earlier walkouts organized by the popular front, the factory has been idle nearly two months in the last six.

Isa Aliyev, chairman of the factory trade union committee, said workers have vowed to remain off the job until the troops leave Baku and popular front members are released from jail.

He said the workers live on their savings and on food donations from sympathizers.

Lithuanians Vote Strongly for Independence Backers; Soviet Crowds Ask Change

By Bill Keller

MOSCOW, FEB. 25—The Communist establishment suffered a double blow today as protesters across the country thronged the streets in a defiant call for a share of power while one republic, Lithuania, voted to end Communist rule.

In at least 20 cities from the Baltic Sea to the Sea of Japan citizens braved an official scare campaign, registering their impatience and anger with President Mikhail S. Gorbachev's pace of change through quiet demonstrations.

The peaceful rallies, the first nationwide independent show of strength by the country's prodemocracy opposition, were held to promote insurgent candidates in next Sunday's elections for control of the three largest Soviet republics—Russia, the Ukraine, and Byelorussia—and to demand an Eastern European–style round table with the Kremlin on a transfer of power from the Communists.

Lithuania held its vote on Saturday, the first multiparty contest in the Soviet Union since just after the Bolshevik Revolution. As expected, the voters soundly rejected the Communists and a gave the Lithuanian parliament a strong mandate for independence from the Soviet Union.

Sajudis, the Lithuanian independence movement, swept 72 of the 90 seats decided in the new 141-seat parliament. Sajudis candidates are expected to win more seats in runoff elections scheduled for March 10 in the 51 districts where no candidate received a majority of the vote.

The 72 seats are enough to guarantee a majority in the Baltic state's new parliament. The Sajudis slate was a mix of prosecession Communists, independents, and newly legalized Social Democratic, Christian Democratic, and Green parties.

Only 29 of the winners were Communist Party members. Of those, only seven belonged to the loyalist group that pledged allegiance to Moscow.

The Communist Party has not given up its legal monopoly in the rest of the country, but the party regulars face challenges from nonparty members and Communist insurgents, many of them fighting uphill races against machine tactics and news blackouts.

Voters also went to the polls in the Moldavian republic, where the first free elections under Soviet rule were expected to benefit another front seeking autonomy from Moscow. No results were available today.

The protest rallies across the Soviet heartland may prove to be an even greater humiliation to the Communist Party than the loss of Lithuania, because the authorities used everything from warnings of bloodshed to an appeal by the Russian Orthodox Church to keep people at home.

The scare tactics surely reduced the turnout, but in Moscow, at least, they left many residents wondering, What is this opposition that has Mr. Gorbachev so frightened?

AUTHORITIES: YOU DON'T FRIGHTEN US; YOU'RE JUST FRIGHTENING YOURSELVES was the message an elderly protester scrawled on cardboard and wore around her neck as she moved through a crowd that was predominantly mainstream and middle-aged.

Judging from photographs made from above, about 50,000 people jammed into a stretch of Moscow's broad garden ring road, although the police claimed that twice that number turned out, and organizers inflated the figure by several times.

Soviet press agencies reported crowds ranging from a few hundred in Tashkent, the capital of Uzbekistan, where the rally was banned, to tens of thousands in Minsk, the Byelorussian capital. Major cities in most regions of the Slavic vastness reported preelection gatherings in the thousands.

In Moscow, the attitude toward Mr. Gorbachev in the speeches and crowd remarks varied from disappointment to bitterness. Participants scorned the Soviet leader as a halfhearted reformer, as a captive of a Stalinist system, and as out of touch or hungry for power.

"Oh, I am so sick of him," said Tamara N. Zveryeva, a pensioner, when asked about Mr. Gorbachev's proposal to fashion himself a more powerful presidency. Wordy and arrogant was her verdict.

Then she relented a bit and added: "We have to admit it is tough for him. He took on all this himself, and he is still the only Communist leader we can trust."

The main purpose of the rally today was to tout candidates for the Russian parliament who have been endorsed by a makeshift alliance of prodemocracy groups inside and outside of the party.

But hostility to the Communist Party was unusually open, in some of the speeches and in placards waved above the crowd. C.P.S.U., NUREMBERG AWAITS YOU, said one. CORRUPTION AND THE PARTY ARE TWIN BROTHERS, said another.

The only party functionary who dared to climb aboard the podium, placed in the bed of a truck, was the ideologically ambiguous Communist chief for the Sevastopol neighborhood of Moscow. He was booed and heckled.

Sergei Kuznetsov, a dissident journalist released last month from a jail in Sverdlovsk, delivered one of the angriest speeches, denouncing Lenin as a "totalitarian" and Mr. Gorbachev as his heir.

"What can we expect from a round table between democratic forces and a criminal government?" he asked, to loud applause.

Other candidates called on the Communist Party apparatus at all levels to step down.

The attendance here was noticeably smaller than at a similar rally outside the Kremlin walls three weeks ago, but that event was officially encouraged as a warning to hard-liners on the eve of an important gathering of the Communist leadership.

This time, although the marchers got a last-minute permit from the city, the authorities pulled out all stops to frighten the public into staying away.

Schoolteachers warned children to stay indoors, nurses at Moscow hospitals were told to brace for injuries, and in many workplaces employers hinted that the day would be a violent one.

Official television and newspapers publicized appeals for calm from the Communist Party, the Council of Ministers, the parliament, the police, and the artistic unions, but refused to give the demonstration's organizers a chance to explain their purpose.

Circulars distributed anonymously in Moscow, and repeated as rumors by some Communist Party officials, warned that the opposition planned to seize power by force. Saturday night's main television news program featured a senior prelate of the Russian Orthodox Church, who invited "believers and nonbelievers" alike to begin an Easter fast today.

"On fast days," the prelate, Metropolitan Pitirim, an official favorite, solemnly intoned, "we try to go outside as little as possible. We go to church or stay home in front of the icon."

Gorbachev Sees Havel and Agrees to Speed Withdrawal of Troops
By Francis X. Clines

MOSCOW, FEB. 26—The Czechoslovak President, Vaclav Havel, and the Soviet President, Mikhail S. Gorbachev, agreed today on a faster timetable for the Soviet troop withdrawal from Czechoslovakia as well as an end to cold war intelligence cooperation directed against Western nations.

The treaties were announced by the two governments as Mr. Havel, a playwright and outspoken anti-Communist, sardonically commented that Czechoslovak railroad workers would see the Soviet troops to the border for nothing.

Under the timetable signed by Foreign Ministry officials from the two nations, all 73,500 Soviet troops are to be gone by July 1, 1991, 23 years after the Kremlin used a Warsaw Pact invasion to crush liberalization in Czechoslovakia. The first Soviet troops and tanks have begun their pullout from Frenstat pod Radhostem and Krnov, on the Czechoslovak border with Poland, the Associated Press reported.

"Mr. Gorbachev and I agreed that the best way to deal with the dark pages of our past is to look forward," the Czechoslovak leader said at a news conference this evening after private talks with the Soviet President.

Gorbachev Forces Bill on Presidency Past Legislature
By Francis X. Clines

MOSCOW, FEB. 27—Under fierce prodding from President Mikhail S. Gorbachev, the Supreme Soviet gave initial approval today to his proposal to secure greater executive powers through the institution of a popularly elected presidency.

In an angry, intense session that culminated in a virtuoso display of Mr. Gorbachev's power to dominate the legislative process, the Supreme Soviet, the standing parliament, yielded to the hard-driving leader and sent the emergency proposal on to the Congress making a law.

"Calm down, calm down, calm down," Mr. Gorbachev said, glaring around the Kremlin hall as he took over the microphone for a long, obviously heartfelt denunciation of the chamber's nascent opposition minority and its often stinging criticism of the proposal.

"Life itself dictates quick action on this matter," he said, closing off debate in a chairman's fiat that soon produced a vote of 306 to 65 to send the proposal on to the 2,250-member Congress of People's Deputies, the final step in the legislative process. Mr. Gorbachev scheduled an emergency session of the Congress for March 12 and 13.

Moscow's Maverick with a Purpose
By Francis X. Clines

MOSCOW, MARCH 2—Boris N. Yeltsin, the virtuoso in the evolving Communist art of campaigning against Communism, is in the thick of it again with a bold election stratagem to craft a shadow presidency for himself, the better to challenge the nation's President, Mikhail S. Gorbachev.

Mr. Yeltsin, the former Moscow party chief who has become a leader of the Soviet parliament's opposition, has been roaming the troubled heart of this nation, the Russian republic, campaigning for near-certain victory on Sunday as a candidate for the republic's parliament.

He hopes to use this as a springboard to be chosen as republic president and chief executive of what he intends to turn into a showcase alternative to Mr. Gorbachev's foundering plan of national renewal.

"This is a chance to form a core of legislators with a better, far different, more progressive outlook directed at the deeper life of Russia," said the ubiquitous politician, who has been pioneering a Western political touch, using his much-sought coattail power to travel around the republic and be photographed with like-minded candidates for their campaign pamphlets.

Delighted, he slaps his palm to symbolize the insurgents' collective handbill and pantomimes pasting the challenge squarely on a campaign wall, beaming as if at the Kremlin wall: Yeltsin redux.

"I am undergoing personal *perestroika*," he declared with impish ebullience, appropriating Mr. Gorbachev's patented buzzword for change to describe his chesslike move at jumping from Moscow, where he is currently a deputy in the national parliament, and challenging Mr. Gorbachev obliquely from the grassroots.

Mr. Yeltsin is perhaps the best-known candidate in the elections on Sunday, when the most populous republics—Russia, Byelorussia, and the Ukraine—vote for local officeholders and members of republic parliaments.

Mr. Yeltsin's choice is impressive, for Russia contains three-quarters of the land and almost half the population of the Soviet Union. It also includes more than a fair share of popular unrest over the failed economy and national anxiety over sagging morale.

And his timing seems impeccable, for the change of Soviet politics begun by Mr. Gorbachev is fast coming to focus on a struggle for power between the traditional fortress, the central government, and the separate republics epitomized by Russia, newly awakening to promises of some autonomy.

Mr. Gorbachev himself has provided a new flashpoint for this issue by demanding the emergency creation of a popularly elected national presidency with greatly increased executive powers, a role tailored to his strategy of shifting his seat of power from the party to the government.

Mr. Gorbachev hurriedly moved the measure establishing this proposed presidency through the Supreme Soviet standing legislature this week. But the plan is being denounced by opposition critics, led by Mr. Yeltsin, as a betrayal of *perestroika*'s promise of balanced self-government.

"We must make Russia and all the republics more independent and at the same time give the center government a good push to become more progressive," said Mr. Yeltsin, an avid politician who garnered daredevil fame in 1987 by being cast from the ruling Politburo for criticizing the party establishment, a role he has since honed into an open challenge of his onetime mentor, Mr. Gorbachev.

"The critical mass is growing," said Mr. Yeltsin, who started his move from his old power base in Sverdlovsk, at the nation's working backbone in the Urals, where he first rose from factory worker to party prodigy.

His strategy is to bring enough insurgents into the Russian parliament to stop the central party's anti-Yeltsin campaign there and guarantee his success in the deputies' election of one of their members as republic president.

"It's not that I need a higher post," protested Mr. Yeltsin, looking delighted after a day at his current job as the unofficial opposition leader in the National Congress of People's Deputies.

It was a day in which Mr. Gorbachev could not resist criticizing his chief antagonist by name for suggesting that some of the nation's many scattered, dispirited Russians, increasingly criticized in other ethnic republics, might want to come home to Mother Russia to create progressive new cities.

"So far Mr. Gorbachev cannot easily pronounce the word 'opposition,' " Mr. Yeltsin said of the Soviet leader's thin-skinned performance in pushing the presidency bill to initial passage. In that confrontation, Mr. Gorbachev dismissed the minority opposition as "demagogues" for having questioned his devotion to power sharing.

"He is getting very nervous," said Mr. Yeltsin, who feels that Mr. Gorbachev's pride is getting in the way of democratization. "I can read between the lines."

The outlook is that Mr. Gorbachev will win approval of his enhanced presidency by mid-March, although Mr. Yeltsin is among those who argue that the alarmed dissenters in the 2,250-member national congress might prove large enough to stop Mr. Gorbachev short of the 1,500 votes he needs.

If the Soviet leader prevails as usual, Mr. Yeltsin sounds hardly at a strategic loss. He is pointing to the "last chance" roundup for the Communist Party to reform itself and renounce its power monopoly in June at the critical party congress.

And should that fall short? "Then the party splits," said Mr. Yeltsin with a calmness resembling the sweet anticipation of a man who expects to be a kind of president-in-waiting by then.

In Moscow it looked like disintegration, but in Vilnius the sense that prevailed was of creation and rebirth.

Parliament in Lithuania, 124–0, Declares Nation Independent

By Bill Keller

VILNIUS, LITHUANIA, MARCH 11—Lithuania tonight proclaimed itself a sovereign state, legally free of the Soviet Union, and named the leaders of a non-Communist government to negotiate their future relations with Moscow.

The Lithuanian parliament voted 124 to 0, with nine abstentions and absentees, to restore the independent statehood ended by Soviet annexation 50 years ago. The Lithuanian Communist Party, which won only a minority of seats in parliamentary elections last month, joined the non-Communist majority in the vote and in an outburst of songs and embraces that followed.

"Expressing the will of the people, the Supreme Soviet of the Lithuanian Republic declares and solemnly proclaims the restoration of the exercise of sovereign powers of the Lithuanian state, which were annulled by an alien power in 1940," said a resolution passed late tonight. "From now on, Lithuania is once again an independent state."

It was not immediately clear what the full implications of the Lithuanian action were. According to Lithuanian leaders, Mikhail S. Gorbachev, the Soviet President, has indicated a willingness to negotiate the conditions of independence. But there was no immediate reaction to the declaration of independence either from Mr. Gorbachev or the Soviet government.

Tass, the Soviet press agency, issued a factual report of the Lithuanian action without comment. Reports on national television were similar.

Hundreds of Lithuanians gathered outside the parliament building, singing national hymns and chanting independence slogans, as the legislators changed the name of the Lithuanian Soviet Socialist Republic to simply the Lithuanian Republic and ordered the hammer and sickle replaced by the old Lithuanian coat of arms.

At one point, people in the crowd outside used screwdrivers to pry the copper Soviet insignia from the front of the building, to a roar of approval.

But behind the united front, many legislators and ordinary citizens voiced deep worry about how Moscow would respond to this precedent-setting breach in the union. The most common fear was a wave of economic reprisals that could produce fuel shortages and unemployment, threatening the state with chaos.

Other legislators worried that such a dramatic act of defiance, especially on the eve of an important Soviet congressional gathering, would weaken President Gorbachev, who has so far generally acquiesced to Lithuania's drive for freedom.

Before approving the law completing the political break with Moscow, the parliament elected as Lithuania's new president Vytautas Landsbergis, a soft-spoken music professor who led the proindependence movement called Sajudis from an eclectic band of dissidents to a legislative majority.

By a vote of 91 to 38, the Sajudis-dominated legislature elected Mr. Landsbergis over Algirdas Brazauskas, the Lithuanian Communist Party leader, whose personal popularity has soared since his party broke with the Soviet Communist Party in December, but not enough to overcome the Communists' association with decades of occupation.

Mr. Landsbergis urged the 3.7 million citizens of the republic to be calm and united as they enter a period of tense negotiations aimed at persuading Moscow to treat them as a friendly neighbor. On Monday the parliament is to consider an appeal to Mr. Gorbachev asking for withdrawal of the more than 30,000 Soviet troops based in Lithuania and the speedy repatriation of Lithuanian men serving in the Soviet army.

"We cannot ignore the interests of our neighbors, particularly our neighbors to the east," the new Lithuanian president said. "But we will not be asking for permission to take this or that step."

Though there was no official reaction from the Kremlin, members of the parliamentary opposition in Moscow sent a message of congratulations, and Sergei Kovalyov, a human rights advocate and former political prisoner recently elected to the Russian republic's parliament, came here to applaud Lithuania's move.

"A lot of Russians will say, 'We liberated you from the Germans; we helped you industrialize,' " Mr. Kovalyov said in a brief address to the parliament. "None of them will say that we deported half of the Lithuanian people to Siberia."

The decision in Vilnius led to a period of extended crisis. A day after the vote President Gorbachev called the move "an alarming step." A day after that he termed it "illegitimate and invalid." By the end of March, a military convoy of more than 100 tanks was pointedly sent into Lithuania. Over the next few months the skirmish over independence was to follow a zigzag course with the Lithuanians first counting heavily on pressure from abroad to win their demands and then backing off just a bit on their timetable. At the same time Gorbachev, ever mindful of how the withdrawal of Lithuania or its Baltic neighbors could enflame nationalist aspirations all through the Soviet Union, kept insisting on a slow, orderly, and measured pace.

Parliament Votes Expanded Powers for Soviet Leader

By Francis X. Clines

MOSCOW, MARCH 13—The full Soviet parliament voted overwhelmingly today in favor of Mikhail S. Gorbachev's plan for a strong presidency and ended the Communist Party's seven-decade monopoly of political power in the Soviet Union.

The decisions opened the way for a popularly elected chief executive eventually, although the first person to hold the new post will be chosen by parliament, probably later in the week, and is likely to be Mr. Gorbachev. Some legislators, however, upset at some of Mr. Gorbachev's parliamentary tactics, threatened to try to block his election.

The presidency bill was approved by a vote of 1,817 to 133, with 61 abstentions. Much of the opposition bloc in the Congress of People's Deputies, the parliament, was won over by concessions by Mr. Gorbachev. The opposition had demanded that the Soviet leader's new powers be more limited and subject to oversight.

The overnight concessions apparently eased many of the doubts expressed previously by critics concerned that the new presidency might usher in a new dictatorship.

The changes came in a long day of political bargaining and fencing.

"This decision is the most significant in the history of our government," Mr. Gorbachev said in steering the presidency bill through the Congress. Mr. Gorbachev is chairman of the Supreme Soviet, the standing legislature, and has been called "president" to indicate his duties.

"This is an important and powerful step on the road to democracy," Mr. Gorbachev declared.

In the past, power in the Soviet Union was controlled by the party, in particular the general secretary, the ruling Politburo, and the Central Committee. Under Mr. Gorbachev—who is also general secretary, or head of the party, and a member of the Politburo—power gradually has been transferred from the party to the government. Today's actions further reduce the influence of the party oligarchy.

"Our Congress, our Supreme Soviet, became really stronger today," said Sergei B. Stankevich, a leader of the opposition group that succeeded in amending the sweeping executive emergency powers to make the presidency more palatable to the Congress.

By nightfall, however, the opposition was outraged at Mr. Gorbachev's autocratic parliamentary procedures and promised a fight Wednesday to stop the remaining important measure sought by the Soviet leader, the transitional appointment to the presidency's initial five-year term.

Mr. Gorbachev reversed normal legislative procedures, winning overall approval of the presidency bill before allowing votes on amendments to further qualify the presidential powers.

Just as the changes today were voted by the parliament, so they could be revoked by a future parliament.

The vote on repealing the constitutional guarantee of the Communists' power monopoly, encompassed in Article 6 of the constitution, was accomplished with barely a complaint from the congressional majority, many of them party careerists loyally following Mr. Gorbachev's prescription for reviving civic spirit and the economy.

The repeal of Article 6 was approved 1,771 to 264, with 74 abstentions. An anti-Communist mood quickly spread among Congress insurgents, who sought without success to offer further amendments to begin rooting out the Communist authorities across the breadth of Soviet institutions.

"Everything is in flux," said Yegor K. Ligachev, once considered the hard-liner in the Politburo devoted to braking Mr. Gorbachev's early democratization moves. "Everything is changing, and pretty quickly, too. We're politicians. We have to take reality into account. But as I see it, this will only rouse us to work even more effectively."

As finally amended, the constitutional amendment establishing the presidency gives the president the power to declare martial and civil emergencies, although this is subject to notification of the troubled locality and oversight by the Supreme Soviet, whose members are chosen from the ranks of the Congress of People's Deputies. Insurgents said they also qualified the post's additional power to issue executive orders by specifying that such power was subject to existing constitutional law.

The president's veto power was also reduced so that once the Supreme Soviet votes an override by a two-thirds vote, the president could not further appeal to the Congress of People's Deputies. In addition, the Committee of Constitutional Control, whose powers include recommending presidential impeachment, would be appointed by the chairman of the Supreme Soviet rather than the president.

The main advantages in the new presidency are to free Mr. Gorbachev of power struggles with the party, eventually provide him the strength of a popular mandate, and afford "working space," said Roy A. Medvedev, a Congress member who is an independent.

"This is the first time we're introducing a presidential form of government, and we can't know in advance how it will function," Mr. Medvedev said.

Soviet Insurgents Voted into Power in the 3 Main Cities

By Francis X. Clines

MOSCOW, MARCH 19—The emerging political opposition scored a series of triumphs across the Soviet Union in election results released today, winning majorities over the Communists in the Moscow, Leningrad, and Kiev city councils and electing significant numbers of insurgents in republic parliaments.

Early results from the latest local and republic elections showed that the fledgling opposition movement received a large-scale vote of confidence on Sunday from Soviet voters intent on registering their displeasure with seven decades of Communist Party domination in their communities.

Nationalist opposition movements continued to make progress in Estonia and Latvia, where separatist candidates did well, and in the Ukraine. There, the Ruk grass-roots political movement scored majority victories in Lvov and in Kiev—the Ukrainian capital and third-largest Soviet city—and claimed a sizable bloc in the republic's next parliament.

Insurgents are planning early tests of their newly won power in light of the results, in which the Communist Party suffered the embarrassment of losing majorities in the country's three main cities.

In Moscow, Interfax, a press agency of Radio Moscow, said insurgents won 281 of the 498 seats in the city council. Opposition leaders in the capital plan to pass laws that would take control of local television and one of the city's newspapers from the long-entrenched Communist patronage machine.

The outcome of such challenges is far from certain, but leaders of the opposition say a grass-roots stratagem must be pursued issue by issue and job by job if the Communist monopoly on power is ever to be truly broken.

Ilya I. Zaslavsky, a leading strategist in the insurgents' Moscow victory, appears ready for that challenge in turning the 498-member city council into an instrument for change. Among the initial issues he and other leaders of the grass-roots opposition plan to settle are whom the new majority might try to name as the city's mayor. No candidates were immediately mentioned as Moscow dissidents celebrated their victory.

The Soviet parliament has repealed the constitutional requirement that the Communist Party have a monopoly role, leaving the opposition the formidable task of defining itself and building power bases in a country whose campaign finances and news media remain largely party controlled.

The voting on Sunday was for thousands of local and republic posts in the Russian republic, the Ukraine, and Byelorussia, three republics where runoff votes were needed, and in Latvia and Estonia, where the first round of local elections was held.

Among the most closely watched opposition tactics was the one pursued by Boris N. Yeltsin, the onetime Politburo ally of President Mikhail S. Gorbachev who survived a party purge to become one of the country's best-known insurgent leaders.

Mr. Yeltsin, pursuing his own grass-roots opposition strategy, won a seat two weeks ago in the Russian republic's parliament, preparatory to trying to win majority endorsement in the new parliament as president of the republic, a prime showcase in which to further develop his anti-Gorbachev image.

Election results gave no firm indication of the parliamentary voting in the Russian republic that would show Mr. Yeltsin's chances, although insurgent candidates were reportedly doing well.

Long-entrenched Communists suffered some of their most stinging defeats in Leningrad, the nation's second city. Dissidents there grouped under the insurgent opposition umbrella called Democratic Elections '90 took 54 percent of the city council seats and 80 percent of the city's seats in the republic parliament, according to various reports, including one from the official Tass press agency.

The mayor of Leningrad, Vladimir Y. Khodyrev, survived on the city council only by arranging to run in a weakly contested outlying neighborhood.

In Byelorussia, insurgents directly defeated key party leaders in council races in Minsk, the republic's capital, the government newspaper, *Izvestia,* reported.

In Kiev, candidates backed by the nationalist Ruk took control of the city council with more than half the seats, and made strong gains in the Ukrainian parliament, Reuters reported, adding that the Ukrainian Communist Party leader, Vladimir A. Ivashko, was elected to parliament.

In Lithuania tanks arrived, and the mounting tension was conveyed in a succession of headlines.

Moscow's Forces Step Up Pressure Across Lithuania
By Esther B. Fein

VILNIUS, LITHUANIA, SATURDAY, MARCH 24—The Soviet authorities sent a column of tanks and paratroopers rumbling past an all-night session of the Lithuanian parliament early this morning, in what witnesses described as the strongest attempt yet to intimidate the republic into abandoning its declaration of independence.

More than 100 tanks and trucks and more than 1,500 soldiers armed with automatic weapons thundered by the parliament building in central Vilnius at about 3 A.M. as legislators worked through the night to complete the creation of an independent government.

The parliament broke off from its work to pass an emergency resolution declaring that it would transfer all authority to its representative in Washington in the event that legislators were arrested or martial law was imposed.

The column proceeded through the town, stopping at an army base inside the city limits after passing the parliament, and there were no signs that the central government was trying to take power in Lithuania, where independence was declared on March 11.

Lithuanian Aides Won't Turn Over Army's Deserters
By Esther B. Fein

VILNIUS, LITHUANIA, MARCH 24—Lithuanian officials refused today to comply with Moscow's demand to turn over hundreds of army deserters, declaring that they would not be intimidated by the Kremlin's theatrical early-morning parade of tanks and military vehicles here in the Lithuanian capital.

Lithuania's President, Vytautas Landsbergis, urged the young Lithuanian men, who fled the Soviet army after their republic proclaimed its independence on March 11, to seek refuge in churches against a surrender deadline of midnight tonight set by the Soviet military.

"We will not sacrifice our sons," said Ceslovas Stankevicius, deputy chairman of the Lithuanian parliament, defiant in the latest standoff over Lithuania's contested sovereignty. "They are citizens of a free country."

Contrary to reports on the Soviet television, Lithuania was anything but chaotic or seething with unrest today. Elections to city, county, and neighborhood councils were conducted calmly throughout the republic, with a turnout estimated at about two-thirds of the electorate.

But Mr. Landsbergis called on the United States and other Western nations to be more vocal in their support of Lithuania "in this dangerous situation," which he characterized as "psychological war."

Soviet Troops, Storming Hospital, Seize Lithuanian Army Deserters
By Francis X. Clines

VILNIUS, LITHUANIA, TUESDAY, MARCH 27—Armed Soviet troops stormed a psychiatric hospital early this morning and arrested a group of Lithuanian deserters from the army who had taken refuge there since the republic's proclamation of independence on March 11, witnesses said.

Some of the deserters were beaten as the troops routed them from the hospital, the witnesses said. Blood stained the stairway, and smashed glass and upended furniture littered the ward that had been the Lithuanians' sanctuary since late last week.

The action against the deserters followed conflicting signs from the Soviet military over the standoff in Lithuania, including the first meeting between Lithuanian leaders and military representatives on Monday.

A doctor who was present during the confrontation at the hospital estimated that about half of the 39 deserters fled down a fire escape.

Awakened at home early this morning, the Lithuanian President, Vytautas Landsbergis, said, "Now we can expect anything, that parliament will also be arrested. The Western states raised hopes that there would not be force. They can say all they want, but Gorbachev does what he wants."

Lithuania Offers to Discuss a Vote on Its Sovereignty
By Francis X. Clines

VILNIUS, LITHUANIA, MARCH 29—Leaders of this republic's embattled independence government sent a signal of compromise to the Kremlin tonight, saying they were ready to discuss the difficult issue of a referendum on secession if President Mikhail S. Gorbachev agreed to talk with them.

The Lithuanian President, Vytautas Landsbergis, conceding that the Kremlin had greeted his pleas for negotiations with a "concrete wall," appeared to be searching openly for a conciliatory note that might entice Moscow to the negotiating table.

"There are no questions that cannot be discussed except the question of Lithuanian independence," Mr. Landsbergis said at a news conference. "The problem of the referendum could also be discussed."

Moscow's Forces Seize 2 Key Sites from Lithuanians
By Francis X. Clines

MOSCOW, MARCH 30—Soviet forces took over the state prosecutor's office in the Lithuanian capital today and seized the printing plant where the republic's main independence newspapers are printed, Lithuanian officials said.

No resistance or injuries were reported in the raids by Soviet paratroopers. But the moves are the most serious so far in a week of steady harassment by Kremlin forces intent on forcing Lithuania to retreat from the declaration of independence approved on March 11 by the republic's parliament in Vilnius, the capital.

The heightened Soviet pressure on Lithuania was reported as the parliament of a neighboring Baltic republic, Estonia, mindful of the independence crisis in Lithuania, approved a slower, more deliberate path toward restoring full sovereignty. The third Baltic republic, Latvia, is expected to pursue its own independence plan next month at a parliament meeting.

The struggle over Lithuanian yearnings and maneuvers for independence dominated the news from the Soviet Union through much of the spring, with the headlines reflecting day-to-day fluctuations in tensions and hopes.

Gorbachev Offers Conditional Talks with Lithuanians (March 31)
Moscow Sends Armored Vehicles Through Tense Lithuanian Capital (April 1)
Lithuanian Leader Softens His Tone Toward Moscow (April 2)
Lithuanians Meet Gorbachev's Aide; Seek to Ease Crisis (April 3)

In the midst of the seething crisis, another summit was announced, raising the question of whether any further advances on disarmament or ending the divisions of Europe were to be linked or held hostage by the events in Lithuania.

U.S.-Soviet Summit Is Planned May 30 with Bush as Host
By Thomas L. Friedman

WASHINGTON, APRIL 5—President Bush and President Mikhail S. Gorbachev of the Soviet Union will hold a five-day meeting in the United States beginning on May 30, the White House and the Kremlin announced today.

The announcement of the summit dates is as much a political statement as a scheduling matter. The decision comes at probably the tensest moment in Soviet-American relations since President Bush took office, largely because of Washington's discomfort with the Kremlin's crackdown on the Lithuanian independence movement.

In talks in Washington over the last two days with Eduard A. Shevardnadze, the Soviet foreign minister, Secretary of State James A. Baker 3d has repeatedly emphasized that suppression of the Baltic drive for independence will seriously damage the superpower relationship.

Nonetheless, the administration appears to have determined that the Kremlin's activity in Lithuania, until now at least, does not require any delay in announcing the summit dates or in holding the meeting. The sessions are scheduled to begin on Wednesday, May 30, in Washington and end on Sunday, June 3.

"I don't have any idea about the private discussions that went on" between Mr. Baker and Mr. Shevardnadze, said the White House spokesman, Marlin Fitzwater. "But I don't think there was any anticipation that the summit would be changed on the basis of the existing situation."

The Baker-Shevardnadze talks are concentrating on overcoming obstacles to treaties limiting long-range nuclear missiles, chemical weapons, and conventional arms in Europe, as well as resolving outstanding economic and regional problems.

Both Soviet and American officials indicated today that the prospects of signing major arms-control initiatives at the meeting appeared to be dim. The meeting was initially scheduled for February. But at their meeting in Malta in December, Mr. Bush and Mr. Gorbachev stated their wish that the get-together be an occasion for signing a Strategic Arms Reduction Treaty, known as Start, or for reaching agreement on all of the accord's major provisions.

Senior American and Soviet officials, briefing reporters on today's talks, indicated that it was highly unlikely that a Strategic Arms Reduction Treaty would be ready for signing at the spring session. Whether even an agreement in principle will be completed by then also remains in doubt.

A senior administration official said that the United States might introduce an important new proposal, either for the current Start negotiations or in the discussion of principles for the proposed Start-2 treaty, which seeks to ban either all land-based multiple-warhead ballistic missiles, known as MIRVs, or those placed on trains.

Soviet officials said that introducing such a ban at this point in the Start talks was not a good idea since it might slow the negotiating process. Several prominent senators have said that Congress would not support the administration's request for both a truck-mounted, single-warhead Midgetman missile system and a rail-mounted MX multiple warhead missile system, and have been urging the White House to pursue a ban on mobile MIRVs with Moscow.

How the setting of the summit dates might affect each side's room for maneuver on the Lithuania question is uncertain.

Some analysts say it could limit Washington's ability to take a tough line with Mr. Gorbachev on Lithuania, should the situation there deteriorate. Walking away from a scheduled summit meeting would be a move without precedent in United States–Soviet relations.

In 1960, President Eisenhower planned to visit Nikita S. Khrushchev, the Soviet leader, in Moscow, but no date had been set when the meeting was canceled after an American U-2 spy plane was shot down over the Soviet Union. In 1968, President Johnson planned to see Leonid I. Brezhnev in October, but again there was no date set when Soviet forces invaded Czechoslovakia that summer, putting an end to the plans.

With the tensions in the Baltic unresolved, nationalistic sentiment was also erupting far to the south.

Soviet Georgians Rally, Demanding Independence but Revealing Disunity
By Francis X. Clines

TBILISI, U.S.S.R., APRIL 8—Tens of thousands of Soviet Georgians packed the streets of Tbilisi tonight for a mournful protest that laid bare not only the republic's increasing hunger for independence but also its badly fragmented politics.

A throng of proindependence demonstrators, including many from neighboring republics sympathetic to the Georgians' anti-Moscow fervor, swirled through the streets to commemorate the "bloody Sunday" of a year ago.

That was the dark event that became a crisis for the Kremlin when shovel-wielding Soviet troops, intent on asserting national authority, killed 19 members of a crowd of peaceful demonstrators last April 9. They doused several thousand more with toxic chemicals.

The victims were mourned tonight as heroes in a tragedy that has pushed Georgia's age-old struggle for viable autonomy to a fiery new intensity.

Its evidence was everywhere. From the statues of Lenin being torn down with impunity across this proud and earthy republic to the open, near gleeful petitioning among tonight's crowds to reject Soviet citizenship and army induction.

But apart from the memorial's unified fervor, the independence drive has been notable for its chronic disunity. The campaign is being organized by a dozen political groups, some openly feuding and each claiming to be the people's true guide to sovereignty.

Debate in the independence movement echoes with passionate denunciations of opponents as "enemies of the people," and with warnings that "neo-Bolshevism" is taking shape in false independence groups bent on keeping the republic frozen in disunity.

Compounding the bitterness is the generational rivalry in Georgian politics between older leaders, who took great pre-Gorbachev risks to protect the language, and younger, more radically spoken sons and daughters who say the Kremlin could have been pressed harder.

The infighting is over the best path to independence for this republic of 5.5 million: through the current militant refusals to recognize anything Soviet or through moderate strategems like using the new democratization to elect independence candidates to all republic seats of power.

"Now we are unified—the April 9 killings saw to that," insisted Georgi Chanturia, leader of the National Democratic Party and a power in the National Forum. This is the Georgians' latest attempt at forging an umbrella group that might unite the disparate forces.

The National Forum is in the forefront of a thus far successful boycott of all government elections for the republic's parliament. Politics has become increasingly polarized, with moderate groups like the popular front, which favors government elections, being denounced as a haven for Communists and as coopted by the Kremlin.

The National Forum is organizing ad hoc elections to be held this fall to press the independence drive in a direction that is not yet clear.

"We have great influence, and the government cannot resist us," said Zviad Gamsakhurdia, a leader of the election boycott and of the plan to vote a separate Georgian congress into being.

As head of the St. Ilya the Righteous Society, he does not say what this congress might attempt, but he insists that its moral power will force the Kremlin eventually to yield independence.

"We are witnessing the modernization of the empire, not true independence," declared Tamara Chkheidze, leader of the Ilya Chavchavadze Society, who sees no profit in boycotting parliamentary elections.

She says she suspects Mr. Gamsakhurdia and others, who have been accorded increasing access to the government-run news apparatus, of being interested in their local patronage building more than independence.

"We really should not miss this moment," Miss Chkheidze warned, foreseeing a republic in deepening disarray the longer elections are delayed.

Beyond the Georgians' own fragmented politics, there are rival eddies of separatism by such equally proud minorities as the Azerbaijanis, Abkhazians, Ossetians, and Georgian mountain people. While the world focused on the 19 deaths here, more than two dozen other lives were lost last year in Georgia's interethnic violence.

If there was one comfort tonight for the Kremlin in the specter of another republic—in this case the birthplace of Stalin—coming to the anti-Soviet boil, it was this continuing evidence of political and ethnic discord, a discord that Moscow is widely accused here of encouraging.

For the demonstration, there were no Soviet troops in evidence. There were only the locally popular police, who were tasked mainly with protecting the capital's giant statue of Lenin from being torn down. Rally leaders intent on showing the world a seriously unified Georgia stressed their view that tonight was not the night for that.

The demonstration was the latest focus in the wave of nationalism that almost daily confronts President Mikhail S. Gorbachev with fresh demands even as he tries to knit greater unity into the greatly troubled Soviet realm.

This evening, a large contingent of sympathizers from the Baltic independence campaigns marched to the scene of the deaths, outside the Council of Ministers building, bearing a sign reading U.S.S.R.: JAIL OF NATIONS. Azerbaijanis, Armenians, and others joined the flag- and flower-bearing flow of Georgians from across the republic.

"The 'red mafia' is the most terrible," said Irina Pkhovelishvili, a woman dressed in black, mourning her brother-in-law with a remark typical for its anti-Moscow intensity.

"This independence movement will continue until we get our freedom," she said, watching the throngs gather. She sat in the city square's now perpetual vigil by loved ones of various Georgians whose deaths a year ago, and in the last decade, have been attributed to the Soviet government's attempt to rein in Georgian nationalism.

As she spoke, people were arriving across mountain roads in bus caravans. The street scene was a mass display of grief, pride, and resolve.

"We have suffered so because you Azerbaijanis are always fighting with the Armenians," one Georgian woman said in greeting to a newly arrived visitor. She called for the region to duplicate "the unity of the Baltics."

"Yes, we agree, there should be a common Transcaucasian home, not all this fighting," the Azerbaijani responded. He voiced what has only been an occasional dream across the nation's southern swath of ancient rivalries and enmities.

The scene tonight was classically Georgian, with political dialogues breaking out across the crowd in the republic's richly distinctive language. Bright spring flowers were brought forth by the armload.

The crowd's political resolve was no less displayed as Georgians closed their wineshops. They soberly renewed their widening call to boycott all things Soviet. The street memorial proceeded in the chill mountain air toward 4 A.M., the hour when the 19 Georgians were struck down a year ago as they and their comrades searched for a way to advance the independence cause.

With hopes of quelling what seemed to be a contagion of nationalistic hopes, Moscow toughened its stance toward the Lithuanians.

Gorbachev Warns Lithuania of Ban on Major Supplies
By Francis X. Clines

MOSCOW, APRIL 13—President Mikhail S. Gorbachev issued an ultimatum to Lithuania today, saying that if the republic does not rescind its strongest independence measures within 48 hours, he will order other republics to start cutting off needed supplies.

In his harshest attempt at pressure so far, the Soviet leader warned the rebellious republic that its independence campaign had degenerated into "an ever tighter knot, assuming the nature of a political dead end."

"Other constituent republics are asking quite aptly why they should continue supplying products to Lithuania at the expense of their own needs," he declared in a letter to the leaders of the Lithuanian government, which declared its independence on March 11 in Vilnius.

Mr. Gorbachev's letter was his strongest turning of the screw in the slow war of nerves that the national government has been waging in its attempt to keep the Lithuanian rebellion from becoming a precedent for other dissatisfied republics to challenge Moscow's sovereignty.

Lithuanians Offer New Compromises to Avoid Blockade (April 16)
Lithuanians Say Moscow Has Cut Main Oil Pipeline (April 18)
Toughening Stand, Moscow Cuts Back Gas for Lithuania (April 19)

The issue was impacting on foreign affairs, since the West was anxious that no crisis be allowed to develop that might derail or delay progress on a comprehensive settlement of cold war issues.

Lithuania Is Asked by Paris and Bonn to Halt Decisions
By Alan Riding

PARIS, APRIL 26—France and West Germany jointly urged Lithuania today to suspend its parliament's moves toward independence and to seek negotiations with Moscow with a view to finding "a solution acceptable to all parties."

The move came in a letter addressed to Lithuania's President, Vytautas Landsbergis, by President François Mitterrand of France and Chancellor Helmut Kohl of West Germany at the conclusion of two days of talks here.

In their letter, the two leaders said a solution to the complex situation in Lithuania "requires time and patience and should be sought through the classic channels of dialogue."

"Without doubt, to facilitate the opening of these talks, it would be helpful if the effects of the decisions taken by your parliament were suspended for a while," they said. "They would lose none of their validity because they are based on the universally recognized principle of the self-determination of peoples."

While Western countries have generally advocated a dialogue between Moscow and Lithuania, this was the first time any of them has specifically called on Lithuania to suspend any of the proindependence actions taken by its parliament.

Lithuania Reports Promising Contact with Soviet Aides
By Bill Keller

VILNIUS, LITHUANIA, APRIL 27—The political impasse over Lithuania's independence appears to be moving closer to a resolution after the intervention of the French and German leaders and backstage contacts between Moscow and the rebellious republic, officials here said today.

The Lithuanian government expressed interest today in a letter from Chancellor Helmut Kohl of West Germany and President François Mitterrand of France proposing that the republic temporarily suspend enforcement of its declaration of independence as a gesture to get substantive negotiations with Moscow under way.

"Perhaps this could be considered as a compromise," said Lithuania's Prime Minister, Kazimiera Prunskiene. "How far Lithuania can get toward this should be the object of discussion in the Lithuanian parliament. I do not think that these two countries have taken a position hostile to the interests of Lithuania."

Mrs. Prunskiene said the idea was "close to something that has already been discussed" by Lithuanian leaders.

As the days lengthened, Gorbachev had a thick menu of problems and challenges to choose from. The Lithuanians were not ready to give up their assertion of immediate independence. Their neighbors in Latvia and Estonia were pressing for sovereignty. Boris Yeltsin was about to run for the presidency of the Russian republic, a post that would give him a power base from which to pressure Gorbachev even more than he was already doing. And if this was not enough, there was the summit meeting with President Bush. Meanwhile, there was an inauspicious May Day.

Gorbachev Jeered at May Day Rally

By Bill Keller

MOSCOW, MAY 1—President Mikhail S. Gorbachev and the Kremlin leadership were jeered today by throngs of protesters who were allowed to march through Red Square at the end of the annual May Day parade.

The Soviet leaders watched in evident amazement from the top of Lenin's mausoleum as a shouting, fist-shaking column milled underneath waving banners that condemned the Communist Party and the K.G.B., and supported Lithuania's declaration of independence.

Chants of "Resign!" and "Shame!" were largely drowned out by the blare of parade music, but foreign visitors who watched from the reviewing stand said they could clearly hear the shriek of hoots and whistles that rose up from the cobblestoned square as Mr. Gorbachev led the others off the mausoleum after enduring 25 minutes of protest.

It was the first time the May Day demonstration, traditionally an orchestrated show of worker solidarity, had been opened to unofficial organizations, and several of the Kremlin officials seemed startled at the vehemence of the angry display.

Since they emerged from Communist rule, the countries of Eastern Europe marked the first May Day without public parades and with few speeches, concentrating largely on private pursuits like picnics and shopping. In Moscow, the tone of the hour-long official demonstration that opened the parade was almost as striking as the unofficial protest.

Organized by Moscow trade unions, it became a show of blue-collar concern about the threats to their security that might come with a market economy.

The banners and speeches warned against unemployment, private property, and unregulated prices, and one placard called for the removal of Prime Minister Nikolai I. Ryzhkov for failing to lift the country out of its economic misery.

The government trade unions, trying to halt a sharp decline in their credibility, have recently staked out a position opposing economic changes that might disrupt the traditional security of Soviet workers.

Mr. Gorbachev's economic advisers say the threat of a worker uprising is the main reason they have pulled back from a "shock therapy" transition to a market economy.

Several Soviet cities, including the capitals of the Baltic republics and the Caucasus republics of Georgia, Armenia, and Azerbaijan, canceled their May Day festivities altogether as holdovers from a discredited past. In Kiev, the Ukrainian capital, the usual worker brigades were joined by demonstrators protesting government handling of the Chernobyl nuclear accident in 1986.

Moscow Communist Party officials announced last week that the annual parade would be thrown open to all comers as a sign of increased pluralism. Officials may also have feared a repetition of last November's Revolution Day, when the official march was upstaged by a huge counter-protest at a soccer stadium.

In another gesture to the new realities of politics in the capital, the insurgent chairman of the Moscow city council, Gavriil K. Popov, a free-market economist, joined government and Communist Party leaders atop the mausoleum today.

The unofficial section of the parade was organized by the Moscow Voters Association, which was instrumental in the takeover of the city government by Mr. Popov and other candidates eager to hasten to demise of the Communist monopoly.

As the crowds of factory workers organized by the unions emptied Red Square, they were abruptly replaced by a scene that has become familiar at protest rallies in the city but must have seemed shocking to the assembled Kremlin hierarchy.

The columns included Hare Krishnas and anarcho-syndicalists, social democrats and anti-Stalinists, and at the front a monk from the Russian Orthodox monastery at Zagorsk who held up a nearly life-sized rendition of Jesus on the cross and called out to Mr. Gorbachev, "Mikhail Sergeyevitch, Christ is risen!"

DOWN WITH THE RED FASCIST EMPIRE! said one placard that bobbed conspicuously before the marble mausoleum where the leadership stood. DOWN WITH THE CULT OF LENIN! read another, its letters painted to simulate bloodstains.

One group of marchers waved the red-green-and-yellow flags of Lithuania and held up signs saying, GORBACHEV: HANDS OFF LITHUANIA, and THE BLOCKADE OF LITHUANIA IS THE SHAME OF THE PRESIDENT.

Lithuania Agrees to Suspend Laws on Independence
By Bill Keller

MOSCOW, MAY 16—The Lithuanian government formally agreed today to suspend all laws it has passed since its declaration of independence on March 11 and to discuss a transition period to full separation from the Soviet Union, officials of the republic said tonight.

The offer, prepared in a closed-door session of the parliament and cabinet, was the Lithuanians' most concerted attempt so far to persuade President Mikhail S. Gorbachev to lift his partial economic embargo and begin negotiations.

The Lithuanian Prime Minister, Kazimiera Prunskiene, was to fly to Moscow on Thursday bearing the government declaration and a letter to

Mr. Gorbachev. It was not clear whether she would be met by Kremlin officials or whether Moscow would accept the gesture as an opportunity to end the standoff.

Mr. Gorbachev would presumably welcome a chance to end the economic sanctions against Lithuania, which could cast a pall over his meeting with President Bush in Washington. That meeting is to begin May 30, about the time that Lithuania expects to exhaust the last of its oil reserves.

To Gorbachev Anxieties, Add Yeltsin Candidacy
By Bill Keller

MOSCOW, MAY 16—With several republics tugging loose around the periphery of the Soviet Union, President Mikhail S. Gorbachev faced a strong challenge today in the heartland of his domain—the vast, rich, and angry republic of Russia.

In the Kremlin this morning, the newly elected Russian parliament convened for what promises to be a fierce struggle over political and economic control of the republic, the nation's biggest and most populous.

The fight was to begin·later this week with an attempt by Boris N. Yeltsin to be elected president of the republic, on a platform that calls for abolishing much of the Kremlin's control over Russian affairs.

Mr. Yeltsin, President Gorbachev's nemesis, was said to have about a third of the 1,068 legislators behind him, but the outcome was uncertain because the Communist Party functionaries expected to compete with him for the job have not generated any enthusiasm.

Supporters of Mr. Yeltsin won a preliminary skirmish tonight by a single vote, managing to postpone the presidential vote until after his main rival, Aleksandr V. Vlasov, had given a report on the sad state of the Russian economy. Mr. Vlasov has been prime minister of the republic for the last 19 months and will presumably be held accountable to some degree for the grim poverty in parts of Russia.

A victory by Mr. Yeltsin would be a personal humiliation for Mr. Gorbachev, who cashiered the maverick Communist from the party Politburo two years ago, and would seriously endanger the Soviet leader's power over the republic that holds more than half his country's population, three-fourths of its territory, and most of its natural resources.

Mr. Gorbachev takes the challenge seriously enough that last Saturday he spent six hours wooing a swing group of lawmakers, and today— though not a member of the Russian legislature—he worked the corridors with a battery of television cameras trailing him.

The Russian challenge comes as Mr. Gorbachev faces continued economic decline, a political impasse over secession moves by the three Baltic republics, and growing doubt about his authority among the people.

The latest indignity came this week when he won the votes of only 61 percent of Communist Party members casting ballots in his race to be a delegate to the July congress of the party he heads. Running in a Moscow district, he encountered surprisingly strong opposition from a watch factory shop foreman supported by a prodemocracy insurgent group.

"He knows the fate of Russia is the fate of the Soviet Union," said Sergei N. Samoilov, one of the 200 legislators invited in for Mr. Gorbachev's lobbying session Saturday. "And it can go two ways: either toward consolidation or toward division."

Mr. Samoilov, who is director of a children's home in Siberia, said Mr. Gorbachev did not criticize Mr. Yeltsin and barely mentioned the three Communist officials whose candidacies for the post have been endorsed by the party leadership. Mr. Gorbachev seemed to recognize that overt pressure would only backfire.

Instead, the Soviet leader listened to grievances and appealed over and over again for unity.

Mr. Samoilov, like many other representatives, said he was unhappy with the choice of candidates, fearing that the election of Mr. Yeltsin would lead to instability but was loath to vote for party-backed candidates associated with Russia's economic decline.

Russia has traditionally been the most powerful and least independent of the Soviet Union's 15 constituent republics. Russians dominated the national hierarchy of the Soviet Communist Party and government, but in exchange, the government of the republic itself was downgraded in status, lacking such separate power centers as its own Communist Party and its own Academy of Sciences.

As non-Russian republics have begun to assert themselves, Russians have begun to demand autonomy over their politics and culture, and most important, over their economies.

"Russia is the heartland of the Soviet Union, but it's also the most mistreated of the republics," Mr. Samoilov said. "All the structures of state administration are missing."

Even Mr. Vlasov, a lifelong party functionary and Gorbachev protégé, told the newspaper *Pravda* on Saturday that he favored "the exclusive right of Russia to dispose of all natural resources."

The republic produces virtually all the Soviet Union's timber and nickel, 90 percent of its oil, and most of its natural gas, aluminum, paper, gold, diamonds, and furs—resources that account for a huge share of the Soviet Union's foreign currency earnings. Most of these resources are controlled by ministries under national jurisdiction.

"The situation in the Baltics and in Russia has led to a lot of people becoming more leftist," said Maj. Vladimir A. Rebrikov of the Moscow police, commenting on Mr. Vlasov's conversion to the idea of economic independence.

Mr. Rebrikov, who said he would vote for Mr. Yeltsin, favors even greater Russian independence, including the right to override any laws passed at the national level.

Several non-Russian republics, including those in the Baltic and the Caucasus mountain regions, have already declared their right to ignore national law, and the prospect that Russia will do likewise, something that appears to have a large following in the Congress, alarms many Soviet officials.

The temporary chairman of the assembly, Vasily Kazakov, said today that 86 percent of the members of parliament were Communist Party members, but many belong to the Democratic Russia bloc, which favors sweeping changes toward democracy and free markets.

The delegations from Moscow, Leningrad, and several other cities include large contingents from Democratic Russia, among them several former political prisoners and dissidents.

The Congress also includes a smaller faction made up of hard-liners and Russian nationalists who would prefer a more authoritarian course for the republic.

Mr. Yeltsin has proposed that the parliament chose a leader for a year or two, and after that time, the republic's president would be elected by popular ballot.

Gorbachev Offers Deal to Lithuania
By Esther B. Fein

MOSCOW, MAY 24—President Mikhail S. Gorbachev said today that Lithuania could be independent in two years if the republic suspended its declaration of independence, Lithuanian officials said tonight.

The officials said they were invited this afternoon to an unscheduled meeting with Mr. Gorbachev, at which he told them that the Kremlin's economic sanctions against Lithuania would be lifted "immediately" and that independence negotiations between Moscow and the republic would begin as soon as the declaration act was frozen.

Despite prodding from Washington and warnings from Moscow, Lithuania has refused to suspend the independence declaration it made March 11, although the parliament voted on Wednesday to freeze legislation enacted after the act of independence if Moscow begins formal talks on the issue.

A spokesman for President Vytautas Landsbergis of Lithuania said his republic's leadership had been briefed on today's meeting and was studying Mr. Gorbachev's proposal.

"Gorbachev said that such a move would in no way threaten us, but would immediately open the door to negotiations," said Nikolai Medvedev, one of four Lithuanian officials who attended the hour-long meeting that was hastily called during a break in today's session of the Soviet parliament. "And he said that once such negotiations were completed, Lithuania could be totally independent as quickly as two years from now."

Yeltsin Is Elected Russian President on Third-Round Vote
By Celestine Bohlen

MOSCOW, MAY 29—Boris N. Yeltsin, the maverick politician who has spent three years fighting the Communist Party establishment, today became president of the Russian republic, overcoming a last-ditch effort by President Mikhail S. Gorbachev to block his election before departing for visits to Canada and the United States.

Mr. Yeltsin, whose popular following makes him a clear threat to Mr. Gorbachev's authority as leader of the Soviet Union, won the presidency of the nation's largest republic on a third round of balloting in the republic's parliament with a final tally of 535 votes, four more than the required majority. His opponent, Aleksandr V. Vlasov, the choice of the party and Mr. Gorbachev, trailed with 467 votes.

When the final count was announced this afternoon to the tense and excited gathering at the Grand Kremlin Palace, deputies rose to their feet to give a standing ovation to Mr. Yeltsin, the former Moscow Communist Party chief who was thrown out of the leadership after a disagreement with Mr. Gorbachev over the pace of change.

Outside the Kremlin gates, hundreds of Yeltsin supporters, waving red-white-and-blue pre-Revolutionary Russian flags and carrying pictures of the new President, gathered to wait for a glimpse of the tall, 59-year-old Siberian, a popular hero who has become a symbol of the promise of real change.

Speaking to reporters after his election, Mr. Yeltsin said he wanted to build relations with Mr. Gorbachev "not on confrontation, but on a businesslike basis, dialogue and talks, on a principled basis, not to the prejudice of Russia's sovereignty and interests."

Mr. Gorbachev, on his arrival in Ottawa for a stop en route to Washington, was asked about the election. The Soviet President said he applauded reports that Mr. Yeltsin had said he was willing to "work fruitfully with the President of the Soviet Union," and then added: "If, however, he is indeed playing a political game, then we may be in for a difficult time. So we will wait and see. Life is richer than any teacher."

Mr. Yeltsin, asked if he expected to receive a message of congratulation today from his longtime foe, said after a dramatic pause, "Yesterday I could not imagine it, but today it would be the politically correct step."

In a brief acceptance speech, Mr. Yeltsin offered to put together a government drawn from different political groups in parliament, including the conservative Communists who fought so hard to keep him from power.

Members of the Russian parliament and several journalists in Moscow said that on Monday night, a group of several hundred members of the Communist Party hierarchy were summoned to a meeting with Mr. Gorbachev and other members of the Politburo for final instructions on maintaining party discipline in the face of Mr. Yeltsin's candidacy. The failure of this final appeal, delivered on the eve of Mr. Gorbachev's departure for North America, served to underscore the party's loss of authority and the rise of Mr. Yeltsin as an alternative force.

Mr. Yeltsin's open challenge to Mr. Gorbachev marks the first time that differences have been aired in public by political leaders in the Soviet Union since the 1920s, in the aftermath of the death of Lenin in 1924. Until Stalin consolidated his power in the late 1920s, there were frequent clashes between factions in the party.

Mr. Gorbachev made a surprise appearance last week before the Russian parliament and delivered a forceful, personal attack on Mr. Yeltsin, whom he accused of attempting to break up the Soviet Union.

The depth of the obvious antagonism between Mr. Gorbachev and Mr. Yeltsin, dating back to Mr. Yeltsin's break with the party hierarchy in October 1987, could lead to a dangerous political stalemate, some Soviets and foreign observers said today.

One battleground is the Soviet government's latest program of economic change, which relies heavily on drastic and unpopular price increases. Mr. Yeltsin has criticized the plan, and today he referred to the "unpopular proposals by the Soviet government to step up economic reform."

Mr. Yeltsin's own economic program is not well defined, although many of his supporters are banking on the competence of the new Russian President's advisers, a group that includes prominent market economists and liberal intellectuals.

His politics, however, continue to worry some members of the Russian intelligentsia. "The fact that Yeltsin reduces everything to social-political issues is very alarming to me," said Dmitri S. Likhachev, the unofficial dean of Russian literary historians and head of the Russian Cultural Foundation, in an interview in Washington.

Mr. Yeltsin's victory, which three days ago seemed a long shot given the strength and resources of his opposition, was attributed by many deputies today to the surge of popular support that came pouring in over the weekend.

"The deputies had to take popular opinion into account," said Nikolai Vorontsov, a member of parliament and the Soviet minister of environmental protection. "There could be no doubt that Yeltsin was supported by a majority of the people."

Outside the main hall, in the ornate czarist chambers of the Grand Kremlin Palace, members of Democratic Russia, the liberal group that led the lobbying for Mr. Yeltsin, greeted each other with giddy jubilation. "We won," said a delighted delegate from the western Siberian oil capital of Tyumen.

Some Yeltsin supporters also attributed his final success to their candidate's public efforts at conciliation. "Boris Nikolayevich showed he is ready to move toward a compromise, to take other points of view into account," said Anatoly Medvedev, a deputy from Moscow, referring to Mr. Yeltsin by his name and patronymic, in the Russian style.

Others said the Communist Party's misguided tactics had granted Mr. Yeltsin success. The party first put up a hard-liner, Ivan K. Polozkov, a party boss from the region of Krasnodar in southern Russia, in the first round of voting, then switched to Mr. Vlasov, the current prime minister of the Russian republic, on the final ballot.

Mr. Vlasov had withdrawn in the first round because of a poor performance in delivering a report on the situation in Russia, politically the most significant of the Soviet republics.

"Mr. Vlasov showed in his report that he is not material to be even prime minister," said Mr. Medvedev, "while Mr. Polozkov is, I am sorry to say, a demagogue, more of the Russophile type."

As Mr. Yeltsin left the Kremlin today, he was besieged by hundreds of supporters, who had kept up a vigil outside the nearby Rossiya Hotel, where many deputies have been staying. Chanting, "Victory! Victory!" the crowd swarmed around the new President, who pledged to press forward for "the renewal of Russia."

"If he hadn't won, the results would have been unpredictable," said Alla Podlesnova, a 51-year-old doctor from Moscow. "Yeltsin is the pride and honor of Russia."

But many in the crowd disputed the notion that Mr. Yeltsin is a rival to Mr. Gorbachev's power. Instead, they said he would provide a needed counterweight to the Soviet leader, a prod toward more rapid change.

"This is not a defeat for Gorbachev," said Sergei Shiskin, a 37-year-old translator from Siberia. "It is a lesson."

Yeltsin Takes Aim at Central Rule
By Celestine Bohlen

MOSCOW, MAY 30—In his first day as president of the Russian republic, Boris N. Yeltsin put the Kremlin on notice today with an aggressive program to free Russia from "the dictates of the center."

Mr. Yeltsin said he expected the Russian parliament to pass a declaration of sovereignty for the Russian republic before President Mikhail S. Gorbachev of the Soviet Union returned from the United States next week.

"This pyramid must be turned upside down," Mr. Yeltsin said, using the occasion of a news conference in the Grand Kremlin Palace to describe his proposal to thwart the nation's strong centralist traditions and to turn power over to the local and republic levels.

The head of the giant Russian republic, the largest and most populous of the 15 in the Soviet Union, the maverick politician poses a formidable challenge to Mr. Gorbachev. Mr. Yeltsin also said at a news conference that the latest plan for economic change presented by Prime Minister Nikolai I. Ryzhkov was doomed.

"I think once you have failed with a program, a government should resign and then a new government should present a new program," he said. He predicted that the new economic plan, presented last week, will be defeated in the congress of Russian members of parliament.

Mr. Yeltsin promised to use his first 100 days to put in place a program for economic autonomy that would allow Russia to contract freely with other Soviet republics for the sale of oil, gas, and other natural resources at world prices.

Mr. Yeltsin said his formula for greater independence for the Russian republic would not weaken but, rather, reinforce the Soviet Union as a federation of autonomous republics. "The more independent the constituent republics will be, the stronger our union," he said.

"There is work to do," he said. "We should reject the previous forms of government that stipulated that everything be done to build up a powerful center."

Besieged at Home, Gorbachev Arrives in U.S. for Summit
By R. W. Apple, Jr.

WASHINGTON, MAY 30—President Mikhail S. Gorbachev of the Soviet Union arrived in Washington tonight for his third visit to the United States and his second summit conference with President Bush, as American officials searched for formulas to persuade him to accept Western plans for a unified Germany and a restructured Europe.

The Soviet leader landed at Andrews Air Force Base at 6:50 P.M. after a flight from Ottawa, where he had conferred with the Canadian Prime Minister, Brian Mulroney. With Mr. Gorbachev was his wife, Raisa.

Mr. Gorbachev is widely perceived in Washington as weakened by a succession of crises at home caused by nationalist tendencies in the Baltic republics and in Armenia, a lack of confidence by the Soviet public in his new economic plan, and the election of a political rival, Boris N. Yeltsin, to the presidency of the Russian republic.

Mr. Bush, his spokesman said, is full of "anticipation and confidence" on the eve of three days of talks, but unwilling to yield on the basic question of full German membership in the North Atlantic Treaty Organization. Mr. Gorbachev also took a stern line on the issue, which promises to be the pivotal question of the meeting that is to open at the White House on Thursday morning.

"The West hasn't done much thinking," Mr. Gorbachev said in Canada, describing American insistence that a reunified Germany belong to NATO as "an old record that keeps playing the same note again and again."

"They try to dictate," he added, "and this will not suit us."

The most pressing and profound issue at the summit concerned Germany. How and when was it to unify? Where would it fit in any new undivided Europe? What were to be the roles of NATO and the Warsaw Pact? And more specifically what was to be done with the largely American NATO forces in West Germany and the Soviet forces in East Germany, if the two countries became one?

Summit Talks End with Warmth but Fail to Resolve Key Issues; the Doubts That Linger
By R. W. Apple, Jr.

WASHINGTON, JUNE 3—For months, senior American officials have expressed confidence that President Mikhail S. Gorbachev would give way, if offered enough inducements, and agree to NATO membership for a united Germany, thus settling the most intractable issue facing Moscow and Washington.

But that confidence is fading fast. After three days of talks between President Bush and the Soviet leader, which produced no real progress on the German question and the shape of post–cold war Europe, top United States policy-makers say they are beginning to believe that Mr. Gorbachev's domestic political situation may be too delicate for him to make such a concession at any time soon, and that a protracted period of ambiguity may result.

"It may well be that the only way he can resolve his dilemma is to string the process out, let Germany go ahead with political and economic reunification, and stall on the military side," said an American official who played a significant role in the Bush-Gorbachev summit conference here. "West Germany would stay in NATO and the Soviet troops would stay in East Germany.

"Unfortunately, with so many security questions undecided, the situation might prove dangerous."

In domestic political terms, Mr. Bush emerged from last week's events with Germany in doubt, Lithuania unresolved, and perhaps a few political problems on the trade agreement. But he will find that easy enough to live with, given his broad popularity. For Mr. Gorbachev, on the other hand, the acclaim he won in the streets of Washington is unlikely to be repeated at home. His public-relations triumph here is not likely to ease his struggle for survival.

At their news conference this morning, the two Presidents made much of the relationship they have built, and a few White House officials say they believe that personal chemistry will eventually dissolve the policy stalemate. Mr. Gorbachev promised not to "put spokes in the wheels" and said negotiations on Germany would continue. The two pledged to meet on a regular basis.

No doubt things have come "a long, long way from the depths of the cold war," as President Bush commented. But there are limits on personal diplomacy, even in an era of good feelings. Between May 1972 and November 1974 four summit meetings took place, and after the fourth one, in Siberia, Gerald R. Ford spoke hopefully of "the spirit of Vladivostok."

But that proved inadequate to overcome fundamental disagreements—the next summit conference did not come until 1979—and the "constructive spirit" of which Mr. Gorbachev spoke may not suffice in the weeks and months ahead.

A protracted debate about the rival visions of the new Europe now seems highly likely, with a substantial possibility that progress in the negotiations in Vienna on conventional forces will prove impossible to achieve and that the summit meeting of the 35-nation Conference on Security and Cooperation in Europe, now scheduled to take place late this year in Paris, will be delayed.

The United States is ready to see that rather inchoate organization gain a more formal structure and a larger role. But the Soviet Union, which belongs to no other important pan-European organization, wants to make it the centerpiece of the new Europe, which is an entirely different matter.

"We are talking about building an all-European security system and casting the issue of German unification, its external aspects, within the context of that larger European security framework," Vitaly Churkin, a senior adviser to the Soviet Foreign Ministry, said in an interview over the weekend.

Many Western European officials, as well as many here, see that idea as "a trap that would give the Soviets a veto like the one they have in the United Nations, in fact if not in law," as a ranking Italian official argued recently. A British diplomat said that an organization with 35 members "would quickly become a talking shop, incapable of making decisions."

But there is some support, among politicians as well as policy experts, for the Soviet idea, or some modified version of it. Hans-Dietrich Genscher, the West German foreign minister, has called for a pan-European "conflict-resolution center," and President François Mitterrand of France supports a loose European confederation.

Leaders of the newly democratic East European countries see the Conference on Security and Cooperation as their only chance for a link to Western Europe, so they too support the idea that something new, beyond NATO and the moribund Warsaw Pact, must be created to handle European security.

Nearly everything about the debate remains murky. One of the things the United States has promised the Soviet Union, to combat Moscow's fear that a unified Germany would be joining an alliance hostile to Soviet interests, is that NATO will be transformed into a more political organization.

Revivifying NATO—giving it some reason for being other than defense against a threat from the East that is rapidly vanishing—is a crucial matter for the United States, Mr. Bush believes, because NATO gives Washington its sole institutional voice in Europe.

But every time in the past that NATO has tried to agree on something other than the common defense against the Soviet Union and the Warsaw Pact, things have gone wrong—whether the question was the Suez invasion in the 1950s or the overflight of United States planes on the way to Libya in the 1980s.

The danger lurking down the road, in the American view, is not the application of a new Soviet noose to Berlin, or even a rancorous Soviet decision to break off negotiations on the German question. The positive tenor of the conversations here seems to make those two eventualities unlikely, at least for as long as Mr. Gorbachev or another reformer remains in power.

For Moscow, the stakes are immense. In the century since 1890, Russia and Germany, the two largest and strongest European countries, have been almost constantly at odds. Now the Soviet Union, already economically weakened, faces the prospect of losing its military power in Central Europe, with no compensating increase in political power, at the very moment when Germany, already economically powerful, stands on the verge of reunification and greatly augmented political influence.

"It's going to require tremendous finesse on our part to manage this kind of unsettled situation," said Robert D. Hormats, a former official of the State Department and the National Security Council. "The analogy to Germany, post–World War I, is very close. We can't afford to isolate them, leave them to brood about losing the cold war, let their economy collapse. If we do, as a last resort, they'll play on neutralist emotions in Germany, which are already too widespread for comfort."

Back in Moscow, the strains on the centralized and federated union were continuing. Just as they eased a bit in Lithuania, they were intensifying in the Russian heartland.

Russian Republic Asserts Its Laws Have Primacy over Kremlin Rule
By Bill Keller

MOSCOW, JUNE 8—The parliament of the Russian federation directly challenged central authority over the largest and richest Soviet republic today by asserting that Russian laws take precedence over Soviet laws.

But the resolution fell short of the two-thirds majority of the full parliament needed to change the Russian constitution, raising doubts among the deputies about whether the declaration would ultimately be put into binding form.

The declaration, which asserts the right to veto any federal law on Russian territory, was approved by 544 members, with 271 voting against and the rest absent or abstaining.

Russian sovereignty is a central plank in the platform of the republic's new President, Boris N. Yeltsin, who advocates a number of measures like the private sale of farmland and republic control of oil and gas resources that would directly contradict federal law.

Mr. Yeltsin has also announced his opposition to the Soviet government's economic plan, which includes price increases on bread and other foods, and it is possible that he would urge the Russian parliament to defy those measures if they are enacted.

Mr. Yeltsin's margin of victory on the question today is indicative of what many lawmakers believe will be a difficult task as he tries to govern Russia with a parliament in which he controls a little more than half the votes.

The statement was adopted as part of a broad, nonbinding sovereignty declaration that is expected to be put to a final vote next week.

Several other republics, including the three Baltic states, have incorporated the right of veto in their constitutions. But a claim of sovereignty by Russia, which encompasses three-fourths of the country's territory—from Europe to the Pacific—more than half its population, and most of its mineral wealth, would raise the issue of federalism to a new level.

President Mikhail S. Gorbachev discounted the prospect of conflict with the Russian republic, saying at a news conference that he was "one hundred percent certain" that its parliament would pass no laws harmful to the creation of a new Soviet federation.

"The Russian parliament has not taken any steps that contradict the constitution of the Soviet Union," Mr. Gorbachev said, possibly alluding to the nonbinding nature of the measure adopted today.

The parliament stood for a rousing ovation after its show of independence today, prompting Mr. Yeltsin to grin broadly and say, "I understand your emotional mood, but the Presidium must remain impartial."

Members of parliament who supported the sovereignty move said their joy was tempered by the knowledge that it would take a two-thirds vote to incorporate the veto provision in the republic's constitution.

Vladimir A. Zhenin, a member of parliament from Mr. Yeltsin's home region of Sverdlovsk, said opponents of veto power for the republic might try to require a two-thirds vote next week on final approval of the sovereignty declaration itself, on the ground that it relates to a constitutional question.

"We can celebrate today's decision, but there are still serious complications ahead of us," Mr. Zhenin said.

He said the measure had been opposed by a bloc of orthodox Communists and party functionaries grouped under the name Communist Russia.

Mr. Gorbachev has generally praised the idea of greater autonomy for republics and has promised to design a new federation to satisfy the republics' craving for greater freedom. A presidential council of representatives from the 15 republics is scheduled to debate this federation plan on Saturday. But Mr. Gorbachev has always insisted on the priority of the Soviet constitution over republic laws.

The first Soviet republic to assert the right of veto over Soviet laws was Estonia, which acted in November 1988.

Mr. Gorbachev denounced the Estonian move and led the policy-making committee of the national parliament in formally declaring it invalid.

The most likely area of conflict between the central Soviet and Russian republic's governments is economic. Mr. Yeltsin and many other Russian politicians have demanded that the republic's oil, gas, coal, and timber be used to raise Russian living standards, and not be sold at subsidized prices to other republics and foreign allies.

In demanding that Russia exercise all rights over its mineral wealth, self-styled reformers like Mr. Yeltsin can expect some support from more conservative legislators who resent the republic's role as the underwriter of the Soviet realm.

But Mr. Gorbachev would presumably be reluctant to lose control of his single greatest source of foreign currency.

Moreover, if Mr. Yeltsin's demands that other republics pay market prices for Russia's oil are enacted, Mr. Gorbachev would face a likely reaction from the poorer republics, like those of Soviet Central Asia.

"I think the party apparatus will use every possibility to make sure things don't come to such a pass," Mr. Zhenin said.

Gorbachev showed his sense of dramatic timing and his penchant for making a virtue of necessity.

Gorbachev Yields on Alliance Roles in a New Germany
By Bill Keller

MOSCOW, JUNE 12—President Mikhail S. Gorbachev today removed one of the main conditions that his country had imposed on German unification. He agreed for the first time that West German troops could remain in the North Atlantic Treaty Organization without a corresponding role for the East Germans in the Soviet-led Warsaw Pact.

His offer, made during a report to the Soviet parliament on his talks with President Bush in Washington, falls short of Western demands that a united Germany be allowed to remain in NATO without conditions.

Mr. Gorbachev proposed that East Germany retain a vaguely defined "associate membership" in the Warsaw Pact, and that a united Germany "honor all obligations" inherited from the two Germanys.

But Mr. Gorbachev's remarks clearly showed that he was striving to find a formula that would allow a united Germany to join NATO, and to prepare his parliament and public opinion for such an eventuality.

In Washington, Bush administration officials assessing Mr. Gorbachev's statement said they were growing increasingly convinced that the Soviet leader was slowly reconciling himself to the idea that a united Germany would be in NATO, provided that Moscow's economic, political, and security concerns are met.

Before Mr. Gorbachev spoke today, Soviet officials had previously suggested various approaches intended to prevent German unification from tipping the military balance in NATO's favor. They had proposed a neutral Germany, joint membership for Germany in both alliances, and the dismantling of the alliances—all ideas rejected by the West.

Today the Soviet leader renewed his call for a broad, general security structure to supplant the two alliances, but he conceded that the rival blocs would continue to exist "for longer than might be imagined."

He again called for "dual membership" for Germany in the competing alliances, but this time it was clear that he was not insisting on an equal membership. The West German army, or *Bundeswehr,* would belong to NATO, he said, while the East Germany army would answer only to the unified German government, not to either alliance.

"United Germany could declare that, for this transition period, it would honor all obligations it inherits from the Federal Republic of Germany and from the German Democratic Republic," Mr. Gorbachev said. "For this period, the *Bundeswehr* would, as before, be subordinate to NATO, and the East German troops would be subordinate to the government of the new Germany."

That proposal would evidently leave a united Germany free to use East Germany's army any way it saw fit—including, as some West Germans have proposed, abolishing it.

The Soviet leader said he had proposed to President Bush that during that period, Soviet troops would remain stationed in East Germany, a condition the West has already accepted, and Moscow would agree to the continued presence of American troops in Europe.

"I told the President that I think that the American presence in Europe, since it fulfills a certain role in maintaining stability, is an element of the strategic situation, and does represent a problem for us," Mr. Gorbachev told his parliament.

Mr. Gorbachev's carefully worded statement on the intricacies of the German question was so murky in places that many diplomats spent the day puzzling over it before recognizing the new elements.

Western diplomats here said Mr. Gorbachev's comments reflected a rapid narrowing of the conceptual differences between East and West on the future of Germany, although the negotiations on concrete proposals remain excruciatingly complicated.

"He is no longer insisting that united Germany can under no circumstances be a member of NATO, something he had said two months ago was absolutely excluded," said one European diplomat.

Soviet Parliament Rejects Increase in Price of Bread
By Bill Keller

MOSCOW, JUNE 14—The Soviet parliament today resoundingly rejected the government's proposal for a steep increase in bread prices this summer, delivering a serious setback to President Mikhail S. Gorbachev's plan to wean consumers from state subsidies.

Although the government has promised to compensate citizens for the first year of higher prices, the parliament, fearing popular discontent, voted 319 to 33 to ask the government to come back with a new proposal in September.

Legislators lined up at the microphones to denounce the price increase as an affront to hard-pressed consumers and as a political blunder by a government that is trying to sell the public on the novelty of a market economy.

The decision casts doubt on the government's plan for more sweeping price increases next January. Raising prices is a central and by far the most widely discussed element of the government's plan to transform the state-run economy.

On Wednesday the parliament approved the government's strategy of breaking up government industrial monopolies by creating joint stock companies, stimulating small businesses, and promoting a commercial banking system. Mr. Gorbachev received the mandate he had sought to begin establishing these market mechanisms by decree, starting next month.

But the government's strategy for slowly dismantling the elaborate price controls met fierce opposition, not only from members of parliament worried about the reaction of consumers, but from market advocates who said the government's pricing policy is absurd.

Raising the price of such a sensitive commodity as bread as the first step seemed almost a deliberate effort to frighten consumers, critics said.

Bread prices have not changed in nearly 30 years, even though the country has increasingly come to depend on expensive imported grain. A typical loaf costs about 25 kopecks, or about 40 cents at the official exchange rate, so low that farmers often feed bread to their pigs because it is cheaper than animal feed.

The government had proposed to triple the price of bread beginning July 1, along with the price of other wheat products like flour, macaroni, cakes, and other bakery goods.

The proposed increase caused special alarm in Central Asia, where bread products make up a huge portion of the sparse diet of large rural families.

Government figures indicate that the price increase for bread products would have cost the average family 40 rubles a month, a heavy blow for a typical two-income family taking home about 500 rubles a month.

The government still plans a general increase in food prices next January 1. Technically this can be accomplished without approval from the legislature, but the government would be reluctant to act without some sign of parliamentary support.

The decision today reflects the government's frustration in trying to win approval for unpopular economic measures. Like parliaments in other countries, the Supreme Soviet finds it much easier to spend money than to raise it, which has led to a virtual hemorrhage in the anemic Soviet budget.

The bread price increase would not have directly helped the budget deficit because the government vowed that "every kopeck"—34 billion rubles a year—would be returned to consumers in the form of compensation checks.

But the price increases on other products next year are to be only partially reimbursed to consumers, with the rest helping to defray the vast government subsidies paid from the budget.

Lithuania Agrees to 100-Day Delay on Independence
By Bill Keller

MOSCOW, JUNE 29—Lithuania agreed today to suspend its declaration of independence for 100 days in exchange for negotiations with Moscow and the lifting of economic sanctions.

The moratorium, which would begin as soon as any talks got under way, was formally proposed by the Lithuanian President, Vytautas Landsbergis. The resolution was approved by parliament by a vote of 69 to 35, with two abstentions.

There was no immediate response from Soviet officials. But Lithuanians said they were confident that President Mikhail S. Gorbachev would accept the compromise as sufficient to end the impasse and to resume delivery of oil and other products that were cut off 10 weeks ago.

"If the members of parliament were not sure that was the case, they would not have approved the moratorium," said Rita Dapkus, a spokeswoman for parliament.

The decision does not resolve the conflict over whose power is sovereign in Lithuania. But it relegates the dispute to a conference table and removes it for now as a source of international embarrassment to Mr. Gorbachev.

Prime Minister Kazimiera Prunskiene, defending the moratorium, said it would freeze the declaration of independence, made on March 11, but would not affect any of the laws enacted later that Moscow found particularly offensive.

These included measures freeing Lithuanian men from the Soviet military draft, putting limits on citizenship in the republic, and laying claim to federal property.

"It is a political statement," she told parliament, and will have no practical effect on the republic's ability to govern itself.

Earlier, Mr. Gorbachev rejected Lithuanian offers to do just the opposite—to suspend the laws enacted after independence while leaving the March 11 declaration itself intact.

Lithuanians, said Mr. Gorbachev, in meetings with leaders of the Baltic republic, had always seemed more concerned with the broader principle of independence than with specific laws.

The independence moratorium sharply divided the Lithuanian parliament and drew a small crowd of demonstrators, who denounced the move as a sellout.

The decisive factor was the endorsement by Mr. Landsbergis, a musicology professor and founding member of Sajudis, the proindependence movement, who had refused until this morning to commit himself to a moratorium.

"Two years ago we chose the peaceful route to independence, the route of negotiations," he said today. "Now the condition for negotiations is a moratorium."

Mr. Landsbergis told reporters that he had decided to support the measure because it was temporary and included conditions to protect the republic's sovereignty against legal maneuvers or the use of force.

The moratorium is to end automatically if negotiations are broken off or if "certain circumstances or events" prevent the Lithuanian leaders from fulfilling their functions.

With the fading of the crisis in the Baltic there was no lack of issues confronting the Soviet leadership either at home or abroad. Domestically, attention was focused on the 10-day gathering of the Communist Party at which 4,657 members were to elect a leader and assess the fate of the organization. At the same time NATO was meeting to draw up its own plans for a new Europe, and Chancellor Kohl was due to come to Moscow. Also, in Houston, the seven richest industrialized countries were debating what, if any, aid should be provided to help the Soviet Union through its painful period of transition.

Soviet Hard-liner Assails Gorbachev on His Leadership
By Bill Keller

MOSCOW, JULY 3—The conservative pillar of the Politburo, Yegor K. Ligachev, roused delegates to the nationwide congress of the Communist Party today by deploring the five years of President Mikhail S. Gorbachev's rule as a period of wavering and "blind radicalism."

His lament for the undermining of old values was reinforced by the chief of the K.G.B. and the defense minister, who both warned against efforts to divorce their institutions from the party.

Vladimir Kryuchkov, the K.G.B. chairman and a Politburo member, ranged afield from security matters to warn against the tendency toward capitalist economics and the growing number of millionaires, and to pledge his lifelong allegiance to the party.

The banner of Mr. Gorbachev's reformers was carried alone today by Foreign Minister Eduard A. Shevardnadze, who declared that the Soviet Union would benefit from German reunification, and said the military had spent the country into ruin. Mr. Ligachev's speech drew thunderous applause from the same audience that on Monday clapped with gusto for the liberal favorite, Aleksandr N. Yakovlev, who helped mastermind many of Mr. Gorbachev's most far-reaching changes in domestic and foreign policy.

There may be no better indication of the reigning confusion in the Communist Party than the enthusiasm generated by two men with such different visions.

In part, that reflects the fact that party leaders are polarized into camps—the hard-liners cheer Mr. Ligachev, the reformers Mr. Yakovlev.

But in the lobby of the Kremlin Palace of Congresses, some delegates, members of the bemused center, said they had clapped for both speeches simply out of a hunger for someone with a clear and decisive program.

"At least these are both clear, distinctive personalities," said Vladimir Zhenin, a delegate from Sverdlovsk. "What people can't understand is Gorbachev, who maneuvers between the two poles. They do not understand this centrist waffling."

The congress, the twenty-eighth since the party was founded by anti-czarist revolutionaries in 1898, comes as the party is being bled by defections and challenged by assertive local and national legislatures.

Mr. Gorbachev's goal is to minimize the splintering of the party and keep a semblance of unity as the congress replenishes the party leadership and revises its platform.

NATO Allies, After 40 Years, Proclaim End of Cold War; Invite Gorbachev to Speak
By Craig R. Whitney

LONDON, JULY 6—President Bush and the other leaders of NATO today issued a declaration to end four decades of cold war by proposing to act jointly with Moscow and other East Europeans in stating that "we are no longer adversaries."

Inviting President Mikhail S. Gorbachev to travel to Brussels to speak with them, the Western leaders promised a new defensive strategy that would make their nuclear forces "truly weapons of last resort." They assured Moscow and the other Warsaw Pact nations that "we will never in any circumstance be the first to use force" and proposed that NATO, the Warsaw Pact, and European states outside the two alliances join in a "commitment to nonaggression."

"Our alliance will do its share to overcome the legacy of decades of suspicion," they said.

NATO's secretary-general will fly to Moscow to discuss the declaration with Mr. Gorbachev, whose own policies are under attack in the Soviet Union. Unspoken in the declaration is a desire by most NATO leaders to give Mr. Gorbachev striking evidence to demonstrate to his critics that his conciliatory policy toward the West is bringing results.

Mr. Bush said at a news conference that he thought the declaration would help Mr. Gorbachev deal with his "hard-liners." But he continued to oppose direct American economic aid to the Soviet Union.

The steps taken today were also aimed at making it easier for Mr. Gorbachev to acquiesce to the unification of the Germanys, something specifically called for in the declaration.

In what was called the London Declaration, drafted over the last two days by their foreign ministers in the palace of Lancaster House, the NATO leaders were clearly trying to speak to history in the same ringing tones as the North Atlantic Treaty sent out from Washington at the height of the cold war when the alliance was formed.

"The Atlantic community must reach out to the countries of the East which were our adversaries in the cold war, and extend to them the hand of friendship," they said, inviting the members of the crumbling Warsaw Pact to join in a declaration solemnly stating that the era of mutually hostile blocs was over. "The walls that once confined people and ideas are collapsing," the allied heads of government said. "As a consequence, this alliance must and will adapt."

In a wide-ranging review of alliance strategy and force levels, the NATO leaders promised to prepare a new defensive approach, using small, multinational light forces stationed far from the former front lines instead of "forward defense." They also pledged to reduce the reliance on nuclear weapons now enshrined in a strategy of "flexible response."

They invited the Warsaw Pact countries to establish a "regular diplomatic liaison" with NATO and agreed to strengthen the role of the 35-nation Conference on Security and Cooperation in Europe.

Significantly, they made a major concession to Soviet fears about a united Germany within NATO, and agreed to set limits on German armed forces as soon as the United States and the Soviet Union signed a treaty reducing their forces stationed in Europe, later this year.

Chancellor Helmut Kohl of West Germany, who was effusive about the support he said he had received all along from Mr. Bush, said that

German troop strength would be one of the topics he would discuss with Mr. Gorbachev when he flies to Moscow on July 15 to try to overcome the Soviet leader's remaining objections to German unification.

The initial reaction from Moscow today was favorable. Mr. Gorbachev told ABC News that he saw "very constructive signs coming out of this summit" and that he was "always ready to go" to Brussels to meet with the Western allies.

Mr. Kohl said today that he would also discuss economic aid to the Soviet Union with Mr. Gorbachev, who sent a letter to Mr. Bush today formally requesting consideration of economic and financial aid for his attempt to transform the Soviet economy, according to American officials. At a news conference, the President said, "I have some big problems with that one" as long as the Soviet Union spent so much on its military establishment and on subsidies for Cuba. But he said he had no objection to a West German decision to provide economic aid.

"As our alliance enters its fifth decade," the Western leaders said in their declaration, "it must continue to provide for the common defense.

"Yet our alliance must be even more an agent of change," they said. "It can help build the structures of a more united continent."

Reaffirming that "security and stability do not lie solely in the military dimension," the allies declared:

"We will remain a defensive alliance and will continue to defend all the territory of all of our members. We have no aggressive intentions and we commit ourselves to the peaceful resolution of all disputes. We will never in any circumstance be the first to use force."

Mr. Kohl and Mr. Bush insisted today that the agreement to give a commitment on manpower levels of a unified German military did not constitute the singling out of German forces. The United States and West Germany have been resisting any repetition of the harsh approach taken by the victorious Allies after World War I, when limits were imposed on German strength and sovereignty. They said the German levels would be set in the context of negotiations involving all the NATO and Warsaw Pact European forces.

After the President, Mr. Bush, the leader who seemed most pleased by what had been achieved here was clearly Mr. Kohl, who for the last two days has held his own background briefings in his own hotel in his own language, while the other leaders were content with common facilities provided by their British hosts.

From the NATO meeting, the action shifted quickly to Houston, where from July 9 the leaders of the Group of Seven industrialized countries were to take up the question of what kind of economic support they would be able to provide for the Soviet Union. Chancellor Kohl, who needed Gorbachev's backing if he was to obtain his dream of a reunited Germany, was willing to give much. The United States was inclined to be far less generous.

Western Aid Issue Sharply Debated by Soviet Leaders
By Bill Keller

MOSCOW, JULY 9—Senior Soviet officials appealed today for Western economic help in moving the moribund Soviet economy toward a free market, but the issue has divided the Soviet Union almost as badly as it has split potential donor countries.

While the seven leading Western industrial powers met in Houston to debate whether to throw a financial lifesaver to President Mikhail S. Gorbachev, liberals and conservatives in Mr. Gorbachev's party differed sharply over what kind of aid to seek, and with what kind of conditions.

Foreign Minister Eduard A. Shevardnadze told reporters today: "Of course, economic help—or, we say it differently, economic cooperation, the supply of credit—of course this will help *perestroika*, democratization, and the humanization of our society."

Some liberals, like the chairman of the Leningrad city council, Anatoly A. Sobchak, warned that large amounts of aid poured into the present system would be wasted. They called instead for Western investment in the form of small, private joint business ventures.

"There should under no circumstances be any large projects," Mr. Sobchak said today during a recess in the Communist Party's twenty-eighth congress, to which he is a delegate. "No money should be given into the hands of the bureaucrats, and no money should be invested into any kind of middleman organization. There should be concrete projects that quickly pay for themselves."

Some conservatives, on the other hand, caution that Western aid would be the wedge of capitalist ideology and would eventually turn the Soviet Union into a colony supplying cheap resources and labor.

Yegor K. Ligachev, the most outspoken conservative in the Politburo, told reporters today that he would oppose any Western aid that was designed to undermine Soviet reliance on state-owned industry and agriculture.

"If conditions are attached to lines of credit, such as making us move to a free market and private property, then Ligachev is against it," he said.

Mr. Gorbachev's aides are generally inclined toward Mr. Sobchak's view—credits and joint investment rather than direct aid, small-scale private ventures rather than large state enterprises, and conditions determined by the business partners rather than by foreign governments.

Confronting Foes, Gorbachev Keeps Party Leadership

By Bill Keller

MOSCOW, JULY 10—Mikhail S. Gorbachev swept confidently to re-election as head of the Communist Party today, after confronting the party's hard-liners with a militant defense of the changes he has ignited in his society.

The party's nationwide congress chose Mr. Gorbachev, who is also president of the Soviet Union, overwhelmingly over the only other candidate who stayed in the race, a Western Siberian party official best known for helping lead a coal mine strike a year ago.

Before the voting today, Mr. Gorbachev shed his conciliatory tone and lashed out in a fighting speech at hard-liners who had vociferously criticized his economic and foreign policies at the congress.

Either they must learn to live with liberty and the free competition of ideas, or the party is doomed, he declared, adding that the party is now in crisis because it has moved too slowly toward democracy and a market economy.

"There is no way to bring back the past, and no dictatorship—if someone still entertains this crazy idea—will solve anything," he thundered.

Although the congress is to continue for a few more days, Mr. Gorbachev seemed to have it now firmly in hand and appeared to have headed off for now any danger of a major split in the party.

He has forcefully tamed the hard-liners and then, with his speech today, reached out to party radicals who want even faster change in hopes of keeping them from deserting the party in huge numbers.

Senior party leaders said today that there was little doubt Mr. Gorbachev's choice for the important new post of deputy party leader would be elected. He is said to have settled on Vladimir A. Ivashko, the centrist leader of the Communist Party in the Ukraine, the second-largest Soviet republic.

Despite outspoken criticism and some calls for him to step down, in the end Mr. Gorbachev easily won his new term as general secretary—the first time the post has been filled by a nationwide party convention rather than by a secretive circle of top leaders.

The main argument used against him today was that it was time for him to choose between the two important jobs he holds—president of the country and general secretary of the party.

Mr. Gorbachev and his supporters conceded that the combination of jobs should eventually be phased out, but not until the more democratic new government structures are firmly in place.

He was elected with 3,411 votes, to 501 votes for Teimuraz G. Avaliani, a party official from the mining center of Kiselyovsk in the Kuznetsk coal basin. Voting against both candidates were 615 other delegates.

Six other candidates were nominated from the floor, most of them close associates of Mr. Gorbachev, but they withdrew.

Mr. Avaliani, a self-educated mining engineer, was summoned by the K.G.B. in 1978 and accused of slander after he wrote a letter to Leonid I. Brezhnev, who was then the Soviet leader, condemning his handling of the economy.

Mr. Avaliani, who was not identified with either the hard-line or radical factions, was elected a local party official after helping lead the strike that made coalfields idle last summer.

Today he expressed sympathy with the miners, who have scheduled a one-day protest strike Wednesday to demand better living conditions and the resignation of the government. But he also warned: "The endless rocking of our already leaky and unstable boat—and I mean the economy—will get us nowhere."

Neither the hard-liners nor the party radicals put up a candidate to challenge Mr. Gorbachev.

Leading conservatives in the party had already endorsed Mr. Gorbachev, fearing that otherwise he would swing to the radical camp and leave them with nothing.

Yegor K. Ligachev, the foremost hard-liner in the Politburo, had hinted that he might be available for some senior party post, but no one nominated him for the top job. Senior party officials said that, at 69, Mr. Ligachev is probably at the end of his political career.

"Rumors of the conservativism of the delegates were a bit exaggerated," said Yuri A. Prokofyev, the Moscow party leader.

The faction calling for more sweeping moves toward democracy and free markets was a tiny minority of the congress delegates from the outset. After their favorite, Aleksandr N. Yakovlev, a close ally of Mr. Gorbachev, declined to be nominated, some of the more radical delegates voted for Mr. Gorbachev, while others scratched out the names of both candidates.

Anatoly A. Sobchak, the chairman of the newly democratized Leningrad city council, said he voted against Mr. Gorbachev on the theory that if he lost, he could devote himself to the presidency without being held back by the party.

"The fact that Gorbachev will still keep the position of party leader will not speed up this process of transfering power to the government and re-creating a state, but it will slow this process down," he told reporters. "It will keep this party in power, along with its traditional forms and methods of working."

Mr. Gorbachev's fiery speech today was clearly designed to prevent the defection of popular figures like Mr. Sobchak, which could further diminish the party's electoral appeal.

Mr. Gorbachev said that while many party leaders were stunned and confused by the new liberties, the party's greatest failing was that it was too slow to recognize the need to abandon the centralized economy and the danger of long-suppressed ethnic grievances.

Echoing a warning issued last week by Boris N. Yeltsin, the populist president of the Russian republic, Mr. Gorbachev said the congress had shown how many Communist leaders are out of touch with the times.

"If any of the delegates, and going by the speeches there are some such delegates among us, came to the congress hoping to take the party back to the old conditions of commands and orders, I must say they are deeply mistaken," he said.

He called on them to stop using authoritarian methods to frustrate the work of elected government bodies, and to enter coalitions with non-Communist parties and political organizations.

"We must put an end to sectarian moods, put an end to this monopoly forever, erase its vestiges from the mind of party workers and all Communists," he said.

"Believe me, the party's success depends on whether it realizes that this is already a different society. Otherwise it will be pushed to the margin by other forces, and we shall lose ground."

Implicitly confronting the military officers who have challenged his handling of foreign policy, Mr. Gorbachev warned that those who work for the state must carry out government policies or resign.

"People ask if our policy not to interfere in the processes in Eastern Europe was correct," he added. "Well, do you want tanks again? Shall we teach them again how to live?"

Three Key Economic Issues Undecided as Meeting Ends
By David E. Rosenbaum

HOUSTON, JULY 11—The leaders of the seven most powerful industrial democracies wrapped up their three-day meeting here today by proclaiming their united goal of fostering worldwide prosperity, but they hardly resolved the three main economic issues that had divided them at the outset.

On trade policy, the leaders at the sixteenth annual economic summit meeting endorsed an ambiguous statement about agriculture subsidies that was finally drafted at 2:30 this morning. It promised to put trade talks back on track, but it allowed all competing sides to assert victory.

On aid to the Soviet Union, they took the time-honored step of politicians unable to reach consensus: they formed a committee to study the situation.

Then, as the congress was winding down came the surprising announcement that the most powerful critic, goad, and gadfly within the party was quitting.

Kremlin Maverick Leaves the Party; More May Follow
By Serge Schmemann

MOSCOW, JULY 12—Boris N. Yeltsin, the popular maverick of Soviet politics, announced today that he was quitting the Communist Party, dealing a sharp new blow to the once-monolithic force even as it struggled to stay united.

The brief announcement by the recently elected President of the Russian republic sent gasps through the vast auditorium of the Palace of Congresses in the Kremlin, where 4,700 delegates have been arguing and maneuvering for 10 days over the future of their badly mauled organization.

Isolated shouts of "Shame! Shame!" competed with a smattering of applause after Mr. Yeltsin declared that he was resigning from the party—in which he once held a seat on the all-powerful Politburo—to concentrate his efforts on running the Russian federated republic, the largest of the 15 that make up the Soviet Union.

The resignation could lead to mass defections and was a serious blow to President Mikhail S. Gorbachev, who had managed to triumph over earlier challenges at the party congress.

Mr. Yeltsin gave no indication that he would form or join another political movement, and his statement included no criticism of the party or its platform. Concluding his announcement, he marched out of the hall, refusing to answer any questions.

Soon after his statement, however, leaders of the Democratic Platform faction announced their intention to create a new "democratic coalition" this fall, effectively breaking with the party. The faction claims about 100 of the 4,700 delegates, but it was not immediately clear whether all its members supported the decision.

Vyacheslav Shostakovsky, rector of the Moscow Higher Party School and one of the faction's leaders, said he and his colleagues had reached the decision because "the congress did not realize our hopes for the separation of party and government functions."

Mr. Shostakovsky said his appeal had been signed by several leading members of the Democratic Platform, including Anatoly A. Sobchak, chairman of the Leningrad city council, Yuri Boldyrev, a prominent member of parliament from Leningrad, and Vladimir Lysenko, who has advocated reforms.

Mr. Yeltsin's announcement came in response to his nomination to the Central Committee of the party, the 396-member body that is chosen to guide the party between congresses.

"In view of my great responsibilities toward the people of Russia and in connection with the move toward a multiparty system, I cannot fulfill only the instructions of the Communist Party," he said, reading from a prepared statement. "As the highest elected figure in the republic, I have to bow to the will of all the people."

The decision by Mr. Yeltsin, long one of President Gorbachev's most nettlesome critics, was not entirely unexpected. He had previously declared his intention to create a multiparty system in the Russian republic, and he has campaigned to eliminate party influence over state administration.

Immediately after his announcement, Mr. Gorbachev, the party leader, said from the dais, "That ends the process logically."

Expected or not, Mr. Yeltsin's resignation was deeply unsettling for a gathering whose members so recently wielded unchallenged power that many of them are unprepared to cede their authority.

To be sure, Mr. Gorbachev himself has fought to loosen the party's grip on Soviet life, and he has shifted considerable power to his other office as president. But he has also said that it is too early to split from the Communists, and he and other top party leaders have publicly professed allegiance to socialism and the party.

Mr. Yeltsin broke that allegiance, not only by declaring that the party took up too much of his time, but by signaling to Soviet citizens that Communism is no longer the only arena for political action. His announcement was broadcast later on national television.

The development was a setback for Mr. Gorbachev, who had succeeded in preventing a schism between hard-liners and reformers at the congress and in imposing his authority on much of the battered party.

Earlier in the day the congress heard a formal announcement of the vote on Wednesday marking the overwhelmingly defeat of Yegor K. Ligachev, the tough-talking leader of resistance to Mr. Gorbachev's reforms, as the deputy chairman of the party.

Mr. Ligachev received only 776 votes to the 3,109 cast for Vladimir A. Ivashko, the Ukrainian leader who was Mr. Gorbachev's choice.

Mr. Gorbachev also seemed set to win approval for his new set of party rules, which grant considerably greater autonomy to the republic party organizations, and for his slate of members to the Central Committee.

The initial reaction from delegates to the twenty-eighth congress seemed to follow their political allegiances. One delegate, clearly hostile to Mr. Yeltsin's politics, declared, "He should have done this long ago."

Others were more sympathetic, agreeing that it was time to separate the functions of party and government.

Yet by simply withdrawing from the party, Mr. Yeltsin once again established himself as the real point man of Soviet politics. It was a role he donned first at the preceding party congress, in February 1986, when he broke new ground in a candid attack on bureaucratism, corruption, and inertia.

Twenty months later, Mr. Gorbachev dropped Mr. Yeltsin from the Politburo, sending him off on an independent and sometimes sensational political path.

Mr. Yeltsin became critical of the pace of change under Mr. Gorbachev and increasingly bold in pressing his attack. In a book published in the West, he described the Soviet leader as "my perpetual opponent, the lover of half measures and half steps."

Theatrical, populist, earthy, and irreverent, the 59-year-old Siberian evolved into a hero of the long-disenfranchised common folk. On May 29 he capped his comeback by being elected president of the Russian republic despite a strong personal campaign against him by Mr. Gorbachev.

In the tumult of the new Soviet politics, nobody was prepared today to predict the ramifications of Mr. Yeltsin's move or of the potential split in the Communist Party posed by the creation of the Democratic Platform.

What the defections underscored was the steady erosion of the party despite its wealth, power, and reach.

The battle seemed no longer to be over the party's policies or direction, but over survival. Much of the day, for example, was devoted to an often rancorous battle over an article of the new party rules that grants broad autonomy to each republic party organization.

2 Top City Chiefs Quit Soviet Party as Congress Ends
By Francis X. Clines

MOSCOW, JULY 13—The Communist Party suffered additional major defections today as the Moscow and Leningrad city council leaders quit the party and insurgent forces began moving slowly toward forming a national opposition coalition.

The departure of two of the most popular opposition figures—Gavriil K. Popov, head of the Moscow government, and Anatoly A. Sobchak, the Leningrad leader—was announced as the party's national congress ended a two-week debate riddled with self-doubt and deepening skepticism about the party's value.

Above all else, President Mikhail S. Gorbachev pressed for party unity until the final moments, praising the delegates and declaring in an interview with CBS News, "Those who reject our socialist past I view with contempt."

"I am not veering from my course," said the Soviet leader, who tightened his grip on the party at the congress. "And I have many supporters."

Mr. Popov and Mr. Sobchak, democratically elected officials who have galvanized free-market moves in the nation's two largest cities, said the party was incapable of leading the nation to democracy and prosperity.

"The twenty-eighth party congress, in which so much hope had been placed among the party and the people, demonstrated the complete inability of the Communist Party to propose to the country a real program for the transition to a new society," the city leaders said in a statement that urged rededicated efforts to create grass-roots political pluralism.

Mr. Gorbachev said he had expected Mr. Yeltsin's resignation. "But I regret it very much," he added, contending that the departure was "no great achievement either for him or for us."

But the departures of Mr. Sobchak, Mr. Popov, and Mr. Yeltsin seem likely to accelerate the party's drop in prestige and the loss of rank-and-file members who have been handing in their membership cards by the tens of thousands in recent months.

As Chancellor Kohl visited Gorbachev another momentous breakthrough was achieved.

Gorbachev Clears Way for German Unity, Dropping Objection to NATO Membership
By Serge Schmemann

ZHELEZNOVODSK, U.S.S.R., JULY 16—The Soviet Union and West Germany agreed today to let a united Germany join NATO and to lift virtually all other remaining barriers to German reunification.

The breakthrough was announced at this spa in the foothills of the Caucasus Mountains by President Mikhail S. Gorbachev of the Soviet Union and Chancellor Helmut Kohl of West Germany after two days of talks marked by unusual displays of harmony and confidence.

Making no effort to conceal his jubilation, Mr. Kohl told West German television, "This is a breakthrough, a fantastic result."

Mr. Gorbachev, who opened the news conference on the accord with a promise of "interesting news," declared, "We are leaving one epoch in international relations, and entering another, a period, I think, of strong, prolonged peace."

The agreement, announced after talks in Moscow and at a mountain hideaway, ends months of maneuvering and sparring between Moscow and the West over German unity. After Moscow's initial resistance to Western demands that a united Germany remain in NATO, a variety of formulas was proposed to enable the Soviets to withdraw from East Germany with dignity and some assurances for their economic and military security.

In the accord, Mr. Gorbachev effectively agreed to surrender all of the Soviet Union's remaining claims as an occupier of Germany and to renounce any restrictions on Germany's sovereignty, including its right to join whatever alliance it prefers.

Mr. Kohl said he had told Moscow that a united Germany would seek to become a member of the North Atlantic Treaty Organization.

In exchange, Mr. Kohl said, the Germans agreed to negotiate a treaty with the Soviet Union covering all aspects of their relations—political, economic, military, cultural, and scientific. No details were immediately available, but officials said the treaty would include provisions for wide economic and technical cooperation.

The Soviet-German agreements make it virtually certain that the Germans will be able to hold all-German elections and to reunite formally by the end of this year.

The Germans also agreed to restrict the future German military to 370,000 troops, compared with about 667,000 now for the two German armies combined. West Germany currently has about 494,000 active forces and East Germany, 173,000.

The Germans also pledged to allow Soviet troops to remain on East German territory for a three- to four-year transition period. Mr. Kohl said Germany would help pay for the maintenance and the withdrawal of the 350,000-strong Soviet force, and that American, British, and French troops would remain in Berlin until the Soviet troops had withdrawn.

The Germans further agreed that no NATO troops, nuclear weapons, or German forces assigned to NATO would be deployed on what is now East German soil during the transition period, and probably not afterward.

"We were unanimous that on the key questions we achieved a far-reaching success," Chancellor Kohl said at the press conference. "This breakthrough was critical because both sides are aware that the historic changes happening in Europe, Germany, and the Soviet Union place special responsibility on us."

The arrangements were designed to satisfy Moscow's concerns over the strength of a future Germany and the problem of repatriating a large military contingent for which the Soviet Union has neither barracks nor jobs.

Officials said details of the agreements would be worked out at various forums, including the "two plus four" talks among the Germanys and the World War II Allies, scheduled to resume on Tuesday in Paris, and the Vienna talks on reducing conventional arms in Europe.

Mr. Kohl said the Soviets had agreed to conclude the series of two-plus-four talks in time for a meeting of the Conference on European Security and Cooperation in November, at which European countries, the United States, and Canada will effectively give international endorsement to Germany's reunification.

The agreement marked a major personal triumph for Mr. Kohl, who sat throughout the press conference with a broad grin across his face. Two weeks after achieving the monetary and economic union of the two Germanys, Mr. Kohl now faces an unobstructed home stretch toward unity.

The two-day display of his personal rapport with Mr. Gorbachev, underscored by the invitation to join the Soviet President in his native regions in southern Russia, seemed certain to strengthen further Mr. Kohl's already strong chances of being elected the first chancellor of a reunited Germany.

Mr. Gorbachev treated Mr. Kohl with an intimacy that no other Western leader has enjoyed with the Soviet President. The two traveled together on a tour of Stavropol, which was long the Soviet leader's home, and then spent the night in a lodge in Arkhyz, a resort in the Caucasus Mountains.

"Our talks were very candid and marked by understanding and personal sympathy," Mr. Kohl said. Mr. Gorbachev said the discussions had been conducted in "the spirit of that well-known German word, *realpolitik.* "

German and Soviet officials agreed that the breakthrough was made possible by the series of meetings of Western leaders in recent weeks, including the European Community session in Dublin, the United States–Soviet summit meeting in Washington, the gathering of the seven leading industrial powers in Houston, and above all, the NATO summit meeting in London. In these meetings, the officials said, the West effectively agreed to eliminate the vestiges of the cold war and to consider ways to help Mr. Gorbachev's program of *perestroika.*

"We could not have reached this agreement without the context in which the visit took place," Mr. Gorbachev said. "In recent months we've had tens of summit meetings, at which all these burning questions touching on the fundamental changes in Europe were discussed."

He specifically referred to the NATO summit in London this month, in which the alliance formally agreed to a reconciliation with the Warsaw Pact, to restructure NATO thoroughly, and to invite Mr. Gorbachev to address it. NATO leaders also gave Mr. Kohl the go-ahead to set a specific ceiling on the size of a unified Germany's forces in his talks with the Soviet President.

"We received an impulse from London, the last meeting of NATO, where important and positive steps were made," Mr. Gorbachev said. "We do not say we applaud everything. Far from it. But a movement began, a historical turn in the development of this very important organization."

NATO's decisions enabled Mr. Gorbachev to tell his nation that Moscow was not giving up positions won through the sacrifices of World War II, but moving to a new stage of cooperation and development.

In comments clearly aimed at his audience at home, the Soviet President tried to argue that a united Germany's membership in NATO would have advantages. "Whether we want it or not, the day will come when the reality will be that a united Germany is in NATO," he said. "And if that is its choice, then it will still make formal arrangements to cooperate with the Soviet Union, and that's to our advantage."

Both Mr. Kohl and Mr. Gorbachev gave credit to their foreign ministers, Hans-Dietrich Genscher and Eduard A. Shevardnadze, who met at least eight times in recent weeks to hammer out the agreement.

The two ministers left directly from their meetings here for Paris to attend the two-plus-four talks. Interviewed on West German television while en route to Paris, Mr. Genscher declared, "The message of Moscow is: Germany will come together this year."

Although the agreement involved a major Soviet concession, it was viewed as a personal success for Mr. Gorbachev, a reflection of the new authority gained through his triumph last week over hard-line forces at the Communist Party congress.

German officials have long believed that Mr. Gorbachev is eager to cultivate relations with a united Germany as the centerpiece of his campaign to revamp the Soviet economy and open it to the West. They have also felt that he was hampered in those efforts by the resistance of Communist hard-liners ranged behind Yegor K. Ligachev.

"He made it clear in private conversations that he now felt cleared for a major reform effort," one senior official said. He said the German offer of a comprehensive treaty played a major role in satisfying Mr. Gorbachev that the Soviet Union would not be locked out of the new Europe that is taking shape with Germany at its heart.

Mr. Gorbachev emphasized repeatedly today and on Sunday that the two Germanys are Moscow's largest trading partners in their respective camps, and that a united Germany is therefore destined to play a major role in the Soviet Union's economic future.

Many of his statements at the press conference seemed intended to allay a widespread feeling at home that Moscow is abandoning the security and influence for which 20 million Soviet citizens died in World War II.

"They accept that the Germans, bearing on their shoulders the lesson of history, a dramatic, traumatic history, have in both their states reached certain conclusions," Mr. Gorbachev said.

"They have shown in their postwar history that they are for democracy, that their policy is that no war should arise from German soil, that they are open to cooperation with other nations. Without this nothing could have happened."

As July gave way to August, Saddam Hussein ordered the Iraqi army to conquer Kuwait. In the initial phase of the operation, foreign embassies in Kuwait City were besieged by the Iraqis. For years Moscow had been Iraq's major arms supplier and the two countries had long had close relations. Yet within two days of the invasion the Soviets joined with the United States in signing a declaration in Moscow that said, "Today, we take the unusual step of jointly calling on the rest of the international community to join with us in an international cutoff of all arms supplies to Iraq." In the months ahead the Soviets not only refrained from using their veto in Iraq's behalf but also joined in a naval blockade and voted for the United Nations resolutions that led to sanctions and war against Baghdad.

Gorbachev Sends a Signal Ending Hesitation at U.N.
By Bill Keller

MOSCOW, AUG. 24—President Mikhail S. Gorbachev warned President Saddam Hussein of Iraq today that the Iraqi leader will face additional international sanctions if he does not withdraw his troops from Kuwait and release foreign nationals under his control.

Mr. Gorbachev's message to the Iraqi leader, reported by the Tass press agency, was a clear sign that Moscow was prepared to support a United Nations resolution authorizing limited military measures to enforce the embargo against Iraq. Members of the 15-member Security Council gathered tonight to begin debating a draft resolution.

Arab diplomats and Soviet journalists here said that despite the Soviets' hesitation to back the use of force, there was now little doubt that Moscow would withdraw its objections to the United States–sponsored resolution in the United Nations Security Council aimed at increasing naval pressure on Iraqi cargo vessels.

"I am 100 percent sure the Soviet Union will either vote for the measure or abstain," said Maksim A. Yusin, the diplomatic correspondent for the government newspaper, *Izvestia.* "A veto can be ruled out."

"It seems to me they are losing patience with the Iraqis," a senior Arab diplomat said.

In what Tass described as "an urgent personal message," Mr. Gorbachev called on President Hussein to begin immediately honoring United Nations resolutions demanding that Iraqis leave Kuwait, restore the ousted government, and assure the safety of foreigners.

"Evading these resolutions will inevitably compel the Security Council to adopt appropriate additional measures," Tass quoted Mr. Gorbachev as saying.

The news agency itself added, "It now depends on the Iraqi side how the Security Council will act."

Moscow has not wavered from its condemnation of Iraq and its endorsement of economic sanctions, but Soviet leaders have consistently pleaded for more time to let the sanctions work before applying new pressures.

During the last week, Moscow has become a crossroads of international diplomacy, with senior diplomats from Iraq and Saudi Arabia visiting this week to compete for the Kremlin's support, and the foreign ministers of Kuwait and Egypt expected within days.

Arab diplomats said one clear signal of Moscow's loyalties in the crisis was the brusque official treatment of Iraq's emissary, Deputy Prime Minister Saddun Hammadi, compared with the warm welcome given the special emissary of the Saudi royal family, Prince Bandar Bin Sultan al-Saud.

Although Moscow has no diplomatic relations with Saudi Arabia, the prince spent hours with Foreign Minister Eduard A. Shevardnadze and other senior officials, and told fellow Arab diplomats afterward that he was satisfied with the Soviet position.

"We have no reason to think they are not serious," said a Persian Gulf diplomat who sat in on some of the talks. "We will give them the time."

In meetings with Prince Bandar and other Arab diplomats, the Soviets argued for delay so that Mr. Hammadi could pass along the Kremlin's mounting impatience to his superiors in Baghdad.

In the meantime, they argued, a few leaks in the embargo would not seriously reduce the pressure on President Hussein.

"They still hope they can influence Iraq, because they feel Iraq has nowhere to go," an Arab diplomat said.

Arab diplomats said Soviet officials also argued for caution because they see a serious risk of a catastrophic war, including the use of chemical weapons.

"There is still a lot of anxiety in this country," Mr. Yusin, the *Izvestia* correspondent, said in an interview. "The memory of Afghanistan is fresh, and when the coffins start coming from the Gulf not everyone will think the goal of stopping the aggressor is noble."

Diplomats and Soviet journalists said another factor in the more moderate Soviet approach was concern about the fate of Soviet nationals in the region, and a desire to evacuate as many as possible before increasing the pressure on Baghdad.

The Foreign Ministry said today that it had completed its evacuation of all 882 Soviet nationals from Kuwait, and was scheduled to begin removing Soviet women and children from Iraq this weekend.

"Soviet citizens in Iraq are not regarded as hostages, unlike citizens of Western countries, but we cannot take risks," Prime Minister Nikolai I. Ryzhkov said on television tonight.

Offsetting the Soviet reluctance to move too quickly against Iraq is a feeling that the Gulf crisis is a test of Moscow's commitment to new principles of international conduct, and the desire for the potential economic benefits that would flow from acceptance in the West.

Early in September Gorbachev and Bush met in Helsinki to jointly affirm their resolve to force Iraq to pull back from Kuwait. But while the Gulf conflict was providing Gorbachev with another opportunity to demonstrate the new Western orientation of Soviet policies, for just about everyone in the Soviet Union, issues of foreign affairs were being dwarfed by the problems of national economics.

The Bread Shelves in Moscow Shops Suddenly Go Bare
By Bill Keller

MOSCOW, SEPT. 3—Moscow consumers today faced a new and ultimate insult, a bread shortage, as the city's bakeries failed before the appetites of residents flooding back into the city from their annual August vacations.

The empty bread shelves prompted ominous reports on the main evening television news program, *Vremya,* and in the government daily, *Izvestia,* which treated the shortage not as a seasonal fluke but as a sign of the continuing breakdown of the state-run economy.

Izvestia deftly alluded to the fact that bread shortages set off the revolution that ousted the Russian monarchy in March 1917.

"I've seen empty shelves in a bread store for the first time in my life," said an irritated Moscow shopper who failed to find his lunchtime loaf at a bakery on Yermolova Street. "They taught us at school that the first revolution began with bread lines."

There were no reports of riots like those that have accompanied the tobacco shortage this summer, but the breadless days seemed certain to give a fresh sense of urgency to an emergency economic plan devised by the economic advisers of President Mikhail S. Gorbachev and Boris N. Yeltsin, President of the Russian republic.

The plan, unveiled today in its 250 pages of detail at a meeting of the Russian parliament, calls for slashing budgets for foreign aid, the military, and the K.G.B., selling state property, and freeing peasants to become private farmers, among first steps in a 500-day march to free markets.

Mr. Gorbachev has not given his public blessing to the plan, saying that details remain to be worked out, but leaders of the Russian republic said the Soviet leader has endorsed the program.

It was prepared under the supervision of one of his economic advisers, Stanislav S. Shatalin. Today two other Gorbachev economic advisers, speaking on the condition that they not be identified, confirmed to visiting Westerners that the Soviet President had approved the Shatalin plan.

While Mr. Gorbachev kept his silence, Mr. Yeltsin's Prime Minister, Ivan S. Silayev, was shown on television tonight describing what he called "the Gorbachev-Yeltsin economic program."

The 500-day plan, to begin October 1, would attack inflation with sharp cuts in government spending, including 10 percent of the military budget, 20 percent of the K.G.B. budget, and 75 percent of noneconomic foreign aid. State property would be sold, beginning with cars and trucks, unfinished construction projects, and some military equipment with civilian uses.

The plan also calls for court suits to reclaim property that is in the hands of "public organizations"—the largest being the Communist Party—for resale to individuals and businesses.

Any member of a state farm would be given the legal right to leave the collective farm, taking with him a plot of land and a share of the common wealth.

By January 1, at least half the state ministries that now oversee the economy would be abolished.

In 1991, state price controls would be gradually phased out, retaining fixed prices only on basic food and consumer goods.

The later stages would bring the further freeing of prices, introduction of wage indexing, the widespread transfer of state-owned factories to stock companies or private ownership, and rapid steps toward making the ruble freely convertible. The ruble, like other soft currencies, is traded in the Soviet Union at rates established by the government, while hard currencies like the dollar, the Japanese yen, and the West German mark are traded freely.

After 500 days, the authors of the plan said, 70 percent of industrial enterprises and up to 90 percent of the construction industry and retail trade would no longer be in state hands.

Mr. Yeltsin is betting that Soviet consumers are ready to accept radical measures to relieve the waves of shortages that have created such a combustible mood in the country.

In recent weeks, tobacco shortages have caused riots in several cities. Spontaneous street protests in Moscow are a daily occurrence as frustrated smokers block traffic or surround empty tobacco kiosks.

Gorbachev Endorses a Proposal for Free Enterprise in 500 Days
By Francis X. Clines

MOSCOW, SEPT. 11—On a day of disarray in the Kremlin, President Mikhail S. Gorbachev finally endorsed a national economic reform plan today but was quickly upstaged as the parliament of the Russian republic rushed the plan to approval to prod the central government to more decisive action.

In the Kremlin, angry members of the national parliament spent the day confronting the Gorbachev government and urging it to make a choice and get the stagnant economy moving toward free-market innovations after months of indecision.

But across town, the legislature of Russia, the largest and richest of the nation's republics, enthusiastically approved the plan of the dominant insurgents to scrap the Communist economic monolith and install a free-enterprise economy within 500 days.

The two actions displayed the heart of the revision struggle in this deeply troubled nation. The national government is anxious about yielding its powerful central economic controls, while the nation's 15 republics are rushing to take the free-market bit into their teeth.

The Russian parliament's vote was 251 to 1. The fast action was engineered by Boris N. Yeltsin, President of the Russian republic, the chief proponent of the 500-day plan and a political rival of President Gorbachev who has struck something of an alliance with the Soviet leader on the economic crisis.

The legislative quickness of Russia, with three-quarters of the nation's land, more than half the population, and most of its natural resources, only added to the sense of frustration among members of the national parliament.

"Where's the program?" said a member of the national parliament in the raucous Kremlin session, as the Gorbachev government failed to meet an earlier promise to resolve its internal disagreement over the economy and present a full-scale proposal today. Demands increased for the resignation of Mr. Gorbachev's Prime Minister, Nikolai I. Ryzhkov.

As he finally committed himself publicly, Mr. Gorbachev appeared to surprise Mr. Ryzhkov. The embattled head of the Gorbachev cabinet has been championing the alternative plan, which would take a slower, far more cautious retreat from central control as the most socially prudent course to free-market changes.

"I'm listening and I can't understand what's going on," a lawmaker said, and soon President Gorbachev stepped in, angrily demanding that the parliament be patient and behave.

"All these charges, insults, innuendo—it smells bad, very bad," Mr. Gorbachev said. "Why are there attempts to corner us today? Wait a little bit. The process is under way."

The critical event in a day of heated, confused Kremlin wrangling was that Mr. Gorbachev, after considerable hesitation, finally committed himself to the 500 days proposal for moving toward free enterprise.

"If you ask me, I am more impressed by the Shatalin program," the Soviet leader said, referring to Stanislav S. Shatalin, an economist who is chairman of a crisis study commission that created an economic revision plan that is faster and presumably more traumatic than an alternative proposal.

"It brings together the republics on the basis of what we need," the Soviet leader said of the Shatalin plan. Mr. Gorbachev has been pressed by the republics for greater sovereignty and has promised them far more initiative in national recovery.

At issue in the choice between the plans was just how much inflation and social disruption each might bring to a nation already reeling from widespread shortages in consumer goods and a state economy stultified by seven decades of central bureaucratic dictates. The Ryzhkov proposal would resist the wholesale denationalization plans of the Shatalin proposal and be slower to ease the existing price and currency controls.

After committing himself at the parliamentary session, Mr. Gorbachev then characteristically sent Kremlin planners back for another attempt at what thus far has proved impossible, blending the Shatalin and Ryzhkov proposals into a single plan.

"The fact that the country's biggest republic will accept our plan will settle everything," Mr. Shatalin said. He insists that the great economic problem can be solved from the outside in, if the republics adopt and enforce the 500-day plan even as the central government continues to struggle indecisively.

Some members of the national parliament complained bitterly that they had been kept in the dark about all but the general direction of the rival plans.

"Shatalin has been working in Mozambique and Ryzhkov in New Zealand," a lawmaker said.

The Shatalin plan, as described by Mr. Yeltsin and his aides, would give the 15 Soviet republics almost total economic autonomy, and the republics would take part in an emergency program to curb inflation and stabilize the economy. The plan would expand the rights of private ownership, create a banking system and stock markets, establish ways to protect low-income people, set selected wage and price controls in its early stages, and include an infusion of imported consumer goods to absorb loose cash.

Eventually, according to the plan, subsidies to industry and agriculture would be ended, most ministries that regulate industry would be abolished, state controls over most prices would end, and farmland, housing, and businesses would be extensively privatized.

Mr. Ryzhkov's plan is a refined version of the program that the Soviet parliament rejected in May. He proposed keeping much more central authority in Moscow, with tighter state controls on prices and property ownership.

Mr. Ryzhkov drew the most anger at the Kremlin session as insurgent lawmakers insisted that, after five years of the Gorbachev government's failure to stir major economic change, he had no credibility.

A Historic Moment Slips By, Overtaken by Other Events
By Serge Schmemann

MOSCOW, SEPT. 12—For an event of such historic dimensions, the signing today of the final settlement between the Germans and the World War II victors seemed almost lost in the tumult of more immediate concerns.

Moscow was gripped by suspense over a grand new economic plan promised by President Mikhail S. Gorbachev. The Germans fretted over the rising cost of unification and braced for the actual moment of unity, now only three weeks off. Americans and Western Europeans were preoccupied by the standoff with Iraq.

And yet the "Treaty on the Final Settlement with Respect to Germany," to give it its full title, arguably had a significance akin to agreements familiar from every high school history text—the Versailles Treaty of 1871, from which a united Germany first emerged, and the Potsdam conference of 1945, from which the Germans emerged severed in two.

Now, after 45 years, the victorious allies were finally resolving the "German Question" and putting an end to the last formal remnants of occupation.

They were restoring full sovereignty to a nation that had savaged Europe a half century earlier. In exchange, the Germans were renouncing all claims to ancestral lands east of the Oder and Neisse rivers lost to Poland and the Soviet Union, restricting their military, and pledging that hereafter only peace would emanate from German soil.

More broadly, the European powers were laying the groundwork for a new European order, with a potent, wealthy Germany at its heart. Perhaps more clearly than any previous event, the treaty demonstrated the retreat of Communism from Europe. Not only the West German mark had gone east—the full Western package of liberal democracy, free-market economy, and the North Atlantic alliance were being voluntarily accepted by the bankrupt rump of the "first state of workers and peasants on German soil."

Yet it was probably the first modern peace treaty that took pains to leave no winners or losers. The Germans, in fact, were insistent that it not be called a "peace treaty" at all, to underscore that it had been achieved in peace. In 1871, by contrast, a united Germany was proclaimed by Bismarck after a war against France, and in 1945 the victors had met in the midst of the smoldering ruins of the Third Reich.

But this, Chancellor Helmut Kohl declared, was "the first unification of a country in modern history achieved without war, pain, or strife."

The statement invited a quick knock on wood, but it did reflect what the six signers—the United States, the Soviet Union, Britain, France, and the two Germanys—all agreed had been a harmonious and creative negotiation.

Secretary of State James A. Baker 3d said the process had created a "new lexicon of openness, cooperation, and partnership," and he went out of his way to praise Foreign Minister Eduard A. Shevardnadze of the Soviet Union.

The very harmony of the process was one reason why the signing of the final settlement could not attract as much attention as economic turmoil or military tension. Despite some eleventh-hour haggling on technicalities and the price the Germans would pay the Soviets, the two-plus-four negotiations never really developed suspense.

The talks, moreover, were not really the locomotive or even the key to German unity. It was really the momentum to reunification touched off by the breach of the Berlin wall and the collapse of Communism in East Europe that had finally compelled the old Allies to resolve the nettlesome "German Question."

In the end, the forces that brought Nazi Germany to its knees and partitioned it 45 years earlier often seemed to be pushed toward a settlement at a pace that they neither set nor really liked.

The Soviet Union, which had, through its own internal reforms, directly empowered the East Germans to shed Communism, found itself especially uneasy at the prospect of losing its premier foothold in the West, and much of the real bargaining was over how to disentangle the Soviets from their enormous commitment to East Germany.

The solution was both bizarre and Solomonic. The Soviet Union was given four years to withdraw its army from Germany, and in the interim the Germans would help pay for the force and finance new housing for the troops when they return home. NATO forces would stay out of East German territory, though they would maintain garrisons in Berlin.

Mr. Gorbachev tried to put a positive twist on the situation, saying that the Soviet troops were now "representatives of a friendly country." Foreign Minister Hans-Dietrich Genscher of West Germany was more blunt: the $7.5 billion deal, he said, was "the price of unity."

It was not a cynical comment from Mr. Genscher. He had been among the first to recognize the promise for Germany held out by the Soviet policy of *perestroika,* or "restructuring," and the large majority of his countrymen shared his view that Mr. Gorbachev was the true midwife of German unity, and deserved a reward.

Military-political technicalities dominated the immediate discussion of the treaty. But if this served to obscure the historic dimensions of the accord, it also underscored its major virtue—that for once in their history, the Europeans were shaping a new order without bloodshed or trauma.

The negotiators seemed to tacitly agree from the outset that to humiliate the Russians or to frustrate the Germans would only undermine European security, and the main challenge of the negotiations became to find ways of avoiding either pitfall.

The initial breakthrough was the decision at NATO's summit meeting in July to forswear any aggressive intentions and to extend a hand of cooperation to the Soviets. That cleared the way for the next major step, the Soviet–West German summit talks at which Mr. Gorbachev and Mr. Kohl agreed on a face-saving way for the Soviets to extricate themselves from East Germany while maintaining influence in European affairs.

The "new European security order" that both East and West have now declared as their goal, in which the two alliances would be replaced by a single conflict-resolving mechanism based on the Conference on Security and Cooperation in Europe, is still a long way off. It will be four years before the last Soviet troops leave East Germany, and both Eastern Europe and the Soviet Union still face great upheavals.

But by making history as quietly as they did, by signing a treaty without undue debate and controversy, the authors of the Moscow treaty may have shown that shaping a new order does not necessarily require a major upheaval.

Soviet Parliament Grants Gorbachev Emergency Power

By Celestine Bohlen

MOSCOW, SEPT. 24—The Soviet parliament granted President Mikhail S. Gorbachev emergency economic powers today, but put off, at his request, answering the critical question of how to move to a free market.

The Supreme Soviet granted Mr. Gorbachev his request for additional authority by an overwhelming vote of 305 to 36, despite warnings from the giant Russian republic that it will not tolerate any infringement of its sovereign rights.

The vote in the national parliament, reflecting the country's vacillating and uncertain political mood, seemed to defy the trend that in recent months has drained power from Moscow toward republic and regional centers.

In an angry, impatient speech, Mr. Gorbachev challenged the lawmakers to give him special powers over the next 18 months to pull the country out of its mounting crisis.

"Everybody agrees that a more effective functioning of government, especially of executive power, is needed," the Soviet President said. "The fact that this hasn't happened has given rise to distress and much criticism."

The resolution approved by the national parliament today would give the Soviet President authority to put into effect policies on wages, prices, finances, and the budget and also the "strengthening of law and order." The Supreme Soviet would have the right to challenge the President's directives, but its approval in advance would not be required.

Parliament today also accepted Mr. Gorbachev's proposal to create a compromise between two opposing views on the country's future economic course, averting a showdown between the more conservative approach advocated by Prime Minister Nikolai I. Ryzhkov and a swifter, radical transition favored by Mr. Gorbachev's top economists.

The compromise, to be worked out by October 15, should include elements of both plans, Mr. Gorbachev told lawmakers today.

"No single plan can be finally adopted," he said. "It is my deep conviction that we have to unite forces at this decisive moment. If we split up, if we clash, we will ruin this historic turning point."

As the Soviet Union heads into a period of wrenching economic change, it also faces unresolved questions about the redistribution of power—between the central government and the republics, between the presidency and the legislature, among newly emerging political factions.

Mr. Gorbachev has put his political skills to the test by trying to accommodate opposing points of view. In the economic debate, he managed to back both sides, defending Mr. Ryzhkov's beleaguered government while seeming to push for the more radical program proposed by one of his top economic advisers, Stanislav S. Shatalin.

In the debate today, Mr. Shatalin compared Mr. Gorbachev to the captain of a football team who tries to fix the game so that both sides win. Mr. Ryzhkov, emerging from the parliament chamber, echoed the same thought by declaring that today's vote had left "no winners and no losers."

But in his bid for additional powers, Mr. Gorbachev also showed impatience for opposing views. In a scathing speech, he scorned his critics, dismissing their objections as "juridical" and their concern about his accumulation of power as "political speculation."

"Some may consider the President's moves wrong, but let the President you have elected on behalf of the country have an opinion of his own and not be a puppet," he said. "I assume the responsibility, and I defend it."

In a day of sometimes bitter legislative debate, members of the national parliament attacked the leadership of the Russian republic for its hasty reaction to Mr. Gorbachev's bid for special powers. Over the weekend, Boris N. Yeltsin, President of the Russian republic, had signed a statement calling Mr. Gorbachev's request "inadmissible," and had warned that any attempts to undermine the republic's sovereignty would be met by countermeasures.

Today, Yuri Golik, chairman of a parliament legal committee, accused the Russians of acting on rumors and misinterpreting the nature of the resolution to expand the President's powers. "They scared themselves and the people," he said.

Mr. Gorbachev and his supporters insisted today that he was not usurping the powers of either the Supreme Soviet or the republics. Nor, they said, does he plan to suspend the work of locally elected institutions—though the Soviet leader last Friday said such action might be necessary "in some cases."

The resolution to grant the President special powers was amended today to extend through March 31, 1992, which corresponds roughly to the 500-day timetable for the transition to a market economy proposed by Mr. Shatalin.

Mr. Gorbachev's request for extra powers today overshadowed the debate over the economy. Gennadi Filshin, a deputy prime minister of the Russian republic, called the move "an attempt to discredit the parliament," while others, like the Soviet Interior Minister, Vadim V. Bakatin, looked at it as an attempt to resolve a mounting legal crisis, "to draw up new rules of the game."

Soviet Market Plan: Who's on First?

By Francis X. Clines

MOSCOW, OCT. 1—President Mikhail S. Gorbachev's extraordinary powers for resuscitating the economy are a week old, and already at least one citizen, Prime Minister Nikolai I. Ryzhkov, has found his stock rising, although mainly as a defender of the traditional central planning authority of Communism.

Deepening the doubt that anything very concrete will soon proceed from Mr. Gorbachev's uncertain plans for escaping to the free market from the collapsing economic maze of Communism, the Soviet leader has used his first executive order to agree to Mr. Ryzhkov's request to keep the central economic plan of the union intact for the next 15 months.

No one knows what real effect, if any, the Gorbachev decree will have in demanding that the separatist-minded republics and insurgent localities stop free-lancing market change on their own and live up to the central plan's contracts for delivering goods and services across the nation. They have long been working on their own agenda of decentralized economic sovereignty as the government repeatedly fails to create a workable plan to revive the economy.

Beyond that, as a statement of his true intent, the President's order is bitter comfort for reformers wanting to see enactment of a firm plan to scrap Communism and switch to the free market across a 500-day period.

For the presidential order appears as finely tailored to the figure of Mr. Ryzhkov as one of his own natty business suits. Mr. Gorbachev's prime minister is the chief opponent of the 500-day plan. And now the presidential decree secures for him the heart of the reformers' targeted 500-day transition and promises him wider authority in this period to enforce the status-quo economic plan of the central planning ministries, the discredited channels of the old Communist monolith.

Although Kremlin demonstrators had demanded Mr. Ryzhkov's resignation as a symbol of the Gorbachev government's economic failure, he not only survives as prime minister but even has powers to take emergency actions with the railroads and other institutions. His cabinet not only endures, said *Kommersant,* the country's leading independent economic newspaper, but has been "mummified" like Lenin.

The old establishment system already appears emboldened by the new decree, and not just because Mr. Gorbachev attributed the ruinous state of the pharmaceutical industry more to the fledgling popular movements for consumer and ecology safety than on the failed stewardship of Communism. There is even an attempt afoot by hard-line polemicists to place the blame for the economic morass on some all-inclusive plot by the country's highly disorganized and still decidedly minor-strength opposition movement.

The main hope for reformers now would appear to be the very contrariness and unpredictability of Mr. Gorbachev on this bedrock issue. Last month he proposed a grand referendum, amid the supposedly urgent economy debate, on privatizing state land. The idea has since appeared to vaporize. Just as suddenly, judging from his current behavior patterns, might the Soviet leader offer some melodramatic reendorsement of the theory—though not necessarily a plan—of a free-market transition.

Mr. Gorbachev's public agonizing over the economy is believable. He needs to find a tool to break the central ministries' soul-deadening economic grip in the long run and proceed to the market. But in the short run, his concern is social stability, which has long been the specialty of the central command system.

As he agonizes, the public waits in ever longer lines for ever shrinking varieties and supplies of goods. Last Saturday, the wait for a winter hat was a Dante-like, five-hour-long snake of compressed, depressed humanity at a neighborhood department store.

Even that vaunted Moscow beachhead of Western marketing, McDonald's, had to double the cost of the "Big Mek" today to almost seven rubles—half the average worker's daily pay—because of the inflationary cost of meat under the now more sacrosanct central ministries' plan.

Izvestia, the government newspaper, scathingly observed that while the leadership dithers nervously over abstractions about the market, the people are learning about it in the real world.

"I have no idea what the free market is," a waiting shopper said on a grocery line. "But I suspect this whole debate is really about how the same old apparatchiks are trying to control this new system and fill their pockets the same way they do now."

The woman presented a fair measure of the level of public cynicism toward Kremlin decrees. She scoffed at Mr. Ryzhkov's precise, dark, expert warnings about food shortages. Only 12,000 tons of winter potatoes in Moscow, 28,000 tons in Leningrad, he intoned in warning a week ago against the 500-day plan. Her point was that here is a central government process whose 70-year-old track record has been devoid of any such mastery over facts, never mind food.

Amid the confusions and contradictions, Gorbachev received another kudo when on October 15 it was announced in Oslo that he had been named the 1990 winner of the Nobel Peace Prize for abetting political change in Eastern Europe and his efforts to help end the cold war.

Gorbachev's Prize; Soviet Leader Is Regarded as a Hero Everywhere but in His Own Country

By Bill Keller

MOSCOW, OCT. 15—Mikhail S. Gorbachev today became the second Soviet champion of democratic reform to win the Nobel Peace Prize, and the second to be denied a national celebration in this country so often out of step with the world's enthusiasm.

When Andrei D. Sakharov was honored in 1975 for his campaign against Communist suppression of human rights, the private joy of the country's freedom lovers was muted by an official chorus of vilification. The official press called the prize "political pornography" and mocked Dr. Sakharov as a Judas who had sold out to the C.I.A.

Fifteen years later, Mr. Gorbachev's moment was greeted with ambivalence in his parliament, widespread indifference on the street, and bitterness from Mr. Sakharov's widow.

Mr. Gorbachev's compatriots generally acknowledged that his award was justified, but said it would not distract attention from ethnic conflict at home or the indignity of the food markets, where a dozen eggs now cost two days' wages.

"I am sure that he deserves the Peace Prize," said Georgi A. Arbatov, director of the U.S.A. and Canada Institute and a member of parliament. "I wouldn't think he has deserved the Nobel Prize for economics."

Mr. Gorbachev got the news from the Norwegian ambassador while he was closeted with aides repolishing a much-postponed program to dismantle central economic controls and create a free market. His plan was scheduled for presentation today but was delayed until later in the week as he tried to strike a balance between radical and conservative variants.

The Soviet leader told a pool of television reporters that he was "thrilled" by the award and would go to Oslo for the presentation ceremony on December 10, "like all other recipients" of the prize. The comment overlooked one notable exception: Dr. Sakharov, who was refused permission to leave the country.

He said the prize reaffirmed the correctness of his policies and would energize him "intellectually, emotionally, and physically."

Mr. Gorbachev's spokesman said he had not decided what to do with the cash prize of about $710,000 that accompanies the award. In the past he has shared foreign awards and book advances with the Communist Party and domestic charities.

While the lack of public celebration had its parallel to the award to Dr. Sakharov, it also formed a stark contrast with the way the Soviet Union responded when two of its citizens, Boris Pasternak and Aleksandr Solzhenitsyn, were awarded Nobel Prizes for literature in 1958 and 1970, respectively. Under pressure and intimidation from the government, both men turned down their prizes after first accepting, although Mr. Solzhenitsyn eventually was able to pick up his award four years later after he was expelled from his native land.

In the Soviet parliament, where a hard-line minority spent much of the day savaging the policies that won Mr. Gorbachev the favor of the Nobel Committee, the announcement was greeted with five seconds of lukewarm applause.

During a rare and freewheeling foreign policy debate with Foreign Minister Eduard A. Shevardnadze, critics charged that Mr. Gorbachev had sapped Soviet strength and prestige by his liberation of Eastern Europe and slashing of the military.

"Even I could defend the interests of the Soviet Union in this way, by making concessions, unjustified concessions," said Col. Nikolai S. Petrushenko, an army propaganda instructor and a maverick in parliament.

Later, in the Kremlin courtyard, Colonel Petrushenko said Mr. Gorbachev's award "reminds me of the times when Leonid Brezhnev used to pin awards on his own chest." He continued: "My opinion is this will not enhance the authority of the President inside the country. This award came from outside."

Other deputies praised the award, while agreeing that it would have little impact at home.

Roy A. Medvedev, a historian once persecuted for documenting Stalin's repressions, said Mr. Gorbachev's peacemaking would ultimately help the Soviet economy by cutting military costs and opening the way for Western aid.

People interviewed outside Moscow's two most prominent tourist attractions, Lenin's Mausoleum and the new McDonald's restaurant, said the award reflected Mr. Gorbachev's standing in the world, but not his dwindling popularity at home.

"The prize is premature, because his work is not finished," said Galina Shefkun, a computer programmer. She suggested that Mr. Gorbachev donate the prize money to buy Big Macs for Moscow children.

"The Nobel Committee just doesn't know what it's like here," a young teacher told the Reuters news agency. "Let them spend a couple of months living like Russians and see how they feel. Is peace only for foreigners?"

Some strollers said the Soviet press and television in recent years had recorded so many man-of-the-year awards and peace honors bestowed on Mr. Gorbachev that no one would pay much attention to another.

Few Soviet citizens appreciate the prestige the world associates with the Nobel Prize, perhaps because the Kremlin has traditionally made light of it.

Indeed, a Soviet reporter for the prime-time news program *Vremya* asked Mr. Gorbachev how he felt about receiving a prize that has traditionally gone to anti-Communists like Mr. Sakharov and Lech Walesa, the Polish Solidarity leader. The Soviet leader skirted the question.

Yelena G. Bonner, Mr. Sakharov's widow and companion in the human rights campaign, declined to comment directly on Mr. Gorbachev's worthiness for the award. But she said it was ill timed, coming with the world near war in the Persian Gulf and the feckless Soviet leadership fiddling over an economic plan.

"It's shocking, the West's blindness to the tragedies our country has lived through during the five years of *perestroika* headed by Gorbachev," she said in a telephone interview.

Mr. Gorbachev released Mr. Sakharov from internal exile in 1986, and for the next two years the dissident and physicist applauded the Soviet leader while goading him to press farther and faster toward democracy.

But gradually Mr. Sakharov grew disenchanted with Mr. Gorbachev, charging that the Soviet leader was accumulating dictatorial power while losing touch with the public mood. Mr. Gorbachev in turn grew resentful of the pressure from the unrelenting human rights advocate, and today reporters extracted from him only the most cursory praise of his predecessor on the Nobel honor roll.

As Miss Bonner saw it, "He said what he had to say, nothing more."

There was not much time for Gorbachev to rest on his laurels.

With His Caution on Economy, Gorbachev May Find Political Center Is a Whirlwind
By Bill Keller

MOSCOW, OCT. 17—Since late July, when President Mikhail S. Gorbachev and Boris N. Yeltsin agreed to join forces in devising an economic program, hopes have soared for a grand political coalition that would lead this country peacefully away from the brink of chaos.

By combining the enormous popular support of Mr. Yeltsin, President of the vast Russian republic, with the Kremlin savvy and world stature of Mr. Gorbachev, the hope was, this coalition might bring the public through the painful transition to free markets and a new national confederation.

With his announcement on Tuesday of a compromise economic program—less radical than the variant adopted by Mr. Yeltsin's republic—Mr. Gorbachev has sharply diminished the prospects of such an alliance with the democratic opposition, and left the two leaders once again on a collision course.

The explanations for Mr. Gorbachev's decision range from psychological to conspiratorial, from power politics to simple prudence.

Is he a master manipulator, a judicious reader of the public mood, a hostage to the conservative forces around him, or simply a wimp?

There is probably some truth in each of those explanations.

Had Mr. Gorbachev unveiled his plan a year ago, it would have been hailed as an act of political daring.

The Soviet leader called for an economy based on free enterprise, private ownership, the phasing out of state controls on prices, and an open door for foreign investors—in short, a repudiation of the economic boot camp that has operated since Stalin's day.

One of the first steps would be draconian cuts in government spending. Economists told Defense Secretary Dick Cheney today that this would include a 20 percent cut in military spending, although this is not spelled out in the plan.

But unlike Mr. Yeltsin, Mr. Gorbachev set no timetable for dismantling the central economic ministries and liberating private business. In the plan was speculation that "the stabilization" of the economy might take from 18 months to two years, suggesting that considerable central controls will remain in place for at least that long.

Mr. Gorbachev's plan is also vague about the economic powers of republics and local governments, while Mr. Yeltsin insists that the republics dominate economic decision making and decide what powers to delegate up to the Kremlin.

Mr. Yeltsin promptly denounced the plan as an attempt to retain "a system the people have come to hate."

After Mr. Cheney's meeting today with a group of economists representing both camps, a senior official in his delegation sighed, "The only thing that was clear about the economic picture is that they have a full-fledged political crisis."

Mr. Gorbachev's plan—presented as a "synthesis" of the Yeltsin plan and a more cautious variant sponsored by Mr. Gorbachev's Prime Minister, Nikolai I. Ryzhkov—is typical of his perpetual quest for the center.

By instinct, and by his political upbringing in the clubby, consensus-oriented world of the Communist Party, Mr. Gorbachev prefers to lead from the middle.

In this case, Mr. Gorbachev has good reason for caution. Even some ardent proponents of change worried that the 500-day timetable in Mr.

Yeltsin's plan was unrealistic, risking runaway inflation, unemployment, and popular upheaval. Perhaps of greater concern to Mr. Gorbachev, the surrender of power to the republics meant the accelerated disintegration of the union.

The sponsors of the more radical plan contend the breakup of the union is already under way, and can only be arrested by mutual agreement.

More important, they argue, the public is more likely to bear the disorder and discomfort that are sure to come as the country gives up the threadbare security blanket of central planning if they have faith in the leaders executing it. Mr. Yeltsin is currently the most trusted man in the country, and any plan that lacks his blessing is likely to encounter popular resistance.

Another theory is that Mr. Gorbachev might have preferred a more radical economic plan, but was held back by more conservative figures around him, especially his dutiful Prime Minister, Mr. Ryzhkov; his Defense Minister, Marshal Dmitri T. Yazov; and his K.G.B. Chairman, Vladimir A. Kryuchkov.

All three men have argued publicly for strong central control of the economy and the political order. A partnership with the radicals would mean replacing the current government with a coalition, and those three men would be high on the opposition hit list.

Analysts in the independent Soviet press have pointed out that Mr. Gorbachev would have strong incentives to protect the three.

Mr. Ryzhkov has been the Soviet leader's main lightning rod, drawing the anger of the radicals and leaving Mr. Gorbachev seeming relatively progressive.

"Responsibility for the crisis situation in the country lies first of all with Gorbachev," said the independent weekly *Karyera*. "To agree to dismissing Ryzhkov would mean admitting it.

"And without the army and the K.G.B., Gorbachev's power will become entirely ephemeral."

Another opposition-oriented newspaper, the Moscow neighborhood weekly *Karetny Ryad*, noted that while Marshal Yazov and Mr. Kryuchkov, both 66 years old, are more conservative than Mr. Gorbachev, they were raised in a tradition of party discipline that tends to keep them loyal to the leader as long as he does nothing too wild. Any successors to those jobs would come from a younger generation, perhaps not so docile.

A somewhat more Machiavellian theory is that Mr. Gorbachev never really intended to join forces with Mr. Yeltsin, but used him as a foil.

Tatyana I. Koryagina, an economist active in the democratic opposition who is skeptical of the 500-day plan, said she believes Mr. Gorbachev played at peacemaking to prod the conservatives in his own government toward more far-reaching changes.

Then he left Mr. Yeltsin stranded, the sole supporter of the most radical plan, which Mr. Gorbachev can portray as a foolhardy invitation to social disorder.

"Yeltsin tried to believe in this common approach, or at least he created a public impression that he believed in it, but political analysts and Kremlinologists have known all along it was an illusion," said Mrs. Koryagina.

The first clear signal that Mr. Gorbachev would not embrace the radical plan came three weeks ago, when he demanded extraordinary new decree powers from the parliament and then used them not to move toward markets but to freeze all existing economic relationships through 1991.

"Now Gorbachev has left the 500-day plan entirely to Yeltsin, hoping he will fail," she said.

Today one of the original authors of the 500-day plan, Grigory V. Yavlinsky, a young economist who had left Mr. Gorbachev's government to become a key Yeltsin economic adviser, offered his resignation, saying the Russian republic's plan to put into effect the radical free-market program was hopeless without the agreement of the central authorities.

Mr. Yeltsin, in turn, has predicted that the Gorbachev plan will fall flat within six months, joining three other failed transition programs that have fizzled in less than a year.

Mr. Gorbachev may win the general blessing of the Soviet parliament as early as this weekend, but the plan will be stillborn without credible support from most of the 15 republics, especially the largest and richest, Russia.

"A drama of political struggle is coming to an end, our little drama in the Kremlin," Mrs. Koryagina said. On the stage stood two men who once seemed possible collaborators, each waiting to see who will fail first.

The pace of politics was uneven. On the vital questions of peace and healing the divisions of Europe there was steady progress bringing accolades for Gorbachev in the West. At home rancor and conflict raged and chaos beckoned.

Gorbachev Signs Treaty in Bonn and Is Hailed for His Unity Role
By Serge Schmemann

BONN, NOV. 9—President Mikhail S. Gorbachev was hailed in Germany today on the anniversary of the breach of the Berlin wall for helping make German unity possible. But the Soviet leader's reduced status was underscored when he appealed to the Germans to be tolerant of the Soviet troops still stationed on their soil.

At a news conference, Mr. Gorbachev also gave a strong reaffirmation of solidarity with the West against Iraq. "The joint action in the United Nations Security Council condemned the aggressor," he said. "We have taken decisive measures, and all efforts to shake this unity are doomed."

The principal reason for Mr. Gorbachev's visit was to sign a treaty of "good-neighborliness, partnership, and cooperation" with Germany that he and Chancellor Helmut Kohl had agreed to as part of the broad package that cleared the way for Moscow's endorsement of German unity.

Mr. Gorbachev became the first foreign leader to make a state visit to the reunited Germany, and the treaty was the first to be signed since reunification on October 3.

The sense of unease was spreading at home. On November 14 the normally passive legislators in the Soviet parliament bolted from their prescribed agenda to demand that Gorbachev address them on the state of the union that many among them contended was on the verge of economic collapse.

"If we do not do something about the situation now, people will take up arms and pour into the streets, and this will not be a military coup but a popular coup," one member of parliament, Lieut. Col. Viktor Alksnis, declared as the lawmakers balked en masse, with members complaining that the day's routine agenda was an insult to the suffering Soviet people.

The next day a group of prominent intellectuals called on Gorbachev to resign if he was unwilling to dissolve his government and form a coalition with non-Communists. "Either affirm your ability to take decisive measures, or resign," the 22 journalists, economists, politicians, and cultural figures wrote in their open letter. Two days after that Gorbachev answered the challenges.

Soviets Adopt Emergency Plan to Center Power in Gorbachev and Leaders of the Republics
By Bill Keller

MOSCOW, NOV. 17—Warning that the country was sliding toward chaos, President Mikhail S. Gorbachev today announced the creation of a new emergency power structure in which he will govern along with leaders of the republics.

The measures, promptly and overwhelmingly approved by parliament, would abolish the post held by Prime Minister Nikolai I. Ryzhkov, who is seen by critics as a chief obstacle to the rapid introduction of free markets.

Mr. Gorbachev said the Federation Council, now a purely advisory body made up of the leaders of the 15 republics, would be transformed into the chief executive agency, a move that would co-opt Mr. Gorbachev's most troublesome rivals into sharing responsibility for the union.

But the final word would belong to Mr. Gorbachev, whose powers would be enhanced by a new security council overseeing the army, the police, and the K.G.B., and by a network of presidential representatives around the country to enforce orders from the center.

"I propose carrying out an urgent fundamental reorganization of executive power in the center by subordinating it to the President, directly to the President," he said.

The Soviet leader also announced that within two weeks the government would announce an emergency food program to supply the public through the winter and dispel fears of hunger. He provided no details.

While Mr. Gorbachev in theory has already accumulated vast powers, his decrees aimed at economic change and civil order have frequently been countermanded by republic and local government or neutralized by the balky government bureaucracy.

The initial reaction was overwhelmingly positive—not only from hardliners alarmed by increasing instability, but also from some of the democratic insurgents, who said it could form the basis for a coalition government of consensus.

But there was no reaction from President Boris N. Yeltsin of the Russian republic, who on Friday called on Mr. Gorbachev to share power with the republics in an emergency anticrisis committee. An aide to Mr. Yeltsin said he wanted to study the proposals and would probably not comment until the next session of the Russian parliament on Tuesday.

Some allies of Mr. Yeltsin said the Gorbachev proposal was close enough to the Russian leader's scheme for a coalition government that it might be acceptable, while others said his suspicions of the Soviet leader run so deep that he could never agree to a subordinate position.

Anatoly A. Sobchak, the Mayor of Leningrad, spoke approvingly of Mr. Gorbachev's reorganization plan. "Practically all of the reasonable proposals voiced yesterday are included in it," he said. Mr. Sobchak has been rumored to be a candidate for vice president or another high post in the new government.

Yuri N. Afanasyev, a radical historian and leader of an opposition bloc in the parliament, said: "This was the calming tonic the Supreme Soviet has been awaiting for so long. What comes afterward is not important. The main thing is that the measures outlined appear to be serious."

But Mr. Gorbachev's sharpest critics among the fractious democratic opposition and representatives from the separatist republics denounced today's moves as a step toward virtual dictatorship.

Marju Lauristin, deputy speaker of the Estonian parliament, said the three Baltic republics would refuse to take part in the Federation Council, which she described as a decoration on an all-powerful presidency.

"We will not participate in any federational institution," she said. "The decision of our people is quite clear."

The changes outlined by Mr. Gorbachev were interrupted by hearty applause and later approved by a vote of 316 to 19, with 31 abstentions.

It was a sharp turnabout from the mood Friday, when parliament and leaders of many republics berated Mr. Gorbachev when he showed up for an emergency speech on the state of the union bearing no dramatic new proposals.

A close aide to Mr. Gorbachev, Georgy K. Shakhnazarov, said the introduction of direct presidential rule had been in the works for some time, but the impatience of the legislators on Friday had convinced him to move sooner.

"He was going to move in this direction sooner or later," Mr. Shakhnazarov told reporters. "Yesterday served as a turning point, and it pushed him to do this."

After his chilly reception in the parliament on Friday, Mr. Gorbachev reportedly had a general conversation in the afternoon with Mr. Yeltsin. Last night he discussed the state of the union with Communist Party leaders at a meeting of the party's governing Politburo, according to Vladimir A. Ivashko, the deputy party chairman.

Mr. Shakhnazarov said Mr. Gorbachev planned to put most of the new scheme into effect by decree in a matter of days. It would remain in force until enactment of a new "union treaty" that Mr. Gorbachev has proposed as the basis for a redesigned Soviet federation.

With many republics skeptical or flatly opposed to his draft of the new union, the prospects for approval were murky at best.

Mr. Gorbachev's measures announced today would leave the parliament intact, but would dissolve much of the existing executive branch. The position of prime minister would be abolished, and his cabinet, the huge Council of Ministers, would be demoted to a "working apparatus" of the new leadership, according to Mr. Shakhnazarov.

Mr. Ryzhkov, who has been Mr. Gorbachev's loyal but increasingly unpopular prime minister since 1985, said he did not know if there was a place for him in the new scheme, but other deputies predicted he would retire from government.

Mr. Yeltsin, for one, has insisted he would take no part in a coalition government that included Mr. Ryzhkov. Mr. Gorbachev in his speech underscored the need to recruit "new, enterprising people with a modern mentality."

Mr. Ryzhkov told reporters he was informed of the plan just 20 minutes before Mr. Gorbachev's speech.

The current Presidential Council, an advisory body organized by Mr. Gorbachev eight months ago and made up of longtime confidants, economists, and representatives of the working class and the arts, is to be disbanded.

Although his aides expressed high hopes that most republics would agree to take part in the more powerful Federation Council, they left little doubt that Mr. Gorbachev would hold the ultimate authority.

"The President will have the last word, but I think 90 percent of the decisions, if not all, will be made on the basis of consensus," Mr. Shakhnazarov said.

In theory, enlisting the republic leaders as partners in power would prevent the sort of impasse that occurred earlier this year, when Mr. Gorbachev adopted a gradual program for introducing a market economy, while Mr. Yeltsin insisted on a crash 500-day program.

It did not take long for Gorbachev's most aggressive critic to declare his dissatisfaction.

Yeltsin Rejects Gorbachev's Reorganization Plan
By Francis X. Clines

MOSCOW, NOV. 19—Boris N. Yeltsin, the President of the Russian republic, today rejected President Mikhail S. Gorbachev's plan for overhauling governmental powers but invited a compromise conditioned on the Kremlin's recognition of the republics' full sovereignty.

The negative reaction of Mr. Yeltsin; leader of the nation's dominant republic and chief adversary of the Soviet leader, heightened the pressure on Mr. Gorbachev to yield further in the current political crisis.

Mr. Yeltsin, in an interview with the Interfax news agency, said Mr. Gorbachev's latest offer to share some powers with the republic leaders would mainly strengthen the President's authority and would "not improve but only worsen the situation in the country."

"Russia, at least, will not accept it," he declared, maintaining his republic's insistence that its own laws have precedence over Soviet laws.

Mr. Yeltsin's sharp attack on Mr. Gorbachev's plan followed developments last weekend that suggested that Mr. Gorbachev had once again gained the political ascendancy.

Mr. Gorbachev yielded somewhat to the republics' pressure for greater self-rule last week when he was confronted by a parliament angry at the nation's slide into economic and political chaos.

He proposed an emergency national government system in which the 15 republics would play a far more active role in Kremlin decisions than their current advisory function but in which he retained the final word on executive decisions.

Mr. Gorbachev made his proposal a day after Mr. Yeltsin had proposed creation of a crisis committee with representatives from the 15 republics, which he said should supplant the government of Prime Minister Nikolai I. Ryzhkov and take over functions like food and fuel distribution. Mr. Yeltsin has also long called for a true coalition government including non-Communists.

Parliament, which is a part of the national government, approved Mr. Gorbachev's general plan by a vote of 316 to 19, with details promised soon in legislative proposals and executive orders.

Mr. Yeltsin made it clear that Mr. Gorbachev's power-sharing offer was not enough for the Russian republic, which includes a majority of the Soviet Union's population and economic resources. The republic has already unilaterally refused to enforce national decrees it finds unpalatable.

The Gorbachev plan, Mr. Yeltsin emphasized, would only seek a republic-union consensus but provided no guarantee of approval by the republics as executive decisions were made final in the Kremlin.

"It is greatly disappointing," Mr. Yeltsin said. "All the proposals of the President are aimed at the strengthening of the center."

Other republics, including Lithuania, Latvia, Estonia, and Georgia, had previously indicated their defiance of the plan. With this criticism from the leader of Russia, the cornerstone of the Soviet nation, it appeared that Mr. Gorbachev did not fully solve his latest crisis with the approval of his plan by parliament on Saturday.

After two quiet days of study of the plan, which drew considerable praise from his own colleagues in the insurgent opposition, Mr. Yeltsin continued to demand that Mr. Gorbachev yield more to the republics. Whether the Soviet President, who was in Paris today, is likely to accede to such pressure from his chief rival is one of numerous questions unanswered so far in this basic struggle over power.

Mr. Yeltsin set his own conditions for a workable solution. He insisted that parliament, which usually follows Mr. Gorbachev's lead, "should first of all make the decision to recognize all the declarations of sovereignty as legal and treat them with respect."

Whether President Gorbachev would agree to reopen the issue and cut a direct deal with the republics remains to be seen. The Soviet leader's other options might be to try to circumvent Mr. Yeltsin's opposition by inviting some of his fellow insurgent democrats into the revised government, or to test the central government's increasingly doubted ability to enforce Mr. Gorbachev's will in some fashion that does not risk aggravating the crisis.

Mr. Gorbachev has been fending off the republics' separatist declarations and protecting his own prerogatives, promising he will soon propose a better national union of decentralized powers. Critics in the republics contend that this proposal is destined to be a mere attempt at maintaining the union government's dominance of political and economic life.

For the meantime, facing plummeting public confidence in his ability to revive the economy and head off anarchy, Mr. Gorbachev has now put forward his emergency changes in the executive branch. These eliminate Mr. Ryzhkov's job, as insurgents have long demanded, and upgrade the Federation Council, the republics' advisory body in the Kremlin, to be the chief executive panel under Mr. Gorbachev and share some of the governing process.

Mr. Yeltsin accused Mr. Gorbachev of carefully denying the republics approval rights over final executive decisions in the new emergency government. Beyond that, he accused the Soviet leader of trying to fashion a new "union treaty" on his own without consulting the republics on their proposals for wielding counterbalancing or even overriding powers.

"We have to speak not about a union treaty but about a union of sovereign states," Mr. Yeltsin said, forcing the separatist issue further. "These are two different things."

Mr. Gorbachev, by failing to consult the republics, is trying to "force" parliamentary approval of his emergency proposals, Mr. Yeltsin contended. He insisted this could only have the reverse effect of stiffening republic opposition to the union's increasingly anxious attempts to reassert its authority.

In the past year, all the republics but Kirghizia have proclaimed far greater forms of self-rule and curtailed ties to the Gorbachev government. The Soviet leader has been juggling the twin crises of economic collapse and disintegration of the union, emphasizing that only a strong national government can maintain social order through the painful transition to a market economy.

East and West Sign Pact to Shed Arms in Europe
By R. W. Apple, Jr.

PARIS, NOV. 19—President Bush and President Mikhail S. Gorbachev of the Soviet Union, joined by leaders of 20 other nations that make up the North Atlantic Treaty Organization and the Warsaw Pact, signed the most ambitious arms-control treaty in history today, pledging to destroy tens of thousands of tanks, howitzers, and other nonnuclear weapons.

"What a long way the world has come!" Mr. Gorbachev exulted.

Having underlined the end of the cold war that divided East and West for more than four decades, the two presidents turned their eyes to the future, taking leading roles in the first session of the three-day Conference on Security and Cooperation in Europe. The 34 participants at the conference—Canada, the United States, and all the countries of Europe except Albania—hope to draw up a charter for the region.

The Persian Gulf crisis lurked just offstage, and Mr. Bush was quick to press for support in the effort to force Iraq to withdraw from Kuwait by diplomatic or military means. "Success here," he said, "can be neither profound nor enduring if the rule of law is shamelessly disregarded elsewhere."

At the meeting, held at the Kléber International Conference Center near the Arc de Triomphe, the 69 delegates—presidents, prime ministers, foreign ministers, and the like—sat at a hexagonal table surrounding three-foot-high cutout maps of North America and Eurasia that resembled pieces from a jigsaw puzzle for giants. There were 67 men and two women: Prime Minister Margaret Thatcher of Britain and Prime Minister Gro Harlem Brundtland of Norway.

Mr. Bush hailed the treaty as "the most far-reaching arms agreement" ever negotiated. The result of two years of painstaking bargaining in Vienna, the accord was also a bit of an anticlimax. It represents a ratification in the military sphere of what has already taken place in political terms.

The military confrontation between the two alliances has evaporated, the Soviets are preoccupied with domestic economic and political crises, the Warsaw Pact's days may be numbered, and NATO is having trouble finding a new role. And today, in addition to the arms treaty, the NATO and Warsaw Pact leaders signed a declaration saying that they were "no longer adversaries and will establish new relations of partnership and mutual friendship."

The air was thick with comparisons to the Congress of Vienna in 1815, at the end of the Napoleonic Wars, and the Conference of Versailles in 1919, after World War I.

Chancellor Helmut Kohl of Germany said that in building "a Europe of eternal peace" the conferees should look to the French Revolution, the Magna Carta, and the Declaration of Independence for inspiration, as well as the writings of the eighteenth-century philosopher Kant, who he said was an advocate of unity among European states.

In the last two centuries, Mr. Kohl said, "Europe and my country in particular became the epicenter of worldwide catastrophes."

"It is the first time in history that we witness a change in depth of the European landscape that is not the outcome of a war or a bloody revolution," said President François Mitterrand. "We do not have sitting here either victors or vanquished but free countries equal in dignity."

Today's events, five years to the day after Mr. Gorbachev and President Bush first met in Geneva, began with the arms accord.

Mr. Bush said the treaty, signed beneath the glittering chandeliers of Elysée Palace, "signals the new world order that is emerging." President Mitterrand told his colleagues that they were "putting an end to the previous age."

In an era when the continent's problems lie not in conflicting ideologies but in economic and structural problems, like renewed conflicts in the Balkans and even the survival of a unitary Soviet state, large land armies seem irrelevant.

Mr. Gorbachev said in his speech that he wanted to press ahead as quickly as possible with other arms-reduction measures, presumably so that he can husband scarce Soviet resources to help satisfy the pent-up craving for food and other consumer goods.

Back from Paris, Gorbachev shot back an answer to Yeltsin and those who were insisting on decentralizing and even dividing the Soviet Union.

Resolute Gorbachev Offers Unity Plan
By Francis X. Clines

MOSCOW, NOV. 23—Vowing the strongest resistance to altering the current union, President Mikhail S. Gorbachev today outlined his proposal for a redesigned power structure for the Soviet Union and bitterly denounced the contrary views of his chief rival, Boris N. Yeltsin.

"It is my firm conviction that the Union cannot be divided," Mr. Gorbachev declared at a news conference where he summarized his long-awaited proposal for a treaty governing the national union that, by his initial description, seemed unlikely to sway the nation's 15 republics from their fervor for separatism.

Mr. Gorbachev sketched a union treaty that would allow republics the "right of self-determination and withdrawal," but only through a "divorce process" of referendum, consensus, and approval. He repeated his insistence that allowing republics to secede could mean bloodshed.

Lithuania and other republics are already insisting that they have the right to leave the Soviet Union.

But Mr. Gorbachev rejected this and retained in his proposal a cabinet system led by a prime minister as part of the presidential hierarchy, an element likely to bring new criticism from separatists.

Only six days ago, Mr. Gorbachev promised, as part of an emergency transitional plan, to scrap the unpopular cabinet system and elevate representatives of the 15 Soviet republics to a full executive Federation Council to give greater national consensus in his decisions.

The Federation Council remains part of his proposed permanent union treaty, but the cabinet headed by a prime minister is revived. The cabinet has become a symbol to much of the public of the centralized bureaucracy of Communism that has brought on the current political and economic crisis.

The national parliament has voted initial approval to Mr. Gorbachev's emergency transitional plan. But, significantly, more lawmakers began questioning its vagueness today. The parliament voted to direct Mr. Gorbachev to give more details within two weeks, although they did not indicate they had the strength to try to vote the plan down.

The Soviet leader gave no details on how different his new vision of the union in the proposed draft treaty might be from the old, fast-fraying national union. But his sudden announcement of its pending publication only increased the helter-skelter sense of the nation's critical struggles over sharing power and staving off economic collapse.

On the latter point Mr. Gorbachev confirmed that foreign allies were offering emergency food supplies to ease growing concerns here of harsh winter food shortages. He intended to accept "advantageous" offers, he said, while expecting even greater aid eventually in the form of economic expertise and credits for his promised transition to the free market from Communism.

The union treaty is to be considered by the separate republics, a process that Mr. Yeltsin contends has been designed to allow Mr. Gorbachev to try to define the limits of the debate even before he has formally listened to critics.

President Gorbachev bridled as he dismissed Mr. Yeltsin's counter-pressure for sovereignty of the republics over the union as mere political opposition designed to give rise to suspicion that the Soviet leader reels from a "paralysis of power" to indulge "dictatorial" ambitions.

"What we have on our hands is a political fight," Mr. Gorbachev said, promising to be up to this struggle under the limits of the constitution.

His strategy in the enlarging power struggle now is clearly to attempt to demean his critics by insisting that the nation was in such crisis that it "should abandon anything that tends to divide us." This carries the risk of confronting the considerable advantage in popular support that Mr. Yeltsin has over Mr. Gorbachev.

The Soviet leader contended that Mr. Yeltsin, who is leading the fight for decentralized power as head of the nation's dominant Russian republic, actually agrees with up to 90 percent of the Gorbachev reform program but creates differences in his own search for power.

"If Gorbachev says one thing one day, critics say the opposite the next," the Soviet leader said.

"Are there any plans that claim to be a serious challenge to our constructive program?" Mr. Gorbachev asked rhetorically, his tone almost imperious as he belittled Mr. Yeltsin's alternative proposals. "No, we are dealing with a destructive program."

Soviet Army Told to Use Force to Defend Itself in the Republics
By Bill Keller

MOSCOW, NOV. 27—The Soviet defense minister announced tonight in a televised address that the armed forces had been instructed to use force to defend military installations, monuments, and servicemen against threats in rebellious republics.

The defense minister, Marshal Dmitri T. Yazov, who said he was speaking on the instructions of President Mikhail S. Gorbachev, contended that the country's security had been endangered by antimilitary measures in several republics, including what he said were calls for surrender of nuclear weapons to the republics' control.

The measures announced tonight included authorizing local military garrisons to seize control of power, water, and food installations if local authorities carry out threats to shut off supplies.

Soldiers have been authorized to use their weapons if they come under attack from civilians, and the military has also been instructed to intervene to prevent damage to military monuments, Marshal Yazov said.

The defense minister's appearance was the latest sign that Mr. Gorbachev is moving to calm unrest in his demoralized military, which is more than ever an important part of his power base.

Earlier this month the Soviet leader was jeered by uniformed members of parliament, angry about their diminishing prestige and distressed by the spiral of disorder in the country.

The military has been one of the strongest constituencies for Mr. Gorbachev's faltering plan to preserve the integrity of the country by enacting a new "union treaty" binding the 15 republics in a looser federation.

Today, Mr. Gorbachev took his battle for that proposal onto the territory of his chief rival, Boris N. Yeltsin, President of the Russian republic, who has rejected the union treaty unless it is changed to concede the full sovereignty of individual republics.

At the opening today of a special two-week congress of the Russian republic, Mr. Gorbachev personally lobbied to have the treaty included in the agenda, hoping the fractious governing body would overrule Mr. Yeltsin. The Russian President compromised by agreeing to a public "exchange of opinions" on the union treaty, thus avoiding the danger of a full-scale debate and vote.

Although leaders of six of the 15 Soviet republics have already declared they will not sign Mr. Gorbachev's treaty, the Soviet leader said today that only a minority of "loudmouths" opposed it, and he was confident it would ultimately win universal support.

Marshal Yazov offered no elaboration on what specifically had prompted his announcement today. Attacks on the military have taken many forms, from raids on military arsenals by vigilante militias in Armenia, to pervasive draft evading in all republics, to calls in the Baltic republics for the withdrawal of Soviet "occupiers," to plans in the Ukraine and other republics to form independent armies.

Marshal Yazov, in his lavishly beribboned uniform, appeared on the main evening news program and read stiffly from a list of measures he said were necessary to bolster the defense readiness of the country.

He contended that "voices are being raised for transferring nuclear weapons to individual republics" and that "some republics are declaring nuclear-free zones without taking into account the defense and security of the state."

"Under no circumstances will nuclear weapons be scattered throughout the republics," he said. "They were, are, and will remain in the hands of the united Soviet armed forces."

Local officials in some republics have advocated the prohibition of nuclear weapons on their territory, but no republic has proposed taking nuclear weapons into its own hands. Marshal Yazov did not explain what "voices" he was referring to.

As the year drew to a close the fate of Gorbachev's reforms was hanging in the balance. The pulls away from the center were growing stronger. The army was growing restive. Western assistance was being debated, but there were some voices in Moscow alleging that such aid would not come without attached strings. There were strains within Gorbachev's own brain trust. And the food situation, never good, was growing worse. Because so much food was being diverted, Gorbachev on December 2 ordered the creation of worker vigilante committees with unusual powers to monitor the food industry and punish those involved in theft and speculation.

Ten days later President Bush lifted a 15-year-old ban on agricultural credits and approved up to one billion dollars in federal loans to allow Moscow to buy food and other agricultural goods. He also said he would propose that the World Bank and the International Monetary Fund give Moscow a "special association" that would provide assistance and advice in transforming the Soviet command economy into a market-driven sys-

*tem. On December 14 leaders of European Community nations met in
Rome and agreed in principle to give the Soviet Union $2.4 billion in
emergency food and medical aid and technical assistance. The E.C. representatives echoed warnings that Gorbachev must be bolstered against challenges from hard-liners.*

*Welcome as the offers of help from abroad were to Gorbachev, they did
not do much to silence those who were opposing the Soviet leader's idea
of federalism.*

Federation Debate Resembles a Bazaar, and Haggling on Treaty Is Far from Over
By Bill Keller

MOSCOW, DEC. 18—The Kremlin Palace of Congresses rang again
today with the recriminations of a country sounding as if it was coming
apart.

The Moldavians walked out. The Estonian leader calmly reported that
his republic was withdrawing for good from the Soviet parliament. Even
the President of Uzbekistan, no hotbed of separatism, announced his
unhappiness with President Mikhail S. Gorbachev's version of a new
treaty to bind the fractious union.

Behind the confrontational bombast, however, the debate over the
future of the union resembles a great bazaar, where Mr. Gorbachev and
his wayward republics are still in the midst of bargaining.

The buyers state their absolutely final offers, stand up as if to leave,
whisper with their companions, dawdle, and sit back down for another
cup of tea. The seller pulls out a different sample. The haggling is a long
way from over.

So far among the 15 republics, Mr. Gorbachev has no firm takers for
his draft of a union treaty, which spells out the balance of powers he
would like in a revamped (and renamed) "Union of Sovereign Soviet
Republics."

The republics are dissatisfied with the division of wealth and power Mr.
Gorbachev is offering and find his version suspiciously vague.

The most divisive issues involve money and security. Who will own the
natural resources—the oil, gold, diamonds, and timber—and control
their marketing? How much will the republics pay in taxes? Who can be
drafted and for what kind of army? Who will control the police?

Mr. Gorbachev is bargaining with republican leaders who are almost
all trying to find their political balance between national feeling and
attachments to Moscow.

Even the comparatively docile leaders in Central Asia must accommodate the resurgent national pride and anti-Moscow frustration of their constituents. And even the devoutly separatist Georgians and Latvians acknowledge their economic dependence on the rest of the union.

Five republics have already declared that they will not sign any union treaty: Lithuania, Latvia, and Estonia, the three Baltic republics bent on restoring the independent statehood they had between the world wars, plus Georgia and Moldavia, both fired by runaway nationalism.

Of these, only Lithuania, which formally declared its independence last March, refused to send a delegation to the Congress of People's Deputies that is now noisily debating the country's future in the Kremlin.

Two more republics, Armenia and Azerbaijan, are sufficiently bitter toward Mr. Gorbachev that they will be extremely reluctant to sign a treaty. The main issue there is not separatism but the two republics' rival claims to the bloodily disputed territory of Nagorno-Karabakh.

These toughest customers altogether account for 10 percent of the Soviet population.

An additional six republics, Byelorussia and the five Islamic states of Central Asia, are the most likely to sign a union treaty. These republics have managed to suppress, contain, or co-opt nationalist movements, and the Asian republics are heavily dependent on central economic help.

But their leaders cannot be seen to cave in to Moscow too quickly, and they are happy in the meanwhile to accept additional endearments from Mr. Gorbachev—such as the recent announcement that Moscow will double prices paid to cotton farmers in Uzbekistan.

That leaves the two Slavic giants, Russia and the Ukraine, which are essential to any future union.

Ukrainian leaders support the idea of a union treaty, but are unlikely to sign anytime soon. The republic is too polarized, with a strong nationalist movement concentrated in the western half of the republic.

The key is Boris N. Yeltsin's Russia, home for half the Soviet population and most of its natural wealth. The leaders of many other republics are watching closely to see what terms Mr. Yeltsin can negotiate with the center.

"Except for the Baltics, they are all looking at Russia to see how far Yeltsin gets," said a Western diplomat who recently sampled opinion in all 15 republics.

Russia was clearly first in Mr. Gorbachev's mind on Monday when he demanded a popular referendum in every republic on the concept of a union treaty. The referendum proposal is an attempt to circumvent uncooperative republican governments, especially in Russia, where preservation of the union is still a popular cause.

Mr. Yeltsin says he has no desire to fracture the union, but his own version of the proper balance of powers leaves Mr. Gorbachev little to do.

Mr. Yeltsin's popularity remains high, but he is not immune to pressure. He is bedeviled by a troublesome, divided parliament in his own republic, and by a number of ethnic enclaves in the republic's federated structure that are clamoring for their own sovereignty.

While spurning Mr. Gorbachev's treaty as inadequate and premature, Mr. Yeltsin has undertaken his own alternative confederation-building exercise, signing direct two-way agreements with individual republics.

Signing a treaty today with Byelorussia, which promised political non-interference and economic cooperation, Mr. Yeltsin said such agreements were a "horizontal basis" for a reformed Soviet confederation.

Just a few months ago at least 14 of the 15 republics—all but Lithuania—seemed prepared to sign an agreement ceding some economic powers, such as monetary policy and communications, to the center as part of a radical 500-day plan to move the Soviet Union to free markets. The republics would have been independent political states in a kind of economic commonwealth.

Mr. Gorbachev decided this was more freedom than he was willing to surrender and at the last minute stood up to go. But he has not yet left the bazaar.

And, to further complicate Kremlin politics, the man who had articulated and implemented Gorbachev's thinking in the arena of foreign affairs quit, offering a dire caution.

Shevardnadze Stuns Kremlin by Quitting Foreign Ministry and Warning of "Dictatorship"
By Bill Keller

MOSCOW, DEC. 20—Foreign Minister Eduard A. Shevardnadze, President Mikhail S. Gorbachev's closest confederate in negotiating an end to the cold war, abruptly resigned today with an impassioned warning that "reactionaries" threatened his country with dictatorship.

"I cannot reconcile myself with what is happening in my country," Mr. Shevardnadze told his stunned audience at the Congress of People's Deputies, adding that he was weary of defending his policies against hard-liners.

Mr. Gorbachev, who said he was not warned of the resignation, sat frozen on the dais of the Kremlin Palace of Congresses. He still seemed distressed hours later when he took the podium to accuse his colleague in *perestroika* of deserting him at a time of political and economic crisis.

"Now, perhaps, is our most difficult time, and to leave at this time is unforgivable," he said. "This must be condemned."

Mr. Gorbachev disclosed that he had planned to recommend Mr.

Shevardnadze for the new post of vice president, where he could apply his artful diplomacy to healing the country's internal divisions. But Mr. Shevardnadze had already said publicly that if offered the post he would decline.

Electrified by the unparalleled spectacle of a top Soviet official resigning on principle, the Congress voted overwhelmingly to reaffirm the course of Soviet foreign policy and to urge that Mr. Shevardnadze reconsider. The foreign minister's spokesman, Vitaly Churkin, said the decision was final.

Mr. Shevardnadze said he would stay on until the Supreme Soviet, the standing parliament, approved the change. The parliament is not expected to meet before the new year.

Some legislators wondered if Mr. Shevardnadze might return to his native Georgia, where as Communist Party chief he had a reputation as a ruthless fighter of corruption and an early economic liberalizer. The republic is currently under control of a separatist government that regards Mr. Shevardnadze as a foe of Georgian nationalism because of his close ties to Mr. Gorbachev, who is a Russian.

Mr. Shevardnadze's announcement today seemed especially addressed to the bickering supporters of reform—perhaps including Mr. Gorbachev himself—as a warning to unite against those pressing for a return to authoritarian rule backed by force.

"The reformers have gone into hiding," Mr. Shevardnadze said, his voice taut with emotion. "A dictatorship is approaching—I tell you that with full responsibility. No one knows what this dictatorship will be like, what kind of dictator will come to power, and what order will be established."

Mr. Shevardnadze spoke angrily and without notes, and except for allusions to a few outspoken critics of his policies he did not spell out what he regarded as the threat to democracy.

Although his resignation was clearly a major political problem for Mr. Gorbachev, Mr. Shevardnadze stressed that his devotion to Mr. Gorbachev and his policies remained strong, and voiced no criticism of the Soviet leader's plan, now before the Congress, to enlarge his presidential powers.

No one among numerous legislators and officials interviewed today said they believed Mr. Shevardnadze's speech meant dictatorship was imminent, in the sense that there would be some early return to the tight controls of the past.

Now in his sixth year of an enterprise that has remade the world order, Mr. Shevardnadze has for some time seemed tired and frustrated by the sniping of hard-liners who blame him for the contraction of Soviet power.

One of the hard-liners who provoked Mr. Shevardnadze's wrath, Col. Viktor I. Alksnis, hailed Mr. Shevardnadze's departure as a triumph for those who want order restored.

"Personally I am very satisfied," he said.

Today Mr. Shevardnadze lashed out at critics who have accused him of putting the Soviet Union at risk of war by siding so closely with the United States in the Persian Gulf crisis. He also defended the government's policies in favor of unification of Germany against those who he said had accused him of "unilateral concessions."

The President's spokesman, Vitaly S. Ignatenko, rushed to tell reporters that there would be no changes in the foreign policy course that Mr. Shevardnadze helped draw up and execute.

"Our foreign policy does not change in one minute," Mr. Ignatenko said. "It does not depend on one person."

Mr. Shevardnadze has been a target of personal invective from those who view the retrenchment of Soviet power as a humiliation.

Over the last year he has been openly attacked in the Communist Party and the Congress for tolerating the reunification of Germany and the collapse of satellite governments in Eastern Europe, for rushing the military forces home to languish in squalid tent cities, for negotiating arms treaties with the West that cut disproportionately into Soviet missiles and tanks, for accepting food aid from the West, and most recently for following too closely the American lead on policy in the Gulf.

Mr. Shevardnadze has fought a fierce battle in public, and reportedly inside the leadership, to keep his country aligned with the American-led alliance that is isolating Iraq.

A hard-line parliamentary faction, Soyuz, has complained despite numerous reassurances that Mr. Shevardnadze is risking having Soviet troops drawn into a war in the Gulf to protect American interests.

"Charges are made that the foreign minister plans to land troops in the Persian Gulf, in the region," Mr. Shevardnadze said today, in a tone of exasperation. "I explained that there are no such plans. They do not exist. Nobody is going to send a single military man, or even a single representative of the Soviet armed forces there."

Mr. Shevardnadze took the podium today because members of the Congress had demanded he justify the Foreign Ministry's record, but instead he handed his prepared text to Mr. Gorbachev and turned to the hushed legislators, his face red with emotion.

He did not spell out in detail whom he regarded as the "reactionaries" menacing the country, but he referred to "boys in colonel's epaulets" who had heaped insults on his work.

The obvious targets included two maverick army colonels, Colonel

Alksnis, a military electronics specialist from Latvia, and Nikolai S. Petrushenko, a propaganda instructor, who have used the parliament as a platform to lobby against Mr. Shevardnadze's performance and to press for more authoritarian leadership.

One consequence of the political skirmishing was that the hard-liners were revealing themselves more openly.

K.G.B. Chief Warns Against West's Aid to Soviet Economy
By Bill Keller

MOSCOW, DEC. 22—The chairman of the K.G.B. today warned the Soviet Congress to be wary of foreigners offering to help the Soviet economy, suggesting that Western businesses and governments represent a hidden danger to the country's security.

The K.G.B. chief, Vladimir A. Kryuchkov, charged that economic contacts were often a pretext for compiling strategic information about Soviet industry and resources, for cheating unwitting Soviet partners, and for imposing an alien capitalist outlook.

"There are attempts from abroad to exert overt and covert pressure on the Soviet Union and to impose doubtful ideas and plans to pull the country out of the difficult situation," he said in a speech to the Congress of People's Deputies. "All these efforts often screen a desire to strengthen not so much us, but their own position in our country."

The chief of the Soviet intelligence and security police agency renewed his call for "decisive measures" to contain ethnic violence, saying the country "will not escape upheavals with more serious and painful consequences."

"Warnings are sounded that if we take decisive measures today to restore order, this will mean we wittingly agree to spill blood," he said. "But respected comrade deputies, isn't blood already being spilled?"

Mr. Kryuchkov's mistrust of the West is well known, but his speech today, filled with admonitions of subversion and economic sabotage, was his broadest attack on what he portrayed as creeping capitalism in the country.

His comments were in striking contrast to President Mikhail S. Gorbachev's assiduous courtship of Western economic support.

Eager to calm the political furor, Gorbachev chose a politician of the old school as his deputy.

Gorbachev Names a Party Loyalist to Vice Presidency

By Bill Keller

MOSCOW, DEC. 26—President Mikhail S. Gorbachev chose a colorless but loyal Communist Party functionary today to fill the new Soviet post of vice president, his chief deputy in managing state affairs and his stand-in if Mr. Gorbachev cannot serve.

Mr. Gorbachev's choice, Gennadi I. Yanayev, presented himself as "a Communist to the depths of my soul" and an unwavering supporter of Mr. Gorbachev's programs. His nomination is to be put to a secret ballot of the 2,250-member Congress of People's Deputies on Thursday.

The choice sent a flabbergasted murmur through the Kremlin Palace of Congresses.

Many members, including some close to Mr. Gorbachev, had conjured up their profile of a probable vice president: a non-Russian to unite the country, a person of popular stature or at least a winning public figure to repair Mr. Gorbachev's diminished prestige, and someone with a reformist reputation.

Mr. Yanayev, who is 53 years old, is of Russian heritage, is unrenowned outside Communist Party circles, and is regarded as a hardworking apparatchik not associated with any particular innovations or causes.

His speech today, which stressed the need for law and order and rejected economic "shock therapy," was in keeping with Mr. Gorbachev's recent drift toward a conservative position.

After two nationally prominent candidates had publicly spurned the post, Mr. Gorbachev appears to have turned, as he has often done for important appointments, to a man steeped in Communist Party discipline and with a background not unlike his own.

Like Mr. Gorbachev, Mr. Yanayev (pronounced ya-NYE-yeff) has never stood for competitive public election. He was appointed to Congress in a seat reserved for trade unions.

The Soviet leader rebuffed suggestions from the hall that he offer a choice of candidates, and debate was cut off after a short series of orchestrated testimonials.

If Mr. Gorbachev died or was otherwise unable to serve, the Vice President would serve as acting president until a nationwide presidential election could be organized, which under the constitution must happen within six months.

Aleksandr Mr. Yakovlev, a law professor and parliamentary leader, said, "Either you choose a man with appeal, charm—that's not the case here—or you choose your own man, reliable."

Mr. Gorbachev "has chosen a devoted person who will share his views and work as a team," he said. "That's good for the President. Will it be good for the country? That depends not only on the Vice President but also on the President himself."

The political sniping did not stop as Yeltsin launched a painful attack on Gorbachev's coffers.

Russia Cuts Share of Soviet Budget
By Bill Keller

MOSCOW, DEC. 27—President Mikhail S. Gorbachev, still reeling from a week of reversals, faced a major new political crisis today after the huge Russian republic voted to slash its payments to the federal budget.

Mr. Gorbachev told the Congress of People's Deputies that the confrontation left the country without a budget four days before the start of the fiscal year and threatened the nation with economic collapse.

The Russian republic's parliament, led by its President, Boris N. Yeltsin, voted Wednesday night to contribute only 23.4 billion rubles to the Soviet budget for 1991, less than a tenth of the total the Kremlin has sought to keep the state-run economy functioning.

Normally Russia contributes about half of the federal budget, which is proposed at 261 billion rubles next year.

"If we set out on this road, it will destroy everything we have done," Mr. Gorbachev said. "Everyone will then live by the principle 'Every man for himself.' This would mean the breakup not only of the economy, but of the Soviet Union."

The clash with the nation's largest republic was the latest in a series of political trials for the Soviet leader, beginning with the departure of his invaluable foreign minister, and continuing today with an embarrassing first-round defeat of his candidate to be the country's first Vice President, Gennadi I. Yanayev, who was confirmed in a second round of voting.

As the Congress adjourned tonight after 10 days, the budget impasse cast serious doubt on its main accomplishments, the reorganization of the government to confer expanded constitutional powers on Mr. Gorbachev and the endorsement of a new union treaty to hold the federation together.

"If the state doesn't have a budget, if it doesn't know where its money is coming from and where it is going, then it means things are really falling apart," said Anatoly A. Sobchak, mayor of Leningrad and a member of the Congress. "If there is no budget, it invalidates the entire Congress, and means we have been sitting here in vain."

The showdown with Russia over the budget is the most serious conflict in months of feuding over sovereignty, wealth, and power. The republic, which embraces three fourths of the Soviet land mass, more than half its population, and most of its natural wealth, has passed many laws that contradict Soviet law and that Mr. Gorbachev has declared invalid.

Russia, for example, has legalized limited private ownership of land by peasant farmers. Soviet law does not permit land ownership, and Mr. Gorbachev has demanded that Russia reverse its law until it can conduct a public referendum. The mixed signals have left local authorities uncertain whether to grant farmers title to land or not.

Traditionally the federal government has gathered almost all the country's revenue, with most of it collected by the republics themselves and then passed to Moscow. The central government then sends each republic a share for its budget.

The Russian republic insists on the right to set its budget priorities, reducing the emphasis on military spending and other federal priorities.

Gennadi I. Filshin, chairman of the Russian republic's State Economic Committee, gathered members of the federal parliament from his republic today during a break and told them that Russia had been forced to take drastic measures because the Kremlin refused to give an honest account of where the money was going.

"We do not know why the army is getting 46 billion rubles for new weapons when a process of disarmament is under way," he said. "The Defense Ministry will not answer our questions. They give us no figures to justify their budget, no insights into the structure of their budget."

Mr. Filshin said the Russian budget was traditionally made up of leftovers from Kremlin priorities.

"Now for the first time we have built our own budget," he said. "And we are going to put it through. The old way has brought poverty to the Russian people. We are not prepared to live any longer in such poverty. That is Russia's position."

Mr. Filshin told the members of the Congress that by controlling its own budget, Russia would stand a better chance of introducing free-market economic changes, including price increases that the central government cannot enact because it lacks public trust.

Mr. Gorbachev, arriving unexpectedly and in an angry mood, accused Russia of arrogant "economic populism" that could set off a chain reaction among the republics and throw the country deeper into chaos.

"What is Russia?" he said. "It is the union. What is the union? It is mostly Russia. Do you think you are more Russian than we are?"

He snapped at Mr. Filshin, asserting that he showed incompetence, and at one point shouted at the Russian agriculture minister to "take your seat."

Mr. Yeltsin, the obvious target of Mr. Gorbachev's fury today, showed his contempt for the debate by leaving on a business trip to Siberia.

Mr. Gorbachev told the Congress that the contribution offered by Russia was 119 billion rubles less than what the republic contributed in the current year, and asserted that the cutback would endanger not only maintenance of the army but also salaries of workers at state factories, hospitals, education, and pensions.

"If we continue debating in this way we will lose two or three months, and all the people will be out in the streets," Mr. Gorbachev said.

Soviet and Russian officials said Mr. Gorbachev now has two choices.

He can negotiate, hoping to whittle down the huge difference or to reach a compromise covering the first part of the fiscal year. Mr. Gorbachev's spokesman, Vitaly S. Ignatenko, said such negotiations would be easier after Mr. Gorbachev appointed a new cabinet, presumably replacing some of the economic executives who have been at loggerheads with Russia.

Prime Minister Nikolai I. Ryzhkov, regarded by Mr. Yeltsin as a chief culprit in the economic impasse, has been hospitalized after a heart attack, and is expected to be among those replaced.

But today Mr. Gorbachev did not sound as though he was in a mood to haggle with Mr. Yeltsin.

A second choice for Mr. Gorbachev is an attempt to seize the money.

A large part of the 261-billion-ruble Soviet budget comes from taxes and revenues collected by the republics and deposited in banks. Although many banks are now agonizing over their loyalties—to Russia or the center—Mr. Gorbachev probably still has enough control over the banking system to pry the money loose.

But some members of the Congress said that that approach would tie up the budget and deepen the confrontation between Mr. Gorbachev and his biggest republic.

"If we don't find a compromise, which is the only way out, this will lead to chaos and civil war," said Mr. Sobchak. "There will be no explosion. But things will just keep getting worse, because the republics will not obey orders from the center."

1991

*A*s the year began, the crisis and challenges facing the Soviet leaders were both merging and compounding. The attention of much of the world was directed at the looming struggle over Kuwait. A Western coalition, led by the United States and involving some Arab forces, was assembling men and matériel in Saudi Arabia in preparation for an assault. Moscow, which had joined in the Western-led naval blockade of Iraq, was offering Washington its diplomatic backing in the confrontation. But if this effort was somewhat perfunctory it was largely because Moscow was facing a staggering array of overwhelming crises and challenges. The economy was stalling, faith in reforms was ebbing, and open defiance of Moscow's central authority was being expressed in many regions of the country and in many sectors of society. The oldest and boldest confrontation was centered in Lithuania, where the demand for real secession and independence had broad popular support. Gorbachev's policies in the Baltic, which had zigged and zagged between tolerance and repression, now took a sharp turn toward greater harshness.

On January 10, he called on Lithuania to halt its defiance of Soviet authority immediately, and warned that "people are demanding" the introduction of direct Kremlin rule of the breakaway republic. A day later Soviet army troops using tanks and live ammunition stormed the Lithuanian press center and a building occupied by the Lithuanian civilian militia. And on January 13, a Sunday, a column of Soviet tanks plowed through a street crowd of civilians and seized the television broadcast center. At least 11 civilians were killed and 100 more were wounded.

The nationalistic yearnings of the Lithuanians were not squelched.

Lithuanian Dead Buried as "Martyrs"

By Bill Keller

VILNIUS, LITHUANIA, JAN. 16—Mourners by the hundreds of thousands streamed through the streets of the Lithuanian capital today to bury those killed by the Soviet army.

Lithuanians were joined by contingents of ethnic Russians, Poles, and Byelorussians in a solemn show of grief that was also, many in the crowd said, a referendum in support of the besieged government of President Vytautas Landsbergis, still barricaded in the parliament building.

As a river of grim-faced families converged on the neoclassical St. Stanislav Roman Catholic Cathedral for a funeral Mass, Moscow's central television was broadcasting a report by Russia's most popular television journalist eulogizing the army troops for having "saved Lithuania" from the threat of ethnic pogroms.

Lithuanians and Western journalists, many of whom had watched unarmed civilians killed Sunday morning by machine-gun fire and crushed under tanks, watched in disbelief as the reporter asserted that all the victims "turn out, upon checking, to have died of heart attacks and traffic accidents."

Fifteen people were killed in the army crackdown, and nine of them were buried in today's ceremony.

Referring to the troops who stormed the republic's main television tower Sunday morning and seized it from the elected Lithuanian government, he said: "In the future, if there is a grain of justice, the names of those 160 lads, who have been spat upon and slandered, should be engraved in bronze under the tower, for they have saved Lithuania."

The special 15-minute report, repeated tonight after the main news program, strongly suggested that more violence was coming.

The reporter, Aleksandr Nevzorov, a Leningrad television star adored for his dramatic crime reports and swashbuckling exposés, asserted that the Landsbergis government had a plot to "exterminate" Communists and their families, and warned that Vilnius was only quiet "for now."

"Because Lithuania really has decided to drink the fiery cup of civil war," the reporter said, over the apocalyptic strains of Wagner's *Götterdämmerung*, "and there is no way out for those who dare to speak Russian in this land."

No Lithuanians were interviewed in the program.

The first detailed, largely accurate accounts of the violence here emerged in the Soviet press Tuesday and today, after two days when most Soviet papers did not publish. These accounts, which likened the events to a military coup and pointed blame at President Mikhail S. Gorbachev, brought a call today by Mr. Gorbachev for suspending press freedoms.

The official portrait of wide civil conflict in Lithuania was contradicted by the scene of normalcy in Vilnius today.

Except for the parliament building, transformed into a fortress by deep trenches and walls of concrete blocks, and the half-dozen buildings held by Soviet troops, the city was so calm that the police said reports of ordinary crime were the lowest they had been in several weeks.

Stores, businesses, and public transportation functioned normally, and away from the funeral throng that filled the city center, people strolled the streets eating ice cream bars in the cold.

Representatives of Boris N. Yeltsin, the president of the Russian republic, arriving here today to show support for the Landsbergis government, said the fate of democratic movements in Russia and throughout the Soviet Union hinged on the outcome of the confrontation here.

"I do not exclude the possibility that Russia could be next after Lithuania, although perhaps Georgia will precede us," said Pavel Voshchanov, a member of the Russian parliament dispatched here as Mr. Yeltsin's emissary.

Mr. Voshchanov said there were already signs that the Communist Party in Russia was devising a similar scenario, summoning workers to economic protests and creating front groups that could challenge the elected republican government and call in the military to back them up.

Mr. Gorbachev on Tuesday accused Mr. Yeltsin of violating the law by calling on Russian soldiers based in the Baltic republics to refuse to participate in actions against the local population, and by suggesting that his republic was near to forming its own army.

Parliamentary deputies from the republics of Latvia, Estonia, Georgia, Armenia, Azerbaijan, and the Ukraine have also come to show support for the Landsbergis government. In a somber silence broken only by church bells and funeral marches, mourners lined the streets eight deep for more than a mile this morning for the final procession of those killed as they stood with family and friends before army tanks that captured the television tower Sunday morning.

Police estimates of the sprawling crowd ranged from 200,000 to half a million.

"What other referendum do they need?" said Vytautas Zekonis, a 46-year-old electrician from the northern town of Aniksciai, surveying the ocean of people surrounding the cathedral. "Let Gorbachev look at this. There aren't many of us Lithuanians, but we want our freedom just the same as bigger nations."

Nine of the 15 officially reported dead were transported in open hearses along the icy Viliya River and down Gediminas Avenue past flickering candles and a profusion of flowers.

First came the body of Loreta Asanaviciute, 23, who was mangled under a tank and died in a hospital later that morning. The others included a high school senior who was hit by a bullet in the forehead, a recently discharged navy electronics specialist, a mechanic, a shop clerk, and a construction worker.

Their battered and bullet-riddled bodies had lain in state in open coffins since Monday. After a Mass and eulogies that stressed the endurance of Lithuania's will for independence, they were taken to Antakalnis Cemetery and buried at dusk in a copse of fir trees.

"Now our independence is baptized in the blood of martyrs," said Julijonas Steponavicius, the Catholic Archbishop of Vilnius and Lithuania, who was persecuted by the Communists and spent years in internal exile in the 1960s and 1970s.

Archbishop Khrisostom, who heads the Russian Orthodox Church in Lithuania, expressed shame that the killings had been done in the name of Russians, and condemned the authorities in Moscow for permitting violence against blameless civilians.

"Difficult trials await us," he said. "We must bear injustice. We are condemned to recognize the power of those who are unworthy of it."

More than 100,000 protesters gathered in Moscow to denounce the army actions in Lithuania. Following the demonstration Gorbachev, at a hastily convened press conference, declared that the confrontations in the Baltic states did not mark any change in his policies, and he rejected accusations that he had abandoned his reformist course. But within a week the government declared that armed soldiers would join the police in patrolling major cities, and Gorbachev followed up this decree by announcing he had granted sweeping powers to the K.G.B. and the police to search private business premises and confiscate documents to combat "economic sabotage." These measures, together with the bloody military crackdown in the Baltic republics, amounted to a broad and powerful campaign to restore central control over the chaotic and disintegrating economy, society, and nation after several years of experimentation with elements of free enterprise and democracy.

But if by issuing the chilling decrees and applying the brakes on liberalization, Gorbachev was accommodating or appeasing forces in the army and security branches, he was alienating those foreign powers whose help would be indispensable in any campaign to modernize and reform the Soviet Union. This was made clear, diplomatically, when Secretary of State Baker met with Aleksandr Bessmertnykh, who earlier in January, had been named to succeed Shevardnadze.

U.S. and Moscow Postpone Summit
By Thomas L. Friedman

WASHINGTON, JAN. 28—The United States and the Soviet Union announced today that they were postponing the meeting between President Bush and President Mikhail S. Gorbachev that had been scheduled for February 11 to 13 in Moscow.

The official reasons given for the delay were Mr. Bush's reluctance to travel far from Washington during the Persian Gulf war and the inability of the two sides to conclude the treaty on reductions in long-range nuclear weapons that they had planned to sign at the meeting.

Secretary of State James A. Baker 3d and the Soviet foreign minister, Aleksandr A. Bessmertnykh, said the meeting would be rescheduled for sometime in the "first half" of 1991. They made the joint announcement after Mr. Bessmertnykh's talks at the White House with President Bush.

Mr. Baker and Mr. Bessmertnykh presented the postponement as a mutual decision unrelated to the violent crackdown on proindependence demonstrators in the Baltic republics of Latvia and Lithuania. But American officials said the decision was driven largely by the Bush administration's reluctance to appear to be engaging in business as usual with Mr. Gorbachev.

Leading Republicans in the House and Senate warned Mr. Bush last week that a trip to Moscow at this time would be widely opposed in Congress. The White House apparently did not want to stir up a second foreign policy dispute at a time of division in the United States over the Gulf war.

Nor apparently did the Bush administration want to undermine or embarrass Mr. Gorbachev by canceling the summit meeting on account of his treatment of the Baltic republics.

The postponement marked the first time that a scheduled summit meeting between the two nations has been put off since 1960. Moscow canceled a meeting set that year between Khrushchev and Eisenhower after an American U-2 spy plane was shot down over Soviet territory and its pilot, Francis Gary Powers, captured.

The decision was also the most tangible sign that relations between the United States and the Soviet Union, which have steadily improved since the day Mr. Bush took office, are now beginning to cool. Mr. Gorbachev has increasingly failed to meet American expectations that he would shift from a Communist to a market economy and loosen his tight control over independence-minded Soviet republics.

Moscow Assures Bush on Baltics
By Andrew Rosenthal

WASHINGTON, JAN. 29—The United States and the Soviet Union ended three days of talks here today with Moscow promising to withdraw some troops from the troubled Baltic region and Washington renewing its offer to stop the war against Iraq if Baghdad pulls its army out of Kuwait.

Neither statement seemed to constitute a significant change in the public policies of either country. But they allowed both superpowers to come away from the talks, the main purpose of which was to delay the next Soviet-American summit meeting, able to point to language that appeared responsive to issues that were at the top of their agendas.

The Bush administration was able to cite Soviet assurances that it will seek to lessen tensions in Latvia, Lithuania, and Estonia as a sign that Moscow was responding to American concerns about the military crackdown in the Baltic republics, and as justification for Mr. Bush's decision not to cite the situation there as a reason for delaying the summit meeting.

For the Soviet Union, the administration's offer to stop fighting if Iraq promises to withdraw, and then immediately follow up with concrete steps to do that, could help mitigate Soviet concerns that the United States is exceeding the United Nations resolutions on Kuwait by trying to destroy Iraq's offensive military potential.

Kremlin Says Its Extra Troops Have Left Lithuania
By Francis X. Clines

MOSCOW, JAN. 30—Kremlin officials said today that most troop reinforcements involved in the deadly attack on civilians in Lithuania earlier this month had been evacuated. But officials in the republic said there was no evidence yet of an easing in the Soviet crackdown that President Bush has said might be expected.

Two columns of Soviet military trucks left Vilnius, the Lithuanian capital, and caused much interest and speculation. But since the city routinely sees frequent convoy movements because of the many Soviet military bases in the region, there was no firm indication that the government of President Mikhail S. Gorbachev was signaling a retreat from its recent hard-line position on the republic's independence campaign.

Soviet officials declined to specifically relate the truck convoys to President Bush's contention in his State of the Union Message that President Mikhail S. Gorbachev had conveyed a willingness to "move away from violence" through troop withdrawals and renewed negotiations with the republic's independence government.

Lithuanian officials, while saying they would welcome a true improvement in relations, said the republic remained tense and frightened, with Soviet soldiers maintaining their occupation of some important buildings and main roads still dangerous because of night patrols by Soviet soldiers.

The Lithuanian president, Vytautas Landsbergis, counseled President Bush to be wary of Mr. Gorbachev's promises without firm evidence. The Soviet leader had strongly defended the actions of Soviet paratroopers in which 15 civilians were killed in the streets of Vilnius in a tank attack on the Lithuanian television tower.

"It is regrettable that the promises of the Soviet leadership are so often broken," Mr. Landsbergis said of Mr. Bush's optimistic report. "This is why the United States should not be satisfied that it has received promises again."

But as Lithuanians prepared for a vote on full independence, the signals from Moscow were consciously ambivalent. On February 1, Gorbachev eased his hard-line pressure on the independence drives in the Baltic region, appointing delegations to begin a "discussion of issues" with the three embattled republics. Then four days later the Gorbachev government stepped up its police crackdown, announcing a 50 percent increase in army patrols in 86 cities. Though billed as part of a campaign against economic criminals, reformers asserted that the government of President Mikhail S. Gorbachev was preparing to use the anticrime campaign as a political weapon against critics. Meanwhile, in Vilnius the Lithuanians were preparing for their vote with barricades still surrounding their public buildings.

Lithuania Votes Overwhelmingly for Independence from Moscow
By Francis X. Clines

VILNIUS, LITHUANIA, SUNDAY, FEB. 10—Lithuanian voters turned a republic-wide plebiscite into a festival of defiance of the Kremlin on Saturday, affirming their republic's harrowing state of independence 11 months after it was officially declared by their elected representatives.

Several hours after Lithuanians poured into the voting booths on a sunny wintry day, a parliamentary spokeswoman said early this morning that 91 percent of those taking part had voted in favor of Lithuania's becoming an independent, democratic republic. She said 87 percent of the votes had been counted.

The voters, presenting gifts to the polling workers and careful lessons to small children on the fresh history of the day, seemed intent on registering an unequivocal reply to the deadly Soviet military attack on the broadcasting station here last month and all other attempts at dissuasion by the Gorbachev government.

"This is a celebration, a festival, with some voters weeping at their happiness in saying yes to independence," said Danute Puchovishiene, a voting board director busy all day here in the picturesque Old City.

The Kremlin had announced regional military maneuvers beginning on Saturday and President Mikhail S. Gorbachev had angrily declared that the plebiscite was illegal. But voters said this only hardened a resolve that was firmly forged by the Soviet army tank raid January 13, with its toll of 15 dead Lithuanians.

"There can be no doubt about the outcome," said Leonas Chernius, voting chairman at Secondary School No. 9, where 133 voters were waiting as the polls opened at 7 A.M. "I see it in the faces of the people, as if this were a festival."

Lithuanians beamed at the voting boxes. They stressed they were only regaining the independence their country enjoyed for two decades before the Soviet Union forcibly annexed the republic in 1940.

"Independence! We will say this as often as we have to to the Kremlin," said Angela Selumbauskaite, an architect. "Gorbachev came here as a Caesar last year and we could tell from the look on his face he understood we are going to go our own way."

More than two thirds of the eligible voters in this republic of 3.7 million people had turned out by midafternoon, republic officials said, five hours before the polls closed at 8 P.M.

Final official figures are not expected until late today. Republic officials holed up in the barricaded parliament building of the independence government estimated that the margin of approval would provide a new, more intense focus for the nationalism issue that now haunts President Gorbachev across much of the shaky Soviet empire.

The other two Baltic republics, Latvia and Estonia, have scheduled similar plebiscites for the next month. The Russian republic, the largest and most influential part of the nation, is further challenging President Gorbachev by preparing a referendum on the question of instituting direct popular election of the republic president.

Such a course was carefully avoided by Mr. Gorbachev on the national level when he created emergency presidential powers for himself and had parliament appoint him to the post last year.

Direct executive election in Russia, which has a majority of the nation's population and wealth, would provide an inviting and far more formidable opportunity for Boris N. Yeltsin, the popular opposition leader, to engineer a forum for challenging Mr. Gorbachev, the leader who once purged him and still obviously fears his sway over the public.

Now the Soviet leader, even as he attempts to rein in the democratization process he himself initiated, finds himself in something of a battle for a popular mandate. As insurgent democrats in the republics use plebiscites to exert more public counterpressure on the Kremlin, Mr. Gorbachev has posed the contrary issue and scheduled a March 17 nationwide referendum on the simple question of continuing the Soviet Union, the Baltic republics included, in some "renewed" democratic form he has been promising in the face of rising demands for self-rule across the 15 republics.

Yeltsin, Criticizing Failures, Insists That Gorbachev Quit
By Francis X. Clines

MOSCOW, FEB. 19—Boris N. Yeltsin, president of the Russian republic, used a nationwide television appearance tonight to call for the immediate resignation of President Mikhail S. Gorbachev for amassing "absolute personal power" and "deceiving the people" with a failed plan for national renewal.

"He has brought the country to dictatorship in the name of 'presidential rule,' " said Mr. Yeltsin, the highly popular opposition leader. He urged the public to support his demand that Kremlin power be turned over to the new Federation Council, dominated by sovereignty-hungry republics.

The speech, eagerly awaited by a Soviet public increasingly dissatisfied with Mr. Gorbachev's rule, was the most powerful and stinging political assault thus far on the Soviet leader during the most recent period of domestic disarray.

"I warned in 1987 that Gorbachev has in his character a tendency toward absolute personal power," Mr. Yeltsin declared, referring to the year in which he was purged from the Communist hierarchy for being among the first to question the pace of change promised by Mr. Gorbachev's *perestroika* program of renewal.

"I separate myself from the position and policy of the President, and I stand for his immediate resignation," said Mr. Yeltsin, whose aides had been negotiating for weeks with the Kremlin for broadcast time for the appearance, which had repeatedly been delayed.

As leader of the nation's largest and richest republic, Mr. Yeltsin took the opportunity to plead for further broadcast time, saying he wished to address the nation on the eve of Mr. Gorbachev's referendum, scheduled for March 17, on whether the public supports a "renewed" version of the present Soviet Union.

In his speech tonight, Mr. Yeltsin indicated a preference for turning that ballot into a vote of confidence on Mr. Gorbachev and his "anti-people policy," as Mr. Yeltsin put it, carefully turning to his prepared text for his final minutes of directly challenging the Soviet leader and announcing a complete break from earlier attempts at cooperation.

"Gorbachev in his first two years after 1985 gave many of us hope," Mr. Yeltsin said. "Right after that, his active policy of—I am sorry to say—deception of the people began, giving promises he did not really know how to implement. Having given hope to the people, he started to act according to other laws."

There was no immediate reaction from the Kremlin. But in the past Mr. Gorbachev has shown high, sometimes short-tempered sensitivity to the challenge and considerable popularity represented by Mr. Yeltsin, his chief nemesis in the public's eye.

The dickering and doubt over national TV time only increased the public's sense of expectation, and Mr. Yeltsin did not let down his camp as he denounced Mr. Gorbachev for an "abrupt shift to the right, the use of the army in interethnic relations, the crash of the economy, low living standards," and more.

"It is quite obvious that his intention is to keep the word *perestroika,* but not its essence," Mr. Yeltsin declared, "to retain rigid centralized power, and not to give independence to the republics and above all not to Russia. This is where his antipeople policy has manifested itself."

Mr. Yeltsin's unalloyed call for President Gorbachev to step down comes at a time when the Soviet leader has been trying to bolster his administration by resorting more to traditional Kremlin reliance on central planning and military force to maintain order.

Mr. Gorbachev's reputation as a would-be democratizer was tattered last month when he defended the use of Soviet tanks in Vilnius, where 15 unarmed people died in the streets as they demonstrated for Lithuanian independence.

He has since increased the K.G.B.'s powers in the name of fighting economic crimes and has authorized troops to be used as civil policemen in more than 400 cities. This is a step widely considered a precaution in anticipation of the public's distaste for a pending round of steep price increases.

Central authorities, in turn, have been trying to put Mr. Yeltsin on the defensive with an investigation of what the K.G.B. calls improper business dealings. Yeltsin aides say this has been a witch hunt to discredit both Mr. Yeltsin and the free-market policies he has been inviting in Russia despite Mr. Gorbachev's renewed reliance on the central dictates of Communism.

Mr. Yeltsin has been in various struggles with Kremlin authorities lately. These range from the public sympathy he quickly extended to the separatist Baltic republics last month after the Vilnius tank raid, to what Yeltsin aides charge was an electronic bugging room set up by the K.G.B. in the Russian parliament.

The Russian leader has tried to showcase his republic as a more democratic and free-market oriented alternative to Mr. Gorbachev's union government. He has put a second question on the referendum on March 17, asking Russians if they would like direct popular election of the republic's president.

Such a step would underline Mr. Gorbachev's unwillingness last year to stand for initial popular election when he accepted the new national presidency. Even more, it would create a more powerful platform for Mr. Yeltsin to maintain criticism of the Kremlin and to organize a full-fledged political opposition to counterbalance the Communists' continuing dominance of the nation's political patronage and government authority.

"The voters wanted me to cooperate with Gorbachev and I made several attempts," Mr. Yeltsin declared, referring to the period last summer when the two rivals announced agreement on a plan for the fast dismemberment of economic Communism by way of what was then called the 500-day plan of moving to free-market economics. Mr. Gorbachev eventually backed off and reendorsed central planning as a safer alternative in this tense and highly troubled nation.

"I consider that my personal mistake is that I was too trusting," Mr. Yeltsin told the nation. He had the occasional tone of a politician announcing his candidacy, although there seems little practical chance of this under the "superpresidency" powers Mr. Gorbachev had tailored for himself last year in the national parliament.

"I have made my choice and each of you has to make his choice and define his position," said Mr. Yeltsin, reading earnestly from a prepared text in the critical closing minutes after initially answering informally to two questioners on the TV show.

"I made my choice and I will not turn off this road," he said without precisely indicating where he personally thought he was headed.

Gorbachev, who so often had extricated himself from trouble at home by pulling off some deft maneuver abroad, tried to pull off one more such trick by offering a peace proposal that would end the conflict in the Gulf. On February 22, Moscow announced that Iraq had given a "positive" response to a Soviet peace proposal and had agreed to withdraw from Kuwait. But it turned out that the Iraqi response had not been genuine or concrete enough to satisfy the allied forces that two days later began their assault on Baghdad. At that time Soviet officials signaled that they were standing with the U.S.-led alliance, though they hoped that Saddam Hussein would have "the guts" to pull back from Kuwait.

The long-smoldering issue of union was now rapidly rising to the surface. At its heart it related to what was to be done if people in the constituent national republics of the Soviet Union used the democratic powers they were being encouraged to develop to leave the U.S.S.R. How was the center to go about supporting democratic changes while simultaneously seeking to maintain the union?

Moscow Publishes New Plan of Union
By Serge Schmemann

MOSCOW, MARCH 9—Soviet newspapers today published a new draft of the federal treaty that President Mikhail S. Gorbachev hopes will be the cornerstone of a revived union. But almost immediately, his political archfoe, Boris N. Yeltsin, delivered a fiery broadside against the treaty and Mr. Gorbachev.

Mr. Yeltsin, speaking to a rally of opposition forces, urged them to form a "powerful organized party" to battle the Communist Party and the Gorbachev leadership. "Let us declare war on the leadership of the country, which has led us into a quagmire," declared Mr. Yeltsin, the president of the Russian republic.

The developments joined a quickening progression of maneuvers and clashes as Mr. Gorbachev has tried to reimpose his control over the increasingly chaotic and fractured politics of the Soviet Union. The President's major current effort has been to rally the country behind a referendum on unity he has scheduled for March 17.

Though a positive vote is all but a foregone conclusion, it has shaped the coming weeks into something of a showdown among the various contenders in the power struggle. Mr. Yeltsin told the rally that this month and this year would be decisive—"either democracy will be stifled or we'll be able to win," he said.

The evening news program, which has scrapped any pretense of balance in the political fray, did not show Mr. Yeltsin, but it gave considerable time to a stern rebuttal by Mr. Gorbachev's top lieutenant, Anatoly I. Lukyanov, the president of the Supreme Soviet, or parliament, who declared that Mr. Yeltsin's speech raised "great alarm for the fate of the country and society."

Mr. Lukyanov accused the Russian republic's leader of "a direct call to confrontation" and warned that the Supreme Soviet would not let the speech pass without notice.

The proposed "Treaty on a Union of Sovereign Republics" has

emerged as a central focus of the political fray. The agreement is intended by Mr. Gorbachev to replace the 1922 agreement that currently binds the 15 Soviet republics with a looser and less centralized structure. Opposition leaders have charged that the document still leaves too much power to the center.

The draft was reportedly the object of fierce debates, and many points remain open to further negotiation, but Mr. Gorbachev evidently wanted to unveil the document in advance of the referendum.

The draft, a revision of one published last year, proclaims the Soviet state to be a "federative democratic state, formed as a result of a voluntary union of equal republics." It envisions broadened local authority but still entrusts the central government with considerable power over defense, state security, foreign policy, and unspecified "foreign economic activities."

The draft envisions a president elected to a five-year term, serving a maximum of two terms, and presiding over a Federation Council composed of leaders of the republics and a cabinet of ministers. Legislative powers would be entrusted to a two-chamber parliament along the lines of the United States Congress, though the published version presented two alternative versions, reflecting differences on representation.

The treaty would grant the republics the right to secede from the union according to unspecified procedures "set by parties to the agreement."

The draft declared that the new treaty would come into effect on acceptance by the republics, but it set no date. In fact, four of the 15 republics—Georgia and the three Baltic states—have declared that they will not sign it, and several others, including Mr. Yeltsin's huge Russian republic, have expressed strong reservations.

In his speech, Mr. Yeltsin declared that the treaty "was a document being imposed on us." Speaking to an enthusiastic audience, he said he had "dozens of the most serious criticisms of the draft treaty, beginning with its title." He and other critics of the Kremlin have urged a union of "states," not "republics."

Mr. Yeltsin charged that the treaty gave too much power to the center and insufficient protection to private property. Only after prolonged study would Russia agree to discuss it, he said.

Mr. Yeltsin signaled today that he intended to further intensify his opposition to the center. He recalled that the Russian republic had set a deadline of March 15—two days before the referendum—for chairmen of local councils who hold office in the Communist Party to quit one or the other.

The sharp response by Mr. Lukyanov indicated that the Kremlin was prepared to fight every bit as fiercely.

On March 15, the citizens of the Soviet Union voted in a referendum casting either yes or no ballots on the question: "Do you support the preservation of the union as a renewed federation of sovereign republics in which the rights of a person of any nationality are fully guaranteed?" When the ballots were counted the result was not exactly clear-cut.

Soviet Vote: An Affirmation of Disarray
By Serge Schmemann

MOSCOW, MARCH 19—In the end, the first nationwide referendum in the Soviet Union did less to point the nation in any direction than to illustrate its disorientation as Mikhail S. Gorbachev begins his seventh year in office.

Mr. Gorbachev had ordered the vote to secure at least the semblance of a mandate for his efforts to regather the reins of his battered union. But if anything, the vote confirmed the image of the President as a hostage of his own *perestroika,* starting reforms and accumulating mandates only to find his intentions foiled and his control escaped.

As always, there was a bit of pertinent Russian folk wisdom, this one recalled by the weekly *Commersant:*

"I caught a bear."

"Bring him here."

"He won't go."

"Then come here yourself."

"He won't let me go."

That seemed to sum up Mr. Gorbachev's political plight as he and his allies claimed victory in the referendum for the "renewed union" they had put to Soviet voters on Sunday's ballot. They did gain a majority, to be sure, but then all of Mr. Gorbachev's opponents who placed their own questions on the ballot also won—first among them Boris N. Yeltsin, who won a strong mandate to seek direct election to the presidency of the Russian federated republic.

The vote was in effect an endorsement of Mr. Yeltsin's anticenter politics, and thus indicated that while a majority of people still preferred a unitary state, they believed even more in Mr. Yeltsin and his resistance to the Gorbachev center.

Thus, in reaching for a belated popular endorsement, Mr. Gorbachev ceded another layer of power to his adversaries. The upshot was likely to be a noisy squabble over who really won, along with more confusion and division.

Yet the referendum, in its indecisiveness, served at least to demonstrate the state of affairs in a time that some commentators have called the transition to "post-*perestroika.*"

For one thing, it showed that despite Mr. Gorbachev's move to a more authoritarian approach, despite his renewed alliance with old establishments and old orthodoxies, neither he nor the hard-liners around him could fully escape, manipulate, or roll back the processes he had set loose.

For all its weaknesses, including the leading way the question was phrased, the proliferation of secondary questions, and the heavy-handed campaigning, the very fact that Mr. Gorbachev felt compelled to go to a vote was a measure of what he had achieved.

Even among his liberal critics, still smarting at his change of heart, there were those who paused to take stock of his achievements.

Vitaly Tretyakov, writing in the newspaper *Nezavisimaya Gazeta* under the headline "Apologia for Gorbachev, or an Epitaph for *Perestroika,*" compiled a list of 46 positive results of *perestroika*—from dealing a "fatal blow to totalitarianism" to the creation of "redundant systems guaranteeing against a return to the past."

But in the act of weighing Mr. Gorbachev's pluses and minuses, Mr. Tretyakov and commentators like him already were effectively looking past the *perestroika* of Mr. Gorbachev's first six years to what he or his successor would face in the new era.

For one thing, Mr. Tretyakov wrote, "History will not forgive the leader of post-*perestroika* any bloodshed or errors as easily as it forgave Gorbachev the pathfinder of 1985–1990."

In this transitional period in his rule, Mr. Gorbachev cut an ambivalent figure. He was the initiator of reform who now stood as one of its major obstacles. He was the giver of *glasnost* who now wrenched state television back to old habits. He was the harbinger of democracy who accumulated dictatorial powers.

The question was how much of this was Mr. Gorbachev himself and how much the bear with which he had cast his lot—the coalition of technocrats, Communists, military officers, and other hard-liners.

Domestic commentators and foreign diplomats alike raked over the events of the last few months to determine the balance of the new order, to find out how Mr. Gorbachev was doing with the bear he now purported to lead.

Among Westerners, the question was whether the resignation of Foreign Minister Eduard A. Shevardnadze and a series of other developments—the brutal crackdown in the Baltic republics, a reversal or freeze in arms control, the failure to ratify two of the Soviet-German treaties, the belated effort to prevent a ground offensive in Iraq—had marked a worrying retreat from the new thought that had marked Kremlin policy through last fall.

A parade of foreign ministers—Secretary of State James A. Baker 3d and the foreign ministers of France, Germany, and Britain—swept through Moscow to assess the new winds. For the present, all declared themselves satisfied that nothing essential had changed, but the concern was evident.

Among domestic pundits, speculation grew that Mr. Gorbachev was circumscribed in his freedom of action by the hard-liners with whom he had cast his lot. The President's insistence that he was not privy to the decision to use military force in Lithuania's capital on January 12, if true, only deepened the question of who was wielding what powers in the Kremlin.

Mr. Gorbachev's difficulties with the hard-liners were illustrated at the current session of the Supreme Soviet, which balked at ratifying the German treaties and resisted three of his nominees to a new National Security Council, including Yevgeny M. Primakov, the architect of Mr. Gorbachev's recent peace initiative in Iraq, and Valery Boldin, Mr. Gorbachev's chief of staff.

The candidates' only flaw evidently was that they were Mr. Gorbachev's men, and the rejection of his chief of staff seemed an especially strong rebuff to the President at a time when he was campaigning for the referendum and struggling against Mr. Yeltsin.

To many a Soviet citizen, the maneuvering often seemed unseemly and worrying. But like the referendum, at least some of what was happening was an affirmation that the democratization and *glasnost* Mr. Gorbachev had loosed on the land were not likely to be curtailed anytime soon.

For a man grappling with an increasingly assertive bear, however, this was probably not a very comforting thought.

The referendum did little to calm political fevers throughout the Soviet Union, be it the Baltics, Georgia, Moldavia, or even Moscow, where the supporters of Yeltsin were increasingly strident in their attacks and criticism. On March 25, Gorbachev responded to the onslaught by ordering a ban on all public rallies and demonstrations in the capital just as insurgent political groups planned to mount sizable demonstrations of support for Mr. Yeltsin in Moscow during a special session of the Russian parliament. Moreover, to help enforce the ban, Gorbachev ordered the national Interior Ministry today to take over law enforcement on the city's streets from the democratically elected city government. The two camps seemed heading into unavoidable and perhaps violent confrontation.

100,000 Join Moscow Rally, Defying Ban by Gorbachev to Show Support for Rival

By Serge Schmemann

MOSCOW, MARCH 28—More than 100,000 Muscovites defied a strong show of military force and Mikhail S. Gorbachev's ban on public meetings to rally today behind his rival Boris N. Yeltsin.

Chanting "Yeltsin! Yeltsin!" and "Gorbachev, go away!" within sight of the extraordinary cordon of military vehicles, water cannon, and troops in riot gear, the throng demonstrated the embattled Soviet President's inability to suppress the growing shift of allegiance to Mr. Yeltsin, the President of the Russian republic.

As the day drew to a close, the consensus was that Mr. Gorbachev had suffered a serious political setback. Despite the tensions, the evening rallies had an almost festive air as Mr. Yeltsin's supporters realized that they had successfully defied Mr. Gorbachev's most aggressive effort to curb their movement and to rout their leader.

The mass demonstration on Mayakovsky Square, which continued into the evening under a floodlit statue of the revolutionary poet for whom the square is named, concluded a day of high drama and suspense as hundreds of military vehicles clogged the narrow alleys of old Moscow and as the parliaments of the Soviet Union and the Russian federated republic met.

Interior Minister Boris K. Pugo said 50,000 troops had been deployed in the city alongside the police to reinforce a ban on public meetings in the capital for 20 days that was ordered by Mr. Gorbachev, ostensibly to safeguard the Russian republic's parliament from "psychological pressures."

No incidents were reported at the rally, and most marchers appeared to agree with the urgent appeals of organizers not to give the Kremlin the satisfaction of a confrontation with the walls of troops that sealed off the old city center along the inner ring road, the Boulevard Ring.

Within hours after the rallies ended, the cordon was lifted and the troops and trucks left the city's center.

For the rest of the nation, the main evening television news program, *Vremya,* gave preference to members of parliament supporting the central authorities, but the program showed enough snippets of scenes from the streets and from speeches in the Russian parliament for experienced viewers to deduce what had happened.

Mr. Yeltsin's political success was sweetened by the fact that the special session of the Russian parliament, of which he is the elected President, was called by Communist members of parliament to censure him for his demand last month that Mr. Gorbachev resign. The deputies had evidently hoped to portray Mr. Yeltsin as a politician waging a personal vendetta at a time of economic and national crisis.

Instead, the session turned into a show of strength for Mr. Yeltsin as the deputies voted to reject Mr. Gorbachev's ban on rallies and then suspended its session until Friday, after the promised withdrawal of the troops. Mr. Yeltsin, who did not attend the rallies today, said he was pleased with the outcome of the vote.

The mass rally was originally called by Mr. Yeltsin's supporters to coincide with the opening of the special session, which seemed at the time to pose a serious threat to his leadership.

The referendum on March 17, however, in which the Russian federation gave a strong endorsement to a popularly elected president and so showed its support for Mr. Yeltsin, signaled to the Kremlin that the leader was gathering strength. The shift has further been demonstrated by a spreading strike of coal miners demanding the resignation of Mr. Gorbachev.

Then, on Monday, as the parliament session neared, Mr. Gorbachev unexpectedly ordered a ban on all political rallies, and the next day he put the Moscow police under the control of the Kremlin. The Moscow city council promptly branded the usurpation of its powers unconstitutional and renewed its authorization for the rallies.

The scene was set for the political showdown.

Starting Wednesday evening, long convoys of military vehicles began to enter the city. Some were packed with special Interior Ministry and army troops, others were empty vehicles of every description intended to block streets.

By noon Thursday, rows of trucks lined virtually every side street in central Moscow and the approaches to Red Square, and bright red water cannon took up positions on Tverskaya Street, the former Gorky Street.

But if Mr. Gorbachev's thought was to intimidate the "democrats," as the opposition coalition of liberals, reformists, and anticenter forces have come to be known, by the end of the day the show of strength appeared to have backfired.

First the Russian republic's parliament session opened with the adoption of a resolution declaring that Mr. Gorbachev's ban on demonstrations and his decree assuming control over the Moscow police were illegal. The vote, 532 to 286, clearly signaled that displeasure with the Kremlin's open move against the authority of Moscow and the Russian republic ranged beyond Mr. Yeltsin's supporters.

The Russian parliament then sent its deputy chairman, Ruslan I. Khasbulatov, to negotiate with Mr. Gorbachev. Mr. Khasbulatov returned and reported that Mr. Gorbachev had refused to rescind his order, but that the President was prepared to pull out the troops by Friday.

The parliament then voted to suspend its session until Friday morning, in effect declaring that it was not prepared to meet under military siege.

Mr. Yeltsin, chairman of the meeting, marshaled the votes and speakers without any apparent concern. He is scheduled to make a major address later in the session, in which he is expected to announce a new version of the 500-day plan for economic changes in the Russian republic, based on the plan Mr. Gorbachev rejected for the Soviet Union last fall.

At the same time, the size of the military force seemed to cause more indignation than fear. When mounted soldiers cantered through Pushkin Square, many onlookers noted the echoes of czarist soldiers riding into masses of revolutionaries.

The government newspaper, *Izvestia,* whose offices look out over one of the main staging areas of the troops at Pushkin Square, carried a strong indictment of the show of force under the headline "Stop this insanity!"

"The military chains, deployed in advance to prevent any peaceful march onto the square, is a disgrace for the authorities," wrote the author Irina Ovchinnikova. "They demonstrate not power, of course, but powerlessness, fear before their own people, an inability and even unwillingness to talk with them."

As the 6 P.M. starting time for the rallies neared, the government relented, agreeing to let the marchers use two squares that had been intended as assembly points for a subsequent march to Manezh Square, the site of many previous demonstrations and the planned venue for today's rally.

Tens of thousands crowded onto Mayakovsky Square, actually the overpass of Tverskaya Street over the Ring Road, and thousands more gathered on the Old Arbat, a pedestrian mall.

Scores of the white-blue-and-red flags of prerevolutionary Russia mingled with placards under a wet snow as the crowd responded to speakers with cheers or shouts of *"Pozor!"* ("Shame").

"They ripped a piece of living flesh away from us and turned it against us when they sent the military here," said Ilya Zaslavsky, a member of parliament. "But we have scored a victory so great it will enter history. Our session has begun not as they planned."

After about 45 minutes, the demonstrators at Old Arbat spontaneously decided to join those at Mayakovsky Square and marched to them along the Ring Road. When they came into view, the Mayakovsky throng burst into cheers, and the two streams joined just as streetlights came on and as spotlights illumined the giant statue of Vladimir Mayakovsky in their midst.

As they prepared to disperse, they started chanting for Mr. Yeltsin and calling on Mr. Gorbachev to resign.   '

Despite the appeals of organizers, several hundred people walked down Tverskaya Street to Pushkin Square to see the trucks and soldiers barring the way to the center. But by now the mood was festive, and before long the people drifted off.

But the tone was far from festive on *Vremya,* the television news program, which has reverted over the last three months into a platform for the Kremlin. "Tonight we saw the confrontation that is dividing our society," the news reader began, showing brief shots of the soldiers and brief snatches of speeches in the two parliaments.

A commentator said the demonstrations were "nothing new—the same people, the same slogans, the same appeals."

"But we should not diminish the importance of it," he continued. "We cannot fail to see that the appeals for a change in leadership and a change in the system are being heard more and more frequently."

Moscow was the seat of two governments that were increasingly pitted against each other. There was the Kremlin regime of Gorbachev and there was the government of the Russian republic headed by Yeltsin. While Gorbachev was finding himself increasingly besieged, Yeltsin was gaining strength.

Yeltsin Attains Greater Powers in His Republic
By Serge Schmemann

MOSCOW, APRIL 5—Boris N. Yeltsin, the champion of forces arrayed against the central government, capped a week of parliamentary victories today by winning expanded powers to rule by decree in the Russian republic and the establishment of a republican presidency.

The vote came on the last day of a special session of the full parliament of the Russian republic, the largest and most powerful of the nation's 15 constituent republics. The session had been called by the Communists themselves to pillory and possibly unseat Mr. Yeltsin, the chairman of the republic's parliament.

In a week of often tense grappling, however, Mr. Yeltsin wrenched a series of tactical victories from the Communists, helped by party members who broke away to form a "Communists for Democracy" group.

In theory, Mr. Yeltsin could use the new powers under the sovereignty he claimed for the Russian republic last June 12 to countermand President Mikhail S. Gorbachev's decrees, adding a new level of confrontation between the rival politicians. In the absence of an agreement, the delineation of authority between the center and the republics has developed into a major source of political conflict.

In fact, however, Mr. Yeltsin was expected to avoid a direct challenge, in part because this could prove futile or dangerous, and in part because it would be unpopular with an already anxious public.

In his final address to the Congress, Mr. Yeltsin chose a conciliatory tone, declaring that personal differences would not "become a hindrance to businesslike cooperation between the leadership of Russia and the union."

"I thank the deputies for this confidence and assure you that it will be used only for the benefit of Russia and its people," Mr. Yeltsin told the lawmakers. He expressed confidence that the republics would be able to reach a new union treaty, "not because the republics are compelled to do this, but because their wish to live together corresponds to their interests."

The measure, adopted by a vote of 607 to 228 with 100 abstentions, granted to Mr. Yeltsin and to one of his allies, the republic's prime minister, the power to issue decrees "to lead society out of a state of crisis."

The extraordinary powers would remain in effect until June 12, the date set for the republic's presidential election, which Mr. Yeltsin is expected to win. Debate on formally establishing the presidency, however, was postponed until the next meeting of the full parliament, which is scheduled for May.

The measures essentially granted Mr. Yeltsin the independent powers he had sought through a referendum in the republic and throughout the Congress. In his present position as chairman of the Russian republic's parliament, his authority had been circumscribed by the strong Communist bloc.

The full parliament, the Congress of People's Deputies, also granted additional legislative powers to the Supreme Soviet, the smaller standing parliament whose members are chosen from the full parliament's deputies, and to its Presidium.

The tally marked a sizable swing of centrist votes to Mr. Yeltsin, perhaps caused to some degree by growing evidence of Mr. Yeltsin's popularity and even more by evidence of growing economic and social disarray.

Secession Decreed by Soviet Georgia

By Francis X. Clines

MOSCOW, APRIL 9—The republic of Georgia declared its independence today, further confounding President Mikhail S. Gorbachev's uncertain hold on the deeply troubled Soviet nation.

The unanimous decision by the southern republic's parliament was made in a surprise session in Tbilisi, the Georgian capital, nine days after a plebiscite in the republic in which more than 98 percent of the voters favored independence.

The parliament's action was timed to coincide with the second anniversary of the killing of 19 civilian protesters at the hands of Soviet troops in Tbilisi.

The declaration turned the anniversary day of mourning into a street festival that continued long into the night as Georgians congratulated one another and celebrated a further step in regaining a freedom they counted lost since 1921, when Bolshevik troops first occupied the republic.

But the parliamentary vote was not the final step, as the Georgian President, Zviad Gamsakhurdia, conceded in his celebration speech when he declared that "this act of independence is not a de facto withdrawal from the Soviet Union." He said it would have to be followed in the next two or three years by a series of legal steps to fully establish self-rule.

Still, for President Gorbachev, the declaration was another blow against his campaign to preserve the Soviet Union as a nation of heavily centralized authority and not as the federation of largely sovereign or independent republics that a dozen separatist movements are demanding of him.

Georgia is a proud, ancient land of five million people, many of whom have long made clear their animus toward Communism and the Kremlin's central rule. Its long-established, long-suppressed independence drive gained considerable momentum in elections last year, when the Communists lost control of the parliament to an insurgent coalition led by Mr. Gamsakhurdia.

As a practical matter, the declaration did not radically alter the current state of confusion over power sharing between the Kremlin and the republics, and in fact only compounded it.

Modern Georgia is an economically shaky land, clearly dependent to some degree on aid from Moscow. It recently became a hotbed of Soviet nationalist clashes, with the Georgian majority represented by the Gamsakhurdia government trying to put down a separate independence claim within its borders by the no less ancient South Ossetian minority of 65,000.

More than 60 people have been killed in South Ossetia in factional fighting as Mr. Gamsakhurdia has demanded that Mr. Gorbachev withdraw Soviet troops dispatched to the region, in northern Georgia, after a state of emergency was declared by the Soviet parliament.

Warning that the Soviet Union faced economic collapse and a paralysis of power, Gorbachev offered a package of anticrisis measures that combined calls for strict discipline with a stepped-up transition to a market economy. He demanded a moratorium on strikes and demonstrations for the duration of the one-year program and called for restoring the chain of authority, arguing that the squabbling republics were threatening to bankrupt the central government.

The most obvious immediate responses to the proposal were acts of defiance. Tens of thousands of workers rallied in Minsk, the capital of the historically docile republic of Byelorussia. Leaders in Georgia, who had declared the republic's independence at about the same time that Gorbachev was issuing his plan, now called on their ethnic kinsmen to begin striking. Siberian coal miners, who were already on strike, intensified their demands.

In the middle of the month, Gorbachev took another trip abroad, this time to Japan and Korea. In Tokyo he implored Japanese lawmakers and industrial giants today to give investment and aid to help the Soviet Union avoid what he said was a "disintegration" of its economy. For their part, the Japanese leaders listened politely to one of his speeches, praised his sincerity, and then expressed misgivings about making sizable investments now. In South Korea, Gorbachev did better. He and President Roh Tae Woo agreed to negotiate a mutual cooperation treaty and to multiply trade tenfold over the next five years in an effort to assist the Soviet Union's faltering economy.

It was another remarkable reversal for the Soviet Union which had for so long supported North Korea in Communist solidarity.

Soon after his return Gorbachev was to demonstrate the same kind of realism in his dealings with his main political foe and rival. On April 24, after a secret meeting with Yeltsin, Gorbachev yielded significantly to the Soviet republics' demands for power sharing as he promised revisions of his highly unpopular price and tax programs and announced a new agreement with the major republics for a "radical enhancement" of their role in governing.

A Cease-Fire of Chieftains

By Serge Schmemann

MOSCOW, APRIL 24—The secretive meeting President Mikhail S. Gorbachev held this week with leaders of nine republics at a retreat somewhere outside Moscow resembled less a conference of government leaders than a peace conference of warring chieftains exhausted and scarred by inconclusive battle.

Accordingly, the joint statement they produced seemed more a cease-fire than a plan of action. But as such, it may prove to be far more significant than the torrent of speeches, decrees, recriminations, and crisis programs that has gushed from the Kremlin and the republics' capitals for much of the last year.

So far, little information has emerged about the session or how it was conceived, except that debates were reportedly fierce and the declblic's parliament, agreed to sit at a table with his archrival Mr. Gorbachev; that the leaders met outside any existing structure, and so as equals; and that the joint declaration they issued reflected the first serious stab at a compromise after months of political clashes.

The meeting also marked the first formal recognition of a distinction between republics seeking to maintain a union—essentially the Slavic and the Central Asian republics—and those that have signaled their intent to seek independence, the Baltic and Caucasian republics and Moldavia.

It is already a matter of some dispute who made the greater concessions, or emerged the bigger winner. What is more pertinent, perhaps, is that all of the leaders who attended came weakened and worried, and evidently aware that their only hope in the gathering storm lay in unity.

President Gorbachev was under strong attack from the left and from the right. Right-wing Communists had called a Central Committee meeting to assail his leadership, and strikers and workers across the Soviet Union were demanding his resignation. He had just returned from his first openly unsuccessful foray abroad, a trip to Japan.

Mr. Gorbachev's popularity at home was at rock bottom, offering little chance that he could put into effect the "anticrisis program" of economic reforms and disciplinary measures introduced by his government this week.

Like Mr. Gorbachev, Mr. Yeltsin had just received something of a drubbing abroad. His was in France, where officials in Paris and at the

European Parliament in Strasbourg made it clear that they still intended to regard Mr. Gorbachev as the sole Soviet leader.

Even in his own bailiwick, Mr. Yeltsin was recognizing that all his popularity did not really outweigh Mr. Gorbachev's powers. Mr. Yeltsin could, for example, claim the support of striking coal miners, but he has no way of satisfying their demands.

Mr. Yeltsin was also beginning to taste some of his own medicine as portions of the Russian federated republic, like Tataria or Yakutia, insisted on gaining greater control of their resources, echoing Mr. Yeltsin's challenge to Mr. Gorbachev.

The prime minister of the Ukraine, Vitold P. Fokin, and his counterpart from Byelorussia, Vyacheslav F. Kebich, had their own problems. Both republics are suffering from spreading wildcat strikes by workers angered by the steep price increases introduced in early April, and both face demands for dissolution of their parliaments.

The Central Asian and Azerbaijani leaders, for their part, saw little economic perspective for the future, outside union with the Slavic republics.

The leaders also felt the growing public dismay at the spectacle of politicians and parliaments feuding while the economy collapses. And so they all gathered at a dacha, or country house, somewhere near Moscow, with no publicity and, according to their aides, minimal notice.

The catalyst, it appeared, was the new challenge to Mr. Gorbachev from the far right in the Communist Party, which had summoned the Central Committee to a meeting today in a bid to unseat him.

The challenge had two effects: it forced him once again to seek a truce with the left, and it demonstrated to the opposition that a genuine threat still lurks to the right of Mr. Gorbachev.

In the end, the Soviet leader made quick work of the challenge. Participants at the Central Committee session said he listened calmly to the charges of the conservatives, then said that if those issues were to be put on the agenda, the Committee should suspend its discussion of crisis measures and prepare for another meeting in three weeks. The proposal was voted down by a solid majority.

Mr. Gorbachev also capitalized on the attack from the right to portray himself as the embattled champion of the center. The plans of "radicals" on both left and right were "fatal," he said, adding, "The greatest danger of the moment is that they have come together, despite what would appear to be irreconcilable mutual hatred."

He said both sides were demanding the resignation of the Soviet Union's parliament, President, and government—and that, he said, he would never allow.

There is no telling whether the cease-fire between Mr. Gorbachev and the republic chiefs will develop into a more permanent truce, or whether they will resume their warring. Mr. Gorbachev has made tactical shifts before, and his feud with Mr. Yeltsin runs deep.

But there are reasons to believe that the cease-fire could hold. For one thing, the statement showed a common awareness of the gravity of the crisis and a realization that no solution is possible without political peace. The declaration said the speakers had emphasized that leading the country out of the crisis "should be placed above everything else at this crucial time."

Furthermore, the statement reflected important compromises by both sides.

Simply by meeting the leaders outside the Federation Council, Mr. Gorbachev recognized their claim to sovereignty. That point was emphasized by the declaration, which said that measures to overcome the crises "are inconceivable without radical enhancement of the role of union republics."

Mr. Gorbachev also conceded that the price increases and taxes ordered by the Soviet government were ill conceived, and agreed to alter them with the assistance of the republics' governments. Most notably, he agreed to lift the 5 percent sales tax, popularly known as the "President's tax," on a range of unspecified necessities.

The republics' leaders agreed to support emergency economic measures and, more significantly, to call for an end to strikes and to declare that demands for the overthrow of existing authorities were "intolerable."

Speaking at the Central Committee meeting, Mr. Gorbachev said the debate at the dacha had been fierce and long. But if the agreements are kept, he said, "this could be the beginning of a break in the developing situation."

A gentlemanly truce of sorts had been concluded in the tug-of-war between Gorbachev and Yeltsin. As part of the deal, Yeltsin obtained tangible gains, while Gorbachev was able to repair his damaged reputation among liberals, reformers, democrats, and democratizers.

Kremlin Transfers Coal Mines to Control of Russian Republic
By Serge Schmemann

MOSCOW, MAY 6—The Soviet government transferred control of the Siberian coal industry to the Russian republic today, marking a milestone in Boris N. Yeltsin's campaign to wrest economic and political authority from the Kremlin.

After months of conflicting claims by the central government and the republics, with resulting confusion over ownership and control of natural resources and industries, the agreement on the mines represented the first sizable transfer of an important industry from the national government to that of a republic.

Before today's accord, Mr. Yeltsin, president of the Russian republic's parliament and principal political rival of the Soviet President, Mikhail S. Gorbachev, had complained that Russia effectively controlled only 16 percent of its wealth.

The transfer of control was a principal demand of strikers who have sharply reduced output at vital mines in Siberia.

The Russian radio said the agreement covered more than half the coal mines in the Soviet Union, including primarily the Kuznetsk Basin in central Siberia, but also the Sakhalin Basin in the Far East and the Rostov mines near the Ukraine. The Soviet Union is the world's largest coal producer, and coal ranks as one of its primary sources of energy.

Details of the transfer were not immediately known, except that regulation of the mines would pass from the Soviet Coal Industry Ministry to the Russian Fuel and Energy Ministry.

Mr. Yeltsin pledged to give the mines considerable economic autonomy, suggesting that instead of quotas and deliveries set by the central authorities, the mines would eventually negotiate direct agreements with customers.

Coming immediately after a truce declared 10 days ago at a meeting between Mr. Gorbachev and the leaders of nine republics, including Mr. Yeltsin, the transfer seemed to foreshadow a new pattern of power sharing between Moscow and the 15 increasingly assertive republics that make up the union.

Mr. Yeltsin also announced today that he had reached agreement with Vladimir A. Kryuchkov, the chief of the K.G.B., to form a Russian version of the security and intelligence agency. Details of the division of responsibilities were not immediately known, but the agreement marked another step in the decentralization of power.

Yeltsin Now Says Gorbachev Is Ally
By Esther B. Fein

MOSCOW, MAY 11—After months of criticizing President Mikhail S. Gorbachev as a virtual dictator, the Russian republic's leader, Boris N. Yeltsin, said in an interview published today that Mr. Gorbachev was in fact "an ally" of the democratic movement.

Mr. Yeltsin said that by signing an agreement with nine of the 15 Soviet republics that calls for a major power shift from the center to the constituents, Mr. Gorbachev had demonstrated that he "today is clearly in favor of reforms, which is very important and which makes him our ally."

The statement by Mr. Yeltsin, which was reported by the independent Interfax news agency, confirmed the significant turnaround in the often tempestuous relationship between Mr. Gorbachev and Mr. Yeltsin, once close political allies who have contested one another bitterly over the pace and style of change in the Soviet Union's difficult path toward a more democratic political and economic system.

Soviet Republics Are Said to Agree on Crisis Program
By Francis X. Clines

MOSCOW, MAY 16—The Soviet government announced today that 13 of the nation's 15 republics had agreed on the details of an emergency plan to steer the nation out of economic crisis. The plan includes budget cuts, fresh assurances for skeptical foreign investors, and a new effort to ban strikes.

"We let down many of our partners and punished ourselves most of all," said Prime Minister Valentin S. Pavlov, who resolved to revive the tattered economy now that greater agreement had been reached with most of the balky, sovereignty-minded republics.

He said only Georgia and Estonia did not take part in this week's negotiations. Even independence-minded Lithuania found the talks inviting enough to retain "observer" status, he said.

Details are not expected to be published until next week, and while Soviet officials at a news conference conceded that past plans had gone awry, they insisted that this one was different for the level of input from the republics.

[The Soviet economy faces a decline in output of 10 percent, an inflation rate exceeding 100 percent and a "radically worse" year, American intelligence agencies say.]

Soviet officials promised fast steps toward building economic credibility. Among those are an executive order with a strong strike ban counterbalanced by a plan for wage increases tied to higher worker productivity in some industries, including energy, chemical, and metals. Manufacturers would have greater freedom to sell a minor part of their products on the open market.

The banning of strikes is especially sensitive. President Mikhail S. Gorbachev has already sought to outlaw them by decree, only to find his wishes ignored. Siberian coal miners recently ended a two-month stoppage that left equipment badly damaged, along with the President's prestige.

As described by Mr. Pavlov, the present state of the consensus plan does not answer critical questions like how the nation might deal with the privatization of property as the underpinning of a move to a market economy. He said the parties had agreed to begin in some fashion with properties at the republic level.

But the negotiations at least signaled progress, if only in terms of basic planning and common resolve, on the heels of the "dacha summit" compromise of last month, when President Gorbachev reached a surprise agreement with most of the republic leaders over an outline for economic planning and power sharing. Mr. Pavlov conceded that the past year had seen a cascade of economic disasters, including the mine strike and the government's failure to meet international trade payments.

"Our left hand reached further than our right one," he said, vowing fast repairs, including accelerated parliamentary approval next week of a multinational measure to reassure foreign investors by guaranteeing protection of their investments here and repatriation of their profits.

Part of the recovery strategy involved obtaining help from the West, notably from the United States, where trade concessions were being blocked by a law that prevented the granting of favorable trading terms to any country that prevented its citizens from traveling or emigrating.

Soviets Enact Law Freeing Migration and Trips Abroad
By Esther B. Fein

MOSCOW, MAY 20—The Soviet parliament today overwhelmingly approved the country's first law granting citizens the right to travel and emigrate freely.

It enacted a separate resolution putting the law into effect by January 1993. The delay was the result of widespread misgivings about the country's ability to handle the high costs that will result from the legislation. The law originally proposed was to go into effect a year earlier.

Its passage by the Supreme Soviet removes a major obstacle to American trade concessions and credits, which are sorely needed to help bolster the ailing Soviet economy.

Under American law, the Soviet Union is barred from obtaining most-favored-nation trading status, which fixes the tariffs on a country's exports to the United States at the lowest prevailing rate, and credits from the Export-Import Bank until free emigration is allowed.

The so-called freedom-of-movement bill endured two years of delays in parliament, numerous revisions in committee, and hours of debate about its potential drain on the country's economy and manpower. Only a week ago, the bill was sent back to committee, a move that some feared would delay it at least three months.

In the end, the lawmakers seemed to have decided that the bill's moral consequence outweighed practical considerations, and voted 320 to 37, with 32 abstentions, for its approval.

"This is a sign, finally, that the Soviet Union values human rights, as do people all over the world," said Fyodor M. Burlatsky, editor of *Literaturnaya Gazeta* and a legislator who lobbied for the measure. "It is truly a breakthrough moment for us in building a law-based state."

The new law is likely to cause concern in Western countries fearful of a huge exodus of Soviet people of all ethnic and religious groups. Currently, the only Soviet citizens leaving in any number are Jews and ethnic Germans, many of them headed to Israel and Germany. Those countries may now require visas, thereby limiting the entry of Soviet citizens.

Last year, about 400,000 people emigrated from the Soviet Union, many of them Jews leaving for Israel, and nearly four million traveled abroad on business or personal trips.

Even without a free-travel law, Soviet travel and emigration has soared in the Gorbachev era. In the mid-1970s, the number of emigrants fluctuated between 20,000 and 40,000, and during much of the Reagan administration, the level was well below 10,000 departures a year.

With relations between Yeltsin and Gorbachev verging on mutual respectfulness, the emphasis in Moscow shifted back to foreign affairs. Essentially, Moscow was offering to change its ways, reduce its arsenals, move toward free markets, and guarantee human rights. And the quid pro quo? Though never fully stated it was nonetheless obvious that what was being sought were Western commitments to help finance the cost of massive economic transformation in ways that minimized the risks of social upheaval.

U.S. and Soviets Bridge Gap on Conventional Weapons and Plan for Summit Soon; Bush Hails Accord
By Alan Riding

LISBON, JUNE 1—The United States and the Soviet Union announced today that they had settled their differences on a far-reaching treaty reducing conventional arms in Europe and that they were preparing for a summit meeting, possibly by the end of June, between President Bush and President Mikhail S. Gorbachev.

After a long meeting with the Soviet foreign minister, Aleksandr A. Bessmertnykh, Secretary of State James A. Baker 3d said today's agreement would allow the two sides to step up negotiations on a new strategic arms reduction accord, which is scheduled to be signed at the summit meeting.

Mr. Baker said the two leaders hoped to meet in Moscow to sign the new treaty "at the earliest possible date," but he refused to speculate when the summit meeting might be held.

"We had hoped for it in the first half of 1991," he said. "I can't say we can meet that schedule, but we will work to that end."

President Bush, in a commencement speech at the United States Military Academy in West Point, N.Y., hailed the settlement for "clearing the way for an important step toward a superpower summit."

The summit meeting had originally been planned for early this year, but was postponed at Mr. Gorbachev's request after strenuous American criticism of a Soviet crackdown against the Baltic republics. Progress toward a strategic-arms treaty was also slowed by disagreements over the conventional-weapons treaty.

That treaty, which was hailed as the most sweeping disarmament accord ever when it was signed at a major East-West summit meeting in Paris in November, establishes limits on the number of tanks, armored personnel carriers, artillery pieces, combat aircraft, and combat helicopters that can be held by NATO and Warsaw Pact nations.

In practice, it meant the Soviet Union would be required to destroy thousands of tanks and other weapons and would lose its traditional huge superiority in conventional weapons in an area stretching from the Atlantic to the Ural Mountains.

But soon after it was signed, disagreement arose over Moscow's effort to exclude weapons controlled by its coastal defense, strategic rocket and naval infantry forces, from ceilings imposed by the treaty. The Bush administration responded by delaying a request for congressional ratification of the treaty.

After today's agreement, the timing of the summit meeting appears to depend on early conclusion of the strategic-arms treaty.

"We're thinking of having the team leaders go to Geneva and resume discussions on a more intensive basis than in recent months," Mr. Baker said.

Mr. Baker and Mr. Bessmertnykh also discussed the Soviet request for huge economic assistance from the West, including the possibility that Mr. Gorbachev might attend the July meeting of the seven industrialized democracies in London.

"That question is still under discussion," Mr. Baker said. "The minister outlined what Mr. Gorbachev had in mind if he attended. We now have a better view of that."

France and Germany have said they favor inviting the Soviet President to the Group of Seven meeting, but the United States and Britain have until now been more cautious, arguing that Moscow should spell out its plans for economic revisions before Western aid is contemplated.

But today, Mr. Baker and Mr. Bessmertnykh appeared to have concentrated on reaching agreement on the Conventional Forces in Europe Treaty so that the strategic arms reduction talks, or Start, can resume and set the stage for an early bilateral summit meeting.

There ensued a period of subtle haggling. At a meeting of the finance ministers from the seven most industrialized powers a consensus emerged against granting large-scale assistance to the Soviet Union until Moscow demonstrated its commitment to substantial reform. Then a day after the Paris meeting ended, Gorbachev, delivering his Nobel Peace Prize lecture in Oslo, made another bid for support from the West, warning that the failure of his campaign to restructure the broken Soviet economy would cost the world its best chance yet for a new era of peace. "If perestroika fails, the prospect of entering a new peaceful period in history will vanish, at least for the foreseeable future," Mr. Gorbachev said. What Gorbachev was after was to set a date for a bilateral summit where he would be able to move from the issue of arms reduction and theoretical talk on market economy to measures of practical help. Time was important. He could feel Yeltsin's breath.

Yeltsin Is Handily Elected Leader of Russian Republic in Setback for Communists
By Serge Schmemann

MOSCOW, JUNE 13—Boris N. Yeltsin, the Soviet Union's leading political and economic reformer, swept to victory today in a presidential election in the Russian republic, becoming the first popularly elected leader in Russian history.

In another direct rebuff to Communism, voters in Leningrad called for restoration of the city's original name, St. Petersburg.

With the bulk of votes counted from Wednesday's elections, Mr. Yeltsin tallied about 60 percent of the ballots cast, easily achieving the simple majority needed to win the newly created executive presidency of the Russian federation outright. Like-minded reformers easily won as mayors of Moscow and Leningrad.

For the fledgling Soviet democracy, the election was the first nationally important vote in which individuals, and not slates, were contested. The platforms and backers behind the main candidates suggested that the country was beginning to move toward broad political coalitions as it sorted out the many groupings that emerged in the first flush of democracy.

And in probably the most emotional of the races, an unexpected 55 percent of voters in Leningrad favored the original name given to their city by its builder, Czar Peter the Great.

The referendum is not binding, but the challenge to a name held sacred by old Bolsheviks and war veterans in favor of a name evoking imperial splendor and a westward orientation turned the vote into an emotional contest of ideologies and beliefs.

All in all, the elections in the Russian republic were a major defeat for the Communist Party, which waged a strong campaign to block Mr. Yeltsin, and indirectly a defeat for President Mikhail S. Gorbachev, whose leadership of the Soviet Union and whose policies are the major target of Mr. Yeltsin's coalition.

Mr. Gorbachev did not endorse any candidate, though he did speak out against renaming Leningrad. After voting Wednesday, he said, "I am ready to cooperate with anyone who will be elected by Russians."

Officials said that more than 70 percent of the republic's 104 million registered voters had cast ballots.

The vote was also a ringing endorsement of Mr. Yeltsin and the broad anti-Communist, proreform democratic coalition of which he has emerged as the leader. He was once a close ally of Mr. Gorbachev in the Communist Party Politburo, but resigned from the party last year.

The republic's presidency also gives Mr. Yeltsin a hefty new lever in his dealings with Mr. Gorbachev, which should prove especially important as they move toward a market economy and negotiate a new agreement binding Russia and the other 14 republics that make up the Soviet Union. Mr. Gorbachev has never faced a national electorate, and now must reckon with tangible evidence of Mr. Yeltsin's authority.

One immediate proof of Mr. Yeltsin's new standing was a personal invitation from President Bush to visit the White House next week.

The popular, burly, 61-year-old chairman of the Russian republic's parliament drew strongly in virtually every Russian city, taking Moscow with almost 72 percent of the vote.

By contrast, the candidate actively backed by the Communist Party, former Prime Minister Nikolai I. Ryzhkov, failed to take a single major city and garnered less than 11 percent in either Moscow or Leningrad. Other candidates trailed far behind, none winning more than 4 percent of the vote.

The leaders of the two largest Soviet cities, Gavriil K. Popov of Moscow and Anatoly A. Sobchak of Leningrad, who are both politically close to Mr. Yeltsin and like him seek to bolster their authority by demonstrating popular support, won easily in their respective cities. Each took more than 65 percent of the vote.

Election officials said results from the 98,000-odd polling stations, where paper ballots are painstakingly counted by hand, would not be final before June 22.

Neither Mr. Yeltsin nor Mr. Ryzhkov had any immediate comment on the results. The main evening television news program, which had openly backed Mr. Ryzhkov, reflected the Kremlin's pique at the returns by giving only a bare-bones report on the voting, concentrating more on the technicalities than on the results.

The Communists had tried to deny Mr. Yeltsin the majority needed for victory on the first ballot, and some opinion polls had suggested that this was a possibility. But in the end, Mr. Yeltsin demonstrated once again a keen political instinct, a broad receptivity to his radical reform program, and his personal magnetism.

He crisscrossed the republic energetically and worked at a statesman's image by traveling to France and Czechoslovakia. He also reached for some of the Communists' military supporters by taking a popular Afghanistan war hero, Col. Aleksandr Rutzkoi of the Air Force, as his running mate.

As president of the Russian parliament, Mr. Yeltsin was already the chief executive and in effect the leader of the Russian republic, by far the largest in the Soviet Union with three-quarters of its territory, just over half its population, and the bulk of its resources and industry.

His campaign for a strong, executive presidency was interpreted as a reach for a direct mandate from the electorate and for authority independent of the sharply divided parliament, whose strong Communist minority has often tried to block Mr. Yeltsin's actions.

In Leningrad, the vote was not likely to change the name anytime soon, since Mayor Sobchak has agreed that so important a step must ultimately be endorsed by the Russian and national parliaments, where it could still be blocked.

But the debate during the campaign moved far beyond the question of a name to the very identity of the Soviet state as it wanders in the vacuum left by the disintegration of Communism.

Ordered built in 1703 by Peter the Great and given the Dutch name of Sankt-Peterburg to underscore his hope that it would become a "window to Europe," the city evolved into a center of great majesty and terrible misery. Its name was Russified to Petrograd in 1914 in the early fervor of the war against Germany, and then changed to Leningrad in 1924 on the death of Lenin.

What lay ahead for Gorbachev as the summer deepened was a visit to London to make his case before the leaders of the seven most industrialized powers and then a summit meeting with Bush in Moscow. It was likely to be another difficult passage, and to pave the way Gorbachev lashed out at the snipers within his party.

Gorbachev Says Hard-liners Risk Communist Demise
By Esther B. Fein

MOSCOW, JULY 3—President Mikhail S. Gorbachev has warned that the Communist Party is on the brink of demise and accused hard-liners of destroying the party from within, according to remarks published today in the party newspaper *Pravda*.

The paper said Mr. Gorbachev delivered his sharp criticism on Tuesday, the same day he gave tacit approval through his spokesman to plans by some of his former and present advisers to start a formal "progressive movement" that is being viewed here as the basis for an opposition party.

The combination of this overture to the left and denunciation of the right encouraged speculation that Mr. Gorbachev was contemplating the possibility of resigning as leader of the Soviet Communist Party or, in what would be a far more significant move, breaking with the party and joining the new Democratic Reform Movement.

The movement is being spearheaded by Aleksandr N. Yakovlev, a Gorbachev adviser and a chief architect of *perestroika,* and by former Foreign Minister Eduard A. Shevardnadze, both former members of the policy-making Politburo of the Soviet Communist Party.

Mr. Shevardnadze sent a letter to the Communist leadership today formally declaring his intention to resign from the party, according to a late-night report on the Russian republic's news program, *Vesti.*

Speaking to a commission charged with preparing a new Communist platform to be discussed at a critical Central Committee meeting later this month, *Pravda* reported, Mr. Gorbachev said that through bitter infighting, the Communist Party was "tearing itself apart." He warned that if the situation continues, the party "will lose the political struggle and all elections it will have to face in the near future. It will lose everything."

"The situation—and I'll say it frankly—is critical," Mr. Gorbachev said, adding gravely that "the party cannot remain in its current situation."

As the leaders of the richest nations were flying to London to hear Gorbachev, ordinary Soviet citizens were hoping for some outcome that would arrest and maybe even reverse the declining quality of their lives.

Summit in London; Gorbachev's Big Gamble
By Francis X. Clines

LONDON, JULY 16—In his special plea to the world's industrial powers, President Mikhail S. Gorbachev is attempting one of the most ambitious strategies of an adaptive career: he is trying to move the withered economic heart of the Soviet domestic agenda into the theater of global politics, where he flourishes.

He has no such touch at home, where he faces cynicism toward himself and his reconstruction program. In turning to the world forum, he is seeking a morale lift from the world at large for the sagging national spirit, as much as traditional foreign aid.

With varying degrees of sympathy, the Group of Seven leading industrialized democracies will sit as a capitalist round table to hear out the irrepressible guest from the East, who was reported still pondering and editing his ultimate plea to the economic summit meeting as he arrived tonight.

In an advance token of the Group of Seven's concern, the group announced that it would introduce annual meetings between its chairman and the Soviet President. The group thus created a special status for Mr. Gorbachev, whose chief point in demanding an audience was that the Soviet Union retains superpower potential in a world of intermeshed economies.

But at that, President Gorbachev's credibility was being called into question even before he landed. His advance summary letter to the Group of Seven was criticized by some as being a sweeping but vague mix of free-market promises and imprecise timetables, lacking the substance to right a national economy now estimated by some Western experts to be reeling under an annual inflation rate in excess of 100 percent.

It is a rapidly shrinking economy of plummeting production, ballooning deficit, and lost credibility symbolized by the tattered ruble. It is an economy haunted by the separate pressures from the nation's 15 republics to find greater power sharing and free-market opportunities with Mr. Gorbachev's cooperation or without it.

"The rate of decline is fantastic," said Stanley Fischer, an economist with the Massachusetts Institute of Technology who is involved in pressing on the Kremlin a high-speed plan for a radical free-market shift. Not even in the Great Depression in America was there a rate of collapse to rival what is now taking hold in the Soviet Union, according to Dr. Fischer, who warned that there is no time for further procrastination and well-meaning study by either Mr. Gorbachev or the Group of Seven.

Pact Is Reached to Reduce Nuclear Arms; Bush and Gorbachev to Meet This Month; 7 Powers Give Soviets New Economic Role

By R. W. Apple, Jr.

LONDON, JULY 17—After nine years of negotiation, the Soviet Union and the United States reached agreement today on a strategic arms treaty, the first to mandate reductions by the superpowers, and President Bush immediately agreed to meet President Mikhail S. Gorbachev in Moscow late this month.

Then Mr. Gorbachev, the proud leader of the nation where Communism first flowered, sat down with the heads of the seven most powerful capitalist nations and asked them for help in reforming an economic system that has all but collapsed. Almost 75 years after the Bolshevik Revolution, the Soviet President's pleas represented an admission of economic failure.

Mr. Gorbachev laid his plans before the Western leaders in what another participant described as "an eloquent performance." Officials taking part in the closed meeting reported that Mr. Gorbachev insisted that Soviet progress toward a market economy and private ownership of property was irreversible, but that he made no new proposals.

Nevertheless, Mr. Gorbachev won praise from the leaders of the seven countries—the Group of Seven. Mr. Bush said the Soviet leader had shown "enormous courage" in pushing ahead with reforms.

"It's not going to be quick or easy to implement change in the Soviet Union," Mr. Bush said after the meeting, "but we believe President Gorbachev has made an irrevocable commitment."

Britain's prime minister, John Major, who played host to the group's seventeenth annual economic summit meeting, said: "This has been a day I believe that history may well see as a landmark. It will be seen as a first step toward helping the Soviet Union become a full member of the world economic community."

The Moscow meeting was tentatively scheduled for July 30 to 31.

Under the provisions of the arms treaty to be signed there, the overall number of nuclear weapons in each side's arsenal will be cut by 25 to 35 percent. The American arsenal will be reduced from about 12,000 warheads and bombs to about 9,000, while Moscow's stockpile is to be reduced from roughly 11,000 to roughly 7,000.

While Mr. Gorbachev made no specific requests for immediate financial assistance, officials of several nations said, and left little time for questions, he asked the group to "take a step forward" in developing greater cooperation with his country.

"The ice has started moving; the icebreaker is on its way toward renewal," the Soviet leader told reporters later. But he quickly added, "There is need for movement from the other side," meaning the West.

Mr. Gorbachev came away with the prospect of a bit more Western aid than had seemed likely a few days ago, including pledges of a "special association" with the International Monetary Fund and the World Bank, extensive programs of technical assistance, and an early visit to Moscow by the group's finance ministers to discuss further measures. But he won no promise of major infusions of cash.

In addition, German officials promised that they would invite the Soviet leader to attend next year's economic summit conference in Munich, and President François Mitterrand of France said that he favored ultimately asking the Soviet Union to join the club, making it a Group of Eight.

At the news conference tonight, Mr. Major said the meeting had established "a partnership with the Soviet Union on a new and better footing," as a first step toward Moscow's integration into the world economic system.

Mr. Gorbachev called the three-hour session "one of the most important meetings of our time."

"Today has meant a lot," the seemingly weary Soviet leader said.

"It's been a good day for the United States," Mr. Bush replied.

Merely by winning admission to the forum of capitalist leaders this week, Mr. Gorbachev can claim a victory. But some things that most of the participants would have liked to give him, including full membership now or soon in the International Monetary Fund and greater drawing rights at the European Bank for Reconstruction and Development, were blocked by the United States and Japan.

Mr. Gorbachev had to overcome American opposition and that of hard-liners in his own country to gain an invitation to London. Still, some members of the Gorbachev delegation expressed open disappointment today with what he had achieved. One said that "the Soviet Union doesn't understand Western economics, and the Western nations don't understand Soviet politics."

Still, the arms accord is likely to help Mr. Gorbachev with his increasingly restive people, as it will free scarce resources for domestic concerns.

By the time that the Strategic Arms Reduction Treaty is carried out, probably in 1999, the number of American warheads on weapons that can reach the Soviet Union will drop by about 25 percent, and the comparable Soviet total will fall by about 35 percent. The treaty puts sublimits on various weapons systems and is particularly tough on the Soviet SS-18 missile, the most powerful in either arsenal.

For two days, the prospect of Mr. Gorbachev's arrival here had hung over those attending the conference—the leaders of Britain, the United States, France, Canada, Italy, Germany, and Japan. Today, as his motorcade of Zil limousines flashed across central London from one meeting to another, he utterly dominated the scene, eclipsing and in some cases eliminating debate on other issues.

The summit conference never really came to grips with the environment, referring discussion of global warming and the rain forests to a United Nations conference next year on the subject and thus avoiding an all-out clash between the United States and the Europeans, especially Britain.

On another difficult matter, described by everyone as crucial, the group merely pledged to complete by the end of the year the current round of talks designed to bring up to date the General Agreement on Tariffs and Trade. This is precisely what was promised in Houston a year ago and not delivered.

Mr. Major, who presided over this week's sessions in a bright and breezy way that contrasted sharply with the stern, hectoring manner of his predecessor, Prime Minister Margaret Thatcher, said it had been "a friendly and very frank summit." He added, "People did speak their minds clearly and comprehensively and on occasions in an unforgettable way."

Much of the groundwork was laid before today. Secretary of State James A. Baker 3d and Aleksandr A. Bessmertnykh, the Soviet foreign minister, had resolved all outstanding questions on the all-important arms treaty, except one technical issue, at a series of meetings in Washington that ended Sunday. That related to the definition of a new missile, in terms of its throw weight, or destructive capacity, for treaty purposes.

White House aides said Mr. Bessmertnykh asked this morning for a meeting with Mr. Baker just before Mr. Bush and Mr. Gorbachev were to meet for lunch at the United States ambassador's residence. A senior American official said the foreign minister brought new proposals, and after a flurry of conferences, the President and his advisers agreed that the final obstacle had been overcome.

Mr. Bush and Mr. Gorbachev spent most of their lunch discussing economic and other matters, then slipped into an adjoining room to ratify what had been agreed to on arms.

Beaming, the two men met briefly with reporters, Mr. Gorbachev saying that his country was "ready to give our hospitality to the President of the United States and Mrs. Bush." He had sought the Moscow meeting for the last year.

"Before you change your mind, we accept with pleasure," replied Mr. Bush, who had held out for the treaty as a condition for making the trip.

Neither side was willing to specify what the final arrangement was, because neither wanted to appear to have made the final concession, lest it be seen as soft by the legislative hard-liners in Washington and Moscow, whose backing will be needed if the treaty is to be ratified.

British and American experts said the difficulties in reaching agreement were more political than military. The Soviet Union is believed to be developing a more advanced, more powerful version of one of its missiles.

The administration wanted to head that off, remembering the deployment of the SS-19 after the 1972 antiballistic missile treaty. Critics of the 1972 agreement charged that its negotiators had failed to get tight enough language.

At his meeting with the Group of Seven, Mr. Gorbachev made no specific requests for monetary aid.

"He really was trying to explain more what was going on inside the Soviet Union, what the pressures were, what he was up against in terms of history, if you will," Mr. Bush reported. "He really stopped short of what some predicted might be on his agenda."

Mr. Major reportedly opened the meeting by telling the Soviet leader: "You are among well-wishers. The challenges you face are formidable, but the opportunities are limitless."

He said candidly, however, that the West expected reform in property rights, market prices, the breakup of state monopolies, and the establishment of a Western-style legal system.

Mr. Gorbachev, in turn, spoke of the need to dismantle barriers to the Soviet economy, including trade restrictions and lack of access to loans.

Daniel Bernard, the French spokesman, described the Russian's presentation as a "particularly rich" 30-minute speech that dealt with the relationship of the Soviet republics to the central government in Moscow and with his own reform intentions.

A British official said Mr. Gorbachev's explanation of his economic policies today was not significantly different from the plan detailed in a 23-page letter he sent to the seven leaders last week.

According to one official, Mr. Gorbachev's one-hour opening statement this afternoon and his remarks at the news conference tonight were not "very specific on details."

He left unclear, this official said, the answers to such questions as exactly how the Soviets intended to privatize state-owned enterprises and liberalize controlled prices.

"There was movement in the right direction," an official said, adding that Mr. Major would try to get clarification during his talks with Mr. Gorbachev here Thursday.

In a briefing tonight, Mr. Gorbachev's chief spokesman, Vitaly S.

Ignatenko, disclosed few details of the private discussions today. He did say that Mr. Gorbachev had discussed the need to create a stabilization fund to bolster the ruble, as a way to more quickly complete the conversion of the ruble on international currency markets. However, he did not seek Western aid for such a fund. "Today was not the occasion" for that, Mr. Major explained.

Mr. Ignatenko said Mr. Gorbachev spoke at length about the relationship between the central government and the republics, and assured Western leaders that he had a mandate to speak for all the Soviet Union in his attempts to press forward with an agenda of economic reform.

A six-point program of assistance was ultimately agreed on, but some of the points struck economists as imprecise and redundant, an attempt to make a small package look bigger. The Western summit partners committed themselves to these goals:

- Setting up the special relationship with the International Monetary Fund and the World Bank, leaving it up to the institutions and the Soviet Union to negotiate the terms.
- Urging other international organizations to make their knowledge and skills available to Moscow.
- Offering technical assistance to help the Soviets exploit energy resources, improve food distribution, increase nuclear safety, make their transportation system more efficient, and convert military industries to civilian ones.
- Helping expand trade with the West and with Eastern European nations.
- Sending Mr. Major to Moscow before the end of the year to check on the progress of reform and, if appropriate, to recommend further Western aid.
- Sending the finance ministers' group to Moscow very soon.

Chancellor Helmut Kohl of Germany, which has supplied most of the Western aid to the Soviet Union in the last year, had hoped for bolder action. But he spoke of "a good start."

Mr. Mitterrand said "we must, really must, reach out," and his aides said that he, too, would have liked to do much more to help the beleaguered Mr. Gorbachev than was agreed to in London.

It was turning out to be a good month for Gorbachev. He had gained the sympathetic ear of the only sources of real assistance. He was about to host President Bush. There was even some progress on a treaty that would reconstitute the Soviet Union by changing its basic federal formula.

Gorbachev's Plan on Power Sharing Wins Wide Assent

By Francis X. Clines

MOSCOW, JULY 24—President Mikhail S. Gorbachev announced today that he had reached agreement with most of the country's republics on a draft treaty for a drastically decentralized system of power sharing in the Soviet Union.

By achieving a draft accord with nine of the 15 Soviet republics, Mr. Gorbachev has achieved a significant political success on the eve of an important Communist Party Central Committee meeting and next week's meeting in Moscow with President Bush.

Given Mr. Gorbachev's urgent efforts to encourage Western and Japanese investment and economic aid, the unity treaty will make it easier for Mr. Bush and other leaders to discuss such help more concretely. One problem in the past has been uncertainty by foreign governments and companies whether such funds should be given to the central government or the separate republics.

The Soviet leader said the proposed treaty, one of the keys to his hopes for the political and economic reconstruction of this battered nation, would settle all major differences between his central government and the republics except the precise system of tax sharing.

The taxation formula is supposed to be worked out in special negotiations within the next day, said Mr. Gorbachev, who was obviously delighted to announce progress toward liberalizing the nation as he faced a week of Communist Party intrigues and superpower summitry.

The White House said today in Washington that on his trip to the Soviet Union next week President Bush would address the Supreme Soviet of the Ukraine and meet with members of the emerging democratic movement in Moscow.

The party hierarchy gathers in private session on Thursday to again vent their frustration at how the Gorbachev strategy is undoing their power monopoly. On Tuesday, President Bush arrives to seal the strategic nuclear weapons treaty as the latest success in the Soviet leader's disarmament compromises.

For all his optimism, Mr. Gorbachev still faces a series of obstacles to his hope for fast final approval of a new union treaty. There is the insistence by some republics such as the Ukraine to put off republic parliamentary debate until September, and there is the thorny taxation issue as well.

Boris N. Yeltsin, President of the Russian federation republic and a key figure in the attempted compromise, stressed in remarks that the tax dispute—how much the central government coffers would yield to the republics' desire to control the revenue flow—was a critical issue that had not been worked out.

Speaking on the eve of a Communist Party Central Committee meeting that is expected to again criticize his courting of Western economic alliances, President Gorbachev nevertheless pronounced the negotiations a success. In particular he hailed the decision of Armenia, one of the six republics that originally boycotted the treaty talks, to rejoin the discussions this week.

Mr. Gorbachev emerged early this morning with the announcement after a final 12-hour burst of negotiations that capped a three-month process of seeking compromise with the restless, sovereignty-hungry republics on a blueprint for a new Soviet Union.

He hailed the treaty as "a very deep reforming of our federation and a serious redistribution of powers in favor of the republics."

"The most important thing is that we have finally reached agreement," the Soviet leader declared this morning. He said the next phase in the process is that the treaty would be open for signing after additional consideration by the nine republics that negotiated it with him.

Having scored an advance with the union treaty, Gorbachev advised his weakened party to streamline itself and jettison beliefs, symbols, and traditions that had become increasingly burdensome.

Gorbachev Offers Party a Charter That Drops Icons
By Serge Schmemann

MOSCOW, JULY 25—President Mikhail S. Gorbachev today proposed a new charter for the Communist Party that rejects some of its most hallowed principles, even the sanctity of Marxism-Leninism.

Speaking at the opening of a two-day session of the party's Central Committee, Mr. Gorbachev, who is both President of the Soviet Union and general secretary of the party, criticized "fundamentalists" in the party and threw his lot in with reformers seeking to replace the militant utopianism of old with a broad social democratic platform.

Declaring that the Communist Party would "lose any claim to participate in political life if it stepped away from the course of reform," he also called a full party congress for November, at which both the new program and his leadership would be judged. The unexpected move seemed to preempt an expected assault on Mr. Gorbachev from party hard-liners, who have used past party meetings to demand his resignation and criticize his policies.

The proposed program also stood to bolster Mr. Gorbachev's credentials as a reformer before the visit here by President Bush next week. Western leaders declared a readiness last week to help the Soviet Union, but have been looking for concrete evidence of progress before committing substantial funds.

Introducing the draft of a new "party program," Mr. Gorbachev declared that previous programs "set goals not so much in accordance with reality, but with the then-popular understanding of the Communist ideal." The result, he said, was "raw ideology" irrelevant to the concerns of society.

He noted that there had been proposals to drop the name Communist and rename the party as a socialist or social democratic party. But he said any changes in the name should await the November congress.

The new program, he said, bases the party's goals on the experience of *perestroika,* on transforming the Soviet Union into a democratic federation of sovereign republics, on introducing a market economy, and on integrating the country into the global economy.

Reaching to the very heart of the old ideology, Mr. Gorbachev declared, "In the past the party recognized only Marxism-Leninism as the source of its inspiration, though the tenet was utterly distorted to suit the pragmatic needs of the day, becoming something of a collection of canonical texts."

"Now it has become necessary to include in our arsenal of ideas all the riches of our own and the world's socialist and democratic thought," he said.

It would have been inconceivable even just a few years ago for the head of the Soviet Communist Party to denigrate Marxism-Leninism and to suggest that the party could be run with competing ideologies. One of the frequent forms of denunciation in the past was to accuse someone of falling under the influence of "bourgeois ideology."

Mr. Gorbachev said many participants had probably noticed that the program barely mentioned the creation of a Communist society, once the central goal of Marxist ideology.

In the original thinking of Marx and Engels as modified by Lenin, a society would go through different transitions until it reached the state of Communism, which was the theoretical goal of the party. Its basic features were supposed to be the end of private property, of any social classes, and of the state, and it would follow a system of "from each according to his ability, to each according to his needs."

"Our experience, and not only ours, does not give enough grounds for believing that this aim can be realistically achieved in the foreseeable future," Mr. Gorbachev said.

He also made these points in outlining the new draft program:

● On a market economy, once considered incompatible with socialism, he said, "The entire world's experience of the past decades points to the conclusion that it is not possible to achieve the principle of each according to his work without a market economy."

● On class struggle, Mr. Gorbachev declared, "The time has long come to acknowledge that the epoch when the masses had no means of improving their lot except by storming the Bastille or the Winter Palace has gone into the past."

● On religion, he said a member of the party had the right "to freely profess his own views, to be an atheist or a believer." In the past it has been forbidden for any party member to be anything but an atheist.

● On party discipline, he said the party no longer required, as it did in the time of revolutionary struggle, "iron discipline, essentially on a militarized structure."

There had been speculation that Mr. Gorbachev himself would leave the party. Instead, he has evidently chosen to try to reshape it into a broad social democratic force and to stem the tide of departures.

Underscoring the urgency of the effort, Mr. Gorbachev reported that party membership fell by 4.2 million in the last 18 months, and was now estimated at its 1973 level of 15 million.

A day later the party approved Gorbachev's program recasting the former "vanguard of the proletariat" into a broad-based "party of democratic reforms." Three days later President Bush arrived in Moscow to explore the shape of relations between the two superpowers.

Bush Is Pledging to Accord Soviets Best Trade Terms
By R. W. Apple, Jr.

MOSCOW, JULY 30—Proclaiming the onset of "a new age of promise" at the start of his fourth summit conference with President Mikhail S. Gorbachev, President Bush promised today that he would seek as soon as possible to put the Soviet Union on equal footing with the United States' other trading partners.

"We have good reason to hope," Mr. Bush said. "One by one, the cruel realities of the cold war flicker and fade and a new world of opportunities beckons us forward."

Mr. Bush said he would ask Congress to grant Moscow preferred tariff terms, known as most-favored-nation status, which Mr. Gorbachev has long sought as evidence of economic normalization between two countries that for decades led rival trading blocs. The President's action provided a political tonic for the beleaguered Soviet leader, though a largely symbolic one; the Soviet Union produces relatively little of interest to American buyers.

Mr. Bush also met with Boris N. Yeltsin, the newly elected President of the Russian republic. Mr. Yeltsin declined to meet Mr. Bush and Mr. Gorbachev together, but he gave significant support to Mr. Gorbachev's attempt to give the Soviet republics more power by announcing he was ready to sign a new union treaty changing the power relationship between the Kremlin and the republics. He said he and Mr. Gorbachev reached agreement this morning after they worked out a complicated tax-sharing solution.

Mr. Bush offered sharp words about Moscow's attempts to rein in the rebellious Baltic republics and about its continuing aid to Cuba.

Speaking in the vaulted, richly embellished St. George's Hall, the largest room in the Kremlin, surrounded by the insignia of celebrated Russian military units, Mr. Bush praised Mr. Gorbachev for "instituting reforms that changed the world" and said that he had won Americans' "respect and admiration for his uncommon vision and courage in replacing old orthodoxy."

Bush and Gorbachev Sign Pact to Curtail Nuclear Arsenals; Join in Call for Mideast Talks
By R. W. Apple, Jr.

MOSCOW, JULY 31—President Bush and President Mikhail S. Gorbachev of the Soviet Union signed a far-reaching treaty today that is designed to scale down their nations' stocks of long-range nuclear weapons, then joined in a bold bid to stage a comparably momentous Middle East peace conference in October.

The two leaders inscribed their names on the 700-page arms reduction treaty at a solemn 30-minute ceremony in St. Vladimir's Hall in the Kremlin. The treaty still needs approval by the legislative branches in both countries, but with the signing, after nine years of negotiation, Mr. Bush said, "We reverse a half century of steadily growing strategic arsenals."

Declaring the arms race over, Mr. Gorbachev commented, "Thank God, as we say in Russian, that we stopped this."

A joint statement issued by the two Presidents said they "will work to convene in October a peace conference designed to launch bilateral and multilateral negotiations."

The signing of the arms treaty, so long awaited, was all but overshadowed by the Presidents' decision to join in calling for the equally long-sought Middle East peace conference, in which Israel has not yet agreed to take part. Clearly, they hoped their announcement would prompt the Israelis and Palestinians to overcome their differences over the composition of a Palestinian delegation at the projected conference.

"This historic opportunity must not be lost," Mr. Bush said.

Secretary of State James A. Baker 3d is to fly to Jerusalem on Thursday "to obtain Israel's answer," Mr. Bush said. By limiting the language of the statement to saying they would "work" to convene a conference, they avoided an ultimatum to Israel that would have resulted if a firm date had been announced.

Aleksandr A. Bessmertnykh, the Soviet foreign minister, is to follow Mr. Baker's visit a bit later, carrying papers to open full diplomatic relations between the Soviet Union and Israel. Moscow has said that could be done only when peace talks were agreed to.

Mr. Bush, who announced on Tuesday that he would ask Congress to approve favorable new trade terms for the Soviets, continued to press for economic reform as a condition for large-scale United States assistance.

"You must define your own branch of democratic capitalism," he told an attentive group of fledgling Soviet businessmen in a breakfast speech. "People must be free—to work, to save, to own their own homes, to take risks, to invest in each other, and, in essence, to control their own lives."

Mr. Gorbachev, for his part, has been pressing the United States to ease restrictions on high-technology exports to the Soviet Union.

The two leaders spent much of the day at a government retreat 20 miles west of Moscow, known as Novo Ogaryovo, discussing political issues that still divide their nations. On the agenda were Cuba, the size of the Kremlin military budget, and the Baltic republics' desire to be independent. There was no indication that the talks were anything but cordial, and Soviet television showed the two leaders smiling, tieless and wearing pullover sweaters.

But what made this week "a dramatic time," as Mr. Gorbachev put it, was the Strategic Arms Reduction Treaty, known as Start, and its symbolic termination of the race by the United States and the Soviet Union to amass weaponry with which to blow each other up.

Start will reduce the superpowers' stocks of long-range missiles and bombers by about a third. But that will take them back only to roughly the level where they stood as negotiations began in Geneva in 1982 on this, the last of the major arms-control agreements conceived in the tensions of the 1970s and 1980s.

Nonetheless, it is the first agreement ever that calls for the two nations actually to reduce their holdings of the most deadly weapons, instead of merely reducing the rate at which those holdings have expanded.

Mr. Gorbachev spoke in soaring terms of the Start treaty, describing it as "a moral achievement" and asserting that it marked the "dismantling of the infrastructure of fear that has ruled the world." He added, "Normal human thinking will now have to replace the kind of military-political thinking that has taken root in the minds of men."

Mr. Bush, less triumphal, said it "represents a major step forward for our mutual security and the cause of world peace." He emphasized that "neither side won unilateral advantage over the other."

The Soviet Union will be required to cut its ballistic missile warheads by more than 35 percent, to about 7,000 warheads from about 11,000; and the United States will have to trim its ballistic missile arsenal by about 25 percent, to roughly 9,000 warheads from about 12,000. The Soviets will also have to destroy half of their heavy SS-18 intercontinental ballistic missiles; the United States has no weapons in that category, and under the treaty is not permitted to build any.

Complicated verification measures, including snap inspections at strategic weapons emplacements, are expected to ease the treaty's approval. Leaders in the United States Senate and the Soviet parliament have predicted relatively little opposition.

There have been two previous strategic arms treaties between the Soviet Union and the United States. The first was signed by President Nixon and Leonid I. Brezhnev in 1972, limiting the expansion of nuclear arsenals. A follow-up, drafted by Mr. Brezhnev and President Carter, was never approved by the Senate.

The summit over, as Gorbachev went on holiday to the Crimea, an old colleague issued a mystifying warning.

Ally Who Soured on Gorbachev Warns of a Stalinist-Style Coup
By Francis X. Clines

MOSCOW, AUG. 16—Aleksandr N. Yakovlev, an estranged confidant and reform strategist of President Mikhail S. Gorbachev, quit the Communist Party today with a warning that party reactionaries were planning a vindictive Stalinist coup d'état.

Mr. Yakovlev's departure had been expected for months. But he left with a melodramatic flourish, cautioning the nation that while the party leadership was losing influence, it was nevertheless "making preparations for social revenge, a party and state coup."

He offered no details or names and made no estimate of the hard-liners' chances of success as the nation prepares for a new stage of political reorganization. A proposed union treaty is to decentralize the Kremlin's power, shifting more authority to the republics and speeding electoral and constitutional change.

In recent months, Mr. Yakovlev's influence with Mr. Gorbachev had waned despite their early years mapping the *perestroika* and *glasnost* strategies together. He resigned from the President's staff this summer after directly challenging the party as a cofounder of the Democratic Reform Movement, a loose opposition vehicle intended to offer a nation-wide political alternative to Communism's remaining influence.

Mr. Yakovlev's role in this new insurgency movement caused the Communist hierarchy to recommend his expulsion from the party on Thursday. He responded today with his preemptive resignation, complaining that his "human dignity has been offended" and that his party rights were violated.

Mr. Yakovlev, 67 years old, has spent most of his career in party and government work. He made an earlier coup warning in January, when, in defending the Gorbachev program, he said he saw a threat of a new sort of coup by party middle managers and grass-roots bureaucrats bent on sabotaging reform.

"We are going to pass over from nonfreedom to freedom without bloodshed, without total violence," he predicted then. But in his newest warning, he said the party leadership was "getting rid of the democratic wing in the party and preparing social revenge."

Turning in his party card, Mr. Yakovlev said, "I would like to warn society that an influential Stalinist group has formed within the leadership core of the party, speaking against the political course since 1985 and slowing social progress in the country."

He made no mention of Mr. Gorbachev, who as general secretary is the head of party. The Soviet leader has shown a greater willingness to challenge the party's hard-liners, even successfully dictating a more liberal party charter last month at a meeting notable mainly for muted complaints and challenges to Mr. Gorbachev.

Then, on the nineteenth of August, the citizens of the Soviet Union awoke to learn that Gorbachev had been toppled, setting off a chaotic period of revolutionary ferment which would see Communism crumble in the Soviet Union in less time than it took to die in East Germany.

DAY ONE

Gorbachev Is Ousted in an Apparent Coup by Soviet Armed Forces and Hard-liners: Accused of Steering into a "Blind Alley"
By Francis X. Clines

MOSCOW, MONDAY, AUG. 19—Mikhail S. Gorbachev was apparently ousted from power today by military and K.G.B. authorities while he was on vacation in the distant Crimea.

The announcement by "the Soviet leadership" came as Mr. Gorbachev was about to proceed into a new era of power sharing with the nation's republics.

The sudden announcement this morning stunned the nation and left it groping for information as Kremlin officials declared a state of emergency.

The apparent removal of Mr. Gorbachev, six years into his *perestroika* reform program, came three days after his former confidant and reform adviser, Aleksandr N. Yakovlev, left the Communist Party, warning of a coming coup d'état.

The Soviet news agency, Tass, cited Mr. Gorbachev's "inability for health reasons" to perform his duties as President.

Vice President Gennadi I. Yanayev was assuming presidential powers under a new entity called a State Committee for the State of Emergency. Its members include Vladimir A. Kryuchkov, chief of the K.G.B., and Dmitri T. Yazov, the defense minister.

The shocking announcement said the committee, in assuming powers, had found that "a mortal danger had come to loom large" in the nation and that Mr. Gorbachev's reform program has gone into a "blind alley."

The committee contended the reforms had caused "extremist forces" to threaten the nation and leave it "just a step from mass manifestations of spontaneous discontent."

The scene on the streets of Moscow was calm at the hour of 6 A.M. when the announcement was made. Later in the morning, as the city approached a new work week, Muscovites heading downtown could see 10 armored personnel carriers moving a few miles north of Red Square toward the Kremlin. But there were no crowds or other signs of public reaction.

In fact, the public has been noticeably calm, even passive, in recent weeks as Mr. Gorbachev and the republic leaders prepared fresh plans to speed the nation to greater constitutional and democratic reforms.

The emergency committee's announcement contended that increasing domestic instability in the Soviet Union was "undercutting its position in the world."

"We are a peace-loving nation and will unfailingly honor all assumed commitments," the emergency committee declared. "Any attempts at talking to our country in the language of *diktat,* no matter by whom, will be decisively cut short," the committee added in language reminiscent of the cold war.

The Tass announcement insisted the state of emergency would be "temporary."

It said that Mr. Yanayev stated that "all power in the country" had been transferred to the committee.

Kremlin announcements said that Mr. Yanayev issued a statement vowing that "in no way" did the removal of Mr. Gorbachev mean "renunciation of the course toward profound reform" in Soviet life.

However, the shift in power to central Kremlin authorities came after days of complaint from central government authorities over what was to have been a new phase in Mr. Gorbachev's democratization program. On Tuesday, the leaders of the nation's 15 republics were scheduled to begin signing a new union treaty to shift considerable power away from the Kremlin and into the republics.

Kremlin authorities, including Anatoly I. Lukyanov, criticized the text of the union treaty, citing "how dangerous" the draft treaty could prove unless it was further amended.

Mr. Gorbachev was last seen two weeks ago, shortly after his meeting with President Bush at the start of his vacation.

Mr. Yakovlev, the former colleague and strategist, said in his announcement Friday that while the party was losing influence, it was still making "preparations for social revenge, a party and state coup."

Today's announcement, made through the traditional means of the Kremlin-controlled news media, stunned the Soviet public. It signaled that an attempt was being made to bring under heel Mr. Gorbachev's historic series of democratization reforms.

The occasion was eerie with the trappings of past Kremlin intrigues: classical music flooding the airwaves, interrupted by periodic readings by a monotoned announcer of the attempted change in power.

In the first hours following the emergency announcement, armed guards outside the state broadcasting studio here were denying entry to news professionals working at Radio Russia, one of the new *glasnost-*era independent news-gathering outlets.

This indicated that the Kremlin committee that announced emergency powers might try and curtail independent information and open debate about their move.

There was no immediate means of estimating the chances of success of the Kremlin hard-liners' move to resolidify central powers. The largest open question was whether the republics, so intent lately on gaining greater self-rule, might resist in some fashion.

President Boris N. Yeltsin of the Russian republic was certain to be highly critical in his role as the populist leader of the political opposition.

No immediate comment was available from Mr. Yeltsin, who had led the latest compromise agreement with Mr. Gorbachev to further democratize the nation.

No details were offered on Mr. Gorbachev's alleged failing health, nor was there any comment permitted in government-controlled press accounts from the democratic opposition groups that had taken root in the past two years.

Beyond President Gorbachev, the announcement was a particular blow to the leaders of the republics who have been intent on securing greater local authority from the Kremlin through the pending union treaty.

Chief among these was Mr. Yeltsin, an avid supporter of the union treaty who had warned last weekend that the current "archaic" central cabinet government in the Kremlin had to be removed if the treaty were to succeed or else the cabinet would "continue to crush us."

Moscow Fears It Awoke to a Nightmare
By Celestine Bohlen

MOSCOW, AUG. 19—As a dozen tanks rolled through Mayakovsky Square, kicking up a cloud of exhaust in the moist evening air, Alla Mikhailovna, in the capital for a visit with her seven-year-old son, stood on the sidewalk and cried.

"It is horrible, just horrible," said the 43-year-old geologist from Tashkent, who identified herself with her given name and patronymic, in the Russian fashion, but declined to give her last name. "I am so sad for my country. What will come of this? Where will it end? War? It is just so frightening."

Across this bedraggled city, people struggled through the day, trying to figure out what had happened to them overnight. They had awakened to find their president mysteriously gone, purportedly for "health reasons," a new State Committee for the State of Emergency in control, and military vehicles roaming the city.

As the day wore on, doused by heavy rains, many Muscovites knew no more than they did when they listened to the first terse bulletins on the state-controlled television and radio. But what they knew was enough to make them stiffen with anxiety.

"We woke up to the noise of tanks on the streets," said Slava Ivanov, a 45-year-old driver. "Beyond that, I still don't know anything concretely.

Where is Gorbachev? Where is Yeltsin? All I know is nothing good can come from tanks."

Several thousand people turned out to demonstrate against the "putschists"—as they were calling the new government that ousted Mikhail S. Gorbachev—to upbraid the young soldiers sitting in their tank turrets, and to rally in defense of the Russian federated republic's government.

As evening fell, barricades made of tree trunks, bathtubs, and vehicles were erected around the Russian government buildings on the banks of the Moscow River, as people prepared for an all-night vigil in anticipation of an army attack.

But elsewhere, a strange silence seemed to fall on the population as people went about their business—some with worried looks on their faces, others acting as if nothing more had happened than a change in administration.

"We can't figure it out," said Mikhail Argutinsky, a chauffeur. "It is a putsch, but somebody had to bring things back into order."

His wife, Anna, was not sorry to see Mr. Gorbachev gone. "Of course, he is not the only one to blame," she said, "but all I know is before him, we lived better."

With no information except what was being released by the people in charge, the city seemed to split in two. At Manezh Square, near the Kremlin, and outside the Russian government building where Boris N. Yeltsin had called demonstrators to come and protect the republic's elected leadership, the crowd swarmed with rumors, tips, and some pieces of real news, hand carried out of the building and read aloud over bullhorns.

But in other parts of the city, people had to make due with sources that seemed a throwback to an earlier era—leaflets glued to the walls of pedestrian tunnels, foreign radio stations, and the old standby, word of mouth.

"They have closed the papers, but that's not so important," said Vladimir Sluzhekov, a reporter, as he stood by a surging crowd of demonstrators. "The radio—that's what hurts. Without the radio, no one knows what's going on except the people who are right here."

By evening when about 25,000 people had already converged on the Russian government building, long after pictures of protesters swarming over tanks had flashed on screens around the world, Margarita Selvova, a 63-year-old pensioner, emerged from her apartment off Moscow's main ring road to ask if and where people had gathered to protest the coup d'état.

"It is a terrible situation," she said. "It happened in 1917 when the

Bolseviks took over. In 1937, my uncle and my father were shot, and my mother arrested. Now it is happening again, but people can't imagine it. We are a very unhappy nation."

Driven by an instinct developed during countless prodemocracy meetings, several thousand people flocked to Manezh Square outside the Kremlin walls by late morning, arriving in time to block a column of armored personnel carriers that had pulled up alongside the Moskva Hotel.

Galina Viltsina, a 55-year-old primary school teacher, came to the square as soon as she heard from a taxi driver that a "fascist coup" was under way. She tried to talk a young soldier into getting down and joining the people in the square, but to no avail. "He does not know anything; he does not understand anything," she said. "I did not argue with him. I talked with him like his mother, like a teacher."

Aleksandr N. Chikunov, a 42-year-old engineer, came as soon as he heard the news on the radio. He had switched channels looking for one of Moscow's alternative stations, only to find them broadcasting the same official bulletins.

Mr. Chikunov, a veteran of the invasion of Czechoslovakia, tried to share his own experience with the young soldiers. "I entered Prague in 1968 and I still have an ill conscience about it," he said. "I was a soldier then, like these guys. We were also sent like they are now, to defend the achievements of socialism. Twenty-three years have passed, and I still have an ill conscience."

By midafternoon, as a thunderstorm began to darken the sky, the crowd from the Manezh Square had moved towards the Russian Republic Building, leaving the square empty for tanks and armored personnel carriers to circle through.

Tanks had also appeared at the White House—as the hulking Russian Republic Building is nicknamed—lingering long enough for Mr. Yeltsin to urge reporters at a press conference that they leave the building while they still could. The tanks drove on by.

Mr. Yeltsin came out briefly, and spoke unimpeded from the top of an armored vehicle that was parked near the building. Later, Ruslan I. Khasbulatov, acting chairman of the Russian parliament, took the bullhorn, telling the crowd, "Our only power is our people, our compatriots, you, our dear Muscovites."

"You have seen what shapes fascism may take," he said. "Only this word can be used to call an attempted coup d'état realized last night by our Soviet junta.

"We do not have radio or TV any longer; practically all communication channels are cut. Faxes do not work. But I do not think it will last long, provided there is a mass support of Muscovites, Leningraders, and other big cities. We shall wipe out this junta."

Confusion broke out at the back of the building when three military buses, with drawn curtains, pulled up in the parking lot. Word went out that the OMON, the "black beret" troops that had been used in the assault in Lithuania last January, were arriving. As people streamed toward the buses, a few women started yelling "bastards," until someone else said these troops had actually been summoned by Mr. Yeltsin to guard the building. "They are ours," a voice said in the crowd.

"But how do we know whether to trust them?" asked a young woman with doubt and fear in her voice.

Many people said they had awoken to events that had caught them completely by surprise. Mr. Yeltsin, for example, was out of town, returning home from Kazakhstan.

But Sergei I. Grigoryants, editor of *Glasnost,* a newspaper that had been the first to test the limits of the new policy of free speech, came to the realization today that he had in fact been given a warning last night, whose significance he did not immediately grasp. "The windshield in my car was broken, so that I couldn't drive in," he said. "Nothing was stolen from the car, not even the cognac."

This morning, the newspaper's offices were blocked and the phone lines were out of order, Mr. Grigoryants said.

Vitaly G. Urazhtsev, a deputy in the Russian parliament who is also chairman of a group of insurgent army officers known as Shield, was arrested this morning as he made his way to the Russian Republic Building. His father said Mr. Urazhtsev was released five hours later. The father said that he had been with his son when they were picked up and that no reason was given for the arrest.

When Oleg D. Kalugin, the former K.G.B. agent who broke ranks with his old bosses and was elected a deputy in the Soviet parliament last year, drove away from his home this morning, he saw two K.G.B. cars following him. He stopped and went over to one of them. "I asked them what they were doing," he said. "They told me they were protecting me. 'From whom?' I asked."

Coup Sets Yeltsin at Center Stage
By Celestine Bohlen

MOSCOW, AUG. 19—As Mikhail S. Gorbachev was deposed today, attention turned quickly to the one dominating figure left on the Soviet political stage: Boris N. Yeltsin, the first elected president of the Russian republic, an ex-Communist who has made a second career out of doing battle with the Communist Party and who is arguably the most popular politician in the Soviet Union today.

The crowds outside the Russian federated republic's government building in Moscow today repeatedly chanted Mr. Yeltsin's name, pleading with him to come out for a speech or at least show his face at the window. When he appeared at a noon press conference, he was greeted by applause from Soviet journalists present, who did little to hide the hopes they have pinned on him.

Even people who in interviews on the streets were clearly shedding no tears over Mr. Gorbachev's political demise said they were looking to Mr. Yeltsin for the future—and not to the group of men associated with the K.G.B. and the military who are now in charge.

"I am not sorry about Gorbachev personally, but the movement he represents," said Aleksei Drinochkin, a 27-year-old graduate student. "If someone progressive like Yeltsin had come in, I would be happy."

At his press conference this morning, Mr. Yeltsin—just back from a trip to the republic of Kazakhstan—read out an address to the citizens of the Russian republic, the nation's largest, with the kind of feisty vigor that many Russians want in their leader, especially now that the republic's policies of market reform and political liberalization are threatened.

As he did with Mr. Gorbachev, when the two men were locked in a series of political duels, Mr. Yeltsin today heaped scorn on his new opponents. "What can you expect from this group?" he said, spitting out their names. "They could not even find a single half democrat."

"Democrats," the term used by many supporters of radical change to describe the liberal opposition across the Soviet Union, today seemed united in their support of Mr. Yeltsin's call for a general strike and civil disobedience against the *diktats* of the new Soviet leadership. By the end of the day, the mayor of Leningrad, the deputy mayor of Moscow, and other republic leaders had swung into formation behind him.

But today, as he marshaled his forces for a head-on conflict with the new Soviet government, Mr. Yeltsin found himself stripped of his most powerful weapons: the Russian television station and radio, which have become the best platform for his populist crusade against the Communists. Even Mr. Yeltsin's fax line, another tool in the battle for the dissemination of information, had been cut, an aide said this morning.

It was Mr. Yeltsin's signature on the proposed new union treaty that apparently most alarmed the conservatives in the party's Central Committee, as signaling the demise of the heavily centralized system of government that has been the source of their power.

Mr. Yeltsin, who stunned even his supporters last spring when he called for Mr. Gorbachev's resignation in a televised speech, put the party on the defensive this summer when he banned the party from the work-place.

Although two of his old colleagues on the Politburo—Eduard A. She-vardnadze and Aleksandr N. Yakovlev—had warned that a government takeover was in the offing, Mr. Yeltsin was caught off guard by this morning's news.

But he was the first to publicly condemn the "unconstitutional and unlawful" coup d'état, and issued an order countermanding the Kremlin committee's first set of decrees. He also issued an order putting Soviet government agencies under Russian control.

Outside of Mr. Yeltsin and Mr. Shevardnadze, people who had become known as supporters of fundamental change were not heard from today. Mayor Gavriil K. Popov of Moscow made no public comment, a rare instance of his not being available to speak out in a crisis.

Although there were rumors early in the day that Mayor Anatoly A. Sobchak of Leningrad, another prime supporter of change, had been removed, he was reported later at Leningrad's city hall criticizing the coup.

There was no further comment today from Mr. Yakovlev, the onetime close Gorbachev aide who fairly predicted the coup last week when he quit the Communist Party, accusing hard-liners of planning to take re-venge.

Some of Mr. Yeltsin's other recent strong supporters, like President Nursultan A. Nazarbayev of Kazakhstan, did not immediately endorse his call for a general strike.

Mr. Yeltsin is the rare Soviet politician to make a successful comeback. Brought from the industrial city of Sverdlovsk to Moscow in 1985 by Mr. Gorbachev, he was tossed out of the Politburo in 1987 for chiding Mr. Gorbachev for his slow pace of reform.

He returned to politics in 1989 with a mandate from Moscow voters, and last May was elected chairman of the Russian parliament. This spring, in the first elections ever held in Russian history, he won the presidency with a landslide vote.

Mr. Yeltsin left the Communist Party in 1990, and has since refused to join any other party, including the Movement for Democratic Reform headed by Mr. Shevardnadze.

As they chart out their response to the coup d'état, Soviet liberals are counting on both the pull of Mr. Yeltsin's popularity and the widespread contempt many people feel for the Communist Party. But how organized the liberal opposition can be in a country where the party is still dominant outside the big cities is another question.

"They don't have to be organized for the general strike," said Father

Gleb Yakunin, a deputy in the Russian parliament. "I think it will happen spontaneously. Even 24 hours of unjammed Western broadcasts will be enough for Yeltsin's decree to be brought to the ears of people all over the country. We are proud of our president."

K.G.B.-Military Rulers Tighten Grip; Gorbachev Absent, Yeltsin Defiant; West Voices Anger and Warns on Aid
By Francis X. Clines

MOSCOW, AUG. 19—The engineers of President Mikhail S. Gorbachev's ouster from power moved quickly today to reimpose hard-line control across the nation. The coup leaders, dominated by the military and the K.G.B., banned protest meetings, closed independent newspapers, and flooded the capital with troops and tanks.

Boris N. Yeltsin, President of the Russian federated republic, who has often been at odds with Mr. Gorbachev, became one of his strongest supporters today, seeking to rally resistance to the Soviet leader's overthrow by climbing atop an armored truck and calling for a general strike on Tuesday to protest the move as an unconstitutional act, a coup d'état.

By nightfall, Mr. Yeltsin had some of his own Russian republic troops and armored combat vehicles moving to his headquarters, and some positive responses were heard to his call for a strike, notably from coal miners and auto workers in Siberia. The scene was set for a possible confrontation between troops loyal to Mr. Yeltsin and those under the command of the national authorities.

One death was reported, that of an unidentified driver said to have been killed in Riga, Latvia, one of the places under military control.

The nation was startled after Mr. Gorbachev, who had been on vacation in the southern Crimea since August 4, was ousted from power the day before he was due to return to Moscow to sign a new union treaty. The landmark accord would have begun a program for speeding constitutional reforms and limiting the Kremlin's ability to dictate the life of the country.

Mr. Gorbachev has been increasingly unpopular at home, in large part because of the country's profound economic troubles, and has been sharply criticized even by many of his former supporters.

Still, there was general disbelief here in Moscow at the coup plotters' assertion that Mr. Gorbachev was ill and therefore had to be relieved of power.

Mr. Gorbachev's exact whereabouts were unknown. There was one report that he had been placed under house arrest in a naval hospital in Sevastopol in the Crimea.

The group now in charge is dominated by security and military leaders, and some top political figures, all of whom had strong disagreements with Mr. Gorbachev's democratization and economic-reform programs. This reform process had the further effect of doing away with the need for Communist Party supremacy.

The new ruling group calls itself the State Committee for the State of Emergency, or, in Russian, *Gosudarstvenny Komitet po Chrezvychainomu Polozheniyu.*

"Over the years, he has got very tired and needs some time to get his health back," contended Vice President Gennadi I. Yanayev, who said he had taken over as acting president, and who directed a news conference at which he defended Mr. Gorbachev's overthrow and his assumption of presidential powers as necessary in the current state of economic and political crisis.

Mr. Yanayev used the news conference, broadcast to the Soviet people, to also announce a series of measures aimed at winning popular support. These included stronger anticrime moves and improved housing.

The group also said it would continue basic reform programs, but its first decrees—like imposing what amounted to martial law in Moscow, Leningrad, and the Baltic republics, and closing the most independent press and television voices—contradicted the pledges to continue on the Gorbachev path.

Mr. Yanayev was asked what legal authority allowed the creation of the emergency committee, which is composed of eight Communist Party, military, and intelligence figures noted for their hard-line inclinations.

He responded that "sometimes there are critical situations that call for immediate action" and that, in any case, the Soviet parliament would eventually approve the action in a special session on August 27.

Mr. Yeltsin, addressing a protest crowd of more than 20,000 Muscovites, decried the Gorbachev ouster as a lawless Kremlin putsch.

But the Yanayev committee, warning that it was prepared to "dismantle" agencies resisting its authority, cautioned him against carrying out his "irresponsible" resolve to lead a general strike.

In Moscow, all of the major independent newspapers, which had been in the vanguard of the more open press typical of recent years, were ordered shut pending "reregistration." But printers at the government newspaper, *Izvestia,* though free to publish, announced that they would not work.

Throughout the morning, tanks and armored personnel carriers lumbered to critical crossroads of the city, four of them spinning wildly in a circle outside the Bolshoi Theater in a roaring display of force that left passersby crying, "Shame!"

Several angry Muscovites ran into the road to retrieve chunks of the ripped-up macadam. "The final sourvenirs of freedom," one man remarked.

Mr. Yanayev defended the necessity for the tanks, troops, and a series of toughly worded orders aimed at overruling, where necessary, the centers of insurgent political power that might contradict the Kremlin's new special orders.

The state of emergency would not be general throughout the nation, he said. The Emergency Committee spared such eastern republics as Uzbekistan and Kazakhstan, traditionally more obedient to Kremlin authority. But Leningrad and Moscow, centers of the opposition politics encouraged by six years of Gorbachev reforms, were among the first to receive state-of-emergency notices.

Reformist politicians in both cities, the Soviet Union's largest, sought to rally opposition. A large crowd began a night vigil outside Mr. Yeltsin's headquarters in the Russian Republic Building on the downtown bank of the Moscow River. Soviet tanks had been stationed there, with their crewmen leaning and watching casually through a long day, occasionally chatting with an angry civilian or joking with others.

Three of the tanks were suddenly turned around, as if in a nighttime lark, after Yeltsin loyalists said they had taken control of the vehicles. The Yeltsin supporters also claimed the defection of a score of Soviet paratroopers. But rumors abounded that the Kremlin forces might choose the time before dawn to make some confrontational move on the building.

Later, 30 more armored vehicles pulled up, and their crews turned out to be Russian troops loyal to Mr. Yeltsin. The crews, trailed by seven ammunition trucks, vowed to defend the building. The Soviets kept their distance.

Thus, ingredients of confrontation were gathering. A report from Leningrad said that Mayor Anatoly A. Sobchak told a crowd of about 2,000 outside city hall that the coup leaders first tried to press Mr. Gorbachev into signing his assent to his removal and, when he refused, placed him under house arrest in his dacha in the Crimea.

A close aide to Mr. Yeltsin reported that he sought to telephone Mr. Gorbachev at the dacha early Monday. The official said someone answered the phone and, when asked to summon Mr. Gorbachev for Mr. Yeltsin, responded: "We have been asked at this end not to disturb him."

The former Soviet foreign minister, Eduard A. Shevardnadze, dismissed the talk of Mr. Gorbachev's ill health as a pretext for a coup provoked by hard-line officials fearful over the pending shift of power from Moscow to the republics, a change Mr. Gorbachev had negotiated with republic leaders.

The negotiations had produced a new treaty for a redesigned Soviet Union, and the first signatures were expected Tuesday at a Kremlin ceremony suddenly canceled in the wake of the coup.

"We were expecting it to happen," Mr. Shevardnadze said of the coup. "Unfortunately, Mikhail Sergeyevitch did not draw the necessary conclusions," he said, adding that there was confusion to be cleared up, including whether Mr. Gorbachev might have known of the looming plot.

"I'm not inclined to defend him," he said of his former mentor and friend.

DAY TWO

Sporadic Mutinies Rack Soviet Army
By Bill Keller

MOSCOW, AUG. 20—The Soviet military has been shaken by sporadic mutinies in the wake of the coup here on Monday, with individual servicemen and some entire units defecting to defend anticoup forces rallying around President Boris N. Yeltsin of the Russian republic.

The defections were apparently limited in number and left the coup committee with the overwhelming balance of power.

But the defections reflected deep ambivalence within the demoralized Soviet military after years of retrenchment and plummeting prestige, and Yeltsin supporters said they raised doubts about the ability of the military to sustain an extended campaign of force against its own citizens, although the defense minister, Dmitri T. Yazov, was among the original members of the coup committee.

Mr. Yeltsin, the most authoritative figure among the elected leaders defying the coup, tried today to shake the Defense Ministry's hold on its troops even more, decreeing that all Soviet military forces on the territory of the huge republic subordinate themselves to him and promising legal protection for those who defy the coup plotters.

The units that rallied to Mr. Yeltsin included 10 tanks from a base outside Moscow, which stood guard today outside the Russian parliament building, its troops feasting on fruit and sandwiches brought by pro-Yeltsin demonstrators.

Senior officers loyal to Mr. Yeltsin said there were mutinies against the Defense Ministry at the Leningrad Naval Base and at a prestigious paratrooper training academy in Ryazan, and added that units in the Kamchatka Peninsula and on Sakhalin Island had refused to go along with the junta that took power early Monday morning.

Col. Gen. Konstantin I. Kobets, a 36-year army veteran who serves as chairman of the State Defense Committee of Mr. Yeltsin's Russian government, said in an interview that two other units that defected on Monday—a paratroop regiment from Ryazan and a motorized battalion from Sevastopol—had withdrawn today after their commanders were replaced.

Across the Russian republic, local units of the Interior Ministry police force and the K.G.B. were also reported to have professed loyalty to Mr. Yeltsin and disavowed the coup, which was conducted with support of top Soviet police officials.

"A split in the armed forced is not only possible, to some extent it is already under way," said Aleksei Pankin, a specialist in military affairs for the magazine *Mezhdunarodnaya Zhizn.* "The military is demoralized, and there are sharp divisions between the officer corps and the general staff."

Col. Gen. Aleksandr K. Ovchinnikov, first deputy chief of the political administration of the armed forces, sought to stem reports of divisions in the military in an interview tonight on state television.

"Rumors are being spread that a number of generals have been arrested, that others have committed suicide," the general said. "They are completely unfounded. They are simply lies and slander."

Surrounded by imploring crowds who rallied against the takeover on Monday near Red Square, the young soldiers manning a column of armored vehicles cracked open their automatic rifles to show that they were empty of ammunition.

"If they order you to shoot us, will you do it?" a woman asked one young Russian. "No, I will not," he answered, eyes downcast.

Asked his assessment of the situation, a private gazed down from his perch atop an armored personnel carrier: "This," he said, slapping the vehicle, "this is not right."

But another soldier, after listening to the crowd plead the cause of democracy, said that after the recent years of economic decline and ethnic conflict, the country was in danger of disintegration.

"If it was three years ago, I'd be with you," he told the protesters.

Outside the Russian parliament building, a lieutenant in the mutinous tank division said he personally felt the takeover was "illegal, in principle." But he said he came over to Mr. Yeltsin because "I obey the orders of the batallion commander, and the order of the commander was to deploy here."

No one can say with confidence that the army will disobey orders to shoot. Soviet conscripts are intensely indoctrinated, and in previous confrontations—in Lithuania, in the Georgian city of Tbilisi, in the taking of the Azerbaijani capital, Baku—they have obeyed orders to attack protesters.

Gorbachev Reportedly Arrested in the Crimea
By Serge Schmemann

MOSCOW, AUG. 20—The overthrow of President Mikhail S. Gorbachev began at 4 A.M. Monday when two tractor-trailers manned by the K.G.B. blocked the runway of the airfield near his summer home in the Crimea, said a Soviet official who said he had detailed information from sources that he did not disclose.

The official, Sergei B. Stankevich, Moscow's deputy mayor and a prominent proponent of change, said Mr. Gorbachev and his closest advisers apparently remain at his dacha at Foros, on the southern tip of the Crimean peninsula, blockaded by an armada of ships and troops.

The information, if correct, left little doubt that Mr. Gorbachev had been the victim of a coup, and was not ill, as the coup's leaders continued to assert. Anatoly I. Lukyanov, the chairman of the Soviet parliament, reportedly told the Russian federated republic's vice president, Aleksandr Rutskoi, that "Mikhail Gorbachev's condition is still grave."

Mr. Stankevich described the events over the maverick radio station Moscow Echo. He did not say where he had received his information, but the details suggested that it had come either from intercepted radio traffic or from within the military.

"These are sparse notes, but they provide the chance to see that a state crime has been committed by a group of people," he said.

Bare-Fisted Russians Make Their Stand
By Celestine Bohlen

MOSCOW, AUG. 20—Inside the "war room" on the third floor of the Russian parliament building, commanders of the republic's forces spent the afternoon poring over maps of Moscow and a floor plan of the 12-floor building, plotting how to stave off an anticipated attack by Soviet army and Interior Ministry troops.

Their attire told the story of Russia's patchwork defense. Two men wore Soviet army uniforms, another the World War I uniform of the Don Cossacks. Others, with pistols at their hips, were in camouflage suits, issued by a security firm called the Bells.

The rest wore either suits and ties or beat-up jeans or baggy pants—just like the hundreds of volunteers who by early evening were ringing the building in a human chain.

The men in the war room were collecting whatever help was being offered. The phones rang with calls from citizens, one reporting an airlift of 35 light tanks at an airfield off Leningrad Prospekt, another advising of a construction battalion moving through the Solntsevo Region southwest of Moscow.

Workers at a joint-venture concern called offering to bring a truck-load of food, while someone in Krasnoyarsk wanted to know what was going on.

Vladimir Nezhinsky, deputy administrative officer of the Russian Defense Committee, got a tip from a contact at Moscow city hall that a curfew would be declared in the city this evening and that the Soviet army troops would be pulled out. Mr. Nezhinsky worried that, if true, this would leave a vacuum for the Spetsnaz, or special forces, to move in for the kill.

(After nightfall there were reports of armored personnel carriers and tanks rattling through Moscow's streets, all seemingly converging on the center of town, the Associated Press said. But by dawn Wednesday there had been no concerted attack.)

Boris N. Yeltsin, the President of the Russian republic, was in the building most of the day, issuing orders to tighten the republic's defense. In a speech to the crowd outside, he said his government was taking precautions "because the junta that seized power will not stop short of any steps to hold it."

"These actions are not aimed against Kazakhstan or Uzbekistan, but against democratic Russia," he said. "The state of emergency has been imposed only where the leadership is democratic, mainly in those regions. This makes it clear against whom this putsch was made."

Mr. Yeltsin urged the crowd to stay calm. "Don't provoke the military," he warned. "The military has become a weapon in the hands of the putschists. Therefore we should also support the military and maintain order and discipline in contact with them."

As the day wore on, the building, known familiarly as "the White House," battened down for the battle that everyone was sure was coming.

Guards on the barricades tried to stop women from entering the building. Witnesses said members of the government of Mr. Yeltsin's Russian federated republic were issued pistols, while some but not all of the men guarding the building's entrances were given bulletproof vests, helmets, gas masks, and bottles filled with gasoline.

One box filled with those Molotov cocktails stood in a corner of the war room, just in case. "If the tanks come, we'll throw them out there," said Viktor Gurov, a 36-year-old member of the Bells security company. "If any one of them asks for it, I will toss him the whole box."

Given the situation, the mood in the room was remarkably relaxed, even upbeat. Outsiders would be occasionally shooed away, only to be allowed to drift back later. Over an internal sound system came the steady drone of "Radio White House," the voice of the Russian government, which has been transmitted continually on a ham radio frequency.

(The A.P. reported that at the height of the confrontation, bursts of automatic weapons fire could be heard up and down the riverbank flanking the building.)

Asked why they had come, everyone in the room answered with the same feelings. "We have come to defend our lawful government," said Mr. Gurov. He said about 50 employees of the private security firm had volunteered to help defend the White House, along with dozens of private detectives from the Alex Agency.

"I know one thing," said Col. Gen. Konstantin I. Kobets before there were any reports of clashes. "We will stop them at the farthest point, and not let them reach here.

"We are completely certain of this," said General Kobets, who was named the Russian minister of defense today. "We have the people behind us. Tonight we will turn the course of events."

A Soviet army officer, who defected this afternoon from the army general staff building, said he came because of his concern for the future of his three children. "I serve in military intelligence," said the 37-year-old lieutenant colonel, who would not give his name. "I know what real democracy is, what democracy is worth."

No one at his office knew he had come, he said, adding that if they did, he could be arrested or threatened with trial for desertion, as had already happened to a fellow officer. But he said he discarded his fears and made no attempt to hide his identity.

"I specifically decided to come in uniform to give these people moral support," he said.

Outside, the building had been ringed with barricades, some of which looked like junk piles. At the back of the funnel-shaped building, a row of buses was positioned to block the back gates, draped in the red-white-and-blue flag of the Russian republic.

The crowd that gathered on the streets before nightfall looked through the barricades that had also been strewn across access streets and the nearby bridge spanning the Moscow River. As the barricades grew larger there was no longer any of the excited confrontations that could be seen on Monday when people swarmed over tanks, overturned trolley buses and in Manezh Square, dismantled the water cannon on top of a truck and then rammed it with a cherry picker.

Instead, the tanks in front of the White House, abandoned by one unit that had defected to the republic's defense, were strewn with flowers and occupied by young boys. On the front arc of the coiled human chain protecting the building, where volunteers stood with their arms linked, an Orthodox priest came to lead the men in prayer.

No firearms were visible, but people had sticks, rods, and broken paving stones. "Of course, we could not hold them off for more than five minutes," said another commander. "This is mostly symbolic."

It drizzled and people sat under umbrellas around fires, listening to foreign broadcasts and an independent local station, Moscow Echo, that has managed to stay on the air on an unauthorized channel. Farther away from the building, the paramilitary atmosphere gave way to one more reminiscent of Woodstock.

DAY THREE

Resistance to Soviet Takeover Grows as Defiant Crowds Rally for Yeltsin

By Francis X. Clines

MOSCOW, WEDNESDAY, AUG. 21—The leaders of the Kremlin coup, facing increased opposition, responded on Tuesday with a curfew and fresh armored movements in Moscow that provoked clashes with angry civilians.

The midnight violence, in which at least three people were killed defying the military curfew, occurred after a long, anxious day in which large crowds sought to protect the headquarters of Boris N. Yeltsin, President of the Russian republic.

As the Kremlin sought to press home freshly assumed powers, Mr. Yeltsin intensified his spirited holdout against the junta of military, K.G.B., and Communist Party figures who deposed President Mikhail S. Gorbachev on Monday.

Mr. Yeltsin drew cheers from tens of thousands of Muscovites through the day and into the night with his calls for the resignation and criminal trial of the eight-member Kremlin group that staged the overthrow.

The coup leaders showed signs of disarray, with the announcement that Prime Minister Valentin S. Pavlov had been hospitalized and rumors that Defense Minister Dmitri T. Yazov had been replaced. The Yazov report could not be independently confirmed and was denied by a Kremlin official.

"Aggression will not go forward!" Mr. Yeltsin shouted to a throng of at least 30,000 gathered at midday outside the Russian federated republic's parliament. "Only democracy will win."

The new Kremlin leaders demanded that Mr. Yeltsin cease his call for nationwide resistance and, in ordering an 11 P.M. curfew, dispatched scores of tanks and armored troop carriers moving about the city in an attempt to intimidate civilians.

Similar movements were reported in the Baltic republics, which first confronted Kremlin authority two years ago with independence demands. Republic officials there said they feared nighttime violence and attacks on their government centers from union troops. But the Kremlin insisted that public order, not provocation, was the troops' mission.

Huge throngs of anticoup crowds gathered in Leningrad to hear words of support for Mr. Gorbachev.

Through the day, the new leaders found their continuing series of executive orders and urgent announcements running up against a passive and increasingly resistant national audience.

Some of the leaders of the major republics began issuing statements of unequivocal opposition after their initial wariness of Monday. For example, President Nursultan A. Nazarbayev of Kazakhstan ended his watchfulness with a strong denunciation of the coup as illegitimate and a usurpation of power.

Aleksy II, Patriarch of the Russian Orthodox Church, also questioned the new leadership's legitimacy and called on Soviet soldiers to restrain themselves as they took up positions in civilian neighborhoods across the city.

"Bewilderment creeps in the conscience of millions of our fellow citizens who begin to question the legality of the newly formed State Committee for the State of Emergency," the Patriarch, a highly popular religious leader, said in a statement that called on the national parliament, not the coup leaders, to restore stability.

While thousands protected Mr. Yeltsin's parliament building Tuesday night and into this morning, an armored troop carrier stopped in a confrontation two blocks away on the city's main ring road and, witnesses said, three civilians were killed.

One man sought to climb atop the sealed vehicle and fell to his death under the wheels, according to witnesses. They said a second man was crushed against a barricade when the armored vehicle careened to escape, hitting a parked bus as a third man was crushed.

A crowd that had been watching soon responded angrily with gasoline bombs and rocks, leaving the armored vehicle aflame, along with two other buses.

That was the first reported incident of violence and death in the first two days of the coup. A standoff marked by fright, uncertainty, and growing popular resistance marked most of the day.

Mr. Pavlov was said to have been incapacitated Tuesday, allegedly having suffered intense hypertension.

Doubt seemed universal at the coup leaders' assertion that Mr. Gorbachev had suddenly fallen into poor health. Mr. Yeltsin demanded that physicians from the World Health Organization be allowed to examine him.

Mr. Gorbachev's exact whereabouts remained unknown, although rumors abounded that the coup leadership had him spirited back to Moscow from the Crimea, where he dropped from sight after the group made its move. But fresh information had him still under house arrest in his vacation home near Yalta.

"We're seeing the agony of the old regime," said Oleg D. Kalugin, a Soviet lawmaker and K.G.B. defector, in predicting the coup committee would be forced to retreat. "These are the old guys, simply crazy," he said.

The nation suffered a tense, unpredictable day under the new regime, with fresh rumors every hour. Russian republic officials reported the resignation of Defense Minister Yazov, leader of the armed forces and a critical figure in the coup committee.

That was quickly denied by the Kremlin, which was ringed with dozens of armored vehicles and hundreds of riot troops waiting near the Bolshoi Theater.

On Tuesday night, the roar of tanks on the move could be heard repeatedly, and rumors intensified that the Kremlin might attempt a military attack on the Yeltsin headquarters. That was denied by Kremlin officials, but tension was high, with Muscovites watching from their windows as scores upon scores of armored vehicles swept through the main roads after the II P.M. curfew began.

Outside the Russian Republic Building, where the white marble walls were bathed in the glow of searchlights, crowds were ignoring the curfew and lugging tree limbs, railroad tracks, and concrete chunks to strengthen their barricades in defense of Mr. Yeltsin.

Some of the tank troops seemed at least as anxious as the public.

"What do they know, they're not from Moscow," a city policeman said after one tank bumped into another in some late-night confusion on the city's main ring road, mostly deserted except for the passing armored vehicles.

The Kremlin coup committee made no appearance on Tuesday, restricting itself to fresh executive orders, broadcast on state-controlled television, demanding that all remaining news outlets in the print and electronic media operating in the republics submit to central authority.

But here in the capital, independent news outlets stayed open, using fax machines and at least one small-power radio station operating thus far beyond the Kremlin's notice.

The city's elaborate subway system, an ideal conduit for information, was papered with anticoup pamphlets, and riders gathered in crowds to read President Yeltsin's exhortations to resist the coup committee.

"They will find themselves in the dock," he told the midday rally, sounding a theme repeated during the day that it would not be enough to see the coup leaders retreat from power, that criminal action was required.

The coup committee sought to enforce its authority by designating a state of emergency in selected areas, like Moscow and Leningrad, where insurgent political opposition has been the greatest threat to the Communist status quo. Military officers were reported showing up at city halls and other bases of legitimate local authority and announcing that they were in charge in behalf of the Kremlin's emergency committee.

The violence that flared after dark capped a long, anxious day in which President Yeltsin's workers stayed barricaded within the Russian parliament building, alarmed at various times by rumors of impending attack.

The deaths tonight in the armored-truck incident and the gasoline bombs thrown from the crowd at the ring road went largely unnoticed by the far larger throng two blocks away at the Russian parliament.

Outside the building, Eduard A. Shevardnadze, the former foreign minister who is attempting to create a democratic alternative movement to the Communist Party, appeared. He chatted casually with the waiting Muscovites and congratulated them for defending the elected Russian presidency.

"Your tomorrow will be better," he said. "The future is with you. I salute you."

The crowd thanked him and maintained their watch.

And then, on the fourth day, the coup fizzled.

After the Coup; a Thick Russian Porridge; "Not the Way to Do a Coup"
By Francis X. Clines

MOSCOW, AUG. 21—The Kremlin junta's sense of cliché was unfailing to the end.

Facing defeat, the anxious men of the sagging coup d'état reportedly fled for the airport to seek sanctuary elsewhere. One report said some went to the warmth of distant Kirghizia, while others hastened to the Crimea and the uncertain mercies of the man the junta had made their captive, President Mikhail S. Gorbachev.

A beige Volga limousine with antijunta policemen from the Russian federation followed in pursuit. The Volga's mission was to catch the junta. But the outer road was crowded with more than 100 tanks, spewing mud chunks and moving as ingloriously in retreat as the junta.

The Volga finally arrived at the locked V.I.P. gates at Vnukovo Airport, and an uncooperative guard rebuffed the pursuing plainclothes police agents.

"Who are you? Where are your papers?" the guard demanded in the timelessly intimidating tone of authority figures, big and small, that seem to stipple this weary, resilient land from one end to the other.

Instantly, a large man stepped from the Volga, pointed a machine gun at the chest of the guard, and said in a clear, slow tone, "Open the gates."

The gates were opened. The junta was gone. But Moscow was delivered nonetheless. The people were free once more to wonder about their longer-running crises and not have to suffer the inconvenience of snaking their food-store lines around tanks and armored cars and boyish-looking riot troops from the outer provinces.

"That's not the way to do a coup," sniffed Andrei Alepin, a 25-year-old Muscovite. "You remember how it was in Chile: fast and energetic. Ours was a thick porridge, a Russian idiocy."

The young man, standing by one of the antijunta street barricades, talked as if there were an aesthetic to totalitarianism and the masses were the connoisseurs.

"Look who they were," he said of the coup members. "The K.G.B. minister, the interior minister—those who have all the power in their hands. Who else do you want?

"That night was theirs," he said of the predawn on Monday when the coup leadership struck.

"They could have done all they wanted, but they did not," Mr. Alepin declared, sounding almost regretful. "Yeltsin remained free. They thought they could scare him by just the sight of tanks."

The man's amusement was widely shared in this redoubtable gray city at the very thought of Boris N. Yeltsin, President of the Russian federated republic and savior of Mr. Gorbachev, ever being intimidated by the mere loud noise of tanks in a city that once rebuffed the armies of Napoleon and the Nazis.

Moscow's strength is its ability to absorb abuse, and in the long, bloody shadow of Russian history the effect of this two-and-half-day coup might eventually rate as a dark amusement. This morning, as the riot troops broke camp outside the Bolshoi Ballet and were trucked off and as the columns of tanks retreated from the city, the noise seemed like the growlings of the Great Oz caught alone behind his imperious curtain.

"Either we shall live like the rest of the world, or we shall continue to call ourselves 'the Socialist Choice' and 'the Communist Prospect,' and live like pigs," said Aleksandr Rutskoi, Vice President of Russia, bidding good riddance to the junta.

The catharsis that the rest of the watching world might have sensed here today was not necessarily shared by the majority of Muscovites, who could spare no time for barricade watch this week.

"What do we care?" one man said, waiting in his car at a gas station line. "We live in Russia, not the Soviet Union."

Others could not contain their mirth at the flight of a junta whose members seemed to share so much of the special blandness that, in the eyes of ordinary people, marks a career spent at Communism. There was open laughter in the city at the reams of condemnations of the junta that poured forth so late and so sheepishly from party and government figures who had silently kept their heads down for the last two days.

The entire Presidium of the Soviet parliament, for example, broke their silence and finally issued a statement condemning the coup today, after the tanks left town. The lawmakers contended that they had firmly reached such a consensus in the first hours of the coup and only bothered to publicize it later.

Muscovites also were marking with small smiles the emergence after a two-day absence of Foreign Minister Aleksandr A. Bessmertnykh. He said that he was genuinely sick, not diplomatically hiding, and that even from his sickbed he was trying to telephone Mr. Gorbachev but could never get through.

Then there was the Communist Party itself, whose leadership emerged this afternoon to declare their fealty to the democratic process and distance themselves from the eight leading party members who staged the coup. The party leadership denounced the coup as "inadmissible," but urged the public to be gentle in applying epithets.

Do not use that word "junta," said Sergei Kalashnikov, a secretary of the party's Central Committee. Rather, the eight members of the coup should be considered people who "made a blunder," he said, adding that there were even some low critics who now might "try to use this situation to strike a blow" against the party's reputation.

In reporting the day's events, the Russian television news program *Vesti,* which had been shut down for two days by the Kremlin plotters, let its joy leak into the news copy. A leering anchor person reported the probable departure of the head of the state broadcast monopoly—"that man beloved by us and treasured by you TV viewers, Leonid Petrovich Kravchenko."

Of all the attempts to mount the antijunta ramparts, none was more imaginatively vindictive than the call of the mayor of Moscow, Gavriil K. Popov.

Not content to simply issue an impassioned denunciation, the mayor jumped right into the duel of decrees that were issued by the junta and its chief antagonist, Mr. Yeltsin, in two days of sweeping orders and counterorders, one null-and-void volley raining down upon another. Mr. Popov put aside imperious sweep in his own city hall decree and struck at the things that really matter to Muscovites.

He ordered all city bureaucracies to see that the water, gas, and electricity at the city apartments of the junta members and all their "collaborators" be shut off as the price of treachery.

One of the last to be heard from today was Yevgeny A. Yevtushenko, the tireless poet. His lyrics, tailored for the flight of the Kremlin junta, were launched to fax machines across the city, squealing and beeping like an electronic lark.

Mr. Yevtushenko sang that "today we are a nation, no longer fools, happy to be fooled.

"Yeltsin rises on a turret, and around him there are no ghosts of past Kremlin rulers, but real Russians, not yet vanished."

A Moscow cabdriver, without benefit of Muse or fax, grunted his own song on the situation in the form of questions as he drove about the rebounding city:

"Did those guys really think they could get away with this?

"Against Yeltsin?

"A bunch of fools like Pavlov, Pugo, and Yazov?

"What can you expect from seventy years of Communism?"

Some Muscovites, those who kept the antijunta vigil again tonight outside the Russian parliament, worked at showing their jubilation to one another and to the increasing number of tourists who began stopping by, climbing over the barricades to take pictures.

But others retained the quiet, usually silent wariness that is the mark of this city's denizens through seven decades of Communism and these 50 hours of its death throes.

"There were more than eight people involved in this," said Ivan Serdikov, watching the tanks retreat into the countryside and wondering what will become of all those the junta stood for.

Mr. Serdikov held the hand of his two-and-a-half-year-old daughter, Polina, and carefully invited her to pay attention to the tanks leaving Moscow.

"I wanted her to see this," he said, as if presenting the girl more of a continuing lesson than a final deliverance. "How all this is going to end, who knows?"

Gorbachev Back as Coup Fails, but Yeltsin Gains New Power

By Serge Schmemann

MOSCOW, THURSDAY, AUG. 22—A coup by hard-line Communists collapsed on Wednesday as abruptly as it began, and President Mikhail S. Gorbachev returned to Moscow early this morning to reassert control.

Mr. Gorbachev landed at Vnukovo Airport on his return from his summer retreat in the Crimea, where he had been placed under house arrest early Monday at the start of the short-lived putsch.

In impromptu remarks to Soviet television that were aired later on a morning news program, Mr. Gorbachev appeared weary but clearly angered by the efforts of the conspirators to get him to surrender power.

"The whole world should know about this, what exactly was being plotted," he said upon arriving at the airport, "and what it is that they did not succeed in getting from me."

Mr. Gorbachev described the coup leaders as "a miserable group" that had tried to "break" him and "to influence his family" by surrounding them with troops and isolating them for 72 hours.

The Soviet President congratulated the Soviet people for having had the "responsibility and dignity" to resist the takeover.

He particularly thanked the President of the Russian federated republic, Boris N. Yeltsin, for standing up to the coup leaders.

Mr. Gorbachev was expected to meet with the Russian leader later today.

Mr. Gorbachev's wife, Raisa, was also shown on morning television disembarking from the plane at the airport while holding a small child wrapped in a blanket. The Gorbachevs left for their country house in a Moscow suburb.

The Soviet President had said in a statement reported Wednesday by the evening television news program *Vremya* that he was "in full control of the situation" and that he would resume his full duties within a day.

The evening program also reported that he had restored contact with the cabinet and the Defense Ministry—both under acting chiefs now that their leaders were disgraced—and to have talked by telephone with Mr. Yeltsin and President Bush.

Only one of the coup leaders—the K.G.B. chairman, Vladimir A. Kryuchkov—was reported under arrest early today. It was the first time a K.G.B. leader had been arrested since Lavrenti P. Beria was detained, tried secretly, and shot in 1953 in the power struggle that followed the death of Stalin.

Reuters reported from Moscow that two other coup leaders, the defense minister, Marshal Dmitri T. Yazov, and Nikolai I. Tizyakov, had been detained, according to Sergei B. Stankevich, a member of the Soviet parliament and an adviser to Mr. Yeltsin. But this report could not be independently confirmed. There were also unconfirmed reports that the other members of the State Committee for the State of Emergency would be put on trial.

The coup crumbled Wednesday as abruptly as it began, without any formal announcement from its leaders, who sent tanks into Moscow on Monday and declared themselves in command.

It seemed simply to fizzle under the disdain of masses rallying to the summons of Mr. Yeltsin, who rose to condemn the coup almost from the moment it became known, and the irresolution of plotters who failed to garner support or even to maintain the loyalty of their forces.

On Wednesday, Mr. Yeltsin declared that the Communist Party had been "the organizing and inspiring force" behind the coup, and the implication was that with its last, desperate rearguard action the once-formidable force that had controlled the Soviet Union for more than 70 years might finally be exhausted.

It remains a question whether Mr. Gorbachev, after his ordeal, will bolt the party he heads, as have Mr. Yeltsin and other former Gorbachev aides.

The awareness that the coup had failed came with the first gray light of dawn, when it became evident that army tanks had not moved against the headquarters of the Russian republic's government in the capital.

Relief spread among the thousands of Muscovites who had spent two drizzly nights at makeshift barricades around the building, called the White House, a wedding cake–like building on the banks of the Moscow River, from which Mr. Yeltsin marshaled the anticoup forces.

Within hours, reports swept through a jubilant Moscow that the members of the Emergency Committee were in flight, and long columns of tanks and armored personnel carriers began to leave the capital, some decorated with Russian flags, to the cheers of jubilant Muscovites.

Like the marchers in Leipzig or the demonstrators in Prague who had brought down Communist regimes through the sheer force of their determination, Muscovites, even those who had not directly taken part in public demonstrations, felt a personal satisfaction in facing down forces that had held them so long in thrall.

"Weren't we great?" exclaimed one woman, capturing a joyous sense that the nation had united to thwart the long-awaited counteroffensive by the forces of the former Communist dictatorship. "Leave, just please leave," another woman shouted at the tanks.

According to the spokesman for the Russian republic's government, the Russian Vice President, Aleksandr Rutskoi, and its prime minister, Ivan S. Silayev, along with other members of the Russian government, flew to the Crimea Wednesday evening and met with Mr. Gorbachev. While they were there, two members of the Emergency Committee—the defense minister, Marshal Yazov, and the K.G.B. chairman, Mr. Kryuchkov—flew there with the chairman of the Soviet parliament, Anatoly I. Lukyanov, and the deputy chief of the Communist Party, Vladimir A. Ivashko.

The spokesman said that in the course of a long talk between Mr. Gorbachev and the Russian delegation, Mr. Gorbachev was informed about the siege and the attempt to seize the Russian republic's headquarters. Mr. Gorbachev received Mr. Ivashko and Mr. Lukyanov but refused to receive Marshal Yazov and Mr. Kryuchkov. Then Gorbachev, who was in good health, after a rest, flew back with the Russian delegation, thanking members of the Russian government and condemning members of the Emergency Committee.

Mr. Kryuchkov flew back with Mr. Gorbachev and the Russians, and was arrested at Vnukovo Airport by the Russian Interior Ministry. Mr. Ivashko, Mr. Lukyanov, and General Yazov were reported to have returned on another plane.

There was no immediate information on other members of the committee, except for Prime Minister Valentin S. Pavlov, who was in the hospital with hypertension. The independent Interfax news agency quoted Mr. Rutskoi as saying that the other members of the coup leadership would be arrested later, and that they would all be tried.

Vremya said Mr. Gorbachev expected that the "adventurists" would carry "full responsibility" for their actions, and the Soviet prosecutor general's office announced it had opened an investigation of the Emergency Committee on charges of committing a "state crime." It was not known if the investigation would extend to others. Wednesday, Mr. Tizyakov was stripped of his job by his organization because of his role in the coup.

But even as Moscow waited for Mr. Gorbachev to reappear, it was evident that the balance of power and the course of the Soviet Union's history had shifted, that the Communists who had fought a rearguard action against change had suffered a potentially fatal blow, that Mr. Gorbachev himself was now beholden to the anti-Communist forces that had rescued him, and above all to Mr. Yeltsin.

Mr. Yeltsin was the indisputable man of the hour, and the advocates of economic and political reform were clearly ascendant.

It was Mr. Yeltsin's dramatic condemnation of the coup virtually at the same time as the rebellion first became known early Monday morning that roused resistance across the Soviet Union and made his headquarters on the Moscow River into a rallying point of the opposition.

The image of Mr. Yeltsin addressing supporters from atop one of the tanks that had come over to his side became the icon of resistance. His statements were published by liberal papers across the Soviet Union and read out at mass rallies from Kamchatka on the Pacific Coast to Leningrad on the Baltic.

Thousands of Muscovites heeded his call and formed a cordon around White House, sealing approaches with makeshift barricades of buses, trucks, and building materials. All across the nation, liberal politicians and supporters of Mr. Yeltsin organized demonstrations and mass meetings.

He issued decrees declaring the actions of the junta unconstitutional and assuming temporary control over all government and security forces on Russian territory.

Addressing the Russian parliament on Wednesday, Mr. Yeltsin declared that it was the defection to his side of several military units that had prevented the junta from interning the Russian government.

Mr. Yeltsin said that instead of obeying the coup leaders' orders, the Tulskaya Division had protected the Russian parliament from attack. He expressed gratitude to the troops and their commanders for their action.

The normally fractious parliament repeatedly rose to unanimously cheer Mr. Yeltsin as he denounced the coup in ringing tones: "This is an impudent coup, unprecedented in the conditions of a genuinely developing democratic society."

One immediate consequence of the curbing of the far-right forces was the virtual certainty that the union treaty, the radically new federal organization that the Communists had tried to block through their coup, would quickly come into effect. The treaty, negotiated between Mr. Gorbachev and nine of the 15 republics, would devolve many of the powers of the center to republican governments in a "Union of Soviet Sovereign Republics."

Flexing his new muscles, Mr. Yeltsin declared that since Mr. Gorbachev had intended to sign the union treaty on Tuesday, he would henceforth consider it in force and was immediately declaring the Russian federated republic economically sovereign and master of all its resources.

The developments also portended an end to efforts to bring the independence-minded Baltic states to heel. Reports from Lithuania, Latvia, and Estonia said that Soviet forces had begun lifting their siege of radio, television, and communications centers, including centers that had been held by Moscow-controlled forces since January.

Elsewhere, the collapse of the coup precipitated frenzied efforts by officials, institutions, and news organizations, many of which had lain low for two days, to demonstrate their disgust with the plotters in a day-long flurry of news conferences.

The Defense Ministry, now under Gen. Mikhail A. Moiseyev, the chief of staff, the cabinet, now under Deputy Prime Minister Vladimir I. Shcherbakov, and the Soviet parliament all issued statements declaring fealty to Mr. Gorbachev.

Leaders of the Communist Party declared that the coup had been "inadmissible" and that from the outset they had demanded a meeting with Mr. Gorbachev, without success. At the same time, a Central Committee secretary, Sergei Kalashnikov, warned journalists against using the term "junta," arguing that leaders of the plot were "people who made a blunder in the estimation of a difficult situation."

Foreign Minister Aleksandr A. Bessmertnykh and Mr. Ivashko, the deputy chief of the Communist Party, separately explained their silence over the past two days by saying they were sick.

Mr. Bessmertnykh told a news conference that Soviet foreign policy would remain unchanged. "It is the same as was formulated by the President of the Soviet Union," he told a press conference.

The tone of official news organs changed radically through the day. *Vremya,* the main evening news program that had toed the junta's line, now portrayed the collapse of the coup as a great triumph for constitutional order and showed long portions of Mr. Yeltsin's speech to the Russian parliament. The Russian republic's radio and television stations, silenced for two days, returned to the air.

The Presidium of the Soviet parliament quickly issued a resolution declaring the removal of Mr. Gorbachev illegal.

The head of the Russian Orthodox Church, Patriarch Aleksy II, pronounced anathema against the leaders of the coup.

Already in the immediate aftermath of the short-lived coup, questions surfaced about its significance for the future of the tumultuous process of *perestroika* that Mr. Gorbachev had launched six years earlier.

In his speech to the Russian republic's parliament, Mr. Yeltsin described the putsch as the last gasp of an order doomed by the union treaty.

"Objectively the new union treaty would strip virtually each of the architects of the putsch of their offices, and herein lies the secret of the conspiracy and the main motivation behind the actions of the parties to it," he said. "Their demagoguery about the fate of the homeland is little more than trickery concealing their personal selfish interests."

In the future envisioned by the union treaty, the central government would lose many of its powers, and it would also be subject to new elections in which Communists would stand little chance of survival.

Communism as a Political Force Is Dead, and the Reformers Gain Strong Legitimacy

By Bill Keller

MOSCOW, AUG. 22—The bungled takeover of the Soviet government left the incumbents of the Communist past discredited, and hastened the demise of the Old Guard that had long been whispering caution in the ear of President Mikhail S. Gorbachev.

Communism as an ideology was already so moribund that even the conspirators did not wave the Marxist-Leninist flag, claiming instead stability as their cause.

Communism as a political force was today's casualty, since the coup debunked Mr. Gorbachev's rationale for clinging to the Communist Party as his power base, in the hope that by doing so he could keep its die-hard partisans in check.

The failed coup legitimized the claim of post-Communist reformers that they are the rightful heirs to power, and invigorated them for the mammoth task of civilizing their country. It also raised the possibility that those who have prevailed may now move against those pillars of the K.G.B. and the military who had conspired against them.

When the euphoria recedes, however, both Mr. Gorbachev and the radicals will still face a fundamental problem that the conspirators were banking on to carry their coup: the public's fear of anarchy, ethnic conflict, and economic insecurity, which has eroded trust in all politicians.

"There was fertile soil for this action," said Arkady I. Volsky, a Gorbachev confidant who now heads an association of industrial enterprises. "People are demanding order. But that order should be established by forces elected by the people, by constitutional methods."

Gorbachev Says Coup Will Hasten Reform; Yeltsin Leads the Celebration in Moscow

By Bill Keller

MOSCOW, AUG. 22—President Mikhail S. Gorbachev, chastened and isolated by his betrayal at the hands of men he trusted, said today that his rescue from the failed coup had taught him that he must join more closely with "democratic forces" and speed the pace of reform.

While elated Muscovites streamed through the streets in celebration of their triumph over the conspiracy, one of the putsch leaders, Interior Minister Boris K. Pugo, killed himself. And the circle of high-level Gorbachev confidants implicated in the plot widened to include the leader of the Soviet parliament, Anatoly I. Lukyanov, who was accused by a high Soviet official of being the coup's mastermind.

But at a news conference tonight, the weary but steely Soviet President refused to join President Boris N. Yeltsin of the Russian federated republic and hold the Communist Party responsible for the rebellion. He reasserted his determination to remain as party leader, declaring that the party could still be purged of "reactionary forces" and made into a vehicle of national unity and reform.

Mr. Gorbachev left little doubt, however, that his 72-hour ordeal had transformed the chemistry of Soviet politics, establishing the anti-Communists who rallied against the coup as the predominant engine of political and economic change.

The Soviet leader spoke with emotion of his strengthened partnership with Mr. Yeltsin, who by galvanizing the resistance to the conspiracy carried out by Communist hard-liners became the ascendant power in the new Soviet politics.

Mr. Gorbachev credited Mr. Yeltsin with the leading role in rebuffing the coup, saying the conspirators finally panicked because of the "implacable position" of the Russian leaders and their followers, including defections in the army.

Today Mr. Yeltsin led the capital in a day of explicitly anti-Communist rejoicing and mapped a mopping-up campaign against the vestiges of Communist power in his own republic.

Mr. Yeltsin, who had been Mr. Gorbachev's bitter rival since the Soviet leader threw him out of the Communist Party Politburo four years ago, has by standing up to the conspirators made himself the most indispensable ally in the Soviet leader's campaign to remake the country.

"So many lies are being told about these two individuals, that it's probably difficult to understand, but we have been bound together by the situation," Mr. Gorbachev said. "We know what the situation is. We know who is who."

One of the most striking impressions during the Soviet leader's 90-minute news conference was a sense of his sudden isolation.

While many of Mr. Gorbachev's original collaborators in reform have quit the Communist Party and remain estranged by his devotion to it, the hard-liners upon whom he relied to run his government, military, and police agencies have proven treacherous.

Today the premier of the Russian republic, Ivan S. Silayev, charged that Mr. Lukyanov, Mr. Gorbachev's friend since they attended law school together in the 1950s and one of his most trusted aides, was "the chief ideologist of this junta."

Mr. Lukyanov was suspended today as chairman of the Soviet parliament pending an investigation.

Mr. Gorbachev said he had met with Mr. Lukyanov, who insisted he had done his best to negotiate an end to the coup, but the Soviet leader sounded as though he needed to be convinced.

The governing presidium of the Soviet parliament announced that Mr. Lukyanov would not preside over an emergency session of the legislature on Monday, which is to include an assessment of his role in the crisis.

Mr. Pugo, named interior minister by Mr. Gorbachev last year, fired two bullets into his wife and then shot himself in the head while the authorities were en route to arrest him, the Russian television news program *Vesti* reported.

The interior minister, one of eight members of the State Committee for the State of Emergency that ousted Mr. Gorbachev on Sunday, died in a hospital. His wife survived but was in grave condition.

All but one of the remaining committee leaders, including Mr. Gorbachev's prime minister, defense minister, and K.G.B. chief, were reported under arrest tonight. Among the other prominent figures arrested for complicity were Gen. Valentin I. Varennikov, the deputy defense minister and commander of Soviet ground forces, and Valery Boldin, the chief of Mr. Gorbachev's administrative apparatus at the Communist Party.

Mr. Gorbachev admitted that he had badly misjudged some of the men he appointed, especially Defense Minister Dmitri T. Yazov and the K.G.B. chief, Vladimir A. Kryuchkov, who the Soviet leader said had held his special trust.

"I see now that it was a mistake, and I'll tell you perfectly straightforwardly because I do not have any problem with speaking the truth, I believed particularly in Yazov and Kryuchkov," he said. "I believed in them."

The aftermath of the coup leaves Mr. Gorbachev with a formidable task in organizing a new government that commands public trust.

One day after he named Gen. Mikhail A. Moiseyev to take over as acting defense minister, the newspaper *Izvestia* published evidence that the general, the armed forces chief of staff, had at least acquiesced in the takeover. The chief of staff of the Moscow military district, Lieut. Gen. Leonid Zolotov, told *Izvestia* that General Moiseyev had issued written orders for the deployment of troops securing parts of the city for the Emergency Committee.

"We must not organize a witch hunt," Mr. Gorbachev warned tonight. "After defeating reaction, we must not follow the same road."

The Soviet leader said he believed that the coup had been timed to prevent the signing of a new union treaty, which would surrender vast authority to the republics.

"There are just a few months to go, and we will have a totally new way of life here," he said, indicating that he remained committed to the treaty. "So that is why everybody was in such a hurry—both those for and those against."

In a televised address to the public tonight, Mr. Gorbachev said the takeover failed because the conspirators "underestimated the main thing—that the people, in these very difficult years, have been transformed."

"They have breathed the air of freedom, and nobody can any longer take that away from them," he said.

"We should not only see the disaster which occurred, but also we have to see this as an enormous opportunity, namely, an opportunity in the sense that our people's true position has been made clear."

Although the Soviet leader spoke with calm resolve of the steps he is taking to set his reform program back in motion, he paused at times to compose himself as he recounted details of his 72-hour ordeal under house arrest at his vacation home in the Crimea.

He said his wife, Raisa, had been badly shaken by the experience.

"She is not feeling well at all, but we think this will pass," he said. "Yesterday we thought, well—anyway, it was hard, and you can understand why."

Mr. Gorbachev said that when his longtime aide, Mr. Boldin, arrived as the emissary from the conspirators with a demand to turn over power voluntarily, he said "to hell with you" and told him that the plot was doomed.

In an earlier interview, upon his arrival back in Moscow early this morning, the Soviet leader said he would have killed himself rather than go along.

While Mr. Gorbachev fielded calls from world leaders and began replacing the arrested members of his government, Mr. Yeltsin basked in the cheers of a roaring throng outside his government building, then sent them on a triumphal march through the city to Red Square.

Tonight thousands gathered outside the K.G.B. headquarters and chanted anti-Communist slogans as a crane sent by Moscow's liberal mayor, Gavriil K. Popov, toppled the statue of the founder of the secret police, Feliks E. Dzerzhinsky.

The Russian parliament voted today to abandon the flag of Soviet Russia, with its Communist hammer and sickle, and restore the white-blue-and-red tricolor of prerevolutionary Russia.

Mr. Yeltsin also announced that he had used special powers granted by his parliament to dismiss the leaders of four Russian provinces who had professed allegiance to the Emergency Committee. All four are hard-line Communists who had battled Mr. Yeltsin's efforts to loosen the party's grip.

The response to the coup has become an instant litmus test for politicians, with the main loser being the Communist Party. The conspirators were all members of the party's governing Central Committee, whose leaders remained mute thoroughout.

"All the anticonstitutional actions by the State of Emergency Committee were tacitly authorized by the neo-Stalinist leadership of the Soviet Communist Party," Mr. Yeltsin charged.

Mr. Yeltsin's allies said measures were in the works to nationalize the party's Moscow headquarters and party papers, including the Communist flagship *Pravda,* that served as mouthpieces for the Emergency Committee.

Mr. Gorbachev, however, said many party leaders, including his second-in-command, Vladimir A. Ivashko, had pressed the conspirators for access to Mr. Gorbachev.

During the coup, the Russian President extended his republic's claim of sovereignty by asserting jurisdiction over all industrial enterprises and other property on Russian territory and creating a new Russian national guard.

Asked about these measures, Mr. Gorbachev, who in the past has challenged Mr. Yeltsin in a war of conflicting decrees, said they were justified, but left the impression that he considered them temporary.

"I think that in the situation, the Russians have acted in the best interests of us all," he said. "And what they have adopted was dictated by the situation."

The failure of the coup also appeared to advance the cause of independence for the three Baltic republics, after months of sporadic violence against secessionist leaders by the Soviet military, K.G.B., and Interior Ministry troops. The army today withdrew from places it had occupied, including the Lithuanian broadcasting center seized in a bloody assault in January.

Latvia and Estonia declared their full independence from the Soviet Union after the takeover was announced, joining Lithuania, which proclaimed its freedom last year. Mr. Gorbachev has repeatedly declared Lithuania's independence claim illegal, while Mr. Yeltsin has endorsed full freedom for the Baltics.

The collapse of the coup left many organizations scrambling to dissociate themselves from charges of complicity.

The K.G.B. today issued a statement insisting that its agents "have nothing in common with the illegal actions by the group of adventurists" and were embarrassed that the agency's head was among the conspirators. The Communist Party's Secretariat announced plans to "discuss the responsibility" of party members who took part.

The official Tass news agency denied reports by independent Soviet journalists that the state news service had advance knowledge of the coup. Tass described as "a lie from beginning to end" the charge published in the nongovernment newspaper *Nezavisimaya Gazeta,* which said the news agency had received texts of the coup leaders' statements 24 hours in advance.

Moscow Crowds Vent Anger on Communists
By Celestine Bohlen

MOSCOW, AUG. 22—The statue of Feliks E. Dzerzhinsky, founder of the Soviet secret police, was lifted off its pedestal in front of the headquarters of the K.G.B. tonight, a victim of an anti-Communist fever that swept this city as thousands of jubilant Muscovites savored their triumph over the coup this week.

Starting with a mass demonstration in front of the Russian federated republic's government building, where they cheered their beaming President, Boris N. Yeltsin, a crowd of almost 50,000 people drifted through the center of the city, waving the republic's newly adopted white-blue-and-red flag, and enjoying the first sunlight of the week.

In the middle of the afternoon, a group spun off up Manezh Square, past the Bolshoi Theater, toward the Lubyanka, as the K.G.B. headquarters is called, where several young men began to go to work on the Dzerzhinsky statue. Starting at the bottom, they painted the word "executioner" around the base. Then they worked their way around the statue's greatcoat and its face, attaching metal wires that they then connected to a small bus parked nearby.

To the cheers of the growing crowd, the amateur team made a first attempt to topple the giant figure, only to be stopped by representatives from the Russian government and Moscow city hall offering their own expert advice and an official sanction of the project.

After lengthy consultation on how to dismantle the statue without disturbing the electrical connections in the subway station below it, four cranes moved in shortly before midnight, lifting the statue up by one arm and laying it on a flatbed truck.

"It's the end of the Communists, of Communist power," said Sergei Kalugin, a 30-year-old Muscovite. "Next, it will be the mausoleum's turn, then Lenin's statue."

After three days of nervous tension, dampened by frequent downpours and the roar of tanks coming and going, people today took to the streets in a holiday spirit, taking turns listening to speeches and standing in lines for ice cream. But as they moved away from the victory celebration at the Russian government building, the mood—while peaceful—became more militant, as people shifted their ire from the eight members of the junta to the whole of the Communist Party, whose tentacles are deeply imbedded in their daily lives.

"We are all sick of the Communists; they have been strangling us for seventy years," said Aleksandra M. Filippova, a pensioner. "We don't have enough food, we have to stand in lines, and go around in slippers because there are no shoes."

Gavriil K. Popov, Moscow's liberal mayor, who ultimately ordered the removal of the Dzerzhinsky statue in retribution for the K.G.B.'s role in the coup and for its "criminal role" during the Soviet era, took another swift blow at the local Communist Party, which has been his nemesis since he took over at city hall a year and a half ago.

In a decree issued today, Mr. Popov ordered the suspension of all activities by all city and local Communist Party offices while an investigation of their role in the coup is carried out. His order, which tonight effectively shut down at least one district party office in the city, called for the sealing of party offices and the cutting of their electricity and telephone lines. An aide to the mayor said tonight the main purpose of the order was to stop party leaders from destroying evidence needed for the investigation.

At the rally on Manezh Square, one speaker cheered the decree, declaring the territory of Moscow a Communist-free zone for the first time since the Bolsheviks took power in 1917.

Led by Mr. Yeltsin, an ex-Communist boss himself who quit the party last year and has recently moved to eradicate it from factories and offices, the victory over the coup this week has provided a fresh impulse to popular anger over the party's influence and power.

The turn against the Communists spread beyond Moscow to the republic of Kazakhstan yesterday, where the republic's President, Nursultan A. Nazarbayev resigned from the once-powerful Politburo and Central Committee, and following Mr. Yeltsin's lead, ordered party bureaucrats out of workplaces.

The anti-Communist mood picked up steam just as President Mikhail S. Gorbachev, in his first press conference since the coup, defended the party and its ideology.

But for people in the streets today, party ideology was secondary to the infuriating privileges enjoyed by the Communist elite, which despite six years of Mr. Gorbachev's reforms, has remained firmly entrenched.

"There is a great confrontation between Communists and democrats," said Nadezhda Itrovna, a 55-year-old Muscovite who came to the celebration today along the barricades around the Russian government building. "The Communists lost, but they could pull themselves together again. We must be very careful, because they are all still in power."

Emboldened by the failure of the coup, Yevgeny Dubrovin handed in his party card today, joining four million other party members—or more than 20 percent of the party rolls—who have quit in the last year. Mr. Dubrovin, an employee of the Soviet Oil Ministry, said he, too, would have quit earlier but, he said, "to be honest, in my job, it would have been a little risky."

Not so today, he said. "Now I am sure it will be fine," he said.

There were people in his office who had openly supported the junta during its brief hold on power, he said, but this morning they stayed quiet and looked gloomy. "But now we know who is who," he said.

Others worried that today's euphoria would only lead to bitter disappointment. "It is a holiday, yes, but mixed with tears," said a 54-year-old employee of the Marine Ministry, "because all the problems we face will still be there tomorrow. Neither the coup nor the victory did anything to solve them."

In front of the Lubyanka, people were determined to strike while the iron was hot. When a member of the Russian parliament, speaking through a bullhorn, warned that a more orderly removal of the Dzerzhinsky statue would take time, the crowd roared back with a chant, "Today, today."

"It has to be today, because people cannot wait any longer," said Valentina Andreyeva, 58, an accountant from Sverdlovsk. "These Communists lie to us all the time, while we work like peasants, like slaves. We go hungry, live from kopeck to kopeck, while they celebrate."

Igor Sukhov, an 18-year-old student carrying flowers presented to him as a veteran of the barricades in front of the Russian government building, said: "We cannot be sure that tomorrow will be as quiet as today. It may not be the most important thing to do, but symbols in Russia have always been very important. And this is a symbol of the K.G.B."

The sight of youths excitedly defacing the most hallowed icon of the K.G.B., under the very windows of the agency that for so many years has cast a dark shadow over Soviet lives, took some people's breath away.

Yevgeny Kuchin, a 19-year-old cadet training to become a Soviet border guard, said, "So many years with one faith, and they are taking it down for no reason." An elderly woman moving through the crowd said, "This leads nowhere."

But it was clear to everyone that the K.G.B., humiliated by the leading role its former chairman, Vladimir A. Kryuchkov played in the coup, was powerless to act. When the people in the crowd looked up at the grand yellow Lubyanka building, they could see an occasional face peering from behind a white curtain. But no one came outside to protest.

In the heat of victory, many began talking wildly about punishment and retribution. People cheered when a member of the Russian parliament announced today that a deputy who had led an attempt to expel Mr. Yeltsin earlier this year was himself going to be expelled for supporting the coup. When someone tonight challenged the removal of the Dzerzhinsky statue, Sergei B. Stankevich, an aide to Mr. Yeltsin, asked for his last name and warned he could be arrested as a provocateur.

With Dzerzhinsky gone, some demonstrators began to talk about the next obvious target.

"Lenin's Mausoleum should be torn down," said Vasily Sergeyev, 30. "He was the first putschist in Russia. He inspired all this. They should all be brought to trial."

Some people listening to the hot rhetoric roiling around them began to worry. "I'm scared," said Masha, a 24-year-old who declined to give her last name. "It reminds me of Germany in the thirties. It's frightening because it is only the beginning of the revolution and nobody can tell how it will end. I hope there is not going to be a witch hunt again."

After the Coup: Yeltsin Is Routing Communist Party from Key Roles Throughout Russia; He Forces Vast Gorbachev Shake-up; Soviet President Is Heckled by the Republic's Parliament
By Francis X. Clines

MOSCOW, AUG. 23—A political shock wave swept through the Soviet Union in the aftermath of the failed coup today as the Communist Party reeled in retreat across the nation and President Mikhail S. Gorbachev yielded to the ascendancy of the Russian President, Boris N. Yeltsin.

Mr. Gorbachev, struggling to regain his leadership role after three days as a hostage to the coup plotted by hard-line Communists, spoke before the Russian republic's parliament. During his appearance, broadcast on national television, he found himself facing an openly skeptical, at times abusive audience. He was scorned by the lawmakers for remaining loyal to the party after the harrowing national ordeal of the last five days.

Mr. Yeltsin, who at times seemed to mock Mr. Gorbachev, spent a dynamic day prodding the Soviet leader for more power sharing and initialing fresh writs to shut down the Communist Party's newspapers and limit its activities on Russian soil. Mr. Yeltsin and other leaders of the Russian republic forced Mr. Gorbachev to replace his whole cabinet and name many replacements loyal to Mr. Yeltsin.

The Russian President's move against the party was reflected across the Soviet Union, as a wave of indignation and demands for change swept from the Baltic republics to central Asia.

The common theme was that, in the wake of the coup, the initiative had shifted to those prepared to confront and erase virtually all the practices and institutions that have dominated the governing of this troubled nation under the Communist system.

The mood of rising anger against the Communist Party and the K.G.B. injected an entirely new energy and uncertainty into the Soviet political crisis. While President Gorbachev warned against a "witch hunt," many officials rushed to join the wave of insurgency and said a full reckoning with the party and the state police was long overdue.

The party's newspapers and offices were being put under lock and key and its political perquisites removed across the land, from Moscow to Kirghizia. Party cells were banned in some hamlets, while Communism's traditional mass propaganda outlets were handed over to presumed reformers. Publication of *Pravda,* the once-dominant party newspaper, was suspended because of its cooperation with the coup leaders.

Though the antiparty drive appeared to be gaining momentum without arousing any discernible opposition, the general uncertainty over the nation's future was if anything heightened by the still-unsettled shape of power sharing between the Kremlin and republics. It was dramatically reflected in the changing relationship between Mr. Yeltsin and Mr. Gorbachev.

The shift of executive power toward Mr. Yeltsin was palpable throughout the day as he moved to end what he described as "the malignant influence of ideological demons."

The husky Russian leader headed off an angry crowd of several hundred demonstrators outside the K.G.B. headquarters by announcing changes in Mr. Gorbachev's cabinet as a sign of resolve to finally begin reforming the infamous organization.

President Gorbachev, who argued that it was unfair to blame all Communists for the coup attempt, found himself on rapidly shifting political ground as crowds, backed up by the local authorities, brought down Lenin statues in the provinces.

Local governments in several regions took action to close down party offices, nowhere more prominently than in Moscow, where the party's Central Committee building, once the repository of total Soviet power, was closed to prevent officials from destroying documents. Groups were formed to protect the building from being overrun by mobs.

Seeking a unity theme, Mr. Gorbachev called on the nation to pursue a power-sharing compact with the republics that Mr. Yeltsin already was executing de facto, acting on the strength of a personal popularity that only grew in his defeat of the Kremlin junta that had held Mr. Gorbachev.

Russian lawmakers made no secret to the watching nation of how clearly they sensed the Soviet leader's dwindling powers. They interrupted Mr. Gorbachev's address with heckling and demands that he join in the rising public clamor to dislodge the Communist Party from its privileged position and explain why he made himself so vulnerable to Communist hard-liners in the cabinet who fought his promises of reform and plotted his ouster.

Firmly on the defensive, Mr. Gorbachev finally drew a positive, rousing response from the chamber by admitting the cabinet's weaknesses and declaring flatly, "This whole government has got to resign."

Mr. Yeltsin, who was in charge of the parliamentary session, repeatedly called attention to his role in saving Mr. Gorbachev from the Kremlin plotters. He even interrupted the Soviet president, demanding that Mr. Gorbachev read aloud some evidence of how most of his own cabinet failed to object to the coup and his arrest in a private session on Monday.

"Here, read this out," the Russian republic's president boomed at Mr. Gorbachev's shoulder.

"I will do this," replied Mr. Gorbachev, seeking to hold his own in this nationally televised tableau of their long-running rivalry. "I'll read it. Let me finish."

Mr. Yeltsin further demonstrated his relative strength when he called on Mr. Gorbachev to acknowledge that they had agreed privately that the next Soviet prime minister should come from the Russian republic. The Soviet leader concurred.

A new prime minister had not yet been named to replace Valentin S. Pavlov, who was on the steering committee of the coup and has been hospitalized under police guard since the coup ended.

(Mr. Pavlov was arrested for his role in the coup, Soviet television said Saturday, the Associated Press reported.)

The first of several appointees in a new national cabinet announced by Mr. Yeltsin to the protesters at the K.G.B. building was Gen. Yevgeny I. Shaposhnikov as defense minister, replacing one of the junta members, Marshal Dmitri T. Yazov. General Shaposhnikov was hailed for refusing to obey orders from the junta.

Gen. Mikhail A. Moiseyev had been acting defense minister for two days, but had come under suspicion for allegedly cooperating with the coup.

Tonight Marshal Yazov made some remarks on Soviet television, the first by any of the conspirators since the takeover failed. "I very much regret what happened," he said.

"In the final analysis, it brings shame on the armed forces," he said, "and I, as the person responsible for the armed forces, am responsible for what occurred."

The new K.G.B. chief is Vadim V. Bakatin, replacing Vladimir A. Kryuchkov, a leader in the coup. Mr. Bakatin, a well-known liberal, had served as interior minister, in charge of the national militia, but Mr. Gorbachev removed him last year in a move to appease hard-line critics.

To fill the post of national interior minister left open by the suicide of Boris K. Pugo, one of the chief plotters, Mr. Yeltsin pushed through the appointment of Viktor P. Barannikov, who until now had held a similar office in the government of the Russian federated republic. In that post he outlawed Communist Party activity within the ministry.

With Mr. Gorbachev's safe return from detention, increasing numbers of government officials have come forward pleading they were not disloyal. Chief among these was Foreign Minister Aleksandr A. Bessmertnykh, who was removed from office today. He said he was genuinely sick during the uncertain days of the coup, and denied that he had been hiding. He said in an interview with ABC's *Nightline* that early in the week he had rejected the coup conspirators' demand that he sign a "terrible document" that was critical of President Bush's response to the coup and United States involvement in internal issues in the Soviet Union.

"If it had been sent that would have been the start of another cold war," Mr. Bessmertnykh said.

General Moiseyev was replaced as chief of staff by Gen. Vladimir N. Lobov, who had served as chief of staff of the joint armed forces of the now-defunct Warsaw Pact. The new first deputy defense minister is Lieut. Gen. Pavel Grachev, a former head of paratroop forces.

In his performance before the Russian parliament, Mr. Gorbachev was applauded at times but generally pressed hard by questioners and hecklers, particularly over his continuing defense of the 15-million-member Communist Party as a useful political organization that was hardly the haven for coup plotters and reactionaries that its critics describe.

In the face of pressure, he warned the lawmakers against "anti-Communist hysteria."

"We must show our maturity and what we have achieved," Mr. Gorbachev said. "You will say that they raised their hand against us, wanted to turn us into meat; they wanted to annihilate us. That is all entirely true."

"But it has to be done according to the law, and so that we all together will be balanced and responsible," he said. "No one should be able to reproach us for carrying out a witch hunt."

But Mr. Yeltsin was not to be denied, and even signed a fresh executive order while Mr. Gorbachev was before the parliament.

"On a lighter note," Mr. Yeltsin said with a big grin, "shall we now sign a decree suspending the activities of the Russian Communist Party?"

And he did, and there was no objection from Mr. Gorbachev, who acknowledged that Mr. Yeltsin's decrees this week had proved potent in building resistance to the coup.

Fielding questions from angry lawmakers, Mr. Gorbachev became angry when asked about assertions that he might somehow have known about the plot in advance, as part of some even grander intrigue. He dismissed this as "sheer invention" circulated desperately by defeated plotters.

Mr. Yeltsin was quite intent on having the Soviet leader read aloud the notes that were taken at the Kremlin cabinet meeting on Monday, in the first hours of the coup. The Russian leader appeared to press this task on Mr. Gorbachev because he wanted him, as much as the nation, to face the treachery that comes of trying to appease hard-liners by giving them Kremlin positions of power.

After some prodding, Mr. Gorbachev finally did as Mr. Yeltsin told him.

According to the notes as read by Mr. Gorbachev, 20 ministers were asked, "Are you ready to take the country out of its crisis? All decisions taken before will not be carried out. Do you agree, or not, to support the Presidium of the Supreme Soviet on the union treaty?

"Do you support this position of the V.K.Ch.P., the Emergency Committee?"

The notes, which Mr. Yeltsin said were made by an unidentified participant, show that most of the ministers either cast their lot with the junta or evaded the question, without speaking up for Mr. Gorbachev.

Mr. Yeltsin looked on as Mr. Gorbachev read the damning list to the nation, giving an official-by-official account of treachery and equivocation. The Soviet president seemed sad and surprised at one or two of those who failed him.

Icons Are Toppled
By Henry Kamm

TALLINN, ESTONIA, AUG. 23—From late afternoon well into the evening, the people of this capital city did something they said they had never done—they flocked to Communist Party headquarters. Then they stood there and laughed.

They stood in a large arc that constantly renewed itself as men, women, and children came and went and stared and pointed at an empty marble pedestal. Until early today, a larger-than-life bronze statue of Lenin had stood there in the familiar rhetorical pose, opposite the entrance to the modern headquarters building.

A crew came this morning and carried out a government decision to remove the statue in the aftermath of the failure of the coup by doctrinaire Communists against the government of President Mikhail S. Gorbachev.

"It was done with respect," said Aino Siiak, a retired economist, her voice full of sarcasm. "A crane came; they put a chain around his neck and took the great philosopher away."

Thousands of people in the Baltic republics commemorated the annexation of their nations by the Soviet Union today, as unrest and protests spread throughout the Soviet Union in the wake of the failed coup.

While in Lithuania and Latvia, the two other Baltic republics, the Communist Party was virtually outlawed today, Estonians expressed their sentiments through a symbolic act.

"Estonians do things slowly," Mrs. Siiak said. "We have no temperament." The way in which she and many others at the scene gave vent to long-suppressed emotions suggested otherwise. Voices trembled and faces quivered as Estonians recalled their sentiments through the tumultuous days that began with the ouster of Mr. Gorbachev on Monday.

"I was exhausted from the events of the last days," said Enno Terk, a 56-year-old mechanic. "I didn't have any sleep. But then I heard this on the radio and I rushed here to see."

The gilt lettering on the pedestal remains. In Estonian and Russian, Lenin is quoted as proclaiming that "Soviet power is the way to socialism." Perhaps imprudently, Lenin concluded that "it cannot be defeated."

How completely socialism, if not Soviet power, has been defeated here was demonstrated in a ceremony held this evening. The people of Tallinn, like people throughout the three Baltic republics, observed the fifty-second anniversary of the signing of the Hitler-Stalin pact as a day of mourning. In a secret addition to the pact, Germany approved a Soviet plan to annex the Baltic republics, which Moscow carried out in 1940.

Gorbachev Quits as Party Head; Ends Communism's 74-Year Reign
By Serge Schmemann

MOSCOW, AUG. 24—President Mikhail S. Gorbachev resigned today as the head of the Communist Party, disbanded its leadership, and in effect banned the once-monolithic party from any role in ruling the vast country over which it had held iron control for more than seven decades.

With Communism under brutal assault across the Soviet Union and his own leadership in shambles in the aftermath of a coup attempt, Mr.

Gorbachev abandoned his efforts to defend party leaders who had obviously collaborated in the putsch and finally dealt the party a fatal blow.

By doing so, Mr. Gorbachev seemed to be seeking some way of remaining a credible political force, something that would have been impossible if he had not repudiated the party.

In a series of terse statements and decrees read on the evening television program *Vremya,* the president also ordered the Cabinet of Ministers, the inner government council, to resign. He then created a committee headed by the premier of the Russian federated republic, Ivan S. Silayev, a close aide of the republic's president, Boris N. Yeltsin, to take charge of the national economy.

This was part of an arrangement worked out by Mr. Yeltsin, who has emerged as the country's leading political figure since the coup attempt.

The committee includes Grigory V. Yavlinsky, a leading advocate of radical economic change in the country, auguring the long-awaited introduction of a sharp turn to a free-market economy. Other members of the committee are Arkady I. Volsky, head of an association of private and state-owned enterprise, and Yuri Luzhkov, a supporter of fundamental change who is head of the Moscow city council.

The moves, announced at the end of another day filled with emotional and fast-paced developments arising from the coup, signaled a virtually complete surrender by Mr. Gorbachev to the liberal and democratic forces who had defied the coup and rescued him.

The actions were accompanied by continued turmoil in the Soviet republics, as Mr. Yeltsin accorded formal recognition to the independence of two more Baltic republics and the parliament of the Ukraine, the nation's second-largest republic, declared its independence and set a referendum for December 1 to endorse it.

Mr. Gorbachev also ordered the Soviet parliament to take all Communist Party property into custody until its future was decided "in strict compliance with Soviet and republican law."

Mr. Communist did not disband the Communist Party, nor did he say he was resigning from the party himself. But in sweeping out its leadership, handing its vast properties to the mercies of democratically elected parliaments, and thrusting it out of all federal government and security organs, he in effect decapitated the 15-million-member organization and left it to find its own place in the new order.

The dramatic gesture followed a broad campaign against the party that had already seen its headquarters sealed in Moscow and across the entire country, its major newspapers closed, and its organization banned entirely in Moldavia and the Baltic republics. Leningrad had sealed off the party headquarters at the Smolny Institute, a site charged with symbolism as the place where Lenin had his first headquarters.

In Moscow, Mr. Yeltsin, the acknowledged leader of the liberal and democratic forces now in ascendance, issued a decree sealing the archives of the K.G.B., the Interior Ministry, and the military.

Mr. Gorbachev's actions came after an emotion-charged day in which tens of thousands of Muscovites turned out to bury three men killed in the coup. The nationally televised ceremonies seemed almost a funeral for the old order.

Against this background, Mr. Gorbachev's announcement, read by a newsreader on the evening television news, had the quality of a full surrender by the old order.

In the statement read over television after he reportedly met with the party leadership for several hours in an undisclosed location, since the Central Committee building was now not in his hands, Mr. Gorbachev based his actions on the party leadership's complicity or silence during the coup.

"The Secretariat, the Politburo, and the Communist Party's Central Committee did not take a stand against the coup d'état," the statement began. "The Central Committee did not manage to take a firm position of condemnation and opposition. It did not inspire Communists to fight against the trampling of constitutional law."

"Among the conspirators were members of the party leadership," it said. "A number of party committees and the mass media supported the action of the state criminals. This placed millions of Communists in a false position."

But the President also defended the rank-and-file membership, as he had done twice since his return from house arrest in the Crimea, in effect appealing to the nation not to carry out a witch hunt against all party members.

"Many members of the party refused to collaborate with the conspirators, condemned the coup, and joined in the fight against it," he said. "No one has the right to blame all Communists, and I, as President, consider it my duty to defend them as citizens from unfounded accusations."

In this situation, Mr. Gorbachev continued, the Central Committee, whose 300 members make up the inner circle of the party, "must take the difficult but honest decision to disband itself."

The fate of republican and local organizations, he continued, "should be decided by themselves."

He then declared: "I consider it no longer possible to continue to carry out my duties as general secretary of the Central Committee of the Communist Party, and I relinquish corresponding authority."

Mr. Gorbachev concluded with the hope that "democratically minded Communists" would work toward the creation of a new party "capable, together with all progressive forces, of actively joining in the continuation of fundamental democratic reforms for the sake of working people."

In a pair of decrees read after the announcement. Mr. Gorbachev dealt what was in effect the death blow to the party.

He ordered an end to all actions by political parties and movements in the military, the security forces, the K.G.B., and the apparatus of government. All members of political parties and political movements, he decreed, could continue their political activities only outside these organs and on their own time.

In a second decree, Mr. Gorbachev ordered parliamentary deputies to take custody of all property of the Communist Party. Its ultimate fate, he said, would be decided according to the laws of the Soviet Union and the republics.

That in effect opened the way for the nationalization of all the party's vast holdings, since Russia and many other republics have already signaled their intention to seize party property. These include innumerable office buildings, luxury hotels, printing plants, residences, and vacation homes, many of which have been put to commercial use in recent years to compensate for falling membership and to earn hard currency for party coffers.

The wealth of a party that argued so fervently at the same time against privatization or private property was a major source of growing public wrath with the Communists.

The death knell of the party as the dominant force in the Soviet Union sounded after a long and tortuous decline during the six years of Mr. Gorbachev's *perestroika,* during which it steadily lost authority but remained entrenched in virtually every branch of the central government.

Only a month ago, Mr. Gorbachev presided at a Central Committee meeting at which virtually every hallowed principle of the party was jettisoned, down to the sanctity of Marxism-Leninism.

All the while Mr. Gorbachev himself continued to cling to the faith in which he was raised, arguing again and again that he was born a Communist and would die a Communist. Even when his closest advisers, men like Eduard A. Shevardnadze and Aleksandr N. Yakovlev, were denounced and quit the party, he remained at its helm, arguing that it could be renewed.

And even in the immediate aftermath of the coup, at his first news conference and in an appearance before the Russian parliament, Mr. Gorbachev declared that he remained loyal to "socialist choice," that not all Communists could be held responsible.

Though long in coming, the stripping of the party of its last grips on Soviet power signaled the end of an experiment that began in the flames of the Russian Revolution and spread to become a dominant historic force in the shaping of the twentieth century, eventually giving in to the corrupting forces of unchallenged power; and under Stalin the Communist Party turned into an instrument of terror, repression, and totalitarian control.

Last in a long line of leaders who believed in the possibility of returning the party to what was seen as its original purity, Mr. Gorbachev came to power in 1985 promising to inject openness and democracy into the party. But the forces he set loose soon began to prey on his own support.

Instead of presiding over the renewal of the party, Mr. Gorbachev ended up presiding over its extended death throes as one after another of its legends and prerogatives fell. In the end, the party turned on Mr. Gorbachev himself, as his comrades engineered the coup.

Finally forced to disband the party leadership and to purge his government, Mr. Gorbachev in effect left himself with no source of power, unless he can find some in the Soviet parliament when it meets next week. But in the rout of Kremlin forces after the coup, it was unlikely that many deputies could be mustered to oppose the steamroller of the Yeltsin supporters.

The inclusion of Mr. Volsky, an ally of Mr. Gorbachev, in the new economic team was viewed as a bow to the President. But Mr. Volsky has also been an advocate of market reform and has maintained close contacts with liberal forces.

The appointment of Mr. Silayev as chairman of a committee to manage the national economy was viewed as a prelude to his nomination as prime minister when the Soviet parliament convenes.

The inclusion of Mr. Yavlinsky signaled that the new government would move rapidly toward the radical reforms that the young economist had proposed in the 500-day plan rejected by Mr. Gorbachev a year ago, and in the program he had prepared more recently with a group of Harvard political scientists. Both plans set a course for the rapid adoption of a market economy, denationalization of state-owned enterprises, and intensified cooperation with the West.

Mr. Gorbachev's surprise resignation as party chief came after Robert Strauss, the new American ambassador to the Soviet Union, presented his credentials to the Soviet leader. He was received by Mr. Gorbachev in the Kremlin, where the two men had a chat. Mr. Strauss, who declined to say what he discussed with Mr. Gorbachev, is expected to return to the United States before formally taking up his position in September.

The day's events followed on an unabating flood of consequences from the brief seizure of power by Old Guard leaders in the Kremlin. In something of a prelude to Mr. Gorbachev's action, Mr. Yeltsin and other republic leaders continued their relentless move against the old order. Having already closed *Pravda* and other party newspapers, Mr. Yeltsin announced late Saturday that he was taking charge of all government communications on Russian territory, including telephones and "coded information," a phrase he did not explain.

Earlier in the day, Mr. Yeltsin had ordered officials of the Russian republic to take custody of all K.G.B. and law-enforcement archives.

That act would further undercut the effectiveness of the central government, since all Kremlin communications would be involved.

In the Ukraine, the parliament decided by an overwhelming vote of 321 to 2, with 6 abstentions, to declare independence, calling a referendum for December 1 to give the measure its certain public support. Even before the referendum, the resolution declared only Ukrainian law valid on Ukrainian territory and the Ukraine sovereign over its resources, in effect stripping a republic of 50 million away from the Kremlin's control.

At the same time, Mr. Yeltsin recognized the independence proclaimed by Estonia and Latvia, as he had before with Lithuania.

Just a week after the coup was first attempted it was clear that the Communist Party and the Soviet system it had imposed were finished. It was similarly obvious that Yeltsin had eclipsed Gorbachev. What remained very much in doubt was the political, economic, military, social, and geographic fate of the Soviet Union.

Soviets' Rush Toward Disunion Spreads; Europe Embracing Baltic Independence; Purge of Military
By Bill Keller

MOSCOW, AUG. 25—Following quickly on the rout of the Communist Party, the unraveling of the Soviet Union itself gained speed today, with one republic after another joining the rush to independence or laying claim to powers of the central government.

One day after the vital Ukraine declared its independence, Byelorussia unexpectedly followed suit, Moldavia announced it would vote on a similar declaration Monday, and Western governments began recognizing the secession of the three Baltic republics.

President Boris N. Yeltsin of the Russian republic, who has emerged in the aftermath of the failed coup by hard-liners as the predominant political figure in the country, said in a television interview that he hoped the mainstay republics would sign a treaty next month reorganizing the country into a looser federation.

But with eight of the 15 republics now asserting or contemplating claims of full independence, there were growing doubts that even Mr. Yeltsin could find a formula to halt the dismembering of this nuclear superpower.

Aftershocks from the abortive coup against President Mikhail S. Gorbachev and the Soviet leader's subsequent abandonment of the Communist Party rolled across the country today.

A presidential spokesman announced that Mr. Gorbachev's military adviser, Marshal Sergei F. Akhromeyev, had killed himself on Saturday night. No evidence has surfaced implicating Marshal Akhromeyev, the former chief of staff of the armed forces, in the attempted coup, but he was instrumental in promoting the military commanders who participated, and he had publicly belittled the danger of a putsch.

The new Soviet defense minister announced plans for a wholesale purge that he said would replace "about 80 percent" of the top command structure with younger officers.

"The people must be younger than we have had, more loyal, and not capable of unconstitutional gambits," said the minister, Gen. Yevgeny I. Shaposhnikov, who as commander of the Air Force defied the conspirators and supported Mr. Yeltsin.

Shake-ups were also anticipated in the K.G.B. and Interior Ministry, following the collaboration of top national security officials in the three-day coup.

(The Speaker of the Soviet parliament, Anatoly I. Lukyanov, who has been accused of complicity in the coup, resigned his post, according to Vitaly S. Ignatenko, a spokesman for Mr. Gorbachev who was quoted on a Cable News Network broadcast.)

Local governments across the country seized Communist Party buildings following Mr. Gorbachev's decree on Saturday, effectively nationalizing the party's wealth. Citizens toppled monuments to Bolshevik heroes, prompting Mr. Yeltsin and other officials to plead for calm.

"There should be no euphoria of revenge," Mr. Yeltsin told a television interviewer tonight. "Otherwise we will lose our self-respect as democrats."

Mr. Gorbachev, who appears to have become essentially a junior partner in a coalition government with Mr. Yeltsin, was reported to be at work on a speech for an emergency session of the Soviet parliament on Monday, which will seek to clarify the murky issue of just who is running the country.

Although the Soviet leader remains commander in chief of the armed forces, and is still formally in charge of the central government, since his return from captivity he has ceded to the Russian president remarkable sway in dictating the shape of a future government.

On Saturday Mr. Gorbachev named Mr. Yeltsin's prime minister, Ivan S. Silayev, to head a committee charged with drastically reshaping the federal government and decentralizing economic powers to the republics.

The four-member committee is dominated by Yeltsin loyalists, who favor slashing central ministries, privatizing state-owned industry, and moving rapidly to a free market.

Mr. Yeltsin said he remains committed to a union treaty that would cede vast powers to the republics.

The Yeltsin team, which once called for Mr. Gorbachev's resignation, now plans to retain Mr. Gorbachev in a scaled-back role, presiding over military and foreign policy and such centralized economic structures as the electric power grid.

"Mikhail Sergeyevitch has not yet exhausted his potential," said Ruslan I. Khasbulatov, chairman of the Russian parliament, in an interview with the independent news agency Interfax. "I don't think that he needs to resign. We, the Russian government, will help him a great deal."

Gorbachev Pleads, but Breakaway Areas Defy Him, Putting Fate of Union in Doubt
By Francis X. Clines

MOSCOW, AUG. 26—President Mikhail S. Gorbachev appealed to the nation today to keep the Soviet Union together, but was all but drowned out by spiraling calls for independence by most of the nation's republics.

The Soviet leader, trying to rebound from the foiled coup of a week ago that has left the country in turmoil, acknowledged at an emergency session of the all-union parliament that the old tightly organized Soviet Union, with power emanating from the Kremlin, could not be sustained. But he urged that the republics seek greater autonomy through a proposed new union treaty with the Kremlin.

But the majority of the nation's 15 republics seemed intent on pursuing independence drives that have exploded in the few days since the failure of the coup and the rise of the public's anger against the central government and its Communist-dominated bureaucracies.

Typical of the reaction at the session of parliament today was a statement by President Levon Ter-Petrosyan of Armenia. "The center is dead," he told the nation watching on television. "The center has committed suicide."

Around the Soviet Union, icons of the past like statues of Lenin continued to be destroyed. Rallies were held in Azerbaijan and other republics calling for an end to ties with Moscow, and moves accelerated for independence in Estonia, Latvia, and Lithuania, the three Baltic republics.

But except for the Baltics, the moves for independence were limited to words, and it was unclear whether or how much these were actual statements of intention to secede or the opening moves in an expected negotiation over the future of relations.

Addressing parliament, Mr. Gorbachev promised new elections for national offices, including the presidency, six months after the signing of the union treaty. He said any republics that did not want to stay in the Soviet Union could then negotiate their secession.

Mr. Gorbachev conceded that he deserved blame for the foiled coup last week by his Kremlin rivals that precipitated the continuing national trauma. Today's anxious, uncertain Kremlin events also included more national cabinet turnovers, the resignation of the chairman of the national parliament, and another suicide, that of the head of the Communist Party's finances, the latest by a ranking Communist apparently unwilling to face the wave of anti-Communist inquiries and censures sweeping the country.

In addition, the 500-member Supreme Soviet, the standing parliament, voted to convene the 2,250-member Congress of People's Deputies next Monday to take up the union crisis, and to see if some compromise can be reached on what this once-powerful superpower should look like in the future.

The corridors of parliament reverberated with the excitement brought on by an unparalleled week of events from the coup to the political collapse of the union.

Anatoly I. Lukyanov, the chairman of parliament who was suspected by some of complicity in the coup, resigned in protest and spent much of the day proclaiming his innocence before reporters in the parliament corridors.

Mr. Gorbachev, struggling to regain momentum lost to the coup and the public's disgust with the central government, offered another plan for reviving the union, including a promised basic overhaul of the K.G.B. But the sovereignty drives in the provinces were fast overshadowing the anxious Kremlin search for compromise.

The surge for independence was complicated by emerging rivalries between Russia, the largest and most powerful of the 15 union republics, and other republics that did not want to be under Russian domination, even in a new, more loosely constructed nation.

Kazakhstan—the nation's second-largest republic in area, which has considerable natural resources but has long been considered a backwater in the Soviet Union—announced its withdrawal from the proposed union treaty.

In immediate reaction to that, the Russian federation, the dominant republic, served notice that it would review its borders with any secessionist republics other than the Baltics. An aide to Boris N. Yeltsin, the President of Russia, said this referred mostly to parts of Kazakhstan and the Ukraine that have heavy concentrations of residents of Russian heritage.

The Ukraine, another major neighbor of Russia, already has an independence drive under way.

The Russian move appeared to be protective in the light of the centrifugal struggle taking over the nation, with dozens of long-postponed border grievances threatening to revive now that the republics will be setting more of their own agenda.

The three Baltic republics, the most European of the Soviet lands, were suddenly gaining official recognition from several nations in their demand to restore prewar independence lost to forced Soviet occupation.

In Uzbekistan, a predominantly Muslim region known primarily for its cotton harvests and long used by Moscow as a showplace of third world development, republic officials began drafting an independence campaign and claimed sovereignty over Soviet military units in the republic.

Kirghizia's President, Askar Akayev, delivered a blistering denunciation of the state of the union, called on parliament to dissolve itself, and "resolutely rejected" the union treaty as needing radical overhaul in the republics' favor. Kirghizia, a largely agricultural area, is also part of Central Asia, which has long been regarded as relatively quiescent in nationalist terms.

Some national and republic leaders professed to be hoping to patch together a rescue plan for the union amid a chorus of contrary demands for a loose federation, a looser commonwealth, or an outright concession to dissolution. The prognosis was not immediately encouraging as four months of negotiations over the union treaty appeared to be coming to naught.

A critical blow for union partisans came today when President Nursultan A. Nazarbayev of Kazakhstan rose to speak amid the confusion and tension of the debate in the Grand Kremlin Palace and announced he no longer could support a new union treaty he had been crucial in negotiating.

Signaling the republic's refusal to be under Russian influence now that the central government was collapsing, Mr. Nazarbayev told the nation, "Kazakhstan will never be anyone's younger brother."

The reference was to the mammoth Russian republic, led by Mr. Yeltsin, which contains more than half the nation's population and much of its economic wealth and natural resources. The Kazakh leader rebuffed Mr. Yeltsin's appeal for a renewed union, one whose government the ascendant Russian leader wants to see heavily staffed by ministers from Russia.

Mr. Yeltsin, a national hero a week ago as he stood up to the Kremlin coup, thus found himself tonight intent on reviving Russia's sovereignty but facing independence drives across both of Russia's major borders. To the southeast was Kazakhstan, suddenly on the move after decades of Kremlin loyalty, and, to the southwest, the Ukraine, the second most populous republic, where an even bolder independence drive continued to gain momentum.

Parliament echoed with harsh and desperate speeches in which politicians railed at one another and pronounced the union a "cadaver" and "a political Chernobyl."

The shocking reversal of fervor for retailoring the union could be seen in the fact that little more than a week ago, Mr. Yeltsin and Mr. Nazarbayev were close colleagues pushing the union treaty. They were preparing to sign the compromise pact in which Mr. Gorbachev vowed to begin a new era of power for the republics last Tuesday, two days after the coup was launched. The pact's promised goal was decentralized democracy, market economics, fresh elections, and a binding constitution and judiciary.

But the separate sovereignty stakes rose rapidly once the coup collapsed and, with it, the Communists' grip on the national institutions in Moscow.

Tonight, Russia was reported reviewing dozens of longstanding border grievances with its neighbors. Principal among these were such sensitive regions as the Crimea, part of the Ukrainian republic, the coal-rich Donets basin, partly in the Russian republic and partly in the Ukraine, and the steppes of northern Kazakhstan, each of which could only compound the current turmoil if they are raised as issues across a new and uncertain landscape of provincial politics.

Across the country, republic situations are shifting helter-skelter, with local leaders vying to show who is strongest for self-rule and for ending ties with Moscow. Underlying issues are complicated even after declarations and referenda on independence.

Communist leaders such as Leonid M. Kravchuk, the chairman of the Ukrainian parliament, have been rushing to shed party images by seeking the leadership in a surging tide of nationalism. The Ukraine, one of the nation's major food and industrial regions, was the first to bolt from the signing of the union treaty because of these local political pressures.

In a long day of speechmaking in the Kremlin that lasted into the night, parliament deputies pilloried the national government, a dramatic turnabout from the last two years in which the Gorbachev Kremlin was backed repeatedly, sometimes sheepishly, by parliament's majority.

Mr. Gorbachev seemed subdued, even wilted as he waited through the early hours of parliamentary haggling for his chance to speak. He soon was more animated on his feet, however, retelling the ordeal of the coup in which he was kept incommunicado for three days in the Crimea by the plotters.

He faced parliament with vows to be far more effective and far less trusting of the Communist Party, whose leadership he resigned Saturday.

"People are saying that I came back to a different country," the Soviet president said. "I agree with this. I may add to this that I am a man returned from the Crimea to this different country who looks at everything—both the past and the present and the future—with different eyes."

Mr. Gorbachev spoke more gently than he had in the past on the subject of letting republics withdraw from the union, saying "businesslike" negotiations should begin once a new union treaty is signed. He also underlined fresh elections as part of the union treaty without, however, firmly specifying there should be one for his own office.

K.G.B., Once a Pervasive Power, Is Quickly Being Brought to Heel
By Serge Schmemann

MOSCOW, AUG. 27—Mikhail S. Gorbachev disclosed today that a full-scale pruning of the K.G.B. had taken place, telling the Soviet parliament that the governing board of the once pervasively powerful security and intelligence agency had been virtually disbanded and its military units reassigned to the army.

The newspaper *Moskovsky Komsomolets* also reported that the entire leadership of the Ninth Directorate of the K.G.B., the division that had been charged with security for top officials and included the men who confronted President Gorbachev at the outset of the coup, had been arrested.

The failure of the attempt to topple Mr. Gorbachev and reverse his policies has inspired and propelled a new campaign to finally bring to heel the K.G.B., the organization probably most closely identified with the horrors of the Stalinist dictatorship.

With revelations that the K.G.B. chief, Vladimir A. Kryuchkov, had been a principal plotter in the aborted putsch and that the agency's elite antiterrorist "Group Alpha" had refused to move against the headquarters of Boris N. Yeltsin, president of the Russian republic, the forces that triumphed over the coup finally moved against the organization whose very initials were once only whispered.

When Mr. Kryuchkov was arrested at Mr. Gorbachev's Crimean retreat after the collapse of the coup, he was flown back separately from other prisoners in the president's plane as an especially dangerous culprit, a testament to the awesome might his organization commanded.

In addition to its armies of agents, the K.G.B. also commanded military units of armor, paratroopers, assault helicopters, and motorized riflemen and border guards, who in the past led such major operations as the combat against Chinese forces in the dispute over borders. According to Mr. Gorbachev's announcement, all these forces have now been placed under military command and control.

Soon after his rescue, Mr. Gorbachev announced that he had named Vadim V. Bakatin, who had previously served as a relatively progressive chief of the Interior Ministry, to take charge of the K.G.B. with orders to purge its leadership, sharply reduce its cadres, break up its powers, and place the agency under political control.

What had made these official moves against the agency possible was the demonstration from the outset of the brief coup that many people no longer quaked before the monolithic organization that had intimidated and repressed them for so long. Already in the aftermath of the coup, the darkened windows of the sprawling K.G.B. headquarters on Dzerzhinsky Square indicated that the agency was finally in retreat.

The K.G.B. combined the foreign-intelligence functions of the Central Intelligence Agency, the domestic policing of the Federal Bureau of Intelligence, responsibilities for controlling the borders, and the role of a "Big Brother" political police. Since Mr. Gorbachev introduced *perestroika* to Soviet life in 1985, several laws had been passed and repeated assertions had been made that the agency's enormous apparatus had been reformed, brought under political control, made more friendly.

Indeed, American intelligence officials reported that the organization had been beset with defections, and both foreigners and Soviets sensed a distinct lessening of surveillance and pressures. K.G.B. officials gave interviews and opened a public relations office; Mr. Kryuchkov even invited the American ambassador to his office for a chat.

The appointment of Mr. Kryuchkov in October 1988 was initially seen by Western intelligence analysts as an attempt to strengthen party control over the agency and to emphasize its foreign functions over its domestic controls. As a K.G.B. general, Mr. Kryuchkov had headed foreign espionage for 10 years.

But foreign diplomats and many Soviets never ceased suspecting that under the new clothing, the K.G.B. still maintained at least the potential for vast surveillance and control.

There was no indication that its staff, estimated at 700,000 plus at least as many informers, had been substantially reduced, or that the reported budget of 4.9 million rubles was anywhere near the truth. The agency also retained its enormous arsenal of special border forces, antiterrorist commandos, and army units under its command.

A former K.G.B. general, Oleg D. Kalugin, joined the ranks of the insurgent movement 18 months ago, and confirmed many of the suspicions. He described Mr. Kryuchkov as an unreformed party apparatchik, and said that the agency continued to infiltrate new democratic organizations, that it continued to have enormous privileges, and that parliamentary controls were ineffective. He also said the organization was riddled with defections.

Despite his efforts at public relations, Mr. Kryuchkov himself began issuing statements and making speeches that reeked of cold war phrases about Western threats and attempts to undermine the Soviet Union. As recently as June, he gave a speech to a closed session of the Supreme Soviet warning of Western intrigues.

Finally, the bungled coup confirmed that Mr. Kryuchkov and the senior leadership had never really embraced *perestroika,* but that the junior ranks had become infused with the new liberties that had spread through society.

In an interview on Saturday, Mr. Yeltsin revealed that Group Alpha had refused to move on his headquarters even after direct threats from K.G.B. officers. And in an interview with Tass, leaders of the commando group said they could have taken the headquarters in half an hour but refused when they concluded that the order was illegal.

Group leaders said that when they were given the order to storm the headquarters, the Russian parliament building, they began asking where it originated. As soon as they realized what it entailed, all subordinate commanders refused to obey.

The decision to disobey "was without precedent for the servicemen, especially for our unit," said Mikhail Golovatov, a former deputy who has since taken over the leadership of the group. "There has never been a case of refusal to carry out orders since the group's formation in 1974."

Mr. Golovatov acknowledged there would have been bloodshed. But the resisters were no match for professionals, he said, adding, "Frankly speaking, we could have fulfilled our tasks in twenty to thirty minutes."

With the party all but dead the key question in Moscow was how far the dismemberment of the Soviet Union would go. Gorbachev, who was fighting to stem the flight of republics from the disintegrating nation, on August 27 threatened to resign if he failed to secure a signing of a revised union treaty by the republic leaders. The most pressing problem concerned the Ukraine, where with the backing of a strongly nationalist population, a government was demanding total independence just like that which was within the grasp of the Baltic states. The difference was that unlike the tiny Baltic states, the Ukraine was a vast and rich territory that had

*formed a part of the Slavic heartland. It provided much of the nation's
wheat, and its coastline sheltered a significant part of the Soviet fleet. Part
of the Soviet nuclear arsenal was also kept on Ukrainian soil. The Ukrainian leader, Leonid I. Kravchuk, in announcing the secession of his land
had at the same time proclaimed a nuclear-free zone calling for the
transfer of nuclear arms to the neighboring Russian republic.*

Soviets Bar Communist Party Activities; Republics Press Search for a New Order
By Serge Schmemann

MOSCOW, AUG. 29—After three hours of anguished debate, the Soviet parliament voted today to suspend all activities of the Communist
Party pending an investigation of its role in the coup. It was an action
that confirmed the demise of the old regime even as the search quickened
for new forms of association and order.

The fate of the party was already sealed before parliament's vote.
Individual republics had closed its offices and seized its vast properties
and funds, and President Mikhail S. Gorbachev had quit as its general
secretary and had called on the leadership to step down.

But parliament was the only national institution with the formal powers to act against the entire organization, and its decision served to
confirm the indictment already passed by the people.

While parliament settled scores with the past, newly unfettered leaders
of the republics searched for interim arrangements to prevent chaotic
disintegration.

A Russian-Ukrainian agreement reached in Kiev in the early morning
after hurriedly arranged negotiations declared it imperative to prevent the
"uncontrolled disintegration" of the Soviet Union and to insure its economic survival and security.

The communiqué seemed to establish a model for interim agreements
among the republics to safeguard the fundamental ties forged over
decades as the tight central controls and Communist-dominated institutions of rule crumbled in the aftermath of the failed coup.

From the negotiations in Kiev, the Russian delegation, led by Vice
President Aleksandr Rutskoi, flew to Kazakhstan for similar talks with
President Nursultan A. Nazarbayev, a republic leader who has demon-
strated considerable authority in Central Asian and national councils.

The day's developments reflected multiple efforts to fill the political
void, to assert local authority, and to prevent chaos. If the actions often
conflicted and even sometimes put the republics at odds, the underlying
search 10 days after the coup attempt still seemed to be for an orderly

transition to a new and yet undefined association of self-governed states.

In parliament, Mayor Anatoly A. Sobchak of Leningrad, who has emerged as a leading advocate of maintaining some form of union and who led a parliamentary delegation that monitored the talks in Kiev, declared that "the former union has ceased to exist, and there is no return to it."

And over the Russian radio, Boris N. Yeltsin, the president of the Russian federated republic, whose heroism during the coup attempt and assertion of Russian power in its aftermath have kept him in the eye of the storm, declared that the center must hold.

"We are maintaining constant contact with President Gorbachev and republican leaders and we are coordinating our actions," he declared in a statement evidently intended to soothe secessionist passions. "I want to state firmly that the collapse of the center is not tantamount to a collapse of the country, let alone Russia.

"I stress, the union center must exist, but there must be a sharp cut in the number of its staff and in the cost of maintaining it."

The center itself worked to regroup. Parliament approved Mr. Gorbachev's proposal to include leaders of nine republics in an expanded Security Council and was expected to approve his nomination of several prominent reformers.

Mr. Gorbachev said the new council would serve as a transitional authority during the reorganization of the union. "Now, however, life demands action," he said.

The interim government under Ivan S. Silayev also met today and discussed urgent measures to stabilize the economy and maintain foreign trade and food supplies.

The suspension of the Communist Party by parliament followed a wrenching debate over what constituted responsibility for the coup. That debate has weaved through the televised proceedings of the legislature since it convened Monday.

Parliament itself has been accused by Mr. Yeltsin and others of complicity through silence, and its debates have been filled with attempts to justify and explain the behavior of various deputies and officials.

The 535-member parliament is expected to conclude by dissolving itself and clearing the way for the full 2,500-member Congress of People's Deputies to name a new legislature when it convenes September 2. The Congress is constitutionally the highest authority in the Soviet Union.

The sharpest debates over the fate of the party focused on an article in the draft resolution that called on the Supreme Soviet to decide whether to close down the party altogether.

Behind it was the question of whether the entire party as an institution was an integral part of the old system that tried to thwart change through the coup attempt and so must be swept away, or, as Mr. Gorbachev and other deputies argued, that at its base it was a reformable organization of well-meaning "workers and peasants."

Born of the utopian Marxism of the last century, the Bolshevik party formed by Lenin was never meant for a democratic role in a multiparty system. Rather, it was meant to be the vanguard of the working class in the struggle against "class oppressors" and to be the chosen elite in the shaping of a new order.

It evolved under Stalin and his successors into a vast and privileged network of institutions that controlled all facets of Soviet life and numbered 19 million members. Even with its powers trimmed by Mr. Gorbachev's *perestroika*, the party continued to exert a powerful brake on any efforts to change the system, and Mr. Gorbachev himself continued to merge the powers of the presidency and party leadership until after the coup, when he finally resigned as general secretary.

"We are talking about the liquidation, not of a party, because the Communist Party has long ceased to be a party, but about a superstate structure, parallel to the structures of power which it illegally usurped," one deputy argued.

But others pleaded against the dismantling of a structure that still provided employment for thousands and held the loyalty of millions.

"Think of the one hundred and fifty thousand people from the party apparatus who are going to lose their jobs," another deputy said. "They are our voters, they will come to us tomorrow and will ask, what are you doing there?"

In the argument that finally tilted the debate, Roy A. Medvedev, the historian and former dissident who returned under Mr. Gorbachev to a prominent position in the Communist Party, declared that liquidating the party would only repeat its own errors. "We cannot liquidate the Communist Party because in people's minds the word liquidation is associated with such facts as liquidation of the Cossacks, kulaks," he said. "It meant either arrest or murder or deportation."

In the end, parliament voted against the article, leaving open the possibility that the party could return in some social-democratic form. But it adopted the balance of the resolution suspending the activities of the party throughout the territory of the Soviet Union, instructing the Interior Ministry to take custody of the party's property and archives and ordering the state prosecutor to open an investigation into its role in the coup.

Even if not threatened with liquidation, the party of Lenin had been relegated to the dustbin of history. The vote was 283 to 29, with 52 abstentions—the highest number of "nays" and abstentions so far in the session.

On the economic front, it was a measure of the general recognition in all 15 republics that they faced uniformly serious economic trials in the months to come that representatives of all 15 attended the first organizational meeting of the Committee for the Management of the National Economy, the acting government formed under Mr. Silayev, the Russian premier.

According to the Interfax news agency, the meeting was told that the climatic conditions in the country were the worst in a decade and that only 25 million tons of grain of the 85 million ordered had been delivered to the state, evidently because collective farms were hoarding in anticipation of higher prices. The committee also heard that supplies of coal and oil were at 80 percent of the norm as the cold months approached.

Attention also focused on the military. Both Mr. Yeltsin and the new defense minister, Yevgeny I. Shaposhnikov, declared that the military must remain centrally controlled regardless of the form the country takes.

"Whatever the destiny of the union—and most likely, in my view, it will be preserved, maybe not in the same form as now, but perhaps along some kind of socioeconomic lines—I just cannot imagine our army being composed of several armies located on the territories of sovereign republics," Marshal Shaposhnikov said.

He also said there was and is no cause for concern about the Soviet Union's vast nuclear arsenal. "Those who now have their finger on the nuclear button are those who are supposed to," he said.

Among the day's other major developments, the Supreme Soviet voted to lift parliamentary immunity from its former speaker, Anatoly I. Lukyanov, a longtime friend of Mr. Gorbachev's who had repeatedly denied accusations that he supported the coup at least by failing to condemn it in time and to summon parliament. The move cleared the way for Mr. Lukyanov to be interrogated and possibly charged, and Tass reported that, soon after, his offices were searched.

The official who made the motion against Mr. Lukyanov, Prosecutor General Nikolai Turbin, then announced his own resignation. Mr. Turbin was in China during the coup, but he accepted responsibility for the inaction of his office.

For many, the most promising development of the day was the joint Russian-Ukrainian communiqué, which lifted some of the tensions raised by the Ukraine's declaration of independence on Saturday and Mr. Yeltsin's subsequent warning that borders between the republics would have to be "reviewed."

The accord may serve as a prototype for cooperation among the republics on key economic and military issues during the search for a new relationship.

The program called for the setting up of temporary structures involving all 15 republics to prepare an economic agreement, to form a collective security system and to take no unilateral actions on military-strategic issues, to avoid measures which would create frictions among republics, to recognize existing borders among republics, to conduct a coordinated policy of radical economic reform, and to confirm their adherence to the Soviet Union's international obligations.

The new search for cooperation was also evident in Moscow as Mr. Yeltsin, who had issued decrees encroaching on central powers, drew back. He withdrew decrees that had imposed Russian controls over Soviet foreign transactions, including those in foreign exchange and precious metals, after foreign bankers expressed concerns.

After the Breakup: *E Pluribus . . .* What?
By Bill Keller

MOSCOW, AUG. 29—The Soviet Union, born of the 1917 Revolution, was pronounced dead this week after a lingering illness. The cause of death was diagnosed as a congenital defect called Communism.

But even as the politicians delivered their funeral orations over the decomposing superpower, a process of reincarnation was under way.

No one could say with any certainty what the Soviet afterlife would look like, what territories would choose to take part in it, what powers it would be given, who would preside over it, or how stable it would be.

Or for that matter, what it might be called. Suggestions in the parlor of parliament, where members today debated the liquidation and reanimation of their state, ranged from the earnest (the Commonwealth of Sovereign States of Europe and Asia, the Euroasian Economic Community) to the facetious (the Club of Crippled Nations, Russia and the 14 Dwarfs).

But even those dry-eyed at the demise of the forced and feeble union agreed that most, perhaps all, of the 15 scattering republics would be reunited in some altogether new configuration by economic necessity, military coexistence, and cultural expediency.

"We are doomed to cooperate," said Aleksandr N. Yakovlev, a prominent lawyer and member of parliament.

The first tendrils of the new collaboration were visible today in President Mikhail S. Gorbachev's decrees creating a National Security Council to coordinate law enforcement and oversee the military "during a period of transition" and establishing a committee to maintain the integrity of communications.

These committees, and others that are sure to come in fields like transportation and energy, do not represent the preservation of the union, but the creation of something new and fragile. Both are to be composed of representatives from the republics, and their power will be limited by their ability to win the republics' consent.

There is a tentative quality to this delicate birth of a new community, since it is taking place in a parliament that has lost its power, under the direction of a president, Mr. Gorbachev, whose only convincing authority is persuasion, under a constitution that six republics have formally declared they do not recognize and that most of the others feel free to ignore.

The only cohesion is consensus. To keep the process from breaking down altogether, Mr. Gorbachev and the leaders of the Russian republic have twice sent delegations to soothe the feelings of republics—on Wednesday the Ukraine, today Kazakhstan—made restive by the ascendancy of Boris N. Yeltsin's Russia.

What keeps the tenuous undertaking in motion is a tacit understanding that none of the 15 scattering republics is sturdy enough to live completely on its own, at least not yet.

For all the heady talk of sovereignty and all the bristle of old suspicions, most citizens recognize that they are bound by common interests that cannot be declared out of existence.

Not one of the republics is ready to join the world economic community on its own, except as a charity case.

Visitors to almost any republic will hear the myth that if only they were freed from the thievery and exploitation of the center they would soon be robust nation-states.

Azerbaijanis speak of themselves as incipient oil sheiks. Tiny Moldavia points to its vineyards and imagines itself the next Bordeaux. Proud residents of impoverished Uzbekistan boast of self-sufficiency, although their main export crop is cotton, and even that colonial industry is threatened by the poisoning of the republic's rivers.

Even the biggest republics are rich, so far, only in potential.

The Ukraine, which claimed its independence last week, has wheat, but lacks the means to harvest it; coal, but the mines are near depletion; the lovely Black Sea coastline, but it is polluted and inadequately developed for world-class tourism.

Russia is a Klondike of natural resources, but the republic staggers under the burden of rusting industry and deteriorating infrastructure.

Most important, there is scarcely a factory in any republic that does not depend on its neighbors for cheap energy, raw materials, or components, not to mention customers. The Soviet Union, Mr. Yakovlev observed, has been "one huge factory."

Thus a feature of the new community will surely be a web of agreements governing trade, currency exchange rates, banking practices, and other rules of the market. At first these may be bilateral treaties, but most experts assume that some functions will be ceded to new superagencies, like those that oversee the economy of Western Europe.

"I think that after a very short time, union republics that are tied up by the unified economy will inevitably ask for the center to have some powers," Mr. Yakovlev said. "Because without it we will not be able to cooperate, to exchange, to survive economically."

Most republics also favor maintaining the integrity of the Soviet military, though they want a greater voice in running it.

The new ministates founded on the ruins of the Soviet Union are likely to have small-scale national guards to defend their territory, a concept Mr. Gorbachev said today was fine with him.

But some kind of collective security is also likely, whether it consists of a broad, NATO-style alliance, as some politicians predict, or bilateral pacts with mighty Russia, as favored by the leaders of Armenia.

The Ukraine, which on Saturday claimed all Soviet military installations on its territory, has already begun backing down. Aside from the alarm at the prospect of a breakaway Ukraine armed with nuclear weapons, the republic was confronted with the cost of being a military power.

"When they calculated how much money would be needed to maintain the 650,000 soldiers based on the territory of the Ukraine, it turned out to be nearly equal to the entire republican budget," said Lieut. Col. Vasily A. Yerokhin, a member of the Soviet parliament. "And that does not count the Black Sea fleet or the strategic nuclear forces."

Politicians in the republics also expect pacts or new superstructures to govern territorial claims, to protect the shared environment, and to apportion the cost of the catastrophes, like the Chernobyl nuclear accident, that have been the Soviet Union's fate.

Another priority for the new community is to protect the human rights gains of the last few years.

Mr. Gorbachev made the Soviet Union a member in the club of civilized nations by freeing political prisoners, allowing a free press, lifting most political limits on foreign travel, and legalizing opposition parties.

Whether the leaders of the new ministates will share his enthusiasm for law and world opinion is a painfully open question. The president of breakaway Georgia, Zviad Gamsakhurdia, has silenced the independent press in his republic and, according to dissidents living in Moscow, has locked up scores of his political opponents.

Moldavian leaders used the attempted Soviet coup last week as a pretext to arrest ethnic minority leaders in that republic, charging them with collaboration.

"Many of the nations of Europe went through their periods of dictatorial power," said Yuri Shcherbak, the deputy prime minister of the Ukraine. "Of course it's entirely possible that we will have some very undemocratic national republics created here."

In a community where almost every republic has substantial minority enclaves of Russians and other ethnic groups, no republic can be indifferent to the internal policies of its neighbors.

As the republics feel their way to a new accommodation, only the most sensitive diplomacy will be able to keep in check old grievances that have festered under artificial union.

"A lot depends on words," said Dmitri S. Likhachev, a revered historian of old Russia, who stressed that such questions as the name of the new entity should not be taken lightly. He favors calling it a "commonwealth" or "community."

"I don't like the word union, because it reminds me of the Soviet Union, which is no longer."

Gorbachev, Yeltsin, and Republic Leaders Move to Take Power from Soviet Congress; Delegates Stunned
By Serge Schmemann

MOSCOW, SEPT. 2—Declaring that the nation was "on the brink of catastrophe," President Mikhail S. Gorbachev and the leaders of 10 republics stunned the opening session of the national Congress today by proposing to transfer all central authority to themselves and an appointed legislative council until a new union can be formed.

The proposal, prepared in arduous negotiations between Mr. Gorbachev and the republics' leaders that ended shortly before the session opened, was a last-ditch attempt to halt the uncontrolled fragmentation of the union before it destroyed the interwoven economies and the armed forces.

Most of the 15 constituent republics have declared some form of independence, eight of them in the two weeks since the failed coup in Moscow.

Under the plan put forth today, a new treaty would be negotiated to form a new kind of Soviet Union, but it was unclear who would do the actual negotiating. In the meantime, the country would be run by three interim councils of indeterminate terms—a kind of parliament to be made up of 20 legislators from each republic; a State Council made up of the Soviet president and leaders of the republics; and an interrepublic economic council consisting of representatives of the republics, including those not wishing to stay in the union.

The maneuver by the presidents surprised and dismayed many of the 1,780 deputies, who were in effect being asked to dissolve their Congress of People's Deputies, the first and highest authoritative assembly elected by the entire Soviet Union, in 1989.

The move also appeared to preempt whatever intentions hard-line legislators may have had of making their own assault on central power. Several officials had warned on the eve of the Congress session that the conservatives would try to regroup, and the reform-minded Democratic Russia movement had mounted pickets on the way to the Kremlin to protest any such attempt.

For the moment, the proposal made today left unclear what powers might remain to Mr. Gorbachev and the central government. But with the republics' leaders likely to be embroiled in their own domestic crises, it suggested that the father of *perestroika* had survived the greatest crisis of his political career and would remain for a time at least at the center of his country's fate.

Neither the president nor Boris N. Yeltsin, the Russian federated republic's president, who sat alongside Mr. Gorbachev on the dais and shared the duties of chairman, made a formal statement today. This was evidently a deliberate act to underscore the fact that the statement read at the Congress this morning by the Kazakh president, Nursultan A. Nazarbayev, spoke for them all.

The Kazakh leader, in his appearance, said he was speaking for Mr. Gorbachev and the presidents of the 10 republics. The agreement, worked out Sunday night and early this morning, described the country as "on the verge of a catastrophe."

Mr. Nazarbayev said the measure had been signed by the leaders of the Russian republic, the Ukraine, Byelorussia, Uzbekistan, Kazakhstan, Azerbaijan, Kirghizia, Tadzhikistan, Armenia, and Turkmenia. He said Georgia had also taken part in the negotiations, but had not signed the measure, leaving the three Baltic republics and Moldavia as nonparticipants.

After he read the statement, the leaders of the gathering announced a break of several hours, during which deputies discussed the proposal in caucuses. Then representatives from each republic rose to declare their support, though some with conditions.

At the end, most deputies seemed to accept the arguments of their leaders that there was no other option left, and the proposal was placed on the agenda by the lopsided vote of 1,350 to 107 with 135 abstentions, auguring its passage with some amendments within the next two days.

The expected move to recognize the independence declared by the three Baltic republics, however, was postponed when Mr. Gorbachev said he had not had time to discuss the matter with the republics' leaders. The hesitation suggested that he was having trouble finding a way to recognize the independence of Estonia, Lithuania, and Latvia without acting on the independence proclamations of other republics.

The Congress also agreed today to limit its session to three days.

The union proposal of the presidents today left a host of questions open, not least among them the authority, financing, and shape of the new structures. What was clear, however, was that it proposed to transfer control over what was left of Mr. Gorbachev's floundering central government to the republics' governments.

"This is a presidential putsch, a real presidential putsch," said Nikolai N. Engver, an economist and member of the Congress. "But thank God this one is without tanks. The politicians would have reached an agreement sooner or later and would have fooled the people into following them. But the dead cannot be resurrected. It's better to be fooled and alive than clear-minded and dead."

Despite howls of protest from some deputies and the dismay of many at the surprise maneuver, a broad sampling seemed to feel that the emergency measure was perhaps the last available means of avoiding social and political disaster.

The structures proposed by the presidents' declaration essentially accepted each participating republic as an equal partner and the master of its internal politics. It was evident, however, that the sheer bulk of the Russian federated republic would guarantee Mr. Yeltsin a dominant role.

Above all, the statement reflected a shared alarm that the vacuum at the center and the cascade of claims to independence would leave republics struggling with one another as their totally intertwined economies—bound together by markets, energy, transport, research, finance, and mutually dependent industries—ground separately to a halt.

The statement by Mr. Gorbachev and the republics' leaders declared that as a result of the coup two weeks ago, "the process of forming new union relations between the sovereign states broke down, putting the country on the brink of catastrophe."

"The situation that emerged in the country after the putsch, if it runs out of control, could lead to unpredictable consequences inside the country and in relations with foreign states," it said.

At the same time, the blow to the right-wing forces had created a "historic chance" to pursue reform and renewal. In these conditions, the presidents asked the Congress to take several steps "in order to prevent further disintegration of power structures" until new forms of government and association are formed and a new constitution is written.

It called for the creation "during a transitional period" of a Council of Representatives that would perform legislative functions and write a new constitution. Each republic was asked to assign 20 members, in effect declaring each an equal participant no matter what its size.

It called for a State Council comprising the Soviet president and leaders of the republics "to decide internal and foreign issues." And it proposed an Interrepublican Economic Committee, also with representatives of each republic on an equal basis, to coordinate economic management and reform.

The leaders further proposed that the republics form an economic union to maintain a "common economic space" and to insure the functioning of the national economy. They also called for a defense agreement to preserve the united armed forces, affirmed Moscow's international agreements, proposed a declaration of citizens' rights, and asked the Congress to support applications by the republics to separate membership in the United Nations.

Soviet Congress Yields Rule to Republics to Avoid Political and Economic Collapse
By Serge Schmemann

MOSCOW, SEPT. 5—Bowing to the reality of a collapsing union and an ultimatum from President Mikhail S. Gorbachev, the all-Soviet Congress voted today to surrender power to a new government largely controlled by the republics.

The action served largely to confirm the collapse of central authority over the 15 constituent republics in the 16 days since the aborted right-wing coup and the increasingly urgent need to restore at least a modicum of order before the centrifugal forces turned uncontrollable.

The major effect of the new central structures approved by the Congress of People's Deputies was to grant sweeping emergency powers for an undefined transitional period to a State Council composed of Mr. Gorbachev and leaders of the participating republics, backed by a largely subordinate legislature and a central Interrepublican Economic Committee to manage the economy.

In so doing, the Congress effectively dissolved itself as the highest legislative authority in the Soviet Union and laid the foundation for a far looser union in which the republics would seem to predominate in deciding the policies and powers of a subordinate and reduced center. A major question remains the extent of Mr. Gorbachev's remaining power and influence. Although his powers seem sharply diminished, it is possible that he might emerge with important powers in the new State Council, particularly if the republican leaders pay more attention to their problems at home.

Under a rough timetable worked out today, the new two-house legislature will convene no later than October 2, and will probably set up a commission to draft a new constitution. It is expected that the new constitution will provide for new elections to the presidency at some future date, at which time Mr. Gorbachev's political future would be decided.

Mr. Gorbachev, who survived the coup only to stand on the brink of losing any viable levers of control, emerged in the interim order with considerably clipped powers and subordinate to the republics, less an executive president than a coordinating manager.

Yet the very fact of his survival, his experience in domestic and foreign affairs, and the familiar determination he displayed at the Congress suggested that he could emerge with a significant role in the new council. Most republic leaders had problems enough at home, and Mr. Gorbachev was likely to be the major conduit for foreign aid.

Whatever the reason, his obvious good humor at the Congress testified to his satisfaction at what he described as a historic moment.

"By determining the principles and mechanisms for the transitional period, the Congress lays the groundwork for a future union of sovereign states," he said before closing the session. "The Congress rose to the occasion at this crucial and, without any exaggeration, historic moment in the development of our state."

For the moment, the arrangement was less a power-sharing agreement than a desperate attempt to create an emergency control center that could combat the incipient chaos and ethnic strife loosed by the coup, prevent the collapse of the economy and the fragmentation of the military.

The law made no attempt to define the scope, functions, or procedures of the new State Council, leaving that to the republican leaders and Mr. Gorbachev to sort out. It was unclear how the republican leaders would be represented in the council and how often the council would meet, whether Mr. Gorbachev, more attuned to Moscow, might rule between meetings with the Russian leader, Boris N. Yeltsin, or would have to check his every action with republican representatives.

The Congress did, however, pass a nonbinding resolution outlining broad principles for the future, pledging to honor existing Soviet agreements with other states, and charging the State Council with "insuring the legal continuity of power and management, guaranteeing a peaceful and orderly transition to a democratic civil society."

The State Council was to hold its first meeting Friday, when it was likely to appoint the Economic Committee—in effect an acting cabinet—and consider emergency economic programs. There were reports that Grigory A. Yavlinsky, the prime advocate of radical economic reform, was readying a preliminary economic plan.

The council was also expected to recognize the independence of the three Baltic states, an issue the Congress avoided taking up for fear of prompting demands by other republics for similar recognition. The Baltics are the only states whose independence has received broad recognition abroad, and while most other republics have also proclaimed independence, all except Moldavia might yet form some new form of association.

The new government was declared a transitional authority until those republics that wanted to could agree on a new relationship, still undefined. The law set no time limits, and deputies talked vaguely of a transitional period of two months to two years.

Besides Mr. Gorbachev, it was also a satisfying moment for those who had struggled for years against a monolithic and repressive system that had held their nation in thrall for seven decades, and who viewed the vote as its final burial.

The eulogy was proposed by Anatoly A. Sobchak, the liberal mayor of Leningrad: "I propose a fitting conclusion to our work by fulfilling the last will of Vladimir Ilyich Lenin and burying him according to the religious and national traditions of our people at Volkovo Cemetery with all appropriate honors."

Lenin had in fact asked to be buried next to his mother and sister in the Leningrad cemetery, but the proposal was quashed by Mr. Gorbachev.

The end did not come easily. For two days the debate at the Congress ranged from bitter resistance against the surrender of power to somber acknowledgment that the old order was out.

At today's session, however, Mr. Gorbachev turned tough. Flanked by Mr. Yeltsin and the leaders of nine other republics, the man who six years earlier first loosed the democratic processes that created this Congress now sternly demanded that it fulfill its purpose by clearing the way for the new era.

Turning away all speakers, demanding silence and obedience in the vast Palace of Congresses, Mr. Gorbachev martialed vote after vote until the deputies balked on a critical paragraph. Twice they denied it a two-thirds majority needed for a constitutional change, when Mr. Gorbachev declared an ultimatum: "We've been talking for three days and we must move foward. Either take this decision and continue on the path, or we will seek new answers."

He did not elaborate, but the glare of the republic leaders made clear that they were the new law in the land with or without the endorsement of Congress. This time, by a margin of scores of votes, it passed—1,606 for, 116 against, 83 abstaining, and 37 not voting.

Critical to the passage was the decision by Estonia and Latvia, despite their independence, to have their deputies take part in the vote. Lithuania withdrew its deputies from the outset.

The rest went easily, and by the time the Congress was called on to vote on a Declaration of Human Rights, no one even asked to speak. The declaration, which includes guarantees of free movement, is nonbinding.

The central action taken by the Congress, the law on transferring power, was in part a compromise. The original proposal from the republican leaders had called for a largely nominal legislature appointed by the republics.

The final version created a two-chamber parliament with a Council of the Republics and a Council of the Union.

The Council of the Republics would have 20 deputies from each republic except Russia, which would have additional deputies from ethnic subrepublics for a total of 52. The catch, however, was that each republic would have only one vote in the Council of the Republics.

In the Council of the Union, seats would be apportioned by quota. Its action would be subject to approval by the Council of the Republics.

The law also lifted a requirement for the Congress to formally dissolve itself. Deputies were allowed to retain their credentials until the end of their term in two and a half years, along with their privileges and immunity, but regular assemblies were canceled.

Substantive powers were granted to the State Council, which was authorized to organize its own work and whose decisions were declared binding. The law said nothing about the relationship between the council and the parliament, empowering the council in effect to rule by decree.

The law called for an Interrepublican Economic Committee to be named by the republics. All national military, security, and foreign-affairs institutions were placed under the control of the council.

The resolution passed by the Congress gave a broad, though nonbinding outline of the new government's goals.

It charged the new leaders with "insuring the legal continuity of power and management, guaranteeing a peaceful and orderly transition to a democratic civil society," and it called for accelerated efforts to negotiate a new union treaty "in which each state can independently define the form of its participation in the union."

The resolution called on republics to reach agreements among themselves on a variety of economic, fiscal, military, and other issues. It pledged to honor all Soviet international agreements, and called for negotiated agreements with republics that wanted to leave the union.

Reporter's Notebook; from Soviet Space Station: Queries on State of the Union

By Francis X. Clines

MOSCOW, SEPT. 6—The astronauts aboard the Soviet space station Mir, having journeyed weightless for the past 18 days above coup, countercoup, and constitutional crisis, beamed down an urgent question today about just how much political disintegration has been taking place below them.

"Is it true that the Russian federation plans to sell the space station Mir?" one astronaut asked the home office. He was rocketed aloft four months ago, when the Soviet Union was really something and even included the three Baltic republics.

"And we're to be sold with the ship?" asked a second astronaut, possibly joking, although in space the line between the sublime and the ridiculous may be as difficult to judge as it is down here among the groundlings of the crisis.

The curious astronauts and a gorgeous view of an apparently serene blue earth were shown on television tonight to a no less curious Soviet nation.

A news commentator could only note that with the separate republics fast claiming independence and old union territory, it is not yet clear whether the republic of Kazakhstan, the site of the main space launching site in Baikonur, might be the new landlord of space station Mir, or whether the withered union government retains title. This was only one of a galaxy of unknowns that has the people of the old Soviet nation as up in the air, in their own way, as the astronauts.

Globes of planet Earth—perfectly round and shiny and now incorrect with their depiction of the old Soviet Union—were selling briskly today in Detsky Mir, the main children's store. There, the continuing steady flow of life was focused not at all on the question of whither the union, but on the question of whence the back-to-school goods sought by all self-respecting families who sense there is enough of a future that little Vanya had best be prepared.

The search for precious notebooks, pads, pens, and bookbags was at least as reassuring a sign of life's continuity as was the freshman class of a new Kremlin government shown briefly on the TV news.

Some of the main faces of the brave new executive collective were the same as before the latest crisis, and the Kremlin backdrop looked as as steady and colorful as the earth behind the astronauts.

In a way, the end of Communism has left youngsters with as much adjustment to ponder as the adults who are rapidly transmogrifying from party members to the lesser mortality of the other 95 percent of this shifting nation.

Now that the seven-year-olds eligible for the *"Oktyabryata"* kiddie corps no longer have the chance to join as party tadpoles, they miss out on one of the really neat Lenin icons, a tiny red star pin depicting the fast-fading patriarch as a lad with a full head of curly hair, truly a collector's item.

This pin is now impossible to find in the black market of Communist kitsch, where Lenin's rule has grown stronger with the death of Communism.

Some laggards in the next age group, the Pioneers, still can be seen on the streets, blasé 10-year-olds in their identifying red scarves, heedless of the iconoclasm going on all about them.

The adaptation seems to have been easier for the next age group, the Komsomol, perhaps since they already were in that nervous age bracket of 13 and 14 years where one's own voice, never mind one's dogma, can crack with change. Komsomol ranks began dwindling over the past two years, as these serious-minded teens sensed the uncertain shape of things to come.

For ordinary people, the sudden promised change from central Kremlin power to the collective power of sovereign republics has made an open question of many of life's details. No one knows yet what will happen to the national military draft, for example, with many republics demanding that their young men not serve beyond their native borders. Likewise, there is no clear idea yet of how much union government will remain and how it will be financed, although it is clear the republics will control the purse strings.

Nothing much is on paper, but the general feeling is that the hybrid of old and new legislatures created to be subordinate to the ruling State Council will not have as loose a mandate for open agenda and unlimited debate as their predecessors. Clearly, the council members wanted to keep the legislature away from the Baltics issue.

President Mikhail S. Gorbachev and the executive members from the republics who took part in today's meeting chose to handle it quickly on this first day of rule, yielding without a great stirring of national debate over the union's loss of three republics.

And what about the Congress of People's Deputies? The 2,000 lawmakers of the old legislative body were last seen heading out to pasture beyond the Kremlin walls Thursday after the leadership prevailed on them to scrap the old government and legislature in favor of something new. The one victory they won, besides a two-and-a-half-year salary buyout, was their refusal to formally disband themselves. Theoretically they could convene somewhere sometime to try and discuss something.

President Mikhail S. Gorbachev, exultantly bidding adieu to this elected Congress he helped invent, thanked them for moving the nation forward by millennia: "From B.C. to A.D." is the way he put it before dismissing them and taking up his new government mechanism.

Soviets Recognize Baltic Independence, Ending 51-Year Occupation of 3 Nations
By Serge Schmemann

MOSCOW, SEPT. 6—The Soviet Union's new ruling council recognized the independence of the three Baltic states, Lithuania, Latvia, and Estonia, today at its first meeting.

The move formally freed the three small republics, which were incorporated forcibly into the Soviet Union in 1940 but renewed their drive for independence in the era of *glasnost.* Their campaign was bitterly resisted by Moscow until last month, when central controls unraveled in the wake of the failed coup and a procession of foreign governments granted the Baltics diplomatic recognition.

In matching proclamations for the three republics, the council also called for negotiations on disentangling the complex economic, political, and military ties between the new states and the rest of the Soviet Union.

The declarations were the first action by the State Council, a committee of republic leaders and President Mikhail S. Gorbachev that was granted sweeping emergency powers by the national Congress on Thursday to control the rapid disintegration of the Soviet Union. The proclamations were read later in the day by Foreign Minister Boris D. Pankin.

Other changes continued to reverberate in the wake of the failed coup, with the city of Leningrad winning a battle to change its name back to the original St. Petersburg. The move, approved by residents in a referendum in June, was formally affirmed today in a decree of the Russian federated republic's parliament, the press agency Tass reported.

Soviet Republics Agree to Create an Economic Union
By Francis X. Clines

MOSCOW, OCT. 11—Russia and a majority of the other republics announced their commitment today to soon forming a new economic community devoted to free-market resuscitation of the fallen Soviet nation.

President Boris N. Yeltsin of the Russian federation, the centerpiece republic in the complex plan, led the way in pressing nine other republics for a formal signing of the economic compact as early as next Tuesday.

The Soviet president, Mikhail S. Gorbachev, leading a meeting of 10 republic leaders at the Kremlin, warned that the economic plan represented the people's "last hope" for decisive action toward national reconstruction after the harrowing failed coup and collapse of the central government in August.

"Peoples' patience is at a breaking point," Mr. Gorbachev cautioned, according to the press agency Tass.

The news that Mr. Yeltsin was back from vacation and recommitting Russia to the economic plan immediately bolstered proponents of the free-market community.

In his absence for the last two weeks, critics of the plan came forward in his own cabinet to warn that Russia, the nation's dominant republic, would be slighted in creating such an economic community from the dregs of the Communist Soviet Union.

But Mr. Yeltsin reaffirmed his view that the plan for a "common economic space" of trade, currency, banking, and customs procedures was the only hope for the crippled Soviet nation to turn itself toward reform and a chance of joining the global free market.

The most Mr. Yeltsin offered to critics, according to initial reports, was the possibility of a common banking system less central in nature. That was in concession to an apparent sensitive point among the now sovereign republics still fearful of echoes of the central monolith that marked Communism's handling of the economy.

The republics, meeting together as members of the new State Council emergency government, also followed through on earlier agreements to reshape the K.G.B. state police into separate new agencies to protect against the possibility of a return to central state police terror.

Ukraine Refusing to Join Agreement on Soviet Economy
By Francis X. Clines

MOSCOW, OCT. 17—Demanding unhampered sovereignty, officials of the Ukraine announced today that they would not join other republics on Friday in signing a proposed new economic pact intended to create a free-market association from the shambles of the Soviet Union.

The resistance of the Ukraine, a critically important republic of 52 million people, had been clear for months. But the warning from Kiev officials that the proposed agreement constitutes a threat to Ukrainian independence deepened the already considerable doubts that the separatist republics might ever be able to muster enough unity to forge a new economic association.

"History has given us a chance to become an independent nation, and we do not want to continue to be a colony," Ivan Pliusch, first deputy chairman of the Ukrainian parliament, told the public tonight on Ukrainian television, insisting that only a drastically revamped economic arrangement might attract the Ukraine's support.

President Mikhail S. Gorbachev is scheduled to be host of a signing ceremony on Friday evening in the Kremlin at which a majority of the 12 remaining Soviet republics are said to be prepared to sign a commitment to create a "common economic space."

In this, the republics would agree to negotiate free-market banking, currency, trade, and customs standards that Western governments say are critical for any chance of reviving the battered Soviet nation and making it a candidate for economic assistance and entry into the global market.

Officials of the Russian federation, the most important republic in any attempts at national reconstruction, said they would sign without the Ukraine.

"I do not know if the Ukraine will survive without Russia, but I definitely know Russia will survive without the Ukraine," Vice President Aleksandr Rutskoi of the Russian republic said in response to the Kiev announcement.

Russian officials maintain that their republic is the chief engine of the agreement and that Russian resolve can see it through to prevent inter-republic trade conflict and a total collapse of the remnants of the Soviet national system.

But Boris N. Yeltsin, the Russian republic's president, and other proponents of the economic agreement concede that the Ukraine is the most important participant after Russia, for the two depend heavily on each other's cooperation for economic balance. Together, the two republics accounted for about 70 percent of the economic output and population of the Communist Soviet Union, which began crumbling after the failed hard-line coup in August.

Nearly a fifth of the total Soviet population lives in the Ukraine, while Russia has about 150 million. The Ukraine's 232,000 square miles of territory contains some of the most bountiful agricultural land and productive factory and mining regions in the nation. Russia, with two-thirds of the Soviet land mass, contains most of the nation's natural wealth and productive capacity.

Attempts to mollify Ukrainian objections are likely at some point. But the future shape of the Soviet nation remains as cloudy as ever on the eve of the signing ceremony.

The occasion was intended in part to exhibit to the world a revived spirit of resolution to prevent the further slide of the Soviet nation toward political and economic oblivion.

Some nationalist-minded officials in the Ukraine insist that a Ukrainian-Russian agreement might serve the two giant republics just as well. Kiev opponents have a long list of objections about the proposed economic pact, starting with the central banking and currency standards that Western officials and other proponents of the agreement insist are important requirements of any viable economic union.

"This will open the road to a new political union," Mr. Pliusch declared, warning that the economic treaty amounted to a "blackmail" attempt at reviving the hated centralized structures of the Communist monolith.

Mr. Gorbachev and Mr. Yeltsin and other proponents deny this, insisting that the economic pact would have only the minimal central structures needed for a free market that the republics themselves would oversee.

The question of reviving some sort of formal political ties among the republics was to be left to the future once the economic association was under way, according to the emergency transition plan approved by the republics last summer amid the crisis that followed the coup.

After 74 years of Communism, the politics of any proposal touching on the subject of the union are risky and imbued with demands in the Ukraine and other republics for total home rule and independence. Ukrainian nationalists stress they have been waiting for centuries to indulge the sort of yoke-free independence now within their grasp, from creating a special currency to forming a Ukrainian army for national defense.

The Ukraine, which proclaimed its independence after the Bolshevik Revolution, became the scene of some of the fiercest fighting in the civil war that occurred in the years after 1917. It was conquered by the Bolshevik forces and became one of the original republics of the Soviet Union.

Nationalist competitiveness in the Ukraine has been heating up among rival politicians focusing their energies on the December 1 presidential election, the first ever in the republic.

Yeltsin Is Telling Russians to Brace for Sharp Reform
By Serge Schmemann

MOSCOW, OCT. 28—Declaring that the time had come to act "decisively, sternly, without hesitation," President Boris N. Yeltsin of the Russian republic told his people today to brace for drastic reform and proposed to take personal charge of the republic's government.

Speaking grimly for more than an hour to the Congress of People's Deputies, the highest assembly in the Russian republic, Mr. Yeltsin de-

clared his intention to lift price controls by year's end, to sharply accelerate the privatization of agriculture and light industry, to stop financing
central ministries and all foreign aid, and to bolster the ruble.

"If we enter on this path today, we will have concrete results by the
fall of 1992," he said. "If we do not take a concrete step to break the
unfavorable course of events, we will doom ourselves to poverty, and
doom a state with a history of many centuries to collapse."

To the surprise of the deputies, Mr. Yeltsin proposed assuming the
vacant post of Russian prime minister himself, thus combining chief
executive and administrative functions in the Soviet Union's largest republic and taking on himself full responsibility for the reforms and whatever backlash they will provoke.

Speaking somewhat incongruously before a bust of Lenin that still
stands in the Grand Kremlin Palace, Mr. Yeltsin asked the Congress for
additional powers to shape the top echelons of the government.

Arguing that regional elections would be a "luxury" at this time, he
proposed to postpone elections. "It is impossible to hold vast election
campaigns and simultaneously carry out deep-going economic changes,"
he said.

His aides have privately expressed fears that if elections were held now,
foes of change could mount a successful fear campaign, electing regional
officials who would block economic reform. The fears seemed to be supported by election results in Poland, which seemed to show a strong
backlash against economic "shock therapy."

Initial reactions from the Congress suggested that Mr. Yeltsin's proposals would be adopted. Even his political adversaries seemed to welcome his proposal to assume personal leadership of the government,
apparently because nobody else in the republic has the stature to weather
the dislocation and discontent of the shock therapy that he proposed.

The Russian leader invited other republics to enact similar reforms, but
he declared that Russia would not tolerate any further foot-dragging and
was prepared to go it alone.

Referring directly and indirectly to the Ukraine, which has decided to
form its own army and to introduce its own currency, Mr. Yeltsin said
Russia preferred to create one central bank for the entire ruble zone and
to maintain a single military. But he said that if necessary, Russia would
form its own central bank and its own army.

*The issues defining the life and fate of what had until recently been the
Soviet superpower were increasingly economic in nature. The sense of
economic collapse was looming ever more seriously. The group of seven
most industrialized nations pledged assistance to stabilize the reeling*

union. As the month opened the Russian parliament overwhelmingly approved Yeltsin's emergency blueprint to free consumer prices in what was envisioned as a painful transition leading to economic recovery. Four days later, Gorbachev warned that the dissolving nation was facing a serious shortfall in this year's grain harvest and stood at the edge of an "abyss." At the same time Gorbachev reported that the Ukraine had decided despite misgivings to join the economic union he had proposed to take the place of the old centrally run system.

Yeltsin's Decrees Seek Full Charge of Russian Assets
By Celestine Bohlen

MOSCOW, NOV. 17—With a burst of new decrees issued over the weekend, Boris N. Yeltsin has moved to assert the Russian republic's dominance over the foundering Soviet economy, proclaiming control over Russia's dwindling reserves of oil, gold, and other precious metals and opening its doors to foreign trade.

The package of new measures, officially announced early today, would lift most controls over imports, exports, and foreign-currency transactions on Russian territory and allow the value of the ruble—now fixed by the Soviet central bank though widely traded on the black market—to float according to market rates, starting January 1.

The floating of the ruble would sharply reduce its value, but would greatly improve the climate for foreign investment by allowing investors to take their profits in cash instead of having to resort to cumbersome barter arrangements.

With his latest flurry of decrees, Mr. Yeltsin appears to be undercutting a union economic agreement signed early this month by President Mikhail S. Gorbachev and the leaders of nine of the 12 remaining Soviet republics.

The agreement recognized individual republics' sovereignty over their own economic output, but it provided for a single currency administered by a Soviet central bank.

Efforts to coordinate policy continue to be hampered by unilateral decisions, as each of the republics stakes out turf and takes measures to assure its own survival. Since the failed coup attempt against Mr. Gorbachev in August, Mr. Yeltsin has steadily sought to expand the power of his giant republic, filling the vacuum created by the disintegration of Soviet state authority and the erosion of Mr. Gorbachev's influence.

With his decrees—issued in the name of the Russian republic's government, which under his current special powers is effectively under his personal control—Mr. Yeltsin again showed his determination to drive the pace of economic reform not only in Russia but also beyond its borders.

But the Russian leader's ability to dictate change has come under question in recent weeks, as his decrees, like those of Mr. Gorbachev, are swallowed up in the growing economic and political confusion.

Last week, for instance, his parliament overruled his effort to impose emergency rule in a troubled Muslim region, Chechen-Ingushetia, forcing him back to the negotiating table with Chechen separatists.

The new package of decrees and government resolutions made no mention of Mr. Yeltsin's proposal last month to lift controls on consumer prices. This sharply increased the cost of most goods, from food to computers, as Russians rushed to protect themselves from expected hyperinflation.

The Russian president, however, seemed to anticipate the social strains of his economic policy. Among other steps, he raised minimum salaries to 200 rubles a month—the average salary is 350 rubles a month—and pay for certain state employees 90 percent.

Russia's announcement that it would liberalize the rules governing foreign trade came just after Ivan S. Silayev, head of the interim Soviet economic council, moved to lift a number of restrictions on foreign trade across the Soviet Union.

But Mr. Yeltsin's measures, which would allow all registered Russian companies to engage in foreign trade and Russian citizens to hold hard-currency bank accounts, go further.

Russia controls 90 percent of Soviet oil production. Officials of the republic, worried about meeting the needs of their people as winter approaches, are now calling for a review of all existing oil-export licenses, and have frozen the granting of any new ones until December 1.

The measure would impose quotas on all exports beyond Russian borders. The production of oil, one of the links that still binds the economies of the republics, has been steadily falling. The resolution calls for strict controls over illegal bartering of oil for other products, arrangements that have become commonplace as oil-producing regions in Russia search for contracts to supply their people with desperately needed goods.

According to the newspaper *Kommersant,* Russian authorities are also concerned about mounting prices paid for Russian oil on the Moscow Oil Exchange. This is seen as an attempt by other republics, in particular the former Baltic republics and the Ukraine, to unload unwanted rubles before issuing their own currencies.

Mr. Yeltsin this weekend also carried out a long-threatened move to wrest control over gold, diamonds, and other precious metals mined in Russia from the Soviet authorities. He declared that the production, processing, sale, and storage of these metals would fall under Russian jurisdiction, with local producers to be paid 25 percent of their value in hard currency.

The status of Soviet gold—of which 67 percent comes from Russia—has become a hot political topic in recent days, after reports that the country's supplies have been steadily depleted by Soviet officials in their anxious search for foreign currency reserves. Grigory A. Yavlinsky, an economic adviser to Mr. Gorbachev, recently announced that Soviet gold reserves had shrunk to 240 tons, from 2,050 tons in 1953.

In a newspaper interview Friday, Aleksandr Orlov, who heads an audit commission of the Soviet parliament, asserted that there were no gold reserves left in the Soviet central bank.

"Our specialists have analyzed the gold situation," Mr. Orlov said, "and come to the conclusion that the Soviet state bank is bankrupt."

The newspaper *Izvestia,* following the trail of Soviet gold, last week presented documentary evidence that five tons of "hard-currency freight"—gold and platinum—had been taken out of the country in the last six weeks.

There was no clear answer available on the gold question, with various officials contradicting each other and Soviet credibility facing increasing doubt in world markets. A loss of gold reserves would reinforce doubts about Moscow's ability to service its $68 billion foreign debt.

As Gorbachev's plans were dissolving he brought back Eduard A. Shevardnadze to head a Foreign Ministry, whose duties and responsibilities were as vague and undetermined as the confines of the central state that Gorbachev was seeking to salvage. That effort was dealt a serious blow when on November 27, the Bush administration tilted away from its earlier support of the Soviet government deciding to recognize an independent Ukraine "expeditiously" if the citizens of the republic voted for separation in a scheduled referendum. Hurt by the White House decision, Gorbachev condemned it as an unwarranted interference in the internal affairs of the Soviet Union. Within hours, Gorbachev was to suffer another serious blow.

Russia Blocks Gorbachev on More Deficit Financing; Spending by Soviets Halted
By Celestine Bohlen

MOSCOW, NOV. 29—The Soviet Union, virtually out of money, was forced to stop payments from its central bank accounts today after the Russian republic, led by President Boris N. Yeltsin, struck another crippling blow to the central government of President Mikhail S. Gorbachev by refusing to authorize another round of deficit spending.

Coming two days after President Bush disclosed that the United States was prepared to quickly recognize the Ukraine's independence, the decision by Mr. Yeltsin not to bail out Mr. Gorbachev's foundering government dramatized the difficulty that Mr. Gorbachev has in getting support for the union even from those inclined in the past to support it.

And in another sign of the crumbling center, Mr. Yeltsin's Russian government announced it was taking over temporary control of the Soviet Foreign Ministry Building and embassies abroad because the Soviet government did not have the money to keep them going.

The fiscal crisis reached a breaking point over an emergency appropriation, sought by Mr. Gorbachev, that would have authorized a 92-billion-ruble deficit to carry the Soviet government through to the end of the year.

Without permission to print more money, the Soviet State Bank is running out of cash to pay salaries and bills, and meet other financial commitments, the bank's chairman said tonight on the main Soviet television news program. As of Thursday, the bank's reserves were down to three billion rubles and today payments had to be halted on central government accounts, said the bank chairman, Viktor Gerashchenko.

Mr. Gerashchenko, whose bank has been chosen for a takeover by the Russian government, blamed the "sad situation" on political maneuvering by a few Russian delegates, and urged the parliament—now adjourned until Tuesday—to meet Monday and authorize the money. Mr. Yeltsin directs the Russian delegation.

Although the upper chamber of the revamped Supreme Soviet, the nation's parliament, approved the budget authorization on Thursday, the lower chamber was unable to muster a quorum, leaving the issue in a state of parliamentary confusion.

"For some reason, several deputies—mainly those representing the Russian federation—took a position of political maneuvering and twisting and indecision," said Mr. Gerashchenko. "In this connection, the debate on the issue was intentionally broken off. What we have is the torpedoing of important decisions."

But the Russian government is adamantly refusing to set off inflation with more freshly minted rubles at a time when prices are already spinning out of control. The Russian government, by far the wealthiest of the republics, has cut off financing to about 80 central government ministries and has taken control of the money supply and the Soviet Union's most important commodities, including oil, gold, and diamonds.

In the meantime, the Russian government moved elsewhere to take advantage of the Soviet government's growing weakness. The Russian federation today claimed temporary control over the Foreign Ministry and all Soviet embassies abroad, arguing that without funds, the central government was not equipped to handle the responsibility.

"The step has been taken to prevent the failure and disintegration of our foreign service, or to be more precise, of its infrastructure," a Russian Foreign Ministry spokesman, Mikhail Kamynin, told the Associated Press.

Those showdowns illustrated Mr. Yeltsin's power, which looms larger as Mr. Gorbachev's authority continues to shrink. But while opposed on some issues—like the emergency budget—the two men remained linked in their efforts to prevent the country from a slow slide to ruin.

Earlier this week, the republics refused to initial a proposed union treaty as Mr. Gorbachev had hoped, and this weekend, the Ukraine, the second most powerful republic after Russia, is expected to cast its vote for independence, casting a shadow over Mr. Gorbachev's efforts to rescue the union and Mr. Yeltsin's efforts to protect Russia from the pending collapse.

Mr. Yeltsin, whose republic controls most of the Soviet Union's resources and holds a commanding position here in the capital, has not been reluctant to use his advantages. A commentator on *Vesti,* the Russian television news, today seemed to echo the Russian government's thinking when he said, "If the Soviet government cannot pay, then it would be logical to hand over its property to those who can."

"If the Russian parliament declares a war on the union parliament, it won't be a long one," wrote a correspondent in this evening's *Izvestia* newspaper, making the point that without the Russians, the Soviet parliament—which seats representatives from only seven of 12 remaining republics—would simply cease to function.

According to *Vesti,* 80 percent, or 72 billion, of the requested 92-billion-ruble deficit would be financed by the Russian republic, which, said the commentator tonight, means "you and I will have to pay this money to the central government."

The commentator said that although a budget freeze will pose a hardship for millions of state employees, Russia, already flooded by unwanted rubles dumped by other republics, cannot afford more inflation just as its program of radical economic change is about to go into effect.

Starting on Monday, rubles will no longer be exchanged for dollars and other hard currencies at tourist rates fixed by the State Bank. Instead, the value of the ruble will hover closer to current black-market rates. Now, at official tourist ruble rate, one dollar is worth 47 rubles, whereas street vendors are offering 80 rubles to the dollar.

Mr. Yeltsin's reform program, which also envisages price liberalization at an unspecified date, has set as its first goal restoring the stability of the ruble, which has become increasingly worthless as inflation rises daily.

In an interview published today in the newspaper *Izvestia,* Mr. Yeltsin sounded a note of alarm.

"I am greatly concerned over uncontrolled intervention of money into Russia," he said. "Tens of billions of rubles are flowing in the republic."

The Russian president said he would press the State Council, of which Mr. Gorbachev is chairman, to consider transfering the Soviet State Bank to Russian control "because under the current situation we need some kind of protection."

One of Russia's greatest fears is that the Ukraine is moving inexorably toward setting up its own currency.

"Russia might introduce its own currency only as a response to the same step taken by the big republics—the Ukraine, for example, which would deal a serious blow to the Russian finance system," he said.

He also said Russia would not sign a political union treaty unless it is joined by the Ukraine.

"The situation for Russia will change radically and, as a response measure, we would have to introduce our own currency, do something about the army," he said.

December marked more than just the end of a year. It saw the end of the Soviet state; the bankruptcy, dismemberment, and extinction of a superpower. Just as there were few if any experts who six months earlier had foreseen so rapid an end, there were now few if any who imagined how a single united Soviet state could linger past winter. Like the daily inscriptions on the charts of a mortally ill patient, the daily headlines graphed the final days of what had been one of the most powerful states and empires in history.

Yeltsin to Finance Soviet Payroll to Avert Bankruptcy
By Serge Schmemann

MOSCOW, NOV. 30—Faced with the imminent bankruptcy of the Soviet government, President Boris N. Yeltsin of the Russian republic agreed today to finance the Soviet payroll for the immediate future and to guarantee sufficient credits to meet the minimal needs of the Kremlin.

The eleventh-hour agreement was reached at a meeting of Mr. Yeltsin and his top economic advisers with the Soviet president, Mikhail S. Gorbachev, and the head of the Soviet State Bank.

Today's agreement marked a recognition by Mr. Yeltsin that however keen his desire to halt the growing and threatening flood of rubles, it was simply not possible to choke off an all-union government that still formally sustains a large portion of the national economy, ranging from the military to the scientific and academic establishments.

At the same time, Mr. Yeltsin's action underscores that real control over Mr. Gorbachev and his government has efectively shifted to the

Russian government, which has signaled its intention to barrel ahead with radical economic change with or without the rest of the former union.

Ex-Communist Wins in Ukraine; Yeltsin Recognizes Independence
By Francis X. Clines

KIEV, UKRAINE, DEC. 2—Leonid M. Kravchuk was pronounced the winner today in Ukraine's first presidential election, and his republic's popularly endorsed independence received swift recognition from the neighboring Russian republic.

"Ukraine has been born," proclaimed Mr. Kravchuk, a 57-year-old Communist Party official who converted to nationalist politics as the party collapsed this summer. "It is a great historic moment."

Following quickly on the confirmation of his victory, Mr. Kravchuk moved to reassure foreign countries anxious about the status of the Soviet nuclear missiles still based on Ukrainian soil. He proposed that the four Soviet republics with strategic nuclear weapons form a "collective management" to control and eventually destroy them.

Mr. Kravchuk made no mention of a role for the Soviet government in such a system, demonstrating determination to achieve the full independence that almost 90 percent of Ukrainians approved in a referendum Sunday.

Rapid recognition of that independence was assured when the evening news on Russian television reported that Boris N. Yeltsin, the Russian republic's president, was recognizing the new state. Poland, Ukraine's neighbor to the west, also declared its readiness to recognize it, and Canada, with a large Ukrainian population, indicated that it would soon follow suit.

Russia's recognition assured that other republics would quickly follow suit, seeming to dash whatever hope the Soviet president, Mikhail S. Gorbachev, still nurtured of shaping some form of new union any time soon.

"The Russian president declared his recognition of Ukraine's independence in connection with the democratic expression of the will of its people," the late-evening news program *Vesti* announced. "Boris Yeltsin expressed his conviction on the possibility and the need to quickly establish new interstate relations between Russia and Ukraine, to include diplomatic relations."

Mr. Gorbachev, for his part, continued to express hope that Ukraine would still join in a union. The President's spokesman said Mr. Gorbachev telephoned Mr. Kravchuk to congratulate him on winning his five-year term, and declared that Ukraine's independence gave it "additional freedom of action and choice concerning its participation in the new union of sovereign states."

Results of the presidential election, which was held simultaneously with the referendum on independence, showed Mr. Kravchuk first in a field of six that included some of the republic's most popular nationalists. He won 55 to 60 percent of the vote, initial figures released today indicated.

Declaring Death of Soviet Union, Russia and 2 Republics Form New Commonwealth
By Serge Schmemann

MOSCOW, DEC. 8—The leaders of Russia, Ukraine, and Byelorussia declared today that the Soviet Union had ceased to exist and proclaimed a new "Commonwealth of Independent States" open to all members of the former union.

In a series of statements issued after a two-day meeting at a Byelorussian government retreat, the leaders of the three Slavic republics declared void all efforts to create a new union on the ruins of the old one. But they called for the creation of new "coordinating bodies" for defense, foreign affairs, and the economy that would have their seat in Minsk, the capital of Byelorussia, and decided to maintain the ruble as the common currency.

They declared that the "norms" and activities of the former union ceased as of the moment of signing, and that the new commonwealth assumed all international obligations of the Soviet Union, as well as control over its nuclear arsenal.

"The U.S.S.R., as a subject of international law and geopolitical reality, is ceasing its existence," the leaders declared.

The action essentially stripped President Mikhail S. Gorbachev of his office and authority, and the immediate question was whether the tough and tenacious Soviet leader would resist—and if he did, whether the military or other levers of power would support him.

The three cofounders of the new commonwealth—President Boris N. Yeltsin of Russia, President Leonid M. Kravchuk of Ukraine, and Stanislav Shushkevich, chairman of the Byelorussian parliament—were scheduled to meet on Monday with Mr. Gorbachev and with Nursultan A. Nazarbayev, the President of Kazakhstan and the unofficial spokesman for the Muslim republics of Central Asia.

Mr. Gorbachev had no immediate reaction. But in a taped interview with French television broadcast today, he argued fervently that the consequences of dismantling the union would make the war in Yugoslavia "a simple joke by comparison."

The Central Asian republics had all indicated an interest in retaining some form of union, and it was not immediately clear why Mr. Nazarbayev was excluded from the Byelorussian declaration, or how he would respond. Arriving in Moscow today, he declared that he was still in favor of preserving an association, and at least in maintaining joint control over the nuclear arsenal.

The predominantly Slavic republics declared that they drew their authority to dissolve the union from the fact that they were its original cofounders. They and the Trans-Caucasus republic, later divided into Georgia, Armenia, and Azerbaijan, were cosigners of the original 1922 treaty that created the Union of Soviet Socialist Republics.

The "sphere of joint activity" assigned to the new commonwealth, however, resembled the functions that Mr. Gorbachev had sought for his new "union of sovereign states": responsibility for foreign policy, development of a "common economic space," "customs policies," transportation and communication systems, the environment, and the battle against organized crime.

One major difference was that the three core Slavic republics, which together account for 73 percent of the population and 80 percent of the territory of the Soviet Union, were now inviting other republics to join, not to negotiate, a new association.

It was a stance certain to irritate the Muslim and Caucasian republics, but also one that stood to curtail the endless bickering that characterized interrepublican negotiations since the coup.

Another major difference was that the move to Minsk and the formal disbanding of the old union cleared the slate of old structures and bureaucracies, freeing the participating republics of the need to haggle with Mr. Gorbachev and the old ministries over the new order they meant to shape.

But the approach had its own dangers. If Mr. Gorbachev was one potential source of resistance, others included the potent military-industrial complex and the trade unions, which could feel threatened by new masters dedicated to reducing the budget.

Resistance could also come from national parliaments and nationalist movements, especially in Ukraine, which could see in the agreement a trick to revive the old union under a new sauce.

Yet the commonwealth appeared to be the most practical compromise. It disassociated itself from Moscow, it created a core of the most important republics, and it blocked the disintegration that threatened to destroy critical intrarepublican economic ties.

The agreements called for coordinated economic reforms, echoing fears in Ukraine and Byelorussia that the impending reforms in Russia would create havoc with their prices. They declared the ruble to be the currency of common commerce, and they called for mutual agreement before any new currency was introduced, responding to Russia's fear that a separate currency in Ukraine would flood Russia with excess rubles.

And they declared the Chernobyl disaster site a common responsibility, touching on the fears of all three republics that the damaged nuclear power plant would be left untended.

The leaders pledged that existing borders would remain open and unchanged, and they vowed to respect each other's sovereignty and "observe international norms of human and national rights."

On an issue that has raised considerable anxiety abroad, the leaders said they had decided "to preserve the joint command over the common military-strategic space and the single nuclear arms controlling body." There was no immediate indication, however, how the control would be shared.

Outlining the responsibilities of the central authority they proposed to form in Minsk, the agreement said: "The parties regard the following as the sphere of joint activity: the coordination of external political activity, the formation and the development of the common economic space, the European and Eurasian markets, the customs and migratory policy, the development of the transportation and communication systems, protection of the environment and ecological security, and the struggle against organized crime."

In a statement announcing the creation of the commonwealth, the leaders said that talks on forming a new union treaty had reached an impasse, while the withdrawal of republics from the Soviet Union had become a "fact of reality." The statement placed the full blame for the economic and political crisis at Mr. Gorbachev's feet, pointing out "the center's shortsighted policy."

The three leaders said the new commonwealth would be open to all members of the Soviet Union, "as well as other states sharing the aims and principles of this agreement."

A separate statement on joint economic policy declared that "preservation and development of close economic ties that have taken shape between our states is vitally important in order to stabilize the situation in the national economy and create preconditions for economic revival."

The key provision called on the three republics to coordinate their economic reforms, indicating that Ukraine and Byelorussia would follow Russia's lead in releasing prices and the ruble rate. The agreement, however, raised doubts that Mr. Yeltsin could follow his announced timetable, which called for prices to be freed on December 16.

Gorbachev Rejects Move to Discard Kremlin Role; U.S. Keeps Link to Moscow

By Serge Schmemann

MOSCOW, DEC. 9—President Mikhail S. Gorbachev today rejected the right of the leaders of Russia, Ukraine, and Byelorussia to dissolve the Soviet Union, adding to the uncertainty over the fate of the Soviet lands.

"The fate of our multinational country cannot be decided by the will of three republican leaders," Mr. Gorbachev said in a statement read on the evening television news. "This question can be resolved only through constitutional means with the participation of all sovereign states and taking into account the will of their peoples."

He said the proclamation of a new "commonwealth of independent states" by the three Slavic republics should be treated as only a proposal, to be discussed alongside his proposed new "union of sovereign states" by republic parliaments and a full Congress of People's Deputies.

Under the Soviet system, ultimate power lies in the Congress, which in practice delegates its responsibilities to the Supreme Soviet, or legislature, of the Soviet Union. But since the failed coup attempt last August, the central Soviet government has disintegrated and increasing power has fallen to the various republics and their leaders.

There is no obvious body such as the United States Supreme Court to decide differences between the central government and republics, and therefore any decision may have to be worked out politically rather than judicially.

Demonstrating that he did not intend to vanish quietly from the political stage with his vestigial union, Mr. Gorbachev declared that the Slavic leaders' annulment of Union laws was "illegal and dangerous," and the speed with which they proclaimed the new commonwealth "baffling."

Gorbachev Vying for Army Backing over Yeltsin's Bid

By Celestine Bohlen

MOSCOW, DEC. 10—As President Mikhail S. Gorbachev's waning authority headed for a critical and perhaps final test in the Russian parliament on Thursday, he and President Boris N. Yeltsin of Russia appeared today to be vying for the support of the Soviet military, ultimately the key to any power struggle.

As they did, the parliaments of Ukraine and Byelorussia today firmly rebuffed Mr. Gorbachev's efforts to keep the Soviet Union alive by ratifying the treaty that their leaders signed with Mr. Yeltsin on Sunday to create a commonwealth of former Soviet republics.

Stressing Mr. Gorbachev's title as commander in chief of the armed forces, the press agency Tass tonight reported that the Soviet president met this afternoon with military officials at the Defense Ministry, while the Russian press agency said Mr. Yeltsin would be meeting Wednesday morning with regional commanders.

5 Asian Republics Join Slavs in Plan for Commonwealth Replacing the Soviet Union
By Francis X. Clines

MOSCOW, DEC. 13—The five central Asian republics agreed to join the new Commonwealth of Independent States today, conclusively rebuffing President Mikhail S. Gorbachev's protestations and all but sealing the end of the Soviet Union.

The decision, reached in a meeting in the Turkmenian capital of Ashkhabad, 1,500 miles southeast of Moscow, means that eight of the 12 Soviet republics are now in accord on the commonwealth plan, and the four others have expressed interest in joining.

The agreement considerably dampens the threat of political divisiveness between the old Soviet Union's western Slavic majority and eastern Islamic minority. It also groups together the four Soviet republics with nuclear capability under weapons-control treaties. One of those republics, Kazakhstan, is joining the commonwealth's three cofounders, Russia, Ukraine, and Byelorussia.

In addition to Kazakhstan, the second-largest republic in area, the others that agreed to join the commonwealth today were Kirghizia, Tadzhikistan, Turkmenia, and Uzbekistan. The five republics embrace about 18 percent of the land that remained in the Soviet Union after the Baltic states became independent. The five republics' combined population of about 50 million is equivalent to 18 percent of the people in the country, including most of the non-Slavs.

President Gorbachev had warned that interrepublic conflict would be a likely result of abandoning the union in favor of a commonwealth of fully sovereign republics.

But the President of Kazakhstan, Nursultan A. Nazarbayev, in announcing the Asian republics' accord, made a point of rejecting Mr. Gorbachev's views as having "nothing to do with the real state of affairs."

Mr. Gorbachev, who had drawn early support from Mr. Nazarbayev in his fight against the commonwealth, thus appeared totally isolated and was pronounced out of touch by his fellow politicians as they prepared for a highly uncertain but rapidly evolving future without the union.

The Asian republics' action further teased the question of when President Gorbachev might resign his post at the shrinking Kremlin power center. He said Thursday that this was a step he would be obliged to take if the republics rejected his invitation to revive the union.

Yeltsin Sweeps Up Crucial Remnants of Withering Union
By Serge Schmemann

MOSCOW, DEC. 19—President Boris N. Yeltsin of Russia set about swallowing up the remnants of the Soviet state today, taking control of the Foreign Ministry, the K.G.B., the parliament, and even Mikhail S. Gorbachev's presidential office, down to his dollars and his phones.

Neither Mr. Gorbachev nor Foreign Minister Eduard A. Shevardnadze, who has served only a month since his return to the union government, had any immediate comment on the moves. Officials at the Foreign Ministry said they had received no advance notice, and it was unclear whether Mr. Gorbachev had.

It is unlikely, in any case, that anyone will try to evict Mr. Gorbachev before he is ready to leave on his own. Officials in the Foreign Ministry acknowledged that the move in itself was not a surprise, since Mr. Yeltsin had already given notice to Mr. Gorbachev that he intended to shut down the union government by the end of the year.

But it was hard to resist the impression that in transferring to himself all of the President's apparatus—the Kremlin, the staff, communications, and all other property and resources, "including those in foreign currency"—Mr. Yeltsin was adding indignity to the drama of Mr. Gorbachev's imminent exit.

The signs from the Kremlin were increasingly that Mr. Gorbachev would resign after the summit meeting of republic leaders in Alma-Ata, Kazakhstan, this weekend. There, the five Asian republics and maybe two others are expected to formally join Russia, Ukraine, and Byelorussia in the commonwealth the Slavic republics proclaimed on December 8.

The Asian republics, Kazakhstan, Kirghizia, Turkmenia, Tadzhikistan, and Uzbekistan, decided to take part in the commonwealth last Friday.

Mr. Gorbachev said in an interview with *Komsomolskaya Pravda* that he would decide his fate after the Alma-Ata conference.

Excluded from the meeting, Mr. Gorbachev still seemed to consider it his duty to instruct the republic presidents on the need for unity. In a letter addressed to the meeting, which was published in *Izvestia* and described by Mr. Gorbachev over television, the President declared that it was still his "moral and political right" to let the new leaders know his views.

He proposed that the best name for the new league would be Commonwealth of European and Asian States—a name originally proposed two years ago by Andrei D. Sakharov, and at that time universally dismissed. Mr. Gorbachev also urged the republics to maintain, at least for a while, a single citizenship, to preserve their economic agreements, and to retain a unified military and foreign policy.

Asked if his post would be liquidated, Mr. Gorbachev replied, "We are beginning a new life, and let it be so."

11 Soviet States Form Commonwealth Without Clearly Defining Its Powers
By Francis X. Clines

ALMA-ATA, KAZAKHSTAN, DEC. 21—Eleven former republics of the Soviet Union formally constituted themselves today as the Commonwealth of Independent States, dedicated to reversing their slide toward economic and political chaos.

Putting aside seven decades of central dictatorship, the republic leaders meeting in the Kazakh capital, near the Chinese border, negotiated and signed a broad commonwealth agreement that guarantees their separate sovereignties but leaves unsettled such important issues as how to create an acceptable system of command to administer common military policy and nuclear weapons control.

The top governmental body will be a council of heads of state and government, assisted by committees of republic ministers in key areas like foreign affairs, defense, and economics.

Full operations are promised to begin no later than January 15, after ratification by the 11 republics' parliaments. The Baltic states, which regained independence in September, are not participating, nor is Georgia, which instead sent an observer to the talks.

To emphasize their resolve to move beyond the Kremlin, the commonwealth leaders preemptively accepted the resignation of Soviet President Mikhail S. Gorbachev, even though it has not yet been submitted.

Their evident urgency to see him leave was reflected in their decision to promise, "with respect," a generous pension once he is in retirement.

"We respect Gorbachev and want him to go gently into retirement in December, as he himself wants," said President Boris N. Yeltsin of the Russian federated republic, who is head of the biggest and most powerful of the new commonwealth's constituent parts and who has been Mr. Gorbachev's chief reform antagonist through the last four turbulent years.

"We do not want to carry on the tradition since 1917 of burying our heads of state and having to rebury them later or having to pronounce them criminal," Mr. Yeltsin said. "A civilized state should end this practice."

There was no direct reaction from Mr. Gorbachev, who has suffered a breathtaking fall from power and grace since the failed coup in August. But in an interview with CBS News, he indicated that he would resign shortly after receiving official notification of the results of the Alma-Ata meeting.

"As soon as I receive official documents and see that the commonwealth is a reality, within a few days I will then take my decision," Mr. Gorbachev said. The Soviet leader said that for the meantime, he and the defense minister remained in control of the "nuclear button."

Mr. Gorbachev, who initially denounced the commonwealth as illegal and dangerous, today spoke of the new association as an accomplished fact. But he warned Americans that they too faced a difficult transition, saying: "I don't think the transformation will be easy and simple from one partner, the Soviet Union and its leadership. Now you have to deal with ten new politicians."

Today was the first full working session of the expanded commonwealth. It is designed to be the vehicle for the survivors of the fallen Soviet empire to head toward free-market prosperity and full democracy. It grew out of the founding body announced 13 days ago by Russia, Ukraine, and Byelorussia, the three Slavic republics, when they met in Byelorussia and pronounced that the Soviet Union had ceased to exist.

The meeting today went a considerable step beyond, for not only was the new association enlarged and sealed with pledges of peaceful collaboration, but also the heads of state began settling some differences.

In a joint declaration, the leaders set forth their intent to "build democratic states ruled by law and to develop relations between them on the basis of mutual recognition of inalienable right to self-determination, equality, noninterference in each other's internal affairs, renunciation of the use of force or threat to use force, or economic or other levers of pressure."

The agreement next must be submitted to the republics' parliaments for ratification. Once they certify this with authorities in Byelorussia, the commonwealth is under way.

The leaders also yielded to President Yeltsin's view that Russia should take over the Security Council seat in the United Nations held until now by the Soviet Union. The Russian foreign minister, Andrei Kozyrev, said later that this was critical for the general nuclear control strategy of eventually seeing Russia succeed the Soviet Union as the single guarantor of disarmament.

The broad-stroke agreements constituted an important political accord but left almost every difficult, concrete issue to be decided later, including such basic matters as the economy and government financing, the precise scope of the new coordinating agencies, borders, and citizenship.

The agreements signed today did not specifically mention a common currency or the ruble, but spoke of adherence in principle to the agreement from the Byelorussia meeting, which did call for a common currency. Today's agreements also noted that some republics had expressed reservations on the Byelorussia agreement.

The refining of the agreements was left to the uncertain hands of the republic parliaments.

In line with this, the four republics with long-range nuclear missiles on their soil—Russia, Byelorussia, Ukraine, and Kazakhstan—again insisted that they were in agreement on joint weapons safeguards, and they issued a statement to this effect. This issue is a central one being pressed by the Bush administration and other governments as one of the prices for early recognition of commonwealth members.

"This document will answer all the questions being asked by other states," said Kazakhstan's President, Nursultan A. Nazarbayev. The Bush administration has various questions and uncertainties and wants to send nuclear disarmament specialists next month to see to some of the problems.

The document may not prove entirely reassuring, for Kazakhstan appears to be continuing to insist that it be treated on a par with Russia rather than joining Ukraine and Byelorussia in eventually ceding nuclear controls to Russia.

And republic leaders could not agree immediately on the related issue of a new military command. This focuses on the precise design of a permanent defense council that is to administer commonwealth military policy.

Such important commonwealth members as Ukraine are especially insistent that the new defense council offer no opportunity to revive central totalitarianism, nor conflict with republic plans to form separate armies.

The commonwealth members put off the military command issue, scheduling it as the topic of a meeting December 30 in Minsk, the Byelorussian capital, which is to be the commonwealth headquarters. As a temporary measure, the republic carried over until the end of the year the central remnant of the union's Defense Ministry, led by Gen. Yevgeny I. Shaposhnikov.

The commonwealth agreement was signed in the heart of this snow-decked mountainside city north of the Chinese border. The ceremony was held at the House of Friendship, a bulky exercise in socialist overdesign, where legions of republic leaders, ministers, and patronage retinues showed up for the new post-Communist round table, smiling and squinting in the TV lamplight of world attention.

The commonwealth members held a news conference this evening, seated by small freshly minted flags of their sovereign republics under a huge bronze-toned medallion that still bore the hammer and sickle of Communism.

On the issue of approval by the republics' parliaments, various sorts of political flurries are expected. The Ukraine parliament, which is wary and nationalistic about the commonwealth, has underlined its right to withdraw. Ukraine's lawmakers, passing the earlier commonwealth agreement after the Byelorussia meeting this month, made some adjustments in the agreement before approving it.

Gorbachev, Last Soviet Leader, Resigns; U.S. Recognizes Republics' Independence
By Francis X. Clines

MOSCOW, DEC. 25—Mikhail S. Gorbachev, the trailblazer of the Soviet Union's retreat from the cold war and the spark for the democratic reforms that ended 70 years of Communist tyranny, told a weary, anxious nation tonight that he was resigning as President and closing out the union.

"I hereby discontinue my activities at the post of President of the Union of Soviet Socialist Republics," declared the 60-year-old politician, the last leader of a totalitarian empire that was undone across the six years and nine months of his stewardship.

Mr. Gorbachev made no attempt in his brief, leanly worded television address to mask his bitter regret and concern at being forced from office by the creation of the new Commonwealth of Independent States, composed of 11 former republics of the collapsed Soviet empire under the informal lead of President Boris N. Yeltsin of Russia.

Within hours of Mr. Gorbachev's resignation, Western and other nations began recognition of Russia and the other former republics.

"We're now living in a new world," Mr. Gorbachev declared in recognizing the rich history of his tenure. "An end has been put to the cold war and to the arms race, as well as to the mad militarization of the country, which has crippled our economy, public attitudes, and morals. The threat of nuclear war has been removed."

Mr. Gorbachev's moment of farewell was stark. Kremlin guards were preparing to lower the red union flag for the last time. In minutes, Mr.

Gorbachev would sign over the nuclear missile launching codes for safe-guarding to Mr. Yeltsin, his rival and successor as the dominant politician of this agonized land.

Earlier today, Mr. Yeltsin told his Russian parliament that "there will be only a single nuclear button, and other presidents will not possess it."

But he said that to "push it" requires the approval of himself and the leaders of Ukraine, Byelorussia, and Kazakhstan, the four former republics that have strategic nuclear weapons on their soil.

"Of course, we think this button must never be used," Mr. Yeltsin said.

Out in the night beyond the walled fortress as Mr. Gorbachev spoke, a disjointed people, freed from their decades of dictated misery, faced a frightening new course of shedding collectivism for the promises of individual enterprise. It is a course that remains a mystery for most of the commonwealth's 280 million people.

"I am very much concerned as I am leaving this post," the union President told the people. "However, I also have feelings of hope and faith in you, your wisdom and force of spirit. We are the heirs of a great civilization, and it now depends on all and everyone whether or not this civilization will make a comeback to a new and decent living."

In departing, the Soviet leader took comfort in the world's supporting his singular achievements in nuclear disarmament. But even more, he firmly warned his people that they had not yet learned to use their newly won freedom and that it could be put at risk by the commonwealth, which he fought to the last.

"I am concerned about the fact that the people in this country are ceasing to become citizens of a great power and the consequences may be very difficult for all of us to deal with," he declared, implicitly arguing that his union could have remained a superpower despite the cold war's end, which he helped engineer.

"We have paid with all our history and tragic experience for these democratic achievements," Mr. Gorbachev said, assessing centuries of suffering across serfdom and revolution, "and they are not to be abandoned whatever the circumstances, and whatever the pretext. Otherwise, all our hopes for the best will be buried."

Mr. Gorbachev's stringent gaze and strong caution to the now dismembered nation were in contrast to the smiling ease displayed during this transition day by President Yeltsin, chief heir to this land's political and economic chaos.

"The people here are weary of pessimism, and the share of pessimism is too much for the people to handle," Mr. Yeltsin declared in an interview with CNN. "Now they need some belief, finally."

Mr. Yeltsin made a point in the interview of sending Christmas wishes to his listeners today as the West celebrated the holiday, although the Russian Orthodox Christmas is not until January 7. Mr. Yeltsin also took care in addressing the outside world to stress that commonwealth leaders had agreed to fulfill the disarmament commitments made by Mr. Gorbachev.

"I don't want the international community to be worried about it," President Yeltsin said, vowing that there would "not be a single second after Gorbachev makes his resignation" that the missile codes would go astray.

The weapons are only one item in a long list of needed precautions that the commonwealth republics must attend to if they are to establish credibility in a decidedly skeptical world that has watched the Soviet Union reverse its totalitarian course and collapse in a matter of a few years.

Mr. Yeltsin is first among equals in the 11-member commonwealth. This is a very loose political association resorted to by the former Soviet republics because of their disenchantment with the very notion of union and their need, nonetheless, for some common arrangement that might ease the escape from post-Communist destitution.

The commonwealth members are free to decide their individual economic and political plans. But they are pledged to a common military command for joint defense needs and to certain economic denominators as well, including the hope of a resuscitated ruble as their common currency.

Russia has already taken the lead in economics as well as defense, with the giant republic of 149 million people bracing for Mr. Yeltsin's first steps toward free-market reform next week. Sweeping price rises are to be legalized on January 2 as an end comes to much of the consumer-goods subsidies that Communism maintained to make its regime minimally palatable.

Mr. Yeltsin made a point in his CNN interview of expressing some displeasure at the limited amount of aid that has been extended by the outside world.

"There has been a lot of talk, but there has been no specific assistance," he said, offering a small smile. He quickly offered an explanation that with the union collapsing for the last year, willing nations probably found no clear address to which to donate.

"Now everything is clear, and the addressees are known," he said, beaming as if in invitation. "And I think that this humanitarian aid will step up now."

He offered the same hint of mischief in dealing with the fact that Secretary of State James A. Baker 3d waited until he headed home from an initial visit before talking quite pessimistically of the commonwealth's chances.

"Mr. Baker, when he and I had a four-and-a-half-hour meeting here in Moscow, Mr. Baker never told me that," Mr. Yeltsin said. "So those who doubt as to the success of the commonwealth should beware and not be so pessimistic," he advised. "We are sick and tired of pessimism."

In leaving, Mr. Gorbachev had no kind words in the televised speech for the commonwealth and never mentioned Mr. Yeltsin.

He reviewed his own campaign to preserve a drastically revised union. It would have accepted the sovereignty the republics gained after the hard-line Communist coup failed in August. This led to the fall of the Communist Party and, tonight, of the union's most prominent defender, Mr. Gorbachev.

"The policy prevailed of dismembering this country and disuniting the state, which is something I cannot subscribe to," Mr. Gorbachev told the nation, his jaw set forward firmly in defeat as the presidential red union flag gleamed its last behind his right shoulder.

As Mr. Yeltsin deftly acquired the Moscow remnants of the Union's powers and real estate across the last few weeks, the huge red union flag atop the Kremlin's domed Council of Ministers building had waved mainly as a symbol of Mr. Gorbachev's holdout resistance to the commonwealth.

The flag was lowered from its floodlit perch at 7:32 tonight. A muted moment of awe was shared by the few pedestrians crossing Red Square.

"Why are you laughing at Lenin?" a man, obviously inebriated against the winter cold, suddenly shouted in the square. He reeled near Lenin's tomb.

The mausoleum was dusky pink against the evergreen trees outside the Kremlin walls. Within, for all the sense of history wheeling in the night sky, the embalmed remains of the Communist patriarch still rested.

The drunk was instantly shushed by a passerby who cautioned that "foreigners" were watching and he should not embarrass the reborn Russia.

"Foreigners?" laughed another Muscovite. "Who cares? They're the ones who are feeding us these days."

In the Gorbachev era there were countless moments of floodlit crisis and emergency solutions hurriedly concocted and rammed through in the Kremlin. Previously, Mr. Gorbachev prevailed and often proved brilliant in his improvising. Tonight, though, he was the executive focus for the last time and he seemed brisk and businesslike, a man containing himself against defeat.

In an interview with CNN later, when asked about his plans, he said he would not comment now on the "many proposals and offers" he had received. He said he would "have to recover a little bit, relax, take a rest."

"Today is a difficult day for Mikhail Gorbachev," President Yeltsin said a few hours before the Soviet President resigned, when the Russian leader was invited to describe Mr. Gorbachev's main mistakes along the difficult road of reform.

"Because I have a lot of respect for him personally and we are trying to be civilized people and we are trying to make it into a civilized state today, I don't want to focus on these mistakes," Mr. Yeltsin responded.

End of the Soviet Union; the Soviet State, Born of a Dream, Dies
By Serge Schmemann

MOSCOW, DEC. 25—The Soviet state, marked throughout its brief but tumultuous history by great achievement and terrible suffering, died today after a long and painful decline. It was 74 years old.

Conceived in utopian promise and born in the violent upheavals of the "Great October Revolution of 1917," the union heaved its last in the dreary darkness of late December 1991, stripped of ideology, dismembered, bankrupt, and hungry—but awe inspiring even in its fall.

The end of the Soviet Union came with the resignation of Mikhail S. Gorbachev to make way for a new "Commonwealth of Independent States." At 7:32 P.M., shortly after the conclusion of his televised address, the red flag with hammer and sickle was lowered over the Kremlin and the white-blue-and-red Russian flag rose in its stead.

There was no ceremony, only the tolling of chimes from the Spassky Gate, cheers from a handful of surprised foreigners, and an angry tirade from a lone war veteran.

Reactions to the death varied widely, according to *Pravda,* the former mouthpiece of the empire: "Some joyfully exclaim, *'La commedia è finita!'* Others, heaping ash on their heads, raise their hands to the sky in horror and ask, what will be?"

The reaction depended somewhat on whether one listened to the ominous gunfire from Georgia, or watched spellbound the bitter if dignified surrender of power by the last leader of the Union of Soviet Socialist Republics, Mr. Gorbachev.

Most people vacillated. The taboos and chains were gone, but so was the food. The Soviet Union had given them pitifully little, but there was no guarantee that the strange-sounding "Commonwealth of Independent States" would do any better.

As for Mr. Gorbachev, public opinion polls indicated a virtually universal agreement that it was time for him to move on—not because he had failed, but because there was nothing more he could do.

It was perhaps a paradox that the ruler who presided over the collapse of the Soviet Union was the only one of its ill-starred leaders to leave office with a measure of dignity intact. It was possible that history would reach a different verdict, but among many thoughtful Russians, it was to his undying credit that he lifted the chains of totalitarian dictatorship. Whether he could also have saved the economy was another question.

"Gorbachev was unable to change the living standards of the people, but he changed the people," *Komsomolskaya Pravda* wrote in a sympathetic farewell that seemed to capture the dominant mood. "He didn't know how to make sausage, but he did know how to give freedom. And if someone believes that the former is more important than the latter, he is likely never to have either."

Another man might have done things differently. But it was difficult to conceive that any of those then available—the conservative Yegor K. Ligachev, the rough-hewn Boris N. Yeltsin, the bureaucratic Nikolai I. Ryzhkov, or the scholarly Eduard A. Shevardnadze—possessed just that blend of reformer and ideologue, of naïveté and ruthlessness, that enabled Mr. Gorbachev to lead the Communists to the edge of the cliff.

"Gorbachev was a true instrument of fate," declared Viktor Yerofeyev, a writer and literary critic. "He had just enough intelligence to change everything, but not enough to see that everything would be destroyed. He was bold enough to challenge his party, and cautious enough to let the party live until it lost its power. He had enough faith in Communism to be named its head, but enough doubts about it to destroy it. If he had seen everything clearly, he would not have changed Russia."

Mr. Gorbachev struggled to the end, and beyond it, to keep the union alive. But in the end, it was by letting the union die and by stepping aside that he gave a new lease on life to the great Eurasian entity, whatever its name.

Measured against its own ambitions, the U.S.S.R. died a monumental failure.

It had promised no less than the creation of a "Soviet new man," imbued with selfless devotion to the common good, and it ended up all but crushing the initiative and spirit of the people, making many devoted only to vodka. It had proclaimed a new humanitarian ideology, and in its name butchered 10 million of its own. It envisioned a planned economy in which nothing was left to chance, and it created an elephantine bureaucracy that finally smothered the economy. Promising peace and freedom, it created the world's most militarized and ruthless police state.

Promising a people's culture, it created an anticulture in which mediocrity was glorified and talent was ruthlessly persecuted. An entire department of the K.G.B. existed to wrestle with art, trying first to co-opt any rising talent "to the service of the state" and if that failed, to muzzle or exile it. The roll call of repressed or exiled artists is a stunning indictment:

Mandelstam, Malevich, Pasternak, Solzhenitsyn, Rostropovich, Brodsky, and so many more.

In the end, promising a new life, it created an unspeakably bleak society—polluted, chronically short of everything, stripped of initiative and spirituality. While the bulk of the nation stood in line or guzzled rotgut vodka, the Communist elite raised corruption to new heights. The likes of Leonid I. Brezhnev and his cronies pinned endless medals on one another and surrounded themselves with a peasant's notion of luxury— grandiose candelabras, massive cars, vast hunting estates, armies of syco- phants, secret hospitals filled with the latest Western technology.

And yet the Soviet Union was also an indisputable superpower, a state and a people that achieved epic feats in science, warfare, even culture.

Perhaps all this was achieved despite Communism, not because of it. Yet by some combination of force and inspiration, the system begun by Lenin and carried out by Stalin unleashed a potent national energy that made possible the rapid industrialization of the 1930s, the defeat of Nazi Germany in the 1940s, the launching of the first Sputnik in the 1950s, the creation of a nuclear arsenal in the 1960s and 1970s. Even now, for all the chaos in the land, two astronauts, Aleksandr A. Volkov and Sergei Krika- lev, continue to circle the globe.

In culture, too, both the "thaw" of Nikita S. Khrushchev in the 1960s and the *glasnost* of Mr. Gorbachev offered testimony that the enormous creativity of the nation was as tenacious as the people.

And in sport, the tangle of Olympic medals and international victories were a tacit source of national pride even among the staunchest critics of the Communist regime.

It is easy now, gazing over the smoldering ruins of the Soviet empire, to enumerate the fatal illusions of the Marxist system. Yet the irresistible utopian dream fired generations of reformers, revolutionaries, and radi- cals here and abroad, helping spread Soviet influence to the far corners of the globe.

Until recently, rare was the third world leader who did not espouse some modified Marxist doctrine, who did not make a regular pilgrimage to Moscow to join in the ritual denunciations of the "imperialists."

Much of it was opportunism, of course. In the Soviet Union as in the third world, Communism offered a handy justification for stomping on democracy and keeping one party and one dictator in power.

Yet it was also a faith, one strong enough to survive all the injustices done in its name. Lev Kopelev, a prominent intellectual now living in Germany, recalled in his memoirs how prisoners emerged from the gulag after Stalin's death firmly believing that at last they could start redressing the "errors" of Stalinism and truly building Communism.

And only last March, Mr. Gorbachev would still declare in Minsk, "I am not ashamed to say that I am a Communist and adhere to the Communist idea, and with this I will leave for the other world."

The tenacity of the faith testified to the scope of the experiment. It was a monumental failure, but it had been a grand attempt, an experiment on a scale the world had never known before.

Perhaps it was the height of folly and presumption that Russia, a country then only at the dawn of industrialization and without a bourgeoisie or proletariat to speak of, would have been the one to proclaim itself the pioneer of a radically new world order.

But Russians have always had a weakness for the broad gesture. The greatest czars—Ivan the Terrible, Peter the Great—were those with the grandest schemes. The greatest writers, Dostoyevsky and Tolstoy, explored ultimate themes in immense novels. The Russian Orthodox Church embroidered its churches and its liturgy in the most elaborate gilding and ceremony.

Nothing happened small in the Soviet era, either. Twenty million died in the war, 10 million more in the gulag. And the pride of place was always given to grandiose construction projects—the world's biggest hydroelectric plant at Bratsk, the world's biggest truck factory at Kamaz, the trans-Siberian railroad.

The czarist merchant wrapped in coats of gold and sable racing in his sleigh by wretched muzhiks in birch-bark shoes translated into the ham-fisted party boss tearing through Moscow in his long black limousine.

Many theories have been put foward to explain these traits. There is the sheer expanse of a country that spans 11 time zones. There is the climate, which imposed a rhythm of long, inactive winters punctuated by brief summers of intense labor. Some posited the absence of a Renaissance, which stunted the development of an individual consciousness and sustained a spirit of collectivism.

Above all it was a nation straddling two continents and two cultures, forever torn and forever fired by the creative clash at the faultline of East and West.

Russians have ever split into "Westernizers" and "Slavophiles," and the death of the Soviet Union had everything to do with the struggle between the "Westernizing" democrats and free-marketeers and the anti-Western champions of powerful statehood and strong center.

The West has always been deemed both attractive and dangerous to Russia. Peter the Great campaigned desperately to open his nation to the West, but Westerners remained suspect and isolated. Communism found nourishing soil in the Russian spirit of collectivism, but its Western materialism proved alien.

Western democracy is foundering here on the same ambivalence. The Soviets plunged wholeheartedly into the plethora of new councils and parliaments inaugurated by Mr. Gorbachev. But their endless debate and inability to organize into cohesive interest groups soon diminished public attention, and at the end the parliaments readily transferred most of their powers to Mr. Gorbachev, Mr. Yeltsin, and other powerful men.

"What remains after the Soviet Union is this Eurasian essence, this unique interplay of Europe and Asia, which will continue to amaze the world with its culture and totally unexpected actions," Mr. Yerofeyev said.

"What was imported in Western Marxism will vanish," he continued. "But Communism will not disappear, inasmuch as the spirit of collectivism is at the heart of this nation. The nation will always say 'we' rather than the Anglo-Saxon 'I.'

"This was Lenin's deftness, that he realized Russia was ready to accept Communism, but needed only 'class struggle' for everything to fall into place. As soon as it had an enemy, the collective consciousness became dynamic."

That spirit was forever captured in the revolutionary posters, with their capitalists in top hats dripping with workers' blood, or the muscular young Communists crushing bourgeois vipers.

Lenin's successors understood this equally well, that it was easier to fire Soviets to enormous feats and extraordinary sacrifice than to organize them for sustained work and steady growth.

The capacity for suffering and sacrifice, whether in the war or in the endless lines today, is something that still awes foreigners. The ability to focus enormous talent and energy on a grand project is equally impressive, and from this came the great achievements in science, weaponry, and construction.

Yet the sloppiness and inefficiency of everyday life make an even stronger impression on visitors. The shoddiness of even the newest apartment block or hotel is shocking. Old houses seem to list precariously in the mud. Wreckage litters every yard. Cars come off the assembly lines half broken.

The planned economy served only to intensify the squalor. It made volume, not quality or inventiveness, the primary measure of production, and it put a premium on huge factories over flexibility or distribution.

The system also gave consumer goods the lowest possible priority, thus institutionalizing shortages and reducing ordinary people to a permanent state of dependence on the state and rude salespeople.

Whether Lenin would have built the Soviet state this way is not certain. Three years before his death, in 1921, he replaced "War Communism" with what became known as the "New Economic Policy" but was in fact a return to a measure of old laissez-faire. The national income rose to pre-Revolutionary levels, but that failed to dissuade Stalin from starting the first Five-Year Plan.

Nonetheless, it was Lenin who became the first deity of the new order. He was a convenient hero. He had died while still enormously popular, and he left behind enough writings on every topic to support whatever position his successors chose to take.

Thus his goateed visage soon became the mandatory icon in every official building or every town square, and his words became scripture. All the powers of science were summoned to preserve his remains forever, and his mausoleum became the spiritual heart of the new empire. His name became an adjective denoting orthodoxy, as in "the Leninist way." Plaques were raised at every building he stayed in, and an enormous temple was built over his childhood home.

The cult seemed only to gain strength with the passing years, as his successors denounced one another and struggled to portray themselves as the one true interpreter of Lenin. Stalin set the trend, killing most of Lenin's comrades as he perfected the machinery of repression, all the while claiming to act in the name of the great founder.

Next, Khrushchev dismantled the Stalin cult and halted the worst of the terror in the name of restoring "true Leninism," only to be overthrown himself. Before long, Brezhnev was the sole heir, and Khrushchev's "voluntarism" joined Stalin's "personality cult" among the heresies of Leninism.

With Brezhnev, the Soviet state passed visibly into dotage. As he grew bloated and incoherent, so did the state. Production fell while an uncontrolled military machine devoured ever-larger portions of the national product. Foreign policy sank into a pattern of stagnant coexistence and fierce military competition with the West, while at home the political police steadily put down the small but brave dissident movement inspired by the brief Khrushchevian thaw.

After 18 years in power, Brezhnev was succeeded by two other old and sick men, Yuri V. Andropov and Konstantin U. Chernenko, and by the time Mr. Gorbachev took the helm in 1985, it was obvious to all that the state was in radical need of help.

Mr. Gorbachev, at 54 the youngest Soviet leader since Stalin, electrified the land almost immediately with the introduction of *glasnost,* or openness. Suddenly the people could talk and think freely, taboos began to crumble, East-West hostilities evaporated, and dissidents emerged from labor camps and exile. The sweet perfume of hope scented the air.

But Mr. Gorbachev's parallel attempts to reform the economy perished on the same shoals as all previous reforms—the thick and privileged Communist party *apparat.* The more *glasnost* flourished, the more it became evident that *perestroika* was foundering, and everything Mr. Gorbachev did seemed to be too little or too late.

Floundering in the end, he lurched first to the left, ordering a radical 500-day reform plan in the summer of 1989, then to the right, rejecting the plan and encircling himself with party stalwarts and letting them use force, then back to the left last spring, opening negotiations with the republics on a new union treaty.

By then it was too late. The rejected right-wingers tried to seize power by force in the August coup, and with their defeat, the republics had no more need for or faith in Mr. Gorbachev or the remnants of his union.

On December 8, the leaders of Russia, Ukraine, and Byelorussia pulled the plug, proclaiming a new Commonwealth of Independent States, and after that it was only a question of time before the breathing stopped.

The union was dead. But the great Eurasian entity on which it fed remained very much alive—as Russia, as a new commonwealth of 11 republics, as a culture and a worldview, as a formidable nuclear arsenal, as a broad range of unresolved crises.

The gunfire in Georgia, the long lines across the land, the closed airports, and the myriad unanswered questions about the new commonwealth—would it confer citizenship? would it remain a single military and economic entity? would it manage transport and communications?—made clear that the legacy of the union would long survive.

Mr. Gorbachev had given people a new freedom. But the Soviet Union had also given them something tangible—the pride of superpower. Whatever their problems and shortages, they had been one of the two arbiters of global destinies, a nation that nobody could intimidate or bully.

Now that was being taken away, too, and how the humiliation would play out, especially in conditions of hunger and poverty, was among the troubling questions for the future.

"The parting with the Union of Soviet Socialist Republics will be long and difficult," *Izvestia* warned. "We must acknowledge that many will not believe or agree to the end of their days with the death warrant written in Minsk and confirmed in Alma-Ata. The idea of superpower has a force equal to nationalism, and in certain conditions it is also capable of uniting millions of fanatic supporters."

INDEX